Against Massacre

HUMAN RIGHTS AND CRIMES AGAINST HUMANITY
Series editor: Eric D. Weitz

Echoes of Violence: Letters from a War Reporter by Carolin Emcke

Cannibal Island: Death in a Siberian Gulag by Nicolas Werth. Translated by Steven Rendall with a foreword by Jan T. Gross

Torture and the Twilight of Empire from Algiers to Baghdad by Marnia Lazreg

Terror in Chechnya: Russia and the Tragedy of Civilians in War by Emma Gilligan

"If You Leave Us Here, We Will Die": How Genocide Was Stopped in East Timor by Geoffrey Robinson

Stalin's Genocides by Norman Naimark

Against Massacre: Humanitarian Interventions in the Ottoman Empire, 1815–1914 by Davide Rodogno

Against Massacre

HUMANITARIAN INTERVENTIONS IN THE OTTOMAN EMPIRE, 1815–1914

The Emergence of a European Concept and International Practice

Davide Rodogno

PRINCETON UNIVERSITY PRESS

PRINCETON AND OXFORD

Published by Princeton University Press, 41 William Street, Princeton, New Jersey 08540
In the United Kingdom: Princeton University Press, 6 Oxford Street, Woodstock,
Oxfordshire OX20 1TW

ISBN: 978-0-691-15133-5

Library of Congress Control Number: 2011934997

British Library Cataloging-in-Publication Data is available

This book has been composed in Palatino LT Std

Printed on acid-free paper ∞

press.princeton.edu

Printed in the United States of America

10 9 8 7 6 5 4 3 2 1

Sometimes we awaken. We realize we have natural duties to Bulgarians or Armenians after they have been massacred, to Soudanese after they have been plundered and enslaved, to South Africans when they revolt, or East Africans when blood begins to flow; and we clamor then for national intervention. It is good that we should awaken, however late. But these ebullitions are too apt to be spasmodic, intermittent, sentimental. And they are so because there is a quite definite question we do not face, and on which there is no clear understanding among us. This question: Is the citizen entitled to look to the nation as the instrument through which, as a matter of settled policy, his cosmopolitan duties and sympathies are to find enactment? Yet this is the question we ought to put—and to answer in the affirmative.
—John MacCunn, "Cosmopolitan Duties," *International Journal of Ethics*, 1899

Sans vouloir tomber dans le piège de l'idéalisme, on essaiera de démontrer que bien des politiques appliquées sont plus inspirées par des visions prédéterminées du monde que par la réalité des faits, même si les situations concrètes semblent justifier les projets suivis.
—Henry Laurens, *Le Royaume Impossible*, 1990

Scrivere storia significa saper collocare nel tempo questioni diverse che sembrano simili.
—Luciano Canfora, *Corriere della Sera*, 2005

Contents

Acknowledgments   ix

Introduction   1

CHAPTER ONE
The International Context of Nineteenth-Century
Humanitarian Interventions   18

CHAPTER TWO
Exclusion of the Ottoman Empire from the Family of Nations,
and Legal Doctrines of Humanitarian Intervention   36

CHAPTER THREE
Intervention on Behalf of Ottoman Greeks (1821–33)   63

CHAPTER FOUR
Intervention in Ottoman Lebanon and Syria (1860–61)   91

CHAPTER FIVE
The First Intervention in Crete (1866–69)   118

CHAPTER SIX
Nonintervention during the Eastern Crisis (1875–78)   141

CHAPTER SEVEN
Intermezzo—The International Context (1878–1908)   170

CHAPTER EIGHT
Nonintervention on Behalf of the Ottoman Armenians
(1886–1909)   185

CHAPTER NINE
The Second Intervention in Crete (1896–1900)   212

CHAPTER TEN
Nonforcible Intervention in the Ottoman Macedonian
Provinces (1903–08)   229

Epilogue   247

Abbreviations   277

Notes   279

Bibliography   345

Index   385

Acknowledgments

I WISH TO EXPRESS my heartfelt gratitude to my three mentors. Philippe Burrin was the first to be aware of my intentions to write a book on the history of humanitarian interventions. His encouragement convinced me to abandon my previous field of research and undertake this intellectual venture. Bruno Arcidiacono and Matthew Leitner rescued me whenever I found myself in a quagmire. In 2002 the Swiss Fonds National de la Recherche Scientifique granted me a three-year postdoctoral fellowship. I first went to the London School of Economics, where David Stevenson welcomed me warmly, and later to Paris. Without this extremely generous grant, it would have been impossible to start this project. I have very fond memories of the passionate discussions over humanitarian interventions I had with Anita Prazmowska, Sue Onslow, Svetozar Rajak, Dejan Djokic, and Peter Siani Davis. I thank my friends Jasna Dragovic-Soso and Ilaria Favretto, who patiently listened to me regarding my latest findings. While in London, I had the privilege to meet and discuss humanitarian interventions with Stevan Pavlowitch, whose wise advice I took into account when researching. I am thankful to the librarians and staff of the London School of Economics, King's College, and University College London for their precious help, as well as to the archivists of the National Archives at Kew. In Paris, the director of the Institut d'Histoire du Temps Présent, Henry Rousso, counseled me on how to navigate through the administrative hierarchies of Parisian archives. The librarians and staff of the Bibliothèque Nubar and the Bibliothèque Nationale François Mitterrand helped me great deal, as did the archivists of the Quai d'Orsay. In Geneva, the Graduate Institute Library's director Yves Corpataux was kind enough to provide me with a copy of all the books I required. Martine Basset found all the manuscripts, pamphlets, and rare publications I needed.

I am grateful to the Royal Council of United Kingdom. From 2005 to 2008, as Research Council UK academic fellow, I worked in the stimulating and enriching environment of the School of History of the University of St. Andrews. Andrew Pettegree, then head of school, allowed me to continue my research undisturbed for almost two years. John Clark helped me to understand how things worked in the Kingdom of Fife and, over a few months, evolved from mentor to friend. Steve Murdoch introduced me to Scottish history, the secrets of rugby, whisky, and humanitarian organizations. David Allan gave me private lessons on Ferguson, Smith, and the Scottish Enlightenment. Riccardo Bavaj, whose office was next to mine, bravely endured my soliloquies on humanitarian interventions. I am grateful to the numerous colleagues who read one or more chapters of this book: Ali Ansari, Michael Brown, Bruce Gordon, Dimitris Kastritsis, Tony Lang, Bernhard Struck, Stephen Tyre, and Michael Bentley, who suggested the title. I thank Lorna Harris for her assistance, as well as Alexia Grosjean and Heike Cavallo, who improved the written English of my manuscript.

Among the colleagues who read parts of this book, I would like to thank Aron Rodrigue, David Holloway, Amir Weiner, Andreas Malaspinas, Christos Hadziiossif, Effie Voutira, Sergio Luzzatto, Guido Abbatista, Marco Dogo, Christian Müller, David Trim, and Jennifer Pitts. Gary Bass sent me the proof of his *Freedom's Battle* at the time I was finishing the first draft of this book. He trusted a perfect stranger! Eric Weitz and Rebecca Gill read the entire manuscript and made precious comments. I can never thank them enough. I am indebted to my colleagues of the International History and Politics Department at the Graduate Institute of Geneva, as well as to the students in my seminars on the history of humanitarian interventions. Some of their comments and my replies to their criticism and challenging questions are to be found in this book. I am appreciative for the constructive reports of the anonymous reviewers and to my editor Ian Malcolm who believed in me since we first met at St. Katharine's Lodge. Ian has waited with great patience for me to be finished with this book. Obviously, the responsibility for what I have written lies entirely with me.

Many people made it possible for me to work in perfect conditions. Dr. Bruno Roche and Pierre Michetti looked after my health. I found inspiration at Roberta's place in Acitrezza. Claudia Franchini's Cornwall Gardens flat, Madame Rolande Cuvillière's apartment at Rue de l'Université, and Giuseppe and Silvana Salvia's house at Prangins were ideal places in which to write, erase, and rewrite. Anna and Daniele made my life easier in every possible way. My brother Raffaele and my friends Antonio Denti, Alexandros Dimitrakopoulos, and Giovanni Distefano were there whenever I needed them. Carla and Annah Andrea helped me to go beyond my congenital cynicism and to seek fragmentary "sentiments of humanity" in international politics. Giovanna always stood by me. This book is for her.

Against Massacre

Introduction

> To be able to talk intelligently about what looks like the
> extraordinary amount of intervention that occurs in the
> present-day international system, or about the seemingly
> original network of contemporary transnational relations,
> it is useful to be able to compare the present system with
> past ones. We may discover that the amount of interven-
> tion today is not at all that unusual and that the network
> of transnational relations is far less original than many
> have claimed.
>
> —Stanley Hoffmann, "Hedley Bull and His Contribution
> to International Relations," in *World Disorders*
> *Troubled Peace in the Post–Cold War Era*, 1988

I BEGAN MY RESEARCH in Geneva at the end of the so-called humanitarian decade (1990–2000) when the subject and international practice
of humanitarian interventions was one of the most controversial matters of discussion in international relations among academics, policy-
makers, and the mass media.[1] As Robert O. Keohane wrote in 2002,
"saying humanitarian intervention in a room full of philosophers, legal scholars, and political scientists is a little bit like crying 'fire' in a
crowded theatre: it can create a clear and present danger to everyone
within earshot."[2] Keohane does not even mention historians, who, with
regard to this topic, have always been conspicuous by their absence.
The only notable exception is *Freedom's Battle: The Origins of Humanitarian Intervention*, published in 2008 by political scientist Gary Bass.[3]

My research looks at the European roots of this concept and international practice during the nineteenth century. I dispute both the assertion that humanitarian intervention is a phenomenon of international relations that appeared after the end of the Cold War and the
suggestion that it emerged abruptly during the nineteenth century. I
investigate when, where, who, how, and for what reasons a humanitarian intervention was undertaken from 1815 to 1914. Through a nuanced historical analysis, I examine the claims of the intervening states
to be aiding humanity, the complexity of state action, the reasons for

intervention as well as for nonintervention, and the relationship between public outcry and state action. My objective is to underscore the distinctive features of this ever-controversial phenomenon and to shed some light on similarities and differences between nineteenth-century and contemporary interventions.

I focus on the political history of humanitarian intervention, which I think of as being a coercive diplomatic and/or armed (re)action against massacre undertaken by a state or a group of states inside the territory of a target state. Its main motivation is to end massacre, atrocity, and extermination or to prevent the repetition of such events. It is an ex post facto event whose objective is to protect civilian populations mistreated and unprotected by the target-state government, agents, or authorities. The adjective "humanitarian" refers to the idea of "saving strangers,"[4] of helping victims, of protecting foreign, apparently innocent, civilian populations.

This research is about the politics and policies of the intervening governments, the European "great" powers, more specifically Great Britain and France. These two powers, together with Russia, were more actively involved than Austria (Austria-Hungary between 1867 and 1918) and Prussia (Germany since 1870) in the interventions that took place within the borders of the Ottoman Empire. Ideally it would have been appropriate to conduct exhaustive research in all the archives of the governments involved, the Ottoman archives included. For multiple reasons related to the time at my disposal and my lack of knowledge of so many different languages, I decided to focus mainly on Great Britain and France. I attempt a *mise en parallèle* rather than a comparative analysis of the role of British and French governments. A number of reasons explain this choice: Great Britain and France both had elected parliaments; the interpenetration of ideas between the two countries is relevant and constant throughout the century, as exemplified by the norms they shared at the societal and international level; British and French diplomats, armies, and public opinion played a crucial role in each of the instances that I examine. I have sought evidence of the existence of a concept and of an international practice of humanitarian intervention in international treaties and diplomatic documents, in parliamentary papers, in various speeches of British and French statesmen, in the press, in the activity of humanitarian lobbies and pressure groups (domestic and transnational), and in the contemporary jurisprudential nomenclature, juridical doctrines, essays, and articles of nineteenth-century thinkers.

The reader of this book must be aware that many other histories of humanitarian interventions await to be written: a cultural and intellectual history of the interventions, a transnational history of the discourses on interventions held by humanitarians in and beyond Europe, a history of the interventions from the perspective of the target state (which can only be written by an Ottomanist) or from the perspective of the victims of massacre and atrocities. Furthermore, it is important to stress that this book does not make the history of the massacres and atrocities that led to the intervention but, more precisely, starts from the accounts of massacres as European observers and diplomats reported them. It was on the basis of those accounts (which might have been accurate or inaccurate, biased or impartial, detailed or vague) that European governments decided whether or not to undertake an intervention to save strangers.

This study leaves aside humanitarian relief and nonmilitary aid, such as the giving of food and medical supplies to a country in crisis—whether because of natural disasters like famine, flood, or earthquake or because of man-made disasters such as war, tyrannical oppression, or revolution. I do not take into account the history of international conflicts having alleged or genuine humanitarian claims and do not examine instances of military interventions to protect a state's own nationals from abuse, which were established practice in the nineteenth century. The British expedition in Abyssinia of 1868 is the archetypal case in point. Its object was to release the British captives whom Theodore, the negus, had detained since November 1863. All the European prisoners were released on April 13, 1868, by an expeditionary corps dispatched from Bombay under the command of Sir Robert Napier. The negus was not deprived of any portion of his territory or forced to make any concession, pecuniary or otherwise. Benjamin Disraeli, then leader of the House of Commons and chancellor of the exchequer, called the attention of Parliament to the "disinterestedness" of British action that did not aim to obtain territory or to secure commercial advantages but was motivated exclusively by moral considerations. Great Britain sought to assess its power and military supremacy as well as its moral supremacy and to vindicate the "higher principles of humanity." The main difference between these interventions and those I deal with here is that the alleged object of the intervention was the protection of strangers. Important similarities among these interventions exist, such as the alleged disinterestedness of the intervening states, their sense of moral superiority, and their utter disregard for the consequences of their actions for other civilian populations. Such was the case in 1900 when the European powers undertook an armed intervention in China to repress the Boxer Rebellion. Their primary goal was to protect European nationals, not Chinese citizens. The intervention indeed resulted in the protection of Europeans and of a number of Christian Chinese from slaughter, but, in the process, hundreds of thousands of innocent as well as combatant Chinese were killed by the expeditionary corps, and many women were raped en route to Beijing.

With the exception of the epilogue, I do not make any reference to "massive violations of the most basic human rights." Such terminology was not in use during the nineteenth century. Today we commonly refer to war crimes, crimes against humanity, genocide, and ethnic cleansing. Of course, none of these concepts existed during the nineteenth century.[5] I found the terms "mass atrocity crimes," "mass atrocities," and "mass crime" equally inadequate for the purpose of this research.[6] As historian Jacques Sémelin points out, the word "mass" announces the exceptional proportions of the crime under consideration, in the sense that it targets a very large group or a mass of individual victims. The expression "mass crime" suggests that a group that very probably enjoys popular support commits a spectacular crime. In this respect, even though the magnitude of the event and its exceptionality are relevant elements to explain humanitarian intervention, "crime" bears a normative assumption inadequate for nineteenth-century humanitarian interventions.[7] On the contrary "massacre," "atrocity," and "extermination"—which I examine more in detail in chapter 1—were three terms commonly used during the nineteenth century.

BEFORE THE NINETEENTH CENTURY

The concept of rights, including natural rights, stretches back centuries, and the idea of a duty to help strangers did not emerge *ex abrupto* during the nineteenth century. Historically, a number of world religions have encouraged assisting others in dire need; Judaism, Christianity, and Islam, for example, justify helping others based on charity and their belief that all humans are created in God's image.[8] As far as Europe is concerned, since the Middle Ages, the pope and the emperor intervened against the princes violating the fundamental rights of their subjects, and jurists and philosophers debated about the concept of the just war. During the Spanish conquest of America, Francisco de Vitoria put forward the principle of the *ius defendendi innocentes a morte iniusta*, the right to defend innocents from an unjust death caused by their own authorities. This jurist considered that a humanitarian war was permissible and just if it was made in the name of the innocent against the tyranny of native leaders or laws, a tyranny consisting, for instance, of the sacrifice of innocent men or even of the killing of innocent men in order to eat them.[9] Such a justification, Tzvetan Todorov argues, did not derive from reciprocity: even if this rule were applied to Indians and Spaniards alike, it was the latter who decided on the meaning of the word "tyranny." The Spaniards, unlike the Indians, were subject and judge of the decision since it was they who selected the criteria according to which the judgment would be delivered; they decided, for instance, that human sacrifice was the consequence of tyranny, but massacre of local populations was not.[10]

During the sixteenth century Alberico Gentili put forward the concept of the aid of the oppressed (*plena est justitia quae defendit infirmos*) and raised the notion of sovereign accountability.[11] In two sections of Book 2 of *De Jure Belli ac Pacis*, Hugo Grotius dealt with the measure of war against the immoral, and the waging of war on behalf of others. Grotius spoke of a legal right rather than a moral duty to come to aid and to wage a war on behalf of the oppressed subjects of another sovereign when the oppressed are powerless. In those circumstances, he claimed, it is open to another sovereign to assert the rights of the oppressed subjects and intervene on their behalf.[12] During the seventeenth and eighteenth centuries the prevailing idea among legal scholars was to restrict as much as possible the grounds for legal intervention of a state in the internal affairs of another.[13] Emer de Vattel criticized Grotius's assertion that a sovereign may take up arms to punish a nation guilty of an enormous transgression of the laws of nature (a nation that treated its subjects with inhumanity). In his view, such a claim opened the door all sorts of abuses. As Samuel Pufendorf did before him, Vattel referred to one possible exception to the principle of nonintervention in the internal affairs of another sovereign state: the case of a third party intervening to assist the oppressed subjects of a tyrannical sovereign. It was only after the oppressed subjects had broken the "political bond" with the tyrant that a third party might intervene on behalf of the oppressed.[14] By the beginning of the nineteenth century the principle of nonintervention in the domestic affairs of another sovereign state had become central in relations between European states. In chapter 2 we shall see that the theory and practice of humanitarian intervention expanded on the edge of this very fundamental pillar of international relations.

The idea that each individual on Earth has some basic rights was central in Immanuel Kant's "cosmopolitan law," which suggested a third sphere of public law, in addition to constitutional law and international law, in which both states and individuals have rights, and where individuals have these rights as "citizens of the Earth" rather than as citizens of particular states. Eighteenth-century philosophes argued that the secular and universal aims of the humanitarian spirit went beyond maintaining and preserving order and aimed to transform, to improve, and to regenerate humanity. The humanitarian ideal of the philosophes was to ban war, impose religious tolerance, forbid torture, improve hygiene and health, promote science, eradicate poverty, develop education, abolish slavery, and recognize that humanity has fundamental rights. The humanitarian spirit, as it emerged in France—in Europe and the Americas—during the late eighteenth century, derived from and developed in an intertwined, sometimes parallel and sometimes opposite, sense to Christian charity and encompassed ideas of secular benevolence (*bienfaisance*) and philanthropy.[15]

The "rights of man" were a centerpiece of the age of democratic revolution. Historian Samuel Moyn claims that those *droits de l'homme et du citoyen* meant something different from today's human rights. For most of modern history, he argues, rights have been part and parcel of battles over the meanings and entitlements of citizenship and therefore have been dependent on national borders for their pursuit, achievement, and protection. In the beginning they were invoked by a people to found a nation-state of their own, not to police someone's else. They were a justification for state sovereignty, not a source of appeal to some authority—like international law—outside and above it.[16] Nineteenth-century British and French cultivated elites included among the natural rights of humanity the rights to life, property, equality before the law, and religious freedom. Some thinkers argued in favor of the universality of these rights, but during the nineteenth century these rights were not universally protected through mechanisms of international enforcement. Arguably, humanitarianism and humanitarian intervention lie alongside the concept of the rights of man, although it would be wrong to draw to hasty conclusions or misleading heroic views of human rights in the nineteenth century.

As a matter of fact, in Britain as well as in France "humanitarian" and later "humanitarianism" were negative terms implying excessive sentimentalism—the kind of sentimentalism that reached back to the Protestant revolution of sentiments in the sixteenth and seventeenth centuries, whose key ingredient was sympathy, the capacity to identify with the suffering of others, which enabled charitable practices to be built on an interior emotional and spiritual foundation.[17] These two terms were kept separated from the terms "human" and "humanity" (*de l'humanité*).[18] Moreover, one should also keep in mind that the roots of nineteenth-century humanitarian movements were remarkably diverse and motivated by radically different principles. In western Europe, national and transnational humanitarianism originated in the politics and philosophy of eighteenth-century liberalism. Throughout the nineteenth century humanitarianism cut across political orientations and was also associated with religious and political projects as diverse as Quaker pacifism, Protestant evangelicalism, Great Power imperialism, Catholic social democracy, and grassroots democratic socialism. The array of activities included under the label "humanitarian practices" was similarly diverse and ranged from aid to poor people and food aid to full-scale military intervention.[19]

As to the late-eighteenth-century campaign in favor of the abolition of the slave trade and of slavery, one can pinpoint a number features that help relate it to nineteenth-century humanitarian interventions. The campaign undoubtedly projected humanitarian actions beyond national boundaries. The abolition movement reveals that men and women whose own rights were assured by their governments could mobilize effectively to assert what they took to be the rights of humanity. The campaigns, and to some extent the military operations undertaken by the Royal Navy, bear similarities to the international practice I deal with in this book. There is evidence that for some early-nineteenth-century political elites the naval operations to end the slave trade represented a useful precedent when discussing the grounds upon which to intervene on behalf of the Ottoman Greeks from a military as well as legal point of view (see chapter 3). If one looks at the modalities of these operations, the British naval actions to end the slave trade were the result of international multilateral agreement, for the Royal Navy acted on an international mandate to suppress the Atlantic and Indian Ocean slave trade. The operations were also the outcome of political actions of influential pressure groups such as the Clapham Sect (or Clapham "saints" as contemporaries derisively tagged the sect), led by William Wilberforce.[20] In the case of the abolition campaign, reformers succeeded in arousing sympathy and awakening moral qualms so powerfully as to mobilize political action that, though certainly colored by self-interest, actually led to actions on behalf of people who were "other" in the fullest sense.[21]

The abolitionists gave birth to the politics of pressure groups, including mass petitions, publication of magazines and tracts, holding of public meetings, appealing to public opinion, and founding of voluntary societies.[22] The importance of public opinion was included in the solemn public declaration of ministers of eight European powers on February 8, 1815, regarding the African slave trade, which now had to be regarded, "by just and enlightened men, in all ages, as repugnant to the principles of humanity and of universal morality." The ministers of the principal European states mentioned that "the public voice in all civilized countries" demanded the suppression of slavery, and that the universal abolition of it was "conformable to the spirit of the age and the generous principles of the allied powers."[23] In fact, however, the trade in slaves and slavery were not universally banned. Military actions had a limited scope and were biased and selective. The British government limited the military action of its navy to the abolishment of the trade in slaves, not slavery itself.[24] The British government's strategy for ending the slave trade was to have such trafficking labeled as piracy, thus making the slaves "contraband" (i.e., property) and justifying its actions because maritime rights governing commerce enabled it to seize and board ships sailing under non-British flags suspected of carrying contraband slaves. The British navy undertook international policing actions against pirates rather than against a target state. The scope of the military action was very limited, with the exception of the destruction of the port of Algiers in 1816 to end the white slave trade in the Mediterranean Sea.[25] Throughout the nineteenth century there would not be a single armed intervention on behalf of African slaves on the African or American continents. British and other European governments did not regard black, non-Christian Africans as human beings whose rights should be protected in the same way as those of suffering Christians were.

The doctrine of the just war, the idea of a right to life for each individual on Earth, the practice of international police action, the organization of domestic and transnational pressure group and other philanthropic societies with humanitarian purposes all existed before the nineteenth century. What was specific to the international concept and practice of humanitarian intervention during that century, when nationalism rose, during the heydays of imperialism, of the struggle of mastery in Europe and beyond? Under what circumstances—if any—did the European powers consider massacre of foreign civilian populations as sufficient motive to undertake a military operation? Can we find examples in the nineteenth century where states looked beyond their own territorial and colonial borders, beyond their own immediate economic and security interests, beyond realpolitik, to demonstrate—by acting to halt or avert new or continuing massacre and atrocity—that they indeed had "purposes beyond themselves"?[26] The purpose of this book is to answer to those questions.

QUESTIONS, ASSUMPTIONS, AND ISSUES

This book focuses on the Ottoman Empire because, during the period examined, the coercive interventions "on grounds of humanity" took place in that empire (the target state) and on behalf of Ottoman Christian populations. The precedent and rationale for these interventions and the parameters of the discourse related to them were inextricably bound up with the image of and geopolitics pertaining to the Ottoman Empire. One of my initial assumptions is that the origins of humanitarian intervention lay in a specific relationship between the European powers and the Ottoman Empire, known as the "Eastern Question." I look at European international relations and the place of the Ottoman Empire within the international system at a time when the European powers increasingly saw it as under their tutelage. To prevent or cure internal disorders in the Ottoman Empire, the European powers took into consideration two solutions: its dismemberment (a radical remedy impossible to enforce for various reasons) or its modernization through the implementation of reforms. In urgent cases, when violent counter-insurgency campaigns undertaken by the Ottoman authorities led to disturbances and massacre, the European powers authorized themselves to intervene militarily in the empire. I analyze whether the intervening states acknowledged the existence of a given threshold (quantitative—the number of people slaughtered—and/or qualitative—the way they were killed, the kind of atrocities perpetrated against them) beyond which a massacre might have triggered intervention. I show whether systemic or local circumstances, political situations, and criteria, *ratione personae* or *ratione loci*, determined a humanitarian intervention or inaction.

A further axiomatic assumption of this book is that a government *always* acts according to a given set of perceived interests. Hence even a truly humanitarian intervention responds to an interest. What dis- tinguishes humanitarian intervention from other kind of interventions is its main motivation, that is, to save strangers from massacre. The intervention can be humanitarian when political leaders, state agents, and policy-makers see saving the lives of strangers as an act of "moral capital,"[27] when it follows a domestic political concern (i.e., the decision of leaders and policy-makers to act according to the demands of public opinion), notwithstanding whether policy-makers empathize with the victims of massacre.[28] As David Forsythe points out, states do care about their international reputation, and "moral" behavior reinforces a positive reputation at home and abroad. Indeed "moral policies" may compel further ethically motivated behavior not originally envisaged by the state. In this way, a humanitarian morality can become politically useful and can reshape state interest in unintended ways.[29]

An intervention can be humanitarian even if it is directed only to saving the lives of a particular group of peoples and ignores the sufferings of other populations. It will certainly be selective and biased, but it can still be humanitarian. On the contrary, if it can be demonstrated that humanitarian motives are a pretext to enhance political, imperial, strategic interests of the intervening state(s), an intervention cannot be qualified as humanitarian. If from a theoretical point of view it is possible to draw clear lines and to define what is or is not humanitarian with respect to an intervention, things are different when confronted with real situations—when for instance, humanitarian and imperialist impulses of domestic constituencies tend to coincide. Was nineteenth-century humanitarianism nothing more than a rhetorical tool, the fig leaf concealing policies in the self-interest of the intervening states? Is it possible to disentangle humanitarian motives from other motives determining the interventions of the European powers?

I examine the motives and modalities of interventions against massacre and deal with some of the aspects related to their effectiveness, outcomes, and (intended and unintended) consequences. We shall see that nineteenth-century humanitarian interventions were generally carried out collectively. Before undertaking the intervention, European powers usually reached a collective agreement guaranteeing the "disinterested" nature of the intervention. Disinterested meant that none of the European powers would seek any unilateral advantage, such as territorial conquest, through their military action. The military operation was not an act of self-defense, nor did it lead to a permanent military occupation or to a peace treaty signed with the target state (which distinguished it from an act of war against the target state). We shall also see what would happen when massacre, atrocities, and extermination occurred but the European powers did not reach a collective agreement, and how far, without such an agreement, some European powers were ready to go to save strangers. As Bass puts it:

> The great powers had to convince each other that their purported mercy mission was not just a foil for imperial expansion. So the intervening states had to impose limitations on themselves. There were a number of established techniques of self-restraint: delineating [the] sphere of justifiable intervention for each of the great powers, delegating to regional powers, putting time limits on humanitarian interventions, restricting the size of the military force, foreswearing diplomatic and commercial advantages from a humanitarian mission, and, above all, multilateralism. All of these devises helped make humanitarian intervention safer.[30]

Undoubtedly, in the early to mid-nineteenth century, the term "humanitarian intervention" would have been meaningless to many individuals this book deals with (see chapter 2). Part of my argument is that the idea of intervention to end massacre began to emerge as a way to protect the right to life of a restricted group of people in the early nineteenth century, prior to the creation of a proper legal definition of the intervention. A legal concept and discourse on states' action intending to assist suffering humanity deprived of the right to life crystallized by the second half of the nineteenth century. It was during the 1870s that campaigners, pamphleteers, journalists, and international legal scholars pointed to historical precedents that had taken place early in the century. European political elites and policy-makers situated and understood early-nineteenth-century interventions in terms of religious and/or political worldviews that could not admit the indiscriminate killing of a religious community. Hence, one of the issues examined in this book is the extent to which the intervening states responded to the suffering of others regardless of their ethnic or religious identity.[31] Did the European powers consider massacre, atrocity, and extermination of any population as an intolerable wrong that needed to be redressed? Did they systematically undertake coercive intervention against massacre? Did they intervene because the Ottoman government showed itself to be unwilling or unable to protect its populations? Or did they intervene because of the widespread sentiment of identity of a great majority of Europeans with suffering Christianity? Was it because non-Christian populations and/or authorities massacred Christians that interventions took place?

If nineteenth-century humanitarian interventions were not based on secular universalism and if they did not systematically transcend boundaries of religion (and therefore both the Christian identity of the victims of massacre and the Muslim religion of the alleged perpetrators are key explaining factors), is it correct to consider these coercive actions as acts of religious imperialism?

It is worthwhile for readers to bear in mind that when Europeans dealt with massacres taking place in the Ottoman Empire, they ignored the appalling record of violations of the right to life in their respective colonies. They forgot, whether deliberately or not, the fact that equality before the law and religious freedom in their own states, let alone colonies, did not exist.[32] European diplomats and acknowledged experts wanted the Ottoman government to legislate for equality and citizenship while, in a former Ottoman territory like Algeria, French authorities ruled in a far more intolerant, discriminating, and despotic way than the Ottomans had ever done. Europeans intervened militarily when the "barbarous" Ottomans used the same "savage" methods to repress insurrection they systematically used in their own colonies. As Bass puts it, the British largely missed the irony of carrying on their debates about Greek suffering during the 1820s while simultaneously discussing how to deal with an Indian mutiny and festering Catholic grievances in Ireland. After Indians massacred Britons in Delhi and Kanpur in the summer 1857, the British sadistically slaughtered Indians by the hundreds, burning old women and children alive, and smearing Muslims with pig fat before killing them. The Earl of Carnarvon, Disraeli's colonial secretary, spoke inside the cabinet for the Bulgarians in 1876, just a few years before he launched widespread brutal reprisals against the Zulus in 1879. In 1876–79, at the height of British public rage over the Bulgarian horrors, an epic drought took the lives of untold millions of Indians. When the Armenian massacres and intervention in Crete took place, the British were at arms against the Boers in South Africa, famous for its barbarities against local populations, white and black.

Humanitarian interventions undertaken by European governments were based on the same basic assumptions of imperialism. The intervening governments and the vast majority of humanitarians involved in the campaigns in favor of intervention were firmly convinced that massacres and atrocities were the direct consequence of the "barbarous" Ottoman government. And, toward the end of the century, imperial racism toward Muslims played a recurring role in moving European humanitarians and some policy-makers to action. The European "most civilized" nations contrasted their "superior" civilization with that of a "barbarous," "uncivilized" target state, prone to inhumanity, whose sovereignty and authority they contested. Since the early nineteenth century the rationale of intervention was saving fellow Christians in the short term and exporting "civilization" (European civilization) in the medium term. We should bear in mind that the Europeans attempted to end the massacre and avoid its repetition, and at the same time they wished to impose their civilization where the intervention had taken place. Many humanitarians who supported imperial expansion at home shared with European leaders few "compunctions about imposing changes on foreign countries," including the Ottoman territories.[33] Any restraint the intervening states showed after an intervention had taken place was related to the political complexity of the Eastern Question rather than to any respect for Ottoman sovereignty. It is in the dichotomy civilization/barbarism, which, as we know, substantially varied between the early nineteenth and early twentieth centuries, that humanitarian and imperialist impulses of Europeans intersected. It was the presumption of superiority of the European civilization that, throughout the nineteenth century, shaped interventions against massacre in the Ottoman Empire.

The end of the ancien régime in France, the extension of suffrage in Britain, the abolition of the slave trade and of slavery in European colonies, and the economic and technological breakthroughs of the Industrial Revolution all lent a conviction even to radical social critics that French or British political cultures were unimpeachably superior to those of the rest of the world.[34] At the beginning of the nineteenth century, theories of progress became more triumphalist, less tolerant of cultural differences and more specifically national. As historian Peter Mandler puts it, a "*civilizational confidence*" began to pervade political discourse in both Britain and France.[35] With Napoleon Bonaparte political power and conquest became justified, sometimes in a missionary manner, in terms of the values of progress and civilization they were presumed to embody. Later the concept of civilization would be increasingly employed as an instrument of political expansion beyond Europe and as the cultural legitimation of European imperialism.[36] The comparatively subtle developmental gradations put forward by eighteenth-century intellectuals, such as Scottish thinkers Adam Smith and Adam Ferguson, were reduced to a crude dichotomy between European civilization and extra-European barbarity or savagery.

For midcentury intellectuals, such as François Guizot or John Stuart Mill, barbarous societies, including the Ottoman Empire, fell outside the community of nations and norms of international law.[37] These views on civilizations reinforced the idea of the European countries' fitness to spread the civilization beyond Europe and to introduce it where, presumably, it did not already exist. Midcentury Europeans saw no harm, indeed saw much good, in an imperial "civilizing mission" over the world's "children" (those peoples who had not yet grown up into civilization) and supported the expansion and consolidation of European rule over non-European subjects primarily on moral bases. The lack of a European *standard of civilization* became one of the justifications for imperial domination of non-Europeans.[38] The civilizing mission claimed to bring the benefits of European social, political, economic, and cultural arrangements to the "dark" reaches of Earth to create humanity where none had previously existed. Non-Europeans became fully human ergo "civilized" (or vice versa) in European eyes by becoming Christian, adopting European-style structures of property rights and territorial political arrangements, and entering the growing European-based liberal international economy.

During the second half of the century, the superiority of the European civilization remained uncontested, though doubts concerning the civilizing character of the imperial and colonial enterprise emerged, in Britain at least, after the 1857 Indian Mutiny and more markedly so after the 1865 "rebellion" in Morant Bay, Jamaica. By the 1870s the failure of the project to modernize and Christianize was widely accepted. As historian Ronald Hyam eloquently puts it, the sympathetic and optimistic fundamental belief in equality and perfectibility of humankind disappeared, and efficiency replaced improvement as the keynote of good administration.[39]

Contrary to Britain, in France, the *mission civilisatrice* acquired a greater currency under the Third Republic. Historian Alice Conklin notes that the notion of a civilizing mission rested on fundamental assumptions about the superiority of French culture and perfectibility of humankind. It implied that France's colonial subjects were too primitive to rule themselves but were capable of being uplifted.[40] The civilizer had duties, moral and humanitarian. Ameliorating (*la mise en valeur*) colonized populations through "superior" French science constituted one aspect of the mission. Abolishing slavery, ending all forms of "feudal vestiges," and eradicating indigenous languages and customs, pestilence, poverty, and ignorance were central to the French understanding of their civilizing mission. The supreme ambition of the civilizing mission was the pursuit of moral progress and was ultimately meant to make men and women out of colonial "savages" and "barbarians" (*en faire des hommes*).[41]

No differently from the case of other European imperialisms, when translated into acts the civilizing mission meant brutal submission, violence, and utter, arrogant disregard of other peoples' most basic rights. Furthermore, whether in their colonies the French presumed to be the bearers of civilization, they often looked at the Ottoman Empire as a feudal, ancien régime–type of government. French rulers committed massacre and atrocities, which, in his 1841 *Essay on Algeria*, Tocqueville argued were justified by France's imperial goal. The French must be prepared to use violence against civilians in ways that would be unconscionable in Europe—to burn harvests, ruin soils, and capture unarmed men, women, and children. The struggle against local Arab leader Abdel-Kader, led by extreme violence, had the full approval of Prime Minister Guizot, the man whose lessons Tocqueville had so much admired. Guizot claimed that humanitarian and philanthropic attitudes would have prolonged the war. In the end the "generous intention of the colonizers" justified a *despotisme du sabre* by France in Algeria.[42] In the European view, the Ottomans lacked any "generous" intention, hence their massacres were totally unjustified. This was the main difference between "civilized" and "uncivilized" rule. Nineteenth-century humanitarian interventions shared with the civilizing mission the firm belief in the superiority of European morality, religious beliefs, and political systems, and the certainty of military and technological domination. One difference did exist. Whereas in the colonies bringing civilization entailed the *despotisme du sabre* and resorting to massacres in the case of humanitarian intervention, the "generous intentions" of the Europeans aimed at ending massacres of fellow Christians. Admittedly, these interventions were selective in the kinds of problems they targeted and in the types of people who deserved to be rescued.

Toward the end of the century a racist "objective scientific basis" would justify the "superiority" of Western culture and Western dominance as being the expression of scientific laws rather than an accident of power politics.[43] In the closing decades of the nineteenth century, "at the height of Britain's imperial power, moral and political justifications of empire receded from the forefront of debates about the nature and purpose of imperial rule. Earlier ethical justifications of empire were displaced as new sociological understandings of colonial societies began to function as *de facto* explanations for imperial rule."[44] By the early twentieth century, in the perspective of the Europeans, "civilization" was a hypothetical basis for global order in a world of hierarchy.[45] When the First World War started a juridical doctrine of humanitarian intervention, though still debated and controversial, had been established and looked back to a jurisprudential corpus that by then was almost a century old.

A last issue I wish to pin down here concerns the role of public opinion. During the nineteenth century some massacres had a greater impact on public opinion and policy-makers than did others. The massacres of Christians by a "barbarous," infidel state clearly aroused the interest of public opinion all over Europe more than did the massacres of Muslims in Central Asia. Massacres of Ottoman Christians attracted sustained interest and attained political significance within the societies of potential intervening states because, in my view, there was a close connection between Christians and compassion during the nineteenth century. In some circumstances those concerned found a way to address their concerns at the domestic and eventually the transnational and international levels. Specific individuals made a priority of massacre and of the political questions related to solving the recurrence of massacre—a priority that lasted beyond initial protests, the setting up of organizations, and institutional commitment. (This was the case with the Eastern Question Associations founded in the aftermath of the Bulgarian Atrocities of 1876; see chapters 6–10). Every European state—even the autocratic Russian government—had to take into account public opinion movements. And in late-Victorian Britain, while not yet a full democracy, the government had to build a consensus not just among elites but also among the middle and working classes. In the case of Great Britain, the growth of domestic mass media and faster communication were vital for the Philhellenes in the 1820s as well as for William Gladstone's campaigners. Whereas during the 1820s the London Greek Committee remained largely an elite group, Gladstone's latter-day supporters had access to more newspapers, with bigger circulation and farther reach. The *Times* had fewer than six thousand readers in 1822 but as many as seventy thousand in 1876. Throughout the century the electorate grew, too. The first Reform Act came in Britain in 1832, followed by the second Reform Act in 1867, which by itself doubled the size of the electorate. The press had to reach almost two million voters. The 1867 franchise reform sent a large number of new voters into the mix, just in time to read the gruesome news of massacres in Bulgaria. Bass argues that this meant more pressure on the British government to act.[46] The hypothesis that public opinion mattered for each and every intervening state seems very sensible indeed. It also seems important to stress the increasing role of the masses with respect to the political life of European states. At the same time, it should be noted that public opinion could be manipulated, as it was in France under Napoleon III, who strictly controlled the French press in 1860 at the time of the intervention in Ottoman Lebanon.

In *Freedom's Battle*, Bass looks at the way freedom at home helped promote freedom abroad, arguing that for the activists who campaigned in favor of intervention, military actions in the Balkans and elsewhere in the Ottoman Empire were intended to promote independence. *Against Massacre* examines the motives of intervention, starting from the assumption that European governments were little interested in freeing Balkan or Middle Eastern populations. As far as those who campaigned in favor of interventions are concerned, this book emphasizes that for some "massacre" figured at least as prominently as "freedom." Other campaigners ignored the issue of bestowing freedom (i.e., independence) or referred to freedom as the rights of Christians to be ruled fairly by a government respectful of their lives, their religion, and their equality before the law. Speaking about freedom at home and abroad, Bass dwells on the force of what he calls "free press" reporting on foreign atrocities. He argues that the new mass media played an increasingly crucial role throughout the nineteenth century as an *ante litteram* CNN. Hence Bass claims that the existence of mass media was the first crucial step toward a humanitarian intervention.[47] For what reasons, on the various occasions this book deals with, when freedom was denied and massacres took place, did humanitarian intervention not take place, despite an impressive mobilization of national and transnational public opinion? It is certainly true that credible information about foreign atrocities coalesced the interests and moral concerns of public opinion, and that without the mass media public opinion would return to worrying about more parochial concerns. Why, then, when reporters emerged as a distinct professional class with some professional standards, did military humanitarian interventions take place less often than in the early nineteenth century, when there were very few professional reporters around?[48]

I will attempt to demonstrate that nineteenth-century humanitarian interventions were not necessarily products of increasing democracy, a free press, and the increasing importance of the principle of self-determination. In fact, the most likely conditions for such an intervention to take place where in the conservative venues of the old Concert of Europe's diplomacy. The rise of international law doctrines on intervention did not bring about an increase of this international practice for a number of reasons, mainly related to the nature and conditions of the international system in the late nineteenth century. It is precisely because of the centrality of the Eastern Question as a key factor for understanding the history of humanitarian intervention that I go beyond the study of intervention in Greece (chapter 3), Lebanon, Syria (chapter 4), and Bulgaria (chapter 6) and examine cases relating to interventions in Crete (chapters 5 and 9) and the Ottoman Macedonian provinces (chapter 10), as well as the 1890s massacres of Ottoman Armenians (chapter 8), a notable case of nonintervention that I consider to be of the utmost importance in understanding the limits of this international practice.

CHAPTER ONE

The International Context of Nineteenth-Century Humanitarian Interventions

> The essence of intervention is force, or the threat of force in
> case the dictates of the intervening power are disregarded.
> It is, therefore, clearly differentiated from mere advice or
> good offices tendered by a friendly state without any idea of
> compulsion, from mediation entered upon by a third power
> at the request of the parties to the dispute, but without
> any promise on their part to accept the terms suggested or
> any intention on its part to force them to do so, and from
> arbitration, which takes place when the contestants agree
> to refer the dispute to an independent tribunal and consent
> beforehand to abide by its award, though it possesses no
> power to compel obedience to its decision. There can be
> no intervention without, on the one hand, the presence of
> force, naked or veiled, and on the other hand, the absence
> of consent on the part of both the combatants. There have
> been instances where one party to the dispute has asked for
> the intervention of a third power; but if both parties agree in
> such a request, the interference ceases to be intervention and
> becomes mediation.
>
> —Thomas J. Lawrence,
> *The Principles of International Law*, 1911

THIS CHAPTER SETS the international context necessary to grasp why humanitarian intervention emerged as a particular kind of intervention and why this international practice took place in a particular geographical area, the Ottoman Empire (the target state), and geopolitical context, when Ottoman Christians were victims of massacre, atrocities, and extermination.

The nineteenth-century international system was answerable to the European powers' *directoire*, which, as historian Bruno Arcidiacono puts it, was an international legal order founded on a substantive principle of legitimacy where peace would be guaranteed by a particular group of states, the "great powers."[1] The ideas behind the *directoire* persisted in the more modest system known as the European Concert, which indicated the propensity of the European powers to consult in order to settle their divergent ambitions and aims. The European Concert was a European order that went beyond the system of weights and counterweights. It was the result of a transitory, conservative, and antirevolutionary consensus among the great powers deriving from the willingness to maintain peace among them and to accept diplomacy as the means to manage crises that might jeopardize peace, but it was not a jungle. European states did agree to use their sovereign rights in a system limited by a whole series of complex balances, by international law, by common diplomatic procedures, by common civilization and values.[2] The Ottoman Empire would formally become a member of the Concert of Europe after the Crimean War (1854–56). Its participation in the Concert was submitted to fulfill certain clauses in the Paris Treaty, which terminated that war. The participation of the Sublime Porte in the Concert lasted only from 1856 to 1878, and during these two decades the European powers intervened twice on grounds of humanity, in two different Ottoman provinces: Syria (1860–61) and Crete (1866–68). With some notable interruptions during the Crimean War and the 1870–71 Franco-Prussian War, Concert diplomacy materially assisted the maintenance of peace until 1908, when the creation of two blocs, the Triple Entente (Great Britain, France, and Russia) and the Triple Alliance (Germany, Austria-Hungary, and Italy), hindered the Concert from functioning.

Great powers regarded themselves as the guardians of peace in Europe and assumed responsibility for the maintenance of order within their neighboring states. The Concert was defined by five rules: (1) only the five great powers, the pentarchy, should decide great European questions, the Eastern Question included; (2) no power should wage war in Europe for territorial gain or promote revolution or unrest within another great power's territory or sphere of vital interest, even in the Ottoman Empire; (3) no international question of vital interest to a great power could be raised without its consent; (4) if a major problem did arise, no powers could refuse an international conference or exclude any other great power from it; and (5) direct challenges and confrontations between great powers had to be avoided at all costs—mainly by referring the quarrel to the Concert.[3] Since decisions had to be voluntary, unanimity rather than majority rule prevailed in European meetings, certainly in those regarding the Eastern Question. A legitimate settlement of any question was impossible if one of the great powers declined to accept it. Collective decisions required elaborate and lengthy preparations.

In this chapter I first examine the term "intervention," by which, in the context of nineteenth-century international affairs, European governments meant an often hybrid politico-military process, a coercive and nonrequested political and/or forcible action of some kind by an outside state (or states), laying at the intersection between peace and war. Then I provide a brief overview of the history of the Eastern Question, the question of the survival or the death of the "sick Man of Europe," and contextualize the meaning of "massacre," "atrocities," and "extermination."[4] I also differentiate between the Capitulations and intervention. The former were special commercial, legal, and religious favors originally granted to the Europeans by the Ottoman sultans in an era when there was no difference between Muslim and civil law in the Ottoman Empire. They allowed extraterritoriality for foreign merchants in Ottoman territory, who could organize themselves according to their own laws, except where disputes arose with Ottomans, and as long as their behavior was not offensive to Muslims. The capitulatory system of legal and economic privileges for citizens of the Christian powers and their Christian clients living in the Islamic state would become a thorn in the Ottoman side, a prime symbol of external interference, compromising Ottoman sovereignty and helping to drive a wedge between Muslims and Christians.[5] The existence of the Capitulations signaled the incompleteness of Ottoman sovereignty in European eyes and in legal fact. We shall see to what extent military interventions against massacre built on the Capitulations.

THE CONCEPT AND PRACTICE OF INTERVENTION IN NINETEENTH-CENTURY INTERNATIONAL RELATIONS

Since at least the Congress of Vienna, European statesmen distinguished the concept and practice of intervention from an act of war. The Holy Alliance of 1815 put forward the principle of armed intervention in the internal affairs of other sovereign states to restore legitimate monarchs thrown out by insurgents. When late-nineteenth-century legal scholars looked back at the nineteenth-century *historique de l'intervention*, they mentioned the anchoring of warships at visible distance off the shores of the target state or naval blockade. They disagreed on some aspects related to the practice of intervention, though there was wide consensus on the intervention being a coercive action, limited in scope and duration.[6] Cases of intervention encompassed actions to enforce treaty rights and obligations; to prevent hostile acts; to preserve the balance of power; to maintain or establish political institution; to prevent intolerance and anarchy, and to enforce reparation for injury to life and property.[7]

In 1860, by the word "intervention," British international legal scholar Montagu Bernard meant the interference, forcible or supported by force, of one independent state in the internal affairs of another. The views of Bernard on intervention were based on the jurisprudence and the history of European powers' relations of the previous fifty years. In his view, intervention was an exceptional circumstance. The fundamental principle of international relations was the principle of nonintervention, which precisely forbade interference in the internal affairs of a sovereign state. By the internal affairs of a state, Bernard meant its legislation and government, so far as they concerned other states or their subjects.[8] Bernard's definition was widely shared by other prominent lawyers such as T. J. Lawrence (see the epigraph at the beginning of this chapter). European statesmen and international lawyers acknowledged that an extensive use of forcible intervention could disrupt the international system. For that reason they viewed armed intervention as an exceptional occurrence and referred to it with the utmost circumspection, fearing that at any moment an intervention might degenerate into a war.

By 1815 European publicists spoke of states or nations as legal and political bodies that governed a people, principally according to the concept of the national state, with a defined territory and ruled by sovereign state power.[9] By sovereignty nineteenth-century Europeans meant the possession by a European country of the recognized trappings of independent statehood and immunity from outside scrutiny or sanction. The *pendant* to the principle of sovereignty was the rule of nonintervention in the affairs reserved exclusively to a state's competence through the threat or use of armed force. This principle, largely developed by Vattel in the mid-eighteenth century, also encompassed every other form of compulsion that crossed over the boundaries of what was legally permissible with respect to the competences of another state, whether involving economic, financial, or other means.

In principle, European governments respected other European states' sovereignty and the principle of mutual nonintervention in each other's internal affairs. In the European multipolar international system, intervention took place when the major powers were in agreement. Major powers were moved by a variety of considerations, not uniquely determined by the balance of power.[10] On the one hand, states intervened in the internal affairs of their neighbors (especially "small" states) because they feared that domestic developments elsewhere could undermine their own security, either by increasing the chance of interstate conflict or by undermining the legitimacy of their own regimes. The military interventions of the Holy Alliance after 1815 were determined precisely by these fears. Contemporaries—including the British government, which harshly contested the legality and legitimacy of this kind of military operation—did not view these interventions as wars (and never labeled them "humanitarian").[11] On the other hand, values related only loosely to material or security interests prompted states to pressure others to change the way in which they treated their own subjects or citizens, as in the case of Great Britain's commitment to the abolition of the slave trade.[12] The slave trade did not in any direct way threaten the political or territorial integrity of Britain, yet British governments committed treasure, arms, and lives to secure its total abolition.

The early-nineteenth-century police actions of the British navy to end the slave trade—whose ambiguous aims were outlined in the introduction—contrast with the willingness of European great powers' governments not to undertake coercive actions in each other's metropolitan and colonial territories to change the way they treated their subjects or citizens. After the Napoleonic wars, in order to maintain peace, the European governments ruled out the possibility of any exception to the principle of nonintervention, whether to prevent intolerance and anarchy or to enforce reparation for injury to life and property. So when massacre took place within the boundaries of one or the other European powers, no military intervention followed. This happened when Russian authorities brutally repressed Catholic Poles' insurrections in the 1830s and 1860s, when pogroms of Jews took place in the late nineteenth and early twentieth centuries, when tens of thousands of women and children died from disease and hunger in British Boer War concentration camps in 1901, and when the German authorities suppressed the Herero rebellion in the colony of South West Africa by a deliberate policy of tribal extermination through relocation, resulting in over sixty thousand deaths.

The nineteenth-century international system and international law established a discriminatory hierarchy between European and non-European states based on the principle of the alleged superiority of European civilization with respect to all others. The sacrosanct norm of nonintervention in the internal affairs of a sovereign state applied only to the European "civilized" nations. European states, along with the United States, represented the community of "civilized states," which enjoyed full membership in the so-called Family of Nations (these are concepts further explored in chapter 2). Non-European states, the Ottoman Empire included, were not members of the club of civilized nations. The Ottoman Empire was beyond the pale of civilization; in the view of the European governments it was a barbarous or, at best, half-civilized state whose sovereignty the Europeans neither recognized nor respected, not even during the period 1856–79, when it was admitted to the Concert of Europe. If the rule of nonintervention in a state's internal affairs did not apply to uncivilized states, when, how, and for what reasons did the European powers allow themselves to intervene militarily within an uncivilized state's borders? In the view of civilized Europeans, did events that "shock the conscience of mankind," such as massacre, atrocities, and extermination of fellow Christians, give them a right (legal? moral?) to undertake a humanitarian intervention?

The Eastern Question

During the second half of the eighteenth century, the Ottoman Empire showed remarkable military weakness and even impotence in the face of Russian expansionism and later, when, in 1798, a French expeditionary corps commanded by Napoleon invaded, occupied, and governed Egypt.[13] It was a squadron of the Royal Navy commanded by Horatio Nelson that eventually forced the French to leave Egypt; it had become clear that not only could a European power come and act at will in some Ottoman lands, but only another European power force them to leave. The "terror of the world" had turned into a weak, vulnerable state, which could nonetheless threaten peace in Europe because of its internal disorder. Throughout the nineteenth century the European powers feared that the implosion of the Ottoman Empire might give rise to a general war in Europe caused by the division of its spoils, and they assumed that for the sake of peace it was far better to keep the empire alive (though not necessarily intact). The European powers frequently intervened in the Ottoman Empire for reasons exclusively related to the maintenance of international peace.

For instance, in October 1831 Mohamed Ali of Egypt—a formal vassal of the sultan—dispatched an army under the command of his son Ibrahim into Syria, an Ottoman province. Ibrahim defeated the Ottoman Army and entered Anatolia, where his advance was stopped by a military intervention of Russia and Austria. Sultan Mahmud signed the Convention of Kuthaya (April—May 1833), granting the Egyptian ruler possession of the Syrian provinces and the district of Adana for life. The reward for Russian support was the Treaty of Hunkiar Iskelesi (Unkiar Skelessi), which committed Russia and the Ottoman Empire to render substantial aid and assistance to one another, in the event of an attack on either, and the closure of the straits to foreign warships. In 1839 Sultan Mahmud sent an army into Anatolia; the Egyptian Army defeated it once again. The European powers intervened in July 1840 and signed the London Convention for the Pacification of the Levant. Mohamed Ali was offered the hereditary possession of Egypt and the administration of southern Syria for life in return for his submission to the sultan and the return of the Ottoman fleet, which he refused. British and Austrian fleets imposed a strict blockade on Syria and Lebanon and bombarded Beirut. On October 10–11, 1840, an Anglo-Turkish force, supported by Lebanese rebels, defeated the Egyptians. The British fleet was then dispatched to Alexandria, and Mohamed Ali was obliged to agree to an armistice. The above-mentioned interventions were intended to support and strengthen the Ottoman government. Other interventions took place within the boundaries of the Ottoman Empire against the government of Constantinople and on behalf of Ottoman Christian populations when massacres and atrocities took place.

Throughout the nineteenth century the five European powers saw the Ottoman Empire as an appendix to Europe, subordinated to a more or less restricted tutelage they had put in place (the degree of subordination obviously varied throughout the century, and the preeminent role of the various European powers with respect to Ottoman internal affairs varied as well). To prevent what the Europeans perceived as chaos, anarchy, and disorder generated by internal disturbances, which might have brought war in Europe, the powers considered a range of solutions. Among them was the dismemberment of the Ottoman Empire, a purely theoretical solution. It was nonviable for the simple reason that according to the vast majority of European leaders from 1815 to 1914, this dismemberment would have certainly led to a general war.

A second, less radical solution was the expulsion of the Turks from Europe. Early nineteenth-century European political thinkers and policy-makers such as Benjamin Constant and René de Chateaubriand supported this solution to the Eastern Question. In 1824 the British ambassador, Stratford Canning, professed a secret wish that the expulsion of the Turks "bags and baggage" from Europe might become a possibility, in terms identical to those used later by William Gladstone.[14] During the 1830s Alphonse de Lamartine argued that the Porte should be deprived of its European possessions.[15] And, according to French prime minister François Guizot: "The Turks will go out of Europe. The Christian faith and Christian civilization will not give up their expansive energy." That day "would be a triumph for humanity."[16] Similarly, John Bright, who was as virulently anti-Turkish as his radical fellow Richard Cobden, viewed the "perpetual maintenance of the most immoral and filthy of all despotism" and the necessity of "permanently upholding the Mahometan rule in Europe" as an absurdity.[17] In 1858, in the midst of the "Danubian Principalities Question," Gladstone argued in the House of Commons that "the Mahometan Power in Europe" could not "be permanently maintained." He wished the political decease of the Ottoman Empire through a gentle euthanasia, by helping Ottoman subject populations, as opportunity arose, to obtain that measure of freedom and self-government that would enable them to occupy the territory of the Turks when their reign came to an end.[18]

From the perspective of the European political elites, the problem of this solution of the Eastern Question was that it seemed to increase rather than diminish the likelihood of destabilizing the European system. Moreover, influential Europeans on the spot often viewed Ottoman Christians as being as "barbarian" and unfit for self-government as their Muslim "oppressors." In 1860 the French ambassador at Constantinople, Charles Lavalette, stated that the Ottoman Christians were not ready for self-government and that once the Ottomans disappeared they would start four-century-old quarrels all over again.[19] Throughout the century the favorite option of many European policy-makers remained an increased autonomy of the provinces of the empire on the model of Samos,[20] Lebanon, and Crete. The defeat of the Ottoman Empire in the Russo-Turkish War of 1877 and the resolutions of the 1878 Treaty of Berlin accelerated the loss of territories. By 1908 the Ottoman Empire had lost all its European territories, with the exception of the Albanian and Macedonian provinces. It was only after 1878 that independence replaced autonomy in the writings of a younger generation of European thinkers and policy-makers as a solution of the Eastern Question.[21] The creation of nation-states in the Balkans in 1878 and at the turn of the century had not much to do with the European powers' enthusiasm about the extension of nationalism to the Balkan peoples. In the view of the European powers, independence would provide a group of client states whose stabilization under the supervision and control of the European states would ensure peace and tranquillity in Europe.

A third possible solution to the Eastern Question was the introduction of general political, administrative, and economic reforms in the Ottoman Empire. During the early to mid-nineteenth century, some Europeans thought that the empire could and should be reformed. The idea of reforming the Ottoman Empire as a way of solving the Eastern Question coincided with the period of the *Tanzimat*, a word that in Turkish means reorganization or reform. The *Tanzimat* were a series of laws promulgated by the Ottoman government between 1839 and 1876 and intended to improve efficiency in governance, centralization, uniformity, and professionalism of the central and peripheral administration of the empire. Europeans used *Tanzimat* to mean a whole movement of reforms, including reforms of the Ottoman Army, changes in Ottoman diplomatic procedures, reforms in the administrative machinery of the state, attempts at introducing equal individual citizenship under secular law, and representative government. European governments interpreted the *Tanzimat* as a drive initiated and backed by them to import western European models of government that would improve and "civilize" the Ottoman Empire.[22] Thanks to the implementation of these packages of political, administrative, and economic reforms aimed at establishing "good government" (which should not be confused with an attempt at exporting democracy or a democratic regime), the empire would march "toward civilization," guaranteeing that no further threats to the European system would come from its provinces.[23]

The two major decrees of the *Tanzimat* were the 1838 *Hatt-i Cherif of Gülhane* and the 1856 *Hatt-i Hümayun*, both drawn up in the reign of Sultan Abdul Mejid. The latter decree was a restatement of the values of the former. It went considerably further in its rhetoric of interreligious equality and secularization and its view of a new form of inclusive common identity—patriotic Ottomanism—to replace the traditional theocratic order among the sultan's subjects. The 1856 decree stated that Muslims and non-Muslims should be equal in terms of military service and in the administration of justice and taxation, as well as in entry to schools and public employment. It also stipulated the need for proper adherence to annual budgets of banks, use of European skills and capital, and codification of penal and commercial law. Both decrees were issued in the context of international strife, the first after the Egyptian crisis of the 1830s and the second at the end of the Crimean War. As Bloxham puts it, while sincere in their intent, both had aspects of a public-relations exercise, for it was essential for the Ottoman Empire to retain the support of the European powers to balance Russian influence. Reforms for Christians were vital to this end, though within the empire and the Ottoman elite there was a tension between the need to reform and the desirability of greater equality between Muslim and non-Muslims, and between the need to adapt to the demands of external powers and the desire to retain internal sovereignty.[24]

Whatever the European cure for the "sick Man of Europe" was, the vast majority of European reform schemes was centered on two main points: to rule responsibly in the interest of the governed and to improve the welfare of all subjects, Muslim and Christian alike, by protecting all persons and properties and introducing equality between Ottoman subjects. In the view of Europeans, the Ottoman ruling elites had to become sufficiently responsible for carrying out their imperial duties. This in turn would allow the central government to more effectively control the empire's provinces and generate a virtuous circle beneficial for the local population, for the central government insofar as it would have brought internal order and stability, and ultimately for Europe too. The Europeans attached particular importance to the abolition of the *millet* system,[25]which most saw as a discriminatory and barbarous system that denied the very basic rights of humanity and wanted replaced by the western European concept of political citizenship. Plans Europeans generally put forward recommended that the Ottoman government assume its ruling authority by centralizing administration of the empire, separating the executive power and the administration of justice, securing the jurisdiction of tribunals, and introducing free trade and religious tolerance.

The 1876 massacre of Rumelian Christians, known as the Bulgarian atrocities, became a turning point in the history of the Eastern Question. The 1875–78 "Eastern crisis" convinced the majority of European policy-makers and political elites that the Ottoman Empire was "unreformable." This crisis increased the mistrust of Sultan Abdul Hamid II, the Ottoman elites, and Muslim populations in general toward the Europeans. For impoverished Muslims in both the Anatolian and Arab provinces, the promises of equality emanating from the central government seemed hollow as they witnessed their Christian neighbors continuing to make economic and educational advances, with little corresponding improvement in their own lot.[26] For the Christian elites (at least those in the Balkan area who remained under direct Ottoman rule), the idea of an Ottoman citizenship was no longer a political option that they would seriously consider. The failure of the 1876 constitution to broker a compromise granting cultural and political rights to the various minority religious communities in return for their loyalty to sultan and empire marked the end of the *Tanzimat*.

By the 1880s many Europeans thought that the constitution and the earlier reforms were nothing but diplomatic subterfuges, intended to deceive foreigners while changing nothing in the empire. As European statesmen, diplomats, and observers assessed the lamentable failure of reforms, they focused particularly on the results of centralization and on the failed attempts to achieve equality between Muslims and Christians. In his influential study on the *Tanzimat*, Edouard Engelhardt stated that the Ottoman reforms had been unsuccessful, as had been the gradual application of the principle of equality for Ottoman Muslims and Christians.[27] The Ottoman government, he claimed, had failed to secularize the state and to emancipate it from Islam's "*doctrine primitives.*"[28] Engelhardt argued that once secularization of the state had failed, all other reforms were similarly doomed. The failure of the reforms meant that the Ottoman Empire was virtually at war with Christianity.[29] Refusing the help of "a friendly and powerful friend (France)," the Ottoman government had shown it remained a "*société asiatique*": immutable, idle, and despotic.[30] Toward the end of the century, both

east and west of Constantinople the issue of Christian reactions to Ottoman reforms became complicated because of the growth of nationalist
movements. When, in 1908, the Young Turks reinstated the 1876 constitution with its provisions for equal citizenship, many thought that a
new era of *fraternité* had started. These happy days, for all sides, were
short-lived.

It should be noted that in their analyses of the state of the Ottoman
Empire, Europeans failed to grasp how deeply the empire changed ad-
ministratively, economically, and politically during the mid-nineteenth
century. They also failed to acknowledge that nineteenth-century sultans and Ottoman ruling classes wanted to strengthen their empire,
and that they were keenly aware of the power, wealth, and progress
of Europe in comparison to themselves. It is true that the reforms, as
conceived by the Ottoman authorities, were certainly intended to prevent European interference and to provide a way to attain international
recognition, but they were also serious attempts at introducing western European political governance, laws, education, and equal rights
and duties for all subjects, no matter what race or creed, to the central and provincial administration of the empire. Moreover, European
governments focused on the mistreatment of Ottoman Christians while
largely ignoring the conditions of Ottoman Muslims—both those living
in the empire and those living in the autonomous provinces or newly
independent Balkan states. As the next section discusses, they ignored
the abuses of the Capitulations and the increase in the number of European protégés as factors that might have explained both the failure of
the reforms and the concerns of Muslim populations.[31] Finally, Europeans forgot that Ottoman Christians often came to serve as convenient
scapegoats for the anger that the Ottoman Muslims could only rarely
express against the Europeans themselves.

European leaders and diplomats saw the Ottoman Empire as an empire whose political and administrative organization was in the main
imperial, consisting of a center and provinces, ruling vast areas and
numerous communities of different religions and customs. The Europeans wanted the Ottoman government to rule over its people in the
same "enlightened" way they ruled their colonies. They did not think
that in the short or medium term the empire could become a constitutional monarchy or a representative government, which they viewed as
the best form of government for "civilized" nations, a designation they
declined to give to the empire and its nations.[32] The kind of government
that European experts and policy-makers felt best suited the Ottoman
Empire was a "proconsular despotism."[33] This kind of despotism was
"benevolent," for contrary to Oriental despotism (see chapter 2), it was
informed by concepts such as "public good," "general interest," and
the "rule of law."[34] As John Stuart Mill wrote about British colonies,

benevolent despotism was justified on the grounds that it was necessary to undermine existing, oppressive political structures and social hierarchies, and because the rational capacities of individuals in barbarous societies were so immature that they were incapable of being "guided to their improvement by conviction or persuasion."[35] According to Mill, despotism was a legitimate mode of government in dealing with "barbarians," provided the end was their improvement. As soon as humankind was sufficiently improved, compulsion was no longer admissible. We shall see that the alleged failure to enforce "good government" reforms figured prominently among the factors Europeans put forward to explain the recurrence of massacre and atrocities and the need to intervene to end the killing of innocent people. The alleged failure to enforce reforms also justified in European eyes the maintenance of the Capitulations, another manifestation of the powers' interference in the internal affairs of the Ottoman Empire.

THE CAPITULATIONS

Long before the nineteenth century, the papacy recognized France's diplomatic and extraterritorial privileges, and France became the intermediary in papal contacts with the Porte.[36] Furthermore, France became the protector of the Ottoman Catholics, the Maronite communities of Lebanon, and the Eastern Christian communities of the Ottoman Empire (the Uniate Churches that corresponded to each of the Eastern Churches and allowed converts to practice their traditional rites and liturgical languages, only introducing necessary modifications for conformity with Catholic doctrine). Russia challenged France's preeminence and claimed the right to protect the empire's Orthodox Christians after the Treaty of Küçük Kaynarca in 1774.[37] During the nineteenth century Great Britain became the protector of both the Protestants and Jews of the Ottoman Empire. At the same time the Capitulations became one of the main grounds for European powers' interference in Ottoman internal affairs. Every renewal of the Capitulations broadened the powers' scope for interference until the religious concessions became the foundation upon which the Europeans developed an internationally recognized protectorate of the Christians both in and of the Ottoman Empire.

The Capitulations became a perfect example of European imperialism because religious and ethnoreligious affinities were manipulated to promote and sustain great-power interests in the Ottoman Empire.[38] In 1853 the tsar sent a mission to Constantinople to press for a rectification of recent Ottoman concessions to Latin Christians and their French patrons. Russia insisted on being given unprecedented rights, not simply as regards clergy and places of worship, but with respect to the substantial body of Orthodox believers as a whole. The Ottoman government called for support from the British and French governments, both of which viewed Russian expansionism with considerable alarm. This quarrel, which originated because of an issue related to Russia's alleged right of intervention on behalf of Orthodox Christians as whole, eventually led to the Crimean War. The defeat of Russia resulted in the entrustment of the destinies of the Ottoman Christians to the Concert of Europe. Were nineteenth-century humanitarian interventions the continuation of the Capitulations by other means? Were they the logical consequence of the European powers' protectorate on Ottoman Christians?

The dragoman of the French Embassy in Constantinople, Georges Outrey, admitted that to some extent the origins of humanitarian interventions could be found in the Capitulations system. Outrey admitted that the Eastern Question was born as a religious question and turned into a political question still intimately connected to its religious aspects. Since the beginning of the nineteenth century, Outrey argued, foreign intervention on behalf of Ottoman Christians, which at its origin was based on "*concession particulières*" (i.e., the Capitulations), transformed itself into something different, a "humanitarian intervention."[39] However, as he explained in an unpublished study from 1898, the religious protectorate and the protection of Ottoman Christians were not the same thing. The first was determined by the "special privileges" of the Capitulations. The second kind of protection France and other European powers afforded Ottoman Christians was based on a system of collective intervention by the European powers—which Outrey refers to as " the right of intervention in Turkey"—put into place to guarantee the general protection of the Ottoman Christians. Humanitarian interventions were the consequence of a "gross violations of the rights of humanity" (*violation énorme des droits de l'humanité*).

The Capitulations and intervention against massacre in the Ottoman Empire shared the idea of protecting Christians ruled by a "despotic" and "barbarian" government. The Capitulations were supposed to guarantee security and avoid discrimination against European nationals and protégés in ordinary times. Interventions against massacre were supposed to protect an entire Ottoman Christian community from becoming victims of massacre and atrocities at exceptional times. The occurrence of massacres reinforced the idea held by European diplomats and policy-makers that as long as the Ottoman Empire remained "uncivilized," unable to protect the rights of European residents and European protégés, the Capitulations should be maintained or even broadened.[40] On various occasions, those who campaigned in favor of armed intervention to end massacre, and who often made use of the rhetoric of the Crusades, interpreted the Capitulations as a guarantee of protection of fellow Christians from the "infidel" encompassing a right of humanitarian intervention.[41] In exceptional times of massacre, however, both policy-makers and European diplomats were cautious and refrained from claiming that the Capitulations gave a right of interference in the Ottoman Empire's internal affairs to protect Ottoman Christians. International legal scholars did not see the Capitulations as the legal ground giving the European states a right to intervene upon grounds of humanity. As British legal scholar Robert Phillimore put it, the question of a right of "religious intervention" in the affairs of "an Infidel State on behalf either of Christians *generally*, or of a *particular* body of Christians" did not exist.[42] European international legal scholars as well as policy-makers were fully aware that the nature of the protection the Capitulations offered to specific groups or individuals had nothing to do with undertaking a military intervention on their behalf.[43] Furthermore, whereas the Capitulations were unilateral, diplomatic, nonforcible acts, humanitarian interventions were coercive, often armed, and generally collective actions. The Capitulations were mainly intended to protect nationals living abroad and groups of local protégés, whereas humanitarian intervention was intended to end massacre. The Capitulations—and more particularly the abuses the Europeans made out of these treaties—were the consequence of European imperial rivalries and one of many means to increase the political, cultural, religious, and economic influence of a single power in a given area of the Ottoman Empire, whereas collective humanitarian undertakings in which each power exerted some control on the others hindered the clear appearance of self-interest.

MASSACRE, ATROCITY, AND EXTERMINATION

Nineteenth-century European governments and cultivated elites used the term "massacre" to indicate the loss of innocent human lives on a vast scale caused by a deliberate act.[44] Massacre was an exceptional event, a violent action, though contemporaries did not consider all violence as massacre. It was generally a collective form of action, involving the destruction of noncombatants—men, women, children, or disarmed soldiers. Massacre was a one-sided affair, and those slaughtered were generally perceived as victims or innocents. A massacre implied the death of many people and was distinguished from natural disasters in that the former was understood as an organized process of destruction of civilian lives and properties.[45] The authorities of a state and its agents could directly perpetrate a massacre and could also be unwilling to put an end to massacre or unable to prevent its repetition. In a multi-ethnic state such as the Ottoman Empire, the perpetrators of a massacre could act against a minority for political or religious reasons. During the nineteenth century European political and cultivated elites used the term "massacre" in combination with "atrocity" and, sometimes, "horror." By atrocity, Europeans meant deliberate acts of violence (generally against innocent civilian populations) such as rape, pillage, slaughtering people, burning villages, and destroying religious buildings.

The term "extermination" deserves particular attention. Since 1945 extermination has been intrinsically related to the concept of genocide—a word coined by Raphel Lemkin during 1943–44—which refers to the "intent to destroy" and "deliberately inflict on a human group a condition of life calculated to bring about its physical destruction in whole or in part."[46] During the nineteenth century the word "extermination" (as well as "war of extermination") had a polysemic meaning. It was a synonym of massacre and of the Latin word *exterminare*, by which Europeans meant to extirpate, expel, remove, or displace indigenous populations, usually to allow for the settlement of European colonies. The sense of extermination often approximated a term we use today: "ethnic cleansing," which is clearly an anachronism as far as the nineteenth century is concerned.[47] However, some nineteenth-century authors used extermination to mean something very close to an act of genocide.

Agreeing with both historian Norman Naimark and sociologist Michael Mann, I argue that ethnic cleansing and genocide are two different activities, intentionality being the critical distinction. In the case of genocide, a qualitative threshold is crossed: the aim of genocide is to *"purify and destroy."*[48] The intention of ethnic cleansing is to remove a people and often all traces of them from a specific territory.[49] The goal, in other words, is to get rid of the "alien" nationality, ethnic group, or religious group and seize control of the territory they formerly inhabited.[50] It is unclear whether European political elites connoted extermination with the "intent to destroy." For instance, Lord Palmerston found it inconceivable that the Russian government intended to destroy the whole Polish nation in 1836. On April 20 of that year he wrote:

What I, on the occasion [of Russia's power to exterminate a kingdom, the kingdom of Poland] referred to, said, was this—that it was impossible for Russia to exterminate, nominally or physically, a nation—I did not say kingdom. A kingdom is a political body, and may be destroyed; but a nation is an aggregate body of men; and what I stated was, that if Russia did entertain the project, which many thinking people believe she did, of exterminating the Polish nation, she entertained what is hopeless to accomplish, because it was impossible to exterminate a nation, especially a nation of so many millions of men as the Polish kingdom, in its divided state.[51]

As we shall see, however, many pamphleteers, campaigners, and even diplomats on the spot seemed to refer to extermination as an act of genocide. In their view, the objective of a massacre was to destroy all members of a group, including children, to kill an entire community without allowing even the chance to flee, or to slaughter them after deportation. In fact, sometimes the word "annihilation" was used, as in the case of the Ottoman Armenians during the 1890s and early 1900s.[52] Some (not all) European observers and diplomats sometimes applied the word "annihilation" to mean precisely the "intent to destroy" a whole community carried out by local populations and Ottoman authorities with (and without) the consent of the sultan. As far as the Ottoman government and authorities are concerned, it seems to me that massacres were not acts *génocidaires*.[53]

It should be noted that nineteenth-century humanitarian interventions were sometimes followed by plans to remove the offensive civilian populations. Sometimes the intervening states recommended that the authorities of the target state enforce the removal of populations as a way to avoid the repetition of massacre. These plans and actual policies did not have the full consent and approval of the removed population, very often a Muslim religious minority.[54] Europeans believed that the removal of a population, especially of Muslim religious communities, and the creation of more homogeneous religious or, sometimes, ethnic groups were a solution that would avoid the recurrence of massacre. We shall see how humanitarian interventions related to the emergence of nationalism, for intervention affected both the target state and the populations on behalf of whom the intervention had been undertaken. Furthermore, in the European account of massacres, Muslims always killed Christians, and the fact that Orthodox Greeks, Lebanese Maronites, Bulgarians, Christian Cretans, or Macedonians killed Muslims seldom entered into the equation. Neither did the Europeans note that "the persistent and widespread nature of such atrocities, not only in the Balkans but in other areas of the Ottoman Empire, was, in large part, due to the destabilising interference of the Great Powers."[55]

During the nineteenth century extinction rather than extermination most closely approximated today's meaning of the term "genocide." Europeans used the term "extinction" most frequently with respect to their overseas colonies—for instance, British settlers and the British government used the term in reference to Australian Aborigines. Neither the term nor the act of extinction was condemned or viewed as an appalling crime, unlike in the second half of the twentieth century. The extinction of a "savage" community did not inordinately shock nineteenth-century European statesmen and the public's conscience. With few exceptions, many Europeans considered the extinction of a human community, such as the Aborigines of Tasmania (Van Diemen's Land), to be the "natural" consequence of contact between the "civilized" and the "savage." The extinction of "savage" races had its justification in the view that the savages would soon depart the Earth as a matter of course, unable to adapt to a "superior" civilization and undeserving of normative ethical consideration. No amount of humanitarian sentiment or scientific expertise, even when supported by the correct political will, could come to the rescue of doomed savage communities. Even the most ardent humanitarians could speak only of preventing future violence and of "saving by civilizing the sad remnants of the dying races."[56] Amerindian tribes, as the Tocqueville specialist Jennifer Pitts notes, had either to accept European ways and survive or reject them and accept inevitable extinction.[57] In the perception of the nineteenth-century intervening states, a conspicuous difference existed between the death by allegedly "natural" causes of the Aborigines or Amerindians and the massacre and atrocity of other populations perpetrated by the authorities of the state or by other groups or communities living in that state as a consequence of the inability or unwillingness of these authorities to protect the victims. Especially when the victims were Christians under the rule of an "uncivilized" state, the European powers considered the possibility of undertaking a humanitarian intervention.

.　.　.

The history of the international practice of humanitarian intervention runs parallel to the history of the European account of the failure of Ottoman reforms and of the Eastern Question. This study will show that the European powers intervened militarily on grounds of humanity only on behalf of the Ottoman Christians.[58] The fact that such interventions took place for only a restricted portion of humanity does not make them less humanitarian, at least as long as one finds evidence of a genuine humanitarian motivation triggering them. What remains to be seen is whether saving Ottoman Christians was the unintended consequence of military operations aimed at preserving European stability and the international system by restoring law and order in one or the other disturbed Ottoman province. One also has to assess the European powers' self-interests at the time of intervention and the extent to which they sought individual profit, prestige, imperial expansion, and containment of other powers' regional ambitions.

Before dealing with these issues, I examine the legal doctrines of humanitarian intervention, which were developed in the second half of the century when skepticism about the success of the *Tanzimat* rose after massacre of Ottoman Christians in the Morea (1821–33), Lebanon and Syria (1860–61), Crete (1866–67), Bosnia (1875), and Bulgaria (1876). After these doctrines were elaborated, no humanitarian intervention took place. This is only an apparent paradox, for after 1878 the international system and the political situation in the Balkans and the Ottoman Empire changed so as to hinder humanitarian interventions from taking place even when, as in the case of the Armenians, massacres and atrocities took place on an unprecedented scale.

CHAPTER TWO

Exclusion of the Ottoman Empire from the Family of Nations, and Legal Doctrines of Humanitarian Intervention

> Il est des excès de sauvagerie qui apparaissent intolérables
> à la conscience des peuples européens, formés dans le culte
> de la morale et du droit; ces derniers estimeront toujours
> qu'ils ont non seulement le droit, mais encore le devoir
> d'empêcher de tels écarts, et que c'est pour eux la plus noble
> mission que de porter un germe de civilisation en terre
> barbare.
>
> —Antoine Rougier, "Théorie de l'intervention
> d'humanité," *Revue Générale du Droit International*, 1910

THIS CHAPTER OFFERS a brief sketch based on nineteenth-century British and French writings, articles, memoirs, journals, pamphlets, and reviews. I do not examine the vast travel literature that certainly contributed to shaping a set of images and perceptions of the Ottomans, nor do I pretend to present a comprehensive survey of the image of Turkey in France and Great Britain or to offer an account of what the Ottoman Empire was like, or even how it was seen by those who actually lived in it. I wish to underline that the image of the Ottoman Empire and that of its Christian populations were far from being monolithic. As Edward Said argues, Europeans generally saw themselves as being essentially rational, developed, humane, superior, authentic, active, creative, and masculine, while throughout the nineteenth century Europeans saw the Ottoman Empire and its inhabitants as irrational, aberrant, backward, crude, despotic, inferior, inauthentic, passive, feminine, and sexually corrupt.[1] Throughout the nineteenth and early twentieth centuries, other images of the Turks—some more positive—also existed but were generally dismissed or ignored.[2]

Many late-nineteenth-century international legal scholars, especially those associated with the Institut de Droit International, had a political agenda and were trying to establish a world order that dispensed with the monarchical conservatism of the old order. Even though their doctrines on intervention considerably diverged, they shared a number of fundamental assumptions. First, to them the Ottoman Empire was a barbarous state; hence from a political, moral point of view the interference in the Sublime Porte's internal affairs and even armed intervention in case of indiscriminate massacres was legitimate. The Ottoman Empire belonged to the uncivilized Orient; it was not a member of the "Family of Nations." Second, for some legal scholars the persistence of discrimination between Christian and Muslim subjects reinforced empathy with mistreated fellow Christians. A minority among them shared with campaigners and protesters the idea of a moral duty to help Ottoman Christians directly through armed intervention rather than indirectly through guidance and support given to the sultan for enforcing reforms. Whereas protesters advocated independence for the Christian or "national community" victims of massacre as the logical consequence of liberation from a barbarous regime, the majority of legal scholars preferred not to engage with the thorny issue of the consequences of an intervention. Some argued that interventions should encompass the enforcement of reforms designed by the intervening states to create a more regulated, ordered, and rational (according to European standards) Ottoman administration and to increase the administrative autonomy of the provinces where a majority of Ottoman Christians lived.

The assumption that Ottoman civilization was fatalistic and stagnant, voiceless, feminine, irrational, despotic, backward, and lacking in European moral character or a fully developed concept of the state did not originate from legal scholars. These views had circulated in Europe since the mid-nineteenth century. European thinkers, diplomats and policy-makers included, determined a standard of civilization. The set of criteria assessing the threshold of civilization varied. Some authors emphasized the relation to the socially dominant modes of theology, ascribed racial characteristics, technological superiority, political institutions, family structure, gender relations, economic success, and individual moral and intellectual capacity, or most often a combination of these. Europeans were the unique judges of the *standard of civilization*: they were in the position to decide how, where, and when to admit an extra-European state to the so-called Family of Nations. The Ottoman Empire was generally excluded from the Family of Nations for several reasons. Most often mentioned were despotism, Islam, polygamy, slavery, a corrupt and inefficient state machinery, inability to reciprocate in legal dealings, and unwillingness or incapacity to reform. After the 1870s European writers also mentioned that the Ottoman Empire was under de facto European tutelage and dispossessed of some of the essential features of sovereignty. These views influenced international legal scholars as they developed their doctrines.

DESPOTISM AND ISLAM

Whether combined or taken individually, despotism and Islam were the two most frequently invoked factors that European legal scholars, diplomats, and political leaders put forward to explain what they saw as Ottoman barbarism and the empire's exclusion from the European Family of Nations. Europeans generally believed Islam to engender despotism or viewed Islam and despotism as being two distinct but typical evils of the Ottoman Empire.

The idea of despotism as a regime hindering progress, and therefore civilization, dated back to the mid-eighteenth century. Montesquieu equated despotism to corruption, stagnation (inability to change and stifling of progress), sterility, absence of independent energy (an essential attribute of liberty) and of free inquiry, dead uniformity, and ignorance.[3] Despotism stifled progress by destroying all groups between the ruler and the mass of the people, the aristocracy included. Many nineteenth-century Western analyses of the state of Ottoman civilization directly or indirectly mentioned Montesquieu's definition of Oriental or Asiatic despotism.[4]

In the early nineteenth century the *secrétaire-interprète* at the French Ministry of Foreign Affairs, Panagiotis Codrika, viewed the Ottoman Empire as immutable in its customs, character, and religious principles.[5] Codrika disputed that the Ottoman Empire was part of Europe; to him it was an alien power as far as its links, customs, and religious principles were not part of the European political system based on Christian institutions. The theocratic and despotic nature of the Ottoman regime made this empire, for Codrika, an enemy of Europe because its aim was to establish a *monarchie universelle* for the propagation of Muslim doctrine, the destruction of all other religions, and the enslavement of the non-Muslim populations.

In 1822 Jean Michel Berton wrote that the Turks gave the rigid precepts of the Koran the mark of their sanguinary ferocity and made Islam the instrument of their despotism and the reason for military anarchy.[6] He viewed the Ottoman Empire as being the antithesis of "civilized" (*policées*) nations; it was a ferocious regime delighting in human hecatombs, extreme violence, and oppression, opposed to the "irresistible progress of human spirit," and despising individual guarantees and the basic human rights of honor, liberty, life and property. The Ottoman Empire was a regime "against nature."[7] Turkey incarnated barbarity;

its government was a *pur accident de la force* and its maintenance an *opprobre pour la civilisation*.

René de Chateaubriand—a traveler, an expert on the "Orient," and French minister of foreign affairs from 1822 to 1824—shared Codrika's and Berton's views on the Ottoman Empire. Chateaubriand was among the leaders of the "crusade" against the powers of Tripoli, Tunis, and Algiers. He cried out for the *droits de l'humanité* and adjured his colleagues in the Chamber of Peers to eradicate white slavery (*la honte de l'Europe*). In the early 1820s he supported the Greek struggle for independence by developing the themes of Christianity oppressed by Islam and of the struggle of Christian civilization against Muslim obscurantism.[8] His *Itinéraire de Paris à Jérusalem et de Jérusalem à Paris*, the account of his travels through Ottoman lands, presented Ottoman civilization as inaccessible, mysterious, fierce, and in decline.[9] Chateaubriand wrote in his *Mémoire sur l'Orient* that the export of modernity and Christianity was doomed to fail because the Ottoman Empire was founded on Islam.[10] He viewed Christianity as liberty and as a peaceful, progressive instrument that led to the improvement of society and to liberation from slavery. Christianity, and Catholicism in particular, was superior to Islam (*la fatalité disciplinée de l'Islam*).[11] Working from these assumptions, Chateaubriand condemned complacency toward the Ottoman Empire, for he believed that it would cause the social destruction inherent in the "Mohammedan" religion to thrive.

In two 1829 essays, *Du développement progressif des idées religieuses* and *De la perfectibilité de l'espèce humaine*, Benjamin Constant, a prominent thinker born in Lausanne and educated in Edinburgh, posited that some non-European societies, such as India, Egypt, Ethiopia, and the Ottoman Empire, were utterly "stagnant." Constant identified four pivotal moments in development of civilization in western Europe: the end of theocracy, the abolition of slavery, the end of feudalism, and the abolition of noble privileges in the French Revolution.[12] Non-Europeans, particularly Muslims, were not concerned by these developments, for Islam condemned people to eternal slavery or incurable stupidity. In an earlier impassioned essay published in 1825, *Appel aux nations chrétiennes en faveur des Grecs*, Constant called for French assistance for the Greeks, frequently referring to Ottoman rule in Greece as an example of the horrors of foreign despotism. Constant depicted the Ottoman conflict with its Greek subjects in apocalyptic language as a battle between Occident and Orient, Christianity and Islam, civilization and barbarism.

By the time of the French landing in Algiers, European commentators often portrayed Islam as a religion inspiring bigotry and fanaticism. By the 1830s the most bigoted Christian stereotypes, accompanied by an equally widespread ignorance and refusal to understand Islam, supplanted the understanding of this religion and civilization.[13]

For Manchester economist and member of Parliament Richard Cobden, Islam was the cause of Ottoman ignorance, barbarism, and poverty. Cobden ascribed the cause of all this decay to the Turkish government—a fierce, unmitigated, sanguinary, and lawless military despotism—allied with the fanaticism of a brutalizing religion, which taught its followers to rely on the sword and to disdain all improvement and labor. In his 1836 treatise *Russia*, Cobden suggested that if Russia ever seized the capital of Turkey, it would improve the situation for the peoples of the Ottoman Empire and bring positive changes to its civilization. At the very least the Russians would remove the slave market, ban polygamy, and defeat the plague.[14] Cobden concluded that a society that comprised the entire civilized world would not include Turkey: "Turkey cannot enter into the political system of Europe; for the Turks are not Europeans."[15]

Islam suffered a particularly bad press in France before, under, and after Napoleon III. French thinkers and other expert on the Ottoman Empire and its civilization portrayed Ottoman society (as well as Algerian society, an ex-Ottoman province) as permeated by religion in all aspects of life: personal, social, and judicial.[16] The French could not conceive of Islam as the unifying bond of this segmented, decentralized society, for in their experience religion had long been a divisive force. The French Revolution had ended the idea of society as a spiritual hierarchy headed by a divinely appointed king and had introduced the concept of a secular state. A society wedded to Islam, portrayed as having no dissenting opinion and ruled according to an immutable law by a divinely appointed sultan, where the Muslim religious authorities owned lands and properties and were exempted from taxes, was the negation of all the French secular values. The direct rule of Algeria would strengthen French prejudices against the Ottomans; the so-called barbarous state of that territory and its peoples proved to the French on the spot and in Paris that the Ottoman Empire was an ancien régime.

Under the Third Republic anticlerics, unbelievers, and many Republican French identified religion with reactionary thought and unscientific attitudes and as a barrier to progress. At the same time a missionary critique of Islam developed, as in the writings of Archbishop Lavigerie against slavery in Algeria. In Great Britain too, after the "Bulgarian horrors" of 1876, a conspicuous literature insisted on the endless evils of Islam. Fanny Janet Blunt pointed out that Islam caused "an astonishing apathy and a total absence of the spirit of inquiry and research with regard to everything."[17] Malcolm MacColl argued that the main cause of

Ottoman barbarism was Islam, "the only religion which declares a war of extermination against the whole non-Mussulman world."[18]

POLYGAMY AND SLAVERY

From the beginning of the nineteenth century, Europeans viewed the character, manners, and social habits of the Ottomans and of their sultans as evidence of the moral decline of the empire, of its incapacity for proper individual and social development, hence of its "barbarism." The contrast between Europe and Asia (and the Ottoman Empire) seemed to be most marked in sexual matters. Some Europeans were convinced that most Muslim men were pederasts and sodomites. The Turks were held to be devotees of impalement, one of the few forms of cruel punishment not practiced in the West. The depictions of this implied both unnatural sex and excessive cruelty.[19] Other Europeans portrayed polygamy as incontrovertible evidence of the barbarous nature of the Ottoman Empire and of its inferior civilization.

Contrary to the supposedly solid basis of interlocking self-interests that supported western European societies, Europeans often portrayed Ottoman society as repressing natural feeling. Instead of the balance guiding Europeans as they strove to achieve and develop a worthy society and civilization, Ottomans supposedly alternated between lifeless conformity and unbridled indulgence. To many European observers, gender relations in Asia seemed utterly bleak in comparison to their own domestic familial affections. In those societies, Europeans argued, women were viewed as corrupted beings and love was pure sensuality without friendship or esteem, whereas Europeans valued the positive influence of feminine society: the high and noble passions that excited humankind to deeds of active patriotism and benevolence, and the softer pleasures that ornamented the social circle, owed their existence to the female presence in society.

Europeans alternatively viewed Ottoman women as slaves, which proved that the Ottoman Empire was uncivilized, or as debauched and vicious, which proved exactly the same thing. Furthermore, Europeans commonly believed that abortion was regularly performed on women. Abortion and sodomy were key factors in European observers' explanations for the decline in the Muslim population of the Ottoman Empire and paved the way for the conviction that power in the empire would ultimately fall to the more prolific Greek and Armenian Christian minorities.[20] Needless to say, the very existence of harems epitomized social decadence.[21] A few European travelers and diplomats pointed out that polygamy was obsolete in some parts of the empire, but the largely prevailing idea was that in the Ottoman Empire there was no middle ground between total repression and unrestrained indulgence, between the eunuch, the harem, and genuine feelings of love and affection.[22]

Corruption and the Absence of a Sound Social Structure

Further reasons for excluding the Ottoman Empire from the Family of Nations were the corruption, incompetence, and inefficiency of Ottoman political bureaucracy and the lack of a sound (i.e., European) social structure founded on a thriving landed aristocracy and/or commercial bourgeoisie.[23]

The famous British ambassador at Constantinople, Stratford Canning, often referred to the "uncivilized Turks" as opposed to "civilized Christians" (and Europeans).[24] In the 1820s he compared and contrasted Britain with an empire whose political system had been worn out by a depreciated currency, disordered financial system, mutinous militia and dilapidated fortresses, decreasing population, and stagnant industry.[25] In his private letters, as well as in his official dispatches, he often mentioned the dirty and foul-smelling streets and alleys; he also noted the ignorance of the people, who were disease-ridden and crawling with vermin. The ambassador depicted Muslim officialdom as corrupt and Ottoman justice and administration as arbitrary and cruel: the Ottoman Empire was "rotten at the heart, the seat of corruption is in the government itself."[26] The theme of the corruption would persist throughout the entire nineteenth century. Half a century later the duke of Argyll, a very good friend of Gladstone, a noted Presbyterian, and a prolific writer on the Eastern Question, continually proclaimed the impossibility of carrying out reforms in the Ottoman Empire, which he viewed as a rotten and corrupted state.[27]

Like Stratford Canning and most British statesmen of his generation, Lord Palmerston viewed the Ottoman Empire as a barbarian, uncivilized, and despotic power.[28] He believed that the British constitution and social system, as they existed in 1830, were the best in the world and profoundly disliked the "lawless" and "arbitrary" power the sultan was thought to have. The (mis)use of power made by the Ottoman government seemed to Palmerston to be the opposite of the constitutional sovereign's power subject to the law, respectful of the privileges of Parliament, and acting on the advice of his minister. As any other British statesman, Palmerston believed in a Parliament in which one House comprised the wealthiest landowners, and he considered the supremacy of the landed aristocracy as essential for the well-being of the country. The Ottoman Empire lacked such an aristocracy and such a House. In his view, the Ottoman landed aristocracy lacked the virtues incarnated and propagated by the British aristocracy.[29] Writing in 1851, after spending the previous year traveling in the European Ottoman provinces, Edmund Spencer described the sultan's government as an anomaly, "the complete antithesis of our governments of western Europe," owing to the "absence of all hereditary rank and property."[30]

Europeans often reported the Ottoman officials' inability to secure landed possessions and to collect taxes effectively. Looking at their colonial experiences and achievements and relying on their liberal credo, Europeans believed that the establishment of the conditions for civilization throughout the empire passed through the construction of modern landed elites and industrious peasantries through the exercise of state power.[31] It is scarcely surprising that the British in particular, who conceived of and understood both their metropolis and the imperial province in a hierarchical fashion, harshly criticized the lack of a powerful and morally preeminent landed aristocracy in the Ottoman Empire. To many European observers the sultans were incapable of being the great unifying force of their empire. They viewed the Ottoman imperial hierarchies as not bound by direct allegiance to the monarch, the Ottoman "proconsuls" as incapable of incorporating local aristocracies into the imperial system, and the empire run by corrupted governors who shamed the name of the sultan and disrespected local (Christian as well as non-Christian) elites.

Authors writing in the late nineteenth century confirmed such "anomalies" of the Ottoman Empire. They insisted on portraying the Ottoman government as having never shown itself earnestly desirous of aiding private enterprise by affording disinterested protection to those individuals and communities willing to improve the state of the economy from within the empire.[32] Henry Richard argued that Ottoman Turks repressed all efforts of the population to rise in intelligence, industry, and wealth. [33] Goldwin Smith described the Ottoman Empire as "one of those military empires that has never become industrial. . . . It has never shown the slightest sign of civilisation—political, intellectual, commercial."[34] Edward A. Freeman contrasted the lethargy of the Turks with the "formidable advances in civilization of the Serbs and Rumanians" since they had been given autonomy.[35]

THE CONDITIONS OF OTTOMAN CHRISTIANS

Another reason Europeans advanced to show the Ottoman Empire's otherness relates to the question of the enforcement of reforms briefly sketched in the previous chapter. As we have seen, for many Europeans the reforms should have been centered on the crucial issue of guaranteeing security of life and property to the empire's Christian subjects. During the early *Tanzimat* period (1840s–1850s) some Europeans believed that the Ottoman Empire could be reformed and might eventually enter the Family of Nations. During the late *Tanzimat* period (1860s) and after the 1878 Congress of Berlin, however, Europeans claimed that the Ottoman government was unable or unwilling to enforce the reforms that would allow it to "march toward civilization." The hope and disillusionment about the capacity of Ottomans to become civilized closely followed these changing views on the possibilities for colonial subjects to be uplifted.

In the early nineteenth century Stratford Canning saw himself as guiding the sultan and teaching him how to introduce and implement the reforms. He saw the absence of laws protecting the life and property of Ottoman Christians as one of the factors determining the Ottoman Empire's status as a barbarous country.[36] His recipe for transplanting civilization into the empire was never properly articulated. Instead, he recommended that the sultan remove every grievance that might occasion rebellion among the Christian populations of the empire, every injustice that might invite foreign intervention, every barbarity that hindered the cordial sympathy of the Porte's Western allies.[37] Canning insisted that Ottoman law courts stop employing brutal violence and torture and accept Christian evidence against Muslims. He wished that aggression and gratuitous outrage against Christians would stop. He suggested that the Ottoman ruling elite enhance the "civilizing process" in the key areas of wealth, education, and granting of Ottoman Christians the place they deserved within the empire's social hierarchy rather than humiliating or constantly debasing them.

For a short time after the decree of *Gülhane* on November 3, 1839, some Europeans thought that it was indeed possible for the Ottoman Empire to become civilized. They highlighted that the decree guaranteed the security of life, honor, and property, called for public trials, and abolished confiscation for all subjects of the sultan as well as vaguely referring to the duty of all Ottoman inhabitants, including the Christians, to serve in the army. The decree established a Supreme Council of Judicial Ordinances charged with creating laws for the security of life and fortune and compiling a penal code. In the early 1840s some Europeans hoped that the millet barriers would eventually be broken down and be replaced by a multinational brotherhood of all Ottoman subjects, introducing the Western concepts of a secularized state and of citizenship. But, as historian Carter Findley notes, in a state that remained officially Islamic and committed to the *shari'ah*, it was no understatement to say that new laws would be required to implement equality between Muslims and non-Muslims.[38] In fact, fierce internal opposition from conservative ministers, provincial governors, ordinary officials, Muslim clergy (*ulemas*), and even the high clergy of the Christian millets hindered the reforms from being carried out. For different reasons these powerful groups opposed the direct relationship between the individual and the state based on rights and obligations that stemmed from the individual's status as citizen of the Ottoman state.[39] When the first, unavoidable disappointments about the implementation of reforms emerged, European writings were quickly pervaded by pessimistic comments on the possibility of success of such a process.

In 1844 Guizot wrote that everywhere in the Ottoman Empire the Turkish tendencies for violence, fanaticism, arbitrariness, and anarchy had not been prevented by the promises of and failed attempts at reforms. Reforms were the result of European constraint or an incoherent and sterile imitation of it. They were not spontaneous attempts on the part of the Ottomans; under those circumstances progress could not be real or durable.[40] Guizot viewed the Ottoman civilization as bound to destroy itself because of its vices. The dismemberment of the empire, which he referred as "*une Pologne musulmane*," would have led to great disorder in Christian Europe. Given the impossibility of curing an empire that would never become part of the European order, Guizot chose to focus on the best policy for Europe, which he thought was one of a patient conservatism aimed at delivering Christian populations from Ottoman oppression.[41] To Guizot it was clear that the Ottoman Empire was beyond the pale of civilization and that it needed European tutelage, an idea that would be further developed after 1878.

One of the outcomes of the Crimean War was the Ottoman Empire's admission to the Family of Nations enshrined in the 1856 treaty. Article 7 stated that the Sublime Porte agreed to participate in the advantages of the public law and system of Europe. It was an admission *sub condicione*, the condition being that the empire improved the living conditions of the sultan's Christian subjects, as mentioned in article 9. This article also mentioned Sultan Abdul-Mejid's edict on the amelioration of the welfare of all his subjects without distinction of religion or of race promulgated on February 18, 1856, known as the *Hatt-i Hümayun*.[42] The latter made promises requiring implementation by more specific regulation. The edict implied the removal of millet barriers and the substitution of a common citizenship for all peoples of the empire, but it was contradictory for it still reorganized the empire along the lines of the millet. Muslim populations were opposed to the *Hatt-i Hümayun*. Provincial notables, administrators, and Muslim religious elites resented the foreign pressures that had led to the edict. The higher Christian clergy generally felt that the *Hatt-i*'s provisions undermined their supremacy in the administrative affairs of their respective millets and opposed its enforcement. Christian laymen approved of the prospect of having a greater voice in the control of millet affairs but resented the idea that equality also meant performing military service. Finally, Ottoman Christians did not hesitate to complain that the Ottoman government violated their rights and freedoms, referring to the earlier privileges granted to them under the old millet system. By backing Ottoman Christians' complaints, the European powers allowed them to evade the provisions of the new laws and their responsibilities as citizens.

If confidence in the Ottoman authorities' capacity to enforce the reforms ever existed, it was short-lived.[43] Prince Albert of Great Britain claimed that under the pressure of the moment, the Ottoman government might issue benevolent decrees but never implemented them. Edmund Hammond, who ran the Eastern Department in the British Foreign Affairs Office, believed the Ottomans to be "wilfully incorrigible." Austen Layard, one of Stratford Canning's zealous supporters, a well-known archaeologist, and future British ambassador at Constantinople, agreed with this view. Lord Aberdeen hated "the barbarians" and grieved that his country should ever again be found on their side. In 1857 Lord Cowley, the British ambassador in Paris, reported Napoleon's conviction that the Ottoman Empire could not last, that "Mohammedanism and civilization cannot coexist and that it would be a blessing for the world in general were the Crescent everywhere replaced by the Cross." Europe as a whole, and not any one of its constituent powers, the French emperor argued, must supervise the Ottoman administration if it proved to be incompatible with the progress of civilization.[44]

During the 1860s a number of inquiries led by the European consuls on the spot determined whether the conditions of Christians in the Ottoman Empire had improved.[45] Even though they revealed that conditions had in fact improved, the prevailing idea in Europe was that the 1856 edict had remained a dead letter. European policy-makers and intellectuals ignored the results of these detailed reports because they were published concomitantly with the recurrence of massacres of Christians—in 1860 in Lebanon and Damascus and in 1867 in Crete. European studies on the reforms in the Ottoman Empire published in the 1860s argued that a successful introduction of reforms was possible, not autonomously but as the result of paternalist regeneration, as tutelage and full obedience to European precepts.[46] By the 1870s European experts no longer believed that the Ottoman Empire would ever be raised to the status of a fully civilized power.[47] The idea of a European tutelage was often mentioned through a scheme for a centralized and sound bureaucracy under the supervision of France (or Russia or Great Britain, according to the "expert's" nationality) to show the Ottoman Empire the way toward civilization.[48]

The Eastern crisis of the 1870s, settled in Berlin in 1878, confirmed to the overwhelming majority of Europeans that the Ottoman Empire was not a member of the Family of Nations. By the 1880s European international lawyers and statesmen argued that the Ottoman Empire was under European tutelage: *la Turquie est en tutelle*.[49] The Institut de Droit International explicitly questioned the Ottoman Empire's eligibility for full legal personality, which in turn opened the door to all sorts of questions pertaining to the applicability of the principle of nonintervention to the Ottoman Empire.[50]

THE MAIN CRITERION FOR INCLUSION IN THE FAMILY OF NATIONS

International legal scholars were well connected with the European intellectual-cum-political stratum and generally shared the views other European thinkers and experts about the exclusion of the Ottoman Empire from the Family of Nations. For instance, in 1894 Cambridge law professor John Westlake, in a chapter entitled "The Equality of States in Civilisation, and the Protection of Subjects Abroad," claimed:

> Throughout Europe and America, *if we except Turkey*, habits occupations and ideas are very similar. Family life, and social life in the narrower sense of that term, are based on monogamous marriage and respect for women. The same arts and sciences are taught and pursued, the same avocations and interests are protected by similar laws, civil and criminal, the administration of which is directed by a similar sense of justice. The same dangers are seen to threaten the fabric of society, similar measures are taken or discussed with the object of eluding them, and the same hopes are entertained that improvement will continue to be realised."[51]

European legal scholars broadly supported and gave legal recognition to cultural (and, toward the end of the century, racial) differences between Europe and the rest of the world, based on the superiority of European civilization and of Christianity over any other civilization and religion. They integrated cultural distinctions into a hierarchical ordering of stato-national developmental levels measured to the standard of European civilization, which for them represented a universal value.

These scholars assumed European progress and modernity as the natural end point of development and civilization everywhere and could not avoid advocating the conversion of non-Europeans to their system. They saw it as their civilized mission to teach nations to coexist through one international (European) law, a unique religion (Christianity), and one education, while persisting as nations with a European-type government. By the late nineteenth century, international legal scholars accepted without question the division of humanity (and of states) into three spheres: civilized, half-civilized, and barbarous (or "savage").[52] All the powers of the first sphere, who were equals among one other, held the legitimate authority to control those of the other two spheres. Civilized nations had a full, developed order of common, mutual, consensual law based on sovereignty and equality, while the uncivilized, the "people of the wild," and the "ignorant" were able to build only limited forms of organized ruling bodies, if at all.[53]

Both historian Jennifer Pitts and international legal scholar Anthony Anghie have recently suggested that the support of international legal scholars for the theories of civilizational progress had two particularly important results in the construction of ostensible standards for inclusion or exclusion in the nineteenth-century European system. First, these progress narratives enabled European thinkers to argue that non-Europeans were unprotected by the Law of Nations. In theory European states were supposed to respect human moral equality even as they advocated suspending ordinary moral, political, and legal norms in interactions with non-European societies. European thinkers also claimed that the moral duty of the Europeans to assist backward nations and states on their route to advancement required a special treatment of the natives; in other words, they justified the imperialistic and colonial enterprise of European powers. The second important result was that theories of civilization and barbarism, rendered in the late-nineteenth-century scientific idiom of sociology and legal positivism, offered legal and political theorists a means by which to put forward European moral and political norms as universally valid while forestalling inquiry into this assumption.[54] European political and intellectual elites largely agreed with and used international legal scholars' doctrines to argue that European international law was (temporarily) not extensible to non-European barbarous and savage peoples and not binding on Europeans in their interactions with non-Europeans. Positivist jurists overcame the historical facts that non-European states had previously been regarded as sovereign, that, by and large, they enjoyed all the rights accompanying this status, and that their behavior constituted a form of practice and precedent that gave rise to rules and doctrines of international law.[55]

In the mid-eighteenth century European scholars adopted the term the "society of nations" (*la société des nations*, in Vattel's words), by which they exclusively meant the society of European nations. In 1815 the Declaration on the Abolition of the Slave Trade referred to the Europeans as "all civilized countries on Earth," excluding non-Europeans and the Ottoman Empire, and pointed to the moral responsibilities of the civilized nations. Throughout the nineteenth century and beyond, in the view of international legal scholars, European civilized nations or states constituted a commonwealth of nations that were constrained and protected by the Law of Nations. They saw the *Droit public de l'Europe* as the principal instrument of their integration. When facing the external world, Europe was a historical, political, and cultural unity. However, this external unity fractured into separate, secular states when it came to internal matters. Throughout the nineteenth century the *Droit public de l'Europe* encompassed a secularized cultural community founded on Christian heritage, still rooted in religious soil and ideologically linked to Christianity, which remained an essential part of European history, conscience, and civilization.[56] The "civilized nations" order included solidarity between monarchic rulers, the concept of a given political order, dynastic or other domestic constitutional institutions, the professional ethos of a highly developed permanent diplomacy answerable to often-changing political masters, and the readiness to establish certain institutional ties.[57]

In 1824, when the House of Commons discussed whether Great Britain should recognize the independence of the Latin American republics, Sir James Mackintosh, the leader of the Whigs and a distinguished jurist, argued that recognition of a new state as a member of the society of civilized nations "must vary very much in its value according to the authority of the nations, who, upon such occasion, act as the representatives of civilized men."[58] In 1836 American jurist Henry Wheaton asserted that formal recognition of a state's statehood and sovereignty was a "perfectly distinct thing" from the recognition required for membership in the Family of Nations.[59]

Oxford international law professor Montagu Bernard delivered a lecture on the "Principle of Non Intervention" at All Souls' College on December 3, 1860. Before discussing the crux of the matter, Bernard pointed out that the whole fabric of international law was built on two assumptions: states are sovereign or independent (the terms were convertible); and states are members of a community united by a social tie. In his view, the history of civilization was a history of the birth and development of the principle of sovereignty *in Europe*; it was at the root of European nations' highest qualities, of their self-respect, their sense of moral responsibility, their manliness and honorable ambition; it was the vital force that gave them energy and kept them from decay. The doctrine of nonintervention, which according to Bernard applied only to European nations, was therefore a corollary of a cardinal and substantial principle of international law.[60]

Other thinkers and experts in international relations shared these views. Richard Cobden, for instance, advocated the principle of absolute nonintervention with respect to European affairs, although when it came to taking a stance on intervention in the Ottoman Empire, he argued that international law did not apply beyond the pale of civilization, or the Family of Nations. Sovereignty and nonintervention were principles that related only to European states.[61] In 1859 John Stuart Mill published an essay, "A Few Words on Non-Intervention."[62] He, like Cobden, made a distinction between rules that applied to civilized nations and those relevant to barbarous entities, and he clarified the grounds that made intervention justifiable.[63] As far as the international relations of European nations were concerned, Mill ruled out any form of intervention, with the possible exception of whether a nation was justified, in time of civil war, in taking part on one side or another.[64] Mill saw *interference* (or overt intrusion to achieve a specific, limited objective) by a civilized state in the internal affairs of another civilized state as generally unjustified, while *intervention* (a far-reaching, penetrating involvement) rarely sufficed when civilized states intervened in barbarous and semibarbarous ones.[65] Since barbarians did not have the rights normally accorded to a nation, the actions of the civilized toward the barbarous did not violate the Law of Nations. For Mill, criticism of French conduct in Algeria, or that of the English in India, in terms of the principle of nonintervention, or indeed of any customary rule of international law, was mistaken:[66]

> A civilized government cannot help having barbarous neighbours: when it has, it cannot always content itself with a defensive position, one of mere resistance to aggression. After a longer or shorter interval of forbearance, it either finds itself obliged to conquer them, or to assert so much authority over them, and so to break their spirit, that they gradually sink into a state of dependence upon itself; and when that time arrives, they are indeed no longer formidable to it, but it has become morally responsible for all evil it allows them to do.[67]

William E. Hall, author of one of the most influential English-language international law textbooks of the second half of the century, pictured the relations between states as if the states were members of a Victorian social club. In his view, international law was a product of the "special civilisation of Europe," whose principles could not be understood or recognized by countries differently civilized. "States outside European civilisation," Hall argued, "must formally enter into the circle of law-governed countries. They must do something with the acquiescence of the latter, or of some of them, which amounts to an acceptance of the law in its entirety beyond all possibility of misconstruction."[68] For legal scholar Thomas J. Lawrence, admission to the club was conditional on the possession of a sufficient degree of European culture. Before a sovereign state could become a subject of international law, it must possess other marks that, though not essential to sovereignty, are essential to membership in the Family of Nations. In the first place, the state had to have the necessary degree of civilization. The state also had to obtain "a kind of international testimonial of good conduct and respectability; and when a state hitherto accounted barbarous desires admission, the powers immediately concerned apply their own tests."[69] At the end of the century another prominent jurist, Lassa Francis Oppenheim, concurred with his fellow scholars that statehood alone did not qualify an entity for membership in the Family of Nations.

John Westlake mentioned the "anomalous position of the (Ottoman) empire, included on the account of its geographical situation in the political system of Europe, but belonging in other respects rather to the second group of contrasted populations" (i.e., barbarous). "She may benefit by European international law so far as it can be extended to her without ignoring plain facts, but her admission to that benefit cannot react on the statement of the law, which is what it is because it is the law of the European peoples."[70] To illustrate that specific case, Oppenheim spoke of a state that, like some others, was only "for some parts within the circle of the Family of Nations" but "remained for other parts outside" because it was not "completely civilized."[71] In the second half of the century, international legal scholars grew increasingly dubious whether Eastern peoples were capable, to the same degree as Western peoples, of admitting a moral basis of reciprocity with other peoples who do not accept the same religious sanctions. According to Sir Travers Twiss, the problem of reciprocity did not arise with nations grounded in Buddhism or Confucianism, but only with Islamic nations, for the moral code of the Koran had a simultaneous function as a code of international law, which, he argued, prohibited relations of equality and reciprocity between the "house of Islam and infidel countries."[72] At the end of the nineteenth century, international legal scholars such as Frenchmen Ernest Nys, Henri Bonfils, and Paul Fauchille observed that to apply European international law to barbarous nations was to misunderstand the reciprocity underlying it.

In 1883 Scottish international legal scholar James Lorimer compared Oriental communities without internal freedom to immature or irrational individuals deprived of legal capacity—an argument he borrowed from John Stuart Mill, among others—and, echoing Edmund Burke, described the relationship between superior and inferior races in terms of a trust the former had over communities suffering from a "weakness of spirit" that rendered them incapable of full membership in the "civilized community." Lorimer argued that European nations could never recognize barbarous states because such states were burdened by "their criminal intention and the consequent absence of rational will."[73] Starting with these assumptions, Lorimer suggested that the conquest of Algeria by France was not a violation of international law: it was an "act of discipline which the bystander was entitled to exercise in the absence of police."[74] Had Algeria come to respect the rights of life and property, its history would not have permanently deprived it of the right to recognition. According to Lorimer, colonization and reclamation of barbarians and savages were duties morally and juridically inevitable; and where circumstances demanded the application of physical force, they fell within necessary objects of a just war.[75]

To participate in international law required a certain similarity of habits, customs, and procedures. As Lorimer put it, nations with different levels of civilizations could not participate in the international legal system on an equal footing:

> The sphere of plenary political recognition [applies] to all the existing States of Europe, with their colonial dependencies, in so far as these are peopled by persons of European birth or descent; and to the States of North and South America which have vindicated their independence of the European States of which they were colonies. The sphere of partial political recognition extends to Turkey in Europe and Asia, and to the old historical States of Asia which have not become European dependencies—viz., to Persia and the other separate States of Central Asia, to China, Siam, and Japan. The sphere of natural, or mere human recognition, extends to the residue of mankind, though here we ought, perhaps, to distinguish between the progressive and non-progressive races. It is with the first of these spheres alone that the international jurist has directly to deal. [However, he] must take cognisance of the relations in which civilised communities are placed to the partially civilised communities which surround them. He is not bound to apply the positive law of nations to savages, or even to barbarians, as such; but he is bound to ascertain the points at which, and the directions in which, barbarians or savages come within the scope of partial recognition. In the case of the Turks we [Europeans] have had a bitter experience of extending the rights of civilisation to barbarians who have proved to be incapable of performing its du-

ties, and who possibly do not even belong to the progressive races of mankind.[76]

In 1886 Carslake Thompson summarized the criteria of inclusion and exclusion from the Family of Nations. In his view, Europeans conceived of Christendom as an entity transcending and underlying the separate portions into which it could be split up.[77] This multifaceted entity was capable, on occasion, of being welded into one mass for common defense against the infidel. Closely allied to this, Thompson wrote, or perhaps the same thing in a modernized form, was the conception of Europe as congeries of peoples, marked by a common Aryan descent, a common acceptance of juridical notions derived from Roman law, and a common acceptance, not so much of Christian faith as of Christian morality. From these points of similarity, substantial agreement was found on conduct, a European civilization and morality based on the institution of the family, that forbade polygamy and slavery and was, in principle, averse to cruelty and bloodshed.

Thompson noted that the germ of international law lay in the fundamental agreement about the conduct of the European nations as contrasted with others, especially "the Mahometan world." He claimed that when emanating from the mouth of a jurist or statesman, the words "Europe" and "Christendom," if not absolutely synonymous, expressed but slightly differing aspects of the same fact. Whichever aspect was uppermost in a particular jurist's or stateman's mind, the conception of the "Turks as different in religion, and of the Turks as alien in civilisation from the Europe to which the men of the subject provinces belonged, practically always went hand in hand to reinforce one other."[78] Not surprisingly Thompson concluded, to Europeans there was something shocking in the spectacle of any European people being subjected to people of a lower type of civilization, when such political subjection resulted in the persecution of the European religion, a check on the development of the European civilization, or outrages against European morality. All Europeans felt concerned to bring such subjection to an end.

International control by the so-called civilized nations of the rest of humanity was based on what in 1910 French jurist Antoine Rougier called the "natural inequality" among states. Rougier claimed that cultural interpenetration among civilizations comprising different groups was difficult, and that equality was a deception. Using typical Social Darwinist parlance, he claimed that when contact was established between civilizations, the strongest would dominate the weakest. The European domination of Turkey and China and the existence of other religious protectorates, Rougier argued, were examples of a Christian right of control over the Muslims, of the white man over the nonwhite man.[79]

LATE-NINETEENTH-CENTURY DOCTRINES OF HUMANITARIAN INTERVENTION

Legal scholar Simon Chesterman recently claimed that at the beginning of the twentieth century the status of humanitarian intervention as a legal doctrine was unclear and that fundamental differences can be seen in its normative status. Chesterman has disclosed the lines of demarcation between those who confidently asserted a right of unilateral humanitarian intervention, those who confidently rejected it, and those who held that international law could or should have little to say about the matter.[80] On one aspect there was full agreement between all legal scholars and European policy-makers in the first or second half of the nineteenth century: humanitarian intervention was not an option as far European affairs were concerned, especially when massacre, atrocities, and extermination took place within the boundaries of another great power.[81]

The terms "intervention for humanity," "intervention on the grounds of humanity," "intervention on behalf of the interests of humanity," and to "remove abhorrent conditions" appeared in the English-language literature in the mid-nineteenth century. Wheaton's 1836 treatise cites the "interference" of the Christian powers of Europe in aid of Greek insurgents against the Ottoman Empire as an illustration that international law authorized "such an interference . . . where the general interests of humanity are infringed by the excesses of a barbarous and despotic government."[82] These terms seem to have a longer history in French. For instance, an 1821 pamphlet by Russian diplomat Comte Boutourlin called for a "war in the name of humanity" of "European society as whole" against the Turks in Greece.[83] "Civilized and Christian Europe" had to intervene on behalf of "humanity against barbarity."[84] Massacres, atrocities, and extermination—three words the author copiously used, as well as annihilation (anéantissement)—of the Greeks were a question of civilization, of the droit des gens as well as a simple, universal moral issue.[85] The Greeks had a natural right to life (right to subsist) and to fight against a "barbarous" and "Infidel" oppressor who was beyond the "social European pact." In Boutourlin's view, as Europe had acted to abolish the slave trade, it had now to end the massacre of fellow Christian Greeks. Christian Europe had a right of prosecution and conviction (vindicte publique). If one of the European states refused to take action, it would be responsible for "criminal" treachery toward the European social pact.[86] Collective intervention (which Boutourlin also refers to as a war) was the only adequate means to ensure that violence and massacre would not recur.

Humanitarian Intervention as a Legal Right

A minority of scholars argued that humanitarian intervention existed as a legal right. Some of them justified it as a quasi-judicial police measure against the crimes of a sovereign, and others characterized it as a defense of the rights of the oppressed. Not surprisingly, some sided with the protesters during the Bulgarian atrocities campaign. In 1876 Gustave Rolin-Jaequemyns argued that as the Europeans had abolished the slave trade, in his view one of the most glorious undertakings of the civilized powers, so they should end massacre and slave trade of "white" women and children as practiced by the Ottomans.[87] E.R.N. Arntz argued that the Ottoman Empire had no right to harm its (Christian) population as it liked. He claimed that the respect of another state's sovereignty did not entail its liberty to plunder, slaughter, hang, and burn. In such cases the human conscience would be in favor of the legitimacy of intervention.[88] Arntz defined humanitarian intervention as occurring in the following instance:

> When a government, acting fully within the limits of its sovereign rights, violates the laws of humanity, either by measures contrary to the interest of other States, or by excesses of injustice and cruelty which profoundly injure our morals and our civilisation, the right of intervention is legitimate. In effect, although the rights of sovereignty and independence of States are important, there is something which is even more important. It is the law of humanity, or of human society, which must not be offended. Just as in the State the liberty of the individual is restricted and must be restricted by the law and by the morals of society, the individual liberty of States must be limited by the laws of human society.[89]

By law of humanity (*droits de l'humanité*), Arntz and Rolin-Jaequemyns meant the right to life, property, security, and equality before the law violated by an uncivilized state. By "measures contrary to the interests of other states" they meant measures that an "uncivilized" state, such as the Ottoman Empire, could commit against the interests of the European states. Moreover, the way the definition is articulated shows that uncivilized states could offend European morals and civilization while the opposite was not even contemplated as a working hypothesis. Civilized states could take action only as long it was collective in order to nullify the potential advantage for any single power and prove the disinterested and morally justified nature of the intervention.

Some writers referred to the burdens that power and civilization imposed on the bearer,[90] or, as in the case of George de Martens and Edwin Borchard, asserted that intervention by the civilized powers was in principle legitimate, when the Christian population of the Ottoman Empire was exposed to persecutions or massacres. In those circumstances, common religious interests and humanitarian considerations justified intervention. However, as Edwin de Witt Dickinson specified, those very motives for intervention were not applicable to relations between civilized powers.[91]

Other scholars who claimed that a legal right of humanitarian intervention existed were Henry Wheaton, Theodore D. Woolsey, Georges Streit, Louis Vie, and Antoine Rougier.[92] The latter wrote an often-quoted article in the *Revue Générale de Droit International Public* in 1910 in which he defined the theory of humanitarian intervention as the attempt to find a juridical basis to the right of one state to exercise international control over the internal acts of another state that are contrary to the laws of humanity.[93] Rougier recognized that whereas in national law the offender would be arrested and punished for disorderly conduct, the international society could not so easily be rid of the culprit. It was necessary either to assume the burden of the administration of the territory where the violation had occurred or to constrain the unworthy sovereign (target state) to reform. Rougier's laws of humanity were a supreme legal rule: the right to life, the right to liberty, and the right to legality.[94] Each time the human rights of a people were ignored by their governments, one or many states could intervene in the name of the society of nations. The intervening states might demand that the questionable acts of public power be annulled. They might prevent the recurrence of such acts and when necessary, take measures intended to momentarily substitute their sovereignty for that of the state being controlled. Rougier specified that if a government violated the laws of humanity not just any power could claim a right to intervene. He excluded unilateral intervention and accepted the rightfulness of a collective action under two conditions: disinterestedness and the greater authority or "superior civilization" of the intervening states.[95]

According to Rougier, every state of the community of so-called civilized states had to recognize as obligations the ideas of order and justice, the existence of a regular government, and the protection of the human rights of its inhabitants. The community of civilized states could not admit to membership a state without a government or one that had a barbarous government. Governments failing to acknowledge the human interests of their citizens committed what Rougier called a "misappropriation of sovereignty (*détournement de souveraineté*)." In such a case, the members of the international community (the European states only) had to intervene to control this government. The sovereignty of the guilty state would be temporarily replaced by foreign sovereignty, either to fulfill the function it neglected or to prevent analogous weaknesses from occurring in the future. Rougier asserted that this control would be of lesser or greater measure depending on whether the concerned states were of equal or unequal culture. If the states were equally developed, the control would be momentary and occasional, for civilized powers were presumed to commit only "accidental mistakes." When a barbarous state violated "human solidarity," and when this violation was long lasting or permanent, civilized powers would take recourse in a more drastic form of control in order to prevent, rather than repress or repair, the evil. In such a case the humanitarian intervention would become tutelage. This, wrote Rougier, was what had happened to the "half-civilized" Ottoman Empire.[96] In his view, massacre in Greece, Syria, Crete, Bulgaria, and Macedonia was the consequence of the uncivilized state of the Ottoman Empire, and intervention on grounds of humanity had been the response of civilized European states.[97]

Among those who revived the idea of an intervention on behalf of the oppressed, there was a tendency to confine it to the geographical area of the Ottoman Empire and to link oppression with barbarous government. Johann Caspar Bluntschli held that a state is authorized to intervene to ensure respect for individual rights and international law, but only where these had been violated in internal conflict within a state and constituted a general danger. The Ottoman Christians, he wrote, being an oppressed minority (*minorité opprimée*), had successfully provoked foreign intervention several times.[98] Civilized nations had a particular responsibility in developing the "common rights of humanity" and were the "guarantors of international law."[99] In 1894 John Westlake, Whewell Professor of International Law at Cambridge, wrote that the existence, in geographical proximity to international society, of a state "which was not bound by its rules"—he clearly was referring to the Ottoman Empire—would be a source of intolerable inconvenience and danger to the members of society. Westlake considered anarchy and misrule as legitimate grounds for intervention.[100] In that respect his doctrine was not dissimilar from Edward Creasy's legitimization of interventions when a race was "grievously oppressed" by a power of a different race.[101]

Other legal scholars restricted the right of intervention on humanitarian grounds to situations where civil war had broken out[102] or acts of rebellion led to the political bonds between sovereign and citizens being broken.[103] Although they mentioned humanitarian motives—notably in the desire to "stay the effusion of blood," these scholars related humanitarian grounds for intervention with other motives, such as averting a "general danger" (Bluntschli and Frantz Despagnet), "prolonged unrest" (Augustus Heffter), or "public order" (for William O. Manning).[104]

Proscription of Humanitarian Intervention

Those who opposed a right of humanitarian intervention also fall broadly into two camps. The first recognized an absolute right of nonintervention, either on the Hobbesian basis that subjects hold no rights vis-à-vis their sovereign, or more commonly because any intervention on their behalf—no matter how great the moral claim—was incompatible with sovereignty.[105] For legal scholars such as Despagnet or Joseph Jooris, interventions in Lebanon and Syria (1860–61) and in Crete (1866–68) were the consequence of the Ottoman authorities' nonenforcement of the clauses of the 1856 Treaty of Paris, not instances of humanitarian intervention.[106] The 1878 Treaty of Berlin compelled the Porte to protect the life and security of its Armenian populations against the Circassians and Kurds. Hence, according to Despagnet, the possible motive of intervention would not have been humanitarian but a consequence of the disrespect of the sacrosanct principle *pacta sunt servanda*. Despagnet was among the very few jurists who analyzed the legal context of nonintervention during and after the massacres of Ottoman Armenians from 1886 to 1896 and of the intervention of European powers in Crete in 1896 and in the Ottoman Macedonian provinces. In his view, none of these was a humanitarian intervention.[107]

Despagnet concurred with other scholars that European interventions in the Ottoman Empire were determined by the latter's material and moral degeneration. In his view, the Ottoman Empire's sovereignty was diminished, nominal at best. The Ottoman Empire clearly was under European tutelage, and it survived only because Europeans could not agree on its dismemberment. Despagnet criticized the theory of a right of civilization, claiming that it opened the door to all sorts of abuses under the hypocritical cover of a disinterested civilizing mission. He underscored that powerful states did not tolerate any observation à propos their domestic politics. Russia, he wrote, could have replied to the U.S. observations about the 1903 pogroms of Kishinev by mentioning the lynching of black Americans (*lynchage des nègres en Amérique*). Foreign intervention, even when triggered by apparent humanitarian reasons, achieved only platonic objectives and was always superseded by the self-interests of the intervening states, whatever moral motives might have been put forward to justify it. [108] This is why he strenuously opposed it.

A larger group of legal scholars countered the moral arguments in favor of a right of humanitarian intervention with the practical danger of its abuse. [109] Robert Phillimore noted that the general interests of humanity was defensible as an accessory motive, but as a "substantive and solitary justification" of intervention in the affairs of another country it could not be admitted into international law since is manifestly opened to abuses, "tending to the violation and destruction of the vital principles of that system of jurisprudence." [110] The interference of Great Britain, France, and Russia in the affairs of Greece, Phillimore argued, was vindicated on three grounds: complying with the request of one party, staying the shedding of blood, and affording protection to the subjects of other powers who navigated the Levant (the eastern Mediterranean Sea). For many years neither the Ottoman government nor Greece had been able or willing to prevent the excesses springing out of this state of anarchy. [111] According to Phillimore, the third ground unquestionably justified the intervention to redress the evil complained of. [112] He denied, however, any existence of an alleged right of intervention on religious grounds, as put forward by the Russian government in 1854 and in 1877, and in his works he did not mention Lebanon and Syria or Crete as possible instances of humanitarian intervention.

Humanitarian Intervention beyond the Realm of International Law

Other scholars put humanitarian intervention in the Ottoman Empire outside the realm of international law entirely. Historicus, alias Sir William Harcourt, expressed this in an often-quoted passage published in 1863: "Intervention is a question rather of policy than of law. It is above and beyond the domain of law, and when wisely and equitably handled by those who have the power to give effect to it may be the highest policy of justice and humanity." [113]

This author mentions Greece as a case of intervention to put an end to the uncivilized methods by which it was conducted. "The battle of Navarino may have been an untoward event, but it was the natural and almost inevitable consequence of a forcible intervention to prevent the Turkish government from reducing its subjects to submission." [114] Herman Rodecker von Rotteck held that intervention should be considered as a violation of the law, but sometimes excused or even applauded. [115]

William Hall explains the apparent political and juristic acceptance of humanitarian intervention as reflecting "considerations of sentiment to the exclusion of law." Hall's position is that no such intervention is legal unless "the whole body of civilized states have concurred in authorising it." Where such authorization is not possible, he argues that such measures, "being confessedly illegal in themselves, could only be excused in rare and extreme case in consideration of the unquestionably extraordinary character of the facts causing them, and of the evident purity of the motives and conduct of the intervening state."[116] For Lawrence, ordinary rules of international law did not impose on states the obligation of "preventing barbarity" on the part of their neighbors. At the same time, international law did not condemn interventions for such a cause if they are undertaken with a single eye to the object in view and without ulterior considerations of self-interest and ambition. In Lawrence's interpretation, motivation and the nature of the massacre had a capital importance.[117] In the 1911 (and 1916) edition of his textbook, Lawrence mentioned the 1860 intervention of the "Great Powers of Europe" to "put a stop to the persecution and massacre of Christians in the district of Mount Lebanon," arguing that their proceedings were worthy of commendation, though they could not be brought within the strict letter of the law.[118] Lawrence did not explain whether the only jurisprudential case he referred to was beyond the realm of international law because the Ottoman Empire was beyond the pale of civilization, did he refer to any other instance of intervention.

Collective Intervention

Lassa Francis Oppenheim, in a passage that, as Chesterman notes, remained unchanged through five edition of his work, doubted whether there was a rule admitting "interventions in the interests of humanity" but did mention that "public opinion and the attitude of the Powers are in favour of such interventions."[119] Oppenheim concluded that such a right may be recognized at some point in the future but restricted it to collective intervention by the powers:

> Many jurists maintain that intervention is likewise admissible, or even has a basis of right, when exercised in the interest of humanity for the purpose of stopping religious persecution and endless cruelties in time of peace and war. That the Powers have in the past exercised intervention on these grounds, there is no doubt. Thus Great Britain, France, and Russia intervened in 1827 in the struggle between revolutionary Greece and Turkey, because public opinion was horrified at the cruelties committed during this struggle. And many a time interventions have taken place to stop the persecution of Christians in Turkey. But whether there is really a rule of the Law of Nations which admits such interventions may well be doubted. Yet, on the other hand, it cannot be denied that public opinion and the attitude of the Powers are in favour of such interventions, and it

may perhaps be said that in time of the Law of Nations will recognise the rule that interventions in the interest of humanity are admissible provided they are exercised in the form of a collective intervention of the Powers.[120]

. . .

In 1900, looking back at the history of Europe since Westphalia, American scholar W. E. Lingelbach claimed that "intervention to prevent intolerance, anarchy and insecurity to life and property has been very common, though there has been little uniformity in the practice. Here perhaps, more than anywhere else, motives for intervention are complex."[121] In Lingelbach's view, moral and religious causes for intervention joined "commercial' ones, for religious persecution is attended with excessive cruelty; anarchy and crime shock the moral sense "of the civilized nations" but also jeopardize "commercial interests and render life and property insecure." He argues that the oldest form of intervention was based on religion. During the seventeenth and eighteenth centuries, with Europe divided into two hostile camps, a practice of intervention grew based on religion. During the nineteenth century, intervention on religious grounds was rare; however, Lingelbach argues, "there is a feature of this kind of intervention which is peculiarly a growth of the present century. The moral sentiment of civilized peoples in modern times has been frequently aroused and governments have been forced to intervene in case where intolerance has become apprehensive and cruel."[122]

However, Lingelbach, who pertains to the category of scholars who argued in favor of a right to intervene, conflated the idea of rescuing strangers with suffering Christianity, and, as many other scholars, he only mentions examples of interventions on behalf of suffering Christians. According to him,

> intervention on humanitarian grounds is recognized, though it appears that national self-interest has usually been too powerful to allow intervention for humanitarian reasons solely. The precedents show that the stronger motives based on political and economic interests are usually necessary to induce states to intervene. Indeed intervention under this head is always based on a number of different but closely allied grounds, and as such is considered legitimate.[123]

In 1908 René Pinon argued that humanitarian interventions were inspired by an abstract religious, philosophical, and humanitarian ideal. During the Crusades, humanitarian intervention aimed to rescue fellow Christians; during the nineteenth century, intervention underwent a major change because of the progressive secularization of politics in

Europe. However, Pinon admitted, nineteenth-century humanitarian intervention had not entirely erased the feeling of solidarity among Christian peoples facing non-Christian peoples despite, since the French Revolution, *le droit des peuples* and *le droit de l'humanité* having been added on to the old Christian ideal.[124]

Whatever views on the existence of a right of humanitarian intervention they might have had, international legal scholars agreed that humanitarian interventions were about stopping massacres, extermination, and particularly shocking atrocities, such as rape and outrages on women and children. The concept of humanitarian intervention as developed in juridical doctrines was certainly not disentangled from political considerations, especially those related to collective security. A prominent scholar such as Oppenheim argued that humanitarian interventions were dictated "no less by sentiments of humanity than by the interest for tranquillity in Europe."[125] This jurist had no difficulty in accepting the practice of humanitarian intervention as long as it happened beyond Europe, in one or the other Ottoman provinces. Oppenheim noted that when "the whole body of civilized states have concurred in authorizing it," risks of abuse decreased. When a single power, such as Russia in 1853, attempted to assert a right to intervene unilaterally on behalf of Christian subjects persecuted by the sultan, the result was a general war (the Crimean War) in which Great Britain and France sided with the sultan in defense of Turkish sovereignty and independence. The restriction to interventions against massacre outside Europe was related to inherent risks for general peace and security. What mattered to the majority of legal scholars was that interventions should be based on the highest possible moral ground—the moral duty of civilized nations to enforce respect for the rights to life, liberty, and the rule of law—especially when these rights were massively violated by a barbarous government. In the European perspective, military humanitarian interventions were a "noble action" and a special manifestation of the civilizing mission.[126] The paradox and contradiction of nineteenth-century humanitarian intervention concerns the European governments' violations of the very same humanitarian principles they proclaimed to uphold and resolve to enforce vis-à-vis the Ottoman government. The Europeans did not admit that the Ottoman Empire might have their same "generous" intentions when it ruled over Christian minorities. They never admitted that the brutal enforcement of colonial policies determined by their generous intentions often resulted in massacre and atrocity similar to those committed by the Ottoman authorities against their Christian populations.

CHAPTER THREE

Intervention on Behalf of Ottoman Greeks (1821–33)

> La conséquence de l'extermination des Hellènes serait grave pour le monde civilisé.
>
> —François Réné de Chateaubriand,
> *Itinéraire de Paris à Jérusalem et de Jérusalem à Paris*

THIS CHAPTER EXAMINES European powers' politics with regard to and military intervention in Ottoman Greece from 1821 to 1833. It looks at various massacres that did not lead to a humanitarian intervention and other events that eventually led to the famous battle of Navarino, which, retrospectively, was portrayed as the first instance of modern humanitarian intervention, the *coup d'essai* of a state practice that would crystallize throughout the century. We shall see to what extent the 1827 intervention was a "humanitarian intervention" against the incidence of a prototype of "ethnic cleansing," as scholar Vahakn Dadrian claimed in his history of the Armenian genocide.[1]

THE INTERNATIONAL AND LOCAL CONTEXT

The Congress of Vienna (1815) put an end to the Napoleonic era and set up the basis of a new international order. From 1815 to 1822 the major European governments (Great Britain, Austria, Russia, Prussia, and France, which had been readmitted to the international system with the status of "great power") regularly met to solve problems that could threaten the newly born international system. The Congress system coexisted with the Holy Alliance (a treaty signed by the three Eastern European monarchies, Prussia, Austria, and Russia), which attempted to preserve the status quo by intervening militarily in various European countries where monarchs were overthrown or seriously threatened by insurgents.

Insurrection in the Ottoman province of the Morea (today's Peloponnese) had taken place in 1770 and had been harshly repressed by the Ottoman Army. At the turn of the century, mainland Greece inhabitants had many grievances against their local government; the peasants considered the amount of taxes they had to pay as oppressive and

arbitrary, especially since 1808 when Ali Pasha of Ioannina and his sons ruled the Morea, parts of Rumelia, and much of Albania. In 1820 relations between the Ottoman government and Ali Pasha deteriorated to the point that the Ottoman Army attacked Ioannina. Khurdish Pasha, the newly appointed governor of the Morea, entered in Ioannina in January 1822. Ali's head and those of his sons were shortly after exhibited in Constantinople. At the same time Alexander Ypsilantis became the leader of the Filiki Eteria (Friendly Association Society), a secret nationalist association created in September 1814 by Greek expatriates in Odessa. The association was active in the Danubian Principalities of Moldavia and Wallachia and aimed at importing revolution in Greece from abroad. In 1821, when Ypsilantis was arrested while attempting to cross the Austrian frontier, the Greeks of the Morea had already started their insurrection.[2]

In December 1821 the most prominent leaders of the insurrection promulgated the Constitution of Epidaurus, the aims of which were to create an effective government that would balance the interests of the competing Greek groups. The constitution was also supposed to impress foreign powers by showing that the Greeks were a "civilized" people deserving to be helped by other civilized and Christian nations. In the short term, the government did not achieve any of these objectives and was not recognized as such by the European powers. The powers gathered at Verona in October 1822 to discuss, among other matters, the insurrection in Greece turned away a delegation of Greek leaders unheard. The British government opposed any action by the European allies in Greece, choosing a policy of strict neutrality toward the "Greek Question."[3]

In 1822 and 1823 the Greeks won many battles and conquered Athens and Nafplion (Nafplio), but the Ottoman Army was far from being defeated. In 1824 the sultan enlisted Mohamed Ali, pasha of Egypt, against the Greeks. This pasha disposed of a modern army and navy that had demonstrated their force crushing a rebellion in Crete in April 1824. Ibrahim Ali, son of Mohamed, and his troops landed on mainland Greece in February 1825. Their target was Navarino, which they took on May 30. By the end of the year, with the exception of Nafplion, the Egyptians entirely occupied the Morea. We shall see how this military occupation eventually led to the European powers' intervention in 1827.

NONINTERVENTION ON BEHALF OF MUSLIM CIVILIAN POPULATIONS OF GREECE

Historians have often emphasized the harsh reprisals and repression enacted by the Ottoman government and by Muslim civilian populations in the Greek provinces while overlooking the context of the earlier Greek insurrection when Christian-Orthodox slaughtered at least ten thousand Muslim men, women, and children in the space of a few weeks.[4] Previous Ottoman harsh repression and reprisals largely explain the violent context of the insurrection. In fact, Greek insurgents started by murdering Ottoman civil servants, especially tax officials, and when the context of the war exacerbated they rounded up, marched out of town to convenient places, and eventually slaughtered entire Muslim populations of the Ottoman provinces of the Morea and Thessaly. The insurgents set fire to houses of Muslim families living in small communities, with their corpses inside, and burned down or destroyed Muslim fortified buildings (*kule*) as well as peasant farmhouses to prevent the return of those who had found refuge in the Ottoman fortresses scattered around the country, such as the Acropolis of Athens. Insurgents killed the civilian inhabitants of the towns of Kalavryta and Kalamata despite the fact that they had surrendered to the Greek leaders on the promise of being spared. The Muslim civilians of Laconia were massacred in the streets after they had already abandoned their villages. In Tripoli (Tripolitza) Turkish inhabitants of all ages and both sexes were not spared.[5] In Messolonghi most Muslim men were murdered, and some women became enslaved by rich Greek families. The Muslims of Vrachori were killed after having first been tortured. Greek insurgents also killed local Jews, who were often perceived as infidels or enemies.[6]

Despite full awareness of these massacres, the European powers decided not to intervene or, more likely, did not even think of intervening on behalf of Muslim civilian populations of the disturbed Ottoman provinces, for several reasons.

First, European political leaders and diplomats viewed these events as a typical case of popular insurrection, not necessarily different from other insurrections taking place elsewhere in Europe, such as the Neapolitan insurrection against the Bourbon monarchy. Second, the Ottoman government did not request any foreign help to rescue the Muslim population of its Greek provinces. Third, even if the Ottoman Empire had been a member of the Holy Alliance (something not even remotely possible, for this was a uniquely Christian venture), the European powers' intervention would not have been based on humanitarian grounds and undertaken to save Muslim civilian populations; it would have been a military counterrevolutionary operation in favor of the Sublime Porte. Fourth, from the perspective of the potential intervening powers, the responsibility for protecting Muslim civilians living in the Morea was entirely that of the government of Constantinople. Finally, British and French public opinion, with few exceptions, did not show any sympathy for Muslim populations of Greece.

During the early 1820s public opinion remained overwhelmingly weighted in favor of the Greeks, especially when the "horrors" of Smyrna (Izmir) and Chios supplanted the memory of previous massacres of Muslim civilians.[7] Accounts of the atrocities committed by Greek insurgents can be found in the memoirs of some Philhellenes who volunteered and discovered, once they reached Greece, that the Christian insurgents were as brutal and barbarous as the Muslims.[8] The journal of a British Philhellene, W. H. Humphreys, portrayed modern Greeks as "debased, degraded to the lowest pit of barbarism." They treated Muslim and Jewish civilians "like animals to be exterminated" and recorded a particularly dishonorable act when defenseless Muslim refugees, mainly women and children, where murdered in a gorge and others were butchered, burned alive, horribly mutilated, and their corpses disfigured.[9] Nonetheless, these accounts did not have much of an impact on public opinion.

Nonintervention on Behalf of Christian Civilian Populations at Smyrna (Izmir) and Chios (1821–22)

The massacre of Muslim civilian populations led to tragic consequences for Ottoman Greek communities of Constantinople, Smyrna, and Chios. In early 1821, when news of the insurgency reached the government of Constantinople, the Islamic religious authorities called on all faithful Muslims to avenge the killings committed by the Christians. Subsequently hundreds of Orthodox Christians, not necessarily Greeks, living in Constantinople and other Ottoman cities and provinces became victims of mob fury. In March 1821 the Greek Orthodox patriarch, Gregory V, and other prominent representatives of the clergy circulated an encyclical excommunicating any man who took part in revolution against the sultan. Despite his publicly proclaimed allegiance, the Ottoman authorities hanged the patriarch at the gate of his own palace at the end of April 1821 and let his body and those of a number of bishops be dragged through the city and thrown into the Bosphorus.[10]

European governments and public opinion were fully informed about the reprisals. The first lines of *Des Grecs, des Turcs, et de l'Esprit public Européen* are: "Infidels are slaughtering Christians on European soil, civilized and Christian Europe keeps silent. Does Europe adhere to these massacres or is it frightened?"[11] The French press gave plenty of accounts of persecutions of the Greek Orthodox populations, of profanations of churches and holy reliquaries, and of murders of priests and church dignitaries. In May 1821 the newspaper *Le Constitutionnel* reported the Ottoman authorities' alleged decision "to slaughter all the Christian subjects of the Ottoman Empire" and expressed the wrath of the Christian world at the purported existence of an Ottoman plan to "wipe out Christianity from the face of this earth."[12] In June local Muslim populations and authorities of Smyrna plundered the Greek quarter of the town and killed hundreds of Christians. At the same time, in Kydonies (Aivali), Ottoman authorities killed hundreds of Greeks and sold the survivors as slaves.[13] No humanitarian intervention followed this massacre, the extent of which did not cause, in the short term, an inordinate shock to European governments or public opinion.

After the massacre European consuls at Smyrna sent a joint letter of protest to the Ottoman governor pointing out that the European merchants of the city had a guarantee of the sultan's protection and had brought great wealth to the town. The merchants threatened to leave if disorder continued and thereby cause the collapse of the trade upon which Smyrna depended. This collective diplomatic action (which did not threaten any further action) was intended to protect European merchants and their trade, not local civilian populations. The European governments acknowledged the Ottoman government's right to repress the revolt using arbitrary, indiscriminate, and violent retaliation against innocent civilians who paid the price of the actions committed elsewhere by other Ottoman Christians.

The Russian government considered the possibility of intervening militarily in Smyrna, putting forward humanitarian motives. Interestingly, the government of St. Petersburg did not refer to a breach of the Treaty of Küçük Kaynarca.[14] Instead, the Russian ambassador at Constantinople, Sergei Stroganov, sought a collective (i.e., European) condemnation of the execution of the patriarch, of the massacres of Christians at Smyrna, and of the sale of women into slavery. Russia appealed to the other European powers to prevent the "specter of a religious war." The Russian ambassador proposed that his European counterparts send ships of war to Constantinople to protect the Christian population there. Stroganov argued that if the excesses of the Turks against the Greeks continued—if the Turks continued exterminating the Greek nation (s'ils ne tendent qu'à exterminer la nation grecque)—Russia could not remain an immobile spectator of these profanations and cruelties.[15]

When the British ambassador at Constantinople, Strangford, refused to agree to this proposal, the Russian government abandoned it, showing itself not be ready to act unilaterally on behalf of the Christians. On that occasion the British foreign secretary, Castlereagh, did not deny that "humanity shudders at the scenes" of atrocities committed by the "fanatic and semi-barbarous" Ottomans, although he made it clear to Tsar Alexander I that humanitarian considerations would jar the consecrated structure of Europe to the core and must be subordinated to the maintenance of this structure. The massacres at Constantinople and Smyrna showed that unilateral intervention was not an option, and as far as collective intervention was concerned, humanitarian motives were clearly subordinated to the maintenance of the international system.

The massacres at Chios, or Scio as the island was universally called at that time, followed shortly after those at Smyrna. No individual calamity was to arouse so much genuine sympathy and compassion among the "civilized nations" of the world, and such an upsurge of indignation against those who had perpetrated the disaster, as that which struck Chios.[16] The Chians enjoyed special political and administrative privileges within the Ottoman Empire, and the initiative for the revolt had actually emanated from their neighbors, the Samians. In March 1822 the Greek insurgents' leader, Lykourgos Logothetis, and 1,500 men from Samos anchored off Aghia Eleni.[17] They pillaged Muslim establishments and even Greek ones, stripped the domes of the mosques of their leaden roofs, depredated the area, and loaded their ships with booty. On April 11 Captain Pasha Kara Ali's 4,000-man-strong fleet reached the island. Logothetis and his men disappeared as quickly as they had arrived.[18] The vast majority of Christian Chians suffered all sorts of atrocities. The inmates of the hospital, the madhouse, and the deaf-and-dumb institution were inhumanely slaughtered. Some civilians were indiscriminately butchered, and eyewitnesses spoke of appalling scenes of streets strewn with the dead bodies of old men, women, and children. Two thousand Chians who had sought refuge in the monastery of Nea Moni were killed, as were three thousand at Aghios Minas. Some luckier Chians found refuge in European consulates, and Greek ships coming from Psara, Samos, Hydra, and Spetses eventually rescued some other Chians. The arrival of a Greek fleet provoked the final reprisal against the survivors who had gathered in the village of Tholopotami. Before the massacre between 100,000 and 120,000 Greeks had been living on Chios; by the end of it there were 20,000; many had perished, others fled or became slaves. On May 25 Strangford wrote to Castlereagh that Turkish ferocity in Chios had been carried "to a pitch which makes humanity shudder." [19]

After the massacre, the British ambassador protested to the government of Constantinople, particularly highlighting the taking of slaves. The Ottoman authorities replied that Christian powers had tolerated slavery for centuries, purely for gain and without sanction of religion, and added: "Why do not the Christian Sovereigns interfere to prevent the Emperor of Russia from sending his subjects into Siberia?" Castlereagh presented to King George IV Strangford's painful recital of massacres and atrocities on Chios. On July 9 the king asked the ambassador to express to the Ottoman government, in the most pointed terms, the grief with which he had perused those painful details. With regard to Greek merchants held hostages in Constantinople, the king made it clear that his government was not legally able to place them under British protection and consequently could not consider himself called upon, or even entitled, to protest at their fate. Castlereagh felt that the atrocity of the hostages' execution had "filled the British nation with horror and disgust." [20] He instructed Strangford to leave no effort untried to awaken the Porte to "the fatal consequences of such scenes perpetrated in the midst of their capital and under the very eye of the Representatives of civilized nations." The ambassador had to inform the Ottoman government that if such deeds of blood were repeated, Great Britain would withdraw its missions to stop them from being almost approving witnesses of acts for which no "human offences can furnish a pretext, much less a justification, and which, if repeated, must stamp the Council of the State that tolerates them, with the reproach of the most ferocious and hateful barbarism." [21] However, this unilateral and genuinely humanitarian diplomatic action was certainly not a step leading to further coercive actions or military intervention.

During the summer of 1822, British newspapers published the details of the massacres of Chios, and in Parliament Castlereagh and Prime Minister Liverpool were questioned on the conduct of the government, among others by Wilberforce. The latter spoke of driving back "a nation of barbarians, the ancient and inveterate enemies of Christianity and freedom, into Asia."[22] In the House of Lords, Earl Grosvenor spoke of intervening in favor of the Greeks in the same way the British navy had intervened against the slave traders. In reply Liverpool and Castlereagh pointed out the Ottoman government's right to repress an insurgency and mentioned that to intervene might have threatened peace in Europe. They held to the policy of noninterference they had put forward since the beginning of the Greek insurrection. It was on July 16, 1821, in the midst of the crisis in Smyrna, that Castlereagh wrote to the tsar that it was imperative to maintain the European system, as consolidated by the treaties of peace.[23]

The British minister had no difficulty admitting that Turkey "with all its barbarisms, constitutes, in the system of Europe, what may be regarded as a necessary evil. It is an excrescence which can scarcely be looked upon as forming any part of its healthful organization; and yet, for that very reason, any attempt to introduce order by external interference into its jarring elements, or to assimilate it to the mass, might expose the whole frame of our general system to hazard." To Castlereagh the Ottoman government and people had given themselves up to "a fanatic madness, and to a blind spirit of internal and exterminating warfare." An intervention at that juncture would have charged the intervening states—particularly Russia, which was the power most willing to act—with the perils and burdens of a military occupation, to be effectuated not among a Christian and "tractable, but amongst a bigoted, revengeful, and uncivilized population." Castlereagh thought it not possible to deliver the Greeks from their sufferings and preserve the system of Europe at the same time. Moreover, even though he did not deny sympathy and compassion for the Greeks, they had been the aggressors on the present occasion.[24] In a letter to the British ambassador at St. Petersburg, Sir Charles Bagot, on December 14, 1821, Castlereagh reiterated that the policy to pursue was that of noninterference. Governments, he argued, were not permitted to regulate their conduct by the counsels of their hearts, and any statesman had to provide for the peace and security of those interests immediately committed to his care.

Moreover, the foreign minister was unconvinced that the Greeks were ready for independence:

> I am by no means persuaded were the Turks even miraculously to be withdrawn (what it would cost of blood and suffering forcibly to expel them I now dismiss from my calculations) that the Greek population, as it now subsists or is likely to subsist for a course of

years, could frame from their own materials a system of government less defective either in its external or internal character, therefore, be tempted, not even called upon in moral duty under loose notions of humanity and amendment, to forget the obligations of existing treaties, to endanger the frame of long established relations, and to aid the insurrectionary efforts now in progress in Greece, upon the chance that it may, through war, mould itself into some scheme of government, but at the certainty that it must in the meantime, open a field for every ardent adventurer and political fanatic in Europe to hazard not only his own fortune, but what is our province more anxiously to watch over, the fortune and destiny of that system to the conservation of which our latest solemn transactions with our Allies have bound us.[25]

By "the cost of blood and suffering to forcibly," Castlereagh might have been referring to the costs incurred by the Greek insurgents (and possibly European powers) to defeat the Ottoman Army. It is not clear whether he hinted at the creation of a religiously (or ethnically) homogeneous Greek state when he referred to the expulsion of Muslim civilian populations. On the contrary, what is very clear is that despite "moral duty under loose notions of humanity and amendment," the British government decided to prioritize the *raison d'état*.

Lord Liverpool argued that the cruelties of the Ottoman government had been committed against its own subjects: the Greeks. And, as a matter of fact, Great Britain had no right "to interfere in a matter occurring between a foreign government and the subjects of that government."[26] On the contrary, Robert Grosvenor argued that Britain had a right to interfere with foreign independent nations in order to prevent the continuance of the slave trade; hence, Britain had a right to intervene against the Ottoman Empire, a state that kept enslaving the Greeks. The prime minister saw no similarity between the naval action to end the slave trade and the idea of an intervention on behalf of the Greeks. His foreign secretary also distinguished between international intervention by the "great powers" acting for the general good, as in the case of the slave trade, and the intervention of individual powers whenever they thought their own interests threatened.[27] To Castlereagh the only possible justification for limited intervention was if threats to the safety and security of Europe could be established beyond all reasonable doubt. When he replied to Wilberforce in Parliament he said that the latter, a friend of peace, now advocated the cause of war.

It must be admitted that Grosvenor, Wilberforce, and even the Russians had a hard time defining the scope and modalities of the kind of intervention they had in mind.[28] Stroganov did not say how anchoring of

European warships off Constantinople's shores would have persuaded the Ottoman government to stop committing atrocities. This is a further element explaining why, in the end, massacres in Constantinople, Smyrna, and Chios did not trigger a military intervention on grounds of humanity. Nonetheless, the history and memory of these events would become important in the discourse of Philhellene circles, groups, and movements, national and transnational, which sprouted up everywhere in Europe. Admittedly, the main objective of the Philhellenes was the independence of Greece. To them the intervention against massacre was necessary to reach that objective. Hence, these campaigners highlighted massacre and atrocities to arouse sympathy for the Greeks at the domestic and international levels. Castlereagh committed suicide shortly before the Congress of Verona in 1822.[29] In a statement from 1823, the new foreign secretary, George Canning, stated that with respect to the Greek Question, Britain would continue to observe strict neutrality.

BRITISH AND FRENCH PHILHELLENES AND THE ISSUES OF MASSACRE AND INTERVENTION

Philhellenes directly contributed to keep the Greek Question alive in Europe. I am not entirely convinced that they can be considered humanitarians, and even if they can, some qualifications are needed. Philhellenes were a heterogeneous group of philanthropists, adventurers, and speculators who contributed in various ways to the Greek cause. They provided financial aid for humanitarian purposes, employment, and protection for the poor; they promoted education or decided to take up arms and fight alongside the Greeks. Some of them were MPs, policy-makers, or politically influential individuals. Others, such as Lord Byron, legitimized the Greek cause in the eyes of the European public through their own direct participation in it. When Byron landed in Greece, many Romantic readers of *Childe Harold's Pilgrimage* instantly espoused the Greek cause. However, as Saree Makdisi notes, when Byron wrote this work in 1812, his Philhellenism was ambivalent and probably misunderstood by many of its readers.[30]

The London Greek Committee, founded in March 1823, campaigned intensely on behalf of the Greeks, although at the same time it became the locus for opposition to the politics of the Holy Alliance in support of liberty, free trade, and republican government for Greece (if not Britain).[31] Similarly, in 1825 French Liberals and Doctrinaires founded the French Greek committee, the Société Philanthropique en Faveur des

Grecs, or Comité Grec, and did not hesitate to embrace Philhellenism as part of their political package.[32] The Comité Grec was the offspring of the earlier Société de la Morale Chrétienne, an organization that professed to have humanitarian goals, which reveals the interpenetration of liberal political thought with the Christian religious sources of the committee itself. French Philhellenes created an outlet for their political energies, which had been repressed by the Restoration's ambient conservatism.[33] The committee attracted public attention, collected funds for the war, and organized numerous social events—bazaars, balls, concerts, and exhibitions—eagerly attended by fashionable French society. As in the case of its London counterpart, the Comité Grec aimed to convince Parisian elites that something had to be done for the Greeks. After the intervention of Navarino, French ruling elites appropriated those events for defending the cause of the Greeks, giving "moral capital" to and primarily benefiting themselves. It became the occasion for all to sing together of the military glory of France, Ultras and Liberals alike.[34] To commemorate French military action in Greece, paintings were commissioned portraying soldiers as the liberators of the Greeks, which was absolutely false but quite useful for internal consumption and to present the French as the rightful castigators of the Turks.

Inspired by the successful precedent of the antislavery campaign, the London Greek Committee used the politics of pressure groups. At a time when reliable news from Greece was scarce, the committee understood the importance of public opinion and systematically sent letters to the editors of the major publications, from the *Times*, *Chronicle*, and *Herald* to the *Literary Gazette*.[35] The committee's paper struggle was limited by the constraints of publishing: the delay and cost of mail and, most annoyingly, the price of printing. The large number of MPs and prominent personalities on the committee facilitated communication between the committee and the government and explains how this tiny group of people proved to be so influential. Bass notes that the committee crassly exploited the free-mail privileges of its MP members, jamming other letters in with those of an MP and sending correspondence through MPs.[36]

In Great Britain and France the public debate ignited by the Philhellenes revolved around a number of intertwined themes, all related, in one way or another, to intervention. One of them was the rescue of the Greeks from "bondage and destruction," as unsurprisingly pointed out by antislavery leader William Wilberforce—one of the most prominent members of the London Greek Committee—at the Commons.[37] Across the channel Chateaubriand presented the enslavement of Greek civilians as a serious violation of international laws on the slave trade. Like

Grosvenor, he argued that these laws applied to the Ottoman Empire even though the latter had not signed any formal agreement or treaty, for the Greek enslavement was a "crime against the liberty of men." In his speech in the Chamber of Peers on March 13, 1826, Chateaubriand proposed to amend the French abolitionist law by replacing the words *"trafic connu sous le nom de la traite des noirs"* with *"trafic des esclaves."* He saw the selling of white Christians as slaves in the bazaars of Asia and Africa as a monstrous anomaly. He did not want to diminish the horror of the black slave trade, though in his opinion the trade of white Christians was a "crime against civilization" (i.e., a religious, civil, and political crime). At least, Chateaubriand argued, black Africans were transported to a "civilized country" where they found Christian religion, whereas the white, "civilized" Christian Greeks were sold to "barbarity and Mahometanism." This was a "crime before the tribunal of God" and that of "civilized nations" (*nations policées*).[38]

To justify intervention, some Philhellenes put forward the question of Ottoman sovereignty over Greek lands. Chateaubriand's 1827 new edition of the *Itinéraires* contained a *Note sur la Grèce*, which contested the idea that the Ottoman Empire was part of Europe. Turkey, he wrote, was an alien power, which did not recognize European laws and customs (*le droit politique de l'Europe*) and ruled according to Asiatic customs (*le code des peuples de l'Asie*).[39] The Ottoman Empire's sovereignty, he argued, extended to its Muslim provinces, not to its Christian provinces. Chateaubriand also pointed out that the Greeks had a fleet and an army, minted coins, promulgated laws, and had a de facto government—a Christian, "civilized" government—which proved that the political bonds between the Ottoman sovereign and his Greek people had been broken; therefore they should be considered as two distinct powers. He used a Vattelian argument to demonstrate that the Ottoman government, by its insupportable tyranny, had brought on a national revolt against it. Therefore any foreign power that was asked to do so could assist the oppressed subject. Chateaubriand also added that for the mere fact of being Christians, European intervention against the Ottoman Empire was justified. Europe should have preferred a people behaving "according to the regenerating laws of Enlightenment" to a people that "destroys civilization everywhere."[40]

Among the pamphlets widely circulated by the London Greek Committee was the 1823 *Report on the Present State of the Greek Confederation, and Its Claims to the Support of the Christian World*, by Edward Blaquiere. The report emphasized the illegitimacy of Ottoman rule over Greece and the enormous suffering and degradation of the Greeks, living an existence deprived of the security of life, liberty, religion, and property.

He put forward many arguments to justify intervention on behalf of the Greeks. First, the modern Greeks were the direct descendants of the ancient Greeks, whose art and literature formed the basis of European civilization. Greece had a legitimate constitutional government and the main elements required for state formation: a people, a territory, and a government.[41] Second, Europeans were entitled to play the role of educators in Greece and would benefit from the commercial advantages that would result from future intercourse with Greece, as well as the certainty of its opening a new and profitable market for European produce. Third, and more important, Greeks were Christians, burdened and oppressed by the infidel. In his view, Great Britain had a duty to support the Greek cause because a Christian community was threatened with "extermination." To strengthen his argument, Blaquiere also made a deliberate reference both to extraterritoriality (the Capitulations) and to the Crusades. Finally, he deliberately minimized the atrocities committed by the Christians against the Muslims. He even legitimized massacre of Muslim civilian populations of Greece, claiming that earlier actions of the Turks had justified the subsequent actions of the Greeks.[42]

Rev. Thomas S. Hughes, who had been among the prerevolutionary tourists in Greece, published two powerful pamphlets: *An Address to the People of England in the Cause of the Greeks, Occasioned by the Late Inhuman Massacres in the Isle of Scio* (Chios) in 1822, and *Considerations upon the Greek Revolution* in 1823. Hughes, a priest and Tory from Cambridge, virulently called for the "extermination" of the Turks, "the most weak, contemptible, vice-stained tyrants that ever polluted the earth on which they trod, vilifying and degrading the fairest part of the creation." "There are some races whom it is a human duty to suppress," he added, "since they have utterly degenerated from the laws of nature, and have in their very body and frame of estate a monstrosity . . . , they are common enemies of mankind . . . disgraces and reproaches to human nature."[43] J. M. Berton (encountered in chapter 2) argued as virulently as Hughes that the European powers had to intervene against the Ottoman Empire. This was a case of "legitimate self-defence against the aggression of a ferocious despotism."[44] According to Berton, the European cabinets should not tolerate the attempted annihilation of Christianity and the extermination of Christians in a European region. They were not supposed to tolerate a monstrous anarchical military system, that of bloody despotism. Even if this was a case of rebellion against a sovereign and evidence of the betrayal was gathered, the Ottoman state should have identified and condemned the culprits. To massacre a population en masse was utterly unjustified.[45] Europe should have intervened against the Ottoman Empire in defense of the cause of a "developing civilisation" and against a "decrepit barbarity," which itself was an anarchical and anti-Christian usurpation.

Philhellenism also led to the emergence of new artistic representations of both the Greeks and the Turks, which enhanced empathy and compassion for fellow Christians throughout Europe. Some famous paintings, such as Eugène Delacroix's painting *Scènes des massacres de Scio*, exhibited at the Paris Salon of 1824, powerfully and vividly illustrated the massacres and atrocities perpetrated against civilian populations. The painting shows Greek women, children, and older people as innocent victims of "evil barbarians." The dichotomy Christians/ Muslims, civilized/barbarians so manifestly apparent in this painting would quintessentially embody all the arguments of the discourse justifying intervention against massacre throughout the nineteenth century.

Delacroix's *Massacres of Scio* was a unique representation of the massacre. In fact, it presented great affinities with J.M.W. Turner's 1822 watercolor study for an illustration of Byron's *The Giaour*, entitled with a verse from the poem, *"Tis living Greece no more."*[46] On May 17, 1826, when rumors of the "barbarization project" spread all over Europe (see next section), the painting exhibition Au profit des Grecs opened in Paris. Delacroix sent two paintings, one of which was *La Grèce sur les ruines de Missolonghi* (fig. 1), completed in just three months. As art historian Nina Athanassoglou-Kallmyer puts it, the painting is an allegory of defeated Greece pleading with Europe for assistance. Greece is personified as a handsome woman (motherland) in despair, her face in tears, her dress disheveled (plausibly evoking rape), who emerges half-kneeling among ruins and gruesome human remains (the atrocities) on the shore of ravaged Missolonghi (Mesolongi). Her stance and gesture are both demonstrative of her plight and appealing. The woman's direct gaze and outstretched hands make an appeal for human, not divine, aid; her eyes are not raised to heaven, and there is no cross, no bishop, no angel, no Christ. In the distance behind her, standing erect upon crumbling city walls, is a black Oriental holding the Crescent flag (an illusion to the Egyptian Army and an ingenious and culturally charged contrast to fair Greece), raising the standard of Islam.[47]

Between 1821 and 1827, when an armed intervention eventually took place, the images, the daily press (at a time when the Liberal newspaper *Le Constitutionnel* had eighteen thousand subscribers), pamphlets, and hundreds of books spread the idea that Islam had aggressed against Eastern Christendom, that Christians were the innocent victims or martyrs of the Muslims, and that Europe should have undertaken a modern crusade to rescue the Greeks as an act of "civilization" against "barbar-

ity." In my view the Philhellenes succeeded in keeping the question of intervention on behalf of the Greeks alive and turned it into one that could bring policy-makers moral capital. It should not be forgotten that some policy-makers were themselves Philhellenes or close to these circles; they were either devout Christians or close to more secular philanthropic circles. Finally, many policy-makers acted on political calculation and opportunism. I do not claim that the actions and campaigns of the Philhellenes alone explain the events of 1827; these actions favorably combined with changed political circumstances, which made intervention possible.

Egyptian Military Occupation of the Morea and the "Barbarization Plan"

While the Philhellenes campaigned at home or engaged as "freedom-fighters," the sultan's army remained far from defeated. The Greek insurgents still needed external financial and military help to achieve their goal. In January 1824 a number of Greek deputies with powers to contract a loan arrived in London. On February 19 the Greek deputies signed a loan agreement with the issuing house of Loughman, O'Brien, Ellis & Co., and on the following day the loan stock became officially available for purchase by the public.[48] Lord Byron and Colonel Leicester Stanhope became commissioners of the loan's issuing houses; they were in charge of the loan distribution and worked with the Greek insurgents. In Missolonghi they planned an attack on Naupactus, a Turkish stronghold; Lord Byron accepted the command of the expedition. He was to be seconded by Greek captains as well as European officers, along with an artillery corps of volunteers from England led by William Parry. They spent a lot of money to little effect and did not carry out the planned military attack. Byron died suddenly on April 19, and the British army recalled Stanhope in May. The issuance of a second loan secured the services of Lord Cochrane (acting in his private capacity) as commander of the Greek naval forces.[49] By the summer of 1826 the value of the bonds of both the first and second loan had fallen terribly, and recriminations about the handling of both loans were flying in London, fueled by press campaigns in *The Times* and in William Cobbett's *Weekly Register*.[50]

The Philhellene agitation in London and financial disaster of the Greek bonds had political consequences for the British government's decision to change its policy toward the "Greek Question." The latter also took into account the Ottoman Navy's increasing inability to provide protection for British commerce, as seen in the recrudescence of piracy in the eastern Mediterranean. However, the factor that more than any other brought the British government to consider the possibility of an intervention in Greece was the military involvement of Mohamed Ali, pasha of Egypt. His son Ibrahim occupied the Morea in February 1825. The military occupation of that region was unacceptable to Russia, which now consented to the complete independence of Greece and considered the possibility of waging war against the Ottoman Empire. Canning feared that the Egyptian occupation of the Morea would create a new power, threatening British interests in the eastern Mediterranean and trade with India. The foreign secretary feared even more a Russian intervention on the side of the Greeks, which could result in the creation of a Greek satellite state of Russia. According to Canning, the British government had two options left: to become allies with Egypt and the Ottoman Empire against Russia or to act alongside Russia and impose a compromise settlement of the Greek Question. He preferred the second option, which, in turn, explains why when in September 1825 a Greek delegation in London presented him with an "Act of Submission" placing the Greek nation's existence under the protection of Great Britain he rejected it, aware that its acceptance would have rendered any future cooperation with Russia impossible.[51]

In October 1825, without an explicit order from his government, the Russian ambassador in London, Christopher Lieven, showed Canning a document on Ibrahim's "barbarization project." The document claimed that Ibrahim was to keep whatever part of Greece he should conquer, and that his plan for disposing of his conquest was to remove the whole Greek population, carrying them off into slavery in Egypt or elsewhere, and to repeople the country with Egyptians and others of the "Mahometan religion."[52] As a consequence, Russia's intervention was almost inevitable, for there could hardly be a more flagrant breach of the Treaty of Küçük Kaynarca. The ambassador, who knew British politics very well and was certain that the British public would never tolerate the barbarization plan, found that the reading of this document would have sealed the cooperation between the two countries on the Greek Question.

Lieven provided the British government with alleged evidence encompassing killing, forced displacement, and enslavement of Greeks. These unverified rumors provided Canning with a ready-made platform for cooperation with Russia, a justification for diplomatic action based on supposedly solid humanitarian ground, the guarantee of support from British public opinion, and the highest moral reason for a diplomatic intervention, exploitable on both the domestic and international levels. Additionally, indignation against Ibrahim Pasha diverted attention from the Ottoman central government, which also suited the cabinet of London. In a dispatch dated January 9, 1826, to his cousin, Stratford Canning, who had recently been appointed ambassador at Constantinople, the foreign secretary wrote:

> I think I see, what you will give yourself joy, if not credit, for having shewn me (though to do justice you state the facts only without drawing the inference), a new ground of interference much higher than any that we have yet had open to us—I mean the manner in which the war is now carried on in the Morea—the character of barbarism and barbarization which it has assumed. Butchering of captives we have long witnessed on both sides of the contest. . . . But the selling into slavery—the forced conversions—the dispeopling of Christendom—the recruiting from the countries of Islamism—the erection in short of a new Puissance Barbaresque d'Europe—these are (not topics merely but) facts new in themselves, new in their principle, new and strange and hitherto inconceivable in their consequences, which I do think may be made the foundation of a new mode of speaking if not acting (I am cautious in my exposition because I am only now mediating aloud to you, not instructing or even deciding) and one which I confess I like the better because it has nothing to do with Epaminondas nor (with reverence be it spoken) with St. Paul.[53]

The Egyptian occupation was certainly rough and repression was pitiless. There were wholesale massacres when places like Missolonghi were stormed, extreme cruelty in the treatment of prisoners, and the enslavement of women and children. However, as Stratford Canning's biographer, Stanley Lane-Poole, revealed in 1888, it was deliberately "rumoured"—by the Russians—that Ibrahim Pasha intended to exterminate the population, or at least to transplant and expatriate them, and fill the country with Egyptians and Arabs. Contemporaries such as Wellington insisted that the Egyptian general had been defamed, an argument Canning did not retain.[54] Furthermore, previous instances of religious resettlement following widespread massacre had not produced any effect on European cabinets. That had been the case when, in 1822, vast numbers of Asiatic Turks poured into Chios, seemingly revealing the Porte's intention to replace the missing, banished, or exterminated Greek population of the island with Muslim settlers.[55] We shall see that even though contemporary policy-makers knew that there was no deliberate policy of extermination, the alleged "barbarization project" would prominently appear among the motivations for European intervention in 1827 and 1828. Curiously, even after the publication of Lane-Poole's book, European international legal scholars would still use Ibrahim's "war of extermination" as the perfect jurisprudential example of an intervention against massacre.

From Mediation to Armed Intervention
(April 1826–October 1827)

In March 1826 the Duke of Wellington went to St. Petersburg, officially to congratulate Nicholas I on his enthronement, as Tsar Alexander had died on December 1, 1825. The real goal of his mission, however, was to reach an understanding with Russia on the Greek Question that would avoid the undertaking of an armed intervention. On April 4 Wellington, Lieven, and Russian foreign minister Karl Nesselrode signed the Protocol of St. Petersburg. This protocol disclaimed any views of aggrandizement of the two powers and offered their mediation, not as a consequence of Ibrahim's barbarization plan, but on the Greek delegation's Act of Submission to Britain. An agreement was reached on Greece becoming a tributary dependency of the Ottoman Empire, autonomous but allowing the sultan "a certain share" in the nomination of its rulers. Local Christians would acquire all Muslim property in Greece, which supposed that the local Muslim population would be forced to leave the new suzerain territory of the sultan. Not surprisingly, after the Russian and British governments signed the protocol, they turned a deaf ear to the Porte's protestations that no plan to deport the Greek population of the Morea existed.[56] Then Britain and Russia asked the governments of Austria, France, and Prussia to share in the work of "peace-making" (as we would put it today) in Greece and to enforce the April 1826 protocol. The Austrian chancellor Klemens von Metternich bluntly refused to coerce the Ottomans on the question of Greece. The Prussian government obediently followed the decision of Vienna. Only France showed a willingness to cooperate.[57]

The French cabinet, headed by the Ultra Jean-Baptiste de Villèle, had supported the noninterventionist line dictated by Austria and Great Britain and strictly followed the French Catholic authorities that had posited the purported heresy of the Orthodox Church as its main reason for dismissing the cause of the revolutionaries. Moreover, the Ottoman Empire was a long-time ally of France, and France wanted to extend its influence in the eastern Mediterranean. French relations with Egypt were more than friendly since it was in Marseilles that two frigates and a brig of war had been secretly built for Egypt. In the meantime, the French government was maneuvering to place the Duke of Nemours on the Greek throne. Upon the failure of this project, and to keep Great Britain and Russia in check, France signed on to the Protocol of St. Petersburg.[58]

On July 6, 1827, France, Great Britain, and Russia signed the Treaty of London, along the lines of the St. Petersburg Protocol of 1826. "In the Name of the Most Holy and Undivided Trinity," the three powers, "penetrated with the necessity of putting an end to the sanguinary struggle," offered their mediation. They were concerned by the consequence of "all the disorders of anarchy," by the fresh impediments to the commerce of the states of Europe, and by acts of piracy that exposed the subjects of the contracting parties to grievous losses and rendered necessary measures. The treaty mentioned the three governments' desire to put "a stop to the effusion of blood, and of preventing the evils of every kind which the continuance of such a state of affairs may produce" and their intention to combine their efforts to reestablish peace between the contending parties "by means of an arrangement called for, no less by sentiments of humanity, than by interests for the tranquillity of Europe."

The treaty also contained three secret articles outlining the consequences that would follow a rejection of the European powers' offer of mediation. They remained secret for all of six days before being published in the *Times*. These articles stipulated that in case the Ottoman Porte should not, within one month, accept the mediation, the European powers would enter into commercial relations with Greece and take "immediate measures for forming a connection with the Greeks" (this being a formal recognition of Greece as a political entity). The three European powers declared to the contending parties that they intended to exert all efforts to reach an armistice, without taking any part in the hostilities. Admiral Edward Codrington's instructions made it clear that he had to be particularly careful that the measures he might adopt against the Ottoman Navy did not degenerate into hostilities.

The three ambassadors at Constantinople presented the terms of the treaty to the Sublime Porte on August 16, 1827. Sir Codrington and H. de Rigny (who would be later joined by Lodewijk Heiden for Russia) presented them to the Greeks at the end of the month. The Greeks accepted the armistice on September 2; the Ottoman government, now aware of the secret clauses contained within it, rejected it. In the meantime, the European admirals agreed to joint action, as taken individually their forces were inferior to the Ottoman ones. The British and French vessels began their action by intercepting every seaborne supply of men and arms destined for use against Greece, and they decided not to use force unless the Ottoman-Egyptian ships persisted in forcing their passage. Because of the Sublime Porte's formal rejection of the armistice, on September 4 the three European powers stipulated a protocol according to which the allied fleet was to protect, in cooperation with the Greeks, all of the part of Greece that had taken an active and continued part in the insurrection. This area was defined as the territory south of Volos in the East to north of Missolonghi and included the islands of Euboea (Evia), Ydra, and Spetses. Any Ottoman ship that did not voluntarily removed itself from this area, including Navarino and Methoni, would "incur all the chances of war."[59]

THE NAVAL BATTLE OF NAVARINO (OCTOBER 1827):
A HUMANITARIAN INTERVENTION?

A combined Turkish and Egyptian fleet anchored in the Bay of Navarino on September 7, 1827. The French fleet anchored in Navarino on September 22, where it found its British allies. Three days later the admirals Codrington and de Rigny met Ibrahim. It was expected that Ibrahim would receive new instructions around October 15, and the admirals believed he would not move during the intervening twenty days. Thus, the majority of the French and British ships sailed away to patrol other sectors of the coast or to obtain provisions. The Russian fleet, under the command of Admiral Heiden, eventually arrived on October 13, when the three admirals sent a joint ultimatum to Ibrahim. The latter was furious that the Greeks had destroyed a flotilla of seven Ottoman ships at Itea in the Gulf of Corinth. He decided to undertake an operation around the area of Kalamata, ravaging the country, destroying the habitations, and burning the olive and other fruit trees. Ibrahim attempted to force passage with his ships stationed at Navarino Bay to head for Patra. On October 20 and over three days and nights, the European powers reacted and defeated the Turco-Egyptian fleet. No less than 6,000 Ottoman sailors perished, but not a single allied ship was sunk. The allies suffered minor losses, for in fact only 174 of their men died in action.

When we look at the modalities of the intervention at Navarino, the humanitarian rationale seems unconvincing. The battle did not save strangers or bring immediate relief to Greek civilian populations—not even to the mass of refugees, including women and children—of Kalamata starved by Ibrahim's troops. The naval intervention did not relieve Greek civilians' miserable sanitary conditions; it was provisions and relief sent by private charities, mostly American, that saved civilian populations from starvation and plague. Had the intervention been against massacre, it should have followed evidence (which did not exist) of the enforcement of the barbarization plan in early 1826. When the military intervention took place, the alleged "ethnic cleansing" plan had been going on for almost two years. Humanitarian motives for intervention on behalf of Christian civilians, which had been so obviously evident in 1821 (in Constantinople and Smyrna), 1822 (in Chios), and 1825 (in the Morea), were questionable in 1827. Even if we consider Navarino as an intervention aimed at preventing the repetition of future massacre or extermination, its modalities were ill-conceived. In fact, Ibrahim had twenty thousand infantry and four thousand cavalry stationed in the Morea, enough military power to further devastate the areas under Egyptian occupation and to perpetrate new massacres. The admirals lacked the necessary military strength to prevent them. Only massive ground forces could have protected the lives of civilian populations of the Morea. A European expeditionary corps would eventually land in the area only in late August 1828.

Navarino's immediate result was to make it impossible for diplomats to go back. Greece was now certain of its independence, but the fighting had not yet ended. The battle of Navarino hardened the attitude of the Ottoman government, which continued to refuse allied mediation or the recognition of the Greeks as anything but rebels. This eventually transformed the intervention into a full-fledged war between Russia and the Ottoman Empire, which started on April 14, 1828, and ended in Russian victory and the signing of the peace treaty of Adrianople on September 14, 1829. After Navarino, Metternich ironically described the position of the three intervening powers as one mediating power, Russia, at open war with the Porte, with half of its squadron engaged in a hostile blockade of the Dardanelles and the other half in a pacific blockade of the Greek coast; a second power, France, engaged in "amicable hostilities" by land with a nominal vassal of the sultan, but neutral at sea; and a third power, Great Britain, neutral but an ally and accomplice of the other two.[60]

The French Occupation of the Morea (1828–33)

On July 9, 1827, during the Conference in London, the French plenipotentiary had obtained a mandate for France to send an expeditionary corps to the Morea in order to remove the Egyptian troops occupying that territory. This was not to be a war of conquest; the French government had not asked for any compensation and claimed to be genuinely disinterested. The French expeditionary corps, initially at least, was to be joined by British forces.[61] The British cabinet eventually refused to join the French when the Russo-Ottoman War began, fearing a hostile reaction in Parliament. While the French gathered some fourteen thousand men in Toulon under the orders of Lieutenant-General Nicolas Joseph de Maison, the French consul at Alexandria, Bernardino Drovetti, urged Mohamed Ali to end the enslavement of a large number of Greeks who had been taken to Egypt. The consul was supposed to convince Mohamed Ali to remove Ibrahim's army by threatening a strict blockade of Alexandria.

On July 19, 1828, a protocol signed by the three intervening powers (with the acquiescence of Prussia and Austria) authorized armed intervention by France and defined the objects of the expedition. The Russian and British governments accepted the expedition on the proviso that France would withdraw its forces as soon as the Egyptian Army was out of Greece unless Ibrahim went north, in which event France could station a military corps on the Isthmus of Corinth to prevent his return. A joint note of the three European powers informed the government of Constantinople that their decision was the consequence of the "war of extermination" that had taken place in the Morea.[62] The powers did not consider the intervention an act of war. Moreover, the target entity was Egypt, a vassal of the Ottoman Empire, not an independent state. The entire operation was confusing from the diplomatic, juridical, and military point of view, for the European powers were moving in unknown political realms. They wished to avoid the consequences of a general war. Hence, when it seemed clear that Mohamed Ali wanted to avoid armed confrontation, the European diplomats reached a swift agreement with the pasha stipulating that the Egyptian Army would withdraw from Greece and that the Greek slaves would be freed. Given that the pasha did not want to appear to withdraw voluntarily from the Morea for fear of offending the sultan, a stratagem was devised. A fleet would sail from Egypt to Greece, nominally with supplies, but actually returning the Greek captives and slaves, which would be intercepted by an Anglo-French squadron and "persuade" Ibrahim's army to embark in exchange for its original cargo. English and French ships would escort and convoy the Egyptian troops back to Alexandria. Ibrahim would temporarily keep possession of four main fortresses in the Peloponnese.

The French undersecretary for foreign affairs, Maximilien de Rayneval, claimed that the mission's objective was "the reestablishment of peace in Europe" by inducing the sultan to accept the Treaty of London.[63] The instruction to General Maison made it clear how to ensure that no further troubles would occur in those disturbed regions. The French expeditionary corps' discipline was deemed indispensable when dealing with the (Christian) population of a devastated country.[64] To avoid the repetition of massacre in the future, the French troops were to make sure that no Muslim civilians would stay in the Morea, the territory that was about to constitute the bulk of the new—religiously cleansed—Greek state. Foreign Minister Auguste de la Ferronays stated that the objective of the intervention was "to chase the Turks out of the places they would hold in Greece after the departure of the Arabs [the Egyptians]."[65] The French oversaw the displacement of circa 2,500 Muslim survivors of previous massacres, who were transferred to Smyrna onboard French vessels on November 5, 1828, inaugurating a state practice that would become as common as it was tragic throughout the nineteenth century.

The French expeditionary corps landed on August 28, 1828, and by the end of that year the Morea and the Cyclades were in fact under a three-power protectorate. The French military supervised the return of enslaved civilians to their homes and guaranteed the removal of Egyptian soldiers. On October 4 Ibrahim himself left the Morea. The withdrawal was complete, apart from the 1,200 Egyptian soldiers in the fortresses. Historian David Brewer writes that in a final charade, the fortress garrisons were instructed by Ibrahim not to fire on the French and surrendered to them after mock attacks. General Pellion tells a different story. He claimed that because of the extremely slow withdrawal of Ibrahim's troops, and because of the worsening sanitary conditions of the French troops, General Maison decided he had to remove *"de gré ou de force"* (whether they liked it or not) the fortress garrisons.[66]

The French occupation of the Morea was a collective intervention implemented by French troops in the name of Europe. The European powers mandated the French Army corps; the latter did not act on an individual basis, instead executing a plan previously agreed with all the other powers. The mandate was clear, and it was plain that none of the powers would benefit individually from the intervention. The British and Russians opposed French plans for the liberation of Greece and strictly watched every French military move.[67] As we have seen, the intervention did not end the massacres or war between the Greeks and the Ottoman Empire; it did not save strangers. At the same time, European (French) troops were not neutrals and cannot be viewed as *ante litteram* peacekeeping forces. They were in the Morea to check and control the withdrawal of the Egyptian Army, ready to intervene against the Egyptians and even the Ottomans if necessary. Their peace-enforcement mandate was very limited, for the French troops could not stop the Greeks from waging war in western Greece and in Attica (and this was never their intention).

The presence of the French troops spared the surviving civilian populations of the Morea the consequences of the final stages of the Greek war of independence. The French expeditionary corps' duties went beyond the traditional role of an occupying army. For instance, when the Egyptian soldiers embarked, Russian, French, and British commissioners checked that they did not kidnap women and children. Unfortunately, the European commissioners did not take into account the wishes of the local populations. Some women wanted to follow the Egyptian soldiers, preferring life in the harem to the extreme poverty of the Peloponnese. As would happen in analogous instances throughout the nineteenth century, the French forces had to face all sorts of problems intrinsically related to a new kind of military operation. For instance, they returned the Greek slaves from Egypt, but no United Nations high commissioner for refugees or International Committee of the Red Cross awaited them in the Morea. Once back in Greece, many displaced children could not find their families and were then sent again to Egypt.[68]

After the withdrawal of Ibrahim's army, General Maison left a *brigade d'occupation* (about 5,300 men), under the command of General Virgile Schneider, in the Morea. In the name of the alliance, the brigade had to maintain law and order. Its garrisons were in Methoni and Navarino. French troops reconstructed roads and fortresses and tried to organize relief, and local populations gratefully remembered the occupation. In his classic work on Greece, George Finlay defined the French expeditionary corps in the Morea as "a pioneer army" whose activity exhibited how an army raised by conscription ought to be employed in time of peace, in order to prevent the labor of men from being lost to their country.[69] French soldiers were supposed to offer the Greeks some rudimentary elements of defense and administration; they were on an *ante litteram* state-building mission. In Nafplio, under the direction of General Camille Alphonse Trézel, they founded an officer's military school where the French taught two Greek regiments, and they built barracks for the embryonic Greek Army.[70]

Finally, it should be mentioned that the French government also had a secret agenda, which was certainly not humanitarian and went against the collective agreement. A small number of French military remained in Greece until 1833 because Polignac hoped to use the complete withdrawal of the expedition as a bargaining point with England in his newly adopted venture, the Drovetti plan, which sought to employ Egypt to conquer the Barbary regencies. Further evidence of the desire of some French authorities to capitalize on the expedition was given by General Schneider's recommendation just before General Charles Gueheneuc replaced him on October 28, 1831. Schneider proposed to the Duke of Dalmatia, then the French foreign minister, that France should officially establish a colony in Greece. The duke refused to have the government sponsor such a colony but raised no objection if French families moved to Greece on their own initiative and at their own risk.[71]

. . .

On February 3, 1830, a new Treaty of London turned Greece into the first independent state in the Balkans. Diplomatic negotiations among the European powers lasted until 1833 and concerned the boundaries of the new state and appointment of a monarch. The independence of Greece was not the intended consequence of the military intervention Navarino or the direct result of the actions and pressures of the Philhellenes, but the accidental outcome of the European powers' converging interests. Navarino was a last-resort measure following a failed attempt of mediation between two belligerents. It was a collective military intervention. It was not a war, nor was it a peaceful transaction between the European powers and the Ottoman Empire. The intervening states considered that the intervention would have beneficial effects on their trade, would put an end to piracy in the disturbed areas, and would be beneficial for peace and tranquillity in Europe, and it was fully approved by their respective public opinion or parliaments. The Russian idea of defending Orthodox Christians was not incompatible with a liberal project of self-determination promoted by French and British Philihellenes, opposed for a long time by the governments of London and Paris. The intervention was not primarily designed to save the lives of strangers even though the humanitarian motive was not entirely absent. Ibrahim's barbarization project was fabricated, but massacre, atrocities, and the appalling living conditions of civilian populations of the Morea were real. Massacre and atrocities solidified the idea of a just intervention and came after the events of Constantinople, Smyrna, and Chios. Hence, humanitarian, self-, and collective interests combined together and made the intervention possible.

The intervention of Navarino was first labeled *"d'humanité"* in the late 1820s, when official documents designated it a consequence of the "war of extermination" (*guerre d'extermination*) taking place in Greece.[72] The international conference of the signatory powers held in London on April 8, 1830, spoke about the "frightful calamities for humanity," which made the Greek Question one that the Ottoman Empire could not deal with alone but one that had been internationalized.[73] In 1830 it was politically useful for the French, British, and Russian representatives to underscore the imperative duty of humanity (*devoir impérieux d'humanité*), which had led to the intervention. This was the best way to emphasize the exceptionality of such an intervention and underpin that it remained subordinated to collective security imperatives of the intervening powers. Even if based on fabricated evidence, the intervention at Navarino would become a precedent, especially as far as the conditions and modalities of intervention were concerned. During the second half of the nineteenth century, many international legal scholars and other international affairs expert retrospectively argued that Navarino was the *coup d'essai* of the international practice of humanitarian intervention. In 1866 Augustus Granville Stapleton, the private secretary of George Canning wrote:

It was not until the mode in which hostilities were conducted by the Turkish general, Ibrahim Pasha, became at variance with the recognized rules of civilized warfare, so as to give every European State a right of war against Turkey, that he entertained the idea of a forcible intervention. It was evident that the Pasha was carrying on a war of extermination—wherever there was the slightest resistance, he massacred all the males, and sent the women and children into slavery in Egypt. He was laboring to blot out of existence a whole Christian people, and to establish a new Barbary State on the shore of the Mediterranean, in the very midst of Europe. Mr. Canning held this to be a casus belli, giving all nations a right to interfere by force, and accordingly he consented to the Greek treaty, which admitted of a forcible interference, if necessary to prevent the consummation of this atrocious design.[74]

Stapleton, in his quality of private secretary must have known the truth about the "barbarization project." It is not very clear if, in his view, uncivilized warfare gave a right to intervene or to wage a war only when instances of massacre, atrocities, and extermination took place within the boundaries of the Ottoman Empire or everywhere in the world. In 1876 many campaigners wanted a second Navarino, to end the Bulgarian atrocities; their concerns about humanity focused on Christians living on the fringes of Europe. In 1880 Sheldon Amos, speaking of the events in Greece, wrote that "Gross acts of inhumanity, properly precipitate intervention."[75] At the turn of the century, Oppenheim wrote that the powers intervened in 1827 because public opinion was horrified at the cruelties committed during the struggle. In 1926 André Mandelstam quoted the treaties of 1830 to corroborate the idea of an intervention going beyond the "sound" self-interests of the intervening powers and of a *devoir humanitaire*.[76]

More recently, legal scholar Ian Brownlie dismissed the characterization of the intervention at Navarino as an instance of humanitarian intervention. In his view this is ex post factoism. He argues that the government of the day did not refer to a legal justification for intervention, and that publicists and historians have ascribed numerous motives to the action. He too concludes that the substantial motive of the intervention was the prevention of racial extermination in the Morea, which cannot be discussed in "terms of a legal concept which probably did not exist at the time."[77] From the point of the historian, the particular conditions of the 1820s international system favored the intervention of 1827–33. The intervention took place only because the population to be rescued was Christian. In my view, throughout the nineteenth century religion would remain an important and discriminating element determining when and on behalf of whom intervention could take place. Intervention in Greece enhanced the claim of European powers to possess the moral high ground that allowed them to intervene for humanitarian purposes in the Ottoman Empire. Furthermore, the Greek Question showed that under certain circumstances, policy-makers could not entirely overlook the emergence of a substantial domestic political constituency in favor of intervention. Finally, governments proved quick to utilize the moral claims of public opinion in their stated interests and successfully used the arguments of public opinion to promote state action and enhance their "moral capital."

CHAPTER FOUR

Intervention in Ottoman Lebanon and Syria (1860–61)

> The time is fast approaching when the imperative claims of Christianity and humanity must and ought to absorb all others in the much vexed Eastern Question.
> —C. H. Churchill, *The Druzes and the Maronites under Turkish Rule from 1840 to 1860*, 1862

THE LOCAL AND INTERNATIONAL CONTEXT BEFORE THE INTERVENTION

Before the intervention of 1860, Mount Lebanon (also known as the Mountain) was an autonomous administrative Ottoman entity distinct from the province of Syria, comprising nearly 200,000 inhabitants.[1] Numerically preponderant, the Christian Maronites inhabited the northern and central regions of Mount Lebanon.[2] They were also numerous in the mainly Druze area of Jezzine and similarly formed an enclave in the town of Dair al-Qamar. The Druze were a splinter group of Sh'ia Islam, sufficiently far removed from Muslim doctrine to be sometimes considered a different religion. The Greek Orthodox community, also known as Orthodox Melkite, was the second largest in Lebanon and settled mainly in the Kura district, the coastal region south of Tripoli. The Greek Catholics (Uniates), also known as Catholic Melkites, were concentrated in Zahleh. The Sunni, Shi'a, Metwalis Muslims, and Bedouins were scattered in various locations both north and south. In Mount Lebanon local Druze and Maronite notables served as intermediaries between the Ottoman authorities and the urban population they spoke for and controlled. The autonomy of Mount Lebanon depended on a network of alliances among leading Druze and Maronite families and on a chain of clan loyalties that cut across sectarian lines and took precedence over loyalty to village, district, or church.[3]

From 1831 to 1840 Egyptian military occupied Lebanon. Ibrahim Pasha conquered Syria in the name of his father Mohamed Ali of Egypt and ruled it with long-lasting consequences. The Egyptian occupiers practiced classic divide-and-rule politics, using the Druze against the Maronites, and encouraged the influx of missionaries, travelers, and economic and industrial prospectors from Europe. In July 1840 a

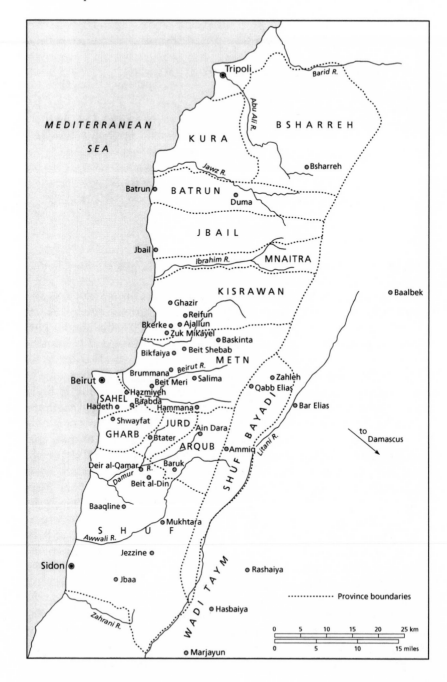

MEDITERRANEAN
SEA

Tripoli

Barid R.

Abu Ali R.

B S H A R R E H

K U R A

Bsharreh

Jawz R.

Batrun

B A T R U N

Duma

J B A I L

Jbail

Ibrahim R.

M N A I T R A

K I S R A W A N

Baalbek

Ghazir

Reifun

Bkerke   Ajallun

Zuk Mikayel

Baskinta

Bikfaiya   Beit Shebab

M E T N

Brummana   Beirut R.

Beit Meri   Salima

Zahleh

Beirut

Hazmiyeh   Qabb Elias

SAHEL   Baabda

Hadeth   Hammana

Bar Elias

Shwayfat

JURD   Ain Dara

to
Damascus

GHARB   Btater

ARQUB   Ammiq

Deir al-Qamar   R.   Baruk

Damur

Beit al-Din

Baaqline

SHUF BAYADI

Litani R.

Mukhtara

S   H   U   F

Awwali R.

Jezzine

Sidon

Jbaa

Rashaiya

WADI TAYM

Hasbaiya

Zahrani R.

Marjayun

·············· Province boundaries

| 0 | 5 | 10 | 15 | 20 | 25 km |

| 0 | 5 | 10 | 15 miles |

British-sponsored coalition made up of Russia, Austria, and Prussia ended the Egyptian occupation and restored Ottoman sovereignty. The price the sultan had to pay for European help was a considerable increase in European agents' presence and interference in the affairs of Lebanon. In December 1842 a dual *kaim makamate*, or governorship, was established under European supervision. After revision in 1845 this administrative scheme remained in place until 1861. It divided the Mountain into two self-governing districts, each with its own district governor (*kaim makam*): the northern district under a Maronite, and the southern district under a Druze.[4]

France had traditionally been the protector of the Maronites. It staked out an early claim to the loyalty of the Maronite Christians at the time of the Crusade of Saint Louis (1147–49), who had rewarded them with the title of "French-men" in return for their services to him.[5] Since the eighteenth century the French government had instructed its diplomats to intercede on behalf of the Maronite nation whenever it became involved in disputes or trouble. The Capitulations treaties signed by the French and Ottoman governments did not include the possibility of a military intervention organized by the French government in defense of the Maronites of Lebanon or of French missionaries. Protection was a discreet diplomatic action, an intercession undertaken by French consuls with local Ottoman authorities. Unlike France, Britain had had no toehold in Syria before 1840.[6] In the early 1840s Palmerston played with the idea of a "special relationship" with the Druze, a vision made more attractive by the missionary dreams of converting the Druze to Protestantism and using them as the base from which to spread religious influence, parallel to French influence over Roman Catholics and Maronites.[7] After 1840 British and French religious, commercial, and political rivalries affected the stability of these Ottoman territories. British and French agents looked upon local populations, especially the Christians, as their clients and protégés and began to play a role that went beyond the protection of religious matters of the previous centuries. As a consequence, the traditionally privileged classes of the region, whether Druze in Mount Lebanon or Sunni on the Syrian coast and in the interior, increasingly perceived the Christians who benefited from trade with Europe as a threat to their own status.

Among other factors to be taken into account when examining the conditions that brought about the massacres of 1860 is the role of the *Tanzimat*, which further destabilized the region. For instance, the introduction of the 1858 Ottoman Land Code allowed Europeans and their protégés to buy up both urban real estate and agricultural land. These newcomers often bought property from impoverished Muslim notables, especially in Damascus. The new laws, under which Christians could testify against Muslims, created further discontentment among the Muslims. By 1860 tension was high, and the Muslim population would have happily ejected the European consuls dwelling in their midst, though instead they moved against local Christians, who were an easier target.[8]

After the Crimean War Russia's policy with respect to the Eastern Question changed. The 1856 Treaty of Paris abolished Russia's privileges in the Danubian Principalities. Russia lost territories in Bessarabia, and its influence was excluded from the lower Danube area. The Black Sea was neutralized and opened to merchant ships of all states. The treaty also dealt with the question of the protection of Ottoman Christians. Now Russia could not pretend to be the only protector of these communities, not even in the Balkans. Even though Russia aimed at overturning the Treaty of Paris, it remained a member of the European Concert. In the short term Austria was the biggest loser of all, for it paid the cost of its support for the western European governments during the Crimean Wwar and, as a consequence, lost that of Russia. Austria found itself isolated during the Italian and German crises of the late 1850s and 1860s, which explains its minor involvement in the affairs of Lebanon and Syria.

The coming to power in France of Louis Napoleon, who was first elected president in 1848 and then, after a coup in late 1851 and a plebiscite eleven months later, became the Emperor Napoleon III, added an element of instability to the international system. He wished to unravel the settlement of 1815, to construct a new European order, and to increase its influence in the East Mediterranean. One way of doing so was by supporting nationalists. This, at least theoretically, meant a foreign policy directed against the Sultan. When massacre took place in Lebanon, Napoleon used the press, publishing (or censoring) news at his convenience. French public opinion was thoroughly informed about the events in those Ottoman provinces mainly thanks to pro-French Maronite clerics in Lebanon and Syria who supplied abundant information. French newspapers such as *Le Moniteur* (controlled by Napoleon III), *Le Constitutionnel* (considered representative of the views of Thouvenel, the minister of foreign affairs), and *Le Siècle*, gave biased accounts of the massacres. This flow of biased information certainly contributed to arouse genuine feelings of French public opinion on behalf of innocent Christian populations allegedly slaughtered by the Druze with the complicity of the Ottoman authorities.

Great Britain at midcentury was a commercial power like no other. In 1860 it generated about a quarter of all world trade, more than twice as much as the next most important country, France. Its commercial interests were spread more widely than those of continental powers.[9] As far as European affairs are concerned, British statesmen aimed at the preservation of the equilibrium created in 1815 and 1856. Maintaining equilibrium via diplomacy was the first best option of Great Britain, a naval power whose land forces were modest. Within eight months of the Treaty of Paris, Britain declared war on Persia and dispatched an expedition from India to drive the Persians out of Afghanistan. In 1856 British forces also bombarded Canton to punish the Chinese for having impounded a small boat flying the British flag. In May 1857 a mutiny broke out in India when Indian soldiers (sepoys) at Meerut in the North-Western Provinces rose against their British officers, killed a number of them, set the cantonment alight with the help of local inhabitants, and then departed rapidly southward. The mutiny quickly became a revolt, and serious unrest spread from Meerut to Benares (although many other areas of the Indian subcontinent were not involved with it), an area the British forces lost control of for several months. The atrocities committed by the rebels were seized upon with enthusiasm as providing carte blanche for every kind of countercruelty. The events at Cawnpore in June and July 1857, when, despite a safe conduct pass, British soldiers were shot and some two hundred women and children hacked to pieces, caused an outcry and revulsion unusual even in so emotional an age.[10] Atrocities on the British side were no less extreme, and in their repression the British forces did not make any attempt to separate the guilty from the innocent. To British public opinion it seemed that in India "the jaws of a pagan hell had been opened before them with the express aim of destroying both colonial rule and Christian civilization." Indians were regarded as "monsters," and newspapers dwelt lovingly upon every atrocity and were adept at discovering rape where none had taken place.[11]

The rebellion had serious consequences for the way Britain viewed its role as a "civilizer" as well as the way Britons viewed "barbarian" peoples or "uncivilized' governments. Doubts concerning the emancipatory and civilizing character of colonial rule emerged after the 1857 Indian Mutiny and more markedly so after the 1865 "rebellion" in Morant Bay, Jamaica. As we shall see, massacres in Lebanon three years after the events in India confirmed to the Europeans what "barbarians" were capable of doing. The British government and its European counterparts gathered further evidence of the consequences of an inadequate and inept imperial rule, for the Ottomans—contrary to what Great Britain did in India—would be unable to put an end to the rebellion and the ensuing massacres and atrocities.

European "Gentle Crusaders" and Their Perception of Local Populations

An articulated set of images and perceptions of Syria and Lebanon had circulated in Europe since the end of the eighteenth century, thanks to the works of orientalists, painters, and poets. They had brought impressions of Lebanon and Syria into the homes of European cultivated elites. In the writings of Alphonse de Lamartine and in the paintings of David Robert's *Ruins of the Temple of the Sun at Baalbec* (1861) and Edward Lear's *Beirut and Mount Lebanon* (1858-59), these Ottoman provinces evoked an Eden on earth, a timeless biblical land, and a mountain refuge that was stagnant owing to Islamic Ottoman domination.

Early-nineteenth-century European writers became prophets of the cultural redemption and religious salvation of Mount Lebanon. They exuded confidence in European cultural, political, technological, and military hegemony. They narrated and judged with the experience of the native (this was a direct consequence of their "scientific" approach to nature and the people they encountered), though such authenticity was tempered by the "superiority of a European who looks down from the height of Christian civilisation."[12] In the words of historian Ussama Makdisi, these Europeans saw themselves as "gentle crusaders." They portrayed Mount Lebanon's populations as waiting to be "regenerated" and reconnected with the evolutionary "stream of Time" from which they had been kept apart by Ottoman despotism and by Islam.[13] For some of them, such as French intellectual and politician Lamartine, a European colony had to be established "in the heart of Asia" in order to bring "modern civilization."[14]

In the mid-nineteenth century, Europeans portrayed Mount Lebanon as a place inhabited by two rival sects, the Druze and the Maronites, where the "fanatical' and "antimodern" Turks cunningly upset the math of reform and harmed the Christians.[15] Europeans invented the mythology of the tribes of Lebanon. They imagined, portrayed, and experienced the Druze and Maronites of Mount Lebanon as separate entities.[16] Makdisi does not suggest that religious communities did not exist or that travelers' accounts were false or fabricated, but instead that they were conceptualized in certain terms that did not correspond to the way the inhabitants of Mount Lebanon perceived themselves. These views penetrated public opinion before massacres occurred and determined the way public opinion and European parliaments reacted to them.[17]

British and French authors who wrote about the massacres, such as Charles Henry Churchill, Louis de Baudicour, Henry Guys, François Lenormant, Eugène Poujade, Baptistin Poujoulat, and "Saint" Marc Girardin, viewed massacre alternatively as the consequence of "native tribalism," of the "barbarism" of Turkish rule, or of the impossibility to "regenerate the Turks." They all agreed on Christian superiority with respect to Muslims.[18] When massacres took place, Churchill and Lenormant (author of many articles published in the Catholic newspaper *L'Ami de la Religion*) claimed that European governments were not bound by the principle of nonintervention in their dealings with the Ottoman Empire.[19] These authors were convinced that, as in the case of the Philhellenes for Greece, something had to be done to stop the massacre. They put forward the idea that the regeneration and reconnection of local populations with "civilization" might well entail an intervention on grounds of humanity, and they described events in Lebanon and Syria as the indiscriminate and brutal slaying of Christians at the hands of the Druze. As had been the case during the intervention in the Morea, on both shores of the channel "humanitarian champions" organized public meetings to support the idea of an intervention and humanitarian relief. Lord Shaftesbury sponsored the Ladies' Association for Social and Religious Improvement of Syrian Females. French Catholics organized various relief missions. The French Catholic deputies presented in Parliament a number of petitions from the Maronites of Lebanon and Christians from Damascus demanding the military intervention of French troops "to protect them."[20] As in the 1820s, French people spontaneously wrote poems on the *Massacres de Syrie* in which they showed how deeply they had made the themes of "Turkish barbarism" their own, and they often fell into the rhetoric of the Christian crusade against the infidel. In these poems the Druze (who came to be called Muslims) intended to exterminate the Christians and to achieve this plan raped women, enslaved civilians, and murdered children. [21]

THE MASSACRES

A great deal of distortion, exaggeration, and extravagant claims characterized the description of events made by European men on the spot. Some have been saddled with responsibilities that cannot be justified by known historical evidence.[22] The following account does not intend to shed light on what really happened. Rather, it tells the story as various men on the spot reported it to European capitals, for the decision of the European governments to intervention was based on those accounts.

On July 15, 1858, a native mob at Jeddah fell upon the Christians in their midst; among their victims were the French consul and the British vice consul. A Franco-British squadron bombarded the town eleven days later. This incident had repercussions beyond Jeddah for it increased the fanatic zeal of the Christians, especially the Maronites of Mount Lebanon, who had been promoting a second civil war using the money received by the Europeans in the first civil war to buy firearms and ammunitions. In the months preceding the massacre, the European consuls engaged Bishop Tobia, whose sinister influence as a promoter of the clashes against the Druze was notorious, as a missionary. This confirmed the Druze and Muslim suspicions of a conspiracy formed by the Christians, in particular the Maronite clergy, backed by interested European governments, to despoil them of their land and goods. The Maronites initiated disturbances, though the Druze, who were far superior in military tactics and discipline, retaliated as ferociously as their opponents. In March 1860 a series of skirmishes occurred in the mixed districts of southern Lebanon. In the last two weeks of May, dispatches from the British and French consuls mentioned sectarian murders, random and unpredictable, occurring among the civilian populations of Lebanon. The leaders of the warring religious communities increasingly fomented and even led the revolt.

Consular reports from the months of May, June, and July 1860 mention the looting and burning of villages; the sacking of monasteries, churches, and mosques; a number of forced conversions; the slaughter of children, women, and older people; and the rape and abduction of women and young girls.[23] French consular reports did not spare morbid details, such as the burning of women after being bathed in the blood of their children. Consular dispatches asserted that the two district governors were incapable of putting an end to the disturbances and accountable for the events taking place in Lebanon. The consuls pointed out that there was no adequate police or Ottoman military presence to stop the pillage. It was precisely the lack of a police force that later became one of the catalysts for European intervention; the intervening powers claimed that the Ottoman Empire (the potential target state) was responsible and unable—or unwilling, as the French government put it—to end the massacre. According to the Europeans, the temper of the Ottoman Fifth Army Corps appeared only when the Druze showed a winning hand. Both the irregulars and the regular soldiers, who were chiefly Syrian recruits, took advantage of the situation to settle old scores with the Christians.[24]

European consuls gave precise information and figures concerning the number of Christians killed and slaughtered. They were not as precise about the number of Druze killed during the civil strife. They unanimously acknowledged that Druze were better organized militarily and almost systematically defeated the Maronites. European consuls often pointed out that because of the disturbances, the survivors from the inland districts fled toward the coastal cities, such as Sidon. There they were refused admittance by local authorities and hid as best they could in caves and gardens around the town and along the coast. According to European eyewitness accounts, local Muslim and Druze bandits killed 250 to 300 people. An eyewitness, British colonel Charles Henry Churchill, described the events that took place at the gates of Sidon as "pure butchery":

300 bodies soon strewed the sea-beach and the gardens round about. The shrieks of the women and children rent the air. Some were slain; numbers violated. The young girls were hurried off by a mingled horde of Mohammedans and Metualis, who mysteriously appeared and pounced upon them like vultures on their quarry. The Druzes scorned to touch such offal. Several Catholic convents and nunneries . . . were invaded, robbed and pillaged with similar treachery. The nuns were turned out nearly naked into the fields, and in some instances suffered personal violence. The monks who failed in secreting themselves or escaping were pitilessly slaughtered; some speared in derision at the foot of their altars.[25]

Violence in the coastal towns of Jaffa, Haifa, Acre, Sidon, Tyre, Tripoli, and Beirut decreased or stopped when, in mid-June, British and French ships anchored off the coast. Marines landed a number of times to protect British or French nationals and protégés, as well as a number of Christian refugees. Even before the fighting began in earnest, European forces were braced to step in. On May 25 a French war sloop and a small British ship, HMS *Firefly*, cruised near Beirut. The fifty-two-cannon Russian frigate *Vladimir*, carrying six hundred troops ready to land, was clearly visible from the Lebanese capital.[26] On June 13 a French squadron anchored in Beirut. The French ambassador at Constantinople, Charles Jean de Lavalette, informed Camille de la Roncière, commander of the frigate *Zénobie*, that his duty was *"avant tout une tâche d'humanité."*[27] In the coastal areas of Lebanon in a single day, a single British warship, the *Mohawk*, brought 600 Christian fugitives, mainly women and children, from the towns of Deir-el-Qamar, Tyre and Sidon. That warship had previously transported to Beirut 1,700 refugees and would transport hundreds more refugees in the following days.[28]

The motive of these operations was undoubtedly humanitarian even though they were mostly directed at protecting European nationals and their commercial interests. In Beirut panic seized the Christian communities, who were convinced that the fate of other Lebanese Christians awaited them, with the result that hundreds of them, including leading merchants, fled to Malta and Alexandria.[29] In the end, the rescue operations saved only a minority of refugees and did not stop massacres going on in the inland. They also had unintended consequences, generating further humanitarian crises when thousands of civilian refugees abandoned the villages of the interior with the intention of reaching these towns, hoping to be rescued by the Europeans. They were Maronite, Greek Orthodox, Greek Catholic, and even Muslim. Despite the efforts of the European consuls, who set up a joint fund to relieve the refugees, the latter were often victims of other refugees who were looting just to be able to survive. The arrival of new waves of refugees worsened hygienic and sanitary conditions, provoking the death of many of them. Refugees became victims of thieves, brigands, and the local government's irregulars, who "molested, plundered and ill-treat the unoffending and panic-stricken Christians."[30]

Throughout the month of June 1860, in inland towns and villages, massacre, atrocities, and, as Churchill put it, a "war of extermination" continued. On June 3, according to French sources, the Druze massacred a group of 975 Christian civilians of Hasbaya.[31] The number of refugees, mostly widows and children who had lost their male relations and were without the means of subsistence, was said to amount to between 3,000 and 4,000.[32] In the battle of Rashaya 900 Christians perished. The dispatches reaching the European capitals gave detailed accounts of males butchered in cold blood, houses burned, churches pillaged, and altars defiled. Many refugees from this town reached Damascus in a state of absolute destitution. By the end of June, the European consuls, especially the French, highlighted what they saw as the obvious complicity of the local Ottoman authorities with the Druze. Noel Moore drew attention to the impossible task for Christian churches and private charity to assist the mass of refugees. Like his French counterpart, he demanded the setting up of a commission of inquiry to examine into the conduct and responsibility of the Ottoman authorities. Captain J. A. Paynter of HMS *Exmouth* believed that the European powers would have to take some energetic steps to end the war, something that French on the spot fully agreed with. The main difference between the reports and dispatches of British and French consuls was that the latter stressed the "barbarity" of the Druze, portraying the Maronites as innocent victims of massacre and atrocity, whereas the former insisted on the importance of ending massacre as soon as possible.[33]

Massacres occurred in Zahleh on June 14 and at Deir el-Qamar on June 20 and 21. Consul James Brant from Damascus wrote to Russell that it was difficult to get a simple narrative of facts from persons "who cannot speak without exaggeration under ordinary circumstances, and who in the present exciting times seem to have lost all power over their imaginations." The consul had incontrovertible evidence of the severe distress of the survivors, almost all women and children, and that emigration, when practicable, went on.[34] A British eyewitness, Cyril Graham, had good reason to believe that in Deir-el-Qamar 1,100 to 1,200 males perished in one day. He reached that town a few days after the massacre. Almost every house was burned, and the streets were crowded with dead bodies, most of them stripped and mutilated in every possible way. Through some of the streets Graham's horse could not pass for the bodies were literally piled up. Most of the civilians he examined had many wounds, and in each case the right hand had been either entirely or nearly cut off. He saw one poor creature, on his knees, who had been cut down as he appealed to the mercy of his murderers; he saw bodies without heads and heads lying alone about the place; "all lying unburied, to be devoured by the hyenas and wild beasts."[35]

On June 30, 1860, Consul Moore wrote to the British ambassador Sir Henry Bulwer that the approximate estimate of the civil war in Lebanon resulted in 150 Christian villages burned, 500 Christians killed, 5,500 massacred, and 75,000 affected ("sufferers") by the war. The last category included those whose property had been plundered, those whose houses had been burned, which in the consul's view constituted the vast majority, and those who had been made widows and orphans, amounting to 15,000. The two last classes were houseless and destitute wanderers, subsisting on charity. Some 23,000 Christians subsisted on public charity in the towns of Beirut and Djouni alone. The Druze losses were "comparatively insignificant." They had had about the same number of killed in warfare as the Christians, while their losses in burned houses was "very inconsiderable."[36]

Civil war in Lebanon extended to Damascus when Christian refugees arrived in the city. According to the British consul James Brant, refugees in Damascus numbered no less than 3,000; most of them were Maronite peasants and Greek Orthodox, including many widows and children. All these people overcrowded the city, especially its Christian quarter; most remained without shelter, begging in the streets of the city.[37] On July 8 or 9, after a minor incident, a violent mob moved toward the Christian quarter. At least 20,000 Druze and Muslims, not necessarily Damascene, poured into town for days. Ottoman forces initially tried to stop the angry mob. Some soldiers then joined the rioters, and the local authorities simply melted away. Foreign consulates and European missions were an early target of the enraged mob. The plunder and killing at Damascus continued for eight days and nights. No less than 2,000 Christians died during the riots and an unknown number of Jews were killed,[38] plus a few foreigners and an unknown number of refugees.[39]

European Governments' Reaction and the Motives of their Intervention

Starting in late May 1860, the French consul at Beirut, Stanislas Bentivoglio, sent numerous, detailed dispatches to Lavalette containing information about massacres and atrocities. The latter agreed with his European counterparts in the Ottoman capital on the strategy to adopt with respect to the disturbances in Lebanon. In mid-June 1860 European ambassadors at Constantinople decided that what mattered above all else was that they act in the interest of humanity and to rule out any disagreement among them. They had to act either collectively or individually, though as far as possible *de concert et d'accord* with local authorities, to put an end to the effusion of blood and to reestablish peace.[40] On June 27 the European consuls wrote to the Druze chiefs a joint letter, whose bearer would be Cyril Graham. The tone of the letter accused the Druze of "pillage, massacres, and devastation," which the European consuls highly disapproved. They held the Druze responsible for any act directed against the Christians, their villages, or their properties and energetically charged them to make peace with as little delay as possible, and to recall the bands acting in the areas of Damascus and Lebanon.[41]

By the end of June, Lavalette confidentially wrote that he was in favor of a military intervention on behalf of the Maronites and against the Druze and the Ottoman local authorities, followed by a political and administrative reorganization of the province.[42] Foreign Minister Edouard-Antoine de Thouvenel, newly appointed in January 1860 and an experienced diplomat who knew the Ottoman Empire well because he had been ambassador to the Porte between 1855 and 1860, expressed grave concern over the violation of the "French-protected Maronites'" most sacred rights and over the likelihood of massacres of Christians elsewhere in the Ottoman Empire if nothing was done to prevent them. He was mainly concerned about the consequences for international peace and security of extended disturbances in various Ottoman provinces. Thouvenel sought juridical legitimacy for intervention in the Capitulations but realized that these treaties did not give France any right to undertake a unilateral military intervention in an Ottoman province. If France wished to intervene militarily in Lebanon, it needed to internationalize the question. For that reason Thouvenel drew the attention of his European counterparts to the unprecedented scale of massacre and the likelihood of similar events taking place in other Ottoman provinces. In his international correspondence the minister emphasized the need to undertake an action in the interest of humanity rather than uniquely on behalf of Maronites, aware that focusing exclusively on the Maronites would look less suspicious to his British and Russian counterparts.

Before the Europeans could reach a decision and make a move, the Ottoman authorities successfully brought the Maronites and Druze together to sign a peace treaty, and they reprimanded their own officials for not keeping the peace. On July 8 the sultan appointed Fuad Pasha as envoy-extraordinary to Syria with full powers over both civil and military matters in the region, along with 15,000 to 16,000 men and supplies of wheat.[43] Fuad left Constantinople on July 12, reaching Beirut five days later. His mission was both punitive and humanitarian: he was in Syria to punish those who had committed crimes, to provide relief for destitute families with compassion and equity, to help rebuild towns and villages, and to reestablish order and local trust in Ottoman rule. Fuad strenuously attempted to avoid any European diplomatic and/or military intervention in Lebanon and Syria. He might well have succeeded had the massacre of Damascus not occurred.

In fact, when on July 5 Thouvenel met with the British ambassador in Paris, Henry Cowley, the latter rejected the French proposal of a joint monitoring of the Syrian coast with warships and the appointment of a European commission to investigate events in Lebanon. At the same time, however, the British government instructed the vice admiral commanding the British naval forces in the Mediterranean to proceed forthwith to the coast of Lebanon and Syria and to act with the British consul in affording protection to the lives and property of "British subjects and Christians residing on the coast from massacre." In execution of this duty, if necessary, the vice admiral could land the marines from the ships under his command.[44] Cowley seemed unconvinced by the possibility that violence against Christian populations might spread to Aleppo and into Asia Minor. Prime Minister John Russell shared this point of view and did not see the necessity to undertake a large-scale intervention, which in his view might have threatened peace in Europe. Russell believed that the representatives of the European powers at Constantinople might find a general and permanent pacification of Syria and Lebanon by pressing the Sublime Porte to take every measure to end to the deplorable state of affairs in Lebanon and Syria.[45]

On July 17 Thouvenel informed Russell that the latest massacre in Damascus had created further duties for all European cabinets.[46] Thouvenel feared that whatever power the European consuls on the spot might be entrusted with, it would not be enough to protect the Christian population. He also doubted that the dispatch of Ottoman troops would suffice to stop the effusion of blood. It was clear that the Porte had no authority left, and that the whole country was in a state of anarchy. In Thouvenel's view, in order to satisfy the principles of justice and order and to establish a durable state of things, it was imperative to suppress the insurrection and to oblige the Druze to lay down their arms. It was necessary to repair "frightful calamities" (a term that had been used in 1827 to justify the intervention against the Ottoman Empire in its Greek provinces) and to prevent their recurrence. Events in Damascus made Thouvenel's words sound very convincing. These events had persuaded European policy-makers that further massacres might occur elsewhere in the Ottoman Empire despite the peace agreement between the Maronites and Druze in Lebanon. The British government could no longer contest the reports of atrocities and allegations of the connivance of the Ottoman authorities and soldiers in the massacres of Christians.

The French minister argued that intervention was necessary because the French consulate and property had been sacked and because "Muslim fanatics" murdered Christians, including French missionaries.[47] In the minister's view, any one of these atrocities was sufficient reason to warrant. However, wishing to avoid any misunderstanding on the nature of the intervention, Thouvenel and Napoleon felt that events in Syria "required a more active intervention on the part of Europe."[48] For that reason the minister sought the support of all the other European powers, claiming that, as in 1842 when France had helped to create Lebanon's administrative system, this intervention did not threaten the independence of the Ottoman Empire.[49] Finally, he pointed to public opinion, which would not brook the continued supineness of Europe in the presence of such disasters.

Thouvenel's plan was to send a collective European and Ottoman commission of inquiry to Lebanon and Syria to ascertain the circumstances that had brought about the conflict. This commission would determine the share of responsibility of the leaders of the insurrection and of the agents of the local administration, as well as the compensation due to the victims. It would also study, for the purpose of submitting them to the approbation of their governments and of the Porte, the arrangements that were to be adopted, with the view of averting new misfortunes. Thouvenel planned to send further troops and disembark them at different points along the coast of the disturbed districts, something that Britain, Austria, and France were already doing. These troops, Thouvenel asserted, would strike terror into the aggressors and restore confidence to the Christian populations. Moreover, to stop the insurrection in the heart of Lebanon, a contingent would be held ready to act according to circumstances. This expeditionary corps would aid the Ottoman Army and, "thanks to its moral authority," would reassure the population and have a beneficial influence on the attitude and conduct of the Ottoman functionaries.[50]

Thouvenel made it clear that before any occupation of Ottoman soil took place, the consent of the Ottoman government should be obtained. As Lavalette explained to the sultan's vizier Ali Pasha, the motive of the intervention was the manifest impotence of the Ottoman authorities, which had engendered massacre and atrocities and made foreign help necessary in order to avoid the collapse of the Ottoman Empire. Furthermore, France had a duty to fulfill and had to respect the opinion of the French public, who "would ask account of the blood shed by the Christians, whilst we stand idly." Hence, having done so much to protect the Ottoman Empire, it would be impossible for France to be "impassive spectators of so many murders and massacre."[51] If the British government agreed with this plan, Thouvenel thought it possible to form, without delay, an understanding with the other cabinets of Europe and with the Porte, and to consult as to the quickest means "of obtaining the satisfaction *due to humanity, and of assisting in the re-establishment of peace in Syria.*"[52] The intervention would thus be collective in principle, and the European troops, sent with common objects, would only execute a commission entrusted to them by the European powers.

After the massacre of Damascus, British prime minister Russell realized that a conspicuous part of British public opinion favored an intervention. At that stage he had many good reasons to be more actively involved in the Lebanese crisis; none of them was humanitarian. First, he deeply distrusted French politics and policies. Second, he feared the consequences of a possible Russian-French alliance and intervention, especially if the Druzo-Maronite truce was broken and new massacres took place.[53] However, given that he could not openly reveal these concerns, to justify the change in British foreign policy spoke on July 23 of the frightful character of the massacre, where 5,500 people had been killed and 20,000 more, including the widows and children of the murdered, were now wandering in a state of famine. The prime minister admitted that while these dreadful scenes were going on, the Ottoman authorities appeared to have been inactive spectators or accomplices in the work of massacre. Hence, "indignant at this want of humanity and of energy," the British government had accepted a proposal of the French emperor to send European troops to Syria "to prevent further excesses."[54] Russell specified that his government very reluctantly sanctioned the use of foreign forces in the interior of Syria, for it could provoke a "fiercer fanaticism among the Mussulmans," retard the pacification process, and lead to grave international difficulties. For these reasons Russell desired that the intervention should be undertaken only when the necessity was clearly proved, and that it should cease as soon as that necessity no longer existed.

The Paris Conference and the Modalities of the Intervention

In late July Thouvenel set up a conference aimed at obtaining the Porte's explicit assent to an intervention by foreign troops in one of the sultan's provinces; this was essential in order to clarify that the intervention was not an act of war against the Ottoman Empire.[55] The first protocol found the juridical legitimacy of the intervention in the Treaty of Paris of March 30, 1856. The main argument was that article 9 of that treaty, which guaranteed the rights of Ottoman Christians, had been violated in Syria. Thouvenel found the political legitimacy for intervention in the continued unrest, which threatened the integrity of the Ottoman Empire and therefore peace in Europe, and requested that the Ottoman government re-create the conditions under which Christians had lived before the massacres.[56] The second protocol, dated August 3 and signed on September 5, embodied the conditions for intervention in Syria, a protocol of disinterestedness and the declaration of the sultan claiming he wished to stop the effusion of blood in Syria.[57]

The seven articles of the second protocol stipulated that a European military force of up to twelve thousand soldiers would be sent to Syria to help reestablish order; France would provide half that number. The European powers would allow sufficient naval forces to monitor the Syrian coast so as to ensure its tranquillity. (By August there were no less than twenty-two warships from "great" and "small" European powers, Greece and Sardinia included.) The Ottoman government would cover the army's subsistence and supplies insofar as it was able. The European expeditionary force would stay in Syria for no more than six months, which the powers believed to be sufficient time to pacify the area. General Charles de Beaufort d'Hautpoul, who had served in the 1830s as chief of staff for Ibrahim Pasha—the alleged executioner of the "barbarization plan" of the Morea—during the Egyptian campaigns in Syria, was named commander in chief of the French expedition.) His mission was not to conquer or occupy any territory but rather was "remedial and temporary," a response to public outcry and to the profound pity inspired by the misery of the Christians of the East. France was to act in the name of all the signatories, and in conjunction with the Ottoman authorities, to defend the best interests of the Ottoman government. Beaufort was not to march on Damascus unless he was certain he could do so usefully and without any risk.[58]

The European powers mandated the French expeditionary corps to undertake the military operation when—as French consul Bentivoglio confidentially admitted—Fuad's army had already obtained very satisfactory results and restored order. The consul was particularly worried about the nature of the French contingent's actions, given that their inaction would almost be ridiculous. What would they do, Bentivoglio wondered, given that the Ottoman authorities were already acting with unsuspected energy?[59] Moreover, Thouvenel and Napoleon III presented the nature of the action of the French expeditionary corps under a completely different light in their discourses for internal consumption. The French emperor stressed that the little army corps was to act as a mobile column that could bring justice anywhere in the country. It would catch, judge, and punish the guilty, return to the Christians their confiscated goods, disarm the Druze, and force on them reparations as indemnity to the victims of the insurrection. The expedition was supposed to appear to be an obvious act of justice.[60] The *Moniteur* claimed that the mission was another in a long line of France's responsibilities in the East that had begun with the Crusades. By humanitarian intervention, French policy-makers meant to bring progress, development, industrialization, and the civilization of *"idées chrétiennes"* to the Islamic world.[61] Contrary to the spirit of the international protocol signed in Paris, once in Lebanon Beaufort hoped to punish the guilty Druze. Clearly sharing the point of view of his emperor, he suggested to his officials that the Christians should feel no guilt, as they were the "innocent" victims of misguided Druze and Muslim leaders. However, once the expeditionary forces landed in Lebanon on August 16, 1860, Beaufort was forced to stick to the letter of his mandate, for the other European powers monitored every single move and decision of the French commander. The expeditionary corps never reached or occupied Damascus, nor did it engage in major military action. Fuad Pasha alone restored law and order and peace. Thouvenel and Napoleon's hopes to use a multilateral action to achieve the aims of French foreign policy were dashed.

Paradoxically, by sticking to the letter of the mandate, the French expeditionary corps accomplished various humanitarian tasks, which Beaufort viewed with contempt. As in the Morea in 1828, the French contingent initiated a number of activities in Syria and Lebanon, such as the burial of corpses and the cleaning of streets.[62] French troops monitored the return of civilian populations to their villages, supervised the reconstruction of the destroyed properties, and attempted to oversee the distribution of food and other aid coming from Europe. The French commander did not grasp the importance of the success of such activities for what we would call today the peace-building phase of the intervention.

In January 1861 Napoleon III argued that to achieve their *œuvre d'humanité* the French troops should stay in Lebanon until its reorganization was completed.[63] The French and the British quarrelled about what we would call the most appropriate "exit strategy." Thouvenel requested a six-month extension of the French mandate and put forward a simple question: What would happen if a massacre occurred again when the French troops had evacuated Lebanon? Would the few marines on British warships be able to stop it? The French minister did not mention that the Ottoman Army was now massively present in Lebanon and Syria. He did not point out that if new disturbances took place simultaneously in various areas of Lebanon and Syria, the tiny expeditionary corps would be as inadequate as the British marines

on the coast. The British government initially vetoed the French proposal, arguing that the frightful massacres that had filled "all Europe
with terror" were over. The prime minister argued that to augment
the European force, and maintain it in Syria with a view to prevent
fresh outrages, would be to alter entirely the original purpose the sultan and the European powers had intended for the force. Russell was
afraid that a longer occupation would soon degenerate into a transfer
of the local government of Syria to the European powers. Thus, instead
of being a useful example, the European occupation would become a
precedent for further occupations in Bulgaria, Bosnia, and other provinces and would lead the way to a partition of the Ottoman Empire. For
this reason, the British government wished to see the government of
Syria restored to the authorities named by the Porte as soon as possible.
Russell admitted that "no security, it is true, would be thus obtained
against a recurrence of the conflicts of Dru[ze] and Christians; but as
long as the two races exist in the country no permanent security can be
obtained."[64]

The discussions between French and British policy-makers show how
similar the issues involving the duration, scope, and consequences of
humanitarian intervention are to those debated in the 1990s and 2000s.
The French were ready to assume extensive administrative and military
duties and full responsibility when they intervened. The other powers
had good reasons to fear that France's agenda went beyond the rescue
of the civilian population. They wished to keep the military operations
as short as possible, though an abrupt end of the intervention, if massacres were likely to occur again, would have meant a failure hard to
explain at home and further, expensive commitment in the disturbed
Ottoman provinces. But how were they to determine beyond any reasonable doubt that massacres would not occur again?[65] In March 1861
the Europeans agreed that the French troops would leave on June 5,
and that Great Britain would maintain its warships on the Lebanese
coast and, if necessary, land soldiers to protect British and Christian
civilians as well as the Druze population.[66] The rationale behind this
diplomatic solution was anything but humanitarian: it was the best option to keep Napoleon happy, to check the French imperial ambitions
in the eastern Mediterranean, and to find an appropriate exit strategy
through the work of a European commission. The latter dealt with the
question of refugees and humanitarian aid, the assignment of responsibility and indemnities, and supervision of the work of the Ottoman ad
hoc tribunals.[67] Finally, the European commissioners set the bases of the
Règlement of June 1861, which would be negotiated between the European ambassadors and the Sublime Porte at Constantinople to guarantee peace and stability in the disturbed provinces.

FROM SHORT-TERM RESCUE TO LONG-TERM PROTECTION OF CIVILIAN POPULATIONS

On September 26, 1860, Fuad Pasha met the members of the newly instituted European Commission in Beirut: Lord Dufferin represented Great Britain, the consul general at Alexandria Mr. L. Béclard represented France, E. P. Novikow was the Russian commissioner, von Rehfues represented Prussia, and P. von Weckbecker represented Austria.

The Question of the Refugees

The first "question" the European commissioners attempted to solve was the case of the thousands of refugees amassed in Beirut. The local authorities, the Ottomans, and the Europeans all lacked the modern-day experience in dealing with relief and refugee-related issues. They found it extremely difficult to channel energies and resources. The Ottoman government sponsored a relief program, though it desperately lacked the funds to enforce it. This scarcity of resources led the Ottoman authorities to exact money and supplies from the Druze, which they gave to the Christians, with the obvious consequence of causing great resentment among the Druze. The lack of funds led to starvation in Deir el-Qamar and elsewhere in Mount Lebanon and further increased the number of refugees in Lebanese coastal towns.

As in almost any humanitarian crisis, the available human and material resources were limited and not always used in the best possible way. The refugees, especially Christians and Druze of the mixed villages, were reluctant to return to their destroyed villages, fearing a repetition of the massacres and wrongly assuming they could indefinitely rely on relief.[68] In fact, when the French troops departed, many Christians who had returned to their villages headed back to the coast once again.[69] This situation made restitution and reconstruction processes almost impossible tasks. Furthermore, in some areas reconstruction began after lengthy Ottoman government and European Commission decisions were made. In those areas where French troops were active, they tended not to cooperate with the Ottomans, sometimes proceeding on their own with the disinfection and clearing of towns and the rebuilding of roads and houses.[70]

The twenty-first-century reader will not be surprised to note that not all aid destined for Lebanon and Syria found its way to the refugees, and that relief committees publicly denounced all sorts of embezzlements. For instance, as far as Catholic relief is concerned, it seems that only 10 percent of the relief earmarked for nuns and Jesuit monks reached them, with widows and orphans receiving less than 1 percent of what charities in France had sent them.[71] Predictably, political, economic, and religious interests became entangled with humanitarian aid. European businessmen who had invested heavily in the silk industry of Lebanon and Syria insisted on Ottoman complicity in the massacres in order to press the Sublime Porte that much more firmly for indemnity.[72] Some, such as the Marseilles Chamber of Commerce, organized charity concerts for the refugees and donated more than 40,000 francs. Other humanitarian charities adopted religious selectiveness. Abbé Lavigerie, director of the Bureau de l'Oeuvre des Écoles d'Orient in Paris, was in charge of subscriptions to aid "victims of Druze fanaticism and Turkish complicity in Syria." He received more than 900,000 francs from all over Europe and the Holy See. Jesuits, Franciscans, and Lazarists shared in the distribution of this aid in the field.[73] In London a number of lords set up a committee in favor of the Eastern Christians that was ready to send "charity ambassadors, in charge to distribute Bibles, money, to save orphans, to build orphanages, in order to lay the foundations of future Maronite Protestantism."[74] The American mission in Lebanon provided relief to native Protestants and their dependents, and an Anglo-American Committee (formed under the presidency of the British consul, Noel Moore) acted on an explicitly nonsectarian basis. This committee dispensed cash, clothing, and modest amounts of bedding to refugees—mostly Christian women, men, and children as Druze, Muslims, and Jews did not come forward for any aid.

The European commissioners in Beirut decided to centralize the distribution of humanitarian aid in order to make it more effective and constituted a central relief committee (*comité directeur*), which received its impulse directly from the commission, coordinated the use and distribution of donations, estimated the cost of rebuilding houses, and used these estimates to determine relief distribution but would stay clear of assessing damages. The commission received and evaluated reports of Fuad Pasha's relief efforts in Mount Lebanon, including the distribution of grain and other necessities, the restitution of stolen goods, and all other aspects of government-sponsored relief. It kept up pressure on local authorities with continual inquiries about how many people were actually benefiting from relief, how many houses and villages had been rebuilt, whether relief was interrupted, and if so, where and why, and whether Christians were returning.[75] The central relief committee accomplished a great deal, for three reasons: Fuad did not mind this particular European interference; European commissioners were genuinely committed to this purely humanitarian mission; and they wished to show the public at home that something was being done to relieve the refugees. However, by October 1860 the resources available for relief by subscriptions from Europe had dried up. They had concretely helped some refugees (mainly Christians) on the coast, but not those remaining in the war-torn inland districts.[76]

Assignment of Responsibility

The European commissioners distinguished between three categories of criminals: those responsible for the massacres (easier to identify in Damascus than in Mount Lebanon), the leaders of bands, and common criminals. In the commissioners' minds, these categories existed to differentiate between those who caused the civil war and those who simply were swept up in its violence. Those in the first category were thought to be most guilty. As historian Leila Tarazi Fawaz puts it, assigning ultimate responsibility for the war "would influence decisions regarding the future of Syria and the share various communities would have in the political settlement under consideration."[77]

In Damascus legal terror began on August 3, and in a few days almost a thousand people had been arrested. The accused were delivered to an extraordinary tribunal made up of Ottoman functionaries brought in from Constantinople. The international commissioners set up a fact-finding commission and the consulates drew up lists of all those whom they knew to have taken part in the insurrection, but in the end an Ottoman tribunal judged alleged culprits according to Ottoman law.[78] According to the French consul in Damascus, Maxime Outrey, the Ottoman tribunal was too indulgent with regard to the abominations that had occurred. In his view, the Ottoman way of dealing with justice would not guarantee the tranquillity of the region and the safety of local Christians.[79] Outrey's views were contradicted, however, by the fact that 167 men were executed by August 20, including 57 hanged and displayed for days in the bazaars, streets, and town gates of Damascus. The extraordinary tribunal at Damascus kept carrying out sentences until early 1861. Hundreds were sentenced to forced labor; hundreds more were sentenced to death and executed. By punishing the perpetrators of the massacre of Damascus, Fuad intended to prove that the Ottoman government was "modern," was "reformed," and resolutely condemned massacres, which were contrary to "the principle of civilisation current in the world."[80] As historian Ussama Makdisi puts it, this was crude terror intended to silence the population, an imperial policy set out to "discipline" the masses of Syria. The terror masked an essentially reactionary goal: to banish the subaltern from politics once and for all, and to reconstitute the broken lines of hierarchy by recovering Europe and the *Tanzimat* from popular understanding.[81]

The European commissioners did not once question the guilt of the Damascenes condemned by the extraordinary tribunal. They were more than ready to place responsibility for the massacre on local Ottoman authorities without even raising the question of the Ottoman government's role. After all, if, on the one hand, the Europeans wished to avoid the repetition of massacre, on the other hand they also wanted to keep the Ottoman Empire alive.[82] Fuad understandably opted for a lenient approach. He would not admit that Ottoman officials were responsible for the massacre and instead blamed the Syrian people, who had allegedly cultivated sectarian animosities. Fuad only decided on the death penalty for the governor of Damascus, Ahmad Pasha, and his officers because of very strong pressure from the European commissioners.

Restoring order in Mount Lebanon proved to be more difficult than in Damascus. First of all, the administrative chaos that followed the massacres and lack of funds generated further problems. Local police who had not been paid for thirty-four months looted and threatened civilian populations, both Druze and Maronite. The European and Ottoman plan of relief, restitution, reconstruction, and assessment of responsibility became a vicious circle because of the issue of punishment, on which Europeans disagreed completely. The French commissioner Béclard clamored for extreme punishment of both the Ottoman authorities and the Druze leaders. Dufferin claimed that even in committing fearful enormities, the Druze had only carried out the same "policy of extermination," albeit to an excessive degree, that the Maronites had undertaken at the start of the quarrel. The British commissioner also wondered whether the abominable crimes that had occurred should be judged taking into account the customs of local populations rather than the standard of European "civilized countries." In his view, "the standard of European civilization" was not altogether applicable in Lebanon and in Syria, and some allowances needed to be made for the force of circumstances and of "inveterate tradition."[83]

The commissioners eventually reached a consensus on a moderate level of punishment for the Druze, who naturally considered the sentences against them harsh and unjustified. Fuad Pasha set up extraordinary tribunals at Beirut and Muktara (Moktara) to judge the accused Druze. The Ottoman government's real intention was to use the extraordinary tribunals to put an end to the feudal structure of Lebanon once and for all, and to modernize the province. Dufferin quickly understood Fuad's plans and argued for clemency toward the Druze, whom Great Britain needed in the region in order to counterbalance French influence with the Maronites.[84] French observers commented on the trials of Druze as a travesty of justice. In the end, Druze elites paid the highest price for the massacres in Lebanon.[85] Assigning responsibility for the massacres proved to be a political rather than a humanitarian endeavor. Above all, the outcome was the result of political compromises.

Consequences of the Intervention: The *Règlement* of June 1861

The intervening powers considered the question of political and administrative reform of Mount Lebanon to be intrinsic to the intervention itself. They argued that in a reformed province massacres were unlikely to occur. Needless to say, reforms that had to be imposed by European powers would be beneficial for local populations, for the Ottoman government, and for peace and tranquillity in Europe.

It proved difficult to reach an agreement, for each of the intervening powers had its own views on the nature of the reform to be introduced. On June 9, 1861, the ambassadorial conference at Constantinople produced a sixteen-article draft that the Porte accepted. The *Règlement et Protocole Relatifs à la Réorganisation du Mont Liban* was a constitutional document that made Lebanon a *Mutasarrifiyya* (governorship). Lebanon would be ruled by a Christian—the term was deliberately vague—governor (*mutassarif*), not a local Maronite, brought in from outside, immediately subject to Constantinople, and removable after three years. The governor had extensive powers, except over the courts. Criminal cases fell under the jurisdiction of the central authority, and Lebanese commercial litigation under the Ottoman tribunal in Beirut. An Administrative Council composed of elected Christian and Muslim members was to assist the governor and had to be consulted if Ottoman troops were to be called into active duty. A volunteer police force not to exceed in number seven per one thousand people was established, and the governor had the right to use this force to disarm the population if necessary. The rest of the Ottoman province's territory lay beyond the scope of the arrangement. This *Règlement* was modified in 1864, with the governor to be retained for five years, and remained in place until the First World War.[86]

It is worth mentioning that on March 31, 1861, the European Commission debated the question of the displacement and resettlement of populations according to religious lines and the creation of religiously homogeneous areas in Lebanon. Just how these "civilized" Europeans intended to solve the question of Lebanon emerged very clearly. According to the commissioners, the "humanitarian" resolution of the Lebanese question rested on a simple (albeit wrong) assumption that two different societies had always existed in Lebanon: the Druze and the Maronites. The displacement of populations and their resettlement on a sectarian basis was the best possible solution the commissioners could think of. They referred to a plan of *"désagrégation"* or ethnic/religious separation of Christians and Druze. They pointed out that in a civilized context men of all origins and religion should be able to live side by side; but given the state of civilization of local populations, this temporary and empirical solution was the only one guaranteeing the continued existence of local populations. The commissioners went into the details of the planned transfer and exchange of populations, which aimed primarily to avoid the reoccurrence of massacres. They deemed such an operation useful, urgently commanded by humanity, and, in their view, no obstacle could justify its repudiation.[87] The displacement of populations should have been carried out as rapidly as possible, for many of the civilians involved had not yet returned to their villages and had lost all their property. Under these circumstances, these refugees would have accepted any solution as long as their lives were guaranteed. However, the European powers could not agree on the administrative division of the Lebanese territory, and they lacked the political willingness and the means to responsibly carry out such an ambitious plan. Moreover, precisely because Druze and Maronites did not constitute two entirely different and opposed societies, and because many of them preferred to live in their original villages, they were very reluctant to agree to such a plan, and in the end the commissioners abandoned its enforcement.

. . .

Intervention in Ottoman Lebanon and Syria had a genuine humanitarian dimension: to avoid the repetition of massacre. In July 1860 one of Thouvenel's confidential reports mentioned that the intervention in Lebanon was not about political rivalries. French ambassador Lavalette concurred that the priority was to end pillage, fire, and massacre. When military action restored tranquillity to the Christians and forced salutary terror on the Druze and their Muslim accomplices, it would be necessary to think about the necessary reorganization of Lebanon.[88] It is indisputable that the European powers' collective intervention was "disinterested," for they did not seek territorial acquisition, exclusive influence, or any commercial concession for their subjects that might not be granted to the subjects of all other nations. However, it would be naïve to believe Napoleon's proclamation: *"Quel intérêt autre que l'humanité m'engagerait à envoyer des troupes dans cette contrée?"* It is abundantly clear that the French motives for the intervention were not exclusively humanitarian. French prestige and influence in the Middle East, the completion of the Suez Canal, defending the Syrian silk trade, and diversion of the French public's attention from home affairs (the dismemberment of the Papal State had been harshly opposed by the Empress Eugenie, and its results alienated the sympathies of the Catholics in France) were all issues of great concern at this time.[89] Napoleon III certainly dreamed of Lebanon as a second Algeria in the Mediterranean, but the French troops respected—or were forced to respect—their mandate; the French emperor was revisionist, though not to the extent that he used the intervention as a pretext for war.[90] As Gary Bass pointed out in *Freedom's Battle*, multilateral action prevented the self-interest of France to prevail, though economic, military and imperial interests sapped the intervention. It is certainly true that public opinion exerted pressure on governments in favor of intervention. In terms of the minds and deeds of European policy-makers, the role of public opinion seems to be less relevant than the full compatibility between a duty of ending the massacre of Ottoman Christians and securing general peace in Europe. In 1860, as in the case of Greece, the agreement of the European powers triggered the intervention.

The particular perception of the Ottoman Empire in Europe contributes to the explanation of the nature and modalities of the intervention. The biased accounts of the massacres reinforced the view of many Europeans that the Ottoman Empire was a "barbarous," "fanatic" empire where anarchy prevailed. The twenty-one year-old Dufferin, who had no direct experience whatsoever of Syrian and Lebanese societies and cultures, alighted in the region with his own baggage of *idées reçues* and civilizational prejudices, as this comment of his epitomizes:

> It is to be remembered that this is a country of vendettas; in the war carried on between the *barbarian tribes* which inhabit it, usages prevail as horrible as those which disgraced the Middle Ages of Europe. . . . Beneath the full blaze of modern civilization we find in Syria habits of thought and practices prevailing for which the only historical parallel can be found in the books of Moses. That the Christians are not to be exempted . . . from the number of those subject to these savage influences cannot be pretended. A mere cursory perusal of the official accounts of the murders, feuds, and wars which have deluged the Mountain with blood during the last twenty-five years proves too lamentably how little influence their religion has had in mitigating the ferocity with which the traditional customs of the country have imbued them. The cruel manner in which they have taken advantage of the first opportunity afforded them to massacre old men, women, and children.[91]

The intervention in Lebanon and Syria would become a precedent mentioned by late-nineteenth- and early-twentieth-century statesmen and scholars in dispatches as well as in confidential correspondence related to other "humanitarian" crises, and in the press as well as in pamphlets of many campaigners. By the beginning of the twentieth century, the intervention in Lebanon and Syria was systematically discussed, integrated, and sometimes contested among the jurisprudence of humanitarian intervention, and it still is included in contemporary international law textbooks. European policy-makers mentioned the intervention and the subsequent scheme of reforms as possible political solutions in other disturbed areas in which Ottoman Christians lived, such as Crete (1868), Rumelia (1876), and Macedonia (early 1900s). During the 1870s intervention in Lebanon and Syria was compared and contrasted with nonintervention on behalf of the Bulgarians and systematically referred to as yet another proof of "Ottoman barbarity" and evidence that the Ottoman Empire did not belong to the Family of Nations.

The intervention of 1860–61 highlights a number of features of intervention against massacre. First, the European powers dealt with the Ottoman government as a sovereign entity only as long as it served the purpose of making it clear that the intervention was not an act of war. Ottoman sovereignty was meaningless to them when it came to impose a solution to avoid the repetition of massacre. Second, to the intervening states (and to the Sublime Porte too) it was very clear that the intervention was an international practice distinguished from a war. Third, in the view of the intervening states the intervention was humanitarian, for its objective was to end massacres of Ottoman Christians in Lebanon and Syria. The European powers clearly identified the Maronites (and the Greek Orthodox in Damascus) as the victims of massacre and held the local and central Ottoman authorities as well as the Druze responsible for the massacre. If the British government insisted on including the Druze among the victims of massacre, this has to be understood as an attempt to counterbalance the French government's action in favor of the Maronites.

Fourth, throughout the crisis the Ottoman Christians— the victims of massacre—were the passive recipients of rights, though they were not involved in the process that would have modified their lives after the frightful events of 1860. The European commissioners in Lebanon, the diplomats in Constantinople, the leaders in European capitals, and the Sublime Porte all seemed to know what was best for them and the nature of the political and administrative reforms to be enforced in the Ottoman provinces. Fifth, the military and political intervention of 1860–61 occurred far too late to put an end to civil war and massacre. The Europeans, especially the French, overlooked the fact that disturbances had subsided before the expeditionary force reached Lebanon, thanks to Fuad Pasha. It is certainly true that the expedition positively contributed to preventing any repetition of the massacres and brought peace and stability to the Ottoman provinces. The intervention encompassed a short-term rescue and long-term protection phase, which culminated with the 1861 *Règlement organique*. The social, economic, juridical, and administrative reforms the "gentle civilizer" enforced (and proposed, including the failed plan of *désagrégation*) were an intrinsic part of the intervention deemed indispensable to bringing peace, progress, and civilization to Lebanese "tribes." The decisions taken on behalf of local populations were the result of a compromise between the European powers that did not involve an accurate analysis of the well-being of the local populations.

Sixth, the tandem work of the expeditionary corps and the European Commission was a dysfunctional novelty. However, the creation of a multilateral ad hoc commission was an innovation related to the emerging international practice of humanitarian intervention. Contrary to what some readers might think, the story of peace-building and peace enforcement following a humanitarian intervention is older than the 2001 *Responsibility to Protect* report. In 1860 a group of intervening states attempted to solve postconflict problems, offering what they thought to be long-lasting solutions intended to improve the well-being of the civilian populations. The intervening states implemented a *campagne de charité* clearly biased in favor of the Christians.[92] They protected Christian survivors as best as they could, helped with the reopening of schools and churches, nourished the refugees, and worked together with civilian inhabitants to reconstruct the houses and fields of the Mountain. They viewed assignment of responsibility and indemnity as an intrinsic part of the intervention. They conceived humanitarian intervention not as a "hit-and-run" operation but as a complex operation encompassing a perhaps rudimentary peace-enforcement process based on implementation of a comprehensive set of reforms.

A final point relates to the British and French fleets' actions of June 1860. French and British ships were clearly visible along the Lebanese coast, not to mention the impressive Russian ship-of-war *Vladimir* and its six hundred troops ready to land. These European forces refrained from intervening and limited themselves to small-scale sporadic operations, for their respective governments had not yet reached an agreement; this shows that the European powers shared the same concept about the modalities of a humanitarian intervention and the risks involved with it. Preventive unilateral humanitarian intervention was not an option for nineteenth-century European powers. And in any case, as we have seen, the landing of a few would not have been sufficient to stop the massacres in Lebanon or in Syria.

CHAPTER FIVE

The First Intervention in Crete (1866–69)

> La Russie est elle bien fondée de parler des droits de
> l'humanité outragés quand pour maintenir ses droits en
> Pologne, elle a écrasé une nation qui demandait aussi son
> indépendance, quand elle tirait sur des femmes et un peuple
> sans armes dans les rues de Varsovie, quand elle a exilé en
> Sibérie des femmes portant le deuil de leurs pères et frères,
> quand enfin elle se conduit d'une manière aussi barbare
> qu'elle le fait en ce moment vis-à-vis des tribus abkhases!
> —Grand Vizier Ali Pasha to the French
> chargé d'affaires at Constantinople, July 1867

THIS CHAPTER FOCUSES on the motives of the European powers' multi-lateral intervention of 1867. As we shall see, the British government opposed any forcible action to save strangers, not deeming massacre and atrocities serious or tragic enough to undertake an armed humanitarian intervention. The British put forward a perfectly sensible argument that any rescue operation would have worsened rather than improved the situation of civilian populations. Even if the humanitarian concern might have been genuine, it is clear that the British government had other motives. It was determined not to help Christian Cretans—whose militancy was seen as a manifestation of the ambition of Russia and Crete—for it feared a new explosion of the "Eastern Question."[1] The other European governments, led by Russia and France, did intervene allegedly to the save the lives of strangers. British policy clearly shaped and affected the modalities of this intervention and makes this case different from that of Lebanon and Syria.

THE CONTEXT OF THE CRETAN MASSACRES

The Cretan Christian revolt of 1866 came as a consequence of the Ottoman attempt to enforce the *Tanzimat*. As elsewhere in the empire, efforts by the government of Constantinople to impose equality exacerbated the relations between Muslims and Christians. For Ottoman rulers and reformers, matters were further complicated in Crete by the fact that local Christians were the majority of the population.[2] During the early stages of the insurrection, the Cretan assembly proclaimed itself to be faithful to the sultan. The assembly made several demands: to be relieved of the exorbitant duties levied on food since 1858; to improve the island's means of communication; and to put an end to the undue interference on the part of the governor (*vali*), Ismail Pasha, in the election of the members of Demigerondia (Consultative Council). The assembly also asked for new olive oil stores. It desired an improvement in local tribunals and schools; the opening of natural ports; the liberty of worship by virtue of the provisions of the *Hatt-i Hümayun*; and an end to the baneful practice of seizing hostages. Finally, Christian Cretans wanted a less centralized system that could speed up the adjudication of civil and criminal cases.[3] The sultan replied in May 1866 by dispatching to Crete 2,520 troops and four mountain howitzers. On June 2 more Ottoman warships, bringing a further 5,700 men, arrived in Crete to restore order.[4] European diplomats feared that a massacre might soon take place, whereas the Ottoman government wished primarily to avoid being accused by the Europeans of passivity. Recalling what had happened six years earlier in the Lebanon, the Sublime Porte wanted to avoid further European interference in the empire's internal affairs.

The context of the Cretan crisis differs from the case of Lebanon and Syria in several respects. Whereas in the case of Lebanon nationalism was not an issue at stake, the Cretan crisis, from August 1866 onward, revolved around the question of the union of the island with Greece. By 1866 Italy had largely achieved its independence, Austria would be defeated against Prussia, and nationalism was to become one of the main features of the Eastern Question in the Balkans and beyond. Contrary to the case of Lebanon, the Cretan revolt was internationalized from its inception. Foreign volunteers fought in Crete to liberate the island from the alleged Ottoman yoke, and the Greek government fomented and armed the revolt. If the Maronites could only count on the sentiments of Christian solidarity, Philhellenes reactivated their solidarity and transnational lobbying networks on behalf of the Cretans, underscoring the precedent and epics of the 1827 intervention of Navarino.

Philhellenes' accounts of Crete imagined a mythical link or common thread (*fil-rouge*) connecting all the Cretan revolts into a unique nationalist movement, from the first in 1769 onward.[5] Just as European travelers' accounts had fabricated the mythology of the tribes of Lebanon, they depicted Cretan Christians as an independent tribe defending their island's freedom against Ottoman occupiers. Contemporary accounts portrayed the Christian and Muslim communities of Crete as if they were living in two different worlds when, on the contrary, the two communities had innumerable ties.[6] These accounts never mentioned that local Christians deliberately converted to Islam. European writers preferred to point out that Christian men embraced Islam only as a way of entering the military, and that Christian women often converted to be rid of their husbands or to claim a portion of their fathers' or husbands' estates.[7] Europeans viewed the Cretan Muslims as "renegades" who would revert to Christianity when the island was united with Greece. Charles Wood noted that the Muslims of Crete were almost entirely composed of islanders who, for the most part, possessed Greek names, spoke Greek, and managed only few words of Turkish. Cretan Muslims were generally depicted as "fanatical from a national point of view, but they are not devout in religious things." Wood wrote that a minority of Muslims, known as the "Bengazis" or "Aripides," with very dark complexions were imported as slaves into Crete from Libya by the Turks. They had been freed at the request of foreign consuls during the first half of the nineteenth century. These "blacks" were seen as "the lowest caste of the Cretan population."[8] Public opinion, especially in France, often set the legal context of the intervention within the legal framework of the 1856 Treaty of Paris. According to this view, the alleged Ottoman government's nonrespect of the clauses concerning the improvement of the living conditions of Ottoman Christians gave Europe the right to intervene or even the duty (*devoir impérieux*) to protect them (as well as Muslims) from "the worst government they have ever had."[9]

At the time of the Cretan crisis, Prussia and Austria were busy fighting each other, and Russia, which had harshly repressed an insurrection in Poland in 1863, was expanding into Central Asia and remained a revisionist power as far as the Treaty of Paris was concerned. The Cretan crisis represented an interesting opportunity for Russia to recover its leading role in the Balkan Peninsula. In France, Napoleon III's foreign policy still wavered between supporting nationalist movements and countering British supremacy in the Mediterranean. This led France to occasionally and inconsistently support the Sublime Porte and Balkan nationalist movements. As for Great Britain, it aimed to protect its interests in the Mediterranean and chose to sustain the Ottoman Empire by supporting the enforcement of reforms and ignoring nationalist movements.[10] During the 1860s imperial affairs with multilayered repercussions for domestic politics affected British policy with respect to the "Cretan Question." In New Zealand renewed warfare with the Maoris over land rights made it difficult for London to avoid substantial military expenditure. The development of the concept of self-government in Canada did not produce the immediate cash dividend many had expected. British attempts to loosen colonial ties by introducing responsible government and cutting military costs received a dramatic setback when a revolt in Jamaica became the focus of one of the most violent midcentury debates over an imperial matter.[11]

In October 1865 the governor of Jamaica, Edward Eyre, with brutal savagery put down a minor local uprising. Talking wildly of the Indian Mutiny, he introduced martial law: 439 persons were killed, 600 flogged, 354 court-martial sentences passed, and a thousand homes burned down. The initial response of the British government was cautiously to endorse Eyre's actions, but this support soon came under attack from abolitionists and dissenting groups. Within weeks, opinion in Britain had become polarized between those who condemned Eyre as a racialist brute and those who hailed him as a defender of all that was best in Christian civilization. Angry debates took place within and outside Parliament. The affair, by uncovering one of the deepest fault lines bisecting the educated classes, and indeed British society as a whole, rapidly assumed an importance running well beyond the confines of Jamaica or the idea of colonialism.

When Eyre came back to Britain, he was greeted by large working-class demonstrations and by support from a bevy of notables, including Thomas Carlyle (notorious for his views on the "nigger question"), Charles Kingsley, John Ruskin, Alfred Tennyson, and Charles Dickens. Men of letters sided with Eyre and formed the Eyre Defence Committee, whereas scientists such as Charles Darwin, Thomas Huxley, Herbert Spencer, and Charles Lyell joined with a number of radical politicians to set up the Jamaica Committee in opposition to the governor. The committee was initially led by Charles Buxton, son of the veteran antislavery leader Sir Thomas Fowell Buxton, and then by John Stuart Mill. A Royal Commission was also appointed to inquire into the matter. Though its report in April 1866 was cautious, its acceptance of at least some of the atrocity stories diminished the enthusiasm of all but Eyre's most blinkered partisans. The Royal Commission report claimed that initial violence had presented a genuine danger, and that Eyre had been right to react vigorously to prevent the spread of the disturbance. However, the report also concluded that martial law had continued for too long, that deaths had been unnecessarily frequent, that the floggings had been excessive and in some instances "barbarous," and that the burning of so many homes was "wanton and cruel." Faced with this critical report, the British government decided that since Eyre had already been suspended on account of the criticisms, a resolution in the House of Commons deploring the excessive punishments would be an adequate response.

The Eyre controversy reached such peculiar heights because it intermeshed with increasing concern about parliamentary reform. Eyre's friends included many who believed that reform would unleash at home those "primitive" horrors displayed in black Jamaica and Fenian Ireland. The anti-Eyre forces, which represented a regrouping of those who had supported the Union during the American Civil War, wanted to extend the franchise not only on grounds of principle but because a refusal to do so might encourage precisely the violence that their opponents also feared. More generally, the Jamaican revolt occurred at a time when harsh racial attitudes were achieving wider prominence. Older beliefs in humanity's basic perfectibility were fading under the impress of missionary pessimism, ethnographical theories ranking peoples on a "scale of civilization," false readings of Darwin, and the rise of craniology claiming the inferiority of blacks. While such developments undoubtedly produced a new contempt for blacks in colonial lands, they also reinforced the belief that withdrawal was now impossible and that the white man's burden could not simply be put down.

Historian Catherine Hall argues that at stake in the Jamaica debate were issues about the relations between the mother country and its colonies, the place of martial law and the rule of law, and the nature of black people. But also at issue were questions about Englishness itself. The debate over Eyre marked a moment when two different conceptions of "us," constructed through two different notions of "them," were publicly contested. Mill's imagined community was one of potential equity, in which "us," white Anglo-Saxon men and women, believed in the potential of black Jamaican men and women to become like "us" through a process of civilization. Carlyle's imagined community was a hierarchical ordered one in which "we" must always master "them." Between the summers of 1866 and 1867 public opinion swung away from the Jamaica Committee to the supporters of Eyre. By June 1868, when the third, last, and still unsuccessful attempt was made to prosecute Eyre, it was clear that the defense of black Jamaican rights was no longer a popular cause. Only a small core of middle-class radicals was left, led by a disillusioned and disheartened Mill, who relied for support on working-class radicals. A considerable body of opinion had concluded that black people were essentially different from white people and thus could not expect the same rights. British subjects across the empire were not all the same.

The Eyre controversy relates to the Cretan crisis in various ways. On the one hand, the British government hoped that the Sublime Porte would be able to master its populations as the British Empire had done in Jamaica. This would have been enough to guarantee peace and stability in the eastern Mediterranean, which was what mattered most to the British government. To defend the Sublime Porte, British foreign secretary Lord Stanley claimed that the Ottoman government had the same right to put down an insurrection in Crete as England had in India, France in Algeria, or Russia in Poland. Britain "could not complain of the government of the Sultan for doing that which every government in the world, including that of the United States, had done, and would do again when the necessity presented itself."[12] At the same time, the government of London feared that Ottoman "barbarism" might prevail at any moment, and that wholesale massacre of civilian populations might eventually take place. This explains why throughout the Cretan crisis the British government made every possible effort to convince the Sublime Porte not to use the Ottoman Army to put down the insurgency in Crete. The British cabinet was fully aware that the repression would have provided abolitionist, dissenting, and radical anti-Eyre groups in Britain with the argument that the government that had supported a criminal governor in Jamaica now supported a barbarous, criminal foreign government. For this reason the British government happily endorsed British diplomats' statements to the effect that Christian Cretans were uncivilized and as responsible for the bad government of the island as were their Muslim fellow islanders.[13] This argument came to reinforce the idea of the legitimacy of Ottoman repression of the insurrection.

On the other hand, a minority of British Liberals, such as the Duke of Argyll, tried to use the Cretan Question to advance the view that the persistence of inequality between Ottoman Christians and Muslims caused unrest. They thought that autonomy (or independence) for Christian Cretans would enhance the "process of civilization" they believed Ottoman Christian populations to be capable of accomplishing. By putting forward this argument, they hoped to reopen the issue of inequality within the British Empire. They proved unsuccessful, for Prime Minister Benjamin Disraeli easily rebuffed Liberal criticism on humanitarian grounds. He explained the British government's reluctance to intervene in a "clear case of humanity," arguing that any aid to the refugees would lead the Greeks to believe that Great Britain was ready to intervene on the Cretan Christians side. This would compound the problem by encouraging the insurgents to prolong their resistance, ultimately prolonging the humanitarian crisis.[14]

EUROPEAN POWERS' REACTIONS TO THE CRETAN INSURRECTION

Since the beginning of the Cretan revolt, the British government had sought cooperation from France. Paris reciprocated and showed a friendly disposition toward the Ottoman Empire rather than toward the insurgents. In June 1866 British ambassador Lyons and his French counterpart Moustier reported from Constantinople that Greek emissaries had provoked the Cretans into action. For that reason, the governments of London and Paris initially treated Greek reports of massacres and atrocities in Crete with skepticism. The two cabinets went as far as to blame the Greek and Russian consuls in Crete for encouraging the Christians to hold demonstrations against the Ottoman government.[15]

In the meantime, Lyons advised the Porte not to put into action its impressively strong army now in Crete. The foreign secretary reiterated that a massacre of Christians might incite European sympathies in favor of the Christian subjects of the Porte. In the sultan's interest he strongly advised the Ottoman authorities to act justly and kindly toward the Christians.[16] The British and French governments instructed their consuls to do everything in their power to prevent bloodshed on the island.[17]

The foreign minister of Russia, Alexander Gorchakov, noted that the stipulations of a protocol signed by the three protecting powers of Greece (Great Britain, Russia, and France) on February 20, 1830, included the humanitarian motive as grounds for intervention in Samos and Crete.[18] This protocol and the 1856 Treaty of Paris constituted "a moral engagement, binding both the Porte and the Great Powers, and which can in no sense be regarded as incompatible with the internal independence of Turkey."[19] According to Gorchakov, Russia wished to find the best manner of representing to the Porte, in a friendly and conciliatory spirit, the necessity of giving reasonable satisfaction to the Cretan population and of seeking out, in concert with the Ottoman government, the means to arrive at a peaceful arrangement. The tsar considered the Cretan question "a local insurrection, painful for humanity because of the excess, violence, and bloodshed that it might bring about."[20] For the time being, the Russian government ruled out a military intervention in Crete, suggesting instead that the Porte appoint an Ottoman commissioner to show the public the "interest taken by the protecting powers in the well-being of the [Christian] subjects of the Porte."[21]

On August 21, 1866, the Cretan assembly proclaimed *Enosis* (union) with Greece. In response, the Ottoman government, which had in the meantime appointed Mustapha Pasha as special commissioner to Crete, set up a blockade of the island.[22] In less than a month the poorly armed Cretan insurgents were bitterly defeated. News of further massacre of Cretan civilians circulated in the European press. The European cabinets admitted that, if true, these massacres were indeed "a disgrace to humanity," but for the time being they remained skeptical about their accurateness.[23] The insurrection generated a massive influx of Cretan refugees to Athens and other Greek islands, as well as of Cretan Muslims to mainland Turkey. According to the British representative in Athens, Edward Erskine, by the end of 1866 Cretan refugees in Athens alone numbered no less than eight thousand, including many women and children.

European governments reacted to the problem of Christian refugees, bearing in mind the modalities of the naval operations in Lebanon in June 1860. The Russian government, with the full agreement of Ottoman authoritites, instructed its warships to take hundreds of women and children to the island of Syra (Siros), as two Italian corvettes and one Austrian warship. Moustier informed Grand Vizier Ali Pasha that France had a duty to succor refugees. If local authorities displayed no clemency, France would give the insurgents asylum on humanitarian grounds in its consulate or onboard the frigate *Invincible*, which was anchored at Suda Bay. Moustier instructed the French consul at Canea not to give the impression of provoking the emigration of Christians but to help all the same their departure to Greece.[24] By October 1866 four European powers had reacted to the insurrection and alleged massacre of Christian civilians by using their warships and consulates to protect their nationals and protégés, as well as the local Christian population. The intervening governments emphasized that the operation was a nonforcible act aimed at saving Cretan Christian victims of massacre. At that stage, none of the intervening states thought to rescue Muslim victims.

An interesting episode took place in late 1866 when Captain Pym, commander of HMS *Assurance*, transported hundreds of Cretan refugees to the Piraeus. In the account of American journalist and painter William James Stillman, Pym carried out a "work of humanity," taking onboard 315 women and children and carrying them to the Piraeus. Mustapha Pasha had given his permission for the ship to transport the refugees, and Consul Dickson had given the order. Nevertheless, the British government was so resolutely opposed to any involvement in the Cretan Question that it punished the captain and publicly and peremptorily disapproved the rescue operation.[25] Stanley deplored Pym's action, which he believed the Ottomans could have interpreted as the beginning of an intervention on the part of the British government, and stated that Dickson's aid to the half-starved fugitives whose villages had been destroyed was "*a pure act of humanity, without political significance.*"[26] To make his point clearer, when the British minister at Athens, Erskine, requested the sending of humanitarian relief for the refugees in the Greek capital, the Foreign Office bluntly refused. London affirmed that there was no governmental fund from which assistance could be granted to those refugees as they were not British subjects.[27]

The naval rescue operation was genuinely intended to save strangers and, as noted, had the full agreement of Mustapha Pasha, the highest local authority of the potential target state. European powers were attempting to avoid a repetition of massacre and to find a long-term peaceful solution through diplomacy rather than armed force, as evidenced by Lyons and Moustier's suggestion that the Porte should display clemency toward the vanquished and give the Christian Cretans assurances that their administration would be gentle and equitable. [28]

The grand vizier reassured the Europeans, stating that "from motives of humanity, no less than from a sense of the importance of not alienating the friendly feelings of the governments of Europe, [the Porte] had taken every precaution against any excess of severity in putting down the rebellion.[29] On January 17, 1867, Lord Stanley stated that the solution to the Cretan crisis had to be found within the context of Ottoman reforms. He mentioned a "Lebanese solution" for Crete, referring to the administrative *Règlement* of June 1861.[30] Ambassador Lyons and the newly appointed French ambassador at Constantinople, Nicolas P. Bourrée, reinforced to the Sublime Porte that the governments of London and Paris wished Cretan Christians and Muslims to live together in peace and opposed the expulsion, by direct or indirect means, of the Muslim population of Crete.[31] No *désagrégation* plans were put forward, as had happened for Lebanon, or enforced, as with the Muslim civilian populations of Attica and the Morea.

Toward the end of 1866 the Foreign Office reiterated the importance of the Ottoman authorities using every possible means to provide relief for the inhabitants of Crete and to assure families of a means of subsistence. It warned the Sublime Porte that the issue of refugees was about to awaken the sympathies of European public opinion and induce a general feeling of dissatisfaction about the prolongation of the struggle that had immersed helpless inhabitants of the island in misery and want. The Porte, the Foreign Office noted, scarcely needed to be reminded that popular sympathy, extending throughout Europe, would eventually influence European governments. The latter would then be forced to interfere in the general relations between the Ottoman government and its Christian subjects.[32] Lyons insisted that it was essential for the Porte to conduct hostilities in a "civilized manner," for even if acts of atrocity had been committed equally on both sides, "the spectacle would be too shocking to be endured patiently by Europe."[33] Although the Porte heeded the advice of London and Paris, further news of massacre, of the fate of the refugees, and of the defeat of the Cretans combined to seize the attention of European public opinion in sympathy with Christian Cretans.

THE RESCUE OF CHRISTIAN CRETAN FAMILIES

Two events occurred at the beginning of 1867. First, the number of volunteers landing in Crete increased. Among these volunteers there were fully armed Garibaldians, Hungarians, French, and Greeks, whose objective was the union of Crete with Greece. Their strategy was *"tenir bon jusqu'au printemps pour forcer les Puissances à intervenir."*[34] We shall see that Bulgarian, Armenian, and Macedonian insurgents would adopt similar tactics during the final quarter of the nineteenth century. Second, the French government came to the sudden conclusion that the Porte had to give up Crete rather than continue to appease the Christian population by giving some form of local autonomy to the island. The newly appointed French foreign minister, Moustier, declared that the country was already lost to the Ottoman Empire, and that it would be better for the sultan to accept this conclusion. Moustier argued that granting concessions would not permanently reconcile the population to Ottoman rule and might even form a precedent on which every part of the Ottoman Empire could base a claim for quasi-independence; hence, Greece should annex Crete. It was better for the Ottoman Empire "to amputate [Crete] than to allow it to form the nucleus of gangrene, which might spread to every part of the Empire."[35]

This abrupt change in French views on the Cretan Question might have been related to the French government's *Note sur le Hatt-i Hümayoun de 1856* of January 1867. The document indicated what the Ottoman government had to do to enforce reforms. It was divided into sixteen paragraphs, taking into account every sector of Ottoman public administration, and indicated all the areas in which the Ottoman government should immediately take serious action.[36] The French government assumed that there was no room for agreement among Ottoman Christians and that there was no single Christian minority or political class able to predominate over the others. None of them was ready for self-determination.[37] Thus, to avoid the situation where fifteen or twenty "races" would be "scattered in Russian, Austrian, and English dust" the Ottoman Christians still needed the "Turks."[38] The pivot of the French policy was the "Turkish race" (*la race musulmane*), which had to consider the risk of blending with the Christians and thereby renounce its exclusiveness. The French government wanted the Porte to abolish any distinction between Muslims and Christians and achieve the *"fusion des races."*[39] Losing Crete, an island inhabited by a conspicuous Christian majority, might well have strengthened the Ottoman Empire. As Lavalette wrote to his foreign minister, Thouvenel, in 1861 in the midst of the Lebanese crisis, the principle of the *fusion des races* would be difficult to apply where these races where enemies and ignored else besides religious division.[40] In the case of Crete, the union with Greece appeared to the French to be both consistent with Napoleon's pronationalist foreign policy and with the principle of *fusion des races*. For obvious reasons Ali Pasha could not agree to the French solution, among other things because of concern about the fate of almost ninety thousand Cretan Muslims under Christian administration or, even worse, in case of annexation of the island to Greece.[41]

The new course of French foreign policy marked the immediate end of British-French cooperation. The British ambassador in Paris, Lord Cowley, argued that if every part of the empire in which agitation could be fomented was to be considered an incurable sore limb, the process of amputation could be applied continuously until nothing but the trunk was left, which could scarcely be expected to survive after being thoroughly dismembered.[42] The British government's next move was to dissociate itself from any humanitarian operation. London even hindered humanitarian aid coming from Britain to the island and stood firm against the protest of the most active humanitarian group (the Candian Refugees Relief Fund, formed by the bishop of London and other persons of influence, located in central London, and whose spokesman was John Hay).[43] As had happened during the early stages of the Greek crisis of the 1820s, and to some extent during the Lebanese crisis of 1860–61, the British government intended to show the Porte and the other European powers its firm commitment to the Ottoman Empire despite the mobilization of public opinion to the contrary. The British government continued to sponsor local relief operations, such as in the town of Rhetymno, where upwards of two hundred Christians found shelter in Vice Consul G. Calocherino's home. This was a way of drawing the attention of British public opinion and of the other European powers to alternative, more effective, and less risky ways to relieve civilian populations. Consul Dickson proposed to create a mixed European-Ottoman commission charged with receiving contributions in money and kind and supervising their distribution to needy Christians and Muslims.[44]

In February 1867 the Russian government invited the European powers to sign a joint communication to the Porte requesting it to allow foreign warships to remove from Crete any Christians who might want to leave the island in "an act of humanity."[45] In answer, the Ottoman government decided to ascertain whether the situation of widows and orphans was as terrible as European sources and newspapers had depicted it. It dispatched a fact-finding commission that was also supposed to afford relief to distressed families. This step satisfied the British Foreign Office since it would "at once meet the just claims of humanity" and end the interference of foreign powers rescuing the families "of the insurgents."[46] Unfortunately, one month later the Ottoman commissioners had not been able to make any distinct reports to the Porte. To buy time, Foreign Minister Fuad Pasha claimed that the Ottoman authorities would gladly transport within the empire any Cretans keen to leave their country and stated that there were no longer families on the seashore suffering from hunger and cold. Contrary to what European sources argued, Fuad insisted that those on the shore were insurgents unwilling to embark on vessels the Ottoman government had put at their disposal. With the exception of Great Britain, the European powers dismissed Fuad's offer and continued transporting Christian Cretans on their own ships.

During the spring of 1867 the Ottoman Navy showed itself to be completely unable to prevent the landing of Greek volunteers in Crete, as reported by a war correspondent for one of the daily London newspapers who was embedded on the ship *Arkadi*.[47] On land, too, the Ottoman forces were unable to defeat the volunteers. Muslim civilians set up irregular troops (bashi-bazouks, or wearers of the red cap (fez), who, in the words of the French diplomat Outrey were nothing less than armed Muslim Cretans defending their territory against Greek volunteers[48]) and retaliated against the violence of the volunteers with further violence, including the raping of Christian women. The sanitary conditions on the island were now deplorable: typhoid fever hit refugees, volunteers, and Ottoman soldiers alike. With the insurrection far from being over, the suffering of civilians remained an urgent, unsolved humanitarian issue.

On March 28, 1867, the French ambassador proposed to the Porte that it allow the Cretans to decide on their future destiny by vote.[49] The British government, however, resolutely opposed the French initiative. Stanley, unconcerned about the fate of Cretans and possibly dreading what would have happened had this principle been applied in the British Empire, feared that France might take the Ottoman Empire *"en tutelle."* Fuad, content of British support, replied to the French government that the Porte had not the least intention of submitting the sultan's sovereignty over Crete to a popular vote. He stated that the war was entirely against foreign volunteers, with whom the Porte would not consent to any armistice. If the European powers meant to take Crete away from the sultan, they would have to fight another battle of Navarino. Fuad pointed out that the insurgents, almost entirely Greek, were still active because, following the advice of the Europeans, the Ottoman Army had avoided bloodshed. He concluded that had his government repressed the insurrection, it would have been straightforwardly accused of "barbarity" in Europe.[50] Fuad's reference to Navarino, his deliberate attempt to highlight that the Ottoman Army had so far avoided massacre, and his awareness of being easily accused of barbarity show that Ottoman policy-makers viewed the situation in Crete as being analogous to those in Greece (1825–27) and Syria (1860–61). Fuad was clearly attempting to avoid a humanitarian intervention and was fully aware that as long as Great Britain opposed the idea of a collective action on behalf of Cretan Christians, the Ottoman government had a chance to avoid extensive European interference in its internal affairs.

Annoyed at the British refusal, which had paralyzed all efforts to do good, Moustier tried to rally Britain to the side of the other European powers by suggesting that it join in asking the Porte to suspend hostilities in Crete and to consent to the mission of a joint European commission to inquire into the alleged grievances of the people, similar to the 1860 European Commission of Beirut. The French government also prepared a new proposal that proposed to the Porte autonomy for Crete, rather than independence, on the model of the *Règlement* of Samos and Lebanon. If enforced, the solution had the advantage of ending the insurrection, with both the Muslim and the Christian Cretans spared from vengeance, and fulfilling the *principes d'humanité*, which motivated the French government.[51] The British opposed this new proposal.[52] In response, the Sublime Porte agreed to send an Ottoman commission to inquire into the alleged grievances of the people, stating that a necessary preliminary to any concession was the end of all activities by the volunteers in Crete.[53]

By June 1867 fighting on the island had turned into a stalemate. The impasse seemed destined to last very long unless the Ottoman Empire deployed its army or the European powers undertook a full-fledged armed intervention. The Ottoman government refrained from deploying its army because it would have provided the justification some of the powers were waiting for to intervene. And Great Britain would certainly not consent to a large-scale intervention in Crete. Hence, the governments of France and Russia informed the Sublime Porte that their warships would enhance the protection of any Christian family who wanted to expatriate because of the insurrection by transporting them away from Crete.[54] In June 1867 Russia informed London that Britain's self-imposed restraint should not hinder the other powers from following *"the impulse and sentiment of humanity."*[55] The Russians stated that the Cretan affair required each cabinet to consult its own conscience, and the moral action of one of them should not become a cause of discord or mistrust for the others. In other words, the intervention in Crete was not to be interpreted by Great Britain as an act threatening the European order. Russia's unique objective was to ensure safety for the women and children fleeing from

> acts of fanaticism and vengeance to which they would fall victims, did no one come to aid them in their distress. If this measure of rescue had not yet obtained the concurrence of the Government of Her Britannic Majesty, it will none the less recognize the inviolability of a right of asylum, of which England, when she will, knows well how to set an example. Under the influence of the same sentiment of humanity, Europe will not remain an unmoved spectator of the system of extermination with which Omer Pasha threatens to strike a population

which he is alike incapable of conquering and pacifying. If he hoped to reduce it by famine, the Christian world would not tolerate it.[56]

When the British ambassador at St. Petersburg asked Gorchakov what would have happened if the Ottomans had opposed the rescue operation, he laconically answered that it was intolerable for Russia (and Europe) to look patiently on while Ottoman troops were perpetrating "atrocities."[57] The Russian government's official motivation for undertaking naval operations was to save the lives of women and children distressed by the target state's incapacity to restore peace and by an attempt at "extermination" (through famine). The latter was an allegation not supported by sufficient or incontrovertible evidence. There are also other inconsistencies related to the motives of intervention the Russian government put forward. First, the incapacity to restore peace was the consequence of the Porte following the advice of the European cabinets not to act against the insurgents, not of its unwillingness to put down the insurgency. Second, the Russian government claimed that because of Omer Pasha's policy, it had a moral rather than legal duty to intervene. However, as the epigraph at the beginning of this chapter recalls, the grand vizier reminded all European cabinets that even while speaking of "rights of humanity," Russia had crushed the Polish rebellion, shooting women and children and deporting Polish women to Siberia, and had more recently acted in a "barbarous" way against Abkhazian populations. In 1863 the other European powers had not rescued a single Polish woman or child: What about the moral duty of Europe in that case? How could the Russian government talk about "rights of humanity"? Third, despite the alleged duty to intervene, the Russian government decided not to deploy adequate military force to end the insurgency and ensuing alleged massacres. We know that St. Petersburg could not officially admit that the British stance hindered the undertaking of such a military operation; it could not openly declare that despite an ongoing "war of extermination," intervention on a vast scale could not take place in Crete for it would have threatened the international system, and that in the end Russia was not ready to go to war to defend Christian Cretans. It is perhaps for this reason that the document did not use the word "intervention" and referred to the old right of asylum, under which a person (a single individual) may be protected by another sovereign country for political opinions or religious beliefs in his or her own country.

Russia and the other intervening powers continued to seek the consent of the Ottoman government to dispel any doubt about the nature of the operation. The Russian ambassador at Constantinople, Nicholas Pavlovich Ignatiev, pressed Grand Vizier Ali Pasha to officially consent to the removal of women and children from Crete on Russian warships. To prove that the relief operation was purely humanitarian, when Commodore Boutakoff landed in Rhetymno, he first paid a visit to the Ottoman lieutenant general and then visited the houses of the Ottoman Relief Commission. Ali Pasha eventually promised that the local authorities would not interfere with any measures the commanders of these vessels might adopt "for mere objects of humanity."[58] The Ottoman military in Crete had no option but to let the refugees go. Any detention or, worse, killing of these groups of civilians would have very likely precipitated further intervention based on now "incontrovertible" evidence of Ottoman "barbarous" behavior. Austrian, Prussian, and Italian warships joined the French and Russian in cruising along the coasts of Crete and took measures for the safety of noncombatants.[59] All the intervening powers acted extremely cautiously and carefully avoided carrying out any act directed against the Ottoman authorities and soldiers. Napoleon III and his naval minister instructed the French admiral in Greece to go ashore in Crete and only to collect women and children and older people.[60] The French dispatched the warships *La Renommée*, *La Sentinelle*, and *Promethée* "for the purpose of removing homeless victims of the war, whenever it should be advisable."[61] Admiral Simon entered Cretan harbors to "save the victims who might be wandering on the coast, and to convey them to Greece." In the meantime, anxious to avoid any misunderstanding concerning the nature of the rescue operation, the French chargé d'affaires, Outrey, gave notice of his decisions in an unofficial letter to the grand vizier asking him to instruct Omer Pasha *"de prêter tout son concours à une oeuvre d'humanité."* For the same reason, Outrey informed his British counterpart, Barron, that the operation was imminent, specifying that Admiral Simon's mission was "purely philanthropic" and would not degenerate into a political intervention In a further internal document Outrey wrote to Moustier that "when one learns about women and children wandering in the countryside, dying out of starvation, the rights of humanity (*droits de l'humanité*) compel us to help them. This is an exclusively philanthropic intervention (*une intervention toute philanthropique*)."[62]

In order for the rescue operation to be morally credible and politically justifiable, France and Russia had to prove that massacres and atrocities had taken place and were still going on. As Canning did in 1825 when he heard of Ibrahim Pasha's barbarization project in the Morea, St. Petersburg and Paris seemed ready to accept as real even fabricated news of massacres. This is not to say that such events did not occur at all on the island; however, rather than acknowledging the complexity of the local situation, Russian and French diplomats decided to believe, or preferred to take as genuine, news from the vice consuls in Crete who, often being of Greek origins, invariably depicted the Muslims as "barbarians slaughtering civilians."[63] Furthermore, they did not pay due attention to the Ottoman complaints, with evidence, that the Greek clipper *Arkadi* (later joined by the ship *Enosis*), while participating in rescue missions, had disembarked new groups of volunteers, something the Ottoman authorities could obviously not tolerate.[64]

It should be underscored that the intervening powers' actions exclusively rescued Christian Cretans and ignored the fate of Muslim Cretans who benefited from Ottoman relief and Muslim charities. During the summer of 1867 the town of Candia experienced a situation quite similar to Beirut's in 1860, though this time the Muslims, rather than Christians, who had fled their inland villages en masse constituted the great majority of the refugees. Within a few months thirty thousand Muslim and seven thousand Christian refugees were overcrowding the town, creating sanitary and relief problems clearly beyond the ability of the local authorities to handle. European powers did not provide adequate relief for the Muslims. In July 1867 the vizier Ali Pasha noted that a truly humanitarian operation should have removed fighting men along with their wives and children. Perhaps rightly, he claimed that he rescue of women and children alone had in fact separated the rebels from an impediment to their movements and encouraged the rebellion. It was for that very reason that in July the Porte attempted to oppose the further transport of women and children from the island, where, according to Ali, they had nothing to fear.[65] This was quickly contradicted by news reporting that families of Cretans concealed in a deep cave had been killed using salt, sulphuric acid, and other combustible matters. In July 1867 Consul Dickson admitted that massacres, atrocities, and the firing and sacking of whole villages now occurred daily and were committed by Ottoman soldiery and especially by the bashi-bazouks against Christian civilians in the interior of the island.[66] Moreover, many families in Rhetymno and Candia were now starving. For all these reasons, the intervening states ignored Ali's decision to withdraw the consent for the rescue operation and continued with their activities. The pace of the operation increased in July when, in less than a month, the French warships alone transported more than 2,500 refugees to Greece.[67]

THE TURNING POINT, AUGUST 1867

Toward the end of August the French government suddenly decided to stop carrying out rescue operations. Paris had gathered evidence that Russian warships were disembarking men and ammunition on the island. The French government feared that the rescue operation could become "*une intervention armée et politique.*"[68] Furthermore, one of the commanders of the French warships reported that of the 480 refugees he had taken onboard, nobody was starving and nobody had witnessed massacres. Some admitted that volunteers had forced them to quit their villages and brought them to the coastal areas.[69]

While dissension in the Franco-Russian camp ran very high, the British government, which could have seized the opportunity to demonstrate the wisdom of its decision not to rescue Cretan families, stood at the center of the most serious domestic political attack against its policy of neutrality and absolute nonintervention.[70] British observers on the spot criticized the strict neutrality that the cabinet had ordered Vice Admiral C. Paget to observe. Lieutenant Murray of the *Wizard* wanted to render a "work of humanity" similar to the French and Russians assistance given to Cretan families by removing them to places of security. He was appalled at the news that an Ottoman naval squadron, including an ironclad ship with Omer Pasha on board, was steaming slowly along the shore, bombarding caves and every nook capable of concealing anyone. The caves at Tripiti, where the Russians had already removed 1,200 persons, were now scarcely recognizable, having been bombarded so heavily.[71] Historian Ann Pottinger Saab notes that although stories of massacres were somewhat camouflaged in the papers laid before Parliament, enough information was presented to alarm the British MPs.[72]

Lord Stanley (now the Earl of Derby) defended the government's policy, pointing out that the Cretans had had a reputation as great liars for two thousand years. He went on to surmise that the tales of cruelty "have no origin except in the imagination of those who relate them." [73] In the Commons, Derby relied on the blanket condemnation that both sides had committed atrocities, "as will always happen in war of this kind, carried on in half-civilized countries and in part by irregular troops."[74] He had little time for either Christians or Muslims. Not long before this he had written in a private letter: "both are fanatics, both intolerant, and in point of civilization, there is little to choose."[75] Many British MPs were unconvinced by Derby's explanation and shocked by the news of the massacres and the appalling living conditions of the refugees. MPs such as Charles James Monk argued that many of the worst atrocities had been perpetrated by local Muslim Cretans, and they pointed out that the Ottoman leadership and Omer Pasha were responsible as they had taken no steps against the aggressors and did not endeavor to prevent the crimes. Monk's solution was a collective intervention to urge either "concessions" or the outright relinquishment of the island to Greece.

On September 12, 1867, a newly re-created Franco-British entente on the Cretan Question persuaded the Porte to announce an amnesty, coupled with an offer of a suspension of arms, which was to expire on October 20, 1867.[76] The Sublime Porte guaranteed that no obstacle would be created to inhibit the departure of those natives who wished to quit the island. The Ottoman authorities would authorize them to emigrate with their families under the conditions that they would give up their interests in everything they possessed on the island and would be unable to return without special authorization from the imperial government. The Porte would maintain a massive army in Crete to preserve peace and would keep the blockade in place to prevent vessels from transporting men and munitions.[77] Following this agreement, European warships took on new waves of Christian Cretans, acting once again with the full agreement of the Ottoman government.

Fuad Pasha, while admitting that generosity motivated the European powers, noted that their action begot results contrary to the humane intention (la pensée humanitaire) that had dictated it. According to Fuad, the Europeans should have focused on saving the twenty thousand individuals spread along the coasts of Greece who, in his view, were too many witnesses to deny before Europe the atrocities the Ottoman authorities were accused of having committed in Crete.[78] Fuad knew that the living conditions of Cretan refugees in Greece were miserable. The situation of the refugees, including the twelve thousand who had descended on Athens, was desperate; many had already died and many more were seriously ill.[79] The Greek authorities and civilian populations of the islands of Syros, Milos, and Corfu and of the towns of Missolonghi and Athens complained when they saw new refugees ready to disembark in their towns, hoping the Greek government would pay for their relief.[80] Since European funds had run out, a serious humanitarian crisis seemed unavoidable. On October 9, 1867, the French chargé d'affaires admitted that to continue the transportation of women and children from Crete to Greece would provoke the worsening of the living conditions of those already in Greece. Shortly thereafter a great number of them would be resettled on Crete itself.[81]

THE DIPLOMATIC SOLUTION TO THE CRISIS

On October 28 the Ottoman government communicated to the European powers its project of administrative reforms for Crete. The Russian government quickly reacted by saying that short of annexing Crete to Greece, there was no solution that Russia regarded as satisfactory.

The French government now claimed that a reorganization of Crete on the basis of the 1861 Lebanese *Règlement Organique* offered the only acceptable solution to the Cretan Question.[82] On behalf of his government, the newly appointed British ambassador at Constantinople, Henry Elliot, supported a "Lebanese solution," insisting on the necessity of protecting the Muslim minority from becoming entirely subject to the Christian majority.[83] A new *Règlement* was eventually enforced in 1868. In the opinion of Fuad Pasha, it epitomized the spirit of progress and liberalism animating the Ottoman government and constituted the greatest concession compatible with the Porte's dignity and incontestable rights.[84]

The reforms the sultan eventually enforced in Crete were very advanced and respectful of both Christian and Muslim rights, though they were not the union with Greece that many Christians now wanted. According to the new scheme, the sultan would appoint a *vali* to run the general administration of the island. The command of the imperial fortress and the troops of the island would fall to a military commander in chief. These two posts would be independent of each other, except in cases of absolute necessity. Two councillors, one Muslim and one Christian, would assist the *vali*. The island would be divided into departments (*sandjaks*) presided over by governors (*mutassarifs*), half of whom would be Christians. The Muslim governors would be assisted by Christian assistants (*mouavins*) and vice versa. The *vali* would work together with an adminisrative council consisting of the two councillors, the chief magistrate, the Greek metropolitan, the finance minister (*defterdar*), and the directors of correspondence (communications). The official languages of the island would be Turkish and Greek. Each *sandjak* would include a local administrative council with six members chosen by the local population (who would all be Christians in *sandjaks* exclusively inhabited by Christians). Tribunals for investigating civil and criminal actions would be constituted at the headquarters of the general government. In the mixed *sandjaks* and districts (*kazas*), tribunals would be composed of Muslim and Christian members chosen by the population (if the population was exclusively Christian, these tribunals would include only Christians). Mixed civil and commercial tribunals would adjudicate all civil, criminal, and commercial actions between Christians and Muslims, and all other mixed disputes. A general council chosen by the population would be instituted at the center of the general government, with two delegates, one Christian and one Muslim for mixed *kazas*, and would meet once a year to study questions relating to public utility, such as the development of channels of communication, the formation of banks of credit, and everything that could serve to promote agriculture, commerce, industry, and public instruction. Finally, the inhabitants of Crete would pay tithes but would be exempt from military service, duties on liquors, and custom duties, while duties on salt and tobacco would be created to compensate for the loss of the latter dues. No other tax would be imposed on the island.[85]

The *Règlement* was an ingenious and progressive piece of imperial administrative administration. For political rather than genuinely humanitarian reasons, the Europeans, especially the British government, mentioned the Muslim minority's interests, whose terrible conditions they had systematically ignored throughout the entire period of the crisis. Before the promulgation of the reforms, the French and British governments asked the Russians to stop the evacuation of Cretans to Greece.[86] French warships undertook the repatriation of Christian Cretan refugees in Greece in September 1868. The French wanted to proceed as quickly as they could, for October in Crete is the month of the olive harvest. The olive oil trade was the most important economic activity on the island, and harvesting traditionally was the task of women and children. With so many women and children now in Greece, a failed harvest would have caused further distress and poverty. Behind this genuine humanitarian concern stood French businessmen with their particular commercial and industrial interests.[87]

A last turn to the Cretan Question was the late 1868 decision by the Greek government to foment rebellion in the Ottoman regions of Epirus, Thessaly, and Macedonia while at the same time attempting to throw the repatriation plan into disarray. With Greece and the Ottoman Empire now on the verge of war, the European powers increased their determination to settle the whole issue as soon as possible.[88] The last thing the European powers wanted was further disorder. At the beginning of 1869 Greece, under European pressure, refrained from sending aid to the rebels in Crete, and shortly afterwards the insurrection completely collapsed. The European powers sanctioned Crete as a privileged province of the Ottoman Empire, and when plenipotentiaries met in Paris they settled the fate of island on their own, excluding Greek officials as well as representatives of the Cretan Christian and Muslim communities.[89]

. . .

Ali Pasha's 1869 *Report on Crete* is an interesting document that explains how the target state interpreted the occurrences of 1866–68. The grand vizier pointed out that the Greek newspapers' lies and calumnies misled European public opinion. European governments had in turn started a new kind of intervention, the *sauvetage des familles*.[90] Ali Pasha claimed that invented stories of massacres of women, children, and older people allowed some of the European powers to transport, under the label of a rescue (*sauvetage*), people whose life, honor, and property were allegedly threatened. He forgot to mention that a number of appalling atrocities had beyond doubt occurred, especially in 1867. In Ali's view, this "philanthropic" intervention, which the Russian fleet carried out for longer than any other power, was in fact a disguised intervention allegedly practiced "in the name of humanity" (*au nom de l'humanité*). He condemned an intervention that had provided all the freedom the insurgents needed as the children, women, and older people were taken away to secure places. Ali Pasha emphasized that a truly humanitarian intervention would not have taken into account the religion of the victims. On the contrary, the European intervention had been biased and unjust, for it had protected only the Christians and disregarded the fate of the Muslim Cretans.

"Was the humanitarian aim of the intervention attained?" asked Ali Pasha. His reply to this rhetorical question was sharp and sagacious: the conditions of the Cretan Christian families—who were, after all, still Ottoman subjects—in Greece, which had fomented the insurgency, were miserable, and the death rate among them was very high indeed. He also deplored the introduction of a new mode of intervention that had rendered the Ottoman blockade of the island ineffective and had hindered Ottoman efforts to restore tranquillity.[91] The grand vizier's analysis showed that the Ottoman government clearly distinguished between humanitarian intervention and war. Even though he resolutely contested that massacres of Christian Cretans occurred from 1866 to 1868, he acknowledged the rationale for intervention that the European powers put forward. One might add to this analysis that the naval operation did not save the victims of massacre who lived inland, far from the island's coasts. Insofar as no landing of ground troops was planned, the rescue operation was ineffective. Historians Robert Holland and Diana Markides have written that the 1866–68 Cretan intervention established a distinctive Cretan "insurrection type": successive phases of agitation and quiescence, a Muslim retreat into the towns, a flow of civilian refugees into various Greek territories, destruction of crops and homes, cordons separating the sides, and a European proclivity to become involved without effecting any resolution of fundamental conflicts.[92]

Contrary to the case of Lebanon and Syria, late-nineteenth and early-twentieth-century juridical international lawyers did not mention the case of Crete among the list of supposedly humanitarian interventions despite the fact that the *sauvetage des familles* aimed at saving strangers and went clearly beyond the old right of asylum. The Cretan case was overlooked perhaps because the naval operation was not directly meant to stop or prevent further massacre. Or perhaps international legal scholars and political analysts viewed that operation as being below the threshold of intervention. After the Eastern Crisis of the 1870s, some authors, such as the Duke of Argyll, portrayed the case of Crete as one in which the British ministers and ambassador at Constantinople had failed to prevent "the work of repressing actual insurrection from being conducted with systematic barbarity." In Argyll's view, the case of Crete was one of nonintervention because of the degree of barbarity attained during that civil war and the many incidents so "shocking to humanity." Even if there had been no serious grievances to justify insurrection in 1867, and even if the war had arisen simply out of the people's desire to reestablish their independence, Great Britain had "a good right" and a duty to require the Porte to act "in a manner consistent with the usages of civilised nations." As in the case of Syria, Britain should have intervened to redress real grievances and to implement reforms in Crete. Argyll contested the British government's refusal to allow the ships of war to transport the Christian families despite being well informed about the "degeneracy," "savage ferocity," and excesses of "half-savage" irregulars and the murder of men, women, and children. In his view, the British government had declined the "offices of common humanity towards the victims of Turkish soldiery" and had abandoned its duties toward Ottoman Christians. Argyll accused the British government of an inexcusable blindness and of reckless partisanship with a government "disposed to massacre as the proper mode of dealing with revolt."[93]

Finally, the 1868 *Règlement* was typically enacted with complete disregard for the political aim of the local populations. From the European powers' point of view, especially that of the British government, the Greek government was no better candidate than the Ottoman Empire to change the state of affairs on the island of Crete. With the possible exception of the Russians, European governments and diplomats did not think that union with Greece would bring "good government" or increase the well-being of either Christian or Muslim Cretans.[94] Despite the renewed activities of Philhellenes around Europe claiming the contrary, in many European government circles the Greek government was heavily criticized for its endemic corruption and the disastrous state of its agriculture and finances. There seemed to be little reason to aid the Cretans to achieve the misery of union with Greece. In the mid-1860s neither the British nor any other European government yielded under the pressure of public opinion. The operation to rescue Christian families had a clear, albeit selective, humanitarian dimension. The British decision not to participate in the rescue operation was determined by political motives, not, as Derby claimed, by humanitarian ones.

Throughout the Cretan crisis, the British government supported, tacitly or even explicitly, swift Ottoman repression of Christians in order to forestall possible intervention by other powers. Britain was keen to discourage Cretan minorities—and any other minority, for that matter—from thinking that they had external support because that might only have furthered separatist ambitions, threatening Britain's self-interests. After the introduction of the 1868 *Règlement*, the island was quiet for almost ten years. The lesson British policy-makers learned was that supporting the Ottoman Empire was the right policy to pursue. In fact, it eclipsed the longer-term ends of encouraging Ottoman reforms and thereby creating a self-sustaining polity. The die of British foreign policy, historian Donald Bloxham writes, was cast through the massacres of Lebanese and Syrian Christians, the Cretan crisis, and the beginning of Russian reassertiveness in the Eastern crisis of 1875—78.[95]

CHAPTER SIX

Nonintervention during the Eastern Crisis (1875–78)

> Does Lord Derby seriously mean to say that if such horrors
> were proved to be necessary in order to keep Russia out of
> Constantinople, such horrors must, therefore, be allowed?
> Are we to give up humanity in order to preserve the "bal-
> ance of power," "Et propter vitam vivendi perdere
> causas"?
>
> —The bishop of Exeter, Frederik Temple,
> in the *Times*, September 16, 1876

THIS CHAPTER EXAMINES the concept and practice of humanitarian intervention during the Eastern crisis of 1875–78. I focus on the insurrection in Bosnia and Herzegovina and on the well-known events of the
Bulgarian atrocities, also known as the "Bulgarian horrors." I examine
the negotiations of the December 1876 Conference of Constantinople,
in which European policy-makers did not agree on the possibility of
undertaking a humanitarian intervention. The conference proceedings
show the kind of peace enforcement (as we would put it today) that
European policy-makers wished to implement in the Balkan provinces
of the Ottoman Empire. The failure of the conference led to the Russo-
Turkish War, which started in April 1877. It is worth clarifying from
the outset that contemporary policy-makers did not consider the 1877
war as an instance of humanitarian intervention, even if humanitarian
motives (the protection of Orthodox Christians) prominently appeared
among the official reasons put forward by the Russian government as
well as Russian Pan-Slavists. We shall see that, as in the case of Crete, the
European powers disregarded Christian national aspirations in the Balkans, not to mention their utter disregard for Muslim victims of various
disturbances. European powers did not fight a *Freedom's Battle* on behalf of Balkan populations but separated the issue of self-determination
from collective action to avoid the repetition of massacre and atrocities. The Bulgarian atrocities certainly were the moment when public
opinion assumed a key role in the formulation of policy. However, I
fully share the point of view of historian Stevan Pavlowitch that public opinion alone did not change British or Russian foreign policy.[1] As

Misha Glenny points out, what public opinion certainly did was to add a new dimension to European politics. Massacres were instrumentalized, so that external perceptions of the Balkans became polarized. The reporting of the Bulgarian massacres triggered a pattern that persists in Western attitudes toward the Balkans to this day: little sympathy is expressed for the victims of conflict if they belong to the national community, which is considered the original aggressor.[2] This was even more clearly the case when the perpetrators were "barbarian" Muslim populations supported by an equally "uncivilized' regime.

From 1875 to 1878 the discussion about intervention was part of a broader discourse for British campaigners as well as for Russian Pan-Slavists, who were a mighty force in the small segment of Russian society that counted as public opinion.[3] Pan-Slavism represented the vanguard of Russian grandeur reemerging after the humiliation of the Crimean War. Profoundly anti-Western, steeped in an obscurantist imperial orthodoxy, Pan-Slavists dreamed of restoring Constantinople as the capital of a Christian empire. This implied the liberation of the Balkan Slavs under Russian guidance and also gave a mighty impetus to its crusading approach toward Islam. Pan-Slavism had supporters within the government, though Tsar Alexander II and his foreign minister, Prince Alexander Mikhailovich Gorchakov, saw it as a dangerous populist movement that encroached on their policy-making prerogatives. After the outbreak of hostilities in the Balkans in 1875, Pan-Slavists were able to put considerable pressure on the tsar and government.[4]

The 1875 Revolt in Bosnia and Herzegovina

The Eastern crisis of 1875–78 took place after Germany's unification, which followed the Prussian victories over Austria in 1866 and France in 1871. The Russian government exploited the latter event by unilaterally releasing itself from some of its obligations under the Treaty of Paris of 1856, which de facto reopened the Eastern Question. Austria-Hungary had lost the power game in central and northern Europe and now faced the prospect of renewed Russian moves into the Balkans. Vienna cast its acquisitive gaze with great urgency on Bosnia and Herzegovina. At the start of the crisis the European powers were not remotely interested in revolutionary struggles in the Balkans, let alone encouraging them. Since 1873 Germany, Russia, and Austria-Hungary had been united in the Three Emperors' League, whose chief aim was to halt the spread of republican and revolutionary ideology in Europe. Although they were hardly friends of the Ottoman Empire, St. Petersburg and Vienna re-

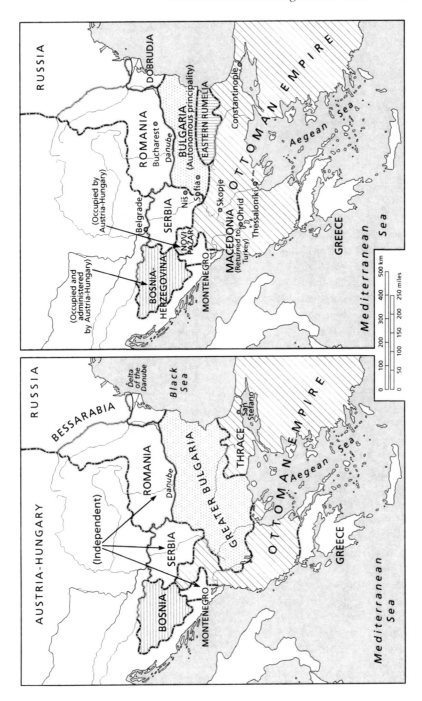

garded the prospect of an armed rebellion overthrowing an established monarchy with considerable reserve. Great Britain was still committed to the status quo in order to keep Russian hands off Constantinople. It was isolated because of the Austro-Hungarian and German alignment with Russia and because France had not yet recovered from the defeat of 1870–71. Because of these shifts in Europe's geopolitics, when the Herzegovinan and Bosnian uprisings broke out in 1875 the Porte no longer saw them as irritating domestic disorders but as an acute strategic threat.[5]

From 1871 unrest had increased throughout Bosnia and Herzegovina. After 1873 it became endemic. In 1874 the crop failed throughout most of the provinces. A bad harvest not only threatened the provinces' peasantry with starvation it also ensured that the tax farmers, ably supported by the gendarmes (zaptiehs) and, if necessary, by the regular army, would pursue their work with even greater zeal. Skirmishes between the Serb peasants and Ottoman troops were followed by retreat into the mountains, and hostage taking became common. An uprising took place in the Nevesinje area of eastern Herzegovina in January 1875. Glenny notes that this rebellion was different from the countless acts of armed resistance in Herzegovina and Bosnia, for it had been at least a year in preparation. It was a matter of weeks before it reached Bosnia. This was "the prologue to the Great Eastern Crisis—the most significant period in nineteenth-century Balkan history, and one that would change the peninsula beyond recognition."[6]

Despite stories of impalement and other "horrors" widely circulated in the press, the British government and a large part of British public opinion were not in favor of the insurgents in Bosnia and Herzegovina.[7] Only a minority of prominent personalities publicly reacted to the harshness of Ottoman repression. Among those people who provided assistance in every legitimate way to the Christian refugees of these areas and endeavored to "end the wrongs committed by the Ottoman government" were Lewis Farley and the Rev. William Denton—two very active figures in the Bulgarian agitation. The supporters of this initiative advocated a foreign intervention, by which they probably meant to internationalize the "Bosnian Question." Another prominent activist was John Russell. In the Times he wrote that he was ready to subscribe 50l on behalf of the insurgents against Turkish misrule, as he had done many decades earlier for the Greeks.[8] The Economist harshly attacked Russell, arguing that it was almost inconceivable that someone who had been both prime minister and foreign secretary had penned such a letter.

The Bosnian Question was internationalized thanks to the initiative of the Austro-Hungarian government. On December 30, 1875, Foreign Minister Julius Andrassy proposed a note, known as the Andrassy

Note, in which he asked the Porte to grant the two rebellious provinces religious liberty and to abolish tax farming. Andrassy wanted the Ottoman government to help the peasants to buy land from their lords and thus reduce the acute agrarian discontent that, in his opinion, had produced the revolt. He suggested setting up a mixed commission of Muslims and Christians to supervise the enforcement of these reforms. The Austro-Hungarian minister's proposal did not hint at or threaten an intervention if the Sublime Porte did not comply with the requests of the note. Recalling the Treaty of Paris of 1856, Andrassy claimed that the sultan needed to formally assure the European powers of his intention to carry out reforms.

All the European powers approved of the note, though the British prime minister Benjamin Disraeli and his foreign secretary Lord Derby felt only contempt for the insurgents, a *"petit peuple à demi barbare."* They opposed autonomy for Bosnia, arguing that autonomy for Ireland would have been less absurd.[9] Great Britain mostly feared the consequences of a Russian and Austro-Hungarian action against the Ottoman Empire. The government saw the situation in Bosnia as being similar to that in Crete, with the difference that Russia and Austria-Hungary—rather than France and Russia—were now the leaders of a European coalition, with Great Britain as usual opposed to taking any action. For the British government, events in Bosnia and Herzegovina were internal troubles that should not concern the European powers.

On May 13, 1876, after the rebels refused the Andrassy Note, the Russian minister of foreign affairs, Gorchakov, met Andrassy in Berlin. In a joint memorandum they proposed that Porte agree to a two-month armistice, a cooling-off period to be followed by negotiations with the rebels. They wanted a list of reforms, the execution of which was entrusted to the European consuls. Among the bases for future negotiation between the insurgents and the Porte, the Austro-Russian agreement mentioned that materials to rebuild destroyed houses and churches should be supplied to the returning refugees, together with sufficient food to support life until they were again in a position to maintain themselves. The two ministers secretly agreed that if the Ottoman Empire were to collapse, Vienna would administer part of Bosnia and Russia would recover southern Bessarabia (a province that had been given back to the Ottoman Empire in 1856, at the end of the Crimean War). If the armistice were to expire unsuccessfully, the Imperial Courts of Russia, Austria-Hungary, and Germany agreed to supplement their diplomatic action by further, nonspecified "efficacious measures" to be taken in the "interest of general peace."[10] This veiled and unspecified threat was unacceptable to the British government. In Lord Derby's view, it was by no means obvious that a two-month armistice would lead to permanent pacification, or that the Ottoman Empire could provide the requisite funds for rebuilding the insurgents' houses and churches and temporarily supply their necessities. In his view, far from improving the situation, the proposals of the Berlin memorandum would have exacerbated the situation by encouraging the rebels to expect the European powers' intervention. As with the Cretan crisis, Derby's considerations might have been correct, though the British minister failed to propose any alternative to this plan. In the end, Britain's position encouraged the Sublime Porte to reject the plan and made a collective European intervention impossible.

It is difficult to imagine what would have happened if Great Britain had agreed to the Berlin memorandum and if the armistice had expired unsuccessfully. First of all, it is not possible to say what the nature of the intervention would have been. If massacre, atrocities, and extermination had occurred, sending warships—a current practice as well as a visible, symbolic, and almost inexpensive action—would have been inadequate in the case of Bosnia. It would have failed to impress the insurgents, and, contrary to the case of Crete, the displacement and protection of refugees would have been a very complex matter. Even if refugees safely reached one the ports of the Adriatic Sea, where could the European powers have transported them given that there was not a country like Greece ready to host them? The most efficacious measures to end massacre would have been the military occupation of Bosnia and Herzegovina, followed by peace-enforcement measures and implementation of reforms. This was a highly risky operation that would have clearly threatened peace in Europe. An operation of such magnitude and complexity was not comparable with the French expedition in the Morea in 1828 or with Beaufort's mission in Lebanon in 1860.

As 1876 dragged on with no solution to the Bosnian conflict, the province of Rumelia—inhabited by a majority of Christian Orthodox Bulgarians—erupted, followed by punitive massacres carried out by the bashi-bazouks. The war party in Serbia was now convinced that the Ottoman Empire was so weak that the time had come to liberate Serbs in Bosnia, Herzegovina, the *sandjak* of Novi Pazar (a special Ottoman zone that separated Serbia and Montenegro), and Macedonia.[11] On June 30 Prince Milan of Serbia declared war on the Ottoman Empire, as did Montenegro shortly after. On July 8, at a meeting held at Reichstadt in Bohemia, Andrassy and Gorchakov agreed that, while their countries would not engage in war, they would, in the event that the Ottoman Empire proved victorious, take such steps as might be required to secure the integrity of Serbia and possibly also the independence of Montenegro and a degree of autonomy for Bosnia and Herzegovina. They also agreed on plans for partition of the Ottoman Empire if it was defeated.

BRITISH FOREIGN POLICY AND MASSACRES IN RUMELIA

In early May 1876 an upheaval took place in the Ottoman province of Rumelia when bands of insurgents killed Ottoman officials and Muslim civilians. According to British sources, Bulgarian émigrés had returned to their native lands to foment the revolt. The excesses committed by the insurgents in the *sandjak* of Philippopolis (today's Plovdiv) were followed by an equally excessive retaliation led by local Muslim populations and the Ottoman Army using irregulars, the bashi-bazouks. On hearing the news that the Bulgarian insurgents had been massacring Muslim civilians, they moved quickly to exact revenge. The Sublime Porte's repression resulted in the destruction of about sixty villages and the killing of twelve thousand people, according to the British government's official statistics. Sir Henry Elliot, the British ambassador at Constantinople, duly reported the disturbances to his government. During the summer of 1876 the British government published a number of *Blue Books*, which were edited versions of the main documents and reports on these occurrences. It is very likely that the permanent undersecretary of the Foreign Office, Lord Tenterden was responsible for censorship of the 1876 documents.[12]

Events in Bulgaria drew attention of the press. Edwin Pears, the Constantinople correspondent of the London Liberal newspaper the *Daily News*, started reporting on the "Bulgarian atrocities" on June 23. Among his articles, Pears published various dispatches by the British vice consul at Adrianople, J. Hutton Dupuis, concerning massacres of Christian Bulgarians. One of these hinted at designs of "deliberate extermination" of this population. The *Blue Books* censored this and other passages, arousing the suspicion that the Conservative government wanted to conceal the truth about the massacres. British Liberals, for obvious political reasons, took the opportunity to attack the government on both moral and political grounds. They claimed that the Porte was directly responsible for a deliberate attempt to exterminate the Christian that could not go unpunished. British politicians, including Disraeli, were fully aware of the causes that had triggered intervention on behalf of foreign Christians in the past, Crete being the most recent example. The prime minister's first reaction shows that, like his political opponents, he situated the question of Bulgaria within the framework of a possible collective European intervention in the Ottoman Empire based on grounds of humanity (i.e., following massacre, atrocity, and extermination). Disraeli did not wish Britain to intervene against the Ottoman Empire. For this reason, he kept claiming that the central Ottoman government was not behind the massacres. He argued that the Porte had not released irregulars in the disturbed district nor given approval to them. From Disraeli's point of view, demonstrating that any massacres amounted to local disturbances would prevent discussion on the possibility of undertaking an intervention. This also explains why Disraeli went as far as calling the atrocities "large extent inventions."[13]

During the early stages of the confrontation in both Houses, for opposite purposes, both Liberals and Tories emphasized the role the Circassians played in the massacres.[14] On July 18 a correspondent of the *Pall Mall Gazette* wrote that 150,000 Circassians had moved into the Balkan provinces between 1860 and 1864 with permission of the Ottoman government when the Russians had compelled them to leave their own country in the Caucasus. These Circassians were portrayed as "half-barbarous savages" and seminomad populations. They were "brigands by nature" and "brigands by art" when they became irregular troops of the sultan (bashi-bazouks) and joined plenty of "Muslim scum" of other provinces.[15] Liberals who wanted to take action against the Ottoman Empire portrayed the Circassians as the perpetrators of the massacres in Bulgaria. Disraeli, however, denied that the Circassians were irregular troops of the Ottoman government and claimed in the House of Commons on July 17 that they were actually victims of the Russians, or their descendants, who in the 1850s had commanded the sympathy and admiration of the House of Commons. In Disraeli's view, Circassians were just defending themselves from attacks by local Christians who had burned down their villages and ravaged their farms. Because the Circassians were an "Eastern population," by which Disraeli meant they were not fully civilized, "scenes took place during this guerrilla warfare of a description from which with our feelings we naturally recoil."[16]

The prime minister's argument was logically irreprehensible and temporarily persuaded part of the press (especially the *Pall Mall Gazette*, the *Standard*, and the *Morning Post*) to take a less unbalanced stance on the issue. Unfortunately for Disraeli, during the month of July the story of the massacres and atrocities in Bulgaria became too sensational to be overlooked.[17] In August 1 Pears and Antonio Gallenga, the *Times* correspondent, published interviews with eyewitnesses, and the provincial newspaper the *Northern Echo* brought gruesome details of the Bulgarian atrocities to the masses.

The Foreign Office instructed the second secretary of the embassy at Constantinople, Walter Baring, to start inquiring about "the atrocities" as early as July 19.[18] Lord Derby asked the Sublime Porte to end the excesses and punish of the criminals. He also urged the ambassador to publicly speak out against the murderers and spare no efforts with the Ottoman government. Contrary to the claims of the *Times*, the *Daily News*, and Liberal MPs, Baring's inquiry was not deliberately turned out as favorably as possible to the Porte. The British fact-finding inquiry aimed at assessing the responsibility of the Ottoman government and determining the accuracy of the accounts of massacre and atrocity. More specifically, Baring had to ascertain the truth of the alleged parading of the heads of murdered women and children by bashi-bazouks and the public sale of women and children. He had to find out how many Bulgarians were in confinement and whether they were victims of torture. He also had to verify whether the story of the burning alive of forty or fifty Bulgarian girls in a stable near Kalofer was true, and whether twenty-five thousand or more perfectly innocent persons had been massacred and sixty to one hundred villages burned.

Baring presented his report confidentially on September 1, 1876, claiming that "the manner in which the rising was suppressed was inhuman in the last degree (the horrors probably surpassing those committed in 1863 by the Russians in Poland)." As to the cartloads of heads, Baring argued that it was utterly untrue that they were ever paraded in the streets of any town, but that the heads of some of a band of insurgents defeated by bashi-bazouks were brought into Sofia on bayonets and poles. It was not true that women and children were publicly sold, but many women had been carried off. The evidence as to torture was conflicting, although there was no doubt that the overcrowding in the prisons of Philippopolis was appalling. Baring was not able to discover anything authentic in the story of the burning of the forty girls. Nonetheless, he concluded that a massacre of some twelve thousand Christians had taken place, that fifty-eight villages in Philippopolis (inhabited by a vast majority of Christians) had been destroyed, but "only" two hundred Muslims had lost their lives. Baring pointed out that the Ottoman government had rewarded Achmed Aga, that no punishment of criminals had occurred, and that two thousand Bulgarian Christians of Rumelia had been detained for alleged complicity in the revolt.[19]

Lord Derby appears to have been horror-struck by the report. On the contrary, despite evidence of massacre, of the responsibility of the Ottoman authorities, and of the unwillingness of the Ottoman central government to punish those responsible for the excesses, Disraeli and Elliot ruled out any possibility of intervening in favor of the Bulgarians of Rumelia on grounds of humanity. Elliot argued: "We may, and must feel indignant at the needless and monstrous severity with which the Bulgarian insurrection was put down, but the necessity which exists for England to prevent changes from occurring here which would be most detrimental to ourselves, is not affected by the question whether it was 10,000 or 20,000 persons who perished in the suppression."[20]

A few days before Baring's report, Disraeli admitted that the massacre was "a horrible event which no one can think of without emotion." But, he said, it was no reason to shift foreign policy. If Britain's treaty obligations to guarantee Ottoman territorial integrity were to be treated "as idle wind and chaff, and if we are to be told that our political duty is by force to expel the Turks to the other side of the Bosphorous, then politics cease to be an art, statesmanship becomes mere mockery." He conceded that there was a "high political and moral duty" to prevent incompetent Ottoman rule, but national security trumped it: "Those who suppose that England ever would uphold . . . Turkey from blind superstition, and from a want of sympathy with the highest aspirations of humanity are deceived. What our duty is at this critical moment is to maintain the Empire of England."[21]

During the autumn of 1876 protesters and Liberal MPs attacked the British government on the main moral assumptions of its foreign policy, and on the bases of Baring's report, which had incontrovertibly proven that massacre and atrocities had occurred, that the Ottoman Empire was responsible for them, and that the Porte was unwilling to take the necessary measure to prevent further massacre. Hence, they claimed, something had to be done. In early September the attacks against the government were reinforced by the publication of Gladstone's pamphlet *Bulgarian Horrors* (see next section) and by the reports on the fate of the many villages and towns published in the *Daily News* by Januarius Aloysius MacGahan, which appeared in collected form on September 11. Particularly appalling was the fate of Batak, where about five thousand civilians, mostly women and children, had perished. In the following eighteenth months, more than three thousand articles denouncing Batak and other atrocities appeared in some two hundred European newspapers. These events played the decisive role in altering perceptions of the Eastern crisis in the capitals of the European powers. Death and atrocity as described by Baring seemed a small matter compared with the details the journalists' accounts provided and with the eloquence of Gladstone's pen. As Thompson pointed out:

> the homes, the surroundings, the individuality of the victims were brought home to the imagination [of the British public], as well as the things they had endured, including the pestilent odour emanating from heaps of cadavers of men, women and little babies, the horrifying view of half-cremated corpses, and the terrifying image of raped girls and women. It is this graphicness of detail and of description, which is the main characteristic of the closing chapter of the story of the atrocities.[22]

The British government's reaction came on September 21 when Derby sent new instructions to Elliot that were immediately made public. In them Derby took note of the "just indignation" of the "people of Great Britain" and characterized the events as "the most heinous crimes that have stained the history of the present century." Such a serious allegation fully justified further action and a European solution to the question, but the minister only ordered Elliot to seek a personal interview with the sultan and to demand that the Porte take steps to rectify the damage.[23]

The pressure mounted on the government was certainly considerable, but what ultimately changed British foreign policy were the Serbo-Montenegrin defeat by the Ottoman Empire and the Austro-Hungarian and Russian agreement of Reichstadt. That the British government did not yield to the pressure of public opinion is shown by the attitude of the British Liberals. During the summer parliamentary session on foreign affairs, Liberal speakers did not mention the possibility of undertaking a unilateral or collective humanitarian intervention. They preferred to focus on the alleged misconduct of the Tory government but refrained from clearly spelling out what should have been done. Sir William Harcourt insisted that "in the name of civilization" it was time to prevent any repetition of the massacres. If the British government could not control "the ferocity" of a "Government tempered by assassination and maintained by massacre," it "had no right to prop up his tottering power."[24] Harcourt concluded by saying that he found it hypocritical for the government of Britain to occupy itself with passing a vivisection bill while being so inert to the miseries of Bulgaria. Derby and Disraeli easily replied to this criticism. The foreign secretary reminded his colleagues that since before the summer he had warned the Porte to make peace speedily in order to avert intervention by the European powers and had protested against the cruelty displayed in the execution of Bulgarian insurgents. Disraeli pointed out that the government, through Baring's inquiry, was ascertaining the facts and working to prevent the repetition of massacres; for the time being, he said, the British government had no need to go any further.

GLADSTONE'S PAMPHLET AND THE QUESTION OF INTERVENTION ON GROUNDS OF HUMANITY

Agitation among the public began during the summer 1876.[25] For many protesters, the issue of a humanitarian intervention was not central. They ostensibly directed their discontent with Britain's foreign policy toward "Turk" and "Tory" or even moderate leaders of the Liberal Party. The agitation provided the focus for a disparate group of Radicals, newly enfranchised voters of the urban areas, the least moderate Liberals, many Nonconformists, and even some High Churchmen who longed to address moral, ethical, and political concerns through effective public action under an inspired leader. Among the protesters must be included those who had organized in and sent relief to the disturbed Ottoman provinces since 1875 and their societies, which by August 1876 had greatly increased their relief work in the Balkans.[26] Historian Ann Pottinger Saab claims that the coalescence of this ill-assorted group around a domestic political issue was very unlikely. They needed a symbolic grievance, a cause that allowed them to protest against religious intolerance, the persecution of Christianity, and the corruption and unresponsiveness of government, without ever having to deal with cases familiar enough to bring out their deep and well-founded disagreements.[27]

Gladstone publicly emphasized the moral rather than the political aspects of the Bulgarian atrocities. He was the ideal icon of the protest movement. His *Bulgarian Horrors and the Question of the East* articulated in strong language the opinion of a great body of British citizens. Gladstone's involvement validated the agitation in the minds of many who needed dramatic leadership, beyond his own customary followers. The commitment of such a charismatic personality to the role of formulator of the beliefs of the protest movement was decisive and made all the difference, as far as public opinion was concerned, when compared with the previous instances of reaction to massacres of Ottoman Christians. However, Gladstone's commitment ultimately proved to be unsuccessful in instigating a military intervention on grounds of humanity.

It would be wrong to think the entire country rallied behind Gladstone. His involvement chilled those Conservatives who had been swept up by the spontaneous outburst of horror when they read about the massacres in Bulgaria.[28] The Conservatives enjoyed significant hard-core support from the army and navy, from high financial circles, rich bankers and commercial magnates, and from large sections of the nobility and the landed gentry. The high-living, hard-drinking county society, which tended to be suspicious of Gladstone at the best of times, was outraged by this new example of his sentimental and ill-judged missionizing and meddling in other people's lives and business. Many members of the Church of England stood with the government, not only because of the ingrained conservative tendencies natural to an established church, but also because of institutionally nurtured mistrust of public enthusiasm.[29] Philo-Ottoman, philo-Disraeli, and philo-Conservative publications were as excoriating and virulent against Gladstone as Gladstone's writings were against the Ottomans and the Tory government.[30]

Furthermore, Gladstone's involvement with the agitation was short-lived, if not ephemeral. Besides his pamphlet, Gladstone's major contribution was his address at Blackheath on September 9, 1876. However, while on one hand this address was made to stir up public agitation about the atrocities, it was also part of the Liberal campaign to capture the Buckinghamshire seat, which his archrival Disraeli had held for three decades before his elevation to the peerage as the Earl of Beaconsfield on August 21, 1876. Following defeat at the polls on September 22, Gladstone refrained from participation in the national antiatrocities campaign, which was anyway beginning to falter. By the beginning of October moderate Liberals had turned strongly against the agitation.[31] By the end of 1876 most Liberals agreed with Granville, the Liberal leader in the House of Lords, on the futility of challenging the government. Hartington, Granville's counterpart in the House of Commons, returned from a trip to Constantinople more aware of the complexities of the Eastern Question and with increased respect for the difficulties it posed for British policy-makers. Gladstone was smart enough to understand that without massive support from the Liberals in the two chambers, it would have been impossible to force the government to change its policy toward the Ottoman Empire. In any case, as we shall see, the government would end up changing its policy in the autumn of 1876.

Various public figures, such as J. Lewis Farley and the Earl of Shaftesbury, appealed to Gladstone. But, as historian Richard Shannon eloquently puts it, Gladstone's voice did not reach the Bosphorus.[32] In early 1876 Gladstone could have been more active—for instance, when Disraeli vetoed the Berlin memorandum of May 1876 and ordered the Mediterranean fleet to Besika Bay outside the Dardanelles. On that occasion he could have proposed an alternative Eastern policy for Britain, for which he had laid the foundations as early as 1858. All he needed to do was to dust off a *Quarterly Review* piece on "The Past and Present Administrations," excoriating Palmerston's Crimean policy, and apply it to the Bulgarians. [33] Gladstone's restraint at this stage was probably the consequence of his respect for Hartington. In late July other prominent personalities, such as Bishop Fraser of Manchester and the Duke of Argyll, insistently pressured Gladstone to speak on the Eastern Question.[34] Malcolm MacColl was about to set out on a self-promoted fact-finding tour of the Balkans with Henry Parry Liddon, canon of St. Paul's, one of the most influential preachers of Britain, and one of the rare members of the Church of England who overtly protested against the government. They requested Gladstone to say something, as did Rev. William Denton and journalist W. T. Stead, editor of the *Northern Echo*.[35] Gladstone's speech at the Commons on July 31, 1876, was not at all what these people expected. He declared himself "not ashamed' to insist on the principle of reconciling any notions of Christian autonomy with strict observance of Turkish territorial integrit,y given that an independent Slav state would be too problematic to contemplate. As far as rumors of extensive and atrocious repression of the Bulgarians were concerned, he declared that this was an aspect on which he did not propose to dwell.[36] Gladstone did not even react to Disraeli's comment on the massacres being imaginary and "coffee-house babble." He did not mention the possibility of undertaking a humanitarian intervention. Of all those who lacked foresight, Shannon argues, it was Gladstone who lacked it most blatantly.[37]

Only in late August did Gladstone fully recognize that the Bulgarian atrocities had sparked a popular reaction, which he could turn to his own political advantage.[38] It took him only a few days to pen *Bulgarian Horrors*.[39] The first 40,000 copies of the pamphlet sold out in three to four days after printing; 200,000 went in the first month.[40] The pamphlet served as the voice of all those who had been shocked by the massacre and were enraged by the nonreaction of the government in London. Gladstone urged the people forward to drive the government, through the vigor of public meetings, into a positive program. He was aware that it was too late to undo the mischief already done but felt that there was still time to redeem the honor of the British name, which had been gravely compromised. The government should end the anarchical misrule, the plunder, and the murders still causing desolation in Bulgaria. He suggested the exclusion of Ottoman authorities from Bosnia, Herzegovina, and Bulgaria. Following the publication of *Bulgarian Horrors*, in a period of less than six weeks nearly five hundred demonstrations took place throughout Britain demanding a repudiation of the government's policy.

The pamphlet was a rehash of articles by American consul general Eugene Schuyler and journalist Januarius MacGaghan, the *Blue Books*, and Gladstone's own speech of July 31, laced with virulent invective against the Turks. *Bulgarian Horrors*, Shannon argues, had no particular literary merit. Even the famous "bag and baggage" phrase was not Gladstone's own but had been coined by Stratford de Redcliffe. The centerpiece of Gladstone's argument was against Disraeli and the Conservative government. Gladstone accused the government of deliberately ignoring the reports of wholesale massacre perpetrated with the authority of a government for which Britain had procured "twenty years of grace" (1856–76).[41] The part of the pamphlet that more closely relates to the issue of intervention is the chapter entitled "The British Fleet at Besika Bay." Here Gladstone argues that moving the British squadron to that bay was not aimed, as officially claimed, at protecting British subjects and the Christians in general, but to encourage Ottoman government to resist.[42] For Gladstone the British fleet at Besika Bay should rather be used "for *purposes of humanity* . . . in concert with other Powers, for the defense of innocent lives, and to prevent the repetition of those recent scenes, at which hell itself might almost blush."[43] This was a clear indication that, in Gladstone's view, the British government should have undertaken a humanitarian intervention. While admitting that a right of humanitarian intervention did not exist, Gladstone stated that "there are states of affairs, in which sympathy refuses to be confined by the rules, necessarily limited and conventional, of international law."[44] However, he did not go into detail relating to the landing of troops and how, in practice, Bulgarians should be rescued.

In the last fifteen pages of the pamphlet, Gladstone formulated the famous "bag and baggage" philippic and demanded the "extinction" of Ottoman "administrative action" in Bosnia, Herzegovina, and "Bulgaria" (a strictly nonexistent entity). To many in Britain, this phrase meant the expulsion of all the Turkish or Muslim civilian populations from Europe, which was the solution put forward by Gladstone's friend the Duke of Argyll.[45] Gladstone had to clarify in a letter to the *Times*, published on September 9, 1876, that he did not intend that the Ottomans should be driven from the Balkans entirely, only from Bulgaria. Even this reply was unclear, so on September 10, in a speech at Blackheath, he explained that only "military and official Turks" should leave Bulgaria. Addressing Sultan Abdul Hamid II in absentia, he said, "you shall retain your titular sovereignty, you shall receive a reasonable tribute, your Empire shall not be invaded."[46] Gladstone stated that in Ottoman European territories the presence of a Muslim element was a "difficulty which had to be grappled with in any satisfactory solution of the problem."[47] In October 1876 Gladstone wrote to Granville that after Bulgaria and Bosnia were granted autonomy, a temporary military occupation on a small scale might be necessary, for purposes of policing, to keep the peace between the Muslims and the Christians. According to Bass, Gladstone presumably envisioned a multilateral peacekeeping mission like the one in Syria in 1861.[48] This is quite plausible, though Gladstone's plan was not particularly original, for this solution to the Eastern crisis was in the air, as we shall see later in this chapter.

NATIONAL CONFERENCE ON THE EASTERN QUESTION

By December 1876 the agitation lost impetus. Its saving element was the idea of a National Conference (or general meeting) based on the precedents of the antislavery and anti–Corn Law agitations. Gladstone deserved no credit for this initiative whatsoever. But, as Shannon points out, just as in the case of his pamphlet, he inevitably became responsible for the situation by the initiative of others.[49]

On November 17 this general convention was held in London. Organizers hoped that the conference would lead to the diffusion of sound information on the various branches of the question throughout the country and to consideration of the best means of promoting the favorable progress of the Eastern Question through the concert of the

European powers. It was aimed at obtaining for the Christian provinces of Bosnia, Herzegovina, and Bulgaria a release from the direct
rule of the Porte, with due guarantees for the equal rights of the non-
Christian population. The conference did not explicitly call for a military intervention on grounds of humanity, and its objective seemed in
line with the instructions issued by Derby to Salisbury for the Conference of Constantinople (see below).

One of the outcomes of the London conference was the creation of a
formal body, the Eastern Question Association, on December 8, 1876.
During the two-day gathering in St. James's Hall, Gladstone spoke for
an hour and a half. Many Liberal MPs attended the meeting, along
with representatives of the Nonconformist and High Church and other
religious groups, the business class, and the working class.[50] Many
members emphasized the moral and personal connection between the
association's aim and the antislavery movement.[51] Prominent also intellectuals joined the cause: John Ruskin and Thomas Carlyle—staunch
defenders of Eyre in 1865–68—now sat with Green, Lecky, Spencer,
Darwin, and many other members of the Jamaica Committee. Carlyle
supportively contributed his immortal phrase about the "unspeakable
Turk." The involvement of Carlyle and Ruskin in the Bulgarian agitation is particularly interesting. Instead of equating Eyre with the Ottoman general Achmet Aga, who had repressed the Bulgarian revolt,
and equating the oppressed Jamaican "Negroes" with the oppressed
Bulgarians, as Gladstone did, Carlyle and Ruskin equated the Negroes
with the bashi-bazouks as ravaging barbarians. Their overriding concern was to support the cause of a stern and just authority—a cause
that, in their view, triumphed in the British Empire—against the powers of evil and degenerate indiscipline and cruelty.[52]

The association failed to stimulate and coordinate local meetings
across Britain, but it published a significant body of material that argued the case for autonomy of the Christian provinces to create maxi-
mum support for whatever issues Gladstone might choose to raise in
Parliament. Historian Ann Pottinger Saab wonders how the published
material—mainly pamphlets—was distributed and how widely it was
read. By comparison with newspapers, it was not cheap. None of the
material sold well; in spite of good authors and inventive distribution,
the publications seem to have reached relatively few people. Nonetheless, the few people whom material did reach were intellectuals, politicians, and jurists embodying a conspicuous part of the nineteenth-
century British cultivated elite. We shall see that the Eastern Question
Association and its members would be very active and quite successful
in involving British elites during the massacres of Ottoman Armenians
of the 1890s, and during the Cretan and Macedonian crises of the 1890s
and 1900s.

The protesters, Gladstone, the National Conference, and the Eastern Question Association put considerable pressure on the British government, even though in the end no humanitarian intervention took place on behalf of the Bulgarians or the Bosnian Herzegovinans. More important, I believe, this public opinion campaign brought about long-lasting changes in the perception of the Ottoman Empire as irremediably "uncivilized' and "barbarian." Finally, it should not be forgotten that the majority of these protesters completely ignored the fate of Muslim populations and that their humanitarianism was biased and selective. The section below illustrates that the protesters concocted and successfully spread a coherent history of the massacres and atrocities against Ottoman Christians and the idea of a right of intervention when inalienable rights of humanity were grossly violated by a "barbarous" regime.

MOTIVES FOR INTERVENTION IN THE CAMPAIGNERS' DISCOURSE

More than international legal scholars, whose main interest was interstate relations, the campaigners' discourse drew attention to the issue of intervention when the Ottoman authorities, who they viewed as the representatives of a barbarous regime, perpetrated gross violations of "inalienable natural rights." Canon Malcolm MacColl, the Duke of Argyll, and James Bryce claimed that the Sublime Porte was unable to guarantee the right to life, honor, religious liberty, and property—the distinctive features of civilization—for its Christian subjects. [53] Hence, they argued, intervention by the European states to put an end to these gross violations was fully justified.

According to MacColl, the Eastern Question was "not a question of religion, but of the elementary rights of humanity and the primary principles of natural justice." MacColl argued that his sympathy with the oppressed as well as his indignation against a great and intolerable wrong would have been "none the less sincere and energetic if the Mussulmans were the victims and the Christians their tormentors."[54] MacColl's main sources were the British consular reports and inquiries of 1860 and 1867 on the "Condition of Christians in Turkey," the message of which he distorted to corroborate his arguments.[55] According to MacColl, the Sublime Porte denied Christians the right to self-defense, persisted in discriminating against them before the law, and, more important, denied their right to life. He particularly insisted on "insecurity of honour" as being a very serious violation of the rights of mankind, even more serious than the insecurity of life, for "the higher the standard of female virtue was the deeper of course was the wrong inflicted by its violation."[56] He argued that the Sublime Porte encouraged outrages against the honor of women. In an article published in the *Times* on September 8, 1876, E. A. Freeman wrote that the Turk was "capable of worse things than even the African or the Red Indian. . . . A good many millions are cowed and kept [in] bondage by the thought of what might happen, not to soldiers, or even to citizens, but to women and children. The Turkish rule is to regard the wife and the daughter as hostages for the obedience of the husband and the father." In a December 1875 *Fortnightly Review* article, Freeman also argued that the revolt in Herzegovina was the consequence of the "foul outrage" (i.e., rape) perpetrated by the Turks on every pretty girl of Ragusa (Dubrovnik). Millicent Garrett Fawcett, a feminist and suffragist leader, argued that the Ottoman Empire was uncivilized because, among other things, it was founded on slavery and torture. (She believed the *Manchester Guardian*'s reports of impalements of Christians in Bosnia to be absolutely true).[57] In her 1877 anti-Ottoman pamphlet, she insisted particularly on the appalling practice of "forcible carrying off of girls and women to the Turkish harems."[58] In chapter 3 I showed that images evoking rape were available to a wide public since the 1820s. However, they cannot compare with the sheer amount of morbid details the European public was exposed to in unprecedented fullness during the Eastern crisis of 1875–78. In the British campaigners' panoply of arguments against the Ottoman Empire and as justification for intervention, the dishonoring of chastity, the debauching of the conjugal union, and prostitution figured quite prominently and undoubtedly touched the most sensitive Victorian nerves.

Legal scholars acknowledged that natural law provided for the equal worth of individuals, irrespective of race or religion, and recognized the existence of norms, the inalienable rights of the individual, of which the individual could neither divest oneself nor be divested.[59] However, they did not argue in favor of a right of intervention stemming from the disrespect of these "rights of humanity."[60] On the contrary, campaigners and protesters assumed that thanks to the moral superiority of Europe, it had a right to intervene on grounds of humanity. As Thompson put it:

> Beyond all question non-intervention is the rule, and interference the exception, but there are cases . . . where a different principle must be established. . . . And if ever there was a nation which had brought itself within the exception it was that which had perpetrated the massacres of Chios, and was yet reeking [of] the slaughter of Missolonghi. . . . After the massacre of Chios the Turks had thrown themselves out of the pale of civilisation; they had proved themselves to be pirates, enemies of the human race, and no longer entitled to toleration from the European family. Expulsion from Europe was the natural and legitimate consequence of their flagrant violation of its usage of war.[61]

Argyll claimed that the European powers had a responsibility to settle the Eastern Question and a moral obligation sealed in the Treaty of Paris.[62] It was a fictitious assumption to assume the "equality of civilization" between the Ottoman Empire and Europe and to extend the advantages of "public law of Europe" to it.[63] To be admitted into the "European Family," the Ottoman government had first to afford to its "own people some tolerable government,—some administrative system recognising the fundamental principles of civilisation, and extending to all classes of her subjects some security of life, religion, property and honour." In article 9 of the 1856 Treaty of Paris, the Ottoman Empire had made a promise to the European powers in that respect.[64] By 1875, Argyll claimed, there was conclusive evidence from all the provinces of the Ottoman Empire not only had the "solemn promises" had not been fulfilled, but also matters in this respect, instead of getting better, were distinctly worse. The lives, property, and honor of families were not secure; in other words, the Sublime Porte did not afford the common rights of humanity to Ottoman Christians.[65] These views could easily be found in the press. For instance, on September 5, 1876, *The Times* reported that Great Britain had "as a matter of international law, the power and the obligation to intervene to see that justice [was] done to the Christian subjects of the Porte. . . . the Sultan [was] no more than a ward in Chancery, subject, as the lawyers would say, to a very strict impeachment of waster if he did not administer the property with full regard to the well-being of all his subjects."[66]

In my view, the greatest success of the protesters was the fabrication of a coherent and teleological history of massacre and atrocities of Ottoman Christians. They underscored the persistence and continuity of extremely inhumane acts perpetrated by the Ottoman authorities and their Muslim populations, such as rape, torture, and enslavement, against Ottoman Christians since the early nineteenth century. Gladstone wrote that massacres were what the Turks always made recourse to whenever they had the power to do so. "What he [the Turk] did in Bulgaria just now, he did then in Chios and in Cyprus [he probably meant Crete]. It is the nature of the wild beast, which cannot be driven out of him, even if you dress him up in tight-fitting clothes and teach him to talk French."[67] These writers, pamphleteers, and campaigners were largely accountable for sketching a history of intervention on grounds of humanity in the Ottoman Empire and the emergence of an alleged right of intervention. They went as far as to reinterpret the events of previous instances of intervention, gave massacres ex-post facto coherence, and created a narrative that distorted historical evidence to support their views. Freeman compared and contrasted the nonintervention in Bulgaria with the instances of intervention in

Lebanon, Damascus, and Crete, and he also mentioned Navarino, "a memorable and glorious day, when the Powers of Europe were united for right and not for wrong . . . joined their forces to crush the might of the barbarian, and to see their brethren free."[68] MacColl spoke of the "premeditated extermination of the Christian race" in Damascus as a demonstration of the Ottoman government's utter disrespect for the right of (and security for) life and recalled that the European powers had undertaken an intervention in Lebanon and Syria.[69]

THE CONFERENCE OF CONSTANTINOPLE

In November 1876, when the Ottoman Army threatened Belgrade, the Russian government, fearful of the consequences of the defeat, delivered an ultimatum to the Porte, threatening a withdrawal of ambassadors if an armistice were not concluded at once. The Porte complied with the Russian request and signed the armistice. Then Lord Derby suggested calling a collective conference at Constantinople to elaborate a scheme of reform for the Ottoman Empire.[70] The British government was ready to participate in the solution of the Eastern crisis and eventually acknowledged that the Balkan crisis might threaten peace in Europe. This was certainly a noticeable change in British foreign policy, but it did not mean that Britain would go as far as accepting the idea of an intervention on behalf of Ottoman Christians if further massacres took place.

The original instruction given to the British special plenipotentiary, Lord Salisbury, on November 20 excluded any coercive or enforcement action against the Porte.[71] In negotiating with the other European powers, Salisbury had to put forward the principle of the independence and territorial integrity of the Ottoman Empire. The European powers should make a declaration that they did not intend to seek territorial advantage, exclusive influence, or any concession with regard to the commerce of their subjects that those of every other nation could not equally obtain. A similar declaration had been made in the 1827 Treaty of London, which preceded intervention in Navarino, and in the Paris *protocol de désintéressement* of August 1860, which preceded the expedition of Beaufort's contingent in Lebanon.

Derby instructed Salisbury to make the Porte aware that the European powers had "a right to demand, in the interest of the peace of Europe" as well as to examine the measures required for the reform of the disturbed provinces. Salisbury's objective was to restore calm to the disturbed provinces because of a manifest incapacity of the Porte to do so. The tone of the instructions was unfriendly toward the Porte, and expressions of humanitarian concern for the "security" of local populations frequently appeared in the lengthy document. Derby's instructions sought a "Lebanese solution" (i.e., a new *Règlement*) for Bosnia, Herzegovina, and Bulgaria and the application of the special statuses of the islands of Samos and Crete as possible bases for negotiation.[72] In the British government's opinion, administrative autonomy for Bosnia, Herzegovina, and Bulgaria would form the best guarantee for the well-being of these provinces and provide respect for the right to life, property, religious liberty, and equality before the law for all populations, irrespective of their faith.

On November 27 new confidential instructions by Disraeli to Salisbury hinted at the possibility of a temporary occupation in the Balkans if the Porte rejected all proposals for reform. Disraeli wanted Russia and Austria-Hungary to be kept out of the Ottoman Empire. Salisbury was supposed to maneuver the Porte into asking for an exclusive British occupation. In December Disraeli changed his mind, deciding that there should be no occupation by anyone, even Britain. His notes for the cabinet meeting on December 22 confirm this was his final decision.[73] During the preliminary meetings of the conference—as the minutes of the first sitting of December 11 indicate—the European delegates made it clear that they were dealing with a collective, European, question: "It is a question which does not interest Russia alone, but the whole of Europe, the general prosperity, humanity, and Christian civilization. May the peace of Europe and the well-being of the Christian populations of Turkey serve as a recompense for the troubles and difficulties connected with the undertaking [of the conference]."[74]

Beyond this general agreement, Salisbury and his Russian counterpart, Nikolay Ignatyev, disagreed on almost everything. The latter had a very sensible point of view on the motives of a military intervention. Ignatyev stated that the occupation of Ottoman territory was not put forward as a *conditio sine qua non* by the Russian government, but that it had been merely suggested as the only measure calculated to meet the pressing necessity, which St. Petersburg foresaw. In fact, the Russian plenipotentiary claimed, the discussions and resolution of the conference could only have a future value, as several months would elapse before any organization that might be decided upon could be brought into active operation. During that time disarmed Christians would have lived in the midst of a considerable population of armed and "infuriated Mussulmans, whose fanaticism had been stimulated to a very high point, and was increasing every day." Ignatyev claimed that his government wanted to avoid a repetition of the massacres, for it seemed likely to him that, when the ambassadors upon the Porte the decisions made by the conference, there would be, either with or without the instigation of the central authority, an outbreak of rebellion by the Muslim populations, which might be followed by terrible results.

Other Russian foreign policy objectives notwithstanding, what Ignatyev described was precisely a short-term humanitarian intervention followed by the implementation of a program of reforms. At the time of their meetings, Salisbury knew that Christians living in the disturbed areas were still ongoing victims of abuses and violence, and that the possibility of further massacres existed.[75] Nonetheless, he stood firm against the possibility of a military intervention as the only means of obtaining reliable security for local populations before the enforcement of the reforms. Even if Salisbury and Ignatyev disagreed, the *procès-verbaux* of the conference reveal that the British and Russian plenipotentiaries largely shared the same concept of intervention, and of humanitarian intervention as an international practice clearly distinguished from war. Ignatyev did not mention war against the Ottoman Empire, and Salisbury spoke of "some sort" of military occupation. When Salisbury rebuffed Ignatyev's plan of intervention, he claimed that a "military occupation" would "incur the risk of calamities as terrible in their character and much wider in their extent than those which [Ignatyev] apprehended."[76]

The European diplomats decided that Bosnia, Herzegovina, and Bulgaria would become autonomous provinces, ruled by a governor-general appointed by the Porte for a period of five years, chosen from among the Christians, on the approval of the guaranteeing powers. The Porte would be compelled to reconstruct churches and houses and to provide the refugees with a means of subsistence until they were able to enjoy their own harvest. A "Native Commission" composed of prominent Christians and Muslims would distribute all assistance. A European Commission would oversee the repatriation of emigrants and the execution of the above-mentioned measures. As far as the province of Rumelia was concerned, the Europeans aimed at ensuring the security of Christian populations by disarming the Muslims, especially irregular troops (and in particular the Circassians), and by exemplarily punishing those guilty of the "misdeeds and massacres" (something the Europeans were perfectly aware the Ottoman government was unwilling to do). The Europeans wished to assure that the Christian victims would be compensated at the expense of the "Mussulman population that took part in the massacres and devastations."[77] European diplomats wanted the Porte to revise the sentences pronounced by the courts in cases where torture had been applied to obtain convictions after the European Commission had verified this. The Ottoman government had to decree a general and complete amnesty to all the Christians of Bulgaria, including those who had been subjected to summary sentences such as exile, "exportation" (displacement), and imprisonment as decreed by various Ottoman commissions for political crimes or on suspicion of them.

The European plenipotentiaries proposed the exclusion of nonnative functionaries from the disturbed provinces and the introduction of the elective principle throughout the area. They put forward the idea of appointing "natives" in charge of the distribution of taxes as well as the replacement of the tithe by an equivalent duty or tax. The Europeans also wanted to introduce local language in the courts and local administrative offices, as had been done in Crete in 1868. They wished Christians to participate in proportion to their numbers and race in the formation of a local militia, and to be involved in the organization of a police force and the concentration of Ottoman regular troops in the fortresses. The European policy-makers also agreed to forbid further colonization of the Balkan provinces of the Ottoman Empire by the Circassians and the resettlement of those already established in Rumelia to the "Mussulman Asiatic provinces of the Ottoman Empire." Quite clearly, all these measures would have made life for Muslims almost impossible in the newly autonomous provinces and would have certainly been considered as unacceptable by the Porte. The last measure would have led to the displacement of thousands of civilians and would have very likely caused a humanitarian crisis of very relevant proportions, which the European completely ignored. The Europeans' utter disregard for the fate of tens of thousands of civilians was also astonishingly myopic, for the resettlement would take place in the Anatolian provinces inhabited by, among others, other Ottoman Christians (Greek Orthodox, Armenians, Assyrians) and would contribute to destabilize the fragile ethnic-religious equilibrium of those regions. To enforce all these measures, which heavily interfered in the internal affairs of the Ottoman Empire, the Porte had to be willing to execute. Who would have enforced the reforms if the Porte proved unwilling or unable to implement them?

According to the European diplomats, an international commission operating in Bulgaria, Bosnia, and Herzegovina would be in charge of controlling and supervising the execution and implementation of the reforms. The Europeans realized that the commission needed to have "a material force sufficient to maintain tranquillity and to cause its decision to be respected."[78] The plenipotentiaries imagined sending an *ante litteram* peace-enforcement contingent of gendarmes (rather than soldiers) to emphasize that their mission was not conceived as an act of war. They agreed that a corps of up to four thousand men be dispatched to Bosnia and up to four thousand to Rumelia. The revenues of Bosnia and Rumelia would pay the gendarmes recruited in various small European countries, such as Belgium. These gendarmes were to act as cadres to facilitate a more concrete organization of the police, with the help of native volunteers chosen from the whole Ottoman Empire. European diplomats supposed that gendarmes would enter a pacified province, but they had no answer to the question of what would happen if that was not the case the contingent of gendarmes had to confront insurgents once again, or even the Ottoman Army.

The conclusions reached at the conference did not amount to a forcible humanitarian intervention. However, the degree of interference by the European powers in the internal affairs of the Ottoman Empire was considerable. The Europeans acted as if the Ottoman government was the target state of an intervention caused by its unwillingness or incapacity to protect its Christian population. They implicitly assumed that Muslim populations were the perpetrators of massacre and atrocities and had to pay the price of the intervention, and that local Christian populations were the victims of massacres and atrocities, which was correct to a certain extent. As the Russian government put it, the decisions reached during the conference were also humanitarian. They were a *minimum irréductible* aimed at the "security of the Christians," and at their "effective and palpable improvement." Ignatyev hoped that the European powers would not "lose sight of the grave responsibility which devolve[ed] upon them before history and before humanity."[79]

FROM THE RUSSO-TURKISH WAR TO THE CONGRESS OF BERLIN

None of the above-mentioned measures was actually enacted. On December 23 the Sultan proclaimed a new Ottoman constitution. Given this allegedly radical change of circumstances, the Porte rejected the European project. The conference broke up on January 20, 1877, and to mark their displeasure the representatives of the six powers agreed to withdraw all their delegates, including the ambassadors. What to do next was by no means clear. The Russian government took the initiative. In March 1877 Ignatyev toured the major European capitals, proposing a new program of reforms whose implementation would be supervised by all the powers. Article 9 of the London Protocol of March 31, 1877, empowered the six signatories "to watch carefully" (*de veiller avec soin*) the manner in which the Ottoman government carried out its promises.[80] It provided for consultation and joint action in the event that the European powers were "once more disillusioned."

The Ottoman government rejected the protocol, and on April 24 Russia declared war to perform what it considered its manifest duty of protecting the Christian population of Turkey from the inhumane treatment to which it was being subjected, though the Russians also clearly desired to acquire new territory in the Balkans and control of the straits. For this reason international scholars in the late nineteenth century did not consider that war as an instance of humanitarian intervention.[81] In November 1877 the Russian armies took the town of Kars, and in December they defeated the Ottomans in Plevna (Bulgaria) and quickly advanced to Constantinople. On March 3, 1878, Russia and the Ottoman Empire signed the Treaty of San Stefano. The clauses of this treaty, which changed the balance of power in favor of Russia in the Balkans and the Caucasus, were not acceptable to the other European powers. Russia, whose army was now weakened and overstretched, had to accept negotiations with all the European powers. To this end, Chancellor Otto von Bismarck of Germany proposed to host a congress in Berlin in June 1878.

During the spring, before the opening of the congress, the powers settled all their thorny issues. The newly appointed British foreign secretary, Salisbury, and his Russian counterpart, Pyotr Shuvalov, signed a secret protocol in which Great Britain recognized Russia's annexation of Bessarabia, Batum, Kars, and Ardahan and Russia agreed to limit the size of Bulgaria. Great Britain and Russia came to an understanding concerning the division of Bulgaria into two separate entities, one an autonomous principality whose Christian ruler was to be elected by the Bulgarians, though it remained a vassal of the sultan, whose suzerainty it had to acknowledge and to whom it was required to pay tribute. The other province, Eastern Rumelia, would be under direct Ottoman administration. On June 6 the governments of Austria-Hungary and Russia agreed that the Russian occupation of Bulgaria should last six months rather than two years and be limited to a force of twenty thousand.

As far as the Ottoman Asiatic provinces were concerned, on May 23 Sir Austen Henry Layard presented the Porte with a draft agreement for the British occupation of the island of Cyprus.[82] On June 4 the Cyprus Convention (or Convention of Defensive Alliance between Great Britain and Turkey) was signed. It stipulated that Great Britain would defend the sultan's Asiatic domains against foreign aggression in return for the introduction of reforms, to be agreed upon later with Britain, for the protection of the Christians and other subjects of the Porte in Asia.[83] This commitment had a bearing on the defensibility of Turkey in Asia. Reform in the provinces inhabited by the Armenians would prevent disturbances that Russia might use as an excuse to intervene. Cyprus was intended to serve, not so much as a base from which British forces could move quickly to Asiatic Turkey, but as "a symbol to Russia and the peoples of Asia Minor of Britain's determination to defend her interests," a symbol all the more effective because of its appeal to the British electorate. These commitments also reflected Salisbury's moralizing imperialism. This was obvious in the pledge of reform, but not in the transfer of Cyprus, which to many Gladstonians and to all foreign powers, including the Ottoman Empire, discredited Britain's frequent pose of unselfishness. What Salisbury had in mind was that Cyprus could serve as a showpiece of the firm yet impartial government that the Ottoman Empire's provinces needed.[84] An anonymous pamphleteer wrote:

> The European powers, as all the world knows, have contracted a special responsibility, not only on ground of common humanity, but of definite treaty engagements. The setting aside of the provisions of the Treaty of San Stefano, and the substitution of those of the Treaty of Berlin, was the replacing of a Turco-Russian by a Turco-European undertaking. . . . It is not only England that has come under special obligations: all the European Powers—signatories of the Treaty of Berlin—have undertaken the most solemn engagements in regard to Turkish reforms. They are each and all partners in a common trust. . . . Of no one Power may this be separately true, as the responsibility is collective rather than individual, but it is certainly true of the European Concert as a whole.[85]

The Congress of Berlin opened on June 13, 1878, and dealt with a number of territorial questions, such as the independence of Serbia, Montenegro, and Romania and the Austrian occupation of Bosnia and Herzegovina, that I will not examine here. As Glenny puts it, Russia and Austria had originally intervened in the Balkans on the pretext of protecting the Christian communities there, and later in order to lend expression to the political aspirations of the Balkan nations. By the time they reached Berlin, these intentions had been forgotten. Andrassy had no difficulty persuading the British and Russian delegations to stick to pragmatic principles and to prioritize geographic and strategic considerations over ethnographic grounds.[86]

According to historian Carol Fink, the Treaty of Berlin also marked a change in the governing norms of European international law.[87] Besides the Christian Armenians (see chapter 8), the other groups who seemed to have acquired new rights and protection, in theory more than in practice, were the Muslims and the Jews of the newly independent states of Serbia and Romania, and of autonomous Bulgaria and Eastern Rumelia. The European powers pretended that the newly independent states of the Balkan peninsula functioned at their *standard of civilization*. They wanted the new Balkan governments to give fair and equal treatment to the minorities living within their territories so as to distinguish themselves from the Sublime Porte and avoid the repetition of the problems affecting that empire. In the case of Balkan Jews, Jewish pressure groups in western European countries proved to be quite successful in convincing the governments in Paris and London that allowing discriminatory policies in Serbia or Romania would have been in complete contradiction to the European policy toward the Ottoman Empire since Navarino (i.e., a policy aimed at guaranteeing the most basic rights of humanity), and that Balkan states' anti-Semitic laws would have singularly contrasted with Ottoman tolerance of the Jews. The powers, however, were certainly not committed to protect non-Christian populations, and no mechanisms for enforcement of the freedom of religion and nondiscrimination principles stated in the treaty were put in place.

The European powers' failure to protect non-Christian populations was particularly striking when it came to the Muslim refugees who had left war zones after the Russian invasion in 1877. By March 1878, when the Treaty of San Stefano brought an end to the war, refugees were clustered in only a few areas: Şumla (Shumen)-Varna, Burgas, the Rhodope Mountains, Gümülcine (today's Komotini), and Constantinople.[88] The Ottoman government evacuated tens of thousands by sea to Anatolia, Cyprus, and Syria, and others passed through Constantinople by land to Anatolia. In July 1878 the Europeans established an international commission for the Muslim refugees of Mount Rhodope. This particular group of 150,000 or so refugees could have destabilized and eventually provoked the collapse of the very artificial province of Eastern Rumelia, threatening the whole settlement of the Congress of Berlin. Thus, the European powers' interest in the matter was not predominantly humanitarian. The commissioners' main task was to organize the repatriation of the refugees, and both the Ottoman and the Russian authorities were supposed to facilitate the work of the commissioners.[89] The returning refugees should have been given back their houses, land, and possessions and should have been free from harassment. In the meantime, as a temporary solution, refugees were to stay in the Rhodope district, which meant providing them with money, hospitals, and orphanages. If the European powers had really wanted to resettle the Muslim refugees, they should have created a permanent commission with full powers, in charge of repatriation and restitution as well as a *"police mixte."*[90] In fact, the Russian occupying authorities did not provide protection for the returning civilians, who were at the mercy of their Christian fellow citizens. Refugees who returned to their homes found them destroyed or in the hands of Bulgarians, with no hope of getting them back. Despite Russian guarantees that the refugees would at least be fed, they were actually left to starve, and local Christian populations did not share the harvest with Muslims. The refugees had no food, no housing, and no land. The French commissioner admitted that Muslim (and Jewish) civilians of Bulgaria and Eastern Rumelia were victims of discrimination and grave mistreatment, which were the result of Bulgarian and Russian policy to "exterminate" the Muslim civilians.[91] The Europeans failed to protect the very basic *rights of others* (i.e., of Muslim civilian populations). In the end, the majority of the Muslim populations of Rumelia and Bulgaria stayed in the southern province of Adrianople, remained in Constantinople, or fled to Anatolia.[92] As far as Ottoman Muslims are concerned, we will see that the displacement and resettlement of populations on a religious (rather than ethnic) basis would be the solution European policy-makers put forward later in the century when new massacres of Ottoman Christians took place.

The protection of Balkan Jews was no more successful. For decades the autonomous governments of Serbia and of the Danubian Principalities of Moldavia and Wallachia, had promulgated anti-Semitic laws, causing misery and distress among the local Jewish communities. The European powers never considered the possibility of undertaking a humanitarian intervention in favor of the Romanian or Serbian Jews, even though consular reports mention "the liberal extinction of the Jewish population in Servia."[93] Despite the nondiscrimination articles included in the Treaty of Berlin, not much would change, especially in Romania, a country that was forced to amend its constitution in 1878 but was not hindered in its persecution of foreign Jews after 1880. If the European powers had wanted to effectively protect the right of others, they should have intervened in Romania. The Treaty of Berlin did not provide any mechanism for the implementation of these measures, nor did it say anything about how to carry out an intervention in case of a state's noncompliance with the rule.[94]

. . .

By the mid-1870s European policy-makers agreed that intervention against massacre could take place within the boundaries of the Ottoman Empire. However, this kind of intervention was entangled with and subordinated to collective security priorities of the intervening states. This explains why no humanitarian intervention took place on behalf of the Bulgarians. As in the case of Crete, the British government's opposition kept any intervention in Bulgaria from occurring. Had the European powers collectively agreed, a humanitarian intervention to prevent further massacres of Christians on the Balkan peninsula could have taken place after the Bulgarian massacres in the spring of 1876. The answer to the question in the epigraph—*Are we to give up humanity in order to preserve the "balance of power"*—is yes. An intervention on grounds of humanity on behalf of the Bulgarians would have threatened the European system and was ruled out by the British government despite the massacres and atrocities that had occurred in the Ottoman province of Rumelia. In 1876 Russia and Austria-Hungary would have undertaken such an intervention, which was fully compatible with their geopolitical interests. They refrained because they were not ready to risk a general war in Europe. In 1877 the Russian government decided to take that risk and declared war on the Ottoman Empire.

The plan elaborated by the European plenipotentiaries during 1876 Conference of Constantinople was quite close to a humanitarian intervention for it encompassed coercive measures to enforce the reforms aimed at avoiding the repetition of massacre in the future. Even though the military occupation was discarded, the amount of interference in the Ottoman Empire's internal affairs was considerable. Humanitarian considerations (the intention of avoiding repetition of massacre, atrocities, and extermination) played a prominent role during the negotiations in Constantinople, revealing a genuine attempt by the European cabinets to prevent further massacres in the future. Undoubtedly the European powers' humanitarianism was biased and selective and wrongly identified Muslim populations as the perpetrators of massacre and at the roots of disturbances and unrest. The Eastern crisis also proved to the Europeans that the Ottoman Empire was irredeemable and utterly incapable of protecting its Christian populations. For this reason, the bilateral and collective treaties of 1878 stated that the European powers would now take responsibility for the Ottoman Christian populations (especially the Armenians) and ensure the enforcement of the necessary reforms.

Public opinion contributed to bringing about a change in British foreign policy, especially when it combined, during the fall of 1876, with defeat of Montenegro and Serbia and the risks of a war in the Balkans, which eventually led to the calling of the Conference of Constantinople. However, public opinion alone would not have been able to convince the British government to undertake a humanitarian intervention. Pro-intervention campaigners in Great Britain, as well as Pan-Slavists in Russia, had a political agenda that went beyond saving the lives of strangers. For the leaders of the agitation, including their reluctant icon, Gladstone, humanitarian intervention—or any other political solution—was an intermediate step toward the liberation of the Balkan peninsula from the Ottoman yoke. For British Liberals, the rationale for their involvement in the agitation revolved around the campaign against the Tories. Liberal leaders did not elaborate the details of a military operation to rescue the victims of massacre, and when it came to reforms their proposals where not really different from those put forward by the Tory government.

CHAPTER SEVEN

Intermezzo—The International Context (1878–1908)

CHANGES, TENSIONS, AND ALIGNMENTS

At least three major changes directly affecting relations between the Ottoman Empire and the European powers took place simultaneously in the late 1870s. First, after the Eastern crisis a majority of European policy-makers considered the Ottoman Empire as "unreformable." The general view across European cabinets and political elites was that reforms were nothing but diplomatic subterfuges, intended to deceive foreigners while changing nothing at home. European policy-makers and international legal scholars recognized the Ottoman Empire as an independent territorial entity, although they did not recognize its domestic sovereignty and authority structures, which they deemed ineffective and "uncivilized." They denied the Ottoman Empire's right to determine autonomously its own domestic authority structures (generally and wrongly referred to as *Westphalian sovereignty*).[1] European governments respected the sultan's authority as long as he ruled over his Ottoman Christian subjects according to the principles of international law (*droit public européen*). When the Porte enforced "*l'arbitraire asiatique*," the European powers authorized themselves to interfere in the Ottoman Empire's internal affairs.[2] They justified their intervention either because they were the "guardians of general principles based on international consensus or simply because they were the protectors of the *droits de l'humanité*."[3]

Second, with the coming to power of Sultan Abdul Hamid II, Ottoman political elites became increasingly reluctant to accept the European powers' interference in their internal affairs. Even though, contrary to what Europeans thought, the pace of internal reforms would continue under the reign of Abdul Hamid, the *Tanzimat* era—intended as cooperation between Europe and the Ottoman Empire—was over. From 1881 the sultan had to accept the establishment of the Administration of the Ottoman Public Debt, which diminished Ottoman sovereignty in various ways.[4] The Sublime Porte's economic weakness forced the Ottoman authorities to accept European intrusion and increased the resentment of the sultan, of the majority of the political elite, and of

Muslim populations. During his reign, Abdul Hamid used his position as caliph to enhance his prestige as spokesman for the Muslim world. He linked the embryonic feeling of Turkish nationalism with non-Turkish Muslims (Pan-Islamism) and led Ottoman ruling elites to identify themselves with the Turkish ethnic group.[5] During the 1880s various decisions taken by the European powers further increased the frustration, resentment, and animosity of the Ottoman political elites and Muslim populations, starting with the humiliating occupation of Bosnia-Herzegovina by Austria-Hungary, followed by the loss of Tunis to France (1881) and the occupation of Egypt by Britain (1882).

Third, for Ottoman Christian elites the idea of an Ottoman citizenship was no longer a political option they would seriously consider. In the final decades of the nineteenth century, Ottoman Christians in the eastern and western provinces of the empire, not merely radical and disgruntled nationalist groups, would seek self-determination. Moreover, the Russo-Ottoman War of 1877–78 led to a misunderstanding among Christian populations of the Ottoman Empire, Armenians included. They were convinced that the insurrectionary formula of the Bulgarians, which had led to the intervention of Russia and to the recognition of the independence of Bulgaria and other Balkan states at the Congress of Berlin, could be applied to their particular case as well. The idea to foment an insurrection—even if its leaders that it would fail and would lead to massive bloodshed among civilians—and to publicize the ensuing atrocities as broadly as possible on the world stage and then wait for public outrage in European countries to translate into a direct and punishing response looked to be shortest way to self-determination. The only problem, notes historian Mark Levene, was that the premise was false. The effect of hitching oneself to the language of human rights self-determination did not in itself improve an insurrectionary ability to gain outside support. What it did, instead, was confirm in the minds of European rulers the already "festering notion that communities in revolt were either stooges, or fifth columnists of interfering and malevolent outside powers intent on sabotaging state agendas."[6]

These three changes are to be taken into account when dealing with increasingly massive and indiscriminate state-approved slaughter of hitherto "protected' Christian communities. These massacres strengthened the Europeans' argument about Ottoman "barbarity," but, contrary to what one might think, they did not foster the idea of rescuing Ottoman Christians through armed intervention. I argue that because of the increased tensions and rivalries, continental and imperial, and new alignments among European powers, there was an increased risk related to these interventions, which hampered their occurrence. Hence, at a time when international legal scholars published their doctrines on humanitarian intervention, when a racist "objective scientific basis" came to justify the "superiority" of Western culture and Western dominance as being the expression of scientific laws rather than an accident of power politics, the practice of armed humanitarian intervention almost disappeared. Despite being at the height of their military power, and despite the fact that various Ottoman Christian populations (e.g., Armenians) were victims of massacres caused directly by the actions of Ottoman authorities or by these authorities' incapacity to maintain law and order (e.g., in Crete and Macedonia), the European powers did not undertake any intervention.

Between 1880 and 1908 the Concert of Europe slowly came to an end. New occasions of conflict, supported by increasingly nationalistic public opinion, gradually turned the international system into a competition. However, competition would not ineluctably lead to war among the great powers.[7] The European powers did not intend to eliminate their rivals. They all would continue to exist, "adjusting their claims against one another from time to time, and extending their influence, sometimes, into areas where, as yet, no equilibrium of forces existed. The most important such area was the Balkans."[8] In fact, before 1908 it was still possible to reach an agreement on the Eastern Question, as had happened during the Cretan crisis and in Macedonia, after Austria-Hungary and Russia had agreed to put the Balkans "on ice" on May 5, 1897.

The foreign policy of France in the 1880s revolved around the idea of recovering the provinces lost in the 1870s. One school of thought was to wage war against Germany, which meant that Paris had to find a powerful ally, the most obvious choice being Russia. An alternative school of thought looked to colonies, social progress, and economic expansion as the main directions of the Third Republic's foreign policy. Those in favor of such a policy generally distrusted authocratic Russia, the oppressor of the Poles.

The so-called Slav Question dominated the foreign policy of Austria-Hungary. The territorial expansion toward the South, a region of crucial political, economic, and strategic importance, would have increased the number of Slavs in the Habsburg Empire, changing the internal balance of power between ethnic groups and very likely increasing the ethnic tensions. Furthermore, a clash against Russia would have been almost inevitable.

After the Congress of Berlin, Russia kept expanding in East and Central Asia. Despite vociferous Pan-Slavs who would keep exerting pressure on Russian foreign policy, St. Petersburg wished for stability in the Near East and distrusted both Austria-Hungary and Great Britain. British imperial interests in Central Asia made Russia quite suspicious about the "responsibilities" of London toward the Ottoman Armenians. The Russian government perceived as a threat the Armenian revolutionary parties in the Ottoman Empire. It feared that they could throw into disarray the Russification programs enforced in the Trans-Caucasian provinces inhabited by large communities of Armenians.[9]

In the 1880s numerous tensions among European powers were defused by the foreign policy of Otto Von Bismarck, the German chancellor. For twenty years he succeeded in maintaining good relations between Russia and Austria-Hungary and keeping France isolated by fostering its colonial expansion. Bismarck was successful in avoiding a European major crisis during the Bulgarian crisis of 1882–85. The latter started when the Bulgarians and Eastern Rumelian nationalists cooperated to achieve the annexation of Eastern Rumelia to Bulgaria.[10] Its consequences would be longstanding, for France and Russia would eventually seek a rapprochement. When deciding on the future of Bulgaria, Bismarck and the other policy-makers did not pay attention to the Sublime Porte. Constantinople viewed the European powers' decision to nominate Prince Ferdinand Coburg as their ruler as completely illegal. Abdul Hamid complied and lost the province of Eastern Rumelia, but in the future he would staunchly refuse interference in any other provinces. The Armenians would pay the price for the lesson the sultan had learned in Bulgaria. It should also be noted that when, in the wake of the Bulgarian crisis, Greece attempted to attack the Ottoman Empire, the European powers agreed in holding Greece back, showing that any territorial aspirations of one or the other Balkan states were a matter that would be decided by the powers according to their interests. In that particular case, they decided that Greece had no right whatsoever to wage a war against the Ottoman Empire.

Bismarck left office in 1890. His web of alliances collapsed shortly thereafter, for his successors had different views on Germany's foreign policy priorities. Germany's renewed territorial, economic, and strategic interests beyond Europe invariably worsened its relations with Great Britain. More important, France emerged from its isolation thanks to its alliance with Russia in 1892. As historian J. M. Roberts puts it, the safeguards against the division of Europe into two camps had gone.[11] The division would become explicit after 1908. From 1890 to 1908 the Ottoman Empire was one of the most sensitive areas of the globe, where the divisions of the European powers met and potentially collided. Hence, in the case of massacres, collective intervention was very unlikely, and unilateral intervention would have almost certainly led to a general war. When the massacres of Armenians took place, a

Franco-Russian diplomatic front and a German-Austrian front built up and made the British government's task of reaching an agreement on collective action impossible. The latter was unwilling to undertake a unilateral armed intervention on behalf of the Armenians because of the military risks involved in such an operation, and because such an action would have irremediably damaged the relations of London with the Sublime Porte. Even worse, it would have favored France in the Upper Nile valley and Russia in the Caucasus, and Germany would have increased its political influence and economic penetration in the Ottoman Empire.

INTERVENTIONS BEYOND EUROPE AND THE ADVOCATES OF THE "ELEMENTARY RIGHTS OF HUMANITY"

In 1898 the United States declared war against Spain and conquered, occupied, and "benevolently assimilated" (annexed) Cuba, Puerto Rico, the Philippines, and Guam.[12] The 1903 treaty with Cuba placed the island under an informal American protectorate that gave Washington the right to intervene on behalf of the Cubans if the government were to prove inadequate for the protection of life, property, and individual liberty. In the Philippines the U.S. government proclaimed that the objective of the war was the liberation of the Filipinos from the iniquities of Spanish imperial rule. However, it soon appeared clear that the U.S. armed forces were waging war against the Filipino nationalists who had initially welcomed the arrival of the United States. The war resulted in approximately 250,000 deaths, the enormous majority of them Filipino civilians.[13]

The motives that inspired the United States to wage war are to be found in the country's attempt to prevent Cuba's sovereignty from being transferred from Spain to anybody else, including radical Cubans vowing revolution against propertied interests. When Spain showed its resolve not to sell the island and was unable to enforce reforms, the United States intervened to halt a nationalistic revolution or social movement that threatened American interests. The U.S. government intended to protect its citizens, trade, commerce, and property rights, and it perceived the anarchy prevailing on the island as a menace to peace. It used humanitarian reasons to justify the war, and the war did end some appalling practices inflicted by the Spaniards on the local population, including the "reconcentration" policies, or the forced relocation of the civilian population to fortified cities and towns in 1896 and 1897.[14]

The U.S. press drew an explicit parallel between the European powers' intervention in the Ottoman Empire (and nonintervention to protect the Ottoman Armenians) and "intervention" in Cuba against Spain. As in Europe, before and during the war public opinion and the press exerted visible pressure on U.S. policy-makers. Since at least 1895 Americans had been reading in the press—especially in sensationalist newspapers—abundant and detailed accounts of atrocities committed by the Spaniards. On May 17, 1896, *New York World* correspondent James Creelman sought to slake his readers' thirst for tales of others' misery: "Blood on the roadsides, blood in the fields, blood on the doorsteps, blood, blood, blood. The old, the young, the weak, the crippled, all are butchered (by the Spanish) without mercy." Historian John Lawrence Tone writes that stories of Cuban slaughter comforted Americans not only by giving them solace in others' misery but also by reinforcing a familiar stereotype of the cruel, lascivious, and lazy Spaniard, historically the key antithesis to the humane, restrained, and industrious Anglo-Saxon, whose burden was to save humanity.[15] The U.S. press regularly accused Spain of infant slaughter and warfare against women. Joseph Pulitzer's *World* warned that "a new Armenia lies within eighty miles of the American coast," and the Chicago *Times-Herald* predicted that without U.S. intervention the slaughter would go on until no one was left in Cuba because no number of civilian dead would be enough to satisfy "the thirst for blood inherent in the bull-fighting citizens of Spain."[16] Major dailies all over the country purchased and reprinted what the so-called yellow press in New York ran. As a result, day after day, Americans received a consistent and relentless tale of massacre in Cuba. It would have been hard to live in the United States, argues Tone, and not have a very clear, though false, idea about what was happening in Cuba. This helps to explain why President William McKinley's war message to Congress stated that the United States was intervening in the cause of humanity and to put an end to barbarities, bloodshed, starvation, and horrible miseries. It also explains why Washington took exactly the same stance toward Spain as the European powers had taken with respect to the Ottoman Empire. In the discourse of U.S. policy-makers, Spain was portrayed as a "decadent," "barbarian," and "uncivilized" power.

The war against Spain was not a humanitarian intervention, although its rhetoric and the dynamics between public outcry and governmental decision-making seemed to work along the same lines on both shores of the Atlantic. By 1900 we also notice, in both western Europe and the United States, an increasing number of movements advocating the rights of non-European, nonwhite, non-Christian populations. However, the success of these groups as well as their universalism and secularism should not be overestimated or overemphasized.[17] Movements such as the Pro-Boers or Congo Reform Association (CRA) in Britain were the result of occasional alliances between small radical groups and evangelical missionaries, who were "humanitarians" on their own terms.[18] Early-twentieth-century humanitarians did not challenge notions of racial and class hierarchy; they did not question imperialism or advocate direct political representation for nonwhite imperial subjects. The intervention humanitarians had in mind was highly paternalistic, and, with the exception of the perspicacious few, humanitarians were largely unwilling to consider that colonialism and settlement—whether Belgian, German, British, or whatever—might actually be inherently incompatible with their lofty aims.[19] Protest movement against human rights violations in the colonies—with the single exception of the Boer case—only really took on a head of steam in cases of the pot calling the kettle black; that is, when the wrongdoer was the colonialist in a competitor country, not one's own.[20]

Similarities between the CRA and the pro-Armenian and pro-Macedonian movements do exist, however, as far as the practices and the individuals involved are concerned. Historian Maria Todorova notes that at the turn of the century the Near Eastern political situation offered the possibility of explaining in simple terms the complex issues that the English colonial metropolis was facing at the time: the uneasiness about Ireland was translated into uneasiness about Macedonia; the vogue about the poor was transformed into a vogue for suppressed nationalities; the feminist movement focused on life in the harems; the remorse about India or the Boer War was translated into guilt about Turkish atrocities.[21] One difference should be highlighted here. The CRA and other, similar movements aimed at changing the colonial practices of "civilized" rulers, whereas the others were directed against a "barbarian" ruler. The first aimed at redressing the "civilizing mission," whereas the second aimed to persuade a reluctant "civilized" power to commit more seriously to ending massacres perpetrated by a "barbarous" regime. Very few campaigners fully understood or shared what cosmopolitan John MacCunn wrote in 1899:

> Sometimes we awaken. We realize we have natural duties to Bulgarians or Armenians after they have been massacred, to Soudanese after they have been plundered and enslaved, to South Africans when they revolt, or East Africans when blood begins to flow; and we clamor then for national intervention. It is good that we should awaken, however late. But these ebullitions are too apt to be spasmodic, intermittent, sentimental. And they are so because there is a quite definite question we do not face, and on which there is no clear understanding among us. This question: Is the citizen entitled to look to the nation as the instrument through which, as a matter

of settled policy, his cosmopolitan duties and sympathies are to find enactment? Yet this is the question we ought to put—and to answer in the affirmative.[22]

The war the British Empire waged against the two South African Boer republics of the Transvaal and the Orange Free State began in October 1899 and ended with the Peace of Vereeniging of May 31, 1902, after seven thousand men on both sides had been killed in action, sixteen thousand British had died of disease, and tens of thousands civilians had perished inside and outside the temporary "concentration camps." The war, which took place at the same time as the Cretan and Macedonian crises, relates to humanitarian interventions in the Ottoman Empire in several ways. First, as far Great Britain is concerned, the military weakness of the British army when faced with bringing a small community of "uncivilized" Dutch farmers to heel was not without consequences. After 1902 British policy-makers' priority would be the reorganization of imperial defense. In that context, any involvement of the British army in Crete or in Macedonia, especially when the motive of a military operation was to save the lives of strangers, would be seriously examined, for the next humanitarian intervention might expose the British army to the same kind of difficulties encountered in South Africa. Second, after the war in South Africa, even the most enthusiastic British imperialists acknowledged that the most urgent matter was the consolidation of the empire. This left little space for interventions on grounds of humanity. Third, the war had exposed the so-called civilizing mission as a complete sham, tarnished the honor of England abroad, and done little to improve the welfare of South Africa's white populations. The "standard of civilization" by which the behavior of civilized nations toward the uncivilized should be measured was now questioned. Were not the "methods of barbarism" the very same methods that had previously triggered humanitarian interventions against the Ottoman Empire? The unasked question relating to the mistreatment of the Boers was the following: were British authorities acting toward Christian Boers (and African heathen populations) as the Ottoman authorities did toward Ottoman Christians?

In this context, the events related to the British and American governments' intervention against the king of Belgium in the so-called Congo Free State are relevant. Apparently they suggest that great powers were ready to intervene to protect nonwhite, non-Christian civilian populations mistreated by a European ruler. They are also important in revealing the role transnational public opinion, aroused by the humanitarian Congo Reform Association, played on both sides of the Atlantic to enhance the governments' decision to intervene. After the decisions made during the 1884–85 Conference of Berlin, King Leopold II of Belgium ruled the Congo Free State. In Europe, Leopold had carved out an image as a philanthropist, a humanitarian crusader whose main interest in Congo was to save the natives from mass depredations perpetrated by Swahili and Arab slave traders in the east and center of the African continent. His real aim, however, was the conquest and hyperexploitation of the natural resources of the Congo basin. The reasons for ruling over the Congolese were related to the now widespread conviction that "dark" and "lower" races were physically, mentally, and culturally inferior to Europeans. Whatever the fate of these peoples in the future, it would be one determined by their European or "white" masters. At best, they would be treated as wards to be "civilized and liberated" from "barbarous customs," as the declaration of the 1890 Brussels Conference proclaimed.[23] At worst, as Scottish anatomist and anthropologist Robert Knox pointed out, they would become extinct.

The subjugation of the Congo was accomplished by coercion and terror, pure and simple. Like other colonial powers, such as France on the Congo River, Portugal in Angola, and Germany in Cameroon, the Congo Free State concession companies set up a forced labor system of exploitation. In the early 1890s Leopold's private African army, the *Force Publique* (a fearsome but poorly disciplined, native-recruited paramilitary gendarmerie of 16,000 men led by some 350 European officers), drove the powerful Muslim slave traders out of the Congo. While Leopold portrayed this as a great humanitarian act, his real purpose was to gain control of the upper Congo River and to acquire more workers. With the mid-1890s rubber boom, Leopold and his licensed concessions now needed more workers to go deeper into the forest in search of wild rubber. Tapping wild rubber was difficult, and Leopold's agents had to use brutal force to get the people of Congo to go into the forests and gather rubber. As more villages resisted the rubber order, Leopold's agents ordered the *Force Publique* army to raid the rebellious villages and kill the people. To make sure that the paramilitary did not waste bullets in hunting animals, the officers demanded to see the amputated right hand of every person killed. Concession companies took hostages, used slave chains, starved porters, and burned villages. It is estimated that before 1908 the killing and ruthless exploitation of civilians resulted in a population loss of ten million people.

By the late 1890s reports regarding the atrocities committed in Leopold's Congo Free State circulated in Europe and in the U.S.A. Early accounts published by Protestant missionaries went unnoticed thanks to the counterpropaganda of Catholic missionaries, the main competitors of Protestants in Congo, and of Leopold's press bureau. In 1896, at the time of the Armenian massacres, the British Aborigines Protection Society appealed in vain to the government to convene an international conference with a view to securing just and humane treatment of the Congolese natives. However, the war against Spain in the United States and the Boer War in Great Britain eclipsed public discussion of the "Congo Question." It was only in May 1903, a year after the end of the Boer War, during a debate at the House of Commons that MP Herbert Samuel called the attention of the government to the misrule of the Congo and described the fiendish acts of cruelty perpetrated on the natives.[24] The result was the adoption of a resolution recalling that the Congo Free State had, at its inception, guaranteed to the powers that its native subjects should be governed with humanity, and stating that no trading monopoly or privilege should be permitted within its dominions.

This marked a decisive stage in what came to be known as the Congo reform campaign, for the motion now committed the British government to action and corroborated the thesis that the Congo Free State was not a fully autonomous state, so its ruler was answerable to the signatory powers of the Berlin Treaty for the way in which he exercised his authority. In August a circular note was sent to the signatory states on the question of the treatment of Africans in the Congo Free State. And, at the same time, the British consul at Boma, Sir Roger Casement, was sent to tour the interior of Congo and to report on the conditions of native populations. In February 1904 Casement's report was published and made a great impression in Great Britain. It gave further evidence that the recent depopulation of the Congo was due to the system of oppression that included forced labor, murder, and mutilation of civilians. Meanwhile, Edmund Morel, a clerk for a Liverpool shipping line used by Leopold to ship out Congo's wealth, with no experience in grassroots political mobilization, funded the Congo Reform Association, whose objective was to assure to the Congolese just and equitable treatment. With Casement's assistance, he began a massive campaign in the *West African Mail* against Leopold's brutality. Week after week, Morel published plenty of stories of Congolese men whose hands had been amputated for having failed to deliver sufficient rubber, or of abused and violated women and children held hostage as a means of forcing their recalcitrant menfolk back to work.

Historian Kevin Grant has recently argued that three ideological branches of British humanitarianism influenced the reform campaign in Congo. The first was trusteeship, which placed theoretical limits on the duration of imperial rule but allowed the administrators to decide when their rule should actually end. The second was evangelical philanthropy. Evangelicals took leading roles in the British antislavery movement and in the development of British overseas missions, which grew dramatically over the course of the nineteenth century. They shared with the advocates of trusteeship a strong faith in the moral and cultural superiority of Christianity and a firm commitment to capitalist development. They believed that they could promote Christian ethics and culture by incorporating foreign peoples into the imperial economy as laborers and consumers. However, in the process of freeing people from bondage and saving souls, evangelicals also instigated social reforms, provoking unrest that imperial administrators wished to avoid. At the turn of the twentieth century, the third ideological branch—the proponents of human rights—challenged these two groups. Two distinct groups advanced a rights-based agenda: the trade unionists and a powerful combination of British merchants who established a strategic alliance with the Aborigines Protection Society. The latter asserted that the rights of British merchants to trade with Africans would guarantee Africans' human rights. Borrowing from the Victorian liberal tradition, this humanitarian lobby argued that "the elementary rights of humanity," as Morel and Casement put it, were based on property ownership, and that the exchange of property through commerce would ensure the fundamental human right of freedom from suffering. Morel and Casement asserted that Africans had fundamental rights to property in their bodies and in the land, and, through the mixing of their labor and the land, to the produce of the soil. Moreover, Africans had their own distinctive cultures that should be respected, which in Morel's view were based on the recognition of essential racial differences. The advocates of evangelical philanthropy and human rights came into conflict over issues of culture and political sovereignty in tropical Africa. Evangelicals generally endorsed cultural reform and political deference, while rights advocates endorsed a significant degree of cultural relativism, as well as political autonomy, for Africans.

Grant argues that it was only in 1906, after missionaries John and Alice Harris joined the CRA and popularized the lantern lecture, where photographs were projected as lantern slides, as a mode of protest, that Morel's radical lobby gained popular support. In the process the campaign was transformed into an evangelical crusade, with many gatherings taking place inside churches or chapels.[25] Within the first two years, the Harrises delivered no less than six hundred public speeches and lantern lectures. Evangelical Christianity, rather than radicalism and the nascent politics of human rights, was the driving force in the humanitarian politics of the British Empire in the early twentieth century.[26] Missionaries set aside Morel's demands for human rights and the preservation of African customs, and although they employed Morel's discourses on property rights and free trade, they refigured these discussions in their "atrocity meetings" in terms of their own evangelical goals of expansion and conversion. This was the triumph not of Morel and Casement's ideas, but of the understanding of imperialism as a civilizing mission based on both commerce and Christianity.

It is worth recalling that before the full involvement of the missionaries with the CRA, the governments of Great Britain and the United States interfered in the internal affairs of Belgium, a small European state, with regard to the treatment of the autochthonous population of Congo. They enforced a concurrent and cooperative diplomatic representation. The language they employed was meant to make Belgium understand that if it did not take heed the emphatic protests of the intervening powers and make an effort to reform the abuses in Congo, the powers might call a conference and ultimately decide to either partition the Congo Free State or place it under some other sovereign. In this respect, the political *démarches* had a clearly coercive nature even though the diplomatic correspondence does not indicate that the intervening governments intended to make recourse to armed force to rescue the Congolese civilian populations. Contrary to Ottoman Christians, the Congolese did not deserve an armed intervention on their behalf, and, after all, Belgium was a "civilized" European country that could not be compared with the "barbaric" Ottoman Empire. Acting in a typical hypocritical way, Europeans and Americans condemned the barbarity of Leopold's henchmen while they committed many of the same atrocities against their own colonial populations elsewhere (the Americans in the Philippines; the British in South Africa; the Germans against the Herero). Belgium finally yielded to the pressure applied by the powers and made reforms, which culminated in its formal annexation of Congo. The outcome of the intervention was thus certainly not humanitarian. Leopold demanded and received a huge cash payment and other benefits in exchange for the "great sacrifices" he had made for Congo. The Congolese had no say in their fate. The Belgian government eliminated the worst abuses against them, although the land, along with its rubber and mineral resources, remained firmly under European control. Later Belgium would do little to improve the well-being of the people or to involve them in administering the colony.

A similar case of diplomatic intervention for humanitarian purposes concerned the "Putumayo atrocities" that took place in the rubber districts of Peru and involved the governments of Great Britain and the United States.[27] In 1907 the Americans and British received information about the inhumane treatment of the Peruvian "aborigines" employed in collecting rubber on behalf of British companies in the Putumayo district on the upper Amazon. In 1912–13 Sir Roger Casement published a report on the exploitation and misery of the indigenous rubber tappers in that area.[28] As in Congo, the British government had sent

Casement to investigate the situation in Peru, and he prepared a number of reports on the appalling conditions there. The Peruvian government and the British companies in control of the rubber district put whatever obstacles they could in the commissioner's way to prevent him and the American consul at Iquitos, Stuart J. Fuller, from procuring full information from the natives, but their reports gave a convincing account of the horrible conditions in Putumayo. Nonetheless, the outbreak of the First World War caused the matter to be dropped.

. . .

At the beginning of the twentieth century, British foreign policy was changing rapidly. Canada, Australia, New Zealand, and South Africa became independent dominions. During the first decade of the century Great Britain reached an agreement for the defense of British interests in the Nile valley and settled its colonial dispute with France. The Franco-British Entente Cordiale of 1904 was a turning point in European relations and in some respects a prelude to the Anglo-Russian rapprochement. In 1906 British capital was involved in a loan to Russia for the first time since the Crimean War. In August 1907 Russian fears of a German-dominated Baghdad railway were decisive, leading Russia and Britain to settle their colonial disputes in Persia, Afghanistan, and Tibet and to agree on the territorial integrity of the Ottoman Empire. By 1908 it was clear that a collective intervention on behalf of Ottoman Christians was unlikely to happen and that the unilateral intervention of one of the European powers would probably have led to a general war.

The year 1908 marked the beginning of the Young Turks revolution in the Ottoman Empire. Opposition to the sultan had been forced underground or abroad, coalescing around those who had been in Paris since the suspension of the constitution of 1877, known as the Young Turks from their journal *La Jeune Turquie*. As the Committee for Union and Progress (CUP), in 1902 they had held a first congress of various groups, including Turks, Albanians, Kurds, Greeks, Armenians, and Jews, united by their wish to remove the sultan, restore the constitution, and save the Ottoman Empire from foreign interference. It was precisely the humiliation and frustration of the foreign powers in Macedonia that eventually precipitated the 1908 coup. Bad harvests in Anatolia put pressure on the European provinces as Kosovo was hit by drought. Shortages directed Albanian unrest against towns and Slav peasants. Rumors that the Austrian Army was coming coincided with troops being withdrawn to deal with mutinies further south and caused concentrations of armed Albanians, which the CUP enlisted. The Young Turks argued that a return to the constitution would dissuade further foreign intervention as more members of the military in Macedonia expressed sympathy for them and their political ideas. The Young Turks believed in their mission to create a modern state based on an Ottoman consciousness. Shortly after the July Revolution, a Parliament was called to represent all the Ottoman provinces, including Bosnia-Herzegovina and Eastern Rumelia. In October, to ward off the reassertion of Ottoman claims, Bulgaria declared independence and Austria-Hungary formally annexed Bosnia-Herzegovina. In the meantime, the intervention of the foreign powers in Macedonia was interrupted and Russo-Austrian rivalry was revived in the Balkans.[29]

In 1909 the sultan's supporters attempted a countermove in Constantinople, which the CUP put down. Abdul Hamid was deposed, imprisoned in Salonica, and replaced with his brother Mehmed V. The question, as Pavlowitch puts it, "was no longer how to reform the Empire, but how to save the state. The gap grew between official Ottoman policy based on constitutional guarantees, and actual CUP practice. Pro-CUP feelings among non-Turkish nationalities in the European provinces turned sour; ruthless authoritarianism gained ascendancy in government."[30] The revolution was largely led by Muslim and, increasingly, specifically Turkish interests. The victorious Young Turks gave little thought to the non-Turkish elements in the Ottoman Empire other than that they must perforce all become Ottomans in a revived and powerful empire.[31]

When in 1911 a Berber rebellion took place in Morocco, the French government, whose influence in that country had grown since 1906, sent an expedition to occupy the capital, Fez. Germany reacted by sending the gunboat *Panther* to Agadir, officially to protect German nationals but in reality to make sure that it obtained compensating advantages for any extension of French influence. The crisis considerably worsened the relations between Germany and Great Britain and increased the pace of the naval race between the countries. The Moroccan crisis opened the last stage of the Ottoman succession problem. Italy, too, sought for compensation for French gains in Morocco, and for the 1908 annexation of Bosnia-Herzegovina by Austria-Hungary (see chapter 10). In September 1911 Italy declared war on the Ottoman Empire and landed troops in Tripoli (Libya). The war spread to the Dodecannese, which was eventually occupied by Italy.

The Sublime Porte closed the straits in April 1912, which alarmed the Russian government. Russia sought an agreement with Serbia and Bulgaria as a way to block an Austro-Hungarian drive to the south and also to offset German influence in Constantinople. The two Balkan countries saw the agreement as a partition treaty: Serbia was to get

Turkish territory on the Adriatic, and Bulgaria was to get Macedonia. Greece joined later, selecting Salonica for its portion. This time, a last-minute attempt to revive joint intervention to force reforms on the Ottoman government achieved nothing, and the first Balkan war began when Montenegro declared war on the Ottoman Empire on October 8, 1912. The war culminated in the defeat of Constantinople. The Treaty of London of May 1913 regulated the new Balkan settlement. The Austrians convinced the powers to create an independent Albania, which cut off Serbia from the sea. The danger that the European powers might be dragged into a general war had been averted because both Russian and Austrian interests had been safeguarded and because the other powers had worked for conciliation and compromise.

A second Balkan war began because the Balkan League fell out over the spoils. This time the final settlement, which took place in Bucharest on August 10, 1913, was made between the Balkan states without the intervention of the great powers. However, both the Bulgarians and the Serbians were dissatisfied with the settlement. The Serbian government was angry about Albania and its exclusion from the Adriatic, blaming Vienna.[32]

German political and economic influence in the Ottoman Empire became almost intolerable to the Russians when, in 1913, a German military mission reorganized the Ottoman armed forces under the supervision of a German general. Sergei Sazonov, the Russian foreign minister, toyed with the idea of seizing the straits by force, but it was decided that this was militarily not feasible. In the end a face-saving compromise was arranged, but it was clear that a new direct clash of interests between Germany and Russia had been added to the other dangers to peace. Less than a year later the First World War began.

CHAPTER EIGHT

Nonintervention on Behalf of the Ottoman Armenians (1886–1909)

> Tous les renseignements confirment ce que je disais
> dans mes dernières lettres sur l'horreur des massacres,
> l'impuissance ou les encouragements des autorités, les
> Kurdes que le Gouvernement n'a pas voulu et ne peut
> plus . . . contenir et sur la misère qui, après les massacres,
> les pillages et les incendies, décime une malheureuse
> population partout traquée, sans abris, sans vêtements, sans
> nourriture, au seuil de l'hiver . . . Si parfois, par un senti-
> ment bien naturel chez les malheureux, des exagérations se
> glissent dans le récit de leur souffrances, les faits que con-
> statent nos agents, de leurs propres yeux, suffisent à justifier
> l'horreur qu'inspirent en Europe ces tristes événements et la
> juste sévérité des pays civilisés pour un Souverain sur qui
> pèse sans aucun doute la responsabilité de la situation.
> —Ambassadeur Paul Cambon, November 1895

THIS CHAPTER STARTS with the failed attempts to implement reforms in the Asiatic provinces of the Ottoman Empire after 1878. It then explores the massacres that took up to 100,000 Armenian lives directly and tens of thousands indirectly in 1894–96 and explains why no humanitarian intervention took place after these events.

The period from the 1870s to 1914 was one of radical change in the character of the Ottoman social order, which saw the "Armenian Question" dragged into the international debate to the distress of the Ottomans. As the Ottoman Empire was pushed more and more out of Europe, the Armenians were increasingly exposed as a major, compact Christian (and European, according to the vast majority of pro-Armenian activists) community in the Asian interior. Moreover, as Bloxham notes, since 1878 unrequited Armenian grievances and aspirations would increasingly be expressed not through the traditional Armenian ecclesiastical hierarchy or through ecumenical political institutions but through nationalist parties.[1] Their very existence intensified Sultan Abdul Hamid II's fear of further territorial loss after those decreed in 1878 during the Congress of Berlin and the loss of Eastern Rumelia in 1886.

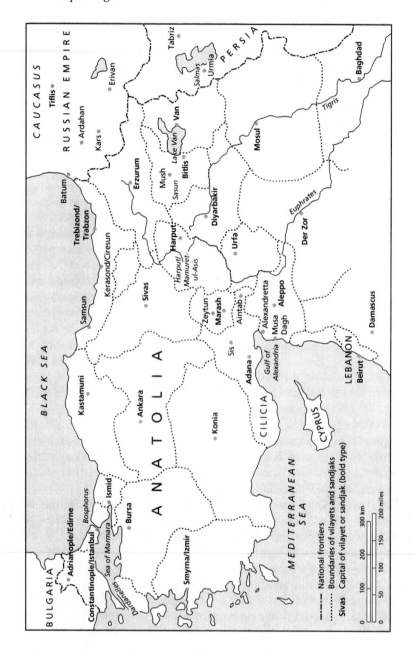

With the Armenian Question we notice a pattern that would be repeated during the Cretan and Macedonian crises. The ostentatious actions of the Armenian political parties were influenced by the desire to regain the attention of external powers—notably Britain, Russia, and France—in the way that seemed to serve Bulgarian so well. Armenian nationalist leaders wrongly thought that acts of massacre, atrocity, and extermination would assuredly be followed by an intervention of the European powers. Hence, it was necessary to let European governments and public opinion know about the repression, the massacres, and atrocities committed by the Ottomans. Armenian nationalists mistakenly assumed that they could achieve as much as other Balkan nationalist groups had achieved, forgetting about the local and international context. They failed to take sufficient account of the different strategic positions and ethnographic distributions of the Balkans and eastern Anatolia, respectively, for in the latter Christians lived amidst a Muslim majority, and in the former, especially in Bulgaria, Muslims were a minority. The nationalists also failed to comprehend exactly what "reform" meant to the great powers. Finally, they did not understand that after the ratification of the Treaty of Berlin, the Ottoman Armenians were in arguably the most difficult position, in no place constituting a demographic majority that would have formed the basis for national separation, and living in precisely the region that Great Britain, the protector of the Armenians, was most determined to see maintained within the Ottoman Empire.[2]

Nineteenth-century western Europeans used the term "Armenians" to mean Gregorians, as well as those people who were members of churches that called themselves Armenians. Gregorians were far more numerous than all the other Armenian Christians combined. There were six provinces (*vilayets*) in eastern Anatolia in which the Armenians formed conspicuous minorities: Erzeroum (Erzurum), Bitlis, Van, Sivas, Kharput (Mamuret-ul-Aziz), and Diyarbakir (Diarbekir). These Ottoman provinces roughly corresponded to what contemporaries meant by "Armenia," though the biggest community of Armenians lived in Constantinople. Contrary to the shepherds and peasants of the East, in the capital Armenians were merchants, shopkeepers, bankers, or civil servants.[3] European governments had no particular sympathy for the Armenians and would have gladly done without the Armenian Question at a time when international relations were troubled by continental rivalries, imperial tensions, and wars. For instance, Charles Eliot, secretary at the British Embassy in Constantinople from 1893 to 1898, portrayed the Armenians as unable to form a national political organization strong enough to hold its own against the adverse circumstances that surrounded them. Armenians were to him like the Poles,

who appeared to possess bravery, wit, and charm. Yet, Eliot wrote, anyone could see that the restoration of the Polish kingdom was impossible, and that the partition of Poland, though it awoke sympathy and
inspired indignation, was due not only to cruel fate, but also to certain
"faults in the national character, such as want of coherence and of capacity of united action." The same applied to the Armenians. Eliot lik-
ened the Armenians to the Jews owing to their aptitude for finance and
commerce; both had itinerant habits and the necessary adaptability to
varying circumstances; both, in spite of outward conformity to ordinary
social usages, remained faithful to their "somewhat forms of religion."
The main difference he saw was that a large group of Armenians "still
dwell in Armenia, little affected by external influences."[4]

These views contrasted with the growing sympathy and interest on
the part of the European for the Armenians and the Armenian Question. After 1878, because Britain's so-called responsibility with respect
of the Ottoman Armenians, the British public's interest ran particularly high, thanks to the numerous articles published by newspapers
such as the *Daily News*. Many inquiries by MPs to the prime minister,
the Foreign Office, and the British Embassy kept the question alive in
Parliament.[5] Before and during the massacres of the 1890s, the strands
of public opinion that supported the Armenians portrayed them as a
more or less compact ethnic, linguistic, and cultural group, occupying
a fairly defined area, within which they were wrongly assumed to be
preponderant over all other peoples.

IMPLEMENTATION OF REFORMS BEFORE THE ARMENIAN MASSACRES

In 1878 the signatory powers of the Treaty of Berlin entrusted a European Commission to determine which reforms to implement in the
European provinces of the Ottoman Empire, leaving no room for the
Sublime Porte to negotiate.[6] As far as the Asiatic provinces of the empire were concerned, and contrary to article 16 of the 1877 Treaty of San
Stefano, article 61 of the Treaty of Berlin stated that the Ottoman government would autonomously implement the reforms. In 1877, with
the Russian Army still occupying the Ottoman territories east and west
of the straits, Russia could effectively guarantee the Armenians' security and monitor the supervision of reforms. In 1878 the situation had
radically changed, for no European army occupied Ottoman territories,
with the exception of Cyprus, and all the powers had an individual right
to call upon the Ottoman Empire to reform the administration of those
provinces.[7] The onerous and exclusive obligation undertaken by Great
Britain in its secret convention with the Ottoman Empire regarding

the island of Cyprus did not provide Britain with an exclusive right over the sultan's Asiatic provinces. In theory, Great Britain could have intervened, militarily if necessary, against the Ottoman Empire if the latter showed itself unable or unwilling to undertake the reforms. In practice, direct control of such vast areas required a financial effort that Britain did not want to make, and an effort in men and resources that it was unable to provide. More important, any such intervention would certainly have meant the end of good relations between London and Constantinople, the consequences of which any British government would have seriously pondered.

In 1878 Salisbury saw a fundamental difference between the Balkan and Asiatic Ottoman provinces. In the former, Christians were the majority; hence an administrative arrangement on the model of Lebanon could be adopted. In the Asiatic provinces, "the Mahometan races, which there constitute an enormous majority of the population," were "unfitted for institutions of this kind, which are alien to their traditions and their habits of thought."[8] The Christians living in the Asiatic provinces, to whom a representative system might perhaps be suited, not only were a minority but were so scattered and intermixed with the Muslims that any separate "machinery of Government" designed for them alone would be faced with the gravest practical difficulties. Bearing in mind his previous experience as India secretary, the reform scheme Salisbury attempted to enforce was based on the principle of improving order, the administration of justice, and the collection of the revenue. His cure for "good government" in the Asiatic provinces of the Ottoman Empire was based on the employment of European supervisors and on the establishment of a gendarmerie organized and commanded by Europeans. Salisbury proposed to set up of central tribunals with jurisdiction over the lower courts, in each of which there should be a European learned in the law whose consent should be necessary in every judgment. He wished to appoint a European tax collector in each *vilayet* (province), who should be accountable for the provincial revenue.[9] Furthermore, it would be "indispensable" that each governor and the judge hold office for a fixed number of years.[10]

In a very sensible document, the grand vizier explained in detail to British ambassador Layard all the difficulties related to the introduction of such a reform scheme.[11] First, it was clearly impossible to constitute the police when the Ottoman government had no means of paying the men employed in it. It would just add to the disorder already prevalent in those areas to raise a force that could become a source of oppression to peaceful people. Second, where would the government find the people who had the requisite juridical and linguistic competences to run the tribunals? Third, because the Ottoman government did not have a proper survey, or cadastre, of the land, it would have had no basis for substituting a fixed rent or tax for the tithes.[12]

In the end, Salisbury's plan was not enforced. A year after the Treaty of Berlin was signed, the living conditions of Armenians had worsened. The foreign secretary appointed new consuls in the Asiatic provinces of the Ottoman Empire in order to verify the actual conditions of the Christian minorities.[13] Their first task was to report on the problems in the areas inhabited by the Armenians and other Christian minorities that were not addressed by the central and local Ottoman authorities. Among them was the arrival of thousands of Circassians who had been expelled from, or voluntarily abandoned, Rumelia and had resettled in Anatolia after the defeat of the Ottoman Empire by Russia and the territorial settlement agreed to in Berlin.[14] Another source of problems was the Kurds, who seemed to have the upper hand everywhere and, in some places with impunity, committed arson, assault, and rape against Christians.

Two years after the Treaty of Berlin, the presence of the consuls had not improved the conditions of the Armenians, had raised Russian suspicions about British ambitions in Anatolia, and had aroused the mistrust of the sultan about a very unwelcome European presence within the boundaries of his empire.[15] The Ottoman government was unwilling to enforce the reforms, and Great Britain was clearly unwilling to coerce it. When the Liberal government came to power in 1880, Granville replaced Salisbury at the Foreign Office and Gladstone became prime minister. It is unlikely that the Porte would have welcomed any suggestion coming from the author of *Bulgarian Horrors*.

During the 1880s the British diplomats on the spot agreed that it was in the interest of humanity to provide for the protection of life and property of the Armenian population.[16] However, a demand for autonomy in Armenia might lead to massacres, which would bring about the immediate interference of Russia. Hence, from the British perspective, even if successful, such an intervention would not necessarily preserve the Armenian "nationality." The British ambassador argued that Russia "would probably never permit an Armenian autonomous or independent State, and any attempt to form one would only end in the absorption of the Armenians into the Russian Empire, and the ultimate extinction of this ancient nation."[17] In 1881 the new ambassador at Constantinople, Lord Dufferin, appointed partly because of his previous experience as commissioner in Lebanon, proposed the appointment of a high commissioner (a solution later adopted in Crete; see next chapter) who would be authorized to oversee the reform process and urge the prompt dismissal of the most notorious governors and officials.[18] That proposal was never implemented. As Salisbury before him,

Gladstone and his government failed to secure the implementation of article 61 of the Treaty of Berlin. The Conservatives under Salisbury came to power in July 1886 and remained in office until August 1892, a critical period in the development of the Armenian revolutionary movement in the Ottoman Empire.

Massacre in Sasun and the May 1895 Reform Program

In late August 1894 news of a brutal repression and massacres that took no account of the age or sex of the victims, including older people, sick people, and children, circulated in British and other European cabinets and newspapers. The massacre took place in Sasun (also called Sassoun or Sasoon, in the province of Bitlis) from August 12 to September 10, 1894. According to the French ambassador at Constantinople, more than seven thousand people perished, whereas British sources speak of ten to twenty thousand Armenians killed and give morbid accounts of pregnant women ripped open, children torn limb from limb, groups of young men bound, buried under brushwood, and burned.[19] In the view of British diplomats, the long-lasting Kurdo-Armenian hostility and local authorities' decision to impose an additional tax, which the Armenian population of Sasun refused to pay, had eventually led to the uprising and massacre.[20] British consular sources dismissed the nationalist activities of the Armenian Revolutionary Party, Huntchak, as having little impact on local villagers.[21] British consul Robert Graves reported that when the Ottomans tried to punish local Armenians, the latter repulsed the first attempt to besiege Sasun. Consequently, Bitlis's governor Tashin Pasha placed three Kurdish cavalry regiments (called *Hamidiye*) under his command.[22] The Fourth Army at Mush (Moush), under the command of General Zeki Pasha, joined them later.[23] Could the European powers have prevented this massacre? What action, if any, did the European powers take after the massacre of Sasun? Did they consider that the massacre of Armenians was likely to be repeated?

The hypothesis that the Europeans were unable to prevent the August–September massacre at Sasun through diplomacy is debatable since all the European governments were fully informed about the escalation of violence in the province. As far as the possibility of a preemptive armed intervention was concerned, we know that there were no precedents for such an international practice during the nineteenth century. The Liberal cabinet and Prime Minister Lord Archibald Rosebery opposed unilateral action as a quixotic idea. The European powers, Rosebery argued, were supposed to protect Christian populations collectively. Hence, from a strictly legal point of view, a concerted and coercive action of the European powers—not necessarily an armed intervention—could have taken place in Sasun before the massacre, given that the British representatives on the spot provided plenty of information indicating that a massacre might well have occurred in that region. As in other instances of massacre examined so far, the first action European powers took was to ascertain what had really happened in Sasun so as not to discredit the Porte's claims. If the occurrence of massacre was verified and evidence of the Porte's incapacity or unwillingness to prevent a repetition was gathered, would the European powers consider undertaking a humanitarian intervention on behalf of the Armenians of Sasun?

The Porte denied that a massacre had occurred, blamed the Kurds for the excesses committed, arrested the Kurdish chief, Hussein Bey, and exiled him to Erzeroum. He was released shortly after his arrest, and Sultan Abdul Hamid presented him with a medal, granted him the title of pasha, and awarded him the military rank of general. This was a way for the Ottoman government to reassert its sovereignty and freedom of action with respect to the events in Sasun. The British instructed Ambassador Philip Currie to send a démarche to the grand vizier protesting the use of Kurdish paramilitary units to put down the uprising. Currie was to remind the vizier of the public outcry generated in Europe by the deployment of paramilitary units in Bulgaria in 1876 and the "great misfortunes" it had caused the Ottoman government. This friendly advice was similar to that which the Foreign Office had sent to the Porte in early 1867 during the Cretan disturbances. On November 2, 1894, Currie presented the Ottoman government with a memorandum on Sasun, based on reports from the British vice consul in Van, C. M. Hallward. The memorandum assumed that a massacre had in fact taken place and held Governor Tashin Pasha, army commander Colonel Ismail Bey, and Mush battalion commander Major Salih responsible for what had happened. Currie asked the Porte for permission to conduct an independent British investigation to determine what had happened in that district.

The grand vizier dismissed the memorandum as unreliable and refused to authorize further investigations on the grounds that the presence of a British official in the rebellious region would revive the uprising, which had now been suppressed. He promised to permit Hallward to travel to Sasun in two months' time. Currie warned the vizier that in the absence of an independent assessment, the British government would not be able to take measures to dispel the wildest rumors circulating in Britain about the massacre.[24] When Abdul Hamid met Currie, he bluntly rejected Hallward's allegations. The sultan too drew a parallel with the Bulgarian case of 1876, noting that when Bulgarian insurgents had circulated stories of massacres, they had achieved autonomous status for Bulgaria. The sultan reminded Currie that it was not possible to establish Armenian autonomy since the Armenian population was not concentrated in a single area and was not in the majority in any Ottoman province. Abdul Hamid made it clear that he was indifferent to reports of persecution and oppression generating European sympathy. He drew a further parallel between the military operation the Ottoman Army had just carried out in the disturbed district of Sasun and the British suppression of native insurgencies in India and Egypt.[25] Abdul Hamid underlined that as Britain had all the rights to suppress insurgency in its empire, so did the Ottoman Empire in its imperial provinces. This was precisely what Derby had claimed when, in 1867, he had defended the rights of the Porte to suppress the rebellion in Crete.

The British government wished to avoid being the only power acting against the Sublime Porte. For that reason, Rosebery tried to stop news of the Sasun massacre from spreading through the country and refrained from publicizing further consular reports on the conditions of the Armenians in Ottoman Asiatic provinces.[26] His attempt failed. By early November 1894 news of the massacre spread in the British press, generating waves of public sympathy for the Armenians and anger at the government's indifference toward and complicity in the massacre. The weekly *Spectator* and *Contemporary Review* accused the Liberal government of having deliberately suppressed news of the massacre.[27] Curiously, Liberals Rosebery and foreign secretary Lord John Kimberley found themselves in a similar situation to that faced by Disraeli and Derby in 1876.

On November 24 the Porte informed the European powers that a purely Ottoman fact-finding commission had been dispatched to Bitlis to investigate the "cruel actions of the Armenian brigands," starting with the assumption that no massacre of Armenians had occurred in Sasun. The British government threatened to publish the Hallward consular reports and informed the Porte that it might invoke article 61 of the Treaty of Berlin and delegate Colonel Herbert Chermside to Sasun to conduct a parallel investigation. Alternatively, the Porte could include a British, a French, and a Russian delegate in the Ottoman commission. On December 7 Grand Vizier Said Pasha reluctantly accepted the European delegation.[28] When the investigation began, the Porte and local authorities hindered the work of the delegation in every possible way. They did not allow British travelers or newspaper correspondents to enter the disturbed districts. Two special correspondents, Emil J. Dillon of the *Daily Telegraph* and F. I. Scudamore of the *Daily News*, managed to run the blockade in February 1895, although it seems certain that Dillon—who dated his letters from Mush—never really went beyond Erzeroum.[29]

The Ottoman police kept a sharp lookout to prevent the Sasun inhabitants from presenting their complaints to the European representatives. They were almost forbidden to leave their district, and those who reached the town were either arrested and sent away or, if accepted as witnesses, kept under the care of the local police, who endeavored to influence their depositions. The three European delegates were constantly obstructed, though despite the difficulties they managed to send reports revealing the appalling details of the massacres.[30] In one report the European commissioners wrote that the Armenians were "hunted like wild beasts" and killed wherever they were met, and if the slaughter was not greater, it was solely due to the vastness of the mountain ranges of that district, which enabled the people to scatter and so facilitated their escape. The report mentioned that the object of the massacre was "extermination, pure and simple."[31] Little information reached the European capitals from neighboring Persia. The British vice consul from Tabreez, who had firsthand information from the Armenian refugees arriving from the disturbed districts, confirmed the accounts of massacres.

Eleven months after the events of Sasun, on July 16, 1895, the European delegation concluded its work after having heard testimony from nearly two hundred witnesses. On July 20 the European consuls concluded that a full-scale massacre of the Armenian population had taken place in Sasun with the participation of regular Ottoman troops. The risk of further massacre persisted as consuls reported that the Armenians of Bitlis, Erzeroum, Trebizond, and Diyarbakir were victims of further harassment and illegal detention.[32] Had the European powers agreed, a humanitarian intervention on behalf of the Armenians could have taken place after July 1895. As in the weeks preceding the July 1860 massacres in Damascus, European sources considered a recurrence of massacre to be very likely. As we know, the Damascus massacre eventually triggered a belated intervention. In 1894–95, however, the conditions for such an agreement did not exist. For different reasons, Germany, Austria-Hungary, and Russia opposed it. As the French foreign minister Gabriel Hanotaux wrote to Paul Cambon, the massacres of Armenians concerned the French government in both humanitarian terms and in terms of France's duties deriving from the Treaty of Berlin. However, the French priority was to avoid any problem with the Russians; hence its intervention would be very limited.[33] The only thing the European powers could agree on during the summer of 1895 was to resurrect the general reform scheme.

In January 1895 the Foreign Office circulated a new program for reforms in the Armenian-populated provinces of Van, Erzeroum, Sivas, Bitlis, Kharput, and Diyarbakir, drafted by Colonel Herbert Chermside. Among other provisions, it called for the merging of the six provinces into one, which would have an established Armenian administrative unit headed by a Christian governor of the powers' choosing.[34] The Russian government disagreed with two principal points in the British draft. St. Petersburg wanted the reforms to be implemented all over the Ottoman Empire, and it fiercely opposed the idea of a large Ottoman province where the Armenians would enjoy exceptional privileges and inevitably attract the turbulent Russian Armenians of Transcaucasia.[35] The French government endorsed the proposal, although it simultaneously expressed its opposition to any coercive measures to enforce it. On May 11, 1895, both Russia and France accepted a substantially edited and diluted version of the British and it was presented to the Porte. The so-called May Memorandum contained the following main points: The number of Anatolian and Asia Minor provinces where Armenian minorities lived was to be reduced. The governors had to be selected and appointed with the semiofficial approval of the powers. A general amnesty had to be proclaimed, releasing Armenian prisoners from custody and allowing exiled and displaced Armenians to return, and the judicial and penal systems had to be reformed. A high commissioner had to be appointed to oversee the reform process, with the approval of the powers. A permanent control commission was to be established, composed of three Christian and three Muslim government officials. The Armenian victims in Sasun, Talvorik (Talori, in Sasun district), and other regions where massacres had been carried out were to be compensated. The right to change religion and Armenians' land titles had to be respected. The living conditions of the Armenian population in other parts of Asia Minor had to be improved. The status of local administration officials and members of the police, gendarmerie, and Kurdish and *Hamidiye* paramilitary forces had to be reviewed. Finally, fiscal administration had to be reformed.[36] The Austro-Hungarian and German governments rebuffed even this diluted plan. The Porte also rejected it, fully aware that disagreement between the European powers played in its favor.[37]

Salisbury returned to power in Britain in June 1895 when he assumed the portfolio of prime minister as well as of the Foreign Office. He had twice failed to introduce reforms in the Asiatic provinces of the Ottoman Empire, first in 1878–80 and again in the early 1890s. For the next five and half months, the course he followed made it clear that to protect the Armenians he was determined to do more than his predecessors

had attempted and more than public opinion required. About his motives he said little, but enough to indicate that they were religious and
humanitarian.[38] In his first dispatch to Currie, Salisbury instructed him
to study the feasibility of deploying the British Mediterranean Fleet,
lying at Beirut some 200 to 300 miles from "Armenia," against the Ottoman Empire to force the government to carry out reforms.[39] For the
first time since the massacre of Sasun, a European prime minister took
into consideration the possibility of undertaking a unilateral humanitarian intervention. In response, Ambassador Currie forwarded to the
Foreign Office a letter from the president of the British Board of Trade
in Constantinople, who noted the impossibility of any such military
intervention.[40]

Other military operations Salisbury had to discard were the occupation of Jeddah on the Red Sea and the occupation of Alexandretta
in Asia Minor. Once landed, the small, possibly inadequate British
troops contingent would encounter many difficulties because of the
scarcity of supplies in the region. Salisbury conceived of yet another
plan, showing his determination to do something about the Armenian
Question. The self-described clever proposal was to transport British troops to provinces inhabited by the Armenians via the river Tigris. Ambassador Currie replied that the proposed expedition would
be impossible to undertake owing to the many shallow points in the
river, which would irremediably damage the warships. In late 1895
the Armenian Question was 1876 turned upside down. France, Germany, and Russia now sustained the sultan, and the British government, supported by public opinion, was in favor of an intervention. In
such circumstances, Gladstone admitted, Britain could do little. Public
opinion had to uphold the government's position and provide national
and moral support for its action.[41] The mighty British Empire appeared
isolated and unable to force the barbarous Ottoman Empire to fulfill
its treaty obligations. By the end of the summer of 1895, it was clear
that the Ottoman government was unwilling to cooperate, that another
massacre would occur, and that European powers would not reach a
consensus on a coercive action to protect Ottoman Armenian civilian
populations.

THE EUROPEAN POWERS AND ARMENIAN MASSACRES,
    SEPTEMBER 1895–AUGUST 1896

Throughout the summer of 1895 British consuls submitted new reports
of massacres of local Armenian populations. They gave detailed accounts of clashes between Muslims and Christians, of Kurdish attacks,

of incitement of Muslims against Armenians by the local Ottoman authorities, and of the spread of the Armenian revolutionary movement.[42] *The Graphic, an Illustrated Weekly* ran continual coverage of the massacres with extraordinary illustrations and astonishing images. In October news of the massacre at Erzeroum prompted the magazine to run what, according to historian Peter Balakian, was one of the most extraordinary pieces of photojournalism of the era.[43]

In Constantinople on September 30, some two thousand Armenians marched to the sultan's residence, demanding an immediate implementation of reform measures. This demonstration, organized by the Huntchak Party, was designed to emphasize the Armenian reform demands more to the European powers than to the Porte. Many of the demonstrators were armed and were obviously expecting trouble, which they found in the form of an organized mob, supported by the gendarmes and the military.[44] The Ottoman gendarmes killed sixty demonstrators and arrested at least five hundred. Mobs attacked Armenian civilians at random on the streets. Queen Victoria and many newspapers expressed their indignation. The British cabinet authorized the deployment of six warships at Lemnos. On October 5 the ambassadors agreed to present a joint memorandum to the Porte. The Europeans cited evidence of the massacres and noted the continued deterioration of public safety in the capital. They warned the Porte to contain the disturbances, which could spread to other parts of the empire, to check "fanaticism" in the Muslim and Christian communities, and to provide security to Christian subjects and foreign nationals. The ambassadors offered their assistance in the reestablishment of public order and declared themselves to be ready to collect and conduct an inquiry.[45]

In October massacres of Armenians took place in Trabzon and Akhisar, where newly resettled Muslim populations from Bulgaria attacked local Armenians. Armed bands of local Muslim civilians and squads of imperial troops ruthlessly slaughtered Armenian male adults wherever they were found. Consul H. Z. Longworth wrote that, caught unaware, these Armenians yielded their life and property with scarcely a struggle, and with piteous submission. This destruction of "many quiet inoffensive and defenceless people" was the first of a series that would have "shocked the whole civilized world."[46] Other massacres followed in Andrin, Angora, Mush, Marash, Bitlis, Gümüshkaneh, Baiburt, and Kharput. In November further disturbances occurred in various villages around Alexandretta (Odjakhli, Uzuli, and Chokmarzvan). Nearly 4,000 Armenians were killed in Gürüm, at least 500 in Kharput, 800 Christian Armenians and Muslims in Sivas, 200 Armenians in Diyarbakir, and 250 in Arabkir.[47] In Zeytoun, in the province of Aleppo, Armenian civilians resisted and fought back. Their resistance eventually forced the Ottoman authorities to accept the mediation offered by the European consuls.[48]

On November 4 the European envoys approved the text of yet another collective note to be presented to the Porte. The note expressed concern over the anarchy prevalent in several regions, threatening Ottoman Christians. In a veiled yet threatening tone, the note mentioned the intervention of 1860 in Lebanon, which should have proved to the Porte that anarchy could not go unpunished. The European powers spoke of a joint action if the Porte failed to take effective measures to address the situation.[49] On November 11 Russian ambassador Alexander Nelidov proposed the joint dispatch of gunboats or lightly armed vessels to the vicinity of the Ottoman capital. He argued that the presence of gunboats would positively affect the positions of the powers vis-à-vis the sultan, stop the spread of the crisis, and prevent recourse to measures involving political complications. Surprisingly, all the representatives of the European powers expressed a generally positive attitude toward the Russian proposal. On November the governments of Austria-Hungary, France, and Italy accepted the proposal, and each dispatched a gunboat with a crew of one hundred men. In the following days Great Britain joined the action. The naval demonstration, as had happened when massacres of Christians took place in the interior areas of Lebanon, was "largely useless" and unable to protect the Armenians.[50] Moreover, it was primarily intended to protect European residents in Constantinople (under the Treaty of Paris, each power had the right to introduce two lightly armed warships, or *stationnaires*, to the Ottoman capital for the protection of foreign colonies).

The Russian government was not ready to go any further to protect Ottoman Armenians. Foreign Minister Aleksei Lobanov-Rostovski noted that contrary to the case of the French expedition in Syria, where disturbances had taken place in a single area, in this case massacres were occurring in various and remote places, and the force of the intervention had to be very significant. Therefore, the sultan should be given more time to restore peace and public order in the country without damage to his authority.[51] The British cabinet rejected Salisbury's idea of forcing the Straits, on the grounds that the French fleet would have been free to sail out of Toulon and attack the British from the rear. It was at this point that the United States chose to quarrel with Britain over Venezuela and the situation in South Africa also worsened. The moment when intervention might have been practicable had passed. Salisbury gave up.

In his letter to Queen Victoria dated January 15, 1896, Salisbury noted that "words were not enough to describe the horrors" concerning the Armenian Question. However, he admitted that Britain would be unable to act alone against the Ottoman Empire.[52] Great Britain needed active Russian military cooperation if it really wanted to undertake a humanitarian intervention. Salisbury reiterated these views in a speech addressed to the Nonconformist Union Association on January 31. He ruled out any current or future British intervention in favor of the Armenians and noted that his government had not undertaken any unilateral obligations on the issue. He argued that the provisions of the Treaty of Berlin were equally applicable to all the signatories, and Britain was not required to do more than other powers. Salisbury said that it was impossible to relieve the suffering of the Armenian population through a military intervention. Britain could defeat five or six sultans on the open seas, but British "ships could not get over the mountains of Taurus."[53]

The Foreign Office received an enormous number of letters, appeals, and protests from the public and from humanitarian and religious groups. Motivated anew by reports of massacres, Gladstone began a fresh public campaign against the "Great Assassin" Abdul Hamid.[54] In mid-December 1895 Salisbury pressured the Duke of Westminster and Gladstone to postpone a rally in support of the Armenian cause and refused to meet a delegation of the British Armenian Society led by the duke. He explained that the government could do nothing more for the Ottoman Armenians. In the meantime, a further massacre occurred in Urfa (or Orfa, one of the *sandjaks* of Alep) at the hands of the *Hamidiye* units.[55] According to French consular sources, at least two thousand Armenians were killed.[56] On January 30, 1896, the European ambassadors at Constantinople circulated an official report on the Armenian massacres. It mentioned that the confirmed number of victims of the massacres was twenty-five thousand, and the total number of victims since the massacre of Sasun was about one hundred thousand.[57] Thousands of Muslim civilians had died as well.

The European powers continued to disagree on the Armenian Question. In June 1896 the French ambassador at London, De Courcel, sent a report back to Paris on Salisbury's dislike of the "detestable Ottoman regime." The British prime minister was horrified by Abdul Hamid's policies. He made it clear that the purpose of British policy with respect to the Armenians was not to "ruin" the Ottoman Empire to protect the self-interest of Great Britain. What Salisbury wanted was a "cleansing operation," an operation of "reparation for all those populations unjustly administrated" by the Ottomans.[58] The French government continued to turn a deaf ear to London, being aware that its Russian ally was extremely reluctant to become militarily involved in the Eastern Question.

While the European policy-makers kept up their discussions, the Armenian political parties—Armenakan, Huntchak, and Dashnak—organized an insurrection in Van that was immediately repressed by the

Ottoman Army.[59] On August 26 a group of thirty-one Dashnak activists, armed with pistols and grenades, took over the Ottoman Bank (actually a Franco-British bank) and demanded that the sultan implement the promised reforms, threatening to blow up the building. These well-known events ultimately led to the further massacre of thousands of Stambouliote Armenians.[60] For once European ambassadors actually witnessed an Armenian massacre with their own eyes rather than reading about it in consular reports. Many of them were deeply shocked. European journalists described the events in morbid detail. Some European diplomats helped civilians who were fleeing the massacre, though they were unable to prevent or stop it. Britain's Ambassador Currie wrote:

> The last few days have enabled me to realise what St Bartholomew's Day was like, and the sights I have witnessed have made a most profound impression upon me . . . The awful cold-blooded barbarity of the mob, which was deliberately organized and armed by the Turkish government, makes one forget the provocation which the Turks undoubtedly received, and long for the punishment of the real authors of these abominations.[61]

SALISBURY'S LAST ATTEMPT TO REVIVE THE CONCERT OF EUROPE

On October 20, 1896, in the wake of the massacres at Constantinople, Salisbury sent a long memorandum to the other powers in a final attempt to revive the European Concert and seek collective agreement.[62] As Bloxham notes, Salisbury expressed his distaste and that of British public opinion for Ottoman rule and pursued "something approximating a genuinely humanitarian policy (albeit one still heavily coloured by sentiments of Christian confraternity), at least in terms of [his] pronouncements."[63] Salisbury's démarche also shows the extent to which a particular practice of humanitarian intervention on behalf of Ottoman Christians had been consolidated throughout the century.

Salisbury claimed that the time had come to resolutely confront the Ottoman Empire, "a dominion which by its own vices is crumbling into ruin."[64] He reiterated the need to preserve the Concert of Europe and to intervene unanimously and in the form of a coalition.[65] The prime minister wrote that, in the interest of general peace, the European powers earnestly desired to maintain the fabric of the Ottoman Empire, at least in that extensive portion of it in which the mixed character of the population made an autonomous Christian government impossible. He made it clear that Great Britain had no self-interest in the matter and did not wish to create an autonomous Armenian province. He reminded his European counterparts that Europe had "to secure due protection in these regions to the Christian subjects of the Porte."[66] The Ottoman government had been unable to provide the elementary conditions of good government for its Christian subjects. The insecurity of the lives and property of the Christian subjects of the Porte was as pronounced as was the misgovernment under which Christians and Muslims suffered unrest and over which the officials were powerless to exercise control. In the prime minister's view, the Ottoman government was "powerless" (i.e., unable) as well as unwilling to stop the "indiscriminate and wide-reaching slaughter of which the Turkish officials, and a portion of the Moslem population under their guidance or with their connivance, have been guilty, has had for its nominal aim the maintenance of the Sultan's Government."

According to Salisbury, the Ottoman government was responsible for massacre, acts of "atrocious cruelty," and acts that today would qualify as ethnic cleansing, such as "driving away a large portion of the classes by whom the industry and trade of the country was carried on." The government of Constantinople was also responsible for the "extermination" of the Armenians (acts that Salisbury distinguished from those aimed at "driving away" the Armenians).[67] His central point was that once the powers reached a unanimous solution, it should be put into operation, regardless of Ottoman sovereignty. Salisbury claimed that a collective intervention was fully justified. The intervention on grounds of humanity would have assured peace in Europe and the territorial status quo of the Turkish Empire and prevented the occurrence of further massacre and atrocity. While Austria-Hungary and Italy promptly agreed, the French and Russian governments opposed the use of force. Thus nothing was done.

Addressing the annual Guild Hall ceremony in London on October 29, 1896, Salisbury ruled out any unilateral act by Great Britain and concluded that only the sultan could achieve the amelioration of the state of affairs in the Muslim and Christian communities in the Ottoman Empire.[68] In private, on October 24, he had bluntly replied to his cousin, Bishop Edward Talbot of Rochester, who had written exhorting him to use "the stick or the threat of it" to enforce reforms in the Ottoman Empire:

What stick? Bombard Yildiz? Our experts assure us that we could not force the Dardanelles without the loss of several ironclads. They may be wrong—but that is what two or three successive "sea-Lords" have told us. When you have done it the Sultan would reiter to Br [sic] which your guns will not reach. You cannot go after him—for he has 200,000 men in and around Constantinople, besides a good many more within reach; and *you* would be sorely puzzled to land 50,000. People talk of stopping the customs at Smyrna. They are already the security for loans; you would only hurt the bondholders. . . . I have argued on the assumption that the other Powers would remain neutral during an attack on Turkey. I am concerned to say that I have adopted this hypothesis, not because I believe it to be true or possible, but for facility of calculation; just as in physics we calculate the action of forces in a vacuum, though a vacuum is actually unobtainable.[69]

Salisbury's last attempt failed. "At the zenith of pro-Armenian sentiment, Britain's ability to help the Armenians was at its nadir."[70] As the *Revue Générale de Droit International Public* put it in late 1896, given the annihilation of the entire Armenian population, we can now talk of the pacification of Armenia. No intervention had taken place because it would have thwarted the European powers' self-interest, and nonintervention had left the Ottoman Armenians in worse condition than before 1894.[71] In the absence of Russian support, and with the Cretan and Macedonian crises still unresolved (see chapters 9 and 10), a solution to the Armenian Question was packed away and left in abeyance.[72]

The decade 1897–1907 was punctuated by a series of massacres of smaller proportions in comparison to those of 1894–96. The Armenian Revolutionary Federation (ARF), in its world congress of 1898, declared that without European intervention it would be impossible to bring to a successful conclusion the struggle to free the Armenian people. Therefore the ARF would be funneled into the task of bringing about intervention through all means. Reforms, the ARF argued, would be granted only to a people up in arms, in protest. To attract European attention, arms and a revolutionary spirit were to be introduced into Anatolia. During the early 1900s the ARF would continue to prepare Ottoman Armenians for "self-defense." Notably it was involved in another insurrection in Sasun in 1904 and tried to assassinate the sultan in 1905.[73]

The 1909 Massacres in the Province of Adana

In 1908, when the Committee for Union and Progress deposed the sultan and took power, it seemed that a new era had begun for the Ottoman Empire, as well as for the Armenians. In fact, a new wave of massacres occurred in early 1909. According to the British ambassador at Constantinople, Sir Gerard Lowther, there had been numerous instances of Kurdish attacks and robberies in the Armenian-populated areas of Mush and Bitlis. On April 13, 1909, disturbances broke out in the city of Adana, the capital of the *vilayet* of the same name and composed of five *sandjaks*: Mersin, Adana, Djebel-Bereket, Kozan, and Selefke. The British vice consul, C.H.M. Doughty-Wiley, arrived in Adana from Mersin in time to witness massacres of Armenians that lasted from April 13 to 16. Despite Doughty-Wiley's warnings and demands, the local administration did nothing to stop the slaughter. The consul estimated that nearly two thousand Armenians perished in Adana and between fifteen and twenty-five thousand perished in the nearby villages. In his report to Lowther, the vice consul categorically rejected the charges of Armenian aggression, noting that the massacres had started simultaneously in several districts of the city. He was convinced that the local authorities were at least aware of the preparations for the massacre. Muslim resentment about the constitutional freedoms given to Christians was a major precipitant, as, inadvertently, were rather ostentatious Armenian nationalistic celebrations of this freedom. Economic jealousy is another explanatory factor, for many Muslim merchants benefited from Armenian losses. According to Bloxham, demographic shifts were also significant, particularly given the backdrop of recent famine at a time when Cilicia had become a reception area for Christians fleeing the 1890s massacres, Muslim migrant workers, and Balkan and Caucasian migrants. Migrants Kurds, Turcomans, and Circassians would all be prominent in attacking Armenians in similar social classes.[74]

When the Young Turks returned to power on April 24, 1909, they deployed the Rumelian regiments from Damascus and Beirut to Adana to restore public order, which, however, only prolonged the massacres as the troops joined in the pogrom.[75] A British eyewitness testified that the Ottoman soldiers attacked the Armenian district, targeting the Mushegh school and Armenian church, where thousands of Armenian residents had gathered seeking refuge. As a result of the "restoration of public order" by the military and local authorities, 4,437 Armenian houses were destroyed.[76]

As soon as news of the massacres reached Constantinople, the European ambassadors made strong representations to the Porte. The British, Russian, French, German, Italian, and U.S. governments dispatched a total of eight battleships to the Cilician port of Mersin. On May 2, by the peremptory orders of the Ottoman government, the bloodshed at Adana stopped, though massacres continued elsewhere in the province. The violence hit the Armenian communities in the Amanus, the valley of the Orontes, Jabal Musa, and Jabal Aqra, as well as Aleppo, where 368 Armenians died. In the Amanus, the majority of the Armenians were slain in the towns and villages. At Antioch, contrary to the solemn assurances of the district governor that no harm would come to the Armenians of the city if they surrendered their arms, local mobs massacred approximately 500, comprising about half the members of the community. When survivors fled to the nearby mountains, their homes and shops were ransacked and burned.[77]

As had happened during the Cretan intervention of 1866–68, European military commanders saved civilian populations. For instance, the refugees from Kasab, assembled at Basit, were transported to Latakia on the French ships *Jules Ferry* and *Niger*. The arrival of the British battleship *Triumph* induced Ottoman irregulars active in the coastal villages around Antioch to retreat forthwith to Antioch. At Antioch, the American missionary Rev. Martin, the British vice consul, Douvek, the Mission des Capucins, and the Soeurs de l'Apparition did everything within their means to alleviate the plight of the surviving Armenians, and the French consul Potton extended his government's protection to the local Armenian community. The crew of the French cruiser *Victor Hugo*, which had arrived in the region of Kheder-Bek, distributed provisions to the beleaguered Armenian population. These and many other individual instances of humanitarian aid or rescue, described in Georges Brézol's and Charles Woods's accounts, did not amount to a humanitarian intervention.[78] Officially, the French rejected the idea of a European intervention to address the consequences of the Adana massacres. The British foreign secretary, Sir Edward Grey, considered a limited diplomatic intervention to be useless and provocative since the Armenians might be encouraged to take actions that would incite Muslims to stage massacres on a massive scale and necessitate a full-scale military intervention by the powers.[79]

While, as Peter Balakian writes, there were heroic bystanders and rescuers like Doughty-Wylie, Lawson, William Chambers, the American Red Cross and other missionaries on the scene, there was no military humanitarian intervention. The irony that the warships of seven nations—Britain, France, Italy, Austria-Hungary, Russia, Germany, and the United States—were stationed just miles away off the coast and did not intervene only highlighted their failure. The views of the Swiss *Journal de Genève* on the massacres of Adana and the nonintervention by the European powers are more nuanced than those of Balakian. Anchoring warships off the Cilician coast was a very ineffective act. Even if marines had landed, they could have protected only the port and some coastal areas. Such a landing might have triggered further massacres in the inland. Hence, the only sensible intervention would have been to land a big army in Asia Minor. Which European power would have agreed to undertake such a military operation to save the lives of strangers? Such an operation would have been a long-lasting military occupation, indistinguishable from a war of conquest. Only one power seemed to have the military capacity (and geographical proximity) to undertake it: Russia. The other powers, the *Journal de Genève* wrote, would have never accepted such a plan. The only thing that one could do to reduce the suffering of these Christian populations (who, the editorial noted, belonged to the same "race" as the Europeans) was to send them money, clothing, and food and to support humanitarian relief actions. This was what the mighty European powers could do on behalf of fellow Christians slaughtered by "barbarian" populations and "half-civilized" rulers.

BRITISH AND FRENCH PUBLIC OPINION AND THE ARMENIAN QUESTION

The British public showed great interest in the Armenian Question, although overall the popular agitation in the 1890s was weaker than it was in the 1870s over the Bulgarian atrocities. Charities, philanthropists, and pressure groups failed to enhance the government action, though this time they were willing to do something against massacre.[80] Armenian societies and émigré groups in Great Britain and France helped to develop a pro-Armenian public opinion movement.[81] Many prominent members of the British political elite, Conservative and Liberal alike, sympathized with the Armenians and demanded forceful actions from the government. The pro-Armenian movement transcended political and even congregational boundaries. Anglicans and nonconformists gathered under the same roof to organize the relief of the Armenians. Transparty meetings and public speeches were numerous. Intellectuals and men of letters actively took part in the debate on the Armenian Question. The Eastern Question Association published the first pamphlet on the Armenian situation in 1877.[82] As had happened on other occasions throughout the century, British poets wrote verses favorably describing the Armenians.[83] Some pro-Armenian authors—above all the Duke of Argyll and Canon MacColl—were self-proclaimed experts on the Eastern Question.[84] The amount and the nature of pamphlets, books, and newspaper articles on the Armenian Question were comparable to those published in 1876 on the subject of the Bulgarian atrocities.[85]

Prominent British public figures joined various Anglo-Armenian societies in the 1890s. The Anglo-Armenian Association was founded by James Bryce in 1893 and was headed by MPs Francis Stevenson and Edward Atkin, the latter of whom later served as chancellor of the exchequer.[86] Another pro-Armenian group politically close to the Tories, the Grosvenor House Association, headed by the Duke of Westminster, was established with Salisbury's blessing. Among its members was MacColl, now canon of Ripon. The International Association of the

Friends of Armenia, founded in 1896, incorporated the Armenian Information Bureau. Its objectives were to disseminate information and literature on Armenia and educate the British public on the subject, as well as to facilitate interaction between the various groups engaged in Armenian relief efforts.[87] The Friends of Armenia, formed in London in 1897, published a monthly called *Friends of Armenia*, with the self-declared objective of the revival of the ancient Armenian nation.[88] In March 1897 this society sent Cambridge University palaeontology professor J. Rendel Harris and his wife, Helen, on a fact-finding trip to Asia Minor. Rendel Harris edited the English translation of one of the most influential books on the Armenian massacres, written in German by Johannes Lepsius.[89] Upon their return to Britain, the Harrises published their correspondence with friends in Britain and missionaries in Asia Minor.[90] This publication added to the general public's knowledge of the situation.

With very few exceptions, as in the case of Bulgaria, these "experts" did not endorse the cause of Armenian independence or show particular sympathy toward Armenian nationalism and nationalist groups. This heterogeneous group of pro-Armenian authors agreed that the Armenians were the innocent victims of massacre and of very serious violations of the rights of humanity. They all held the sultan and his government responsible for a planned "extermination," and for torturing, raping, and dishonoring family life at its very source. Authors close to the Liberals emphasized, more than the others, the similarities between the Bulgarian atrocities and events in the eastern provinces of the Ottoman Empire or in Constantinople. They compared the massacres of Batak and of Sasun.[91] Pro-Armenian publications repeatedly discussed the outrages against and rape of Armenian women as an indicator of the extent of Ottoman "barbarity," and for the same reasons they indulged in morbid details of all sorts of torture and atrocities inflicted on the Armenians.

As far as the question of intervention was concerned, pro-Armenian groups clearly wanted the European powers to intervene. These authors attempted to answer two fundamental questions: What rights did Britain and Europe have to interfere in the internal affairs of the Ottoman Empire? And what responsibilities did Britain and Europe have toward the Armenians? Every analysis of the Armenian massacres invariably mentioned article 61 of the Treaty of Berlin and the Sublime Porte's obligation therein to carry out reforms. In W. T. Stead's opinion, the treaty sanctioned Europe's right to intervene and moral duty to do so.[92] Stead, who extensively quoted legal scholar Rolin Jaequemyns, argued that the Armenians, as well as other Christian populations of the Ottoman Empire, were entitled by the Treaty of Paris of 1856 to consider the sultan's promises of reform at the very least as implicitly guaranteed by Europe. Europe, by the very fact of its having saved the Ottoman Empire from ruin or dissolution, had not only acquired the right, but also contracted the obligation to secure for the Armenians, as well as the Greeks and Bulgarians, the accomplishment of these promises. Articles 61 and 62 of the Treaty of Berlin solemnly warranted, by express international legislative enactment, the right of the Armenians of "Asiatic Turkey" to their lives and the security of their persons and property. And because of the bilateral convention of June 4, 1878 (the Cyprus Convention), Britain had "a special and more direct responsibility" as an ally and associate of the Porte to introduce the necessary reforms.[93]

In France the pro-Armenian (*philarménien*) movement was as vigorous and dynamic as in Great Britain.[94] Just as in Britain, the pillars of the French pro-Armenian movement were part of the pantheon of French idealists: men of letters, poets such as such as Anaïs Caumel Decazis,[95] historians, and publicists, whose intellectual courage was matched by their pathos for what they considered to be supreme issues of humanity, truth, and justice. The vectors of their voices were a number of reviews read by French elites, such as *Le Mercure de France, La Revue Blanche, La Revue de Paris*, and *Le Correspondant*. These reviews published articles by academics such as Pierre Quillard and Paul Passy[96] and by public figures like Anatole France, Francis de Pressensé,[97] Henri Rochefort, Albert Vandal, [98] Victor Bérard, Bernard Lazare, Father Charmetant, Denys Cochin, Pierre Isaac, Albert de Mun, Jean Jaurès, Jules Lemaitre, and future prime minister Georges Clemenceau.[99] Among the most active French *philarménien* groups was the Comité Franco-Arménien.[100] Many of its members had personal ties with members of the French government, and some of them would become editors of or contributors to the review *Pro Armenia*. The chief editor of this review was Pierre Quillard, who met several times with the French foreign affairs minister, Théopile Delcassé, to discuss the Armenian Question.[101] The magazine's editorial board included Anatole France, Clemenceau, Jaurès, and E. de Roberty.[102]

The assumption made by French pro-Armenians that through their actions the government might change its policy and thereby help improve the lot of the Armenian subjects of the sultan proved ill-conceived. The reason for their failure lies not in the methods or aims of the French protest movement but rather in the French government's determination not to interfere in Ottoman internal affairs. Contrary to what happened in Great Britain, French public opinion and the press heavily criticized the government's support for the Sublime Porte. On November 3, 1896, a group of deputies launched an interpellation, demanding an explanation of the rationale behind the government's policy on the Armenian issue. The leaders of the transparty parliamentary action were Denys Cochin, who, thanks to his personal ties to Ambassador Paul Cambon, was fully apprised of the nature of the ongoing massacres; Albert de Mun, the mouthpiece of the Catholic Right; and Jean Jaurès, representing the Socialist Party. Foreign Minister Gabriel Hanotaux defended his policy by replying that the Concert of Europe should work with the Ottoman government to ensure the well-being of the Ottoman Empire, and that "no direct interference" (*immixtion directe*) or threat of intervention would be allowed. He insisted that the proposed reforms should be extended to the entire population of the empire and not be limited to the areas inhabited by the Armenians. Not surprisingly, this was exactly the same point of view held by the Russian government. Supported mainly by the deputies of the center, Hanotaux carried the day by winning a vote of confidence by 402 to 90.

As in Great Britain, public opinion and pressure groups in France transcended traditional political or even religious divisions. Prominent French Protestants, such as Franck Puaux, director of the *Revue Chrétienne*, and Louis Vernes, director of *La Revue du Christianisme Libérale*, were also well-known *philarméniens*.[103] The Catholic Bureau des Oeuvres d'Orient published Father Charmetant's "*martyrologue arménien*," which included all the cases of massacre and even outrages such as the kidnapping of "*jeunes vierges*," a particularly sensitive issue and, to many Europeans, incontrovertible evidence of violation of the *droits de l'humanité*.[104] French pro-Armenian publications portrayed the Armenians as fellow Christians and Europeans thanks to their ancient culture and to the alleged "biological superiority of the Armenian mind with respect to all other Orientals."[105] By qualifying Armenians as "*Grecs d'Asie*," supporters conceptualized the understanding that, except for Caucasian Armenians, they shared a Mediterranean "*européanité*," thus turning these communities into the "*avant-poste de la civilisation européenne en Asie*."[106] This explains why the Oeuvre des Ecoles d'Orient was on the front line of the struggle in favor of the Armenians, together with lay authors such as Bérard, who firmly believed in a more secular *mission civilisatrice*. Transparty parliamentary action was the consequence of what historians Vincent Duclert and Gilles Pécout have called a revolt of the humanist and religious conscience in the face of the extent of the massacres. Politicians from different political backgrounds witnessed the failure of "civilized" countries to implement the promises made in the Treaty of Berlin; they were appalled by the discovery of a criminal governmental policy and puzzled by the inability of the European Concert to act; and, finally, they were irate at the failure of Hanotaux's diplomacy.[107]

The interpenetration and transnational exchange of ideas on the Armenian Question between France and Britain were extensive. In the preface of a work on Armenia, *Les Massacres d'Arménie*, Gladstone was unmistakably echoed in Clemenceau's words: *"qui parlera d'humanité au peuple souffrant d'un gouvernement inhumain."* The themes and tone of public lectures, conferences, books, articles, and pamphlets by French *philarméniens* were very similar to those of their British friends. Pro-Armenian intellectuals and politicians, both French and British, shared the concept and a common language of a corpus of "rights of humanity," which they thought had to be respected everywhere, even by "uncivilized" countries such as the Ottoman Empire. Despite their different backgrounds and ideologies, French deputies, British MPs, other pro-Armenian intellectuals and public figures on both sides of the channel spoke the same language with regard to the process of exclusion of which the Armenians were victims. They spoke of the same intolerable chain (spiral) of physical elimination, and of Ottoman, "barbarian," state violence as demonstrative of the Sublime Porte's and the sultan's responsibility for the massacres. *Pro Armenia* was the most impressive transnational attempt to do something for the Armenians.[108]

Pro Armenia offices in London, Paris, and Rome worked together closely, not in the name of religion but in the name of humanity. They wished to provide some form of European protectorate or supervision to those populations to whom the sultan's government "denied life, liberty, security in property—all the elements of orderly life."[109] In 1904 they published simultaneously a special report of the proceedings of a conference held in London on June 29 under the auspices of the International Eastern Question Association (see chapter 10).[110] Other European transnational groups, such as the Bureau International Permanent de la Paix, also became involved in the Armenian Question and coordinated their common action with the British and French pro-Armenians.[111]

. . .

The European powers' nonintervention in favor of the Ottoman Armenians is important, for it reveals that despite the extent and incontrovertible evidence of massacre, atrocity, and extermination, the nature of the international system prevented intervention from taking place. The horror that these massacres aroused in "civilized" Europe was not enough to trigger a humanitarian intervention. Saving strangers, even Christian coreligionists, was an international practice subordinated to the maintenance of peace and the security of Europe. Salisbury's policy or Hanotaux's response in Parliament revolved around the issue of humanitarian intervention. European political and intellectual elites shared transnational experiences and discourses centered on a number of common principles concerning the most basic rights of humanity or, more precisely, of "suffering Christianity" and the duties of governments in this sphere. However, the ideas, initiatives, and transnational networks and movements did not bring about a humanitarian intervention.

Nonintervention on behalf of the Ottoman Armenians is related to the Armenian genocide, even if there is no straight line connecting the massacres of the 1890s with the genocide of 1915. As historian Donald Bloxham points out, the guiding ideologies of the perpetrators were different, and the earlier killings were not conducted under the same sort of close, centralized authority as their later counterparts. However, both occurred in the key context of the empire's terminal decline, where the 1894–96 killing was a precedent, shaping the mindset of state and victims alike.[112] The European powers' involvement in Ottoman internal affairs was a key element in exacerbating the Ottoman-Armenian dynamic toward genocide, while Turkish sensitivity about external intervention on behalf of the Armenians was a vital contributory factor to the emergence of denial. Armenians held the attention of a large number of their European contemporaries, for "suffering Christianity" was often juxtaposed with the "infidel," "barbarous" Ottomans. The Europeans did not tolerate the massacre of so many Christians; therefore the destruction did not go uncriticized. Frequently the Ottoman leaders responded to external criticism by comparing the Ottoman situation with the record of European colonialism and slavery, but to no avail. The fact that Christian powers ignored the conditions of massacre of Muslims had relevant consequences, even in the case of the Armenians. Protests of Christian powers unaccompanied by substantive action had a detrimental effect on the lives of the Armenians for Ottoman governments and populations that questioned the loyalty of the Armenians. The powers' rhetorical bias toward "suffering Christianity" only confirmed the Ottomans' prevailing sense of embattlement and identification with suffering Islam.[113] Nonetheless, as Bloxham puts it, though the ambit of historical and moral responsibility for the massacres of Armenians extends to the European powers, criminal responsibility remains entirely on the perpetrators. The European powers were not coperpetrators, and the Armenians were not simply victims of European diplomacy. As the epigraph at the beginning of the chapter reveals, the responsibility for the massacres lay with sultan. The French ambassador at Constantinople, Paul Cambon, confirmed the horror of the massacres and the encouragement given to Kurdish authorities by a central government that did not want and could not contain their actions. French agents personally ascertained the misery that after the massacre, pillage, and fire decimated this unfortunate population and left it without shelter, clothing, or food. If sometimes, because of a natural sentiment among these miserable people, some exaggerations had slipped into the accounts of their suffering, the deeds ascertained by the French agents largely justified the horror that these sad events inspired in Europe and the resulting attitude toward the sultan who was, without any doubt, responsible for the situation.

CHAPTER NINE

The Second Intervention in Crete (1896–1900)

> Les canons de l'Europe, qui devraient être tournés contre les
> Turcs qui massacrent, bombarde[nt] les chrétiens massacrés.
> —Count de Chaudordy, *La France*
> *et la Question d'Orient*, 1897

THE SECOND MILITARY intervention by the European powers in Crete took place shortly after the Armenian Question was left in abeyance. This intervention was clearly not an instance of humanitarian intervention, but it deserves attention for it points out the extent to which European governments could act contrary to the wishes of public opinion. The latter accused European cabinets of siding with the oppressors instead of acting against massacre. The purpose of the intervention was to help the Ottoman government restore law and order on the island after an insurgency and to avoid further threats to an increasingly fragile international order. As the British ambassador at Constantinople, Philip Currie, put it, the military occupation of Crete amounted to "placing the island in trust in the hands of the powers." It was an *ante litteram* "peace-enforcement" operation following the Porte's request for intervention by the powers, and it was supposed to give time for finding a political solution to the crisis.[1] The military occupation of Crete shows the unintended consequences of the intervention, especially for Muslim Cretans. This intervention also illustrates that, despite acute tensions and rivalry, European powers could still agree on collective intervention even when the issue concerned the Eastern Question. Surely the initial Ottoman cooperation and the conditions of the military operation contrasted with the Armenian Question.

The political and military commitment of the European powers in Crete was not adequate to the circumstances, for each intervening state was entangled in other crises (e.g., the British in South Africa) or had other, more important interests at stake. The German government was concerned only to show itself to be supportive of the sultan and completely disregarded the fate of civilian populations. Russia and Austria-Hungary wished not to upset the fragile status quo in the Balkan Peninsula, and whatever decision they took on Crete depended on broader geopolitical considerations. The only government that had a clear and declared political interest in the affairs of Crete was Athens, which believed that the time had come to annex the island to Greece and did not hesitate to declare war on the Ottoman Empire in 1897. The European powers' decision to prop up the Sublime Porte frustrated Cretan insurgents, Greece, and in the end the Sublime Porte, for, after the annexation of Bosnia and Herzegovina by Austria-Hungary in 1908, the European powers eventually allowed the union of Crete with Greece.

CRETE DURING THE 1880s AND 1890s

As a consequence of the international settlement of the Eastern crisis, on October 23, 1878, the sultan signed the Halepa Convention, which modified the Organic Law of 1868.[2] According to this treaty, a Muslim or Christian general governor would be appointed for a five-year period. If he were a Muslim, he would have a Christian assistant and vice versa. The General Assembly of Crete was to consist of forty-nine local Christian and thirty-one Muslim residents who would meet once a year, decide on local needs, and use any surplus tax revenues for public services. Greek and Turkish would be the official languages on the island. This constitution was placed under the auspices of the international law of Europe by article 23 of the Treaty of Berlin, which thus gave it an international character. The European powers had the right to supervise the introduction of reforms, although nothing specified the mechanisms guaranteeing their enforcement.

Just over ten years later, in 1889, Christian Cretans revolted because, they claimed, the Porte was not respecting the Halepa Convention. The French government explicitly condemned the Ottoman government's opposition to the "*intérêts de la paix européenne, comme à ceux de la justice et de l'humanité*," but it took no further action.[3] Neither did Great Britain. In August 1889 Salisbury warned Greece that Great Britain could not allow "material intervention" in Crete and declared himself opposed to an intervention by the European powers in favor of the Christian Cretans.[4] The French foreign minister, Eugène Spuller, entirely shared this point of view.[5] The situation on Crete rapidly drifted into anarchy.[6] As had happened in 1867, many Christian Cretan civilians began to seek refuge in Greece. In August 1889 no less than four thousand had fled the island.[7] At the same time, because of the persecutions of Christian insurgents, more than ten thousand Muslim Cretans hastily abandoned their villages and headed to the towns or Ottoman fortresses in a bid for protection. Despite Ottoman relief and generous donations through private Ottoman subscriptions, these refugees started plundering to stave off starvation. The spiral of events triggered by the insurrection inevitably led to greater disturbances in the urban areas of Crete, such as Canea, Candia, and Rethymno, where Muslim civilians appropriated the properties left by Christian town dwellers, as well as in rural areas, where Christian Cretans from the interior likewise appropriated the properties and goods left by fleeing Muslim villagers.[8] In November 1889 the sultan granted amnesty to the insurgents and promised to introduce financial and administrative reforms.[9] No intervention followed the disturbances. Moreover, British consul Alfred Biliotti[10] set up a fact-finding inquiry that ascertained that Greek newspapers were greatly exaggerating reports of massacres and other atrocities, although massacres were not pure imagination: 50 Christians and 42 Muslims had died; 6,640 Muslim and 2,456 Christian private buildings were devastated; 57 mosques and 14 churches were ruined; and 37 Muslim and 115 Christian schools were destroyed.[11]

By the end of the summer of 1895, with the Ottoman government busy dealing with the Armenian Question, a new insurrection started in Crete when the governor adjourned the Cretan Assembly. Thousands of internally displaced Muslim civilians coming from the villages once again entered the towns seeking protection, and thousands of Christians again fled to Greece. As in 1889, the European governments reiterated that they had no intention whatsoever of undertaking an intervention, which they deemed too risky because of the ongoing Armenian Question. In case of massacres, Captain Drury, commander of HMS *Hood*, told Consul Biliotti, protection would be offered exclusively to British subjects by the temporary landing of an armed force.[12] The other European warships in Cretan waters would do the same.

Because of the state of unrest on the island, the Ottoman government requested assistance first from the British and then from the French government. Salisbury replied that Great Britain would assist the sultan's government with a view to pacifying Crete. If the Ottoman government wished it so, Biliotti could mediate with the insurgents, though any European action ought to be collective.[13] On June 24 the six European ambassadors in Constantinople presented a collective declaration to the Porte, known as the Four Points declaration, in which they endeavored to restore tranquillity in Crete on behalf of the Ottoman Empire. They advised the Porte to adopt the following measures: nomination of a Christian governor, revival of the Halepa Convention, convocation of the assembly, and general amnesty.[14] The intervention was the opposite of a humanitarian intervention. It followed the invitation of a government threatened by internal disturbances. From the Sublime Porte's perspective, so utterly opposed to any interference in the Armenian Question, the situation looked very different. First, the province of Crete had a majority of Christians, whereas the Armenians were minorities living in provinces inhabited by a majority of Muslims. Second, the Porte knew that an intervention in Crete had taken place in the past and might well occur again in the future. Third, the sultan's government was aware that the European powers—especially Russia and Austria-Hungary—would not allow the union of Crete with Greece, for it would have destabilized the already fragile European equilibrium, especially in the Balkans. It is plausible to think that the timely request of the Porte to the European powers was a shrewd move to prevent further, more invasive European interference.

On July 3 the Porte accepted Four Points declaration and dispatched 3,200 men from Salonica, 2,400 troops from Kosovo, and four battalions of the Aleppo Army Corps to Crete. The aim of the operation was to avoid the landing of foreign (i.e., Greek) insurgents and to make sure that no supplies (especially no arms) would reach local insurgents. With the Porte's agreement, the European powers set up a blockade of the island, keeping only one port open for the purposes of trade. The European governments agreed that the consuls on Crete should act together and cooperate with the commanders of the vessels already stationed at the port of Canea.[15] Multilateral cooperation guaranteed that none of the powers would unilaterally benefit from the situation. Unfortunately it had the unintended consequence of slowing down the relief initiatives of a number of charities on behalf of civilian populations, for each decision had to be approved by all the consuls.[16]

Greece managed to smuggle arms and to land men on the island.[17] The situation there deteriorated: there was pillaging, murdering, torching of houses and villages, and even the deliberate cutting down of olive trees. In the meantime, refugees continued to arrive on Greek shores; more than 1,200 women and children reached the Piraeus during the summer of 1896. In Rethymno Captain Paget of the British ship *Dolphin* reported that the 2,509 Christian refugees in the town were in a precarious condition and that dysentery and nonmalignant typhoid were rife.[18] They were the lucky ones. According to British vice consul Calocherino, 20,000 Muslim refugees in Rethymno survived in an appalling state.[19] In Canea the situation was so serious that, in mid-August, Blanc authorized that about 1,000 refugees, only 100 of whom were French subjects, at the Roman Catholic and Sisters of Charity convents be housed onboard French ships.[20]

On August 25, 1896, the European powers made a collective proposal to the Porte, inspired by the *Règlements* of Samos and of Lebanon.[21] Three days later, a surprisingly cooperative Abdul Hamid agreed to a "Thirteen Points" project of reform as long as the Cretans would return to lawful behavior. This project included the five-year appointment of a Christian governor general, to be proclaimed by the sultan with the approval of the European powers. It also involved the appointment of a commission, including European officers, to reorganize the gendarmerie, and another commission to reform the judicial system on the island. The European ambassador would monitor the execution of the arrangement in the Ottoman capital, while the consuls would supervise the implementation on the island. Immediate cessation of hostilities and a return to order was the main condition, and any refusal to comply would instantly end mediation by the European powers. The consuls in Crete notified the Christian deputies of the text of the arrangement and called on them to declare their unreserved acceptance of the reforms within three days.[22] On September 4 the Cretan Assembly formally accepted the proposal.

For obvious reasons, this arrangement could not be immediately implemented in full. By the beginning of 1897, dissatisfied Christians agreed on a *levée en masse* for the following spring.[23] On February 5 a fire was started in Canea, which resulted in the majority of the Christian areas of the town being set ablaze. On February 8 a Greek naval squadron was sent into Cretan waters with the announced purpose of saving Christians from massacre and "assisting the revolution" on the island, though Biliotti was adamant that in fact this put local Christians in even greater danger. It certainly threatened to trigger Ottoman reinforcements from other Turkish provinces. A Greek torpedo flotilla under the command of the king's second son, Prince George, was dispatched from Piraeus amid scenes of delirious enthusiasm.[24] On February 16 Colonel Vassos and a thousand (five thousand according to French sources) Greek soldiers landed ten miles west of Canea and occupied the island in the name of King George I.[25] The immediate evacuation of European subjects onto warships, the increased pace of the exodus of Christians to Greece—embarked on Greek warships carrying what the government of Athens claimed to be a unilateral "humanitarian intervention"—and the increased number of Muslim civilians who fled from the villages into the main Cretan towns contributed to the European powers' decision to occupy the towns of Canea and Rethymno and to organize a foreign gendarmerie.[26] Each power monitored the actions of the others, as the instructions to Rear Admiral Edouard Pottier, commander of the French naval division detached to the Levant, demonstrate. On February 6 he received a clear order not to let any other power (i.e., Great Britain) be more active than France "*notamment en ce qui concerne la force des troupes que vous devriez débarquer*," and to protect French interests in Cretan waters.[27]

THE INTERNATIONAL MILITARY OCCUPATION OF CRETE (1897–99)

On February 15 onboard the *Sicilia*—with Italian admiral Napoleone Canevaro acting as senior flag officer—the admirals agreed to land 100 men of each nation to provide temporary protection of Canea. A mixed force of 450, composed of 100 British marines and as many French, Italians, and Russians, along with 50 Austrian seamen, occupied that town.[28] The collective nature of the occupation required a complex, time-consuming, and not fully synchronized multilateral decision-making process. The consuls in Crete acted in concert and referred to the ambassadors or directly to their respective governments; the admirals similarly had to reach a consensus before acting and also had to refer to their respective naval ministries.

The temporary military occupation of Crete was primarily intended against Greece and was taken with the full agreement of the Ottoman authorities. As Holland and Markides put it, "the occupation had not been set in motion to further Christian aspirations, as Greek opinion supposed, but to stuff the genie back into its bottle. Misunderstanding on this point had profound implications. Clarity was not helped by the joint European statement that Crete was to be held *en dépôt* under the Concert's protection. But where was it to be *en dépôt* to?"[29]

If the intervening states did note the suffering of the civilian populations of all creeds in Crete, it was because of the circumstances of the intervention.[30] As the Russian minister Agenor Goluchowski pointed out, the occupation of the island and the simultaneous prohibition for the Ottoman government to send further troops to Crete entailed the European powers' responsibility to protect Muslims Cretans. Without European protection, he argued, Muslims would have been at the mercy of Christians, who would have massacred them.[31] During the early stages of the occupation, the only government speaking of the "sentiments of humanity" or "in the name of humanity" was the Ottoman Empire, which reiterated the occupying powers' responsibility to protect Muslim Cretans and asked the Europeans to extend their occupation to the towns of Rethymno, Candia, Sitia, and Kissano-Castelli.[32]

In the early days of the occupation, the Christian insurgents in Canea attacked the international troops, whom they saw as the agents of the Ottoman government. When an apparent calm returned to the coastal towns, the daily life of the international troops became rather boring. They built tennis courts, some of them drank absinthe to excess, and enjoyed the newly opened European restaurants in Canea.[33] In the meantime, Christians who lived in the inland areas, misinformed by the Greek troops still in Crete and relying on the evidence of their own eyes as to the presence of Greek soldiers, guns, and flags, attacked Muslim positions and sacked, burned, and pillaged the villages of their foes. They paid little heed to the words of the admirals, whom they could not see and whose actions they did not understand. In the district of Selinos, a "fight of extermination" between Christians and Muslims went on for a week before the European admirals decided to extend their protection to the towns of Selinos, Candanos, and Hierapetra by anchoring warships in those bays. In Selinos, as elsewhere, lacking men and resources, the European commanders could only invite Muslim notables to monitor security in town, threatening them with severe repression if Muslim civilians were found instigating disorder. At the same time they notified the Greek commodore that Greek troops would be held responsible if Candanos Muslims were massacred.[34]

With the administration of Crete completely paralyzed and the military personnel utterly incompetent to run it, the admirals quickly realized that the pacification of the island could not be achieved without a greater number of troops and resources. They were fully aware that the success of the military action depended on the political settlement of the crisis.[35] At this stage, the Ottoman government showed itself to be very cooperative. It did not oppose the idea of Cretan autonomy along the lines of the *Règlements* of Samos and Lebanon,[36] or even the reconstitution of the gendarmerie under European command.[37] The political unwillingness to solve the crisis came from the European cabinets, who were not ready to commit themselves in Crete and whose cooperation was shaky and rather limited.

Besides the paralysis of the administration, the occupying troops faced a very complex humanitarian emergency. No less than twenty-five thousand distressed internally displaced people, in great majority Muslims, required food and medical relief. Smallpox was prevalent owing to overcrowding and lack of sufficient cleanliness and sanitary regulations among the refugees; diphtheria was reported as epidemic in Candia, where it also affected the international troops. Provisions were insufficient, and none of the European governments provided Crete with direct financial assistance. Internally displaced Muslims survived thanks to aid from Ottoman Muslim charities and some European charities. Christian families suffered as well; many continued to flee to Greece, and at least eight thousand left the town Candia. In April 1897 the admirals increased the number of troops on the island to a total of 6,570 men.[38] Up to December 1898 (extended under the orders of the high commissioner to July 1899), Crete would be divided into five sectors: the French occupied Sitia; the Italians, Lassithi; the Austro-Hungarians, Kissamos; the Russians, Rethymno; the British, Candia; and mixed detachments occupied Canea. The troops could maintain order, but they could not restore law or improve the living conditions of civilian populations. With very insufficient means, the occupying powers did what they could to enforce some humanitarian policies. Colonel Herbert Chermside (previously consul in the Armenian provinces), the British military commander responsible for the occupation of Candia, reported that some 58,000 people throughout the island were in need of food. In the town of Candia, 31,900 Muslim Cretans were barely surviving (29,000 had come from the province of Candia, and 2,900 from Sitia, Spinalonga, Hierapetra, and Mirabello) and had no resources or money to buy food.[39] The British authorities improved the sanitary conditions of their occupation sector as much as they could, but these short-term measures were mere palliatives, unable to avoid an impending humanitarian catastrophe.[40]

Because of the European governments' unwillingness to solve the Cretan Question since 1897, many diplomats on the spot agreed on a solution to the crisis that, in some respects, anticipated the Greco-Turkish exchange of population of 1922. In Chermside's opinion, "a displacement by emigration of the Moslem inhabitants must inevitably follow the establishment of Christian political and administrative ascendancy in the island."[41] The British commander noted that a similar emigration had taken place in Bulgaria, Dobruja, Serbia, Thessaly, the Caucasus, and Bosnia. The incompatibility between Christian and Muslim Cretans was not, in the view of the European diplomats, one of "race." Cretan Muslims, French consul Blanc wrote, "were as Greek as the Christians, and did not speak a word of Turkish."[42] The hatred dividing them was religious and social, for the Muslims were rich and held the majority of the properties on the island. In his view, thirty-five thousand of the eighty-five thousand Muslim Cretans should have emigrated. By the end of the century, the issue of the "emigration" of Muslim Cretans was commonplace among European military, policy-makers, and "experts." French admiral Pottier wondered if the Muslim families of Sitia (the French-occupied sector of the island) could be displaced to Tunisia. Victor Bérard, one of the most respected and active French experts on Cretan affairs and a strenuous supporter of the *Enosis*, put forth the idea of the permanent resettlement of Cretan Muslims elsewhere within the borders of the Ottoman Empire, probably at Rhodes and Adalia, where Muslim families from the Morea had resettled in the early 1830s.[43] The Porte was not opposed to the removal of the Cretan Muslims (and some local Muslim were in favor of quitting their island themselves), but for obvious reasons of prestige it could not undertake to send ships to assist the emigration of such a large body of Muslims. Moreover, the Ottoman authorities pointed out that such a proceeding would be expensive because the refugees, who were largely rural proprietors, would have to be provided with land and would need money to make a fresh start.[44] The Ottoman government lacked such financial resources and informed the European powers that there were no "empty" lands available in the neighboring provinces of the empire for that purpose.[45]

THE GRECO-OTTOMAN WAR OF 1897 AND ITS CONSEQUENCES FOR CRETE

In April 1897 Greece fostered an insurrection over its border with the Ottoman Empire and ordered a general mobilization of its forces. The Porte responded by declaring war on April 18. Thirty days later the war ended in disaster for the Greeks. The Ottoman Army severely defeated Prince Constantine's troops in Thessaly and Epirus and invaded Greece. The Peace of Constantinople, signed on November 22, 1897, restored the status quo ante bellum and imposed on Greece a war indemnity of one hundred million gold francs. Only the mediation of the European powers saved Greece from military humiliation. As a consequence of this war, the European powers demanded that the Greek government accept Cretan autonomy under Ottoman suzerainty. Athens had no choice but to submit to the request, and some Cretan insurgents leaders, including Eleutherios Venizelos, were hounded out of Crete by their Christian moderate opponents. It was now the Ottoman Empire that refused the conditions imposed by the European powers. The Greek threat having disappeared, the Ottoman government was suddenly much less inclined to accept European interference in its internal affairs.

In January 1898 Crete had still no stable, working administration or government.[46] Salisbury admitted to Courcel that the only reason a general war had not yet started was that Crete was not worth it.[47] The admirals set up a temporary executive committee, officially appointed by the Cretan Assembly. Its duty was to administer those portions of the island that complied with the Cretan Assembly, while the admirals continued to exercise their authority and "humanitarian work" in the districts occupied by European or Ottoman troops.[48] The idea was good on paper only, for it did not convince Muslim Cretans to return to their villages, which in turn made impossible the return of the Cretan Christians refugees in Greece. Colonel Chermside agreed with Biliotti that if no remedy was found before winter 1898–99, the whole population of Crete might be so completely ruined that the sums required to assist them in their distress might be beyond the island's means. This was scarcely a matter for private charity, and to solve it, a large capital sum, such as a loan, was required. The present, wrote the British consul, "was no longer a political question, but has become one of humanity."[49]

In April 1898 Germany and Austria-Hungary ended their participation in the military operations in Crete to mark their support to the Ottoman government and withdrew their ships from the blockade. Great Britain, France, Russia, and Italy thereupon divided Crete into four departments that they each administered, whereas Canea would still be occupied by a joint force.[50] The Council of Admirals' creature, the Executive Committee, was supposed to make contact with the Christian Assembly. This was clearly the precursor of a new administration. Such a shadow government, Holland and Markides argue, would need money, and money was something that Europe had always begrudged. At the end of August the admirals, at Russian instigation, decided to occupy the Dimes, dismiss the Muslim staff, and replace them with Greek subordinates. This took place on September 3 in Canea and Rethymno. The local British authorities warned that "that which is an easy task in Canea and Rethymno became a very dangerous undertaking in Candia" and stressed that there were not enough troops in the town to protect the Christians in the event of a violent backlash. They were overruled.[51]

On September 6 hundreds of Christians and Muslims perished in one of the frequent fights around Candia; some British officers, soldiers, and sailors who attempted to put an end to it were killed by native Muslims and by one or two Ottoman soldiers; Vice Consul Calocherino and his family perished as well. The ensuing massacre of approximately eight hundred Christians ended only when British warships began a blanket bombardment of the town of Candia. In a situation that remained highly explosive, with London newspapers noting that British fatalities in Candia had been more than those suffered by General Kitchener's army at Omdurman and asking for Britain to exact its price, the ambassadors of France, Great Britain, Italy, and Russia presented an ultimatum to the sultan demanding the withdrawal of Ottoman troops from Crete within a month.[52] On October 4 another threatening note stated that if the evacuation of Ottoman forces was not completed by the date fixed, the European powers, freed from every moral obligation respecting Ottoman sovereignty, would take steps to establish a regime in accordance with the wishes of the majority of Crete's inhabitants. In other words, if the sultan decided that his troops were to stay, the Europeans would allow the *Enosis*. The Porte yielded, and on November 28 the last Ottoman troops left Crete.[53] By then, the original sense of the intervention had changed. It was no longer an intervention by invitation, it was no longer collective, but it was not yet a full-fledged war against the

Ottoman Empire. It was certainly not an intervention against the Ottoman Empire. Moreover, after the departure of the Ottoman Army and authorities, the occupying powers became, *nolens volens*, the "protectors of Muslim populations."[54]

The admirals took over the provisional government of the island, delegating a commander for each of the occupied sections and an additional commander in the international zone of Canea. Each commander had the power to enforce all civil acts and collect all dues, including the administration of justice carried out in the name of the admirals.[55] On the provincial level, each of the four powers organized the administration and security of its own sector separately. For instance, in Candia, the British Provisional Administration created a central administration, which appointed district commissioners in charge of disarmament, the administration of justice, police, and finance. It created a number of commissions devoted to solving specific and urgent problems, such as relief, agriculture, mortgage, registration of Muslim property, postal service, and schools.[56] All over the island, European soldiers disarmed Muslim and Christian Cretans and promised the Muslims safety of life, property, and honor and the possibility of returning to their village homes. At the same time they promised the Christians that when all their arms were delivered up, they would be eligible for posts in the administration. Despite these measures, the conditions of civilian populations remained critical.

High Commissioner Prince George of Greece and the End of the International Occupation

The European-run blockade of the island came to an end on 23 November, with the exception of importation of arms and munitions of war. In the meantime, the European powers had taken up the question of the governorship of the island. It took lengthy negotiations to settle the matter, and only on November 26 did they invite Prince George of Greece to become high commissioner in Crete for three years.[57] In spite of objections from the Porte, Prince George assumed his new duties on that day and arrived at Canea on December 21. The Greek government, which had rejected a similar decision in the past, now accepted it, for it was no longer in a position to negotiate with the European powers. The admirals, having handed over the government to the high commissioner, now requested their own recall, leaving only a few foreign troops.

The high commissioner's responsibilities included establishing an autonomous government, creating a national militia, administering justice, granting the rights to conclude conventions and coin money, and conferring decorations.[58] The European powers seemed unwilling to delegate total power to Prince George and maintained the prerogative of organizing the gendarmerie under Italian officers (Carabinieri captain Federico Craveri was the commander of the Cretan gendarmerie, later replaced by Count Balduino Caprini, and then by Egidio Garrone). By January 6, 1899, the commissioner had already nominated a committee of fifteen members entrusted with the mandate of deciding on the constitution. In late March he appointed the first Cretan civil servants to replace the international officers in charge of the provisional administration of the occupied sectors. The transition would be lengthier and more difficult than he expected because of his numerous disagreements with European admirals and consuls.[59] In April 1899 a constitution drafted by Eleftherios Venizelos was promulgated. Crete was by then a hybrid entity, formally under Ottoman suzerainty, de facto under the European powers' trusteeship, though administered by a Greek high commissioner who often referred to the island as a "state." The new constitution gave the Cretan Muslims many good reasons to fear for their future. To them, the appointment of Prince George meant that none of the European powers would administer Crete permanently, and that sooner rather than later Crete would become Greek.[60] They were right.

Prince George almost immediately abolished Turkish as one of the official languages of the island, retaining only Greek. With the concurrence of the European powers, he removed all restrictions on the emigration of Muslims from the island. As Consul Biliotti pointed out, putting a roof over the head of Muslim families would not be sufficient to enable them to start their lives anew. Their Christian neighbors had taken the oxen, mules, horses, donkeys, plows and other agricultural implements of all the Muslim refugees in Candia when they fled their villages. This explained why they were not anxious to return to their villages. Christian refugees were no better off, and they too seemed very reluctant to go back to their villages. The question of refugees was one of money, of reparations and repatriation, similar—though on a larger scale—to the situation the European commissioners in Lebanon and Syria had dealt with in 1860–61. If Muslims did not return to their villages, a great number of Christians who were now in forced exile in Greece would be unable to return to Candia and retake possession of their houses, in which Muslim refugees from the inland villages were now living.[61]

In 1899, despite the efforts of all the occupying forces, very few Muslims had returned to their villages. The Greek government decided to stop providing relief to Cretan refugees in Greece, with the intended result of hastening their return to the island. This decision had cata-strophic consequences for the town of Candia. With Christians return-ing home, the British occupying authorities suddenly had to accom-modate Muslim refugees elsewhere. They called on private British charities, such as the Grosvenor House Committee, to come to the as-sistance of the indigent of both creeds.[62]

Throughout Europe the idea of mass emigration of Muslims looked to be the only possible solution to a developing humanitarian crisis of considerable proportions, despite the fact that European diplomats were fully aware this mass of Greek-speaking Muslims would not feel at home in any other part of the Ottoman Empire. The 1900 census confirmed that emigration of Muslim Cretans in 1899 and 1900 was considerable. Muslim Cretans were now about one-ninth of the popu-lation, as against about one-third in 1881. By the turn of the century, the statistics provided by the British provisional administration of the province of Candia revealed that no less than twenty thousand Muslim Cretans had emigrated.[63]

PHILO-CRETAN PUBLIC OPINION IN GREAT BRITAIN AND FRANCE

As during the massacres of Armenians, the interpenetration of ideas between the two shores of the channel was relevant. Transnational or-ganizations, such as the Bureau International de la Paix, through its directors Frédéric Boyer and Elie Ducommun, addressed a note to the French minister of foreign affairs in favor of Cretan self-determination.[64] Public opinion in France and Great Britain saw the European powers' intervention in Crete as the exact opposite of a humanitarian interven-tion. Pro-Cretan activists assumed that Christian Cretans were victims of massacre perpetrated by the Ottoman government and the local Muslim population. In their view, Christian Cretans were an oppressed population fighting for a just cause; therefore, the European powers should have protected them rather than acting as the gendarmes of Constantinople. The issue of the intervention in Crete was discussed by international legal scholars such as Georges Streit who went as far as to argue that Greece had a right to undertake a unilateral interven-tion on grounds of humanity on behalf of (Christian) Cretans.[65] The great majority of contemporary legal scholars, however, did not men-tion the case of Crete among instances of intervention on grounds of humanity.

Gladstone and other British Liberals denounced the intervention as suppressing the legitimate political aspirations of the Christian Cretans.[66] The House of Commons took great interest in the Cretan Question, and various MPs swiftly linked the events taking place in Crete with the massacre of Ottoman Armenians. Because of the pressure on his government, Salisbury was forced to defend the policy before the House of Lords.[67] After a specific request from Lord Kimberley, he proceeded to publish a series of *Blue Books* on the affairs of Crete.[68] Meetings and subscriptions in favor of the Christian Cretans were held everywhere in Britain. Russell, MacColl, Stevenson, and Herbert Gladstone as well as students, teachers, and university professors all sang the slogan:

> The Concert . . . the concert be hanged!
> The Powers ring of harpies round a sick jackal
> Crete must be free Crete must be free

British newspapers and periodicals were flooded with speeches, articles, poems, and letters in connection with the Cretan Question. The *Manchester Guardian* openly and vehemently supported the union of Crete with Greece and contributed to a revival of the old Philhellene spirit. The Eastern Question Association reinvigorated its role as publisher with a new series of pamphlets evocatively called "Papers of the Greek Committee."[69] The majority of the articles published in the newspapers, pamphlets, and reviews narrated epics of the Cretan Christians against the Ottomans throughout the centuries, some of them contrasting the "Cretan massacres" with those of 1860 in Lebanon and Syria.[70] In 1898 R.A.H. Bickford-Smith, a humanitarian and commissioner of the Cretan Relief Committee, published *Cretan Sketches*.[71] The book portrayed Christian Cretans as "civilized" victims of Muslim "barbarians" who had "destroyed everything."[72]

Ernest N. Bennett a journalist in Crete at the time of the occupation, had a minority opinion on the Cretan massacres. He argued that the interest shown by European public opinion and press toward the Cretan Question attracted a "plague of *specials*" (special correspondents) at Canea—some fourteen by the end of February 1897.[73] A great majority had two main things in common: they were philo-Cretan and anti-Turkish. Their articles were clearly biased against local Muslims, and the information they gathered generally came from a number of "comparatively obscure individuals in Crete."[74] The European correspondents lived in the towns, mainly in Canea. They seldom sought any information from the Ottoman authorities, and they depended largely on the news brought to them by Christians, whose accounts were certainly affected by the destruction of their property. The interpreters employed in Crete were almost exclusively Christians. Bennett's account of atrocities committed by Christians against Muslim civilians in Crete was quite uncommon and sharply contrasted with the phrase "oppressed Christians," which figured ad nauseam in the majority of accounts on Crete. In his view, the very fact of mentioning Christianity was wrong and almost "a desecration of the word Christian to apply it to the Cretans as a means for securing sympathy." The so-called Christians had slaughtered helpless women and children in cold blood and had been led to such infamous acts by their own priests, who were "veritable wolves in sheep's clothing."[75]

In France those who had massively supported the cause of the Armenians were all in favor of the annexation of Crete to Greece and resolutely opposed to the intervention "against" the Christians in Crete. Victor Bérard's book *Les Affaires de Crète*, an anti-Turkish account full of exaggerations and morbid details concerning the massacres, stressed the indignation and shame of watching the European canons keeping up in Crete the work of death carried out by the Turks in the last three centuries.[76] On February 18, 1897, a *"Grand Meeting de protestation sur les affaires de Crète—La politique du gouvernement et la politique socialiste"* was held in Paris. Some days later, in his speech at the Chamber of Deputies, Jaurès claimed that France had engaged in a conflict against its tradition of liberty and honor.[77] On February 23 Cochin evoked memories of Navarino and pleaded for an intervention *"dans un intérêt de pure humanité"* and the enforcement of reforms.[78] He claimed that if the sultan ordered massacres in Crete like those that had occurred against the Armenians, "the blood would fall upon the whole civilized world *(le sang qui sera versé retomberait sur tout le mond civilisé)."* Europe, he said, had a moral duty to carry out a "disinterested" action, to enforce reforms, and to use force if necessary, for "civilized" people had a duty to clean this corner of Europe made filthy by crime. Alexandre Millerand, who took the floor just after Cochin, pointed out that European (French) public opinion strenuously opposed the return of the island to the sultan, and hence this should not be an option. The minister of foreign affairs, Hanotaux, defended the intervention in Crete (and, at the same time, French nonintervention in favor of the Ottoman Armenians), claiming that his government, as well as other European governments, was primarily concerned with maintaining peace in Europe. He pointed out that the presence of the European admirals in Crete was intended to safeguard the security of the Christians. Hanotaux did not deny that horrors and abominations had occurred, although Frenchmen were made to consider the kind of misery that an irresponsible initiative might have led to in Europe. In his view, humanitarian intervention was subordinated to the priorities of European collective security.

. . .

The settlement of the Cretan Question was a political matter that had little to do with the well-being of local populations, Christian and Muslim alike. In 1896–97 the "peace-enforcement" intervention of the European powers in Crete ended the insurgency and the massacre of the civilian population. As Ambassador Paul Cambon admitted, European powers had a shaky and ambiguous attitude.[79] The Europeans' commitment was doubtful, as revealed by the few resources they put at the disposal of their representatives on the spot, which failed to prevent a further massacre from taking place, as happened on September 6, 1898. The occupying powers were unprepared to deal with the administration of the island as well as the sanitary and relief problems caused by the mass of internally displaced civilians.

The temporary protection of Muslim Cretans refugees was an unintended consequence of the occupation, not a planned rescue operation. In the end, the most notable and tragic outcome of the intervention was the massive emigration of Muslim Cretans, who paid the highest price of all. As Holland and Markides put it, the conundrum surrounding British power in Crete is that the naval preponderance meant that Britain could dominate the coastal regions and ports and crucially influence the political fate of the island. But it could not affect what happened in the interior. The British authorities were fully aware of the line separating indifference from an organized attempt by Christian Cretans to wipe out the Muslims. The haphazard harassment of the minority— occasional sequestration of property, destruction of vines, or isolated loss of life—could not be prevented in a society that offered inadequate protection to all. Indeed, insofar as such discriminations encouraged the gradual disappearance of Muslims from Crete, there was an unspoken benefit, since the Cretan Question would quietly disappear with them. But a wipe-out was another matter. It would trigger Ottoman retribution in much of the Balkans and Asia Minor and prove—as in the case of the Armenians—that the British could not help steer a steady course toward pacification even in places where they enjoyed special advantages. As long as the Cretan Question survived, the British were not to be free from the specter of extermination and its wider ramifications.[80]

The lesson European decision-makers learned from the intervention in Crete was how difficult an intervention would be to undertake if widespread massacres took place in Macedonia or elsewhere in the

Ottoman Empire. In 1903 Earl Percy claimed that the European powers had "prevented a war of extermination" by occupying the island. How would the Europeans enforce these measures if a "war of extermination" took place in Macedonia? Who would enforce law and order in towns "comprising a large and fanatical Moslem population" if, as in Crete, the Ottoman Army was asked to withdraw as early as possible?[81] If new massacres occurred, Hanotaux feared, not just a single power but all the powers would be forced to act by a unanimous movement of public opinion and even by a compelling duty to rescue Christian communities.[82]

CHAPTER TEN

Nonforcible Intervention in the Ottoman Macedonian Provinces (1903–08)

> Depuis plus d'un an la commission financière est constituée,
> depuis plus de trois ans les agents civils et les officiers sont
> à leur poste. Qu'ont-ils fait? Où en est l'application du pro-
> gramme de Mürzsteg ?
> —René Pinon, *L'Europe et l'Empire Ottoman*, 1908

THE EUROPEAN POWERS' intervention in the Ottoman provinces of Macedonia has to be examined in the wake of the Armenian and Cretan cases. Like the case of Crete, this was not a full-fledged intervention against massacre but still deserves to be examined for it shows how, by the beginning of the twentieth century, the concept of humanitarian intervention was used and abused in Europe. As wrongly as the Armenians, Macedonian nationalists thought that evidence of indiscriminate massacres and atrocities increased the likelihood of an intervention by the European powers. Macedonian nationalists drew the wrong lessons from previous interventions and did not realize that from the European governments' perspective, nationalism was among the factors preventing humanitarian interventions from taking place.

After 1878 the European provinces (*vilayets*) remaining under direct Ottoman government were Adrianople (roughly corresponding to today's Thrace), Scutari (in today's Albania), Janina (northwestern Greece), and the three Macedonian provinces of Kosovo (Kossovo; main center Skopje or Uskub), Monastir (Bitolja), and Salonica. The population was of an extremely mixed background. The Muslims comprised Turks, Albanians (especially in the western areas), and Pomaks; the Christians mostly comprised Slavs (Serbs and Bulgarians) but also Greeks, Vlachs (Arumanian or Kutzo-Vlach, a minority closely akin to the Romanians, whose millet was recognized by the sultan only in 1905). Gypsies and Jews also inhabited the area; the largest and most important Jewish community lived in Salonica.[1] Ethnically and religiously, Macedonia was even more mixed than Syria and Lebanon. The 1878 Treaty of Berlin had not granted autonomy to the Ottoman Macedonian provinces, even though it was implied in article 23, by which the sultan pledged to introduce into his European provinces laws similar to the Organic Laws of Crete "but adapted to local requirements."[2]

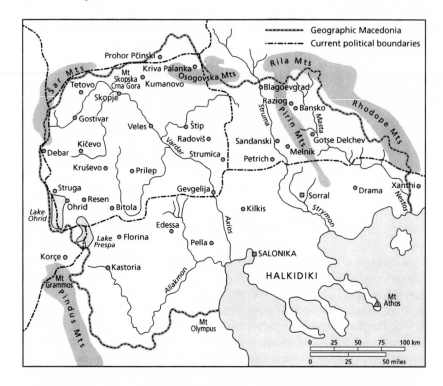

Bulgarian nationalists made Macedonia the focal point of their expansionist projects. Their views clashed with those of Greek nationalists. Toward the end of the century Romanian nationalist propaganda in favor of the Vlach minority came to play a further destabilizing role.[3] The Serbs entered the struggle for influence in Macedonia claiming that the Slav population there was mainly Serbian, that the tradition and culture of Macedonian Slavs was really Serbian, and that the language was closer to Serbian than to Bulgarian. Last but not least, in October 1893 the Macedonian Revolutionary Organisation (IMRO)[4] was founded in Salonica and claimed to work "for the autonomy" of Macedonia.[5] Another revolutionary organization, the Supreme Macedonian Committee (SMC), founded in 1895, acted from Bulgaria. Its initial goal was to achieve autonomy for Macedonia. From their inception these nationalist movements and groups, whether pro-Bulgarian, pro-Greek, pro-Romanian, or pro-Serb, who had already seen the failure of the Armenians, made it clear they wanted to entice the European powers to intervene to the advantage of the Christian population.

Two European powers had a particular and direct interest in Macedonia: Russia and Austria-Hungary. Germany openly defended the integrity of the Ottoman Empire and supported all initiatives undertaken by Austria-Hungary in agreement with Russia in the Balkans. The French government defended its interests and was keen on cooperating with its Russian ally.[6] Great Britain did not really have a Macedonian policy per se as it viewed Macedonian affairs as part of its general policy, whose main targets were to be found in Africa, Egypt, the Red Sea area, and especially India. As long as Russia and Austria-Hungary agreed to freeze Macedonia, none of the other powers were willing to pursue a different policy and cooperation would be possible.

THE UPRISINGS OF 1902–03

On September 23, 1902, the Djumaya uprising commenced when about three hundred men crossed the Ottoman frontier from Bulgaria. At the roots of the uprising were groups from neighboring countries, as it had been the case in Crete, where insurgents came from Greece. The Ottoman forces easily suppressed the uprising by the middle of November. From the outset, discrepancies concerning the nature of the violence, massacre, and atrocities characterized the "Macedonian Question." According to Ottoman sources, about fifteen villages suffered material damage, two hundred people fled to Bulgaria, and thirty-seven were killed. Bulgarian sources tell of twenty-eight villages being completely destroyed by Ottoman regular and irregular forces, over a hundred females violated, an unknown number dead, and three thousand refugees in Bulgaria. For all the actors involved, news and information about massacres and atrocities had a capital importance. For insurgents and nationalist organizations, it was essential to spread information about such events to draw the attention of European public opinion. For the Sublime Porte, denying that massacre and atrocities had taken place was crucial in order to avoid the European powers' interference in internal Ottoman affairs. Finally, for the European powers, assessing whether massacre and atrocities had really taken place was important in deciding what further steps were to be carried out.

Contrary to the early-nineteenth-century cases of intervention, the sources of information in Macedonia were multifarious and difficult to control. Local actors organized campaigns of information that suited their political purposes. For instance, the SMC sent Stoyan Mihaylovski, a local intellectual, on a tour to the European capitals to inform Europe that regular Ottoman troops massacred women and children. Throughout the crisis, the so-called pro-memoria lists were circulated in Europe precisely to arouse public opinion about events in Macedonia, part of the nationalist groups' strategy to exaggerate, distort, and sometimes fabricate news of massacres, atrocities, and extermination in the hopes that pressure exerted by the European public on their respective governments might trigger an intervention in Macedonia.[7] The pro-memoria denounced "the barbaric actions" of Ottoman soldiers, including torture and murder. They also contained detailed lists of demolished villages and accounts of the inhumane conditions of jails or of deportation of convicts to northern Africa or Asia Minor.[8] The Ottoman government's countermove to the pro-memoria was to portray the Macedonian uprisings as marginal actions by a few terrorists. Throughout the Macedonian crisis, the Porte refused to grant the necessary permits for European journalists to travel across the region. Given the precedent of the 1894 massacres in Sasun, this strategy eventually stirred the suspicions of many Europeans.

As in Crete, special correspondents of European newspapers such as the *Times*, *Le Temps*, and *Le Matin* received information through the IMRO staff or from Bulgarian, Greek, or Serbian diplomats. The result was a cacophony of contradictory news, which produced generally unclear accounts of the events occurring in the Ottoman Macedonian provinces. European diplomats, aware of the tactics and propaganda of local and foreign nationalists, distrusted these sources. The newly appointed British consul general in Salonica, Alfred Biliotti, informed the Foreign Office that the majority of peasants who had sought refuge in Bulgaria during the uprising of Djumaya had returned to their Ottoman villages in late January 1903, willingly surrendering their arms and not mentioning instances of rape or even of looting or beating on the part of Ottoman troops.[9] As Biliotti put it, the publication of allegations of massacre and atrocities in Macedonia in 1902 was purely a newspaper campaign, with the object of rousing Europe to intervene on behalf of the Bulgarians. The SMC and IMRO did not deny this, and since the more public opinion was stirred the more chance there was for the agitators to attain their ends, no pains were spared in working up comparatively trifling incidents and opportune rumors into sensational stories. The British consul concluded that the excesses the troops and Muslim peasants had committed, in spite of the earnest endeavors their officers and the civil authorities undoubtedly made to restrain them, were more serious than those that would have occurred under the same circumstances in European states, but they were by no means as serious as they had been portrayed by the IMRO, the SMC, and the Bulgarian authorities.[10] At the beginning of 1903 all European powers discarded the idea of an intervention in the Ottoman Macedonian provinces because the humanitarian motive was far from being persuasive.

Mindful of precedents of European interference, Sultan Abdul Hamid appointed a general inspector for the European provinces of the

Ottoman Empire. Hussein Hilmi Pasha arrived in Salonica on December 8, 1902, and set up a specific program of reforms.[11] Without even letting him have a try, the French consul in Salonica, Louis Steeg, criticized the reform scheme applying expensive and mindless machinery toward resistance rather than progress.[12] According to Paul Cambon, then French ambassador in Great Britain, the reforms were similar to those intended, but never implemented, for the Armenians. Because of their poor record, Cambon, the most philo-Armenian of the European diplomats, was very skeptical about Ottoman authorities' competence to run a sound financial administration, unconvinced about their ability to reform the gendarmerie and their willingness to let Christian subjects work for the public administration.[13] For Cambon, in order for the reforms to be effective, the European powers had to enforce them directly. In his view, the three Macedonian provinces had to become a single autonomous entity, with a Christian governor appointed by the consent of the European powers, a gendarmerie commanded by European officers, and finances administered by European supervisors. Any other attempt at reform would only bring disappointments, disturbances, and insurrection. It would have been, Cambon wrote, the Bulgarian atrocities all over again. This was an analysis of which Lansdowne, the British foreign secretary, fully approved. However, neither Cambor nor Lansdowne had an interest in promoting the kind of interference in the internal affairs of the Ottoman Empire they seem to recommend.

On February 21, 1903, the Russian foreign minister, Vladimir Lamsdorf, and his Austrian-Hungarian counterpart Goluchowski presented the Ottoman authorities with a set of reforms based on the following main points: The Ottoman general inspector was to have his post for a preordained time period in order to carry out his task satisfactorily and to dispose of troops without needing to obtain permission from the central government in advance. The gendarmerie was to be reorganized by foreign officers (as in Crete) recruited from Muslims and Christians according to their share of the population. The government had to take the necessary measures to suppress the crimes and offenses committed during the revolt and to grant amnesty to all political prisoners. Each *vilayet* would have its own budget, the Ottoman Imperial Bank would control the revenues of the provinces, and the tax farming of the tithe was to be abolished. In the view of the two European ministers, when implemented, these reforms would introduce "good-government," bring peace and prosperity, and increase the well-being of all local populations; Europe would in turn benefit from tranquillity and stability in the region. The Ottoman government accepted the reform plan with only minor amendments and began implementing it on February 23, 1903.[14] The European powers did not mention autonomy for Macedonia and did not show any sympathy for Macedonian nationalist movements or reveal any plan for further interference. The reform plan was not intended to undermine what was left of Ottoman authority, which explains why part of European public opinion was dissatisfied with the powers' decisions.

PRO-MACEDONIANS

Massacres in the Macedonian provinces aroused a smaller amount of sympathy among the European public than had the massacres of Armenians. Whereas the Armenians were the archetype of defenseless victims, European newspapers portrayed the Macedonian people as brave insurgents able to defend themselves. The Macedonian Question could not be portrayed as a struggle of oppressor versus oppressed. The European press tended to illustrate it as a succession of unrelated facts, and news reports were published only when they appeared sufficiently exciting (or morbid) in order to awaken readers' interest.[15] Nonetheless, a pro-Macedonian European movement developed in the wake of the precedent of agitation in favor of the Armenians and the Cretans.

French Liberal, Socialist, and Radical politicians, as well as journalists and intellectuals, had shown an interest in the Macedonia since 1901. In 1902 the newspaper *Le Temps* had published several articles on the Macedonian Question, to be followed by other newspapers and reviews, such as *L'Aurore*. French international law reviews also a great deal of interest. The *Revue Générale de Droit International Public* published its first article on Macedonia in 1903.[16] Among the Macedonia promoters and supporters were René Henry in the *Correspondant*, Victor Bérard in the *Revue de Paris*, and Raymond Recouly in the *Revue Politique et Parlementaire*.[17] As had happened for the Armenians, ad hoc reviews such as *La Macédoine (organe des revendications légales pour tous les Macédoniens)* were created.[18]

Among those groups who had previously supported the Armenians and the Cretans, many now defended the cause of the Macedonians, putting forward the same political, civilizational, and humanitarian motives.[19] By awakening the conscience of public opinion, they wished to help those Christian "human beings" allegedly exterminated by Ottoman soldiers who, contrary to the Muslim Turks, belonged to the "civilized races."[20] As journalist Gaston Routier put it, the Macedonian Question had become more than a political question; it was a question of "justice and of humanity."

The pro-Macedonia agitation in France reached one of its highest peaks in early 1903.[21] On February 15 a meeting took place at the Paris theater of Chateau-d'Eau. The convenor was Paul d'Estournelles, a French diplomat and later winner of the Nobel Prize for Peace. Orators announced that their mission was humane and spoke on behalf of all the oppressed of the Orient, and in the name of all the political parties of France.[22] Denys Cochin, de Pressensé, and Jaurès, among others, brought up previous instances of nonintervention in favor of the Armenians to stress the urgent need to do something now in Macedonia. French pro-Macedonians did not speak about the independence of Macedonia, and sometimes they referred back to the Ottoman precedent in Lebanon. The pressure on the French government was strong and visible when a group of pro-Macedonian deputies questioned the government on March 10, 1903, forcing the foreign minister, Théophile Delcassé, to reply to the allegations of inaction. Their point of view was eloquently summarized by de Pressensé, who wrote that Delcassé lacked vigor and was content with a trivial philanthropy a year after crimes had occurred. In his view, it was not enough to condemn the crime after it had been committed or to pronounce eloquent funeral elegies and write epitaphs on victims' gravestones; he wanted the French government to prevent further crimes and punish the culprits.[23]

In Britain many authors who had animated the debate on the Armenian Question now participated in this related issue.[24] The center of philo-Macedonian agitation was the London Balkan Committee, a direct descendant of the Eastern Question Association founded in 1878 in the wake of the Bulgarian atrocities. The Balkan Committee aimed to promote discussions and form opinion "in a way which left no room for the more emotional and crude appeals to which some of Gladstone's followers were wont to resort."[25] As James Bryce, now president of the committee, noted, using the exact words of Routier, the Macedonian Question was primarily one of justice and humanity.[26] The committee's members presented a clear continuity with past associations in men, methods, and ideas. Many, such as MacColl and Lady Frederick Cavendish, had previously been involved in the Bulgarian agitation and had supported the Armenian and Cretan causes. The vice presidents of the Balkan Committee counted a number of bishops, Lord Herbert Gladstone, and the Earl of Aberdeen; the executive committee included H. N. Brailsford, newspaper correspondent and author of a study on Macedonia,[27] archaeologist Arthur Evans, historian G. P. Gooch, and K. C. Westlake, a Liberal and professor of international law at the University of Cambridge, who became the committee's second president (see chapter 2). The committee operated through local branches and held meetings in the large towns, generally attended by mayors, bishops, nonconformist churchmen, MPs, and professional members.[28] It promoted great numbers of petitions to the Foreign Office from established and nonconformist church congregations. Many of these petitions followed a set form and were printed with the name of the church entered in a specific space provided. Nonconformist congregations sent by far the greatest number of petitions; others emanated from public meetings, trade associations, women's liberal associations, whole towns, brotherhoods and so forth. A vast quantity were submitted between September 29 and November 16, 1903, when the Balkan Committee organized over 150 meetings all over Great Britain.

As historian Douglas Dakin writes, the Balkan Committee started off with many preconceived ideas and was not well-informed.[29] Noel Buxton's 1907 book *Europe and the Turks* epitomizes the beliefs of many humanitarians and of many committee members. Buxton was a Liberal, ideologically close to Gladstone, and an active phil-Armenian. He stated that abominations such as those of the Congo (see chapter 7) were the more deplorable because they were performed by Europeans. But those of the Ottoman Empire, he argued, were without exaggeration the "greatest atrocity on the surface of the world, because the sufferers themselves are civilized beings." His book was supposed to enlighten the British public about Macedonia: "the field of the great battle between East and West—between barbarism and civilization." He first illustrated "the great mistakes" of previous British governments with respect to the Ottoman Empire. He argued that it would have been far better for Europe, for local populations, and indeed for the Ottoman Empire to follow Gladstone's "bag and baggage" policy (which he completely misrepresented). Although he never quoted his sources, he mentioned a number of massacres and thousands of victims among Macedonian, Christian, and civilian populations. He also admitted that the rise of nationalism had had dreadful consequences on the local populations. However, in his view the "cause of trouble" was the "Turk," whose government was based "on barbarous ideas," inequality, and cruelty and was inefficient and corrupt.[30]

Buxton's "right plan" for Macedonia aimed at removing the direct rule of the Sultan by establishing a government responsible to the powers. His solution was molded on the Tory Lansdowne's proposal of 1903. He perorated the cause of the Macedonians, which was not so much "a mere matter of relieving pain, as in the case of some famine or earthquake," as it was a matter of "making the barest necessities of decent life, even family morality itself, possible to great populations, and those, too, not ignorant or savage, but of the type which has made civilization." The historic monster of British slavery itself, he wrote, affected directly but 700,000 souls; those whom "Turkish rule degrades in body and in mind are many millions." Buxton concluded his book by suggesting that the importance of public opinion lay in its being the vector of the moral feeling of a nation. According to him, organizations such as the Balkan Committee united all those who could claim personal knowledge of the matter and set themselves to collect information and supply it, through the press and in other ways, to the large number of people, many of them MPs, who asked for it:

> Government is the reflection of public opinion and obeys the public will; influence is increased by organisation, and it is by joining in exerting influence that every man or woman can do some tangible thing to make possible a life of decency and goodwill in a hundred thousand homes. We neglect the claim of those who have fallen among thieves at our peril. Nations equally with persons, must pay dearly for breaking moral law. And by what law are we bound? By the call of common human nature, to aid the victim of cruelty.[31]

The pro-Macedonia movement rapidly acquired a transnational dimension, probably because of the previous experiences of many of its participants. British and French agitators met several times; for instance, the 1904 National Conference on the Macedonian Question held at Caxton Hall in London had a number of French guests, such as Quillard and Bérard.[32] Meetings were organized in Milan and Rome (where Anatole France took part in a demonstration on May 7, 1903), as well as in smaller Italian towns, in Brussels, and in Geneva. The Balkan Committee held a big meeting at St. James's Hall in London on September 29. A month later, on October 25, sixty delegates from Great Britain, Belgium, the United States, Italy, and France gathered in Paris. Participants pointed out that the question of Macedonia was a *question humanitaire* whose purpose was to save the lives of the Bulgarians of Macedonia and to give them good government in that province for the future. On that occasion, de Pressensé spoke of hundreds of villages destroyed or burned; women, older people, and even children slaughtered, tortured, and raped; and refugees tracked down and persecuted. He reminded the audience and the European governments that the aim of the pro-Macedonians was *"singulièrement modeste"*: to convince the Liberal powers of the West (*trois grandes puissances libérales de l'Occident*) to appoint a governor and a system of control and supervision in Macedonia. De Pressensé and his comrades favored a military intervention, the basis of which, in his view, was legal, political, and moral. He recalled that during the Armenian massacres a frightful moral bankruptcy hit European diplomacy. This political and moral failure should not be repeated in Macedonia. The price of inaction in Macedonia meant that "civilization" was a merely hypocritical cover for the struggle for power, and that the *droit des gens* was a paradox for modern humanity. Inaction in Macedonia would show that the "grand Assassin" Abdul Hamid had won against Europe and against the human conscience.[33]

THE TERRORIST ATTACKS OF 1903 AND THE MÜRZSTEG REFORM PROGRAM

Pro-Macedonians did not succeed in convincing the European governments to intervene militarily in the Ottoman provinces, nor did the terrorist attacks of April 28, 1903, on the Ottoman bank of Salonica by young IMRO anarchists. On that occasion, European consuls called on their governments to send warships. The choice of this particular action reflected the official European cautiousness. The consuls hoped to produce a dissuasive effect on the terrorists and to prevent harsh Ottoman repression. They feared a second wave of Bulgarian atrocities in Salonica and hoped that, as in 1860 in Lebanon, the presence of European warships would avoid massacres at least in the coastal areas. The Ottoman authorities hunted down and killed many suspects. Fearing a general uprising, they scoured the Bulgarian quarters of Salonica. They promised protection to the Muslims living in and around the town and did provide it, but at the same time they warned them not to take the law into their own hands. The Ottomans too had learned a lesson from previous massacres. In fact, contrary to what happened in Damascus in July 1860, there was no reaction from the Muslim population, and no massacre of Christians followed.[34] Temporarily, at least, this reinforced the idea among the European powers that there was no need for further intervention in Macedonia.

Having failed to provoke massacre in Salonica, Macedonian revolutionaries persisted in their subversive policy in the province of Monastir. The Ilinden uprising, which started on August 2 (St. Elias's Day), attempted to exploit the absence of the Ottoman troops from Monastir. The latter were stationed in the *vilayet* of Kosovo, where the local Muslim population did not want the reform program. The insurgents and the mob that participated in the insurrection destroyed the properties and goods of the Muslims of Monastir and latter retaliated by destroying neighboring villages inhabited by a majority of Christians. The Ottoman soldiers retaliated, and the IMRO immediately informed the European powers about a number of atrocities committed by Muslims against Christian civilians. European consuls found evidence that the irregular troops were guilty of massacres and atrocities, and there were authenticated cases of brutality on the part of the regular soldiers. However, the uprising did not have the repercussions hoped for by its instigators because members of the European public and representatives on the spot were more shocked by the brutal deaths of innocent people caused by the insurgents than by the atrocities committed by soldiers.[35] The European powers agreed not to conduct an armed intervention and focused on the enforcement of substantial administrative and economic reforms.

Lord Lansdowne, in a note of September 29, suggested that the Macedonian provinces should have a Christian governor, or at least Christian assessors to help the governor if he were a Muslim. Macedonian gendarmerie should have Christian officers, and all irregular forces should be withdrawn from the territory at once. When, three days later, the Russian and Austrian emperors Nicholas II and Francis Joseph, along with their foreign ministers, met at Mürzsteg, a few miles from Vienna, they drew up a program not dissimilar to the British proposal. According to the French international legal scholar Antoine Rougier, the two powers' action benefited from the general consensus of Europe.[36] This collective action was, in Rougier's view, a nonforcible intervention (or *intervention diplomatique*) threatening recourse to sanctions, not to armed force, if the Porte refused to comply and compelled the Ottoman government to implement the reforms.

The Mürzsteg program aimed to supervise the execution of the reforms by significantly interfering in Ottoman internal affairs. The motive of the interference was to restore law and order and prevent further disturbances as well as further massacres. General Inspector Hilmi Pasha was to be accompanied everywhere by two special civil agents from Russia and Austria, who were to bring his attention to abuses and necessary remedies, to convey to him the recommendations of the ambassadors in Constantinople, and to keep their own governments fully informed of affairs in Macedonia. The task of reorganizing the gendarmerie in the three *vilayets* was entrusted to a general of foreign nationality in the service of the Ottoman government. He was given military officers from the European powers to assist him, and, if it was thought necessary, assistant officers and noncommissioned officers. These officers were to supervise, instruct, and reorganize the Ottoman gendarmerie and to monitor the conduct of Ottoman troops, each within a zone of jurisdiction. As soon as a certain pacification of the country had been ascertained, the powers would demand from the Ottoman government a modification of the territorial delimitation of the administrative units for a more regular grouping of the different nationalities. The powers also demanded that the Ottoman government allocate special sums to cover the return home of Christian families who had fled as refugees to Bulgaria or other places and aid the Christians who had lost their property and domiciles. The Porte should pay for the repair of houses, churches, and schools destroyed by Ottoman soldiers during the in-surrection. In the Christian villages burned down by Ottoman soldiers and irregulars, exemption was sought for returning Christians from the payment of all taxes for a period of one year. For Goluchowski the pro-gram included two goals:

1. The pursuit of the programme accepted by the sultan in February [1903], the realisation of which [was] subordinated to the control of the two civil agents representing Vienna and St Petersburg.
2. A humanitarian action to come in aid of the Christian popula-tions which suffered so much from the war and devastations and which were brutalised so much by the revolutionary committees as well as by the Sultan's soldiers. The process initiated by Austria-Hungary and Russia [was] also an action of pacification to restore order, security and to improve the destiny of the Christian popula-tions of Macedonia.[37]

On February 1, 1904, Italian general Emilio De Giorgis arrived in Con-stantinople and undertook his task of reforming the gendarmerie of the three provinces. He was to remain in office, like the civil agents, for two years, though he actually stayed in office until he died in 1908, when he was replaced by General Mario Nicolis di Robilant).[38] As Dakin empha-sizes, De Giorgis achieved exactly what he set out to achieve: the forma-tion of a Macedonian gendarmerie elite. De Giorgis was perfectly aware that the gendarmerie was not a suitable force for suppressing bands of insurgents, a task he considered to belong to the army.[39] Hence, if seri-ous disturbances occurred, this European presence would have almost certainly been useless.

In 1905 the implementation of the reform program, apart from the reorganization of the gendarmerie, which was becoming a respectable though not very important institution, had made very little progress. The humanitarian measures listed above largely remained a dead let-ter. One of the correspondents of the French journal *L'Européen* wrote on May 19: "Trifling relief has been distributed by the Government to the peasants whose villages have been burned, for the rebuilding of their houses. In reality this has been a cruel irony towards the poor peasants, for it is not with sums of from 10 to 20 francs that they can rebuild their burned houses. But what is still more iniquitous is that the bashi-bazouks took from the unfortunate peasants the small charities the benevolent societies bestowed on them."[40]

On January 17, 1905, the governments of Austria-Hungary and Rus-sia proposed to the Ottoman government a financial agreement placing the budget and revenue of the three Macedonian provinces under the strict control of the Ottoman Public Debt Administration.[41] The Sublime

Porte rejected this proposal, as well as Lansdowne's plan to add four European financial experts to the civil agents. On October 5 the ambassadors at Constantinople advised their governments to take coercive action if the Porte did not comply.[42] On October 6 the European powers collectively announced to the Porte that the four delegates would proceed forthwith to join Hilmi Pasha and the two civil agents.[43] A second collective note followed on November 14 demanding the Ottoman government's approval, without delay, of a two-year extension of the reform program and the gendarmerie reorganization scheme, the recognition of the four financial delegates, and the acceptance of the *règlement* governing the action of the International Financial Commission for the three *vilayets* of Macedonia.[44] The Ottoman ambassador in London complained that the powers' demands were without precedent in diplomatic annals, attacked the integrity of the Ottoman Empire, and were incompatible with the treaties guaranteeing it. The Sublime Porte offered yet another compromise, which the European powers did not accept. Thus, the powers undertook coercive action in the form of a naval demonstration and the military occupation of Mytilene and Lemnos.

The initial proposal for coercive action came from Austria-Hungary, with Russia's approval; it quickly obtained the support of France, Great Britain, and Italy. Germany gave only its moral support to the naval demonstration. On November 22, under the command of Austrian vice admiral Ripper, 617 European marines proceeded to occupy the island of Mytilene. On November 26 they occupied the post, the customs house, and telegraph offices. Then the squadron advanced and occupied the island of Lemnos, situated at the entrance of the Dardanelles Strait. On December 5 the Ottoman government substantially gave in.[45]

French jurist Antoine Rougier wrote that the European powers' collective and coercive intervention aimed at obtaining the appointment of the financial commission for Macedonia. It was the consequence of modern international law, which no longer allowed for the idea of absolute sovereignty for the states, as this would render them not responsible for the deeds they committed.[46] In Rougier's view, the military occupation of Mytilene and Lemnos was not an instance of rescuing European nationals or a response to a received offense. The European powers could have invoked "*la raison d'humanité*," for the military action aimed at preventing new disorders in the Balkans, but they did not make recourse to such an explanation because they did not want to excite the local population and nationalist groups. Rougier claimed that the line between coercive measures and war was thin and uncertain, and he eventually considered the European powers' military action of late 1905 as an *ultimatum*, which he defined as a coercive measure replacing peaceful relations between two or more states.

In January 1908 Sir Edward Grey, the Liberal foreign secretary who replaced Lansdowne in December 1905, circulated a secret memorandum among the members of the British cabinet on the state of the Ottoman Empire. Grey emphasized that while there was "nothing that we can do" for the Armenians except to allow the population the right to emigrate, Britain could do something in Macedonia. He wished to ask the other powers whether they would consent to giving European officers executive control over the gendarmerie, and he mentioned the possibility of using a mobile column of gendarmerie against insurgent bands, which from a military point of view was nonsense. He was very skeptical about a second European naval demonstration to secure these measures and claimed not to be prepared to resort to coercive measures for any proposal such as that for judicial reforms alone, which would not pacify the country. If there was to be coercion, it should be for something that would be really effective. In the end, Grey did not put forward a new or more detailed set of reforms or anything like a military operation on grounds of humanity. If the powers did not wish to cooperate, Grey felt Britain had done its duty and concluded, like Salisbury in 1896, that there was nothing more it could do on behalf of the Macedonians.[47]

The Austro-Russian entente broke down in January 1908. The breach was the result of a concession obtained by Austria-Hungary to conduct surveys for a railway through the *sandjak* of Novi Pazar to Salonica, a strip of Turkish territory dividing Serbia and Montenegro that was generally regarded as the Hapsburg Monarchy's imperial route to the Aegean.[48] To Russia this seemed a violation of the agreement of 1897. During the summer the whole question of reforms in the Macedonian provinces became one of purely academic interest, for the Young Turk revolution had broken out in July and a Turkish constitution had been proclaimed in Constantinople.[49] Reports from Macedonia showed that there had been a sudden and complete transformation. The insurgent bands disappeared as if by magic, and the powers concurred that the moment was inopportune for pressing any demands on Constantinople. The revolution led to the withdrawal of the foreign officers, the winding up of the financial commission, and the recall of the civil agents. However, national hatreds in Macedonia still raged, and no guarantee or respect of basic rights of humanity existed.

In July 1908 the Russian foreign minister, Izvolsky, felt able to approach Alois von Ährenthal with a formal proposal for a modification of the status quo that would suit both empires; Austria was to be allowed to annex Bosnia and Herzegovina in return for promising support Russian claims in the Straits. In September the bargain was struck. Unfortunately, the two statesmen disagreed about what had taken place at their meeting. Certainly when they parted Isvolsky did not expect the annexation of Bosnia and Herzegovina without warning on October 5.[50] Russia opposed the Austro-Hungarian fait accompli but was not ready to go to war. Germany backed Vienna because of the Anglo-Russian entente. In the end Austria-Hungary made formal amends to the Turks by agreeing to pay for crown property in the provinces and the crisis was over.[51] Open conflict between Russia and Austria-Hungary in the Balkans had reappeared after being hidden for eleven years. Russia was deeply resentful of Germany and Austria-Hungary and began to rearm in earnest. It was unlikely that it would again allow its prestige among Slav nations to be so jeopardized.[52] Any further cooperation between the two European blocs now seemed very remote.

The Outcome of the Intervention

The European governments knew that massacre and atrocities had occurred in Macedonia. They clearly identified the victims of massacre and their culprits, although, rather than openly targeting the Ottoman Empire for sole responsibility, they held the revolutionary committees as equally responsible. Once the European powers discarded the military option, the governments of Vienna and St. Petersburg informed (threatened) the Sublime Porte (the target state) that not accepting the reform program might induce the signatory powers of the Treaty of Berlin to ask for more invasive requirements. The target state initially accepted implementation of reforms under the powers' supervision. Contrary to the case in Crete, the Ottoman government was fully aware of being the target state. The intervention was coercive but unarmed, with the exception of the naval demonstration and the occupation of the islands of Mytilene and Lemnos; it was collective, with two particular powers playing a more prominent role than the others; and it was "disinterested" (i.e., none of the powers would receive any unilateral benefit from the action). The intervention did not end massacres of civilian populations by using military force, although it aimed at securing the local Christian population's right to life, property, and religious liberty through the enforcement of reforms. As Grey put it in 1908, a full sense of moral responsibility determined British policy, which endeavored to alleviate the suffering of the population, to avert any dangers to European peace, and to bring about the restoration of order and the security of life and property.[53]

The Macedonian struggle was over churches and nationalities, as often between enemy gangs as against the Ottoman Army. There were no precedents of intervention on grounds of humanity when Christians committed massacres against other Christians. Contrary to previous instances of intervention, this time European powers could not accuse the Ottoman authorities of being unable to end a massacre. If we assume that the nonforcible action was intended to prevent further massacre from occurring, one might argue that the European powers' intervention avoided massacres on the scale of those perpetrated against the Armenians. This was not the point of view of the Balkan Committee, which in 1908 claimed that the situation in Macedonia had assumed "proportions of horror" and that the Austro-Russian intervention produced "bloodshed, anarchy, and outrage of every description."[54] In other words, the unintended consequences of the intervention produced massacres on a vast scale. The Balkan Committee emphasized that since 1903, in a country of about a 1.5 million inhabitants, over ten thousand people had been murdered; and the monthly murder lists showed no sign of diminution. By 1908 the main victims were women and children, outrages of every kind were ever more numerous, and the destruction of houses, property, and cattle had been extensive. Nationalist forces from outside Macedonia terrorized villages in order to effect political conversions, while the Ottoman troops raided indiscriminately in pursuit of maintaining order, though in general they avoided contact with armed insurgent bands and found the defenseless villages were easy prey. A vast stream of the local population emigrated to the United States, encouraged in every possible way, so that in the central areas of Macedonia there were hardly any able-bodied men left in many villages, only women and children.[55]

In this respect the intervention was a total failure, not to mention the issues of reparation and reconstruction. Furthermore, when massacres did occur, the European officers could do nothing except photograph the corpses and make a report to inform their governments.[56] The very partial enforcement of the reform scheme arguably enabled the continuation of the war between rival bands. Christian populations wrongly interpreted the reforms as a guarantee of help from the European powers, behind which they would shelter in order to organize their respective movements for independence.[57]

In defense of the intervening states, one could wonder what would have happened had no intervention whatsoever occurred. In his contemporary account of the Macedonian Question, Pinon asserted that the intervention was insufficient to solve the problems of Macedonia—too weak to improve the living conditions of local populations, and especially to obtain their security for life and property.[58] But in the end the reform program was "a compromise between the adventurous politics of intervention and the concrete politics of the interests."[59] Did other solutions exist? It is plausible to argue that if European officers had taken over command of the troops and the European commissioners had had extensive executive powers to suppress rebel bands, they would have more successfully restored security for life and property. However, such a proposal was utterly unrealistic, for Austria-Hungary, Russia, and Germany opposed a military intervention, the Sublime Porte was resolutely against any further encroachment on its sovereignty, and Great Britain was certainly not ready to act unilaterally.

A further aspect of the intervention in the Ottoman Macedonian provinces concerns the work of humanitarians on the ground. In 1903 Brailsford proposed that the refugees and needy populations be assembled in centers under the eyes of European consuls, or "at least of some Europeans," in order to effectively distribute relief.[60] Lansdowne wrote to the British ambassador at Constantinople, Nicholas O'Conor, that the British government should facilitate the relief operation as far as possible. O'Conor pointed out that "no organized system of concentration camps, such as those established in South Africa" would prove practical, but relief could be organized in the towns, to which refugees naturally gravitated. The ambassador wished relief to be distributed without distinction of race or creed, not because his humanitarianism was truly universal, but because he wanted to make it clear that Great Britain was not helping Christians against Muslims (i.e., Macedonian nationalists against the Ottoman government). He also pointed out that the consul's participation should be limited to giving advice to the agents sent specially for the purpose of distributing and administering relief funds.[61]

By October the British ambassador authorized the distribution of relief by the benevolent committees of the Macedonian Relief Society. Mr. and Mrs. Brailsford, Mr. H. Harris, and Mr. Nevinson arrived at Salonica at the end of October to distribute the relief funds subscribed in Britain. Their work was "purely benevolent and charitable" and "limited to the succour of distressed persons, without distinction of race or creed."[62] They were aware that they lacked the means to fully assist the inhabitants of the ruined villages.[63] In the province of Monastir a depot was managed by the Rev. L. Bond of the American Mission, assisted by Mr. Kiria, the local representative of the British and Foreign Bible Society. When smallpox and pulmonary complaints appeared among the refugees congregated in the town of Monastir, a small hospital was opened on premises occupied by the French Sisters of St. Vincent de Paul, who, with the approval of the French vice consul, were ready to act as nurses. The British and Foreign Bible Society provided the necessary funds.[64] In Okhrida the depot was in the charge of Mrs. Brailsford, who also supervised the hospital opened there in November 1903. In Reska an American missionary from Salonica, Mr. Haskell, and

Mr. Tsiko of the Bible Society collaborated to help refugees. In Florina the Lazarist Mission and the Sisters of Charity took care of the sick and wounded before the arrival of the British agents, who distributed blankets and clothing. In the villages of Kastoria, Klissoura, and Biglishta, Mr. Brailsford was kept busy and, with the help of local doctors and three nursing sisters of St. Vincent de Paul, opened a hospital for noncontagious diseases. Another hospital later opened at Monastir. It would be difficult, Consul General Graves wrote, to exaggerate the unselfish devotion of the whole relief staff in the performance of their voluntary tasks, which involved constant hardships and discomfort and exposed the agents to grave risks to life and health. They saved many lives and prevented much suffering and misery. Their mere presence in the disturbed districts acted as a check on potential trouble-makers and an encouragement to the sufferers to have patience and hope for better times when, Graves hoped, European gendarmerie officers would patrol the Macedonian provinces. The British consul noted that work of these humanitarians was carried out

> not affording a shadow of justification for the idea that advantage may have been taken of the opportunities offered for religious or political propaganda. The composition of the staff, comprising British, French, American, and Austrian members, belonging to the Anglican, Methodist, Roman Catholic, and Orthodox confessions, affords sufficient evidence of the groundlessness of any such suggestion. On the whole the relief agents have received due protection and assistance from the Ottoman authorities.[65]

Finally, I would like to mention a November 1903 memorandum by Lord Percy, parliamentary undersecretary for foreign affairs. Percy underscored that giving Crete autonomy resulted in the "voluntary" exile of a large proportion of the Muslim population. If such a solution had been adopted in Macedonia, the numbers involved would have been "infinitely larger."[66] The Balkan Committee put forward a plan of ethnic homogenization for Macedonia based on the "modification of territorial boundaries of the administrative units, with a view to the more regular grouping of the different nationalities."[67] Such a plan would have entailed multiple displacements and exchanges of civilian populations and caused a "humanitarian" tragedy not only for the Muslim populations but also for the vast majority of the Christians, who would have become Bulgarian, Greeks, Serbs, or Arumanians according to decisions made in one or the other European capitals.

Epilogue

> Could civilization (with a capital C) really ever be universal-
> ized, and how far could it be extended?
> —Mark Mazower, "An International Civilization," 2006

Humanitarian Intervention During the Interwar Period

The first world War marked the end of tsarist Russia, of the Hapsburg Empire, and of the Ottoman Empire. It was the first total war of the century, in which soldiers and civilian populations suffered as never before. As the Allies' war propaganda claimed, "civilized" European soldiers now committed massacres and atrocities against other civilized and Christian populations. In 1915 the Bryce report—named for the chair of the Committee of Alleged German Outrages, the same James Bryce so actively involved on behalf of the Armenians and the Macedonians before the war—proclaimed German forces guilty of widespread sadistic outrages during the invasion of Belgium. The alleged victims of the Germans were mainly women and children. The report accused German soldiers of raping women and girls; using civilians as human shields during combat; and cutting off children's hands and ears in front of their horrified parents, just like Leopolod's *Force Publique* had done in Congo a few years earlier.[1] If some of the German outrages were lurid inventions serving the war aims of the Allies, the Armenian genocide was not at all an invention. Not surprisingly, the Allies coined the term "crimes against humanity," referring to the intentional mass killing of innocent Armenian populations on unprecedented scale (at least as far as massacre and atrocities in the Ottoman Empire were concerned). As historian Michael R. Marrus puts it: "in practically every way one could imagine, the War of 1914–1918 transformed beliefs and practices of how states should interact internationally."[2]

The international order born after the end of the First World War and the creation of the League of Nations should have brought perpetual peace worldwide. The new international order would not have allowed humanitarian interventions undertaken by a self-appointed committee of powers allegedly acting in the interest of all members of the Family of Nations.[3] In theory, the League of Nations should have taken on the responsibility of humanitarian intervention as well as the protection of the most fundamental human rights all over the world.[4] The new "Society of Nations" should have given the sanction of social solidarity, on an objective basis, to the hitherto purely sporadic, isolated acts of "altruistic nations acting as enforcers of the law of nations."[5] Being capable of formulating and enforcing international law, the new Society of Nations should have limited national sovereignty, abolished the inequality of states, and hence—as University of Texas professor Malbone W. Graham put it—prevented such "crimes against humanity" as persecution, oppression, uncivilized warfare, injustice, and slave trade. In the long term, the League of Nations would have enforced "the prevention and control of disease, the reduction of the opium traffic, and the mitigation of suffering throughout the world."[6] In this idealistic view, the League of Nations and its members would have taken on the *responsibility to protect* humanity (see below).

In practice, as historian Mark Mazower points out, the new Society of Nations in Geneva still depended on the same civilizational hierarchies that had underpinned so much pre-1914 liberal thought.[7] Even though "half-civilized" states such as Abyssinia, Siam, Iran, and Turkey were now members of the League of Nations, it pertained only to the "civilized nations" to guide "the less, or uncivilized, into the way of national self-realization."[8] The institutionalization of a minority regime and of a mechanism of enforcement of the rights of minorities, however imperfect or flawed, certainly encompassed the idea of protecting the most basic human rights (of European civilian populations). The minority regime was—at least as far as European territories were concerned—an attempt to prevent massacres and atrocities such as those that had victimized the Ottoman Christians in the past. The victorious powers promoted the rights of minority groups as "obligations of international concern"—an echo of prewar humanitarian intervention, but without commitment to act diplomatically or militarily. According to Marrus, relinquishing what might have been their commitments to humanitarian intervention in the preceding era, the peacemakers looked to the League of Nations to speak and act on behalf of them all.[9] The regime bestowed sovereignty upon new European nations; it was selective, partial, and discriminatory as far as it did not apply to Germany or to the victor states.[10] Minority rights were a badge of the new states' secondary status, manifested by their need for tutelage in the exercise of their own sovereignty.[11] To be sure, the victorious powers were reluctant themselves to be bound by such agreements—creating a standing grievance among the "minority states" that festered over the period. Concern about minorities did not mean solicitude for them, and support for them was far from a transcendent humanitarian commitment. For instance, the victorious powers stood passively while hundreds of

Jews were forcibly uprooted and tens of thousands lost their lives in pogroms and other anti-Jewish violence accompanying civil wars and regional conflicts in East Central Europe.[12]

Beyond Europe, the Covenant of the League of Nations set up the Mandate System, which applied only to German colonial territories and to the Ottoman Empire territories beyond the boundaries of the newly independent state of Turkey. As Anthony Anghie notes, the Mandate System represented the international community's aspiration, through the League, to address colonial problems in a systematic, coordinated, and ethical manner.[13] "At the highest level, it embodied the ideal policy of European civilization towards the cultures of Asia, Africa and the Pacific."[14] On paper, the Mandate System consisted of rudimentary normative and institutional processes for the protection of the indigenous populations. In fact, it did not result in a comprehensive body of law that could be denominated international human rights law.[15] It adapted the old concept of trusteeship in a new legal, scientific, and allegedly objective form, instituting a new form of colonial power based not on political but on economic control. Mandate territories were inserted into that economy in a subordinate role. As a result, while those territories appeared to be freed from political control, they remained subject to the control of the parties that exercised power within the international economy.[16] In the ex-Ottoman territories of Syria, Palestine, and Iraq, the enforcement of the Mandate System had given the mandatory powers a chance to enforce the "enlightened" and "modern" reforms they had attempted in vain to impose on the Ottoman authorities. Very rapidly, however, the enthusiasm and optimism left the place, to the disillusionment of local populations, whose subjugation was protracted under French or British rule, and to the disenchantment of the ruling authorities now firmly convinced of the impossibility of exporting "civilization."

The League of Nations never disposed of the political and military capacity to enforce humanitarian intervention worldwide.[17] The ambitious idea of a League of Nations able to select and oversee the work of a single state mandated by the international community, as the agent of the league, to remove "unfortunate conditions violative of the most elementary human rights" never materialized.[18] The League of Nations did not provide for an extension of the Mandate System or a "policy of state-building" in circumstances related to a humanitarian intervention. There was no mechanism entrusting the state-members "either to assume the burden of the administration of the territory, or to constrain the unworthy sovereign to mend his ways."[19] As we know, the newfound international solidarity and increased integration and equality between states as well as the exercise, for the general welfare of humanity, of a new humanitarian intervention were never properly discussed at the League of Nations Council or Assembly. The alleged legality of humanitarian intervention through the development of new and enlightened standards of the social Law of Nations did not become a fruitful means for securing, through the international community, the redress of evils to which previous generations had been indifferent or blind. As Ellery Stowell noted in 1939, the barbarities perpetrated against Jews in several European states showed that intervention against a "great" state was impracticable. Nonetheless, he argued, other means were available and applicable, such as the granting of asylum in missions and consulates. Stowell acknowledged that this measure did not amount to humanitarian intervention and pointed out:

> Humanitarian intervention was of recent, but very vigorous, growth and tended to bind the whole world closer together in defense of elementary principles of justice. It is as yet a toddling infant that becomes stronger every day with the spread of communications. Even if the great development of national self-sufficiency and isolation should continue, this growth of humanitarian intervention will undoubtedly still go on, although it may be at a slower pace.[20]

The extermination of the European Jews and the other horrors of the Second World War proved Stowell's prediction tragically wrong. Moreover, the 1930s abuses of humanitarian intervention by Fascist Italy in Ethiopia (a war waged with the "humanitarian" aim of rescuing local populations from a "barbarian" government) and by Nazi Germany, which justified the intervention in Czechoslovakia on humanitarian grounds (the protection of the Sudeten German minority mistreated by the Prague government), gave to this international practice a very bad press after 1945.[21]

HUMANITARIAN INTERVENTION DURING THE COLD WAR (1945–89)

After the end of the Second World War, the emergence of international human rights law—starting with the 1948 Universal Declaration of Human Rights and the Convention for the Prevention and Punishment of the Crime of Genocide—sanctioned the interference in the relations between a sovereign and its citizens. However, despite the fact that the Charter of the United Nations promotes respect for human rights and for fundamental freedoms for all without distinction as to race, sex, language, or religion (articles 1 (3), 55, and 56), the issue of intervention when massive violations of the most basic human rights take place is ignored.[22] Many reasons explain the vanishing of this international practice for more than four decades. First, as a reaction to the tragic outcome of the Second World War, the UN Charter prohibits the use of force in international relations with the exception of self-defense in response to an armed attack against a state (article 2). The use of force can be mandated by the UN Security Council in case of a threat to, or a breach of, international peace or an act of aggression (chapter 7, articles 39–42). Second, the rapid process of decolonization, which started in the aftermath of the war, sanctioned the ineluctable end of the *standard of civilization* and the absolute condemnation of the idea of interfering in the internal affairs of a sovereign state and of imposing a foreign style of governance. The majority of the newly independent states, many of which had been European colonies, understandably viewed (and still view) the concept and practice of humanitarian intervention as an expression of imperialism. The UN General Assembly, where postcolonial states obtained the voting majority in the 1960s, decided that what constitutes a "threat to the peace" should be interpreted very restrictively. Fearing violations of newly independent states' sovereignty, the General Assembly excluded massive violations of the most basic human rights as legitimate motives of intervention.

The third factor explaining the fading of humanitarian intervention is systemic. The Cold War (1945–89) literally paralyzed the UN security system. The global confrontation between the two superpowers, the Soviet Union and the United States, left little room for intervention mandated by the Security Council. Neither of the superpowers wished to upset the global political order by intervening on grounds of humanity in the other's sphere of influence. Like the European powers during the nineteenth century, both were fully aware of the risks—now nuclear—of such an intervention to the international order. Nonetheless, when each superpower intervened within its sphere of influence, humanitarian considerations and rhetoric were systematically mentioned (the Soviet Union in Hungary in 1956 and Czechoslovakia in 1968; the United States in the Dominican Republic in 1965, Grenada in 1983, and Panama in 1989). As far as the other states of the international community are concerned, either they were still coming to terms with their imperialist or colonial past or they did not want to hear about humanitarian interventions, as in the case of many African and Asiatic countries. When intervention by India in Eastern Pakistan (1971), by Vietnam in Cambodia (1977), and by Tanzania in Uganda (1979) took place, the intervening states cited the threat to peace and their security, faithfully sticking to the letter of the UN Charter and avoiding reference to humanitarian motives, even though, in all these circumstances, massive violations of the most basic human rights did take place and could have been mentioned as a motive for intervention.

Humanitarian Interventions since 1989: A Comparison with the Nineteenth Century

With the end of the Cold War, the controversial concept and practice of humanitarian intervention resurfaced. During the 1990s the end of the Security Council's paralysis coincided with a number of massive violations of the most basic human rights in the context of civil wars or in states whose authority and institutions collapsed (the so-called failed states). On a number of occasions, the Security Council mandated humanitarian interventions. Among the cases of intervention in the 1990s were those on behalf of the Iraqi Kurds in 1991, Bosnia-Herzegovina from 1992 to 1995; and East Timor and Sierra Leone in 1999. Alongside these interventions were tragic cases of *non*intervention (or belated and utterly inadequate intervention), such as the 1994 genocide in Rwanda, war crimes in Chechnya, and crimes against humanity in Tibet. The 1990s were also marked by the controversial 1999 North Atlantic Treaty Organization (NATO) military intervention against the Federal Republic of Yugoslavia on behalf of the Kosovo Albanian population. This intervention was different from all the others, for it was undertaken without the mandate of the UN Security Council, allegedly to prevent an impending humanitarian catastrophe. The 1990s singularly contrast with the following decade (1999–2009) when no humanitarian intervention, notwithstanding the massive presence of UN peacekeepers, took place in the Darfur region of Sudan (2003–04) or the Democratic Republic of Congo, where, between 1998 and 2006, more than four million people were killed—a massive loss of civilian life greater than the estimates for the conflicts in the Balkans, Rwanda, Iraq, and Darfur combined.

The September 11, 2001, terrorist attacks against the United States profoundly affected its foreign policy. War against Afghanistan (since 2001) and the very controversial war and military occupation of Iraq (since 2003)—neither instances of humanitarian intervention—resulted in the military overstretch of U.S. armed forces and, more important, a considerable loss of moral credibility. The Iraq War, the abuse of a humanitarian rhetoric alongside the unsubstantiated allegation of the Iraqi government's possession of weapons of mass destruction, undermined the standing of the United States and Britain as norm carriers. Since 2003, with the possible exception of events currently taking place in Libya (March 2011), these states are no longer able to bear the costs of acting outside the world's institutional framework and or persuade others to act decisively in humanitarian emergencies. The Iraq War has also disrupted the fragile unity within the Security Council at a time when Russia is attempting to recover its global power status and China has considerably strengthened its own status as a global power. Hence, in various circumstances the Security Council has proved unable to take action. Do instances of humanitarian intervention and nonintervention during the last twenty years have something in common with nineteenth-century humanitarian interventions, or is their paradigm entirely new?

The Purpose of Humanitarian Intervention

Today, by humanitarian intervention we refer to an international practice aimed at ending the most serious and massive violations of human rights: genocide, crimes against humanity, war crimes, and ethnic cleansing. Even though the legal concept of genocide or crimes against humanity did not exist at the time, nineteenth-century humanitarian intervention was a coercive international practice at the interstate level to end massacre, atrocity, and extermination and to obtain redress for damages the victims suffered, along with indemnification for material injury and reasonable security for the civilian populations. We have seen that nineteenth-century armed interventions were biased and selective *ratione personae* (i.e., they occurred to protect Ottoman Christians) and *ratione loci*.

Then, as now, the intervening states made very clear that intervention was not an act of war or of military conquest. To be consistent with the stated principles of ensuring the provision of humanitarian assistance and the protection of civilians, and with the disinterested nature of the intervention, the 1990s armed humanitarian interventions have been events of limited duration. Retrospectively, some scholars have viewed the short-term commitment of the intervening states and of the United Nations as one of the main shortcomings of the 1990s international practice and argued in favor of the long-term protection of the victims of massive violations of the most basic human rights. Other scholars contest the appropriateness of armed interventions even if violations of the most basic human rights take place. Noam Chomsky argues that today's humanitarian interventions are nothing else than the replay of the old imperialist record, yet another Trojan horse of the West's neoimperialist tendencies.[23] Those who agree with Chomsky do see many similarities between nineteenth-century and post–Cold War humanitarian interventions. What they contest is precisely the adjective "humanitarian," which in fact conceals the self-interested motives of the intervening states, as was the case during the nineteenth century.

When comparing nineteenth- and late-twentieth-century interventions, Chomsky is certainly right in claiming that the rich and powerful are the inheritors of the colonial systems of global domination. It is also true that the rich and powerful intervened in weak and poor countries, and that the former do not accept any interference in their internal affairs when they massively violate the most basic human rights (as in the case of Russia in Chechnya or China in Tibet). No different from European policy-makers during the nineteenth century, in some circumstances agents of the World Bank and the International Monetary Fund, imbued with neoliberal ideology, might have been presumptuously convinced that after intervention takes place, the liberal democratic model of governance is the key to solve complex postconflict situations of the society where genocide, crimes against humanity or ethnic cleansing have occurred.[24]

In Chomsky's view, it is not merely the fact of intervening militarily that denotes the similarity to nineteenth-century interventions, but the alleged long-term protection of the victims of massive violations of human rights that replicates the "civilizing mission" and the colonial past. For Mahmood Mamdani, a Columbia University anthropologist, the end of the Cold War has led to a shift to post-1945 state sovereignty as a global principle of relations between states. In his view, the basic shift heralds "an international humanitarian order that promises to hold state sovereignty accountable to an international human rights standard."[25] The standard of responsibility, Mamdani argues, is no longer international law but rights. As of 2005 the UN World Summit (see below) adopted this new humanitarian order, claiming the responsibility to protect of vulnerable populations. That responsibility is said to belong to the international community, to be exercised in practice by the United Nations, and in particular by the Security Council, whose permanent members are the great powers. This new order, Mamdani argues, describes as "human" the populations to be protected and as "humanitarian" the crisis they suffer from, the intervention that promises to rescue them, and the agencies that seek to carry out intervention. Whereas the language of sovereignty is profoundly political, that of humanitarian intervention is profoundly apolitical, and sometimes even antipolitical. Hence, Mamdani says, we are witnessing a partial transition from the old system of sovereignty to a new humanitarian order confined to those states defined—by the powerful states—as "failed" or "rogue" states. The result is a bifurcated system, whereby state sovereignty obtains in large parts of the world but is suspended in more and more countries in Africa and the Middle East (Mamdani does not provide us with a list of these states). Rather than rights-bearing citizens, beneficiaries of the humanitarian order are akin to recipients of charity. Humanitarian intervention promotes dependence and heralds a system of trusteeship. For Mamdani, the era of the international humanitarian order is not entirely new and draws on the history of modern Western colonialism, when the leading Western powers claimed to protect "vulnerable groups." When it came to countries controlled by rival powers, such as the Ottoman Empire, "Western powers claimed to protect populations they considered vulnerable, mainly religious minorities like specific Christian denominations and Jews. In lands not yet colonized by any power, like South Asia and large parts of Africa, they highlighted local atrocities—such as female infanticide and suttee in India, and slavery in Africa—and pledged to protect victims from their rulers."[26] Chomsky and Mamdani suggest that the "humanitarian" label in the nineteenth as well as the twentieth century is a mere fig leaf concealing other motives that have nothing to do with saving the lives of strangers. If, for these authors, evidence of continuity is to be found in the imperialism of powerful states, in my view the clearest continuity between humanitarian interventions then and now is in the subordination of these interventions to international peace and security priorities of the great powers.

Humanitarian Intervention and Threats to International Peace and Security

During the nineteenth century, not every instance of massacre, atrocity, and extermination of Christians occurring in one or the other Ottoman provinces resulted in a humanitarian intervention. If the intervention threatened to destabilize the international system, despite the organization of impressive national and transnational public opinion campaigns, the European powers would not intervene to end massacre. Under the conditions of the nineteenth-century international system, before undertaking and intervention, European powers had to reach a collective agreement guaranteeing that none of them would unilaterally benefit from the intervention. Unilateral interventions were treated with bracing skepticism by all the other powers. When Russia tried in 1853–54 to assert a right unilaterally to protect persecuted Christian subjects of the sultan, the move, far from being unanimously applauded by France and Great Britain, provoked the Crimean War and the alliance of these powers with the sultan to protect the Ottoman Empire. Since 1989 the UN Security Council has acted in quite a similar way. When council members did not agree on the terms of an intervention or when massive violations of the most basic human rights took place within the boundaries of one of the major powers, intervention did not occur.

According to the original conception of the UN Charter, international peace means the absence of military conflict between states, and a threat to the peace presupposes the objective existence of a threat of aggression by one state against another. It was hardly the intention of the framers of the UN Charter that human rights violations in the context of internal conflicts should be regarded as a threat to international peace. During the Cold War the deployment of military force under the Security Council's aegis led to simple (first-generation) peace-keeping missions primarily entailing observation and reporting, with only light weapons used for self-defense. The point was to show the UN flag and utilize armed diplomacy to help fighting parties reduce or avoid hostile confrontation. As David Forsythe puts it: "humanitarian matters were excluded."[27]

After 1989 the UN Security Council motivated its resolutions in favor of intervention by considering massive violations of the most basic human rights in the context of civil wars and state collapse as threats to international peace. The UN Security Council asserted under chapter 7 of the UN Charter a right to engage in enforcement actions. As had been the case during the nineteenth century, the process developed inconsistently and selectively, with many double standards, because at times the unwillingness by major powers to spend money was matched by an unwillingness to run risks.

In 1991 the Security Council determined that the Iraqi authorities' repression of the Kurds and the ensuing border crossing of two million Iraqi Kurds threatened international peace. The UN insisted on free access by humanitarian organizations (Resolution 688/1991), demanding that Iraq immediately end the repression and ensure that the human and political rights of all Iraqi citizens be respected. A number of states undertook humanitarian relief operations in northern Iraq, backed by military force. In mid-April 1991 the intervening states—Britain, France, Italy, the Netherlands, and the United States—deployed over twenty thousand troops to protect "safe havens" (this term, under British insistence, was preferred to the more traditional "enclaves" on the grounds that the latter suggested a redrawing of boundaries). In the case of Yugoslavia and its successor states (1991–93), the Security Council considered civil war and serious violations of international humanitarian law another threat to international peace (Resolution 757/1992). The UN was unable to stop a number of massacres of civilian populations, the most tragic being that of Srebrenica (July 1995), where seven thousand civilians were murdered.

The Security Council also considered the humanitarian tragedy resulting from civil war and anarchy in Somalia a threat to international peace and security and authorized a military intervention on grounds of humanity (Resolution 733/1992). Without reference to cross-frontier implications, it acted under chapter 7, authorizing the member states and the secretary general to use all necessary means to establish as soon as possible a secure environment for humanitarian relief operations (Resolution 794/1992). The United States offered to head such an operation. The ambition was to restore hope, peace, stability, and law and order in Somalia. The humanitarian intervention was interrupted in 1995 when none of its aims were achieved.

When, in the spring of 1994, a civil war between the Tutsi and Hutu ethnic groups developed in Rwanda and led to the genocide of the Tutsi, as well as massacres of moderate Hutu civilians, the international community hesitated to intervene despite being fully informed about the tragic nature of the events. In Resolution 918/1994 the Security Council determined that the situation in Rwanda constituted a threat to international peace and security in the region and, under Chapter 7, imposed an arms embargo on Rwanda. Nothing was said about an intervention while the perpetrators kept committing crimes against humanity and genocide. In Resolution 929/1994 the Security Council, again under chapter 7, authorized the member states to carry out a military operation aimed at contributing, in an impartial way, to the security and protection of displaced persons, refugees, and civilians at risk in Rwanda and to use all necessary means to achieve this objective. The twenty-one states that were requested to contribute troops failed to do so. The genocide took place without any attempt being made to stop it. In four months some eight hundred thousand people were killed. American president Bill Clinton and his administration studiously avoided using the term "genocide" with regard to the mass killings of Tutsis in Rwanda and referred to "acts of genocide" to evade its obligations to prevent genocide under the terms of the 1948 Convention on the Prevention and Punishment of the Crime of Genocide.[28] Far too late, French troops eventually undertook a limited military operation. With resolution 955/1994 the Security Council established an International Criminal Tribunal for Rwanda to prosecute people responsible for genocide, crimes against humanity, and other serious violations of international humanitarian law. Thereby the council confirmed that such acts constitute, in themselves, a threat to international peace and security.

In East Timor the Security Council considered the acts of terror against the civilian proindependence population as a threat to international peace and security and, under chapter 7, authorized an international military operation to restore peace. In October 1999 the Security Council authorized the establishment of the United Nations Mission in Sierra Leone (UNAMSIL); six thousand troops assisted the implementation of the agreement under chapter 7, with an explicit mandate to protect civilians under imminent threat of physical force.[29] The Security Council's language increasingly connects massive violations of the most basic human rights to threats to collective security, as was the case during the nineteenth century. However, as two centuries ago, there is no guarantee that massive violation will lead to an intervention, and even when an intervention takes place, it often proves unable to stop the violations.

Ten years after the events in Rwanda, referring to the events taking place in Darfur, the U.S. Congress used the term "genocide." On September 9, 2004, the Secretary of State Colin Powell concluded that genocide was the appropriate term to use.[30] Two weeks later, President George W. Bush repeated the genocide charge during an address to the UN General Assembly.[31] The United Nations acceded to American pressure in October 2004 by creating an International Commission of Inquiry on Darfur. Three months later the commission concluded that the government of Sudan had not pursued a policy of genocide directly or through the militias under its control. The commission did find that the government's violence was "deliberately and indiscriminately directed against civilians." These acts amounted to "crimes against humanity."[32] By then, in a situation reminiscent of the summer of 1895 after the enquiries of the powers with respect of the events of Sasun had taken place, intervention to end crimes against humanity would have been possible and fully justified.

The UN Security Council established the United Nations Mission in Sudan (UNMIS), liaising and coordinating at all levels with the African Mission in Sudan (AMIS), and determined that the situation continued to constitute a threat to international peace and security. However, no armed intervention followed. In 2006 the AMIS, a peacekeeping force consistently hobbled by a weak mandate and inadequate logistical and financial support by Western donors, finally acknowledged the obvious: it was unable by itself to secure hundreds of thousands at risk across an area the size of France. The African Union/United Nations Hybrid Operation in Darfur (UNAMID)—a robust force of twenty thousand troops, six thousand police, and a significant civilian component— began its mandate only on December 31, 2007, more than two years after the International Commission of Inquiry had published its report and when the situation on the ground was no longer an emergency. The force was authorized until July 31, 2010 (SC Resolution, 1769/2007 and 1881/2009). According to UN staffers on the ground, the death rate in Darfur had by 2005 fallen lower than the level normally considered an emergency, and the UN force arrived far too late to end massacre and atrocities. In Mamdani's view, nothing shows that the Security Council is eager to secure a political settlement in Darfur, which in his view is what Sudan needs the most. This situation is, mutatis mutandis, quite similar to the Cretan intervention at the end of the century when none of the intervening powers was committed to securing a political settlement.

An Ex Post Facto International Practice with Unexceptional Outcomes and Unintended Consequences

Then, as now, intervening states viewed military intervention as a last resort. European powers wanted the Ottoman Empire to introduce autonomously the administrative, economic, and political reforms they deemed important, which in their view would have prevented the recurrence of massacre and subsequent intervention. Before undertaking an armed intervention, the European powers used diplomatic pressure and mediation and threatened coercive action in the near future if massacres were not stopped at once. Nineteenth-century humanitarian interventions were ex post facto events that did not prevent large-scale massacre but were modestly aimed at preventing further massacres from occurring. Recent humanitarian interventions too have been ex post facto events. They are caught in the dilemma that Robert Legvold has eloquently illustrated: "To wait until massive numbers of lives have been lost before acting [compounds] the tragedy. Yet, to reach agreement on forceful action in response to warning signs before tragedy strikes promises to be difficult in the extreme, if the evidence is ambiguous, as it is likely to be, and if a sizable number of states, including major powers (like Russia, China and India), start from a strong bias against intervention."[33]

In the last two decades it took an often tragically long time to ascertain facts, reach a political agreement, and intervene militarily when massive violations of the most basic human rights were taking place within the borders of a sovereign state. In the era of television carrying worldwide breaking news, of the Internet, of satellite images providing precise details of what is happening in a single square meter of a troubled area, of supersonic planes and ultrarapid ships, the intervening states showed to be as slow in the fact-finding process and the actual deployment of troops as nineteenth-century European powers were. In a similar way to the European powers in the nineteenth century, the United Nations must raise a military force from scratch for each and every operation, which takes considerable time.[34] The time required to negotiate collective intervention certainly does not work in favor of a rapid rescue operation. As during the nineteenth century, late-twentieth-century civilian victims of massive violations of the most basic human rights have suffered for months or even years before an intervention occurred (when it occurred), with one troubling exception.

Security Council Resolutions 1160 and 1199 of 1998 determined that the humanitarian situation in Kosovo, one of the provinces of the Federal Republic of Yugoslavia, constituted a threat to international peace and demonstrated the need to prevent a humanitarian catastrophe. Those who criticized the intervention stated that evidence of massive violations of the most basic human rights was unsubstantiated.[35] Contrary to the previous 1990s cases of intervention, this time the Security Council did not authorize a military intervention owing to the clear intentions of Russia and China to veto such a decision. In November 1998 NATO threatened the government of Belgrade that it would intervene using force. In March 1999, after negotiations with Belgrade failed, NATO undertook a military operation. The operation lasted until June 1999, when Belgrade agreed to sign an agreement with the member states of the "G8" on the autonomy of Kosovo and on an international military presence in that province. Only after the end of the military operations, *a posteriori*, did the Security Council (Resolution 1244/1999) welcome the agreement and authorize, under chapter 7, an international security presence in Kosovo. Shortly after, Kofi Annan, then United Nations secretary general, acknowledged the failure of diplomacy and evoked circumstances when the use of force may be legitimate in the pursuit of peace but stressed that the Security Council should be involved in any such decision. For the first time since the founding of the United Nations, a group of states, acting without explicit Security Council authority, defended a breach of sovereignty primarily on humanitarian grounds.[36]

How to explain the events of 1999? As in the nineteenth century, intervention is, in part, explained by the memory of past events. First and foremost was the massacre of some seven thousand Muslim males within the United Nations "safe haven" of Srebrenica in 1995 while the UN peacekeepers looked on as spectators. In 1998–99, in Europe as well as the United States, there was a growing perception of a developing humanitarian emergency in Kosovo. Many stories of atrocities allegedly perpetrated by the Serbs against the Kosovo Albanians circulated in the mass media, combined with images showing stream of refugees. These stories eventually solidified public opinion in Europe and the United States with respect to the urgency and legitimacy of an intervention.[37] Part of the story of the 1990s interventions, Mary Kaldor notes, is the way in which political leaders consistently learned the wrong lessons from each intervention, which then contributed to the failure of the next intervention:

> In particular, international policy seems to have swung from inaction or inadequate action to overwhelming force, especially the use of air strikes, and back again. It seems to have been very difficult to chart a middle course. The safe haven in Iraq was initially successful but was not sustained. The intervention in Bosnia was too weak and it was (probably) wrongly concluded that air strikes had been a crucial fac-

tor in the success of the final agreement. The intervention in Somalia was supposed to compensate for the weaknesses of the mandate in Bosnia; however, the US-led force emphasized the use of overwhelming force at the expense of politics. The Somali debacle resulted in the non-intervention in Rwanda, which was probably the most serious failure of the whole period. The need to restore credibility and act forcefully led to the NATO air attacks against Yugoslavia. And the intervention in East Timor was too late.[38]

To this day, intervention in Kosovo remains an exception rather than a meaningful precedent for a new international practice. This point was made abundantly clear by the UN secretary general, a considerable number of scholars, and the political leaders who had authorized the intervention, including U.S. secretary of state Madeleine Albright and British prime minister Tony Blair.

Nineteenth-century interventions' armed responses against massacre varied conspicuously: an expeditionary corps of a single state—France in Ottoman Morea and in the province of Syria—was mandated by all the other European powers. The intervening states could lead simultaneous though parallel rescue operations, such as the naval operation undertaken in Crete in 1867–68. In contrast to a classic war situation, European ambassadors in Constantinople and representatives of the Ottoman government negotiated possible solutions to the ongoing crisis before, during, and after the intervention. The European powers usually sent representatives (commissioners, consuls, or special envoys) to the Ottoman province where the crisis had occurred to ascertain the facts. They set up fact-finding commissions in charge of verifying whether a "just cause" for intervention existed. On some occasions, they gathered incontrovertible evidence of recent massacre, which they might (or might not, as in the case of the Armenian massacres of the 1890s) use as evidence leading to a "last resort" armed intervention. The European powers set up rudimentary ways to monitor troubled areas, such as in the eastern provinces of the Ottoman Empire inhabited by Armenian communities from 1878 to 1885. But in the end, nineteenth-century European powers intervened too late, with too few troops and means or both. The 1827 intervention in Navarino and the following military occupation of the Morea occurred seven years after the massacres of Chios and Smyrna and more than two years after the alleged "barbarization" plan of Ibrahim Pasha had begun. In 1860 the largely useless French expeditionary corps in Lebanon landed after massacres of Maronites and the Damascene Christians took place. In 1866–67 the European powers rescued Christian Cretan refugees, though their displacement was not the most appropriate response to the impending humanitarian emergency, for the rescue operation did not stop the insurgency. In the 1890s the intervention in and military occupation of the same island did not prevent or end the humanitarian catastrophe affecting both the Christian and Muslim communities. The Bulgarians in 1876 and the Armenians in the 1890s and 1900s were not rescued or protected by the European powers. Nonforcible intervention in Macedonia did not end the civil war. Moreover, because of the selective nature of the intervention, the European powers did not rescue Ottoman Muslim "guilty minorities," with the result that these civilian populations left the territories they inhabited, whether on a voluntary or forced basis.

The outcomes of the 1990s interventions are as dubious as that of nineteenth-century interventions. The 1992 intervention in Somalia ended up contributing to an escalation in the levels of violence in a civil war. Instead of providing aid and stability, the intervention had the unintended consequence of becoming the catalyst for further violence. The attempt to get occupying troops out on a strict timetable pegged to political reform did no better in Bosnia after 1995. Much as in Lebanon and Syria in 1860, the deadline had been casually set as a reassurance before the troops went in, and it came to look increasingly unworkable as it actually drew near.[39] Belated French intervention in Rwanda was largely useless; genocide continued during and after the landing of the small French expeditionary corps. According to a five-hundred-page report issued by the government of Rwanda in early August 2008, France actively participated in the 1994 Rwandan genocide by directly supporting the *génocidaire* regime.[40] Some scholars claimed that the airstrike strategy of NATO in Kosovo increased the number of civilians displaced or dead, including hundreds of Kosovar Albanians, aggravated the hatreds between the Serbs and the Kosovar secessionists, and intensified both fighting and killings among them.[41]

During the nineteenth century the armies of the intervening states did not fear the encounter with local rebels. European governments and public opinion felt certain that a Druze or Cretan insurgent would always be weaker and inevitably defeated by a French or British soldier. Nonetheless, to respect the principle of the disinterested nature of the intervention, the European expeditionary corps avoided confrontation with both local insurgents and Ottoman military. Europeans did not worry about losing a small amount of their soldiers. On the contrary, in the interventions that took place during the last two decades, the loss of a relatively low number of troops weighed heavily. In the 1990s the intervening states designed intervention to minimize risk to the military personnel and to achieve the highest possible public acceptance rate for a national deployment in military operations not directly related to traditional notions of national security. For instance, the loss of eighteen U.S. Rangers in Mogadishu in October 1993, their corpses dragged through the dusty street, heavily contributed to President Clinton's decision not to intervene in Rwanda in 1994.

Among the unintended consequences of humanitarian intervention, we might include "reverse ethnic cleansing," as in the case of Bosnia-Herzegovina after 1995 and of Serb and Roma minorities in Kosovo after 1999. The Dayton Agreement of December 1995 brought peace to Bosnia and Herzegovina at the cost of the division of territory, population, and almost every aspect of civil life along ethnic lines. Two years into the peace process, the progress of return of refugees and displaced persons was extremely disappointing. More than two million people—almost half the population—were still dispossessed of their homes. Some six hundred thousand of these were still refugees abroad who had not found a durable solution; many faced the prospect of compulsory return into displacement within Bosnia and Herzegovina. Another eight hundred thousand were internally displaced to areas in the control of their own ethnic group, living in multiple-occupancy situations, in collective centers, or in property vacated by the displacement of others, often in situations of acute humanitarian concern.[42] In Kosovo the KFOR/UNMIK peacekeeping process did not prevent a new phase of ethnic cleansing, a lethal coercive process by which the Serbs and Roma were induced to leave Kosovo or endure the deadly consequences of remaining behind. NATO did not fulfill its responsibility for economic and social reconstruction, including the reintegration of returning refugees, as well as its offers of stability to the South Balkans as a region.[43]

These are examples of poor management of postintervention rebuilding processes by the intervening states and organizations. In the case of nineteenth-century interventions, European powers deliberately encouraged "reverse ethnic cleansing" and the departure of Muslim Ottoman minorities living in the Balkans in order to enhance the creation of more homogeneous religious areas where, supposedly, massacres were less likely to happen. In the nineteenth century the long-term protection of Ottoman Christians invariably meant for the Ottoman Muslim "guilty minority" the denial of basic protections for their lives and properties. The European powers did not cope at all with the issue of reconciliation of ethnic and religious communities. In their view, the best option was the removal or departure of the Muslim communities where they happened to be a minority (as in Greece, Crete, and Macedonia) or the ethnic/religious separation of the rival groups (the plan of *désagrégation* of the Druze and Maronite communities elaborated by the European commissioners in 1861).

The Victims of Massacre, the Target State, and the Intervening States

Nineteenth-century humanitarian intervention took place in a clearly defined geographical area of the globe—the Ottoman Empire—and proved to be a selective practice as far as the humanity on behalf of whom it took place was concerned. Contrary to the European powers, the Security Council does not refer to the lack of civilization of the target state as the explaining factor of genocide, crimes against humanity, and ethnic cleansing. The post-1945 international community is based on the equality of races, languages, and religions among its member states and has developed a formidable institutional presence that did not exist during the nineteenth century. In the 1990s the United Nations intervened militarily to protect Somalis, a black, Muslim population, and NATO did the same to protect Muslim Bosnians and the Muslim Albanian majority of Kosovo. This is a difference between nineteenth-century and late-twentieth-century interventions, which Chomsky and Mamdani overlook, although the "indifference" in the case of Rwanda or the allegation that the genocide was nothing else than the manifestation of typical violence of that region of the world considerably darkens the post-1945 picture.

During the nineteenth century European powers viewed the Ottoman Empire as a "weak" or an *ante litteram* "failed" state unable to perform the tasks of statehood, to protect its (Christian) subjects, to prevent massacre, atrocities, and extermination, and to put an end to these occurrences. Critics of humanitarian intervention argue that the agents of postintervention attribute the lack of development and the occurrence of massive violations of the most basic human rights to the absence of "good (i.e., liberal) governance." This commonplace relies on universal international human rights norms, which makes it appear neutral and potentially applicable to all states. Although 1990s humanitarian interventions occurred within the borders of "weak" (weakened because of ongoing civil war or having a weak internal legitimacy, efficacy, and stability) or "failed" states (because their internal political and administrative systems, both central and peripheral, have collapsed), contrary to the Ottoman Empire, today's weak states have multiple ways, such as the General Assembly of the United Nations, to make the international community aware of the abuses of intervention by powerful states against them. Moreover, late-twentieth-century interventions exhibited what political scientist John Ruggie calls the "qualitative dimension" of multilateralism.[44] These interventions were organized according to, and in defense of, "generalized principles" of international responsibility and the use of military force, many of which are codified in the UN Charter, in UN declarations, and in the UN's standard operating procedures. Despite these changes, equality of race, language, and religion did not really matter when massive violations of the most basic human rights took place within the boundaries of rich and powerful states, as in the cases of Chechnya and Tibet. In this respect not much has changed since the nineteenth century: powerful states at the center of the system are the leading force behind interventionist policy and do not become targets of humanitarian interventions.

As in the nineteenth century, post–Cold War interventions have been determined by the mixed motives of the intervening states. Take, for instance, the intervention to protect Iraqi Kurds. This military operation, which remains an exceptional intervention to protect a community oppressed by its own government, was the result of the special circumstances determined by the 1990 Gulf War. Against a defeated Iraqi army, there was little risk to soldiers' lives in providing humanitarian protection to the Kurds. The Gulf War ensured that forces and logistics were readily and cheaply available. Despite the fact that conditions to protect the Shi'a civilian populations living in southern Iraq were favorable, the intervening states did not create "safe havens" but "no-fly zones." Arguably, the Shi'a needed the same protection as the Kurds received, but in their case the intervening states did not want an increase in Iranian influence in the region.[45] Hence, political, economic, and strategic factors clearly shaped the intervention, which was selective and discriminated against the Iraqi Shi'a. In the end, as the media spotlight began to shift elsewhere and public interest waned, the commitment of Western governments to protect the Kurds evaporated. Finally, it should not be forgotten that the intervention enjoyed initial success in dealing with the refugee problem and alleviating the immediate suffering of the Kurds, but the short-term palliative measures were not replaced by a long-term solution.

A well-known example of a government pursuing its own political agenda while undertaking a humanitarian intervention is that of France in Rwanda in 1994. The French government emphasized the "strictly humanitarian" character of the operation, and French prime minister Édouard Balladur argued that France was obliged to intervene to stop "one of the most unbearable tragedies in recent history." French policy-makers claimed to be responding to an outraged public, but the government covertly pursued its national self-interest. France had a long-standing relationship with the government of President Juvénal Habyarimana, it had supported the one-party Hutu state for twenty years, and it provided troops when the Rwanda Patriotic Front (RPF) threatened to overrun the country in 1990 and 1993. President François Mitterrand was anxious to restore waning French credibility in Africa and fearful that an RPF victory in French-speaking Rwanda would result in the country coming under the influence of Anglophone countries. Paris feared the potentially explosive impact on Zaire (where President Mobutu's dictatorial regime had been a staunch ally of France) of an educated and democratic government in Rwanda. As a result, the French actions were concentrated in the southwestern part of the country on the border with Zaire, where Hutu forces loyal to the ousted government were strongest, and did not provide adequate humanitarian assistance to the mass population of Rwanda.

FROM SHORT-TERM RESCUE TO LONG-TERM PROTECTION OF VICTIMS

Part and parcel of nineteenth century interventions were schemes of reforms the Ottoman authorities were supposed to enforce after the intervention to avoid repetition of massacre. The intervening states were fully involved and committed in what we would refer to as post-intervention rebuilding processes (e.g., durable peace and promotion of good governance and sustainable development). Postintervention offered the Europeans an opportunity to introduce "civilization" in the "barbarous" Ottoman Empire, and the intervening states pretended to know what was best for the Ottoman government and all its population. In fact, these packages of reforms overlooked the Ottoman government's interests, those of non-Christians populations, and the aspirations of local Christian populations, especially when they aspired to self-determination. European powers put considerable effort into the settlement of the question, as well as in ground-level reconstruction efforts. Despite lacking the vast array of institutional tools and specialized agencies and nongovernmental organizations (NGOs) that exist today, the European powers attempted to create better living conditions for Christian communities by repairing infrastructure, rebuilding housing (as in Lebanon), planting and harvesting (as in Crete), cooperating in other productive activities, setting up efficient gendarmeries (as in the Macedonian provinces), reforming the Ottoman financial system, or introducing tax collection.

Europeans in charge of the rebuilding process faced complex situations and were confronted with unplanned and dramatic changes that clearly went beyond the initial scope of the intervention. For instance, they were fully aware that massacres, atrocities, and extermination brought about the question of refugees and what Marcus Cox has defined as "a game of musical chairs, in which it [was] impossible to return one family to its home without causing the further displacement of another."[46] Intervening states learned that humanitarian interventions have a tendency to expand their reach, that extrication is difficult, and that the pressure to deepen involvement in a political direction is great. Since the 1820s, the intervening states were aware that the skills required to put an end to massacre were very different from those required to rebuild peace in an Ottoman province or to feed and protect civilians in an emergency or its aftermath. They realized that soldiers were not trained to provide police services, and, since the intervention in Crete of 1866–68, they insisted on, and sometimes provided the officers for, a gendarmerie.

The duration of the 1990s interventions was as limited and short as possible and left unresolved the question of the settlement of the very issue that brought about the gross violations of human rights.[47] In the early 2000s, because of the flaws and failures of the 1990s, scholars such as Bass, Keohane, Ignatieff, and Wheeler put forward the idea that after the rescue of the victims, a long-term political, economic, social, and military commitment of the intervening states and international organizations should help local actors create a new polity governed by law. These scholars are fully aware that any prolonged participation in the internal affairs of another state arouses the suspicion of many governments all over the world and thus have attempted to find the optimum-size intervention: big and lengthy enough to provide long-term protection for the victims of massive violations of the most basic human rights, but small and swift enough not to be mistaken for imperialism.[48]

Keohane views humanitarian interventions of the next era of world politics as having two phases: destructive and constructive. In the destructive phase, military action ends control over a society by a regime that massively abuses human rights. In the constructive phase, economic aid is provided and efforts to build state institutions are carried out, typically under the auspices of an international organization such as the United Nations. The constructive phase of humanitarian intervention is uncomfortable for postcolonial sensitivities, especially when it is prolonged. It creates a "quasi-imperial situation in which outsiders rule by virtue of force, legitimated by their supposed good intentions and the pronouncements of international organizations."[49] In his view, however, the alternative—leaving resentful occupants of the troubled area to figure out ways to strike back at the rich societies from which the interventions came—is increasingly unattractive owing to the globalization of informal violence wielded by nonstate actors. Hence, Keohane imagines three stages and three different categories of sovereignty that could provide procedures to help regularize movement toward the recovery of full sovereignty for the target state of an intervention, and to avoid the above-mentioned risks. At first, sovereignty may be denied, as in trusteeship arrangements. Then, "nominal sovereignty" could be reintroduced and the country would regain international legal sovereignty—and its seat in the United Nations—whereas domestic authority would still be in the hands of the United Nations or some other outside authority. As the troubled society begins to recover, it would make sense to grant its new state institutions a little bit of sovereignty at a time. The next step, Keohane argues, would be "limited sovereignty," in which domestic governance is for the most part controlled by local people, but the United Nations or another external authority can override its decisions when they are seen to be abusive to human rights or to contradict agreements that have been made. The final stage would be "integrated sovereignty," in which nationals of the state control domestic authority and there is no continually functioning external authority, but there are constitutional restrictions, adjudicated by a supranational court and potentially enforceable by the country's neighbors.[50] Whether the reader of this book shares Keohane's proposals or prefers Mamdani's analysis, the fact is that sovereign states still are the main actors of world politics. We have not yet entered in the "next era of world politics," and the "new humanitarian order" is far from being unanimously accepted or a reality. Hence, the unrelenting tensions between sovereignty and intervention will persist, even when intervention takes place in failed states.

Public Opinion and New Humanitarianism

Nineteenth-century media played a crucial role in stimulating the debate on humanitarian intervention among a receptive and cultivated public opinion. Public opinion coalesced (and coalesces today) around grisly events. We have seen that reporters played an important role after the massacre of Chios, and that the authorities of the target state attempted to censor European newspapers. For the exact same reasons, Bass points out, the Sudanese government is restricting foreign press coverage of Darfur today.[51] But just as the press was inconsistent in its reach, it was also skewed in its coverage, as Mamdani shows in the case of Sudan. The British press in the 1820s was pro-Greek because of its philhellene sources. It was philo-Cretan or pro-Macedonian because of the same sources. But this does not mean that newspaper reporting should be dismissed as just the voice of national bias. It would be hard to argue that British newspapers were covering Greece or Bulgaria because of a deep and abiding British interest in those particular areas of the Balkans.[52] There was surely a biased and selective interest in the plight of Christians over that of Muslims. The accounts of horrors in French and British newspapers or Delacroix's paintings exhibited in Paris had a tremendous impact on public opinion, which is similar to, though on a far smaller scale than, BBC-World or CNN "breaking news" images of Rwandan civilians armed with machetes slaughtering women and children on the side of a road.[53]

During the late nineteenth century, humanitarian groups were successful in heightening public awareness of massacre, atrocity, and extermination of foreign civilian populations and introducing a theme in the domestic and foreign policy political agenda of European governments and parliaments. By the turn of the century, transnational movements such as the pro-Armenians, pro-Macedonians, or the Congo Reform Association showed themselves to be capable of coordinating their actions and initiatives beyond national borders. Today, as in the nineteenth century, media (including Internet social media) and public attention to massive violations of the most basic human rights in the context of an internal conflict seems to be a necessary, but not sufficient, condition for an intervention to take place.

Nineteenth-century humanitarians had a strong political and religious credo, supported humanitarian interventions, and took political positions as far as the objectives of the interventions were concerned that went beyond stopping massacre and atrocity. Nineteenth-century humanitarians pretended to perform "purely" disinterested actions when in fact they were inevitably driven by their own ideology and political agenda. H. N. Brailsford, active in the British Relief Fund in Macedonia, had no compunction in spelling out in disgust his belief in a fundamental difference between the moral standards of London or Paris and those of the Balkans. Without second thoughts about English performance in South Africa, the Indian continent, or Ireland, he wrote that "when the rulers govern by virtue of their ability to massacre upon occasion, where Christian bishops are commonly supposed to organise political murders, life has but a relative value, and assassination no more than a relative guilt. There is little to choose in bloody-mindedness between any if the Balkan races—they are all what centuries of Asiatic rule have made them."[54] Brailsford, like many other humanitarians, was a supporter of the "civilizing mission"; he was a fervent Christian who disdained Muslim "infidels"; he perceived the Ottoman Empire to be the antithesis of the values of modernity and progress that he firmly believed in. Nineteenth-century humanitarians were active in founding or participating in the activities of relief societies; they published and read international affairs reviews, funded the publication of pamphlets and brochures, and organized fundraising and subscriptions to fulfill domestic and foreign humanitarian activities as well as petitions to pressure the government.

During the last quarter of the twentieth century, human rights transnational advocacy groups and humanitarian NGOs, in conjunction with leading foreign policy strategists, established a rights-based humanitarian consensus often referred to as the "new humanitarianism," in contrast with the older generation of humanitarians, typically incarnated by the International Committee of the Red Cross (ICRC) delegates' profession of an apolitical impartiality and neutrality. "Old humanitarians" view the beneficiaries of aid as passive recipients, seek to alleviate suffering, and do not necessarily act to defend violated rights, whereas "new humanitarians" are concerned with long-term human rights outcomes rather than short-term humanitarian necessity. As David Rieff notes, humanitarian relief organizations became some of the most fervent interventionists.[55] Today, new humanitarians are openly radical, political, and campaigning. In this respect, they have something in common with late-nineteenth-century humanitarian campaigners, for they want relief to have long-term political impact and are prepared to see humanitarian aid used as a tool to achieve human rights and political goals.[56] As Fiona Fox put it in 2001, the unelected, often unaccountable, and usually foreign humanitarian becomes judge, juror, and politician in Third World conflicts. Similarly to Brailsford in 1903, the late twentieth century's "new humanitarians," like the Save Darfur Coalition analyzed by Mamdani, reach verdicts on highly complex political crises. Sometimes they are asked to decide which strategy would best deliver peace and stability and to predict the impact of humanitarian aid on the future development of a given conflict.[57]

As Europeans did with Ottoman Muslim civilian populations throughout the nineteenth century and during the early twentieth century, new humanitarians have deemed several populations undeserving of aid, including Rwandan Hutus, Afghans, and Iraqis, because they have been associated with the crimes of their leaders. Perhaps the most striking example, according to Fox, was that of the Serbs in 1999, when it became almost impossible to attract funds to deliver aid programs in Serbia while aid poured into Kosovo and Albania. To many observers, new humanitarians are the heralds of a new form of colonialism, and the specter of multimillion-dollar NGOs ignoring national sovereignty to march into nation-states, supported by Western armies and declaring the correct way to resolve a hitherto local conflict, is surely suspect. Kirsten Sellars portrayed the following image of an operational NGO: "Heeding the impulse to take up the latter-day 'White Man's Burden,' battalions of NGOs marched into Mogadishu, Sarajevo and Goma armed with landcruisers, satellite phones and the latest liberal imperalist orthodoxies. Local governments retreated in their path, and soon many areas in these countries became de facto zones of occupation under the control of humanitarian armies."[58]

According to David Chandler, the human rights movement's progressive agenda is little more than a myth. It may promise empowerment of marginalized peoples, but it works in the opposite direction by enabling Western elites and governments to impose their agenda, by force if necessary. Worst of all, Chandler believes, the human rights agenda is undermining international order by eroding classical international law and expanding the reasons for waging war.[59] The United Nations attempted to respond to the kind of criticism put forward by opinion-makers and scholars like Chandle establishing a Commission in charge to study the responsibility to protect civilian populations victims of massive violations of the most basic human rights.

R2P: OLD WINE IN NEW BOTTLES?

At the UN Millennium Assembly in September 2000, Canadian prime minister Jean Chrétien announced that an independent International Commission on Intervention and State Sovereignty (ICISS) would be established as a response to Secretary General Kofi Annan's challenge to the international community to endeavor to build a new international consensus on how to respond in the face of massive violations of human rights and humanitarian law.[60] Launched on September 14, 2000, the commission sought to find new ways of reconciling the seemingly irreconcilable notions of intervention and state sovereignty. The commission completed its work within a year, and during the fifty-sixth session of the United Nations General Assembly it informed the international community of its findings and recommendations for action.[61] The report, entitled *The Responsibility to Protect* (known as the "R2P"), was published shortly after the terrorist attacks of September 11, 2001. The R2P's main assumption is that state authorities are responsible for the functions of protecting the safety and lives of citizens and promotion of their welfare. The report emphasized a shift of fundamental importance from a definition of sovereignty as the control governments have on their citizen to sovereignty as responsibility. The agents of a state are responsible for their actions and accountable for their acts of commission and omission, and when they show themselves to be unwilling or unable to protect their citizens, the international community becomes responsible for the victims of massive violations of the most basic human rights. The national political authorities are responsible to the citizens internally and, through the United Nations, to the international community.

The R2P should be placed in historical perspective and understood as a way of addressing the major flaws and failures of the 1990s interventions. Not surprisingly, the report strongly emphasizes the "responsibility to prevent" massive violations of the most basic human rights and criticizes the 1990s interventions' lack of attention to the monitoring of situations that might potentially lead to genocide or crimes against humanity. The R2P put forward "the responsibility to rebuild' a society where massive violations of the most basic human rights have taken place, highlighting the poor management of "exit strategies" during the 1990s. When it comes to the crux of the matter, the report merely mentions the six classic criteria of intervention (right authority, just cause, a right intention, last resort, proportional means, and reasonable prospects of success). With the possible exception of the inclusion of large-scale "ethnic cleansing," whether carried out by killing, forced expulsion, acts of terror, or rape, in the list of the most serious violations of the most basic human rights, the report is far from innovative. The ICISS confirms once again that overthrowing a regime should not be the legitimate objective of the intervention, although disabling that regime's capacity to harm its own people is viewed as being essential to discharging the mandate of protection. The R2P views occupation of territory not as an objective as such and claims that there should be a clear commitment from the outset to returning the territory to its sovereign owner at the conclusion of the military phase of the intervention, or, if that is not possible, administering it on an interim basis under UN auspices.[62] As a way of helping ensure that the right intention criterion is satisfied, the R2P suggests that military intervention always take place on a collective or multilateral rather than single-country basis, which was the solution adopted during the nineteenth century by the European powers.

As international legal scholars Laurence Boisson de Chazournes and Luigi Condorelli point out, the R2P does not innovate in any shape or form, with the exception of the terminology, which seems to mark the rejection of the controversial *"droit (ou devoir) d'ingérence."*[63] The report is nothing more than a solemn reconfirmation, framed in a single document, of the rooted principle of the national and international responsibility of protecting all human beings against massive violations of the most basic human rights. What the R2P desperately lacks are the instruments and tools allowing the enforcement of the responsibility to protect when the state's authorities, the international community, and the UN Security Council do not respect their duty to protect the victims of massive violations of the most basic human rights. The report does not answer the question of what to do when a sovereign state is unable or unwilling to protect its own citizens, when peaceful attempts to end massive violations of human rights fail, and, most important, when the Security Council is paralyzed. Should we remain powerless spectators of the killings, or should somebody else (the General Assembly, a regional organization, "available" states) replace the Security Council and trigger the most adequate operations—even military if necessary—to end the sufferings caused by the continuous perpetration of crimes?[64]

The UN Secretary General's High-Level Panel on Threats, Challenges and Change, which reported to Kofi Annan in December 2004, took up positively the ideas put forward by the R2P. In *A More Secure World: Our Shared Responsibility*, the panel's experts proposed that the UN should adopt the emerging norm of the responsibility to protect in cases of "genocide and other large-scale killing, ethnic cleansing or serious violations of international law."[65] Instead, the ensuing secretary general's report *On Larger Freedom* placed the responsibility to protect in the section dealing with freedom to live in dignity, detaching the idea of taking on responsibility from an automatic equation to armed force and to emphasize the need to implement the responsibility to protect through peaceful means.[66] In 2005, when the UN General Assembly adopted the R2P, its more draconian principles were diluted even further.

In September 2005, 191 states committed themselves to the principle that the rule of nonintervention was not sacrosanct in cases where a government was committing genocide, mass killing, and large-scale ethnic cleansing within its borders. As Carsten Stahn puts it, paragraphs 138 and 139 of the 2005 General Assembly's *Outcome Document* are a "rather curious mixture of political and legal considerations, which reflects the continuing division and confusion about the meaning of the concept" of responsibility to protect.[67] States committed themselves to act only on a case-by-case basis through the council, which stands in contrast to the assumption of a systematic duty. The *Outcome Document* also entirely dropped the idea of guidelines for the authorization or endorsement of the use of force by the council and did not firmly state that UN collective security action constitutes the only option for responding to mass atrocities through the use of force. The United States, for example, argued that the *Outcome Document* should not foreclose the possibility of unauthorized intervention, noting that there may be cases that involve humanitarian catastrophes but for which there is also a legitimate basis for states to act in self-defense. The *Outcome Document* also left the door open to unilateral responses through its "case-by-case" vision of collective security and a qualified commitment to act in cooperation with regional organizations. The issue of what should happen if the Security Council were unable or unwilling to act was not discussed.[68] The issue of postintervention engagement was mainly addressed in institutional terms through the creation of the Peace-Building Commission, which was specifically established to address the challenge of helping countries make the transition from war to lasting peace.[69] According to Stahn, since 2005 there is consensus only on what he calls the negative dimension of R2P: the limited ability of the host state to invoke sovereignty against external interference, whereas the issue of whether and under what circumstances states may use force to end large-scale violations of the most basic human rights is still controversial. There is even less agreement on the idea that foreign entities have a positive duty to act, a positive obligation to intervene under the concept of responsibility to protect. Consensus becomes very thin when it comes to defining to whom this responsibility shifts if a state fails to live up to its primary duty to protect citizens living in its territory.[70]

In conclusion, I believe that the current paradigm of humanitarian intervention is not entirely different from that of the nineteenth century. Looking at the number of times responsibility to protect and humanitarian intervention are used with respect to events currently taking place in Libya, it seems the latter is definitely back in fashion or that the former has not yet ousted the latter as predominant terminology. More important, "responsible" interventions to protect civilian populations victims of gross violations of human rights are still subordinated to collective security priorities of the intervening states; they are still the result of mixed motives; their modalities still vary conspicuously though they always take place ex post facto and are led by rich and powerful states within the territories of weaker states; even when they are well-intentioned and genuinely aim at ending massacre, their outcomes are unexceptional, controversial, and produce unintended consequences. Writing the conclusion of this book in mid-March 2011, watching events unfolding in Libya, it seems likely to me that the next armed intervention to protect victims of genocide or crimes against humanity will probably be faced with a stark choice between waiting until massive numbers of lives have been lost or reaching rushed agreement on forceful action in response to ambiguous evidence before tragedy strikes. The next intervention will hardly target rich and powerful states. If Western states intervene in weaker non-Western countries, their deeds are likely to be viewed as a replay of the old imperialist record. If they do not intervene, they will be accused of indifference and racism for doing nothing in the face of massive human suffering. If intervention is limited and focuses on rescuing victims, intervening states will be accused of unwillingness to spend money or take military risks. The long-term protection of victims through durable peace, promotion of good governance, and sustainable development will arouse suspicion among many governments fearing a repetition of the *mission civilisatrice*. As

Alex Bellamy puts it: "Changing the language of humanitarian intervention (from sovereignty vs. human rights to levels of responsibility) has not changed its underlying political dynamics. As such, 'responsibility to protect' language may also be used to inhibit the emergence of consensus about action in genuine humanitarian emergencies."[71]

Today's international community, despite the increasing role of international and transnational nonstate actors, is still a community of sovereign states. Despite the increased social and economic interdependence between states, nation-states are still the chief providers of foreign and domestic security for human populations.[72] The international community has not yet moved beyond the system of Westphalia and has not entirely overcome the idea of state sovereignty. Although all the preconditions for a new era of human rights exist, there are still formidable obstacles hindering its advent. Despite all the relevant changes introduced after 1945, humanitarian intervention has not become legal and has not been legitimized on the basis of universal values or principles, or as the result of the creation of new global governing structures. In 1999 Kofi Annan asked: "If humanitarian intervention is, indeed, an unacceptable assault on sovereignty, how should we respond to a Rwanda, to a Srebrenica—to gross and systematic violations of human rights that offend every precept of our common humanity?"[73] In 2011, as events in Libya seem to demonstrate, this question still awaits a definitive answer.

Abbreviations

A. & P.	Accounts and Papers, general abbreviation for the *Blue Book*. They are referred to under their title, number (if any), and year of publication, the document number.
CP	Correspondance Politique, MAE
CPC	Correspondance Politique et Consulaire, MAE
CRAC	Correspondence Respecting the Affairs of Crete
CRAAT	Correspondence Respecting Reforms in Asiatic Turkey
CRIRAPAT	Correspondence Respecting the Introduction of Reforms in the Armenian Provinces of Asiatic Turkey
FO	Foreign Office Papers, Public Record Office
FCRAC	Further Correspondence Respecting the Affairs of Crete
FCRASEE	Further Correspondence Respecting the Affairs of South Eastern Europe
MAE	Archives du Ministère des Affaires Etrangères, Quai d'Orsay, Paris
PRO	Public Record Office
TNA	The National Archives, Kew, London

SYSTEM OF REFERENCE FOR ARCHIVAL SOURCES

I follow General Information Leaflet 25, "How to Cite Documents in the National Archives," for all Public Record Office documents. As far as possible I follow the same method for the documents of the French Ministère des Affaires Etrangères.

The National Archives (TNA): Public Record Office (PRO), department code, series number, author, possibly followed by organization, recipient, document number, date in day-month-year format, and document title in quotation marks, only if important.

The spelling of Turkish, Greek, Armenian, and Arabic words and names is determined by diplomatic usage. The reader must be aware that the spelling is mistaken, and that a popular and diplomatic usage has been used.

Notes

Introduction

1. United Nations, *The Humanitarian Decade: Challenges for Humanitarian Assistance in the Last Decade and into the Future* (New York: Office for the Coordination of Humanitarian Affairs, 2002).

2. Robert O. Keohane, "Introduction," in *Humanitarian Intervention: Ethical, Legal, and Political Dilemmas*, ed. J. L. Holzgrefe and R. O. Keohane (Cambridge: Cambridge University Press, 2002), 1.

3. Gary Bass, *Freedom's Battle: The Origins of Humanitarian Intervention* (New York: Knopf, 2008).

4. Nicholas Wheeler, *Saving Strangers: Humanitarian Intervention in International Society* (Oxford: Oxford University Press, 2000).

5. Simon Chesterman, *Just War or Just Peace? Humanitarian Intervention and International Law* (Oxford: Oxford University Press, 2001), 30.

6. Jacques Sémelin, *Purify and Destroy: The Political Uses of Massacre and Genocide*, trans. Cyntia Schoch (New York: Columbia University Press, 2007), 323; *Le Massacre, Objet d'Histoire*, ed. David El Kent (Paris: Gallimard, 2005). Gareth Evans has reintroduced the term atrocity in the debate on the *Responsibility to Protect*. See Gareth Evans, *The Responsibility to Protect: Ending Mass Atrocity Crimes Once and for All* (Washington, DC: Brookings Institution Press, 2008).

7. J. Sémelin, "Qu'est-ce qu'un crime de masse? Le cas de l'ex-Yougoslavie," *Critique Internationale*, no. 6 (2000): 143–58.

8. Richard Ashby Wilson and Richard D. Brown, "Introduction," in *Humanitarianism and Suffering: The Mobilization of Empathy*, ed. R. A. Wilson and R. B. Brown (Cambridge: Cambridge University Press), 1.

9. Francis Kofi Abiew, *The Evolution of the Doctrine and Practice of Humanitarian Intervention* (The Hague: Kluwer Law International), 1999, 33.

10. Tzvetan Todorov, *The Conquest of America* (Norman: University of Oklahoma Press, 1999), 149–50.

11. Coleman Philipson, *Alberico Gentili De jure belli, 1612*, Classics of International Law, trans. Rolfe (Oxford: Clarendon Press, 1933), cited in Chesterman, *Just War*, 14.

12. Hugo Grotius, *De jure belli ac pacis*, book 3, 1646, Classics of International Law, trans. Kelsey (Oxford: Clarendon Press, 1925), xxv § 8(3)–(4), cited in Chesterman, *Just War*, 15.

13. Samuel Pufendorf, *De jure naturae et gentium libri octo* (1688), Classics of International Law (Oxford: Clarendon Press, 1934), 8, vi, § 14, cited in Chesterman, *Just War*, 15

14. Chesterman, *Just War*, 18, quotes E. de Vattel, *The Law of Nations: Principles of the Law of Nature, Applied to the Conduct and Affairs of Nations and Sovereign*,

1758, Classics of International Law, trans. Fenwick (Washington, D.C.: Carnegie Institution, 1916).

15. Some historians use the words charity, philanthropy, and humanitarianism interchangeably, and others maintain rigid distinctions. David Owen implies an expanding meaning, reflected in the etymology. Charity reflects Christian principles, philanthropy is not necessarily religious, and humanitarianism, which first appeared in English the 1800s, describes—often derisively—those concerned with the welfare of humankind. See Dean Pavlakis, "The Development of British Overseas Humanitarianism and the Congo Reform Campaign," *Journal of Colonialism and Colonial History* 11 (2010), http://muse/jhu.edu; Frank Prochaska, "Philanthropy," in *The Cambridge Social History of Britain 1750–1950*, vol. 3, ed. F.M.L. Thompson (Cambridge: Cambridge University Press, 1990), 360; Hugh Cunningham, "Introduction," in *Charity, Philanthropy, and Reform: From the 1690s to 1850*, ed. Hugh Cunningham and Joanna Innes (New York: St. Martin's Press, 1998), 2; Donna T. Andrew, *Philanthropy and Police: London Charity in the Eighteenth Century* (Princeton: Princeton University Press, 1989), 5; David Edward Owen, *English Philanthropy, 1660–1960* (Cambridge: Belknap Press of Harvard University Press, 1964).

16. Samuel Moyn, "Human Rights in History," *Nation*, August 11, 2010; and Moyn, *The Last Utopia: Human Rights in History*, (Cambridge: Belknap Press of Harvard University Press, 2010), 29.

17. Samuel Moyn, "Spectacular Wrongs," *Nation*, October 13, 2008, 32.

18. Bruce Mazlish, *The Idea of Humanity in a Global Era*, Basingstoke : Palgrave Macmillan, 2009.

19. Wilson and Brown, *Humanitarianism*, 4.

20. The sect was founded in 1782 by Henry Venn, vicar of Huddersfield; Zachary Macaulay, one of the first governors of Sierra Leone, a London merchant and for fifteen years manager of the Evangelical journal *The Christian Observer*; Henry Thornton, the wealthy banker, member of Parliament for Surrey; James Stephen, the lawyer; and John Shore, governor-general of India from 1793 to 1799.

21. Wilson and Brown, *Humanitarianism*, 10.

22. Howard Temperley, "Anti-Slavery," in *Pressure from Without in Early Victorian England*, ed. Patricia Hollis (London: Arnold, 1974), 27–51; Linda Colley, *Britons: Forging the Nation, 1707–1837*, 2d ed. (London: Pimlico, 2003), 354–55.

23. Wilhem G. Grewe, *The Epochs of International Law: Translated and Revised by Michael Byer*, (Berlin: Walter de Gruyter, 2000).

24. The British Empire outlawed slave trade in 1807. It was only in 1833 that the Whig colonial secretary, Lord Stanley, introduced a bill to abolish slavery in the empire. The abolition of slavery as a domestic institution of property rights was accomplished in each state where it had previously been legal without military intervention by other states.

25. Oded Löwenheim, "'Do Ourselves Credit and Render a Lasting Service to Mankind': British Moral Prestige, Humanitarian Intervention, and the Barbarity Pirates," *International Studies Quarterly* 47 (2003): 23–48; Ann Thomson, *Barbary and Enlightenment: European Attitudes towards the Maghreb in the 18th Century* (Leiden: Brill, 1987), 123–42.

26. Evans, *The Responsibility to Protect*, 17, quotes Hedley Bull's evocative phrase.

27. John Kane, *The Politics of Moral Capital* (Cambridge: Cambridge University Press, 2001), 7. Kane, a political scientist, defines moral capital as moral prestige—whether of an individual, organization, or cause—in useful service. Moral capital is a resource and derives its worth from its value and utility, from the moment when "moral prestige" is mobilized "for the sake of tangible, exterior returns." The concept of moral capital draws attention to the ways that moral distinction can become a source for power in the world, the ways that it facilitates and legitimizes action. Moral capital sustains and enhances the reputation of an actor or actors. A cause that has earned moral capital itself becomes a source of moral capital for other causes, and the association with people or causes that possess moral capital becomes a strategic benefit for moral standing or moral influence.

28. Chaim D. Kaufmann and Robert A. Pape, "Explaining Costly International Moral Action: Britain's Sixty-Year Campaign against the Atlantic Slave Trade," *International Organization*, 53 (1999): 631–68. Kaufmann and Pape argue that costly moral international actions related to the abolition of the slave trade and of slavery were an outcome of a domestic cry for moral reform, motivated mainly by parochial considerations; in other words, the fact of saving strangers was not central to ending the slave trade.

29. Wilson and Brown, *Humanitarianism*, 18.

30. Bass, *Freedom's Battle*, 360.

31. Michael Barnett and Thomas G. Weiss, "Humanitarianism: a Brief History of the Present," in *Humanitarianism in Question*, ed. M. Barnett and T. Weiss (Cornell: Cornell University Press, 2008), 1–49.

32. Alice L. Conklin, "Colonialism and Human Rights, a Contradiction in Terms? The Case of France and West Africa, 1895–1914," *American Historical Review* 103 (1998): 419–42.

33. Bass, *Freedom's Battle*, 344.

34. Jennifer Pitts, *A Turn to Empire: The Rise of Imperial Liberalism in Britain and France* (Princeton, Princeton University Press, 2005), 14–16.

35. Peter Mandler, " 'Race' and 'Nation' in Mid-Victorian Thought," in *History, Religion, and Culture: British Intellectuals History 1750–1950*, ed. S. Collini, R. Whatmore, and B. Young (Cambridge: Cambridge University Press, 2000), 226–44.

36. Stuart Woolf, "French Civilization and Ethnicity in the Napoleonic Empire," *Past and Present* 124 (1989): 96–120. See also Bruce Mazlish, *Civilization and Its Contents* (Stanford: Stanford University Press, 2004).

37. François Guizot, *Histoire de la civilisation en Europe (1828)* (Paris: Hachette, Pluriel, 1985); J. S. Mill, "Civilization," in *Dissertations and Discussions: Political, Philosophical, and Historical* (London, 1869), 1:160–205; Michael Levin, *J. S. Mill on Civilization and Barbarism* (Routledge: Oxon, 2004); Georgios Varouxakis, *Victorian Political Thought on France and the French* (Basingstoke: Palgrave, 2002), 35–37; J. Joseph Miller, "Chairing the Jamaica Committee: J. S. Mill and the Limits of Colonial Authority," in *Utilitarianism and Empire*, ed. Bart Schultz and Georgios Varouxakis (Oxford: Lexington Books, 2005), 155–78.

38. Gerrit Gong, *The Standard of "Civilization" in International Society* (Oxford: Clarendon Press, 1984).

39. Ronald Hyam, *Britain's Imperial Century, 1815–1914: A Study of Empire and Expansion*, 3d ed. (Basingstoke: Palgrave, 2002), 76.

40. Alice L. Conklin, *A Mission to Civilize: The Republican Idea of Empire in France and West Africa, 1895–1930* (Stanford: Stanford University Press, 1997), 1. Contesting the existing historiography, Conklin argues that the *mission civilisatrice* cannot be dismissed as window dressing and claims that republican France invested the notion of a "civilizing mission" with a fairly specific set of meanings that set limits on what the government could and could not do in the colonies. For an interesting criticism of Conklin's study, see Gary Wilder, *The French Imperial Nation-State: Negritude and Colonial Humanism between the Two World Wars* (Chicago: University of Chicago Press, 2005), 6–7.

41. Conklin, *A Mission to Civilize*, 106.

42. Jennifer Pitts, "L'Empire britannique, un modèle pour l'Algérie Française: Nation et civilisation chez Tocqueville et John Stuart Mill," in *L'Esclavage, la colonisation et après . . . France, Etats-Unis, Grande-Bretagne*, ed. Patrick Weil and Stéphane Dufoix (Paris: Puf, 2005), 55–81, at 69; Pitts, *Writings on Empire and Slavery: Alexis de Tocqueville, Edited and Translated by Jennifer Pitts* (Baltimore: Johns Hopkins University Press, 2001).

43. Jack Donnelly, "Human Rights: A New Standard of Civilization?" *International Affairs* 74 (1998): 1–24, at 6.

44. Karuna Mantena, "The Crisis of Liberal Imperialism," in *Victorian Visions of Global Order: Empire and International Relations in Nineteenth-Century Political Thought*, ed. Duncan Bell (Cambridge: Cambridge University Press, 2007), 113–35, at 113–14.

45. Mark Mazower, "An International Civilization? Empire, Internationalism and the Crisis of the Mid-twentieth Century," *International Affairs* 82 (2006): 553–66, at 554.

46. Bass, *Freedom's Battle*, 372–73.

47. Ibid., 25.

48. Ibid., 37. I do not intend to dismiss the importance of the "penny press," though I believe that pamphlets and reviews are equally important and possibly had a greater impact on the cultivated elites, close to the political power, and that European policy-makers paid as much attention to this printed matter as they did to the penny press.

CHAPTER ONE: THE INTERNATIONAL CONTEXT OF NINETEENTH-CENTURY HUMANITARIAN INTERVENTIONS

1. Bruno Arcidiacono, "Les projets de réorganisation du système international au XIXe siècle (1871–1914)," *Relations Internationales* 123 (2005): 11–24; and "Pour une généalogie de la Charte des Nations Unies: la tradition directoriale," *Relations Internationales* 127 (2006): 5–23. In the first article Arcidiacono convincingly argues that the *directoire* was essentially different from the traditional system of equilibrium (the balance of power, a system that sought to

preclude the mastery of one power, prevent the conversion of the system into a universal empire, and reinforce the independence of European states). The pentarchy seemed to be a more effective system to the powers involved in it, for solidarity among them was the best possible guarantee of success; it was also more realistic than other "recipes" in that the "big five" had a manifest advantage. Its principal weakness was that the common interest of the five powers was constantly challenged by their individual ambitions and aims.

2. Richard B. Elrod, "The Concert of Europe: A Fresh Look at an International System," *World Politics* 28 (1976): 159–74, at 171; Paul W. Schroeder, *The Transformation of European Politics 1763–1848* (Oxford: Oxford University Press, 1994); and Georges-Henri Soutou, "Was There a European Order in the Twentieth Century? From the Concert of Europe to the End of the Cold War," *Contemporary European History* 9 (2000): 329–53.

3. Paul W. Schroeder, *Austria, Great Britain, and the Crimean War: The Destruction of the European Concert* (Ithaca: Cornell University Press, 1972), 405.

4. Aslı Çırakman, *From the "Terror of the World' to the Sick Man of Europe":* *European Images of Ottoman Empire and Society from the Sixteenth Century to the Nineteenth* (New York: Peter Lang, 2002), 156–57, 164. The Earl of Crawford might have been the first person (in 1769) to use the metaphor of a sick man to describe the decline of the empire. Tzar Nicholas I pronounced the historical phrase in 1853 to Sir Hamilton Seymour: "Nous avons sur les bras . . . un homme très malade; ce serait, je vous le dis franchement, un grand malheur, si, un de ces jours, il venait à nous échapper, surtout avant que toutes les dispositions nécessaires fussent prises."

5. Donald Bloxham, *The Great Game of Genocide: Imperialism, Nationalism, and the Destruction of the Ottoman Empire* (Oxford: Oxford University Press, 2005), 11–12.

6. Robert Phillimore, *Commentaries upon International Law*, 3d ed. (London: Butterworths, 1879), 1:552–68; Frantz Despagnet, *Cours de droit international public*, 3d ed. (Paris: Librairie de la Société du Recueil Général des Lois et des Arrêts, 1905, §IV, *Historique de l'intervention*, 221–38; Thomas J. Lawrence, *The Principles of International Law*, 4th ed., 2 vols. (London: Macmillan, 1911), 124; P. H. Winfield, "The History of Intervention in International Law," *British Year Book of International Law* (1922), 130–49; Thomas G. Otte, "Of Congresses and Gunboats: Military Intervention in the Nineteenth Century," in *Military Intervention: From Gunboat Diplomacy to Humanitarian Intervention*, ed. Andrew Dorman, T. Otte (Aldershot: Ashgate, 1993), 19–52.

7. W. E. Lingelbach, "The Doctrine and Practice of Intervention in Europe," *Annals of the American Academy of Political and Social Science* 16 (1900): 1–32, at 2.

8. Montagu Bernard, *On the Principle of Non Intervention: A Lecture Delivered in the Hall of All Souls' College* (Oxford: Parker, 1860).

9. Georgios Varouxakis, " 'Great' versus 'Small' Nations: Size and National Greatness in Victorian Political Thought," in *Victorian Visions of Global Order*, 136–58, at 154; Bell, "The Victorian Idea of a Global State," 160.

10. Stephen D. Krasner, "Sovereignty and Intervention," in *Beyond Westphalia? State Sovereignty and International Intervention*, ed. G. M. Lyons and M. Mastanduno (Baltimore: Johns Hopkins University Press, 1995), 228–49, at 233.

11. In 1821 the British government rejected the Holy Alliance's principle of intervention in European affairs and successfully imposed the principle of respecting the principle of nonintervention in cases of internal changes of European governments or constitutions.

12. Krasner, *Beyond Westaphalia*, 233.

13. In the last twenty-five years scholarship has provided abundant evidence that the paradigm of the centuries-long decline and inevitable demise of the Ottoman Empire is mistaken. This paradigm held that Ottoman elites set in motion a long and steady decline that dragged on from the eighteenth to the early twentieth century. Despite some efforts to ape the West, the long-decaying empire ineluctably disappeared with the end of the First World War. Among many others, see the recent publication by Karen Barkey, *Empire of Difference: The Ottomans in Comparative Perspective* (New York: Cambridge University Press, 2008).

14. Stanley Lane-Poole, *The Life of the Right Honourable Stratford Canning: Viscount Stratford de Redcliffe*, 2 vols. (London: Longman, Green, 1888), 1:345–46.

15. A. de Lamartine, *Souvenirs, impressions, pensées et paysages pendant un voyage en Orient, 1832–1833, ou note d'un voyageur, oeuvres complètes* (Paris, 1861). In 1840 Lamartine argued that it was in the interest of humanity to vivify the inert corpse of Islam, not violently but "naturally," thanks to the activity of more productive populations that were not supposed to strangle it. The Ottomans had to let the West join the Orient. They had to let Europe extend its laws, arts, customs, industry, and commerce to the fifteen or twenty peoples who could be found living at the edges of the empire. The Mediterranean, which was neither a French nor an English sea, but a European sea, was to become once again the theater and the vector of an incalculable amount of commerce and ideas. A. de Lamartine, "La question d'Orient: la guerre. Le ministère. Deuxième article, août 1840," in Renée David, *Lamartine: La politique et l'histoire* (Paris, Imprimerie Nationale, 1993), 164.

16. Henry Richard, *Evidence of Turkish Misrule*, Eastern Question Association, Papers on the Eastern Question, no. 1 (London: Cassell, Petter and Galpin, 1876), 8.

17. Kingsley Martin, *The Triumph of Lord Palmerston: A Study of Public Opinion in England before the Crimean War* (London: Hutchinson, 1963), 203–5.

18. Ann Pottinger Saab, *Relcutant Icon: Gladstone, Bulgaria, and the Working Classes, 1856–1878* (Cambridge: Harvard University Press, 1991), 66–71.

19. MAE, CP de la Turquie jusqu'à 1896, vol. 346, Doc. No. 68, l'Ambassadeur à Constantinople Lavalette au Ministre des Affaires Etrangères—Edouard Thouvenel, 18 September 1860: "si les Ottomans ont mérité de disparaître, les Chrétiens d'Orient sont-ils bien dignes de prendre leur place? Sauront-ils mieux ce qu'ils doivent à la civilisation générale de cette Europe dont ils feront, à leur tour, partie? Autant de questions que se posent avec amertume, sans pouvoir les résoudre. . . . Où trouver un terme . . . qui satisfasse, à la fois la justice, la politique, l'humanité?"

20. *Recueil des traités de la Porte Ottomane* (Paris: Amyot, Editeur des Archives Diplomatiques, 1855), 2:399ff. In 1832 the Ottoman government promulgated a special status for the island of Samos. The island had a special political or-

ganization and was placed under the orders of a Christian chief (bey or prince), named by the sultan. A council (*conseil*) composed of members chosen from the local notables administered the island and decided autonomously about religious and commercial issues.

21. Thomas Brassey, *The Eastern Question and the Political Situation at Home* (London: Longmans, Green, 1877); H. A. Munro-Butler-Johnstone, *The Turks: Their Character, Manners, and Institutions, as Bearing on the Eastern Question* (Oxford: James Parker, 1876); Alfred Austin, *Tory Horrors or the Question of the Hour: A Letter to the Right Hon. W. E. Gladstone, M.P.*, 2d ed. (London: Chatto and Windus, 1876); John Boyd Kinnear, *The Mind of England on the Eastern Question: What England Thinks. What England Wishes. What England Can Do* (London: Chapman and Hall, 1877). Among the French authors: Albéric Cauhet, *La question d'Orient dans l'histoire contemporaine (1821–1905)*, préface de Frédéric Passy (Paris: Dujarric, 1905); Max Choublier, *La question d'Orient depuis le traité de Berlin* (Paris, 1897); Étienne Lamy, *La France du Levant* [1900] (London: Elibron Classics, 2003); René Millet, *Souvenirs des Balkans; de Salonique à Belgrade et du Danube à l'Adriatique* (Paris: Hachette, 1891); Charles Sancerme, *La question d'Orient populaire* (Paris: Librairie Ch. Delagrave, 1897); *Solution de la question d'Orient proposée au Congrès de Berlin par un publiciste d'Orient* (Paris: Charles Schiller, 1878).

22. Modern scholarship has convincingly shown that strongly motivated Ottoman reformers were responsible for the bulk of the reforms; they were not puppets of the Western powers and acted to implement their own program and to further their own political cause.

23. In the view of the Europeans, this was certainly not intended as a way to establish a democracy, to support Balkan or Middle Eastern nationalist movements, or to advocate self-determination of the Ottoman provinces inhabited by fellow Christians. During the first half of the century British and French prime ministers and the secretaries of their respective ministries of foreign affairs, as well as diplomats, military, and civil servants on the spot, could hardly be described as democrats. Internal constitutional and institutional reforms in Great Britain and in France (under the July Monarchy as well as under Napoleon III) did not lean toward democracy, and it would be a mistake to think that Europeans dealing with reforms in the Ottoman Empire aimed to impose democratic reforms.

24. Bloxham, *The Great Game*, 32–33.

25. According to tradition, Ottoman subjects were members of a religiously defined community called *millet*. Each millet had its own hierarchy, led in theory by its religious leader, namely, the patriarch of Istanbul for Orthodox Christians and the chief rabbi for the Jews; it administered its own courts for personal status cases and ran its own educational institutions. The Ottoman concept of the millet recognized a theocratic order where the spiritual chief served as arbiter in both secular and spiritual matters. He was high priest, chief administrator, and supreme judge. The sultan guaranteed the lives, property, and liberties of his subjects and allowed them to follow their own religion; in return the subjects had certain restrictions imposed on their rights and were taxed. The majority of nineteenth-century Europeans assumed that Ottoman Muslims formed one community and non-Muslims another.

26. Bruce Masters, *Christians and Jews in the Ottoman Arab World: The Roots of Sectarianism* (Cambridge: Cambridge University Press, 2001), 140–41; Kemal H. Karpat, "*Millets* and Nationality: The Roots of the Incongruity of Nation and State in the Post-Ottoman Era," in *Christian and Jews in the Ottoman Empire, The Functioning of a Plural Society*, ed. Benjamin Braude and Bernard Lewis (London: Holmes and Meier, 1982), 141–69.

27. Edouard Engelhardt was one of the assistants to Jules Ferry, several times French plenipotentiary minister under the Third Republic. Engelhardt wrote frequently for the *Revue générale de droit international public*, and his writings were often translated into English.

28. E. Engelhardt, *La Turquie et le Tanzimât, ou histoire des réformes dans l'empire Ottoman depuis 1826* (Paris: A. Cotillon, 1882), 1:4, 2:299: "le législateur moderne devait avant tout faire disparaître dans l'État la confusion originelle qui identifiait le gouvernement de la chose publique avec la religion."

29. Ibid., 2:324.

30. Ibid., 2:328.

31. Masters, *Christians and Jews*, 7.

32. British experts, diplomats, and political leaders involved with Ottoman affairs never described the settlement colonies of Canada, Australia, New Zealand, and the Cape Colony as a type of constitutional governance that the Ottoman government could apply. They only rarely compared the situation in some of the provinces of the Ottoman Empire with Ireland, a country de facto annexed to Great Britain.

33. In Malta and the Ionian islands, the British ruled disregarding the liberties of local (Christian) populations, which they viewed as singularly unfitted to enjoy any portion of political power. The long rule of "King Tom" Maitland, governor of Malta and lord high commissioner of Ionia, and previously governor of Ceylon, was a typical example of "proconsular despotism." Maitland had autocratic control of the central executive power, while notables and landowners were given more power over administrative and judicial measures in the villages. To Maitland the Ionians were as "uncivilized" as Muslim Turks and other Ottoman Christian populations. See Michael Pratt, *Britain's Greek Empire: Reflections on the History of the Ionian Islands from the Fall of Byzantium* (London: Collings, 1978).

34. Guido Abbattista, "Empire, Liberty and the Rule of Difference: European Debates on British Colonialism in Asia at the End of the Eighteenth Century," *European Review of History—Revue Européenne d'Histoire* 13 (2006): 473–98; Sankar Muthu, *Enlightenment against Empire* (Princeton: Princeton University Press, 2003); J. Pitts, "Jeremy Bentham: Legislator of the World?" in *Utilitarianism and Empire*, 57–93.

35. J. Pitts, "L'Empire britannique" in *L'Esclavage, la colonisation et après*, 58–73; Pitts, *A Turn to Empire*, 143; Miller, "Chairing the Jamaica Committee" in *Utilitarianism and Empire*, 162–66.

36. The most significant of all these capitulatory agreements was that accorded to France on May 28, 1740. It recognized the exclusive right of France to protect those foreign nationals whose countries were without representatives at the Porte and gave permission to all members of "Christian and hostile na-

tions" to continue to visit Jerusalem "under the flag of the emperor of France, with no permission to do so under any other flag." The final article bound future sultans to observe these obligations.

37. Roderic Davison, *Essays in Ottoman and Turkish History 1774–1923: The Impact of the West* (Austin: University of Texas Press, 1990), 29–50. Articles 7 and 14 of this treaty dealt with the protection of Christianity in the Ottoman Empire and with an Orthodox Church that Russia could build in Istanbul. The interpretation of these articles aroused controversy. It was very clear to the Russians, to the Ottomans, and to the rest of the European powers, and it would be as clear for the whole nineteenth century, that Russia did receive some specific rights to act within the Ottoman Empire on behalf of Christians. The rights were three: to build one Russo-Greek church in Istanbul, to make diplomatic representations with respect to that one church and those who served it, and to protect the Christians of Moldavia and Wallachia.

38. Bloxham, *Great Game*, 12.

39. MAE, Mémoires et Documents, vol. 107, *Etudes pratiques sur le protectorat religieux de la France en Orient par Georges Outrey, consul de première classe*, Constantinople, 8 September 1898, 10–13, and 99–104.

40. Despagnet, *Cours*, 395: "La différence absolue de civilisation et de religion entre les peuples chrétiens et les peuples musulmans ou de l'Extrême-Orient entraîne une telle divergence d'idées entre eux, au point de vue de la morale et du droit, que les premiers n'auraient jamais pu s'astreindre à la législation ni au pouvoir arbitraire et despotique des seconds; aussi, presque tous les gouvernements de l'Europe ont-ils passé avec ces derniers Etats des traités qui ont pour objet de soustraire, à peu près complètement, leurs nationaux établis dans ces pays à l'influence des autorités locales."

41. Andrew Wheatcroft, *Infidels: A History of the Conflict between Christendom and Islam* (London: Penguin, 2004), 213.

42. Phillimore, *Commentaries*, 1:620, 460–88. See also William I. Shorrock, *French Imperialism in the Middle East: The Failure of Policy in Syria and Lebanon 1900–1914* (Madison: University of Wisconsin Press, 1976).

43. Thomas J. Lawrence, *The Principles of International Law*, 2 vols., 4th ed., rev. (London: MacMillan, 1911), 1st ed. 1895 (London: Elibron Classics Replica Edition, 2003), 1:254–58; Pasquale Fiore, *Il diritto internazionale codificato e la sua sanzione giuridica*, 4th ed. (Turin: Union Tipografico-Editrice Torinese, 1909), 210–12. Here Fiore claims that the privilege of extraterritoriality is personal and cannot be extended to the point of covering entire consular districts, in which citizens of various states live protected by the Capitulations.

44. Patrick Thornberry, *International Law and the Rights of Minorities* (Oxford: Oxford University Press, 1991), 33.

45. Sémelin, *Purify and Destroy*, 322–23.

46. Convention on the Prevention and Punishment of the Crime of Genocide Adopted by Resolution 260 (III) A of the United Nations General Assembly on December 9, 1948, art. 2. Available at http://www.hrweb.org/legal/genocide.html.

47. Martin Shaw, *What Is Genocide?* (Cambridge: Polity Press, 2007), 49.

48. Sémelin, *Purify and Destroy*, 345.

49. William A. Schabas, *Genocide in International Law* (Cambridge: Cambridge University Press, 2000), 196. Sémelin, *Purify and Destroy*, 345–46, agrees with the views of Michael Mann and Norman Naimark that applying the notion of "genocide" to all destruction/eradication processes raises difficult issues. He believes that the distinction between "ethnic cleansing" and "genocide" is a relevant one. "Ethnic cleansing" and "genocide" are indeed on the same continuum of destruction with the purpose of eradication.

50. Norman Naimark, *Fires of Hatred: Ethnic Cleansing in Twentieth-Century Europe* (Cambridge: Harvard University Press, 2001), 3; Andrew Bell-Fialkoff, "A Brief History of Ethnic Cleansing," *Foreign Affairs* (Summer 1993): 110–23; Benjamin Lieberman, *Terrible Fate: Ethnic Cleansing in the Making of Modern Europe* (Chicago: Ivan R. Dee, 2006); Michael Mann, *The Dark Side of Democracy: Explaining Ethnic Cleansing* (Cambridge: Cambridge University Press, 2005).

51. *Opinions and Policy of the Right Honourable Viscount Palmerston* (London: Colburn, 1852), 314–15.

52. The term "annihilation" (*Vernichtung*) appeared also in the orders General von Trotha gave to repress the Herero of South West Africa. And even though his initial order might not have meant the physical extermination of the entire Herero people, as Tilman Dedring argues, his line of reasoning clearly blurred the distinction between their military defeat and their wholesale destruction. Tilman Dedering, "A Certain Rigorous Treatment of All Parts of the Nations: The Annihilation of the Herero in German South West Africa, 1904," in *The Massacre in History*, ed. M. Levene and P. Roberts (New York: Berghan Books, 1999), 205–22.

53. Sémelin, *Purify and Destroy*, 339: "Some colonial massacres were probably perpetrated with this in mind, like that of the Herero population of Namibia in 1904 by the German settlers. Are there other examples? This is subject for debate, and more research need to be done, particularly on the nineteenth century."

54. It should be recalled that Europe had a long tradition in the forceful removal of populations. Spain got rid of the Jews in 1492, and of the Moors and of the Moriscos, the Moor descendants, in 1606 when, as historian Andrew Wheatcroft puts it, in a final act of ethnic cleansing, they were marched to the seaports and shipped to Morocco. Wheatcroft, *Infidels*, 37.

55. Mark Levene, "Introduction," in *The Massacre in History*, 26–27.

56. Patrick Brantlinger, *Dark Vanishing: Discourse on the Extinction of Primitive Races, 1800–1930* (Ithaca: Cornell University Press, 2003), 3, 36.

57. Pitts, *Writings on Empire and Slavery*, xv, 228–29.

58. Political scientist Martha Finnemore illustrates that the seeds of the ways in which interveners identified with victims to determine who was an appropriate or compelling candidate for intervention lay in the abolition of the slave trade. Finnemore considers abolitionism the first step toward the consolidation of a new set of norms universalizing "humanity" and endowing it with rights. Martha Finnemore, "Constructing Norms of Humanitarian Intervention," in *The Culture of National Security: Norms and Identity in World Politics*, ed. Peter J. Katzenstein (New York: Columbia University Press, 1996), 153–85; and Finnemore, *The Purpose of Intervention: Changing Beliefs about the Use of Force* (Ithaca: Cornell University Press, 2003).

CHAPTER TWO: EXCLUSION OF THE OTTOMAN EMPIRE FROM THE FAMILY OF
NATIONS, AND LEGAL DOCTRINES OF HUMANITARIAN INTERVENTION

1. Edward W. Said, *Orientalism: Western Conceptions of the Orient* (London: Penguin, 1995).

2. James Renton, "Changing Languages of Empire and the Orient: Britain and the Invention of the Middle East, 1917–1918," *Historical Journal* 50 (2007): 645–66.

3. J. W. Burrow, *Whigs and Liberals: Continuity and Change in English Political Thought. The Carlyle Lectures 1985* (Oxford: Clarendon Press, 1985, 116–17); Thierry Hentsch, *L'Orient imaginaire: La vision politique occidentale de l'Est Méditeranéen* (Paris: Minuit, 1987), 157.

4. On the impact of Montesquieu in Great Britain, see F.T.H. Fletcher, *Montesquieu and English Politics (1750–1800)* (Philadelphia: Porcupine Press, 1980 [1939]).

5. Jean Dimakis, *P. Codrika et la question d'Orient sous l'Empire Français et la Restauration* (Paris: Edition Jean Maisonneuve et Presses de l'Université de Montréal, 1986). Codrika held this position at the ministry from 1802 to his death in 1827.

6. J. M. Berton, *Les Turcs dans la balance politique de l'Europe au dix-neuvième siècle ou considérations sur l'usurpation et sur l'indépendance de la Grèce: Suivies d'une nouvelle traduction des Lettres de Lady Montague sur la Turquie* (Paris: La Librairie Nationale et Etrangere, 1822), 7–9.

7. Ibid., 41–42.

8. Laurent Dhorne, "Les conceptions diplomatiques de Chateaubriand," mémoire, Université de Lille, 2000–2001, 95.

9. François-René de Chateaubriand, *Itinéraire de Paris à Jérusalem et de Jérusalem à Paris: Oeuvres complètes de Chateaubriand*, 5 vols. (Paris: Garnier, 1861).

10. Chateaubriand, *Mémoires d'Outre-Tombe* (Paris: Gallimard–La Pléiade), 2:261, 275–76. Also "Congrès de Vérone," in *Oeuvres complètes de Chateaubriand* (Paris: Garnier, 1861), chap. 18.

11. Henry Laurens, *Le Royaume Impossible. La France et la genèse du monde arabe* (Paris: A. Colin, 1991), 38.

12. Benjamin Constant, *Political Writings*, trans. and ed. Biancamaria Fontana (Cambridge: Cambridge University Press, 1988); Pitts, *A Turn to Empire*, 179, 318.

13. Thomson, *Barbary and Enlightenment*, 30–31.

14. Richard Cobden, "Russia 1836," in *The Political Writings of Richard Cobden*, 2 vols. (London: T. Fisher Unwin, 1903).

15. Ibid., 1:206.

16. Patricia M. E. Lorcin, *Imperial Identities: Stereotyping, Prejudice and Race in Colonial Algeria* (London: I. B. Tauris, 1999), 244–49; Sharif Gemie, "France, Orientalism and Algeria: 54 Articles from the *Revue des Deux Mondes*, 1846–52," *Journal of Algerian Studies* 3 (1998): 48–70.

17. Fanny Janet Blunt, *The People of Turkey: Twenty Years' Residence among Bulgarians, Greeks, Albanians, Turks, and Armenians. By a Consul's Daughter and Wife*, ed. Stanley Lane Poole, 2 vols. (London: John Murray, 1878 [Elibron Classics Series edition, 2005]), 2:173.

18. Malcom MacColl, *The Eastern Question: Its Facts & Fallacies* (London: Longmans, Green, 1877), 233–35. Canon Malcolm MacColl was a Scottish Episcopalian priest, a close associate of Gladstone's, equally trusted by Salisbury, and one of the most expert and vigorous British pamphleteers. He was an acknowledged expert of the Ottoman Empire, known for his reports of Ottoman impalements and infanticides that he made during his stay in the Balkans, which we now know to be fabricated. His tendentious and misleading information on these acts of extreme violence would prove very influential.

19. Sir George Campbell, eighth Duke of Argyll, was a Scottish peer who followed Gladstone until the 1890s and was noted for his strong Presbyterianism.

20. Wheatcroft, *Infidels*, 276.

21. M. E. Yapp, "Europe in the Turkish Mirror," *Past and Present*: *"The Cultural and Political Construction of Europe"* 137 (1992): 134–55, at 149–50.

22. F. Bianconi, *La question d'Orient dévoilée, ou la vérité sur la Turquie. Mussulmans, Raias, Slaves et Grecs, Tcherkess et Tziganes* (Paris: Librairie Générale, 1876), 39.

23. P. J. Marshall and Glyndwr Williams, *The Great Map of Mankind: British Perceptions of the World in the Age of Enlightenment* (London: J. M. Dent, 1982), 145–46.

24. Allan Cunningham, "The Sick Man and the British Physician," in *Eastern Question in the Nineteenth Century*, ed. Edward Ingram (London: Frank Cass, 1993), 2:73–107, at 73.

25. Lane-Poole, *Stratford Canning*, 1:392; E. E. Malcolm-Smith, *The Life of Stratford Canning (Lord Stratford de Redcliffe)* (London: Ernest Benn, 1933); Cunningham, "Stratford Canning and the *Tanzimat*," 108–29.

26. Leo Gerald Byrne, *The Great Ambassador* (Athens: Ohio State University Press, 1964), 39.

27. Cunningham, "Stratford Canning and the *Tanzimat*," 112.

28. George Campbell, *The Blue Books, and What Is to Come Next*, Eastern Question Association, Papers on the Eastern Question, no. 12 (London: Cassell, Petter and Galpin, 1877), 49. See also *The Races, Religions, and Institutions of Turkey and the Neighbouring Countries: Being the Substance of Two Lecturers Delivered in The Kirkcaldy Burghs*, Eastern Question Association, Papers on the Eastern Question, no. 3 (London: Cassell, Petter and Galpin, 1877), 19.

29. Palmerston remained foreign secretary from 1830 to 1841 and took over again from 1846 to 1851; he was then home secretary from 1852 to 1855, and finally prime minister from 1855 to 1865.

30. Jasper Ridley, *Lord Palmerston* (London: Constable, 1970), 588; Kenneth Bourne, *Palmerston: The Early Years, 1784–1841* (London: Allen Lane, 1982), 622; George J. Billy, *Palmerston's Foreign Policy: 1848* (New York: Peter Lang, 1993), 17; Peter Mandler, *Aristocratic Government in the Age of Reform: Whigs and Liberals 1830–1852* (Oxford: Clarendon Press, 1990).

31. Edmund Spencer, *Travels in European Turkey*, 2 vols. (London: Colburn, 1851), 1:267.

32. C. A. Bayly, *Imperial Meridian: The British Empire and the World 1780–1830* (London: Longman, 1989), 196–200.

33. Blunt, *Peoples of Turkey*, 1:92.

34. Henry Richard, *Evidence of Turkish Misrule*, Eastern Question Association, Papers on the Eastern Question, no. 1 (London: Cassell, Petter and Galpin, 1876), 1. See also John Holms, *Commercial & Financial Aspects of the Eastern Question*, Eastern Question Association, Papers on the Eastern Question, no. 3 (London: Cassell, Petter and Galpin, 1877).

35. G. Smith, "The Policy of Aggrandisement," *Fortnightly Review* 23 (1877): 303.

36. Edward A. Freeman, *The Eastern Question in Its Historical Bearings: An Address Delivered in Manchester, November 15, 1876*, 2d ed. rev. (Manchester: Taylor, Garnett, Evans, 1897), 17. Freeman was a Liberal and a lifelong enemy of the Ottoman Empire. He traveled to Dalmatia in autumn 1875 and inaugurated a campaign for the relief of Christian refugees.

37. Cunningham, "Stratford Canning, Mahmud II and Muhammad Ali," 39–40.

38. Lane-Poole, *Stratford Canning*, 2:206–14.

39. Carter Vaughn Findley, "The Ottoman Administrative Legacy and the Modern Middle East," in *The Imperial Legacy: The Ottoman Imprint on the Balkans and the Middle East*, ed. Carl Brown, 158–73 (New York: Columbia University Press, 1996) 162.

40. Karpat, "*Millets* and Nationality," 163.

41. François Pierre Guillaume Guizot, *Mémoires pour servir á l'histoire de mon temps* (Paris: Michel Lévy Freres, 1861), 7:261–62.

42. Ibid., 263.

43. It was specifically the work of Stratford Canning, French ambassador Édouard Antoine de Thouvenel, and the Austrian internuncio to the Porte, with the collaboration of Grand Vizier Ali Pasha and Foreign Minister Fuad Pasha. From 1861 to 1871 either Ali or Fuad was grand vizier, with only two brief interludes totaling thirteen months when they were not. During the same time span one or the other of them was foreign minister, with no interruption at all.

44. Emile De Girardin, *Solutions de la question d'Orient* (Paris: Librairie Nouvelle, 1854); Abdolonyme Ubicini, *Lettres sur la Turquie ou tableau statistique, religieux, politique, administratif, militaire, commercial, etc. de l'Empire Ottoman depuis le Khatti-Cherif de Gulkhané (1839)*, 2 vols. (Paris: Libraire Militaire de J. Dumaine, 1853–54).

45. William E. Echard, *Napoleon III and the Concert of Europe* (Baton Rouge: Louisiana State University Press, 1983), 168–69.

46. A. & P., *Condition of Christians in Turkey (1860)*, 1861. Reports received from Her Majesty's Consuls Relating to the Condition of Christians in Turkey, 1860. Presented to Parliament in 1861 (London, 1861).

47. Eugène Morel, *La Turquie et ses réformes* (Paris: Dentu, 1866).

48. Ibid., 165.

49. Ibid., 25.

50. Joseph Jooris, "La Question du Liban," *Revue de Droit International et de Législation Comparée* 15 (1883): 243–53, at 248–49; E. Engelhardt, "Le droit d'intervention et la Turquie," *Revue de Droit International et de Législation Comparée* 12 (1880): 363–88; E. Engelhardt, *La Turquie et le Tanzimât* (Paris: A. Cotillon, 1882), 2:315.

51. Pitts, "Boundaries of Victorian International Law," 72.

52. John Westlake, *Chapters on the Principles of International Law* (Cambridge: Cambridge University Press, 1894; London: Elibron Classic Replica Edition, 2003), 101 (emphasis is mine).

53. James Lorimer, *Institutes of the Law of Nations: A Treatise of the Juridical Relations of Separate Political Communities*, 2 vols. (London: Blackwood, 1883); Antoine Rougier, "Théorie de l'intervention d'humanité," *Revue Générale du Droit International Public* 17 (1910): 469; Joseph Hornung, "Civilisés et barbares," *Revue Générale du Droit International Public*, 16 (1884): 79; 17 (1885): 1–18, 447–70, 539–60; and 18 (1885): 188–206, 281–98. In his 1904 *Le droit international: Les principes, les théories, les faits*, Ernest Nys divided the population of the world into civilized, barbaric, and savage peoples. International law was for him a European creation. No comparison could be made between the multiplicity of juridical relations established among civilized nations and the rare applications of law between them and barbarians and savages.

54. Heinhard Steiger, "From the International Law of Christianity to the International Law of the World Citizen—Reflections on the Formation of the Epochs of the History of International Law," *Journal of the History of International Law* 3 (2001): 187.

55. Pitts, "Boundaries of Victorian International Law," 67–70; Anthony Anghie, *Imperialism, Sovereignty and the Making of International Law* (Cambridge, Cambridge University Press, 2005), 59.

56. Pitts, "Boundaries of Victorian International Law," 68–69.

57. Guizot, *Mémoires*, 4:4–7: "L'Europe est une société de peuples et d'États . . . unis entre eux par des liens moraux et matériels . . . qui tendent aux mêmes fins . . . la Chrétienté. C'est là notre caractère original et notre gloire. Ce grand fait a eu pour conséquence naturelle la formation progressive d'un droit public européen et chrétien. . . . Les maximes essentielles et incontestées du droit public européen sont en petit nombre. Parmi les principales se rangent celles-ci: 1° La paix est l'état normal des nations et des gouvernements. La guerre est un fait exceptionnel et qui doit avoir un motif légitime; 2° Les États divers sont entièrement indépendants les uns des autres quant à leurs affaires intérieures; chacun d'eux se constitue et se gouverne selon les principes et dans les formes qui lui conviennent; 3° Tant que les États vivent en paix, leurs gouvernements sont tenus de ne rien faire qui puisse troubler mutuellement leur ordre intérieur; 4° Nul État n'a droit d'intervenir dans la situation et le gouvernement intérieur d'un autre État qu'autant que l'intérêt de sa propre sûreté lui rend cette intervention indispensable." (Europe is a society of peoples and of states . . . united by moral and material connections . . . who strive for the same goals . . . Christianity: that is our original character and our glory. This great feature made it naturally possible the progressive creation of a European and Christian *droit public* . . . whose essential and uncontested assumptions are few: 1. Peace is the usual state of the relations among European nations. War is an exception, and it must have a legitimate motive. 2. States are fully independent in their internal affairs; each governs itself according to the principles and shapes that suit it best. 3. As long as states live in peace, their governments do not interfere in each other internal affairs. 4. No state has a right to intervene in the internal

affairs of another state, as long as its security makes such an intervention indispensable.)

58. Grewe, *Epochs*, 292–93.

59. *The Miscellaneous Works of the Right Honourable Sir James Mackintosh* (1846), 3:44, cited in ibid., 452.

60. Henry Wheaton, *Elements of International Law: With a Sketch of the History of Science*, 2 vols. (London: Fellowes, 1836), cited in Martti Koskenniemi, *The Gentle Civilizer of Nations: The Rise and Fall of International Law 1870–1960* (Cambridge: Cambridge University Press, 2001), 114.

61. Bernard, *Intervention*, 9 (emphasis is mine). Montagu Bernard was the first professor of international law and diplomacy appointed in Great Britain. His chair was set up in Oxford in 1859 (the Chichele Chair). The University of Cambridge would do the same in 1866 with the Whewell Chair, appointing William Hancourt. The position held by the eccentric Scotsman James Lorimer in Edinburgh after 1862 continued to be a chair in the Law of Nature and of Nations. Sir Travers Twiss, a Foreign Office consultant, taught at King's College London from the 1850s. Bernard was one of the few British jurists who appear to have been familiar with continental, and specifically German publicists', work, and the only one who gave the subject of intervention serious juridical consideration.

62. Donald Read, *Cobden and Bright: A Victorian Political Partnership* (London: Edward Arnold, 1967), 112. See also R. J. Vincent, *Nonintervention and International Order* (Princeton: Princeton University Press, 1974), 45–54.

63. J. S. Mill, "A Few Words on Non-Intervention," in *Dissertations and Discussions*, 3 vols. (1867), reprinted from *Fraser's Magazine* 60 (December 1859).

64. Carol A. L. Prager, "Intervention and Empire: John Stuart Mill and International Relations," *Political Studies* 53 (2005): 621–40, at 628.

65. Vincent, *Nonintervention*, 54–56.

66. Prager, "Intervention and Empire," 622.

67. Pitts, "L'Empire britannique" 55–81; Pitts, "Jeremy Bentham," in *Utilitarianism and Empire*, 57–93. Miller, "Chairing the Jamaica Committee," in *Utilitarianism and Empire*, 163.

68. Prager, "Intervention and Empire," 629–30.

69. William Edward Hall, *A Treatise on International Law*, 8th ed., ed. A. Pearce Higgins (Oxford: Clarendon Press, 1924), 47.

70. Lawrence, *The Principles*, 1:57–58.

71. Westlake, *Chapters on the Principles*, 103.

72. Walter Schiffer, *The Legal Community of Mankind* (New York: Columbia University Pres, 1954), 82.

73. Pitts, "Boundaries of Victorian International Law," 71–72.

74. Alexander Orakhelanshvili, "The Idea of European International Law," *European Journal of International Law* 17 (2006): 315–47, at 319. On Lorimer, see also Arthur Nussbaum, *A Concise History of the Law of Nations* (New York: Macmillan, 1947), 228–30.

75. Phillimore, *Commentaries*, 1:86–87.

76. Orakhelashvili, "The Idea of European International Law," 319.

77. Lorimer, *The Institute of the Law of Nations*, 1:101–2, quoted in Orakhelashvili, "The Idea of European International Law," 318, 325.

78. Carslake Thompson, *Public Opinion and Lord Beaconsfield 1875–1880*, 2 vols. (London: Macmillan, 1886), 1:74–76.

79. Ibid., 76.

80. A. Rougier, "Théorie," 506. See also a series of articles by A. De Lapradelle, "La Question Chinoise," *Revue Général de Droit International Public* 7 (1901): 276–77; 8 (1901): 272–340; 9 (1902): 40–115, 367–405.

81. Chesterman, *Just War*, 35–44.

82. In their lists of jurisprudential cases of interventions on grounds of humanity, some legal scholars encompassed instances of threatening the use of force. Among them a frequently mentioned case was the 1856 mobilization of the British and French in front of the port of Naples. The naval demonstration aimed at forcing the Neapolitan government to free the political prisoners. No military intervention ensued. Early-twentieth-century American legal scholar Ellery Stowell claimed that the language employed in the British, French, and Austrian governments' notes condemning the 1863 harsh Russian suppression of a Polish uprising was so minatory as to seem to threaten war in the event the Russian government should not yield. In a "blundering fashion" and "amidst irrelevant and extraneous verbiage," the European diplomatic notes embedded the arguments necessary to justify action on humanitarian grounds. Ellery Stowell, *Intervention in International Law* (Washington, DC: Byrne, 1921), 101, 112. Stowell (122–23) linked the case of oppression and intervention in Poland in 1863 with that of oppression and nonintervention in Ireland in 1921.

83. Henry Wheaton, *Elements of International Law*, 2:I, §§0, 91, cited in Chesterman, *Just War*, 24.

84. M.L.C.D.B., *Des Grecs, des Turcs, et de l'Esprit Public Européen, Opuscule de 1821* (Paris, Jules Renouard, 1828), 3–6. I warmly thank historian Vangelis Kechriotis, who confirms that the author of the pamphlet was the Russian senator and diplomat Dmitiri Petrovitch comte de Boutourlin.

85. Ibid., 31–32. Boutourlin contrasts "l'Europe civilisée et chrétienne" with the immutable Ottoman Empire "composé monstrueux d'ignorance et de barbarie, ennemi né du christianisme et de l'ordre social . . . et de la civilisation." And, on p. 72: "Il semble indigne de l'Europe chrétienne et civilisée de balancer un instant entre la vue mesquine de petits intérêts commerciaux, ou d'ambition, ou de crainte éventuelle, forcés de se concentrer un moment, et la vue majestueuse et générale de l'humanité entière perfectionnée par la civilisation et par le christianisme, repoussant d'un sentiment unanime les empiètements jusqu'à ce jour trop puissants d'une horde de barbares."

86. Ibid., 6: "la question est ici du domaine de la civilisation entière. Elle est tout en droit des gens, et même en simple morale universelle."

87. Ibid., 96.

88. Gustave Rolin-Jaequemyns, "Le Droit International et la Question d'Orient," *Revue de Droit International et de Législation Comparée* 8 (1876): 338.

89. Gustave Rolin-Jaequemyns, "Note sur la théorie du droit d'intervention: A propos d'une lettre de M. le Professeur Arntz," *Revue de Droit International et de Législation Comparée* 8 (1876): 673–82, at 673–74.

90. Translated by Michael Byers in Grewe, *Epochs*, 495. See also Rolin-Jaequemyns, "Note," 673; and V. Arntz, "Lettre à M. Rolin-Jaequemyns," *Revue de Droit International et de Législation Comparée* 8 (1876).

91. Alfred T. Mahan, *Some Neglected Aspects of War* (Boston: Little, Brown, 1907).

92. Edwin De Witt Dickinson, *The Equality of States in International Law* (Cambridge: Harvard University Press, 1920), 262–63; George Frédéric de Martens, *Traité de Droit International*, 3 vols. (Paris: Librairie Marescq Ainé, 1886), 1:398; Edwin M. Borchard, *The Diplomatic Protection of Citizen Abroad* (New York: The Banks Law Publishing Co., 1915), 14.

93. Theodore D. Woolsey, *Introduction to the Study of International Law*, 4th ed. (London: Sampson, Low Marston, Low & Searle, 1875); Georges Streit, "La question Crétoise au point de vue du droit international," *Revue Générale de Droit International Public* 4 (1897): 61–105, 447–483; Louis Vie, *Des principales applications du droit d'intervention des puissances Européennes dans les affaires des Balkans depuis le traité de Berlin de 1878 jusqu'à nos jours. Étude de droit international public et d'histoire diplomatique. Thèse pour le Doctorat* (Toulouse: Imprimerie Lagarde & Sebille, 1900), 25–26.

94. A. Rougier, "Théorie," 472.

95. Ibid., 489.

96. Ibid., 504.

97. Ibid., 497.

98. Ibid., 469–70.

99. Johann C. Bluntschli, *Le droit international codifié* (Paris: Librairie de Guillaumin, 1870), §478.1.

100. Ibid., §5.1: "L'essence de la civilisation consiste, comme le disait déjà Dante (Alighieri), dans le développement harmonique de l'humanité. Le droit international est un des fruits les plus précieux de la civilisation, car il est, de son essence, une organisation de l'humanité. La prétention des états européens et américains, d'être, plus spécialement que tous les autres, les représentants et les protecteurs du droit international serait absurde, si elle ne se fondait pas sur la civilisation plus avancée de ces états."

101. Westlake, *Principles*, 78–79, 319–320.

102. Edward S. Creasy, *First Platform of International Law* (London: John Van Voorst, 1876), §316, 303–4.

103. Augustus W. Heffter, *Le droit international public de l'Europe: Nouvelle édition revue et augmentée après le décès du traducteur par l'auteur*, trans. Bergson (Paris: Cotillon, 1866; London: Elibron Classic Replica 2004).

104. William Oke Manning, *Commentaries on the Law of Nations*, ed. Sheldon Amos (London: Sweet, 1875).

105. Bluntschli, *Droit international codifié*, §478; Despagnet, *Cours*, 212–13; Manning, *Commentaries*, 97.

106. Nassau William Senior, "Book Review: Wheaton's International Law," *Edinburgh Review* 334 (1843): 365; Richard Wildman, *Institutes of International Law* (London: William Benning, 1849, 62–63); James Reddie, *Inquiries in International Law: Public and Private*, 2d ed. (Edinburgh: William Blackwood and Sons, 1851), 389–404.

107. Joseph Jooris, "La question du Liban," *Revue de Droit International et de Législation Comparée* 15 (1883): 243–53.

108. Despagnet, *Cours*, 231–37. Another exception is E. Engelhardt, "L'Angleterre et la Russie. A propos de la question Arménienne," *Revue de Droit International et de Législation Comparée* 15 (1883): 146–59.

109. Despagnet, *Cours*, 237, 215–16.

110. F. E. Smith, *International Law*, ed. J. Wylie, 4th ed. (London: J. M. Dent, 1911), 63–64. A similar statement is in Thomas Alfred Walker, *The Science of International Law* (London: Clay and Sons, 1893), 151–52.

111. Phillimore, *Commentaries*, 1:442, 568–69.

112. Ibid., 571.

113. Ibid., 572–74.

114. William Vernon Harcourt, *Letters by Historicus on Some Questions of International Law: Reprinted from "The Times" with Considerable Additions* (London: Macmillan, 1863), 14.

115. Ibid., 6. See the next chapter for discussion of this event.

116. Cited in Stowell, *Intervention*, 525.

117. Hall, *A Treatise on International Law*, 343–44.

118. Lawrence, *Principles*, 1:129.

119. Ibid.

120. Lassa F. Oppenheim, *International Law* (New York: Longmans, Green, 1905), 1:186.

121. Ibid., 186–87.

122. William Ezra Lingelbach, "The Doctrine and Practice of Intervention in Europe," *Annals of the American Academy of Political and Social Science* 16 (1900): 1–32, at 17.

123. Ibid., 19.

124. Ibid., 25.

125. René Pinon, *L'Europe et l'Empire Ottoman: Les aspects actuel de la question d'Orient* (Paris: Perrin, 1908), 6–7.

126. Treaty between Great Britain, France, and Russia for the Pacification of Greece. Signed at London, July, 6, 1827.

127. Engelhardt, "Le droit d'intervention et la Turquie," 365.

CHAPTER THREE: INTERVENTION ON BEHALF OF OTTOMAN GREEKS (1821–33)

1. Vahakn N. Dadrian, *The History of the Armenian Genocide: Ethnic Conflict from the Balkans to Anatolia to the Caucasus*, 6th ed., rev. (Oxford: Berghahn Books, 2003), 13.

2. David Brewer, *The Flame of Freedom: The Greek War of Independence, 1821–1833* (London: John Murray, 2003), 61.

3. C. W. Crawley, *The Question of Greek Independence: A Study of British Policy in the Near East 1821–1833* (New York: H. Fertig, 1973 [1930], 14–15.

4. W. St. Clair, *That Greece Might Still Be Free: The Philhellenes in the War of Independence* (London: Oxford University Press, 1972), 1–2; Allan Cunningham, "Lord Strangford and the Greek Revolt," in *Anglo-Ottoman Encounters in the Age of Revolution*, 2 vols., ed. E. Ingram (London: Frank Cass, 1992), 1:188–232; George Finlay, *History of the Greek Revolution* (London: William Blackwood, 1861), 172; Albéric Cauhet, *La question d'Orient dans l'histoire contemporaine (1821–1905)* (Paris: Dujarric, 1905), 32. While the main text is devoted to the Turkish atrocities, in a footnote Cauhet mentions Greek cruelties, such as the

starving of prisoners, the killing of civilians after their surrender, and the massacre of twelve thousand Muslim and Jewish prisoners of Tripolitza [Tripoli] whose children were later sold as slaves.

5. W. Alison Phillips, *The War of Greek Independence, 1821 to 1833* (New York: Smith Elder, 1897), 60–61.

6. Justin McCarthy, *Death and Exile: The Ethnic Cleansing of Ottoman Muslims, 1821–1922*) Princeton: Darwin Press, 1995), 11–12.

7. Jean Dimakis, *La guerre de l'indépendance Grecque vue par la presse Française (période de 1821 à 1824): Contribution à l'étude de l'opinion publique et du mouvement Philhellénique en France* (Salonica: Institute for Balkan Studies, 1968).

8. R. L. Green, *Sketches of the War in Greece* (London: Hurst, 1827); F. Pouqueville, *Histoire de la régénération de la Grèce*, 4 vols. (Paris: Firmin Didot, 1827).

9. *W. H. Humphreys' First "Journal of the Greek Independence" (July 1821–February 1822)*, ed. Sture Linnér (Stockholm: Almqvist & Wiksell, 1967), 62–65. On the Jews: "The Jews, of whom there were a great many in the town and whom [the Greeks] detest[ed] equally with the Turks, shared the same fate" (64). See also M. Raybaud, *Mémoires sur la Grèce, pour servir a l'histoire de la guerre de l'Indépendance, accompagnés de plans topographiques*, 2 vols. (Paris: Tournachon-Molin, Libraire, 1824–25).

10. M.C.D. Raffenel, *Histoire des événements de la Grèce, depuis les premiers troubles jusqu'à ce jour, avec des notes critiques et topographiques*, 3 vols. (Paris: Dondey-Dupré, 1822–28).

11. M.L.C.D.B., *Des Grecs*, 1: "Les infidèles massacrent en ce moment les chrétiens sur un sol européen, et l'Europe chrétienne et civilisée se tait. Est-ce de sa part adhésion ou crainte?"

12. Nina Athanassoglou-Kallmyer, *French Images from the Greek War of Independence 1821–1830: Art and Politics under the Restoration* (New Haven: Yale University Press, 1989), 17.

13. Henri Mathieu, *La Turquie et ses différents peuples* (Paris: E. Dentu, 1857), 311: "A Smyrne même, et sous les yeux des consuls européens, la population grecque en masse fut vouée à la mort. Les notables de la ville et des environs, convoqués par le pacha, pour aviser aux moyens de rétablir la tranquillité, furent massacrés dans le bâtiment de la douane, au nombre de trois cents environs."

14. Roderic Davison, *Essays in Ottoman and Turkish History 1774–1923: The Impact of the West* (Austin: University of Texas Press, 1990), 29–50. According to historian Harold Temperley, the interpretation of articles 7 and 14 of that treaty were developed by usage. Metternich admitted a certain right of interference. Canning qualified it by saying that Russia had a special right of friendly advice on behalf of Christians of the Turkish Empire, but he doubted whether this "right extended to interference on behalf of subjects of the Porte who had thrown off their allegiance." See Harold W. V. Temperley, *England and the Near East: The Crimea* (Hamden, CT: Archon Books, 1964), 467.

15. Crawley, *The Question*, 18.

16. H. Long, *Greek Fire: The Massacre of Chios* (Bristol: Abson, 1992), 31.

17. Philip Argenti, *The Massacres of Chios, Described in Contemporary Diplomatic Reports* (London: John Lane, 1932), 52–95, quotes the report of Céléste Etienne

David, French vice consul in Chios, addressed to Vicomte de Chateaubriand, Ministre, Secrétaire d'Etat aux Affaires Etrangères, D. no. 39bis, Scio, 14 Juin 1824. Ministère des Affaires Etrangères (Paris: Correspondance Consulaire de Scio, 1812–25).

18. Public Record Office (PRO), now National Archives (NTA), files of the Foreign Office (FO), Turkey 78, mainly vols. 108 and 109.

19. Argenti, *The Massacres*, 16, Strangford to Castelreagh Constantinople, May 25, 1822. PRO, FO (Turkey) 78, vol. 108, Doc. No. 73. The French vice consul on Chios, Céléste Etienne David, wrote in exactly the same terms as the British diplomat, but for the poetic tone of his report: "Toute l'Europe a plaint ses tristes destinées. Le bruit sinistre de [la chute de Chios] a retenti dans tous les cœurs ouverts à la Pitié! Quelle catastrophe en effet fut jamais plus terrible? . . . Toute une population innocente périt. . . . Mais que dis-je une partie de cette population (la plus malheureuse peut-être!) doit survivre à ces horribles sacrifices, pour aller, dans un affreux exil, baigner de pleur amers les chaînes de l'esclavage." See P. Argenti, 90–91. Report of Céléste Etienne David, French vice consul in Chios, addressed to Chteaubriand, Ministre, Secrétaire d'Etat aux Affaires Etrangères, D. no. 39 bis, Scio, 14 Juin 1824. Ministère de Affaires Etrangères (Paris: Correspondance Consulaire de Scio, 1812–25).

20. Argenti, *The Massacre*, 25–26.

21. Ibid. The Marquis of Londonderry, secretary of state for foreign affairs, to Viscount Strangford, British ambassador in Constantinople, FO, 9 July 1822. PRO, FO, (Turkey) 195, vol. 33, Doc. No. 6.

22. Bass, *Freedom's Battle*, 69.

23. *Correspondence, Despatches, and Other Papers of Viscount Castlereagh, Second Marquess of Londonderry. Edited by His Brother, Charles William Vane, Marquess of Londonderry*, 12 vols. (London: John Murray, 1853), July 16, Castlereagh to the emperor of Russia, on the affairs of Turkey, 12:403–8.

24. J. W. Derry, *Castlereagh* (London: A. Lane, 1976), 406.

25. Charles K. Webster, *The Foreign Policy of Castlereagh* (London: Bell, 1924), 377.

26. Bass, *Freedom's Battle*, 70.

27. Derry, *Castlereagh*, 190–91.

28. Barbara Jelavich, *Russia's Balkan Entanglements 1806–1914* (Cambridge: Cambridge University Press, 1991), 42–75.

29. Harold W. V. Temperley, *The Foreign Policy of Canning 1822–1827* (Hamden, CT: Archon, 1966), 447–75.

30. Saree Makdisi, *Romantic Imperialism: Universal Empire and the Culture of Modernity* (Cambridge: Cambridge University Press, 1998), 134–37.

31. Frederick Rosen, *Bentham, Byron, and Greece: Constitutionalism, Nationalism, and Early Liberal Political Thought* (Oxford: Clarendon Press, 1992), 6.

32. Athanassoglou-Kallmyer, *French Images*, 10.

33. Ibid., 35.

34. Ibid., 118.

35. Bass, *Freedom's Battle*, 83.

36. Ibid., 84.

37. C. M. Woodhouse, *The Battle of Navarino* (London: Hooder And Soughton, 1965), 75: "It is a disgrace to all the Powers of Europe that, long ere now, they have not made a simultaneous effort and driven back a nation of barbarians, the inveterate enemies of Christianity and freedom, into Asia. . . . I know of no case in which the power of a mighty country like England could be more nobly, more generously, or more justifiably exerted than in rescuing the Greeks from bondage and destruction."

38. Chateaubriand, *Itinéraire*, vol. 5, "Opinion sur le projet de loi relatif à la répression des délits commis dans les Echelles du Levant."

39. Chateaubriand, "Note sur la Grèce," in the 1827 preface to his *Itinéraire de Paris à Jérusalem et de Jérusalem à Paris*. Chateaubriand explains that he viewed the "Note sur la Grèce" and the "Opinion à la Chambre des Pairs" as complements to the *Itinéraire*.

40. Chateaubriand, "Avant-propos de la deuxième édition de la Note sur la Grèce, Deuxième partie," in ibid.

41. Rosen, *Bentham*, 135–36.

42. In a similar manner, another Philhellene, George Waddington justified the massacre of four hundred Turks, after the fall of Athens in 1822, as follows: "If, indeed the signal for murder was really given by the hand of a Sciot, fresh from the scene of the ruins of his country, his eyes yet moist with tears of sorrow and indignation, and the last shrieks of his enslaved family still ringing in his ears, we might also be tempted to suspend in his favour the severity of our condemnation, and to pardon the savage retaliation to which he had been driven by his miseries." G. Waddington, *A Visit to Greece*, 72–73.

43. Ibid., 59.

44. Berton, *Les Turcs*, 49.

45. Ibid., 52–56.

46. Athanassoglou-Kallmyer, *French Images*, 30–31.

47. Ibid., 91.

48. Brewer, *Flame*, 222–23; Rosen, *Bentham*, 276–80; Douglas Dakin, *The Greek Struggle for Independence 1821–1833* (Berkeley: University of California Press, 1973), 120–41.

49. C. Lloyd, *Lord Cochrane: Seaman-Radical-Liberator. A Life of Thomas, Lord Cochrane 10th Earl of Dundonald* (London: Longmans, 1947).

50. Brewer, *Flame*, 294–95.

51. Temperley, *England and the Near East*, 467.

52. Crawley, *The Greek Question*, 49; Temperley, *The Foreign Policy of Canning*, 344–51.

53. Lane-Poole, *Stratford Canning*, 1:395–96.

54. Bass, *Freedom's Battle*, 131; Arthur Wellesley, Duke of Wellington, *Despatches, Correspondence, and Memorandum of Field Marshal Arthur, Duke of Wellington*, 3 vols. (London: John Murray, 1867), 3:362, 393, 398–99; Woodhouse, *Battle of Navarino*, 37. (This monograph is based on the Codrington papers, on the Admiralty and Foreign Office papers.)

55. Argenti, *The Massacres*, 28.

56. Crawley, *The Greek Question*, 55–56.

57. Paul W. Schroeder, *The Transformation of European Politics 1763–1848* (Oxford: Oxford University Press, 1996), 642–53; M. S. Anderson, *The Eastern Question, 1774–1923: A Study of International Relations* (London: Macmillan, 1966), 60–66; and Bass, *Freedom's Battle*, 132.

58. Ministère des Affaires Etrangeres [hereafter MAE], Correspondance Politique [hereafter CP] de la Turquie jusqu'à 1896, vol. 246, l'Ambassadeur à Constantinople Armand Guilleminot au MAE—M. le Baron de Damas, Doc. No. 120, 6 June 1827.

59. Brewer, *The Flame*, 323; Woodhouse, *Battle of Navarino*, 60–62; Bass, *Freedom's Battle*, 139.

60. Crawley, *The Greek Question*, 115.

61. MAE, CP de la Turquie jusqu'à 1896, vol. 256, le Ministère des Affaires Etrangères à M. l'Amiral Henri de Rigny, Doc. No. 31, Paris, 12 April 1828.

62. A. & P., Papers Relative to the Affaires of Greece—Protocols of Conferences Held in London. Presented to Both the Houses of Parliament, May 1830, 83. Protocole de la Conférence tenue au Foreign Office, le 11 Août 1828, Rédaction de la déclaration à la Porte Ottomane au sujet de l'envoi d'un corps de troupes dans la Péninsule Grecque—Annexe A.

63. Vernon John Puryear, *France and the Levant: From the Bourbon Restoration to the Peace of Kutiah* (Berkeley: University of California Press, 1941), 50–58.

64. MAE, CP de la Turquie jusqu'à 1896, vol. 256, le Ministère des Affaires Etrangères à M. le général Maison, Commandant la Division d'Expédition en Morée, Doc. No. 35, Paris, 6 August 1828: "Le but de votre mission . . . est de délivrer la Morée de l'ennemi et la protéger contre 'toute' agression ultérieure. . . . Le Roi vous recommande de maintenir une discipline exacte et sévère. . . . Si la discipline est un des éléments de la force d'une armée, elle devient d'autant plus nécessaire que cette armée doit opérer dans un pays dévasté et qu'elle est appelée à délivrer un peuple sur lequel des calamités sans nombre ont pesé depuis plusieurs années. Les militaires sous vous ordres doivent donc éviter avec soin tout ce qui pourrait contribuer à aggraver les maux d'une population déjà malheureuse."

65. Puryear, *France and the Levant*, 58.

66. Pellion, *La Grèce et les Capodistrias: Pendant l'occupation française de 1828 à 1834 / par le Général de division Pellion* (Paris: J. Dumaine, 1855), 93–94. The French troops were severely affected by diseases such as malaria, plague, and awful hygienic conditions. On page 90 Pellion wrote of the "exhalaison pestilentielles des camps récemment abandonnés par les Turcs, et celles de leurs cimetières, où les cadavres, à peine couverts d'un légère couche de terre, étaient fréquemment déterrés pendant la nuit par les chacals. . . . Faute d'établissements hospitaliers, l'armée françaises entassait ses malades à bord des bâtiments de transport, où ils étaient livrés aux d'infirmiers qu'il était presque impossible de surveiller."

67. Ibid., 127: "L'occupation avait principalement pour but d'exercer une influence morale à l'égard des Turcs; ce but était atteint par le fait seul de la présence du drapeau français sur le territoire grec."

68. Ibid., 93.

69. Finlay, *History of Greece*, 7:28.

70. F. Charles Roux, *France et Chrétiens d-Orient* (Paris, Flammarion, 1939), 145.

71. Puryear, *France and the Levant*, 110.

72. MAE, CP de la Turquie jusqu'à 1896, vol. 247, Guilleminot, Ambassador at Constantinople to MAE, La déclaration collective des trois hautes puissances signataires du traité de Londres, Doc. No. 55, 6 August 1827.

73. A. & P., Papers Relative to the Affairs of Greece—Protocols of Conferences Held in London. Presented to Both the Houses of Parliament, May 1830, note of 8 April 1830.

74. Oppenheim, *International Law*, 1:194; Augustus G. Stapleton, *Intervention and Non-Intervention or the Foreign Policy of Great Britain from 1790 to 1865* (London: Murray, 1866), 32.

75. Stowell, *Intervention in International Law*, 126; Sheldon Amos, *Political and Legal Remedies for War* (London: Cassel, Petter and Galpin, 1880), 158.

76. André-N. Mandelstam, *La Société des Nations et les puissances devant le problème Arménien*, Edition Spéciale de la Revue Générale de Droit International Public (Paris: Pédone, 1926), 8–9.

77. Chesterman, *Just War*, 30.

CHAPTER FOUR: INTERVENTION IN OTTOMAN LEBANON AND SYRIA (1860–61)

1. Alfred Lyall, *The Life of the Marquis of Dufferin and Ava*, 2 vols. (London: Murray, 1905), 1:99–100.

2. Spagnolo, *France & Ottoman Lebanon*, 3.

3. Leila Tarazi Fawaz, *An Occasion for War: Civil Conflict in Lebanon and Damascus in 1860* (Berkeley: University of California Press, 1994), 19.

4. Ibid., 27–28; Gérald Arboit, *Aux sources de la politique arabe de la France: Le Second Empire au Machrek* (Paris: L'Harmattan, 2000); Dominique Chevallier, *La Société du Mont Liban à l'epoque de la révolution industrielle en Europe* (Paris: Geunther, 1971); Masters, *Christians and Jews*.

5. Caesar E. Farah, *The Politics of Interventionism in Ottoman Lebanon, 1830–1861* (London: I.B. Tauris, 2000); Spagnolo, *France & Ottoman Lebanon*, 20; M. Jullien, *La nouvelle mission de la Compagnie de Jésus en Syrie (1831–1895)*, 2 vols. (Tours: Imprimerie A. Mame et Fils, 1898).

6. A. L. Tibawi, *American Interests in Syria 1800–1901: A Study of Educational, Literary and Religious Work* (Oxford: Clarendon Press, 1966), 152.

7. Ann Pottinger Saab, *Reluctant Icon: Gladstone, Bulgaria, and the Working Classes, 1856–1878* (Cambridge: Harvard University Press, 1991), 38.

8. Farah, *The Politics*, 527.

9. K. Theodore Hoppen, *The Mid-Victorian Generation 1846–1886* (Oxford: Oxford University Press, 1998), 155.

10. Ibid., 190.

11. Ibid., 191.

12. Baptistin Poujoulat congratulated Henry Guys, the former French consul at Beirut who wrote an account of his experience in the region: "Vous racontez et vous jugez avec l'expérience d'un homme du pays, mais avec la supériorité d'un européen qui regarde des hauteurs de la civilisation chrétienne." See Poujoulat's introduction to Henry Guy's *Beyrouth et le Liban: Relation d'un séjour*

de plusieurs années dans ce pays (Beirut: Lahd Khater, 1985 [Paris, Comptoir des Imprimeurs, 1850]), 1:viii.

13. Ussama Makdisi, *The Culture of Sectarianism: Community, History, and Violence in Nineteenth-Century Ottoman Lebanon* (Berkeley: University of California Press, 2000), 21.

14. A. de Lamartine, *Voyages*, 3:22, in Guys, *Beyrouth et le Liban*, 39.

15. Makdisi, *The Culture of Sectarianism*, 68–69.

16. Ibid., 23–25.

17. Farah, *The Politics*, 186.

18. H. Guys, *Beyrout et le Liban*, "Mœurs des chrétiens: Ils sont supérieurs aux Musulmans," is the title of chapter 11 of Guys' study on Lebanon. In another of his works, *Esquisse de l'etat politique et commercial de la Syrie* (Paris: Chez France Libraire, 1862), Guys reiterated these views, using as evidence the "barbarity" of the massacres. Charles Henry Churchill, *The Druzes and the Maronites under Turkish Rule from 1840 to 1860* ([London, 1862] Reading: Garnet Publishing, 1994), 54–55.

19. Churchill, *The Druzes*, 8–9, 128–31; F. Lenormant, *Les derniers evénements de Syrie* (Paris: Ch. Duniol, 1860).

20. Farah, *The Politics*, 659, 672.

21. Henry Calland, *Les massacres de Syrie: A Monsieur de Pongerville. Membre de l'Académie Française*, was composed on August 2, 1860. J. L. Courcelle-Seneuil, *Les massacres du Liban: Au profit des Chrétiens de Syrie*, 1860.

22. Farah, *The Politics*, 527.

23. A. & P., Despatches from Her Majesty's Consuls in the Levant, Respecting Past or Apprehended Disturbances in Syria: 1858 to 1860, presented to the House of Commons, 20 July 1860; and Further Papers Relating to the Disturbances in Syria: June 1860 (in continuation of Papers Presented to Parliament, 23 July 1860), presented to the House of Commons 30 July 1860.

24. *The Lebanon in Turmoil: Syria and the Powers in 1860. Book of the Marvels of the Time Concerning the Massacres in the Arab Country by Iskander Ibn Yakq'ub Abkarius*, trans. and ann. J. F. Scheltema (New Haven: Yale University Press, 1920).

25. Churchill, *The Druzes*, 157.

26. Bass, *Freedom's Battle*, 164.

27. MAE, CP de la Turquie jusqu'à 1896, vol. 345, Lavalette to Thouvenel, Annexe à la Dépêche du 13 Juin, No. 7, 13 June 1860: "En 1845, les bâtiments français dans des circonstances semblables à celles au milieu desquelles vous vous trouvez, n'hésitèrent pas à recueillir momentanément à leur bord les malheureuses victims de la guerre civile, sain pain et sans asile par suite de l'incendie de leurs villages. Mon approbation est, d'avance, acquise aux actes de cette nature que vous seriez dans le cas d'accomplir. Il importe que votre présence prouve aux Montagnards que nous ne sommes pas indifférents à leur sort . . . cela suffit quant à présent du moins, à notre politique. Je vous engage, du reste, Monsieur le Baron à être circosnspect dans votre ation, et à éviter, autant qu'il dépendra de vous que nos intentions puissant être travesties et rendue suspectes au gouvernement Ottoman, dont les Agents chercheraient peut-être, à s'en venger sur ceux à qui nous voulons du bien."

28. A. & P., Further Papers, Doc. No. 1, Consul General Moore to Russell, Beirut, 27 June 1860, received 14 July, and inclosure 1 in No. 1, Moore to Bulwer, Beyrout, 26 June 1860.

29. Ibid.

30. A. & P., Further Papers, Doc. No. 2, Moore to Russell, Beyrout, 28 June 1860, received 14 July.

31. MAE, CPC, Turquie, Beirut, vol. 12, consul Bentivoglio to Thouvenel, No. 22, 17 June 1860; consul Bentivoglio to Thouvenel, No. 27, 26 June 1860. See also CPC, Turquie, Damas, Lanusse to Thouvenel, No. 86, 19 June 1860.

32. A. & P., Further Papers, Doc. No. 5, Brant to Russell, Damascus, 28 June 1860, received 20 July, and inclosure Brant to Bulwer, Damascus, 26 June 1860.

33. MAE, CPC de la Turquie jusqu'à 1896, Damas, vol. 6, French Consulate at Damas—Direction Politique—to Thouvenel, MAE, Doc. No. 86, 19 June 1860: "Il m'est impossible, M. le Ministre, de tracer ici tous les actes barbares commis par les Druzes; un seul exemple en donnera une faible idée. Les enfants étaient égorgés en présence de leurs pères et on forçait ceux-ci à boire du sang de leurs enfants avant d'être égorgés eux-mêmes. Mais ces deux villages enclavés dans des districts complètement Druzes et tout à fait isolés des Chrétiens du Liban ne devaient pas seuls subir ces cruelles épreuves. . . . Les Chrétiens réfugiés à Hasbeya [circa 900] furent égorgés comme des agneaux."

34. A. & P., Further Papers, Doc. No. 6, Brant to Russell, Damascus, 2 July 1860, received 20 July.

35. Ibid., Doc. No. 22, Dufferin to Russell, Paris, 4 August 1860, received 6 August, Inclosure in No. 22 (extract), Graham to Dufferin, Beyrout, 18 July 1860. Dufferin trusted Cyril Graham because he spoke Arabic and was personally acquainted with both the Druze and the Maronite populations.

36. Ibid., Inclosure in Doc. No. 13. These findings would be confirmed by *Exmouth* captain J. A. Paynter to Vice-Admiral Martin on July 5, 1860, Inclosure 1 in Doc. No. 14.

37. Fawaz, *An Occasion for War*, 81.

38. Xavier Raymond, "La Syrie et la question d'Orient—I.—Les affaires de Syrie," *La Revue des Deux Mondes* 29 (September 1860): "les Juifs de Damas auront souffert leur part de ces atrocités; mais qui réclamera pour eux? Qui oserait même répondre qu'on ne les accusera pas bientôt d'en avoir profité?," 399–425, at 407. See also part 2, 627–58 (livraison of October).

39. Fawaz, *An Occasion for War*, 259; and Linda Schilcher Schatowski, *Families in Politics: Damascene Factions and Estates in the 18th and 19th Centuries* (Stuttgart: Franz Steiner Verlag, 1985), 89–91.

40. MAE, CP de la Turquie jusqu'à 1896, vol. 345, Lavalette to Thouvenel, Doc. No. 7, 13 June 1860: "Ce qu'il faut, c'est de mettre un terme au pillage, à l'incendie, aux massacres. Lorsque les mesures militaires indispensables auront rendu la tranquillité aux chrétiens qui survivent, et qu'une terreur salutaire aura été inspirée aux Druzes et aux Musulmans, leurs complices, il sera temps d'examiner les défauts de l'organisation de 1842 et d'y porter remède."

41. A. & P., Further Papers, Doc. No. 13, Moore to Russell, Beyrout, 5 July 1860, received 20 July.

42. MAE, CP de la Turquie jusqu'à 1896, vol. 345, Lavalette to Thouvenel, Annexe à la Dépêche du 13 Juinm, No. 7, 13 June 1860.

43. Fawaz, *An Occasion for War*, 106–7.

44. A. & P., Correspondence Relating to the Affairs of Syria 1860–61, 1861, Doc. No. 5, Russell to Mr. Erskine, 12 July 1860.

45. Ibid., Doc. No. 4, Russell to Bulwer, Foreign Office, 10 July 1860.

46. Ibid., Doc. No. 11, Thouvenel to Persigny (communicated to Russell by Persigny, 20 July 1860).

47. Ibid., Doc. No. 13, Cowley to Russell, Paris, 19 July 1860, received 20 July.

48. Ibid., Doc. No. 9, Earl Cowley to Lord J. Russell (received 18 July), Paris, 17 July 1860.

49. MAE, CP de la Turquie jusqu'à 1896, vol. 345, Lavalette to Thouvenel, Doc. No. 25, 18 July 1860.

50. Ibid., Doc. No. 11, Thouvenel to Persigny (communicated to Russell by Persigny on 20 July), Paris, 17 July 1860.

51. MAE, CP de la Turquie jusqu'à 1896, vol. 345, Lavalette to Thouvenel, Doc. No. 31, 24 July 1860.

52. A. & P., Correspondence Relating to the Affairs of Syria 1860–61, 1861, Doc. No. 11 (emphasis is mine).

53. Ibid., Doc. No. 18, Cowley to Russell, received 23 July, Paris, 22 July 1860.

54. Ibid., Doc. No. 22, Russell to Cowley, Foreign Office, 23 July 1860.

55. A. & P., Further Papers on the Disturbances in Syria, 1861, Doc. No. 37, Russell to Cowley, 28 July 1860.

56. Ibid., Doc. No. 59, Inclosure 2, Protocol of a Conference Held at Paris, August 3, 1860.

57. MAE, Mémoires et Documents, vol. 122, Doc. No. 17, Résumé des Affaires de Syrie.

58. Olivier Forcade, "Les premières expériences militaires françaises de l'humanitaire sous le Second Empire: Le moment originel de l'expédition française de Syrie en 1860–61?," *Quatrième Journe Guerre et Médecine—12 mai 2007—Paris*, 1–8, at 3. This historian's sources are the archives of the Service Historique de l'Armée de Terre [SHAT], Fonds G4, carton 1, "Instructions générales du secrétaire d'Etat à la Marine Hamelin au général Beaufort d'Hautpoul, commandant de l'expédition," 2 August 1860.

59. MAE, CP de la Turquie jusqu'à 1896, vol. 346, Bentivolgio to Lavalette, August 1860.

60. Fawaz, *An Occasion for War*, 114–15, quotes a document of SHAT, G4/1 Hamelin to Beaufort, Paris, 2 August 1860.

61. Farah, *The Politics*, 543.

62. C. Rochemonteix, *Le Liban et l'expédition Française en Syrie (1860–1861): Documents inédits du Général A. Ducrot* (Paris: Librarie Auguste Picard, 1921). Father Camille de Rochemonteix, a Jesuit, edited the unpublished documents of General Auguste-Alexandre Ducrot. MAE, CP de la Turquie jusqu'à 1896, vol. 347, Lavalette to Thouvenel, Dépêche Télégraphique, 12 October 1860.

63. A. & P., Correspondence Relating to the Affairs of Syria 1860–61, 1861, Doc. No. 253, Thouvenel to Count de Flahault (communicated to Lord J. Russell by Count de Flahault, January 22), 18 January 1861.

64. Ibid., Doc. No. 172, Russell to Cowley, 7 November 1860.

65. Farah, *The Politics*, 660; Chevallier, *La Société*, 283–84. When, in June 1861, the French expeditionary corps was withdrawn from Lebanon, Catholic deputies opposed the emperor's decision and claimed that *"le départ de l'armée serait suivi dans le Liban de scènes regrettables."* A committee composed of Saint-Marc Girardin, Denys Cochin, Father Gratry, Father Pételot, François Lenormant, Poujoulat, and Lefèvre-Pontalis, who were later joined by Crémieux and Pressensé, addressed a petition to the French Senate asking for the prolongation of French occupation in Syria. They failed. French deputies such as Cochin, Crémieux, and Pressensé would later be actively involved in defending Christians living in the Ottoman Empire, particularly the Armenians of Anatolia.

66. A. & P., Correspondence Relating to the Affairs of Syria 1860–61, 1861, Doc. No. 324, Russell to Cowley, 27 February 1861.

67. MAE, CP de la Turquie jusqu'à 1896, vol. 346, Projet d'instructions pour le Commissaire de sa Majesté en Syrie. Doc. No. 58, Lavalette to Thouvenel, 14 September 1860; Doc. No. 61, 20 September 1860 ; and Doc. No. 72, 26 September 1860.

68. A. & P., Correspondence Relating to the Affairs of Syria 1860–61, 1861, Doc. No. 203, Major Fraser to Russell, 2 December 1860, received 15 December; Doc. No. 218, Dufferin to Russell, 4 December 1860, received 29 December; Doc. No. 219, Inclosure 1, Dufferin to Russell, 4 December 1860, received 29 December, which refers to a letter of Leutenant Colonel Burnaby giving an account of the satisfactory way in which the work of reconstruction had been progressing in the district of Metn.

69. MAE, CP de la Turquie jusqu'à 1896, vol. 348, Lavalette to Thouvenel, No. 1, 1 January 1861; PRO, FO, 78/1627, Dufferin to Bulwer, No. 100, 13 January 1861, in Dufferin to Russell, No. 50, 10 January 1861.

70. Fawaz, *An Occasion for War*, 173.

71. C. Rochemonteix, *Le Liban*, 141–42, 345: Appendice, *Souscription recueillie en faveur des Chrétien de Syrie*; Olivier Forcade, Frédéric Guelton, "L'expédition en Syrie en août 1860–juin 1861," *Revue Internationale d'Histoire Militaires* 75 (1995): 49–62.

72. Farah, *The Politics*, 632.

73. C. Rochemonteix, *Le Liban*, 99–100.

74. Ibid., 103.

75. A. & P., Correspondence Relating to the Affairs of Syria 1860–61, 1861, Doc. No. 168 Inclosure 1, Protocol of the Third Meeting of the Syrian Commission, held at Beyrout, 11 October 1860.

76. Ibid., Doc. No. 182 Inclosure 10, Protocol of the Seventh Meeting of the Syrian Commission, held at Beyrout, 30 October 1860.

77. Fawaz, *An Occasion for War*, 202.

78. MAE, CP de la Turquie jusqu'à 1896, vol. 346, Lavalette to Thouvenel, Doc. No. 72—Annexe à la Dépêche, 26 September 1860.

79. Ibid., Damas, vol. 6, Outrey to Lavalette.

80. Ibid., vol. 346, Lavalette to Thouvenel, Doc. no. 72—Annexe à la Dépêche, *Proclamation de Fuad Pacha*, 26 September 1860.

81. Makdisi, *The Culture of Sectarianism*, 151.

82. MAE, CP de la Turquie jusqu'à 1896, vol. 345, Lavalette to Thouvenel, Doc. No. 49, 22 June 1860; No. 7, 13 June 1860; and No. 13, 17 June 1860. Béclard's comments in TNA: PRO, FO, 78/1628, séance du 29 janvier 1861; see also TNA: PRO, FO 78/1626, Dufferin to Bulwer, No. 40, 3 November 1860; PRO, FO 78/1627, Dufferin to Russell, No. 41, 19 December 1860.

83. A. & P., Correspondence Relating to the Affairs of Syria 1860–61, 1861, Doc. No. 190, Inclosure 1, Substance of an Interpellation addressed by Lord Dufferin to Fuad Pasha, at the Eighth Sitting of the Syrian Commission, 10 November 1860 (emphasis is mine); Inclosure in No. 257, Protocol of the Sixteenth Meeting of the Syrian Commission, held in Beyrout, 29 December 1860.

84. Ibid., Doc. No. 309 Inclosure 4, Protocol of the Twentieth Meeting of the Syrian Commission, held at Beyrout, 24 January 1861.

85. Makdisi, *The Culture of Sectarianism*, 155; MAE, CP de la Turquie jusqu'à 1896, vol. 349, Lavalette to Thouvenel, Doc. No. 55, 17 April 1861.

86. MAE, CP de la Turquie jusqu'à 1896, vol. 350, Lavalette to Thouvenel, Doc. No. 85, 12 June 1861; Doc. No. 90, 26 June 1861; A. & P., Correspondence Relating to the Affairs of Syria (In Continuation of Correspondence Presented to Parliament in April 1861), 1861, Doc. 67, Inclosure 2, Réglement pour l'Administration du Liban.

87. In 1861 the French minister of war, having learned of the flood of Christian refugees, came up with the idea of a displacement of populations. The minister wrote to Beaufort asking for the numbers available and suggesting that the Maronites who so chose be resettled in Algeria instead of emigrating to Egypt and Greece, for Arabic was also spoken in Algeria. And, being sober, industrious, and energetic, as opposed to lazy, indigenous Algerians, they could contribute to the economy by growing wheat, cotton, and tobacco, in keeping with Algeria's agriculture, and at the same time provide a fine element for the population there. In his reply Beaufort stated that, during the 1860 events, large numbers of Maronites and Greeks had fled to Egypt, Asia Minor, Greece, and the Mediterranean islands, but that after the French expeditionary force arrived, "nearly all of them returned." Accordingly, Beaufort saw no point in establishing a colony of them in Algeria, but rather to work for a stable government for them in Lebanon. Should this fail and it became obvious that "Maronites were to be sacrificed to the jealous pretensions of England and the impotent Porte, then I would advocate this measure as a last resort." Besides, most of those likely to leave were Maronites who were not knowledgeable in the workings of cotton fields, their expertise being in tobacco and silk. Beaufort thus saw no advantage in resettling them in Algeria. Farah, *Politics*, 652; Rochemonteix, *Le Liban*, 305–12.

88. MAE, CP de la Turquie jusqu'à 1896, vol. 345, Lavalette to Thouvenel, Doc. No. 25, 18 July 1860.

89. Alyce Edythe Mange, *The Near Eastern Policy of the Emperor Napoleon III* (Westport, CT; Greenwood Press, 1975), 91–92.

90. Rochemonteix, *Le Liban*, 292–94; MAE, Mémoires et Documents, vol. 122, Doc. No. 19, Mémoire du Comte Edouard de Warren, auteur de divers travaux sur l'Inde, adressé à Napoléon III, Nancy, 18 July 1860.

91. A. & P., Correspondence Relating to the Affairs of Syria 1860–61, Doc. No. 190 Inclosure 1, *Substance of an Interpellation Addressed by Lord Dufferin to Fuad Pasha, at the Eighth Sitting of the Syrian Commission, November 10, 1860* (emphases are mine).

92. Rochemonteix, *Le Liban*, 213.

Chapter Five: The First Intervention in Crete (1866–69)

1. Robert Holland and Diana Markides, *The British and the Hellenes: Struggles for Mastery in the Eastern Mediterranean 1850–1960* (Oxford: Oxford University Press, 2006), 83.

2. MAE, *Correspondance consulaire et commerciale 1887–1907*, La Canée, vol. 30, Consulat de France en Crète—Direction des Affaires Commerciales—MAE, M. le Ministre Léon Gambetta, Doc. No. 40, La Canée, 3 December 1881. "Le recensement qui vient de s'opérer en Crète a donné pour résultat un chiffre total de 279.192 habitants, se décomposant, par religion, en 204.781 grecs, 73.487 musulmans, 646 israélites, 254 catholiques, 17 protestants et 7 arméniens. 142.248 mâles et 136.944 femmes." The 1887 Ottoman official census numbered 294,192 inhabitants, of which 204,781 were Christian Orthodox and 88,487 were Muslims.

3. A. & P., Correspondence Respecting the Disturbances in Crete: 1866–67, Presented to Both Houses of Parliament by Command of Her Majesty, 1867, Doc. No. 5, Consul Dickson to Clarendon, 2 June 1866 (received 19 June).

4. MAE, CP de la Turquie jusqu'à 1896, vol. 367, Ambassador at Constantinople Moustier to the Minister Édouard Drouyn de Lhuys, Doc. No. 60, 30 May 1866.

5. John H. Skinner, *Turkish Rule in Crete*, published for the Eastern Question Association (London: Cassell, Petter and Galpin, 1877), 11; E. H. Bunbury, "Crete," *Contemporary Review* 1 (1866): 551–67; Anonymous, *Facts on the Candian Question, and the Hatt-I-Humayoun*, 1867.

6. Molly Green, *A Shared World: Christians and Muslims in the Early Mediterranean World* (Princeton: Princeton University Press, 2000).

7. Masters, *Christians and Jews*, 27.

8. H. Charles Woods, *The Danger Zone of Europe: Changes and Problems in the Near East* (London: T. Fisher Unwin, 1911), 215–16; Victor Bérard, *Les aAffaires de Crète* (Paris: Calmann Lévy, 1898), 89–91. According to Bérard, the Ottoman government had encouraged these "*nègres arabisés*" of Benghazi to emigrate to Crete. They were "fanatical soldiers" of the sultan and of the Ulemas. Cretan Christians repeatedly asked in vain for their expulsion.

9. *La question d'Orient et l'insurrection Crétoise* (Paris: Dentu, 1868), 1–32.

10. Kenneth Bourne, "Great Britain and the Cretan Revolt, 1866–1869," *Slavonic and East European Review* 35 (1956–57): 74–94; Gordon L. Iseminger, "The Old Turkish Hands: The British Levantine Consuls, 1856–76," *Middle East Journal* 22 (1968): 297–316; Ann Pottinger Saab, "The Doctor's Dilemma: Britain and the Cretan Crisis, 1866–69," *Journal of Modern History* 49 (1977), On Demand Supplement, D1383–D1407; Maureen M. Robson, "Lord Clarendon and the Cretan Question, 1868–9," *Historical Journal* 3 (1960): 38–55.

11. Hoppen, *The Mid-Victorian*, 221–25; Catherine Hall, *Civilising Subjects: Colony and Metropole in the English Imagination, 1830–1867* (Chicago: University of Chicago Press, 2002); R. W. Kostal, *A Jurisprudence of Power: Victorian Empire and the Rule of Law* (Oxford: Oxford University Press, 2008).

12. Saab, "The Doctor," D1386.

13. TNA: PRO, FO 881/1462, Turkey, Confidential Prints: Memorandum Island of Crete, 1821–1862, Mr. A. S. Green, 26 September 1866; TNA: PRO, FO 881/1550, Turkey, Confidential Prints: Reports from Her Majesty's Consul in Crete on the Condition of the Island: 1858–62. Originally Doc. No. 1, Inclosure no. 1, in Consul J. A. Longworth, 1 October 1858, 20 February 1867.

14. Saab, "The Doctor," D1385.

15. MAE, CP de la Turquie jusqu'à 1896, vol. 368, Moustier to Drouyn de Lhuys, Doc. No. 87, 22 August 1866.

16. TNA: PRO, FO 881/1499, Turkey, Confidential Prints: Correspondence, Doc. No. 22, Stanley to Lyons, 13 August 1866.

17. A. & P., Correspondence Respecting the Disturbances in Crete: 1866–67, Presented to Both Houses of Parliament by Command of Her Majesty, 1867, Doc. No. 22, Inclosure No. 4, Lyons to Dickson, 22 August 1866.

18. M. Capefigue, *L'Europe depuis l'avènement du Roi Louis-Philippe* (Paris: Comptoir des Imprimeur-Unis, 1845–46), 1:65–67. Summary of the conference held at the Foreign Office on February 20, 1830: "Dans le cas où l'autorité turque serait exercée d'une manière qui pourrait *blesser l'humanité* chacune des puissances alliées—sans prendre toutefois un engagement spécial et formel à cet effet—croirait de son devoir d'interposer son influence auprès de la Porte afin d'assurer aux habitants des îles susmentionnées une protection contre des actes oppressifs et arbitraires" (emphasis is mine).

19. TNA: PRO, FO 881/1499, Doc. No. 47, Gorchakov to Brunnow (communicated to Stanley by Brunnow, 5 September), 20 August 1866.

20. Ibid. "Une insurrection locale déjà pénible pour l'humanité à cause des excès, des violences, et de l'effusion de sang qu'elle menace de provoquer." The English translation is mine.

21. TNA: PRO, FO 881/1499, Doc. No. 35, Stanley to Cowley, 27 August 1866.

22. MAE, Correspondance consulaire et commerciale, La Canée, vol. 28, consulat de France à la Canée, Doc. No. 39, 30 September 1866—Blocus de l'île de Crète.

23. MAE, CP de la Turquie jusqu'à 1896, vol. 368, Moustier to Drouyn de Lhuys, Doc. No. 91, 19 October 1866; A. & P., Correspondence Respecting the Disturbances in Crete: 1866–67, 1867, Doc. No. 85, Dickson to Stanley, 15 October 1866 (received 31 October); MAE, CP de la Turquie jusqu'à 1896, vol. 369,

chargé d'affaires at Constantinople De Bonnières to the Minister of Foreign Affairs Moustier, Doc. No. 120, 5 December 1866.

24. MAE, CP de la Turquie jusqu'à 1896, vol. 368, ambassador to Constantinople to Drouyn de Lhuys, Doc. No. 103, 30 October 1866.

25. William James Stillman, *The Autobiography of a Journalist*, vol. 2 (1901), Project Gutenberg eBook, http://www.gutenberg.org/ebooks/11594.

26. A. & P., Correspondence Respecting the Disturbances in Crete: 1866–67, 1867, Doc. No. 85, Lord Stanley to Mr. Fane, 29 December 1866 (emphasis is mine); TNA: PRO, FO 421/23, Confidential Print South-East Europe, Doc. No. 195*, Erskine to Stanley, 15 December 1866 (received 27 December).

27. TNA: PRO, FO 421/23, Confidential Print South-East Europe, Doc. No. 173, Dickson to Stanley, 17 November 1866 (received 6 December); TNA: PRO, FO 881/1499, Turkey, Confidential Prints: Correspondence, Disturbances in Crete, Doc. No. 152A, Erskine to Stanley, 15 December 1866 (received 27 December); TNA: PRO, FO 421/23, Confidential Print South-East Europe, Doc. No. 199, Stanley to Erskine, 27 December 1866.

28. A. & P., Correspondence Respecting the Disturbances in Crete: 1866–67, 1867, Doc. No. 120, Lyons to Stanley, 28 November 1866 (Received 7 December).

29. TNA: PRO, FO 881/1499, Doc. No. 141, Lyons to Stanley, 30 October 1866 (received 9 November).

30. Ibid., Turkey, Confidential Prints: Correspondence, Disturbances in Crete, Doc. No. 261, Stanley to Lyons, 17 January 1867.

31. Ibid., Doc. No. 262, Stanley to Lyons, 17 January 1867. In contrast, this was the solution favored by the Europeans in the 1890s (see chapter 9).

32. A. & P., Correspondence Respecting the Disturbances in Crete: 1866–67, 1867, Doc. No. 142, Stanley to Lyons, 27 December 1866.

33. A. & P., Further Correspondence Respecting the Disturbances in Crete: 1867, in Continuation of Correspondence Presented to Parliament February 11, Doc. No. 3, Lyons to Stanley, 26 December 1866 (received 4 January 1867).

34. MAE, CP de la Turquie jusqu'à 1896, vol. 369, De Bonnières to Moustier, Doc. No. 129, 12 December 1866; ibid., vol. 368, De Bonnières to Moustier, Doc. No. 113, 21 November 1866; Charles Prolès, *Gustave Flourens: Insurrection Crétoise 1867–1868. Siège de Paris 1870–71* (Paris: Chamuel Éditeur, 1898).

35. A. & P., Further Correspondence Respecting the Disturbances in Crete, 1867, Doc. No. 5, Mr. Fane to Stanley, Paris, 24 January 1867 (received 25 January); ibid., Doc. No. 45, Stanley to Cowley, 13 March 1867; MAE, CP de la Turquie jusqu'à 1896, vol. 369, Bourrée to Moustier, Doc. No. 13, 22 January 1867; and Doc. No. 19, 6 February 1867.

36. Engelhardt, *La Turquie*, 2:6. At the same time as the French note, the Russian government put forward a counterproposal based on the principle of special guarantees within the traditional framework of the millets. Autonomy and decentralization were the keywords of the Russian plan. Lord Stanley rallied to France and agreed that the Russian project would inevitably have led to the dismemberment of the Ottoman Empire. The government of Constantinople fully shared this view.

37. Ibid., 1:219.

38. Ibid.

39. The idea of a "fusion of the races" was far from being new. Back in 1858 Stratford Canning had mentioned that the ideal aim of the decree of 1856 should have been "the fusion of classes, the development of resources, liberty of conscience and improved intercourse with Foreigners irrespective of religion." A. & P., Papers Relating to Administrative and Financial Reforms in Turkey, 1858–61, 1861, Memorandum by Stratford to Redcliffe, 22 October 1858; MAE, CP de la Turquie jusqu'à 1896, vol. 344, Mémorandum de 1860, 6–18.

40. MAE, CP de la Turquie jusqu'à 1896, vol. 348, Lavalette to Thouvenel, Doc. No. 1, 1 January 1861.

41. Ibid., vol. 369, Bourrée to Moustier, Doc. No. 13, 22 January 1867.

42. TNA: PRO, FO 881/1499, Doc. No. 290, Mr. Fane to Stanley, 24 January 1867 (received 25 January); A. & P., Further Correspondence Respecting the Disturbances in Crete, 1867, Doc. No. 8, Dickson to Stanley, 25 January 1867 (received 11 February).

43. TNA: PRO, FO 421/23, Confidential Print South-East Europe, Doc. No. 185, Erskine to Stanley, 10 December 1866 (received 15 December); and No. 208, J. Hay to Stanley, 29 December 1866.

44. A. & P., Further Correspondence Respecting the Disturbances in Crete, 1867, Doc. No. 69, Dickson to Stanley, 13 March 1867 (received 2 April); and Doc. Nos. 70 and 179, Dickson to Stanley, 5 June 1867 (received 25 June).

45. Ibid., Doc. No. 10, Stanley to Lyons, 13 February 1867.

46. Ibid., Doc. No. 44, Stanley to Lyons, 12 March 1867; MAE, CP de la Turquie jusqu'à 1896, vol. 369, Aali Pasha to the Ottoman chargé d'affaires at St. Petersburg, annexe to the Dépêche politique No. 20, 9 February 1867.

47. A. & P., Further Correspondence Respecting the Disturbances in Crete, 1867, Doc. No. 60, Erskine to Lyons, 20 March 1867 (received 30 March).

48. MAE, CP de la Turquie jusqu'à 1896, vol. 372, chargé d'affaires at Constantinople Outrey to Moustier, Doc. No. 143, 6 August 1867.

49. Ibid., vol. 370, Bourrée to Moustier, Doc. No. 47, 27 March 1867; TNA: PRO, FO 881/3579, Confidential Print, Memorandum Respecting the Policy Pursued by Her Majesty's Government with Regard to the Cretan Question, 16 March 1878.

50. MAE, CP de la Turquie jusqu'à 1896, vol. 370, Bourrée to Moustier, Doc. No. 47, 27 March 1867.

51. Ibid., vol. 371, Bourrée to Moustier, Doc. No. 88, 19 May 1867.

52. A. & P., Further Correspondence Respecting the Disturbances in Crete 1867, Doc. No. 98, Stanley to Cowley, 23 May 1867; and Doc. Nos. 156 and 158.

53. MAE, CP de la Turquie jusqu'à 1896, vol. 371, Bourrée to Moustier, Doc. No. 109, 15 June 1867; ibid., vol. 372, MAE to Outrey, Doc. No. 126, 12 July 1867; and Bourrée to Moustier, Doc. No. 131, 16 July 1867.

54. Ibid., Bourrée to Moustier, Doc. No. 128, 10 July 1867.

55. A. & P., Further Correspondence Respecting the Disturbances in Crete, 1867, Doc. No. 186, Memorandum Communicated by Baron Brunow, June 26, 1867 (English official translation; emphasis is mine).

56. Ibid.

57. Ibid., Doc. No. 224, Sir A. Buchanan to Stanley (received August 5), 31 July 1867.

58. MAE, CP de la Turquie jusqu'à 1896, vol. 372, Outrey to Moustier, Dépêche Télégraphique, 20 July 1867.

59. The French had the frigate *La Rénommée*, corvette *Rolland*, and dispatch boats *La Sentinelle* and *Le Prométhée*; the Russians intervened with the frigate *Alexander Nevski*, corvette *Mercury*, and gunboat *Bonabori*; the Austrians intervened with the frigate *Radetzky* and gunboats *Wakk* and *Villebich*; the Italians had the dispatch boats *Authion* and *La Sirena*; the Prussians had the gunboat *Blitz*; and the Americans had the corvette *Swatara*, though it did not embark a single Cretan.

60. MAE, CP de la Turquie jusqu'à 1896, vol. 372, MAE to Outrey, 26 July 1867. "Cette mesure, malheureusement se trouve d'autant plus justifiée que notre consul aussi que ceux d'Angleterre, de Russie et d'Italie écrivent d'un commun accord à leur gouvernements que des massacres ont bien lieu, que l'autorité est aussi impuissante à arrêter ces atrocité qu'elle l'est à réprimer l'insurrection et que l'humanité réclame la suspension immédiate des hostilités."

61. A. & P., Further Correspondence Respecting the Disturbances in Crete, 1867, Doc. No. 225, Mr. Barron to Stanley (received 6 August 6), 23 July 1867.

62. MAE, CP de la Turquie jusqu'à 1896, vol. 372, Outrey to Moustier, Doc. No. 140, 30 July 1867. An unusual situation occurred when, "out of views of humanity," the Austrian frigate *Radetzki* cruised off of Crete to pick up those who were seeking to save their lives. Because this large warship drew so much water there were very few harbors on the island it could even approach, so any refugees seeking asylum had to swim to it to be rescued.

63. Ibid., vol. 371, Bourrée to Moustier, Doc. No. 98, 4 June 1867; ibid., vol. 372, Outrey to the Grand Vizier, Annexe 1, Doc. No. 138, 28 July 1867.

64. A. & P., Further Correspondence Respecting the Disturbances in Crete, 1867, Doc. No. 191, Mr. Ellis to Stanley, 20 June 1867 (received 28 June).

65. Ibid., Doc. No. 212, Lyons to Stanley, 11 July 1867 (received 20 July).

66. Ibid., Doc. No. 218, Dickson to Stanley, 13 July 1867 (received 30 July); and Doc. Nos. 220 and 223, Inclosures 1 and 2 in No. 223.

67. Ibid., Doc. No. 233; Buchanan to Stanley, 14 August 1867 (received 19 August); MAE, CP de la Turquie jusqu'à 1896, vol. 372, Outrey to Moustier, Doc. No. 143, 6 August 1867. Outrey confirmed that since the operations had begun, the French had disembarked 926 women, children, and older people, and no men at the Piraeus.

68. MAE, CP de la Turquie jusqu'à 1896, vol. 372, Outrey to Moustier, Doc. No. 159, 21 August 1867.

69. Ibid., Doc. No. 152, 20 August 1867.

70. A. & P., Further Correspondence Respecting the Disturbances in Crete, 1867, Doc. No. 229, Ellis to Stanley, 3 August 1867(received 11 August).

71. Ibid., Doc. No. 253, Inclosure 3, Murray to Paget, 4 August 1867.

72. As Saab did before me, I compared the contents of the Blue Books with the documents at the TNA: PRO, FO 195/795 and 878.

73. Saab, "The Doctor," D1396–D1397.

74. Ibid.

75. Ibid.

76. MAE, CP de la Turquie jusqu'à 1896, vol. 372, Outrey to Moustier, Doc. No. 178, 11 September 1867.

77. A. & P., Further Correspondence Respecting the Disturbances in Crete, 1867, Doc. No. 257, Barron to Stanley (received 27 September).

78. Ibid., Doc. No. 267, Fuad Pasha to Musurus Pasha, communicated to Lord Stanley by Musurus Pasha, 15 October, Constantinople, 13 October 1867; and Doc. No. 277, Inclosure, Circular letter addressed by Aali Pasha to the Consuls of France, Austria, Italy, and Russia, Canea, 14 October 1867.

79. Ibid., In Continuation of Correspondence Presented to Parliament, 2 December 1867; ibid., 2 February 1867, 1868, Doc. No. 7, Erskine to Stanley, 20 November 1867 (received 30 November); and Doc. No. 41, Inclosure 1, Petition of Cretan Refugees Committee. This committee, which Erskine did not really trust, claimed that the number of Cretan women refugees in Greece was sixty thousand. The committee had requested financial aid from Queen Victoria for the use of the Cretan refugees in Greece, but it was refused.

80. A. & P., Further Correspondence Respecting the Disturbances in Crete, 1867, Doc. No. 278, Erskine to Stanley, 23 October 1867 (received 1 November).

81. MAE, CP de la Turquie jusqu'à 1896, vol. 373, Outrey to Moustier, Doc. No. 186, 9 October 1867.

82. TNA: PRO, FO 881/1589, Turkey, Confidential Prints: Corres. Disturbances in Crete (Continuation of No. 1581), Doc. No. 19, Elliot to Stanley, 15 November 1867 (received 30 November).

83. MAE, CP de la Turquie jusqu'à 1896, vol. 373, Bourrée to Moustier, Doc. No. 208, 20 November 1867.

84. A. & P., Correspondence Respecting the Disturbances in Crete, 1868, Doc. No. 80, Report by Aali Pasha Respecting His Mission to the Island of Crete, Fuad Pasha to Musurus Pasha, 1 April 1868 (communicated to Lord Stanley by Musurus Pasha, 11 April 1868).

85. Ibid., Doc. No. 23, Inclosure, Judicial Organisation for the Island of Crete; ibid., Inclosure in No. 32, Administrative Regulation for the Island of Crete; and Doc. No. 67, Inclosure, Imperial Firman Relative to the Reorganization of Crete—Règlement Organique; MAE, CP de la Turquie jusqu'à 1896, vol. 373, Outrey to Moustier, Doc. No. 185, 2 October 1867.

86. MAE, CP de la Turquie jusqu'à 1896, vol. 374, Bourrée to Moustier, Doc. No. 96, 4 February 1868; MAE, Mémoires et Documents, Turquie, Tome 117, Doc. 18, 1 April 1868; MAE, CP de la Turquie jusqu'à 1896, vol. 376, Bourée to Moustier, Doc. No. 118, 8 June 1868, report of a conversation between the British ambassador and the sultan. See also TNA: PRO, FO 881/1634, Turkey, Confidential Prints: Corres. Disturbances in Crete (Continuation of No. 1581).

87. MAE, CP de la Turquie jusqu'à 1896, vol. 377, Bourrée to Moustier, Annexe au Doc. No. 176, 20 September 1868, "Cette quantité considérable d'huile est prise d'ordinaire par le commerce et l'industrie de Marseille, l'intérêt commercial vient en aide à l'intérêt politique et nous donnera peut être au besoin des raisons d'agir spéciales."

88. Ibid., vol. 378, Bourrée to Moustier, Annexe to Doc. No. 237, 16 December 1868; MAE, Mémoires et Documents, Turquie, Tome 117 Doc. 13-bis.

89. MAE, Mémoires et Documents, Turquie, Tome 118, Doc. No. 3, Affaires de Crète—Conférence de 1869 à Paris, 9 January—18 February 1869.

90. MAE, CP de la Turquie jusqu'à 1896, vol. 375, Bourrée to Moustier, Rapport de S. A. Aali Pacha, Grand-Vézir, sur sa mission dans l'Ile de Crète.

91. TNA: PRO, FO 881/1589, Inclosure in Doc. No. 160, Report by Aali Pasha Respecting His Mission to the Island of Crete, 1 March 1868.

92. Holland and Markides, *The British and the Hellenes*, 83.

93. George Campbell, *The Eastern Question: From the Treaty of Paris 1856 to the Treaty of Berlin 1878, and to the Second Afghan War*, 2 vols. (London: Strahan, 1879; Elibron Classics Series, 2005), 1:114–19, 216.

94. MAE, Mémoires et Documents Turquie, Tome 120, Doc. 7, *Etude sur la Crète par M. Hanotaux*, 16 March 1881.

95. Bloxham, *The Great Game*, 34–35.

CHAPTER SIX: NONINTERVENTION DURING THE EASTERN CRISIS (1875–78)

1. Stevan K. Pavlowitch, *A History of the Balkans 1804–1945* (London: Longman, 1999), 115.

2. Misha Glenny, *The Balkans* (New York: Viking, 2000), 110.

3. Bass, *Freedom's Battle*, 245; Glenny, *The Balkans*, 124–25. Glenny (129) explains that Pan-Slavists cannot be considered a monolithic group of people but rather were an ideological cacophony. See also Maria Todorova, *Imagining the Balkans* (Oxford: Oxford University Press, 1997), 85; Barbara Jelavich, *Russia's Balkan Entanglements, 1806–1914* (Cambridge: Cambridge University Press, 1991).

4. Saab, *Reluctant Icon*, 6.

5. Glenny, *The Balkans*, 101–2, 128.

6. Ibid., 105.

7. R. W. Seton-Watson, *Disraeli, Gladstone and the Eastern Question: A Study in Diplomacy and Party Politics* (New York: Norton Library, 1972 [1935]), 20.

8. Thompson, *Public Opinion*, 1:221.

9. Seton-Watson, *Disraeli*, 22.

10. Sedley Taylor, *The Conduct of Her Majesty's Ministers on the Eastern Question: A Statement of Facts Based on Official Documents* (London: Liberal Central Association, 1877), 28.

11. Glenny, *The Balkans*, 127.

12. A. & P., Correspondence Respecting the Affairs of Turkey, and the Insurrection in Bosnia and Herzegovina. In Continuation of Papers Presented to Parliament, Turkey, No. 2, 1876 (hereafter Correspondence Bosnia and Herzegovina); TNA: PRO, FO 881/2916, Confidential Prints, Atrocities in Bulgaria, Memorandum by Lord Tenterden, 9 August 1876.

13. A. & P., Correspondence Bosnia and Herzegovina, Doc. No. 538, Elliot to Derby, Therapia, 6 July 1876 (received 14 July).

14. Stephen D. Shenfield, "The Circassians: A Forgotten Genocide?" in *The Massacre in History*, 149–62. Between 1860 and 1864 hundreds of thousands of Circassians abandoned their Caucasian lands because of Russian expansionism

and religious cleansing. Their arrival in the Ottoman Empire led to one of the nineteenth century's great "humanitarian crises," which, in Glenny's word, "never even touched European conscience." About 400,000 Circassians sought refuge in Anatolia, Bulgaria, and Macedonia. The Ottoman Empire recruited them as soldiers. Both by decree and by force majeure, Christians were evicted en masse from their homes and villages to accommodate the new arrivals. The refugees began to terrorize parts of the countryside, and thousands of Christians fled into Romania or Serbia. The émigré Bulgarian revolutionaries acquired many new recruits, and some of them were involved in the May uprising.

15. Thompson, *Public Opinion*, 1:311.

16. Ibid., 1:319.

17. Edwin Pears, *Forty Years in Constantinople* (New York: D. Appleton, 1916); James Baker, *Turkey in Europe* (London: Cassell, Petter and Galpin, 1877), 41–46.

18. Baring was a young man who had no knowledge of the Bulgarian language and only a faulty command of Turkish. He was to be accompanied by his father-in-law, a Levantine named Frederick Guarracino who had served for thirty years as a British agent in Asia Minor. In David Harris, *Britain and the Bulgarian Horrors of 1876* (Chicago: University of Chicago Press, 1939), 144–48.

19. TNA:PRO, FO 881/2936B, Confidential Print, Supplement to The London Gazette of Tuesday, the 19th of September, Published by Authority, Report of Mr. Baring on the Atrocities Committed upon the Christians in Bulgaria.

20. A. &. P., State Papers continued, Turkey, Session 8 February—14 August 1877, Doc. No. 221, Sir H. Elliot to the Earl of Derby, Therapia, 4 September 1876, received 14 September.

21. TNA:PRO, FO, 65/939/354, Loftus to Derby, 21 August 1876; Richard Millman, *Britain and the Eastern Question 1875–1878* (Oxford: Clarendon Press, 1979), 148–52.

22. Thompson, *Public Opinion*, 1:334. Glenny, *The Balkans*, 109, writes that there is no doubt that the Turkish irregulars were responsible for terrible crimes. However, this testimony also contains inconsistencies. Had eight thousand been killed in Batak, for example, this would have made of it a middle-sized town, but by MacGahan's own admission it was an extremely remote rural settlement.

23. A. &. P., State Papers continued, Turkey, Session 8 February—14 August 1877, Doc. No. 316, Derby to Elliot, 21 September 1876.

24. Harris, *Britain and the Bulgarian*, 176.

25. Richard Shannon, *Gladstone and the Bulgarian Agitation* (London: Nelson, 1963), 28; Jonathan P. Parry, *Democracy and Religion: Gladstone and the Liberal Party, 1867–1875* (Cambridge: Cambridge University Press, 1986).

26. The National Society for Aid to Sick and Wounded in War (which was to become better known in later years as the Red Cross Society), League in Aid of the Christians of Turkey, Russian Sick and Wounded Fund, Serbian Relief Fund, Lady Strangford British Hospital and Ambulance Fund, Stafford House Committee, Red Crescent Society, Mansion House Fund Relief Committee, Central Relief Committee at Constantinople, and Manchester Relief Fund. Dorothy Anderson, *The Balkan Volunteers* (London: Hutchinson, 1968).

27. Saab, *Reluctant Icon*, 63.

28. Harris, *Britain and the Bulgarian*, 250–53.

29. Saab, *Reluctant Icon*, 125; Shannon, *Bulgarian Agitation*, 205.

30. For an eloquent criticism of Gladstone's pamphlet, see H. A. Munro Butler-Johnstone, who insists on Gladstone's ignorance of Ottoman history, *Bulgarian Horrors, and the Question of the East: A Letter Addressed to the Right Hon. W. E. Gladstone, M.P.* (London: William Ridgway, 1876). Another pamphlet very critical of Gladstone was Henry de Worms, *England's Policy in the East* (London: Chapman and Hall, 1876). See also John Mill, *The Ottomans in Europe* (London: Weldon, 1876; Elibron Classic Series, 2005); Robert Montagu, *Foreign Policy: England and the Eastern Question* (London: Bradbury, Agnew, 1877); James Baker, *Turkey in Europe* (London: Cassell, Petter and Galpin, 1877).

31. Shannon, *Bulgarian Agitation*, 251–61.

32. Richard Shannon, *Gladstone: Heroic Minister 1865–1898* (London: Penguin, 1999), 159; Eugenio F. Biagini, *Liberty, Retrenchment and Reform: Popular Liberalism in the Age of Gladstone, 1860–1880* (Cambridge: Cambridge University Press, 1992).

33. Shannon, *Gladstone*, vol. 1: *1809–1865* (London: Meuthen, 1984), 361–62, quotes E. W. Gladstone, "The Past and Present Administration," *Quarterly Review* (1858): 554 –60.

34. It was on this occasion that the "impalement incident" occurred when MacColl wrote to the *Times* on September 28, 1876. It was strongly denied by the British consul at Bosna-Seraï. A. &. P., State Papers—continued, Turkey, Session 8 February—14 August 1877, Doc. No. 687, 5 October 1876, received 17 October; also Doc. No. 742.

35. Rev. William Denton, *Fallacies of the Eastern Question*, Eastern Question Association, Papers on the Eastern Question, no. 8 (London: Cassell, Petter and Galpin, 1877).

36. Shannon, *Gladstone: Heroic Minister*, 167.

37. Ibid., 168.

38. Saab, *Reluctant Icon*, 77–79.

39. W. E. Gladstone, *Bulgarian Horrors and the Question of the East* (London: John Murray, 1876).

40. Saab, *Reluctant Icon*, 90.

41. Gladstone, *Bulgarian Horrors*, 18.

42. A similar position was taken by George Campbell, *What the Turks Are, and How We Have Been Helping Them: Speech of the Duke of Argyll in the City Hall, Glasgow, September 19, 1876, with a preface* (Glasgow: James Maclehose, 1876), 29: "It is an entire mistake in the public mind that the sending of the fleet to Besika Bay had anything to do with the Bulgarian horrors." The Bulgarian atrocities took place during the first two weeks of May, and the fleet was sent to Besika Bay at the end of the month. Campbell, *The Eastern Question*.

43. Gladstone, *Bulgarian Horrors*, 43.

44. Ibid., 47–48.

45. Thompson, *Public Opinion*, 1:172–73; George Campbell, "The Resettlement of the Turkish Dominions," *Fortnightly Reviewer* (April 1878).

46. Cunningham, "The Wrong Horse?" 232.

47. Thompson, *Public Opinion*, 1:171–72.

48. Bass, *Freedom's Battle*, 280.

49. Shannon, *Gladstone: Heroic Minister*, 191–92.

50. Among the writings of the Eastern Question Association are Henry Richard, *Evidence of Turkish Misrule*, Eastern Question Association, Papers on the Eastern Question, no. 1 (London: Cassell, Petter and Galpin, 1876); George Campbell, *The Races, Religions, and Institutions of Turkey and the Neighbouring Countries: Being the Substance of Two Lecturers Delivered in The Kirkcaldy Burghs*, Eastern Question Association, Papers on the Eastern Question, no. 3 (London: Cassell, Petter and Galpin, 1877); and *The Blue Books, and What Is to Come Next*, Eastern Question Association, Papers on the Eastern Question, no. 12 (London: Cassell, Petter and Galpin, 1877).

51. The Canada Building was the headquarters of the Aborigines Protection Society and the administrative center of the Eastern Question Association movement. F. W. Chesson, a prominent organizer of the later phase of the agitation, was the secretary of the Aborigines Protection Society. F. W. Chesson, *Turkey and the Slave Trade: A Statement of Facts*, Eastern Question Association, Papers on the Eastern Question, no. 7 (London: Cassell, Petter and Galpin, 1877).

52. Goldwin Smith, a representative of the most characteristic spirit of both movements, made a special point in 1876 of looking back to the Eyre case as comparable to the atrocities agitation as an expression of those "two great Liberal sentiments—the love of justice and the love of humanity."

53. James Bryce was a member of Parliament from 1874 and would become one of the leaders of the Liberal Party in the 1880s. He served as undersecretary of state for foreign affairs (1886), founded the Anglo-Armenian Society in 1876 and the Armenian Association of England in 1893, traveled extensively in Armenia, Caucasus, Smyrna, and Constantinople, and founded the Balkan Committee, which became the locus of British pro-Macedonia activities. Bryce was also the author of *Transcaucasia and Ararat*, published in 1877. He was one of the first Western politicians to respond to the 1915 Armenian genocide and was active in forming British-Armenian Red Cross Society and Fund for Relief. In 1916 he published a collection of documents entitled *The Conditions of the Armenians in the Ottoman Empire 1915–1916*.

54. MacColl, *The Eastern Question*, viii.

55. Ibid., 44–45.

56. Ibid., 74.

57. Millicent Garrett Fawcett, *The Martyrs of Turkish Misrule*, Eastern Question Association, Papers on the Eastern Question, no. 11 (London: Cassell, Petter and Galpin, 1877), 1.

58. Fawcett, *The Martyrs*, 10, 11.

59. Rougier, "Théorie," 489; Bluntschli, *Le Droit International Codifié*, §6: "Le droit international, le droit général de l'humanité, réunit les chrétiens et les mahométans, les bouddhistes et les brahmanistes, les disciples de Confucius et les adorateurs des étoiles, les croyants et les non-croyants." See also Henry Sumner Maine, *International Law: A Series of Lectures Delivered before the University of Cambridge 1887 (The Whewell Lectures)* (London: John Murray, 1888), 34; Fiore, *Il Diritto Internazionale*, 288: "I diritti d'inviolabilità e libertà personale possono

essere limitati per ragioni di ordine pubblico, ma non possono essere mai negati del tutto all'uomo a qualunque razza egli appartenga."

60. Thompson, *Public Opinion*, 1:116.

61. Ibid., 117. To substantiate his opinion he quoted Wheaton and John Stuart Mill's article "A Few Words on Non-Intervention," specifically Mill's observation that the rule of nonintervention cannot apply as between a civilized and an uncivilized people because all moral rules imply reciprocity, and there can be no reciprocity with barbarians.

62. Campbell, *The Eastern Question*, 1:xiii; Despagnet, *Cours*, 234: "si l'on a admis la Turquie dans le concert européen et surtout si l'on a garant son indépendance et son intégrité, c'est à la condition que la Porte réaliserait les réformes promises pour l'égalité religieuse et civile de ses sujets, l'administration de la justice, la gestion des finances, les mesures contre la partialité et la corruption de ses fonctionnaires. En fait les interventions dans les affaires intérieures de la Turquie s'expliquent par le non accomplissement de ces réformes toujours promises et toujours éludées."

63. Campbell, *The Eastern Question*, 1:9.

64. Ibid., 15–16.

65. Ibid., 129.

66. Thompson, *Public Opinion*, 1:89–90.

67. W. E. Gladstone, *Lessons in Massacre; or the Conduct of the Turkish Government in and about Bulgaria since May 1876. Chiefly from the Papers Presented by Command* (London: John Murray, 1877), 76–77; Freeman, *The Eastern Question*, 14; Denton, *Fallacies*, 7–8; Campbell, *What the Turks Are*; MacColl, *The Eastern Question*, 51; and Sedley Taylor, *The Conduct of Her Majesty's Ministers on the Eastern Question: A Statement of Facts Based on Official Documents* (London: Liberal Central Association, 1877).

68. Freeman, *The Eastern Question*, 14–15.

69. MacColl, *The Eastern Question*, 280–81.

70. A. &. P., State Papers—continued, Turkey, Session 8 February—14 August 1877, Correspondence Respecting the Conference at Constantinople and the Affairs of Turkey (hereafter Conference at Constantinople), Doc. No. 53, Inclosures 1–4, Reports from Baring Respecting the Proceedings of the Commission at Philippopolis of November and December 1876.

71. Since 1874 Lord Salisbury had been a member of Disraeli's cabinet as secretary of state for India. David Steele, *Lord Salisbury: A Political Biography* (London: Routledge, 2001).

72. A. &. P., Conference at Constantinople, Doc. No. 1, Derby to Salisbury.

73. Robert Blake, *Disraeli* (New York: St. Martin's Press, 1967), 614–15.

74. A. &. P. Conference at Constantinople, Doc. No. 112, Salisbury to Derby, Pera, 22 December 1876, received 31 December, Inclosure 1, Réunions Préliminaires, compte-rendu no. 1–Séance du 11 Décembre 1876.

75. Ibid., Doc. No. 104, Elliot to Derby, Constantinople, 15 December 1876, received 31 December.

76. Ibid., Doc. No. 55, Salisbury to Derby, Constantinople, 7 December 1876, received 15 December.

77. Ibid., Doc. No. 112, inclosure 2, compte-rendu no. 2—séance du 12 Décember 1876, and annexes nos. 1 and 2.

78. Ibid.

79. Ibid., Doc. No. 135, inclosure 3, compte-rendu no. 7—séance du 20 Décembre 1876.

80. Engelhardt, *La Turquie*, 2:178.

81. Woolsey, *American Foreign Policy* (1898), 74, cited in E. Stowell, *Intervention in International Law*, 131.

82. Dwight E. Lee, *Great Britain and the Cyprus Convention Policy of 1878* (Cambridge: Harvard University Press, 1934); Lillian Penson, "The Foreign Policy of Lord Salisbury, 1878–80: The Problem of the Ottoman Empire," in *Studies in Anglo-French History during the Eighteenth, Nineteenth and Twentieth Centuries*, ed. Alfred Coville and Harold Temperley (Cambridge: Cambridge University Press, 1935), 125–42; C. J. Lowe, *The Reluctant Imperialists: British Foreign Policy 1878–1902*, 2 vols. (London: Routledge, 1968).

83. Article 1 of the Cyprus Convention committed Great Britain to pursue the matter of Armenian reforms. In return for its willingness to protect "by force of arms" the Ottoman Empire against Russian territorial encroachments beyond Kars, Ardahan, and Batum, England was allowed to occupy the island of Cyprus.

84. Peter Marsh, "Lord Salisbury and the Ottoman Massacres," *Journal of British Studies* 11 (1972): 63–83, at 71–72.

85. [An old Indian], 186–87.

86. Glenny, *The Balkans*, 145–46.

87. Carol Fink, *Defending the Rights of Others: The Great Powers, the Jews, and International Minority Protection, 1878–1938* (Cambridge: Cambridge University Press, 2004).

88. McCarthy, *Exile*, 77.

89. A. & P., Correspondence Respecting the Proceedings on the International Commission Sent to the Mount Rhodope District 1878 (hereafter Rhodope District), Doc. No. 1, Inclosure 1, Layard to Salisbury, 17–18 July, received 27 July 1878.

90. Ibid., Doc. No. 15, Layard to Salisbury, Therapia, 27 September 1878, received 12 October.

91. McCarthy, *Exile*, 86.

92. Ibid., 83, whose sources are mainly the Foreign Office documents.

93. TNA: PRO FO 881/3188, Consul General Longworth to Clarendon, Belgrade, 12 March 1869, received 18 March; TNA: PRO, FO 881/1509, Confidential Prints, Correspondence Respecting the Condition of the Jews in Servia, 10 April 1867; A. & P., State Papers—Servia-Turkey. Correspondence Respecting the Condition and Treatment of the Jews in Servia, 1867, Doc. No. 15, Stanley to Longworth, 17 March 1867.

94. Thornberry, *International Law and the Rights of Minorities*, 33.

CHAPTER SEVEN: INTERMEZZO—THE INTERNATIONAL CONTEXT (1878–1908)

1. Stephen D. Krasner argues that Westphalian sovereignty has almost nothing to do with the Peace of Westphalia. It was Emer de Vattel who developed the notion of nonintervention. So we ought to refer to Vattelian, or at least

Vattelian-Westphalian sovereignty. Stephen D. Krasner, *Sovereignty: Organized Hypocrisy* (Princeton: Princeton University Press, 1999); Arcidiacono, "Les projets," 11–24; and "Pour une généalogie," 5–23.

2. Denton, *Fallacies*, 5–6.

3. Engelhardt, *La Turquie*, 2:322: "gardiennes des principes généraux basés sur le consensus international, soit simplement comme protectrices des droits de l'humanité."

4. The Public Debt Commission, operated by Europeans, took the proceeds from taxes on tobacco, silk, fishing, alcoholic spirits, official stamps affixed to legal documents, and the entire tribute payments of Bulgaria, Cyprus, Greece, and Montenegro. The Ottomans could not collect either appropriate customs dues or many of their own taxes.

5. Pavlowitch, *The Balkans*, 144.

6. Mark Levene, *The Rise of the West and the Coming of Genocide*, 2:280.

7. J. M. Roberts, *Europe 1880–1945*, 3d ed. (London: Longman, 2001), 60.

8. Ibid., 67.

9. Documents Diplomatiques Français, 1re série, Tome 12, Doc. No. 108, Mr. De Montebello, French ambassador at St. Petersburg. to Mr. Hanotaux, French minister of foreign affairs, St. Petersburg, 27 July 1895: "Le gouvernement actuel, comme celui de M. de Giers, désire avant tout que l'agitation dans les provinces qui confinent à la Russie n'ait aucun prétexte pour persister ; il a constamment à lutter, et il le fait avec la plus grande énergie, contre les comités qui cherchent sans relâche à soulever les Arméniens, sujets de la Turquie ; depuis bien d'années, la Russie est parvenue à empêcher que les mouvements qui se produisaient en Asie Mineure n'eussent un contre-coup sur son territoire."

10. S. Pavlowitch, *The Balkans*, 139–40.

11. Roberts, *Europe*, 89.

12. Louis Martin Sears, "French Opinion of the Spanish-American War," *Hispanic American Historical Review* 7 (1927): 25–44. The French government was particularly critical of U.S. intervention although it remained neutral with respect to the conflict. As for the humanitarian and Christian protestations of President McKinley, these were labeled "sophistry," that "sophistry [for] which the Americans assumes so naturally a sentimental form." Charles G. Fenwick, "Intervention: Individual and Collective," *American Journal of International Law* 39 (1945): 645–63.

13. Paul A. Kramer, *The Blood of Government: Race, Empire, the United States, & the Philippines* (Chapel Hill: University of North Carolina Press, 2006).

14. John Lawrence Tone, *War and Genocide in Cuba, 1895–1898* (Chapel Hill: University of North Carolina Press, 2006), 193, explains that in November 1897 the Spanish government ended "reconcentration," but sickly and staving peasants could not be "deconcentrated" to a burned-out and devastated countryside by fiat, a situation similar to the resettlement of the Cretan internally displaced population at the turn of the century (see chapter 9). On the policy of "reconcentration," Tone argues that this was nothing new or specific to the Spanish occupiers. The United States had practiced a form of reconcentration in its wars with Native Americans by herding them onto reservations (195). *Reconcentrados* arrived in garrisoned towns not only bereft of animals but lacking seed, tools, clothing, and money, a situation similar to that of Damascus and Lebanese

coastal towns in 1860. Furthermore, in areas where the insurgency was strong, a majority of the *reconcentrados* were women and children because the men were with the insurgency or with the Spanish as Volunteers and counterguerrillas, similar to what would happen during the Boer War (see below).

15. Ibid., 218.

16. Ibid.

17. Ann Marie Wilson, "In the Name of God, Civilization, and Humanity: The United States and the Armenian Massacres of the 1890s," *Le Mouvement Social* 227 (2009): 27–44.

18. Events in South Africa deeply touched British population; the conflict unleashed the excitement and bellicosity of the British public even though a tiny minority, derisively branded "pro-Boers," spoke out against the war. On the pro-Boers: John W. Auld, "The Liberal Pro-Boers," *Journal of British Studies* 14 (1975): 78–101; Marouf Haisan, "The 'Historical' Emily Hobhouse and Boer War Concentration Camp Controversy," *Western Journal of Communication* (2003): 138–63; Claire Hirshfield, "Liberal Women's Organizations and the War against the Boers, 1899–1902," *Albion: A Quarterly Journal Concerned with British Studies* 14 (1982): 27–49; Dennis Judd and Keith Surridge, *The Boer War* (New York: Palgrave Macmillan, 2003); Paula M. Krebs, "The Last of the Gentlemen's Wars: Women in the Boer War Concentration Camp Controversy," *History Workshop* 33 (1992): 38–56; Andrew S. Thompson, "The Language of Imperialism and the Meanings of Empire: Imperial Discourse in British Politics, 1895–1914," *Journal of British Studies* 36 (1997): 147–77, at 150–51.

19. Levene, *The Rise of the West*, 239.

20. Ibid., 272.

21. Todorova, *Imagining the Balkans*, 100.

22. John MacCunn, "Cosmopolitan Duties," *International Journal of Ethics* 9 (1899): 152–68, at 160 and 163.

23. Levene, *The Rise of the West*, 238.

24. Kevin Grant, *A Civilised Savagery: Britain and the New Slaveries in Africa, 1884–1926* (New York: Routledge, 2005), 51–52, notes that Morel and Fox Bourne had provided Samuel with statistics, testimonies, and other evidence for his speech, just as they had provided the general arguments employed by all five of the speakers supporting the motion. Samuel and his supporters highlighted missionary testimonies as the most significant evidence regarding exploitation and atrocities in the Congo. Samuel pointed out that he was not one of those short-sighted philanthropists who thought that the natives must be treated in all respects on equal terms with white men. Rather, Samuel asserted vaguely that there were certain rights must be common to humanity: the rights of liberty and of just treatment.

25. Ibid., 6–8, 36.

26. Ibid., 41.

27. Michael Taussig, "Culture of Terror—Space of Death: Roger Casement's Putumayo Report and the Explanation of Torture," *Comparative Studies in Society and History* 26 (1984): 467–97.

28. A. & P., Correspondence Respecting the Treatment of British Colonial Subjects and Native Indians Employed in the Collection of Rubber in the Pu-

tumayo District, Miscellaneous, No. 8, 1912; Report by His Majesty's Consul at Iquitos on His Tour in the Putumayo District, Miscellaneous, No. 6, 1913; Report and Special Report from the Select Committee on Putumayo, together with Proceeding of the Committee Minutes of Evidence and Appendices, 1913.

29. Pavlowitch, *The Balkans*, 181.

30. Ibid., 170.

31. Bloxham, *The Great Game*, 58.

32. Roberts, *Europe*, 213–16.

CHAPTER EIGHT: NONINTERVENTION ON BEHALF OF THE OTTOMAN ARMENIANS (1886–1909)

1. Bloxham, *The Great Game*, 16.

2. Ibid., 38.

3. Arman J. Kirakossian, *British Diplomacy and the Armenian Question, from the 1830s to 1914* (Princeton and London: Gomidas Institute Books, 2003), 145; A. O. Sarkissian, *History of the Armenian Question to 1885* (Urbana: University of Illinois Press, 1938); Roy Douglas, "Britain and the Armenian Question, 1894–7," *Historical Journal* 19 (1976): 113–33, at 113–15.

4. Charles Eliot, *Turkey in Europe*, (New York: Barnes & Noble, 1965 [1900], 122). Eliot's comparison of the Armenians with the Poles and the Jews can also be found in Woods, *The Danger Zone of Europe*, 388, and similar descriptions and comparisons are made in a pamphlet entitled *The Eastern Question and the Armenians* (London, April 1878).

5. A. &. P., Correspondence Respecting the Condition of the Populations in Asiatic Turkey, and the Proceedings in the Case of Moussa Bey, Turkey No. 1, 1890–91; A. & P., Correspondence Relating to the Asiatic Provinces of Turkey 1892–93, Turkey No. 3, 1896; A. & P., Further Correspondence Respecting the Condition of the Populations of Asiatic Turkey, in Continuation of Turkey No. 1 1891, and Turkey No. 1, 1892, Inclosure 3 in Doc. No. 10, Memorandum on the Misleading Views Respecting Armenian Affairs by the Paragraphs Periodically Recurring in Certain Newspapers, in Particular the "Daily News," and upon the Condition of Kurds and Armenians Generally, Vice Consul George Pollard Devey to Ambassador Sir William White, 12 January 1891. On William White, see, Colin L. Smith, *The Embassy of Sir William White at Constantinople 1886–1891* (Oxford: Oxford University Press, 1957).

6. A. & P., Correspondence Respecting Reforms in Asiatic Turkey, 1878 (hereafter CRRAT, 1878), Doc. No. 1, Salisbury to Layard, Foreign Office, 8 August 1878.

7. Manoug Joseph Somakian, *Empires in Conflict: Armenia and the Great Powers, 1895–1920* (London: I. B. Tauris, 1995).

8. CRRAT, 1878, Doc. No. 1, Salisbury to Layard, Foreign Office, 8 August 1878.

9. Steele, *Salisbury*, 138, noted that Salisbury's aim was to introduce British advisers into Ottoman provincial administration with much the same role as the residents at Indian princely courts. Aware that the analogy would not please the Ottoman authorities, he edited references in the *Blue Books*.

10. CRRAT, 1878, Doc. No. 1, Salisbury to Layard, Foreign Office, 8 August 1878.

11. Ibid., Doc. No. 2, Layard to Salisbury, Therapia, 21 August 1878, received 30 August.

12. Ibid., Doc. No. 3, Layard to Salisbury, Therapia, 24 October 1878, received 1 November; and Inclosure in No. 3, Safvet Pasha to Layard, Sublime Porte, 24 October 1878.

13. The appointments included Major Charles B.Wilson as consul general in Anatolia; Captain J.D.H. Stewart, Captain H. Cooper, Lieutenant Herbert Chermside, and Lieutenant Kitchener as vice consuls in Anatolia; Captain Clayton as vice consul at Van; Henry Trotter as consul at Erzeroum; Captain Everett as vice consul at Erzeroum; and Alfred Biliotti as consul at Trebizond.

14. A. & P., Correspondence Respecting the Condition of the Populations in Asia Minor and Syria, Turkey, No. 4, 1880, Doc. No.14, inclosure 1, Clayton to Trotter, Mush, 31 July 1879. See also Doc. No. 63, Trotter to Salisbury, Erzeroum, 7 October 1879, received 26 October, in which Trotter refers to 10,000 families who had given notice of their intention to leave the Russian territory for Ottoman territories. Of these, 3,878 families, or a total of 23,498 people, had already arrived in Erzeroum, and a further 3,263 had been forwarded to their intended destination. Some 884 individuals had reached the vilayet of Van (the towns of Van, Bitlis, and Moush), very few were in Trebizon, Diarbekir, and Kharput, and more than 10,000 were in Sivas, although the latter were Circassians.

15. Bloxham, *The Great Game*, 37.

16. Kirakossian, *British Diplomacy*, 122–23.

17. A. & P., Correspondence Respecting the Affairs of Turkey, Turkey No. 7, 1880, Doc. No. 3, Layard to the secretary of state for foreign affairs, Constantinople, 27 April 1880.

18. On August 23 consuls Wilson and Trotter submitted a memorandum to Lord Dufferin that insisted on the importance of appointing two commissioners for a term of three years to oversee the reform process, with full executive powers in the provinces of Erzeroum, Van, Bitlis, Hakiari, Kharput, Dersim, and Diyarbakir, as well as Sivas, Kara-Hisar, and Tokat districts in Sivas province, Marash district in Aleppo province, and part of the Sis district of Adana province.

19. Documents Diplomatiques Français, 1ʳᵉ série, Tome 11, Paul Cambon to M. Gabriel Hanotaux, Minister of Foreign Affairs, Pera, 14 November 1894; Paul Marsh, "Lord Salisbury and the Ottoman Massacres," *Journal of British Studies* 11 (1972): 63–83, at 74.

20. A. & P., Correspondence Relating to the Asiatic Provinces of Turkey: 1894–95, in Continuation of Turkey No. 3, 1896, and Turkey No. 6, 1896.

21. The Huntchack (Hunchack) Party was founded in 1886 by a group of Russian Armenians in Geneva. A socialist party with a strong Marxist orientation, its members believed that a new and independent Armenia would initiate a worldwide socialist revolution.

22. During the winter of 1891 Sultan Abdul Hamid's government organized a mounted militia, drafted almost exclusively from the Kurdish tribes known as *Hamidiye*. Some thirty regiments were set up and amounted to a total of 33,000

men. In the sultan's intention, the Kurdish militia had to stem the burgeoning Armenian national liberation movement and, wherever possible, alter the ethnic composition in the provinces where the reforms had been scheduled to take place. Moreover, it served as a bulwark against the Russian Army in case of a renewal of hostilities in the East.

23. Robert Graves, *Storm Centres of the Near East: Personal Memories 1879–1929* (London: Hutchinson, 1933).

24. Kirakossian, *British Diplomacy*, 192.

25. Ibid., 193.

26. In 1894 Gladstone, now eighty-five years old, stepped down as leader of the Liberal Party, passing on his portfolio to Rosebery, with John Kimberley as foreign secretary. Rosebery became the prime minister of a very fragile government weakened by a solid opposition and by internal dissensions of the Liberal Party. Rosebery's government lasted only until June 21, 1895.

27. Kirakossian, *British Diplomacy*, 194.

28. NTA: PRO, FO 881/6645, Confidential prints, August 1895, E. Barrington, Summary of Correspondence Relating to the Armenian Question, 29 June 1895; Documents Diplomatiques Français, 1ʳᵉ série, Tome 11, Cambon to Hanotaux, Pera, 19 December 1894; MAE, CP Turquie Jusqu'à 1896, vol. 521, Cambon to Hanotaux, Doc. No. 69, Péra, 2 May 1895.

29. NTA: PRO, FO 881/6645.

30. Kirakossian, *British Diplomacy*, 203.

31. Peter Balakian, *The Burning Tigris: A History of the Armenian Genocide* (London: Pimlico, 2005), 56; Douglas, "Britain and the Armenian Question," 116.

32. On Diyarbakir, see Gustave Meyrier, *Les massacres de Diarbekir: Correspondance diplomatique du vice-consul de France 1894–1896, présentée et annotée par Claire Mouradian et Michel Durand-Meyrier* (Paris: L'Inventaire, 2000). See also Sébastien de Courtois, *Le génocide oublié. Chrétiens d'Orient, les derniers Araméens* (Paris, Ellipses, 2002).

33. Documents Diplomatiques Français, 1ʳᵉ série, Tome 11, Hanotaux to Cambon, Paris, 27 November 1894.

34. Kirakossian, *British Diplomacy*, 200–1.

35. Somakian, *Empires*, 24; Douglas, "Britain and the Armenian Question," 119.

36. Kirakossian, *British Diplomacy*, 209–10; Douglas, "Britain and the Armenian Question," 119.

37. A. & P., Correspondence Respecting the Introduction of Reforms in the Armenian Provinces of Asiatic Turkey (hereafter CRIRAPAT), Turkey No. 1, 1896, Doc. No. 74, Currie to Kimberley, Constantinople, 4 June 1895, received 8 June, and Inclosure in No. 74, "Reply of His Majesty the Sultan to the Proposed Scheme of Armenian Reforms." See also Doc. No. 126, Currie to Salisbury, 2 August 1896 (telegraphic); Doc. No. 130, 3 August 1895, Inclosure 2, "Summary by Colonel Chermside of the Porte's Last Answer."

38. Marsh, "Salisbury," 74.

39. Douglas, "Britain and the Armenian Question," 121.

40. Kirakossian, *British Diplomacy*, 214; Somakian, *Empires*, 26.

41. Shannon, *Gladstone*, 577–82.

42. CRIRAPAT, Turkey No. 2, 1896. See also A. & P., Further Correspondence Relating to the Asiatic Provinces of Turkey, in Continuation of Turkey No. 2, Turkey No. 8, 1896.

43. Balakian, *Burning Tigris*, 129.

44. Bloxham, *The Great Game*, 52.

45. Kirakossian, *British Diplomacy*, 230.

46. A. & P., Further Correspondence Relating to the Asiatic Provinces of Turkey, in Continuation of Turkey No. 2, Turkey No. 8, 1896, Inclosure in Doc. No. 61, Consul Longworth to Currie, Trebizond, 8 February 1896.

47. On the events in Sivas, see the diary of Émilie Carlier, *Au milieu des massacres: Journal de la femme d'un consul de France en Arménie* (Paris: Félix Juven Editeur, 1903).

48. A. & P., Further Correspondence Relating to the Asiatic Provinces of Turkey, Turkey No. 8, Inclosure to Doc. No. 265, Consul Henry D. Barnham, consul at Aleppo, to Salisbury, "Memorandum by Consul Barnham Respecting the Zeitoun Insurrection, 1895–96."

49. Documents Diplomatiques Français, 1re série, Tome 12, Doc. No. 185, Paul Cambon to Berthelot, Pera, 4 November 1895; A. Cahuet, *La question d'Orient*, 450–73; Max Choublier, *La question d'Orient depuis le Traité de Berlin* (Paris, A. Rousseau, 1897), 383–427.

50. "Cronique des faits internationaux. Turquie—La question arménienne—Intervention européenne," *Revue Générale de Droit International Public* 3 (1896): 371–74.

51. Kirakossian, *British Diplomacy*, 245; Dadrian, *History*, 127–31; A. & P., Further Correspondence Relating to the Asiatic Provinces of Turkey, Turkey No. 1, 1896, Doc. No. 110, Sir F. Lascelles to Salisbury, St. Petersburg, 3 July 1895, received 8 July. In the course of conversation, Prince Lobanov told the British ambassador Lascelles that "Russia had always been considered the protector of the Christians in the Turkish dominions, and she would be only too happy to obtain greater securities for their welfare and the protection of their lives and property, but her direct interests on the frontier forbade her to indulge in the philanthropic dreams which seem to prevail in England, whose interests, on account of her insular position and distance from the Armenian districts, were not directly affected."

52. Kirakossian, *British Diplomacy*, 256–57.

53. Andrew Roberts, *Salisbury: Victorian Titan* (London: Phoenix, 2000, 605; Steele, *Salisbury*, 320–30; J.A.S. Grenville, *Lord Salisbury and Foreign Policy: The Close of the Nineteenth Century* (London: Athlone Press, 1964), 24–54.

54. Kirakossian, *British Diplomacy*, 252.

55. A. & P., Correspondence Relating to the Asiatic Provinces of Turkey. Reports by Vice-Consul [Gerald] Fitzmaurice from Birejik, Ourfa, Adiaman, and Behesni, Turkey No. 5, 1896; Documents Diplomatiques Français. 1re série, Tome 12, Doc. No. 265, Cambon to Berthelot, Pera, 6 January 1896.

56. MAE, CP Turquie Jusqu'à 1896, vol. 526, Cambon to Berthelot, Doc. No. 3, Pera, 8 January 1896.

57. G. Thoumaïan, *Les Massacres en Arménie: Rapport officiel des six ambassadeurs à Constantinople. Extraits du "Livre Jaune." Lettres et rapports de témoins oculaires*

(Paris: Comité protestant français de secours aux Arméniens, 1897); A. & P., Further Correspondence Relating to the Asiatic Provinces of Turkey, Turkey No. 1, 1896, Inclosure in No. 543: "Evénements de 1895 en Asie Mineure."

58. Documents Diplomatiques Français, 1ʳᵉ série, Tome 12, Doc. No. 410, De Courcel, French Ambassador at London, to Hanotaux, London, 20 June 1896.

59. Dadrian, *History*, 131–38.

60. Kirakossian, *British Diplomacy*, 263–68; Balakian, *Burning Tigris*, 103–15; Dadrian, *History*, 138–46; A. & P., Correspondence Respecting the Disturbances at Constantinople in August 1896, Turkey No. 1, 1897, Turkey No. 3, and Turkey No. 7.

61. Douglas, "Britain and the Armenian Question," 127. A long, anonymous account of the events of Constantinople is "The Constantinople Massacre," *Contemporary Review* 70 (1896): 457–65.

62. Document Diplomatiques Français. 1ʳᵉ série, Tome 12, Doc. No. 457, Cambon to Hanotaux, Therapia, 25 September 1896, and Doc. No. 465, De Courcel to Hanotaux, 2 October 1896.

63. Bloxham, *The Great Game*, 53.

64. A. & P., Further Correspondence Relating to the Asiatic Provinces of Turkey, Turkey No. 2, 1897, Salisbury to Sir E. Monson, Doc. No. 1, Foreign Office, 23 September 1896, and Doc. No. 2, Salisbury to Sir N. O'Connor (and Mr. Henry Howard in Paris, Sir Francis Lascelles, Sir Edmund Monson, and Sir Francis Clair Ford), Foreign Office, 20 October 1896.

65. These views were largely shared by the members of the British cabinet—for instance, Sir Austen Chamberlain who, since 1895, was civil lord of the Admiralty. Chamberlain's reaction to the Armenian massacres of 1895 reveals his preoccupation with the necessity of British participation in European powers' management. *Birmingham Daily Post*, November 27, 1895, Charles Petrie, *The Life and Letters of the Right Hon. Sir Austen Chamberlain, K.G., P.C., M.P.* (London: Cassell, 1939), 1:71.

66. A. & P., Further Correspondence Relating to the Asiatic Provinces of Turkey, Turkey No. 2, 1897, Doc. No. 2, Salisbury to O'Connor, Foreign Office, 20 October 1896.

67. Ibid.

68. Kirakossian, *British Diplomacy*, 277.

69. Roberts, *Salisbury*, 611.

70. Bloxham, *The Great Game*, 54.

71. "Cronique des faits internationaux. Turquie—La question arménienne—Intervention européenne," *Revue Générale de Droit International Public* 3 (1896): 386–90.

72. Somakian, *Empires*, 31; Georges Brézol, *Les Turcs ont passé là . . . Recueil de documents, dossiers, rapports, requêtes, protestations, suppliques et enquêtes, établissant la vérité sur les massacres d'Adana en 1909* [en vente chez l'auteur] (Paris: Chez l'Auteur, 1911). See also *Massacres d'Adana et nos missionnaires, récit de Témoins* (Lyon: Imprimerie Vve M. Paquet, 1909); Woods, *The Danger Zone of Europe*, especially 120–87.

73. Bloxham, *The Great Game*, 57.

74. Ibid., 61.

75. Balakian, *Burning Tigris*, 146–49.

76. Kirakossian, *British Diplomacy*, 303–4; Balakian, *Burning Tigris*, 149–57; So-makian, *Empires*, 37–44.

77. Avedis K. Sanjian, *The Armenian Communities in Syria under Ottoman Dominion* (Cambridge: Harvard University Press, 1965), 279–82. More than thirty thousand Armenians perished as a result of the 1909 massacres in Adana. *La Cilicie (1909–1921) des massacres d'Adana au mandat Français*, ed. Raymond H. Kévorkian, special issue of the *Revue d'Histoire Arménienne Contemporaine* 3 (1999).

78. Woods, *The Danger Zone of Europe*, 140–41.

79. Kirakossian, *British Diplomacy*, 304.

80. The Armenian Mission of Religious Society of Friends, founded in Istanbul in 1881, was the first British group that carried out charitable, medical, and educational activities in the Armenian-populated regions. Other groups who played significant roles in relieving the Armenians and in keeping the interest of public opinion alive were the British Armenia Committee, the Scottish Armenian Association, and the Armenian United Association and Women's Relief Fund. The association, headed by Madeleine Cole, brought together prominent British women and sent funds to the six Ottoman provinces, raising and disbursing more than 16,000 pounds.

81. Two Armenian periodicals were published in London: *Hayastan* (in English and in French) and *Huntchak*, the organ of the Social-Democratic Huntchak Party. Many Armenian groups and committees were based in London, including the Armenian Patriotic Union, founded in 1888 by Karapet Hagopian. Another group, the Armenian United Association of London, founded in 1898, published an English-language magazine, *Ararat: A Searching on Armenia*.

82. J. W. Probyn, *Armenia and the Lebanon*, Eastern Question Association, Papers on the Eastern Question, no. 10 (London, Cassell, Petter and Galpin, 1877).

83. Balakian, *Burning Tigris*, 125; William Watson, *The Purple East: A Series of Sonnets on England's Desertion of Armenia* (London: John Lane, 1896).

84. The Duke of Argyll published *Our Responsibilities for Turkey: Facts and Memories of Forty Years* (London, John Murray, 1896), which was a follow-up to his *The Eastern Question*, expanding and reiterating his thoughts with respect to the Armenian massacres. Malcolm MacColl, now canon of Ripon, published *England's Responsibility Towards Armenia* (London, Longmans, Green, 1895).

85. See the bibliography for a list of meaningful articles on the Armenian Question published in Great Britain.

86. Bryce had been a prominent member of the Eastern Question Association, and it was natural for him to support the cause of the Armenians within the limits of the Treaty of Berlin. Bryce published *The Case for the Armenians, with an Introduction by Francis Seymour Stevenson, M.P. (President of the Anglo-Armenian Association), and a Full Report of the Speeches Delivered at the Banquet in Honour of the Right. Hon. James Bryce, M.P., D.C.L., on Friday, May 12th, 1893* (London: Printed for the Anglo-Armenian Association, Harrison and Son, 1893). In 1905 Bryce would go to Macedonia as president of the Balkan Committee. AMAE, CPC nouvelle série 1897–1914, vol. 46, Doc. No. 234, Agent Diplomatique de

France en Bulgarie, à M. Rouvier, Président du Conseil et au MAE, Sophia, 24 September 1905. Rouvier reported that Bryce believed an "extermination" of the Christians of Macedonia to be a possibility, which the European powers should have avoided for humanitarian reasons (*sentiments d'humanité et de civilisation*) as well to avoid broader problems (*des complications générales que les appétits de certaines Puissances pourraient déchaîner*).

87. The Bishop of Rochester was president of the association while Lady Henry Somerset was its honorary secretary.

88. Balakian, *Burning Tigris*, xviii; Noel Buxton and Rev. Harold Buxton, *Travel and Politics in Armenia with an Introduction by Viscount Bryce and a Contribution on Armenian History and Culture by Aram Raffi* (London: Smith, Elder, 1914), 124. Noel Buxton was president of the Balkan Committee.

89. J. Lepsius, *Armenia and Europe: An Indictment* (London: Hodder and Stoughton, 1897).

90. *Letters from the Scenes of the Recent Massacres in Armenia* (London, 1897), cited in Kirakossian, *British Diplomacy*, 282.

91. W. T. Stead, *The Haunting Horrors in Armenia* (London: Review of Reviews Office, 1896), 9–10.

92. Ibid., 17; Gustave Rolin-Jaequemyns, *Armenia, the Armenians, and the Treaties*, translated from the *Revue de Droit International et de Législation Comparée* and revised by the author (London: John Heywood, 1891).

93. Stead, *Haunting Horrors*, 21.

94. Vincent Duclert et Gilles Pécout, "La mobilisation intellectuelle face aux massacres d'Arménie (1894–1900)," in *Les exclus en Europe 1830–1930*, ed. André Gueslin and Dominique Kalifa (Paris: Les Editions de l'Atelier, 1999), 323–44.

95. *Les voix explorées de l'Arménie* (Paris: Paul Schimdt, 1897).

96. Paul E. Passy, *La vérité sur l'Arménie* (Paris: Lievens, 1896).

97. Préssensé was a Protestant and a moderate Republican. In 1880 he was secretary of the French Embassy in Constantinople. He later became a journalist and wrote for *Le Temps* from 1888 and for *L'Aurore* from 1898. He would become a member of the French Socialist Party in 1902. His articles were translated into English and published by British reviews, such as *Nineteenth Century*.

98. Albert Vandal, *Les Arméniens et la réforme de la Turquie: Conférence faite par M. Albert Vandal de l'Académie Française dans la salle de la Société de Géographie le 2 Février 1897 sous la présidence de M. Le comte de Mun, député* (Paris: Plon, 1897), 35.

99. G. Clemenceau wrote the preface to *Les massacre d'Arménie: Témoignages des victimes* (Paris: Edition du Mercure de France, 1896). See also G. Clemenceau, *L'Iniquité* (Paris: P.-V. Stock, 1899).

100. MAE, CPC nouvelle série 1897–1914, Turquie, vol. 73, letter of the comité franco-arménien to the French prime minister, 21 June 1897.

101. Ibid., vol. 76.

102. *Pro Armenia*, no. 1, 25 November 1901.

103. Christian reviews such as the *Revue Chrétienne* and *Etudes Religieuses* published several articles in 1896 on the massacres of Armenians emphasizing the fact that Christian coreligionists were slaughtered in various provinces of the Ottoman Empire.

104. Père Félix Charmetant, *Martyrologue Arménien: Tableau officiel des massacres d'Arménie dressé après enquêtes par les six ambassades de Constantinople et statistique dressée par des témoins oculaires Grégoriens et Protestants des profanations, d'eglises, massacres d'ecclésiastiques, apostasies forcées, enlèvements de femmes et jeunes vierges avec carte de la région des massacres* (Paris: Bureau des Oeuvres d'Orient, 1896).

105. Duclert and Pécout, "La mobilisation," 327.

106. Ibid.

107. Ibid., 332, 333: "Comme l'engagement intellectuel, l'intervention politique n'a pas eu d'influence directe sur les massacres d'Arménie, ce à quoi elle était pourtant destinée."

108. As the editors put it in one of the first issues of the review: "*Nous ne parlons au nom ni d'un parti politique français, ni d'un groupe arménien; . . . nous entendons, au contraire, faire oeuvre d'union entre tous les hommes de coeur et de bonne volonté.*" *Pro Armenia*, first year, no. 3, 25 December 1901, 17.

109. London Office of *Pro Armenia*, p. 3; Gilles Pécout, "Une amitié politique méditerranéenne: le philhellénisme italien et français au XIXe Siècle," in *La democrazia radicale nell'ottocento Europeo: Forme della politica, modelli culturali, riforme sociali*, ed. Maurizio Ridolfi (Milan: Feltrinelli, 2005), 81–106.

110. London Office of *Pro Armenia*, *Report of the International Conference on the Situation in the Near East, Held in London on 29th June, 1904 with Preface by Rt. Hon. James Bryce, M.P. (Presiding) and F[rancis]S[eymour] Stevenson, Esq., M.P. Note on the English Movement, by H. M. Massingham. Note on the Historical Background by H. N. Brailsford, and a Brief Account of the Recent Massacres, by G. R. Malloch* (London: Eastern Question Association, 1904). Accounts of previous conferences held in Brussels, Budapest, Geneva, and Paris are to be found in *Pro Armenia*.

111. MAE, CPC nouvelle série 1897–1914, Turquie, vol. 78, Réunion à Bruxelles d'un Congrès d'arménophiles au café de la Tourelle, July 1902. Among the French representatives were Jaurès, de Pressensé, Elie et Elisée Reclus, Lejeune, Nys, Emile Vadervelde, and Clemenceau. The assembly gathered in Brussels created an international permanent committee composed of members of all political parties. The French members of the committee included d'Estournelles de Constant (delegate of the French government at the arbitrage permanent tribunal of La Haye), Lavisse, Denys Cochin, and Marcel Sembat. The British members included, among others, Malcom MacColl and James Bryce. The other members came from Denmark, Belgium, Germany, Holland, Italy, Switzerland, and Austria-Hungary.

112. Bloxham, *The Great Game*, 4.

113. Ibid., 16.

CHAPTER NINE: THE SECOND INTERVENTION IN CRETE (1896–1900)

1. A. & P., Correspondence Respecting the Affairs of Crete (hereafter CRAC), No. 10, 1897, Doc. No. 126, Currie to Salisbury, 14 February 1897.

2. Halepa was the quarter of Canea—today's Iraklion—where the consulates were situated and the bulk of the European community lived. Holland and Markides, *Britain and the Hellenes*, 83–90.

3. MAE, Mémoires et Documents, Turquie, Tome 121, Doc. 3, Note pour le Ministre sur les affaires de Crète du 1er mars 1889 au 1er mars 1890, 5 March 1890; Doc. 7, Note pour le Ministre—Les relations de la France et de la Turquie.

4. CRAC, Turkey No. 2, 1889, Doc. No. 168, the Marquis of Salisbury to Sir R. Morier, 12 August 1889.

5. Ibid., Doc. No. 175, The Earl of Lytton Salisbury, 10 August 1889, received 13 August 13; Inclosure in Doc. No. 202, Commander Brenton to Vice-Admiral Sir A. Hoskins.

6. Ibid., Doc. No. 56, Biliotti to Salisbury, 21 March 1889, received 9 April; and Doc. No. 80, Sir W. White to Salisbury, 18 June 1889, received 28 June.

7. Ibid., Doc. No. 147, Inclosure, Consul H. Lewis Dupuis to Monson, 7 August 1889; Doc. No. 173, Monson to Salisbury, 7 August 1889, received 13 August.

8. Ibid., Doc. No. 216, Inclosure No. 2, Admiralty to Foreign Office, 29 August 1889. The date of the inclosure is 19 August 1889.

9. A. & P., Further Correspondence Respecting the Affairs of Crete, Turkey No. 2, 1890, Doc. No. 135, Inclosure Imperial Firman respecting the Affairs of Crete, 14 December 1889.

10. Roandeau A. H. Bickford-Smith, *Cretan Sketches* (London: Richard Bentley, 1898), 87. This is an 1896 portrait of Biliotti: "The consular corps in the island is a strong one, including Sir Alfred Biliotti for Great Britain; his step-son-in-law, M. Blanc, the portly and jovial representative of France. . . . But Sir Alfred is at all times and in all way 'the boss' . . . Sir Alfred had had his own way with both Turkish and consular authorities. . . . He is as wily as a Greek, as supple as an Arab, and as inscrutable as a Turk." Victor Bérard, *Les Affaires de Crète* (Paris: Calmann Lévy, 1898), 92–94: "Sir Alfred Biliotti, consul d'Angleterre à la Canée, n'est pas un Anglais de naissance, mais un levantin, d'extraction latine, catholique de religion et sujet ottoman."

11. MAE, Correspondance consulaire et commerciale 1887–1907, La Canée, vol. 30, Consulat Général de France en Crète—Direction des Consulats et des Affaires Commerciales—Sous Direction des Affaires Commerciales to Delcassé, La Canée, 30 October 1899.

12. CRAC, Turkey No. 7, 1896, Doc. No. 122, Foreign Office to Admiralty, 25 May 1896; Inclosure 2 in No. 224.

13. Ibid., Doc. No. 130; Salisbury to Mr. Michael H. Herbert–Chargé d'Affaires at Constantinople, 25 May 1896; Doc. No. 200, Salisbury to Dufferin, 1 June 1896; Doc. No. 204, Herbert to Salisbury, 14 June 1896; MAE, CP de la Turquie jusqu'à 1896, vol. 529, Cambon to Hanotaux, Doc. No. 238, 21 July 1896: "notre force en Crète est dans l'entente européenne; il importe de ne pas l'affaiblir par des actions séparées ; elle a suffi jusqu'à présenter et suffira sans doute jusqu'au bout à empêcher l'Angleterre de jouer un rôle prépondérant."

14. CRAC, No. 7, 1896, Doc. No. 243, Herbert to Salisbury, 24 June 1896.

15. Ibid., Doc. No. 413, Courcel to Salisbury, 31 July 1896; MAE, Correspondance politique des consuls jusqu'à 1896, La Canée, vol. 20, Consulat de France en Crète to Hanotaux, No. 45, 6 August 1896.

16. CRAC, No. 7, 1896, Doc. No. 298, Biliotti to Salisbury, 6 July 1896; Doc. No. 321, Herbert to Salisbury, 8 July 1896, received 13 July; MAE, CP de la Turquie jusqu'à 1896, vol. 529, Cambon to Hanotaux, Doc. No. 223, 12 July 1896.

17. CRAC, No. 7, 1896, Doc. No. 474, Monson to Salisbury, 7 August 1896; MAE, CP de la Turquie jusqu'à 1896, vol. 529, Cambon to Hanotaux, Doc. No. 244, 28 July 1896; MAE, Correspondance politique des Consuls jusqu'à 1896, La Canée, vol. 20, Consulat de France en Crète to Hanotaux, MAE, Doc. No. 56, 28 August 1896.

18. CRAC, No. 7, 1896, Doc. No. 459, Admiralty to Foreign Office (received 8 August), 6 August 1896.

19. Ibid., Doc. No. 585, Biliotti to Salisbury, 21 August 1896.

20. Ibid., Doc. No. 413, Biliotti to Salisbury, 12 August 1896.

21. MAE, CP de la Turquie jusqu'à 1896, vol. 529, Cambon to Hanotaux, Doc. No. 231, 17 July 1896; MAE, Correspondance politique et Commerciale [hereafter CPC] 1897–1914, Crète, vol. 7, Document sur l'Ile de Samos de Mars 1868 (servant pour l'organisation future de Crète), vol. 3, Eléments divers extraits des différents statuts des provinces autonomes de l'Empire Ottoman et pouvant servir à une refonte de la situation en Crète, February 1897.

22. CRAC, No. 7, 1896, Doc. No. 582, Herber to Salisbury, 28 August 1896; Inclosure 2 in No. 603, Dispositions que les Représentants des Puissances considèrent comme pouvant être proposées à la Porte.

23. A. & P., Further Correspondence Respecting the Affairs of Crete [hereafter FCRAC], Turkey No. 10, 1897, Inclosure in Doc. No. 52, captain of the Barfleur Custance to admiral Sir J. Hopkins, 15 January 1897; MAE, Correspondance politique des Consuls jusqu'à 1896, La Canée, vol. 20, Consulat de France en Crète to Hanotaux, MAE, Doc. No. 95, 31 December 1896.

24. Holland and Markides, *Britain and the Hellenes*, 91.

25. Documents Diplomatiques Français, 1re série, 1871–1900, Tome 13, Doc. No. 102, Courcel to Hanotaux, London, 12 February 1897.

26. MAE, CPC 1897–1914, Crète, vol. 2, Cambon to Hanotaux, Doc. No. 64 (telegram), 15 February 1897; CRAC, No. 10, 1897, Doc. No. 103, Hopkins to Admiralty, 12 February 1897; MAE, CPC 1897–1914, Crète, vol. 1, Dépêche Télégraphique de la Canée to the Ministry of Foreign Affairs, 11 February 1897.

27. MAE, CPC 1897–1914, Crète, vol. 1, from the Ministry of Foreign Affairs, 6 February 1897.

28. Documents Diplomatiques Français, 1re série, 1871–1900, Tome 13, Doc. No. 152, Sir E. Monson, British ambassador at Paris, to Mr. Hanotaux, French minister of foreign affairs.

29. Holland and Markides, *Britain and the Hellenes*, 92.

30. CRAC, No. 10, 1897, Doc. No. 211, Harris to Admiralty, 26 February 1897.

31. Documents Diplomatiques Français, 1re série, 1871–1900, Tome 13, Doc. No. 187, M. Lozé, French ambassador at Vienna to Hanotaux: "L'Europe . . . ne peut laisser les musulmans à la merci des chrétiens qui les massacreraient."

32. A. & P., Correspondence Respecting the Affairs of Crete and the War Between Turkey and Greece, Turkey No. 11, 1897, Doc. No. 155, Tewfik Pasha to Anthopoulo Pasha, 22 February 1897.

33. Bérard, *Les Affaires de Crète*, 19, 21, and 30: "Deux mille hommes de troupes internationales y gardent les pavillons des six puissances. Les Anglais l'encombrent de leurs tonneaux de bière et de leurs boîtes de conserves. Au

(restaurant) *Concert Européen*, des officiers russes boivent toute le long du jour, sous les fenêtres de la caserne rouge, où Djevad-Pacha, dans le silence et la fumée de cigarettes, attend la lassitude de l'Europe complice."

34. CRAC, No. 10, 1897, Doc. No. 186, Biliotti to Salisbury, 22 February 1897, received 23 February; Doc. No. 232, Biliotti to Salisbury, 2 March 1897, received 3 March.

35. A. & P., Notes Addressed by the Representatives of Great Britain, Austria-Hungary, France, Germany, Italy, and Russia to the Turkish and Greek Governments in Regard to Crete, Turkey No. 4, 1897, Doc. Nos. 1, 2, and 3.

36. Documents Diplomatiques Français, 1re série, 1871–1900, Tome 13, Doc. No. 200, Cambon to Hanotaux, Pera, 15 April 1897. See also Doc. No. 356, Hanotaux to the French ambassador at Berlin, 22 June 1897, which mentions that contrary to the island of Samos, where there probably were 50 Muslims out of a population of 48,000 inhabitants, in Crete 40,000 Muslims had fled from their homes, and the situation, as the German ambassador in Paris Münster noted, was painful and required *"les plus grands ménagements."*

37. MAE, CPC 1897–1914, Crète, vol. 39, Consulat de France en Crète, 8 March 1899; MAE, vol. 91, Cambon to Hanotaux, telegram, 10 March 1897. In 1896 the military attaché had organized three gendarmes companies (255 men in total) under the command of seven European officers. There were eighty Montenegrins, ninety-six Albanians, fifty Christian Cretans, and thirty Muslim Cretans. During the uprising forty-eight Christian Cretans joined the insurgents and the experience was not pursued any further.

38. MAE, CPC 1897–1914, Crète, vol. 92, Répartition des troupes européennes dans les différentes localités, July 1897, October 1899, and January 1901; and vol. 8.

39. Ibid., vol. 7, Consul Paul Blanc to the MAE, Doc. No. 4, 21 March 1897; PRO, FO 881/7250, Turkey, Confidential Prints: Correspondence Affairs of Crete Part I, Inclosure 2 in No. 475, Memorandum, Consul Biliotti, 16 December 1898.

40. PRO, FO 881/7452, Turkey, Confidential Prints: Correspondence Affairs of Crete Part II, Inclosure in No. 127, Lieutenant Clarke to Captain Shaw, governor of Candia, 20 February 1899; FCRAC, Turkey No. 1, 1899, Doc. No. 234, Chermside to Salisbury, 28 February 1899, received 13 March, Report on Sanitary Work in Candia; Turkey No. 5, 1898, Doc. No. 134, Biliotti to Salisbury, 11 March 1897, received 30 March.

41. CRAC, Turkey No. 9, 1897, Doc. No. 8, Chermside to Salisbury, 17 April 1897, received 1 May.

42. MAE, CPC 1897–1914, Crète, vol. 10, Doc. No. 45, Blanc au MAE, 4 May 1897; vol. 19, Doc. No. 20, Blanc to Hanotaux, 1 October 1897.

43. Bérard, *Les Affaires de Crète*, 230–32.

44. FCRAC, Turkey No. 3, 1898, Doc. No. 178, Biliotti to Salisbury, received 13 September, 27 August 1897.

45. CRAC, No. 9, 1897, Doc. No. 8, Harris to Hopkins, 23 April 1897, received 3 May.

46. FCRAC, Turkey No. 5, 1898, Doc. No. 17, Salisbury to Currie, 19 January 1898.

47. MAE, CPC 1897–1914, Crète, vol. 21, Doc. No. 537, Courcel to Hanotaux, 18 December 1897.

48. Documents Diplomatiques Français, 1ʳᵉ série, 1871–1900, Tome 14, Doc. No. 115, Hanotaux to the French ambassadors in London, Rome, and Constantinople, Paris, 1 April 1898 (copy of a circular telegram of Count Mouraieff).

49. FCRAC, Turkey No. 6, 1898, Doc. No. 33, Chermside to Foreign Office, 18 July 1898; No. 5, 1898, Doc. No. 134, Biliotti to Salisbury, 11 March 1897, received 30 March.

50. Ibid., No. 5, 1898, Inclosure 2 in Doc. No. 199, Minutes Meeting of Naval Officers, 8 April 1898.

51. Holland and Markides, *Britain and the Hellenes*, 100.

52. A. & P., Turkey No. 7, 1898, Doc. No. 30, Biliotti to Salisbury; Doc. No. 61, Tewfik Pasha to Anthopoulo Pasha (communicated by Anthopoulo Pasha, 13 September), 11 September 1898. For a complete account of the incident, Doc. No. 135, Salisbury to O'Conor, 26 September 1898.

53. Documents Diplomatiques Français, 1ʳᵉ série, 1871–1900, Tome 14, Doc. No. 380, Cambon to Delcassé, 26 September 1898.

54. Ibid., Doc. No. 425, Courcel to Delcassé, London, 10 October 1898.

55. PRO, FO 881/7250, Turkey, Confidential Prints: Correspondence Affairs of Crete Part I, Inclosure in No. 99, Rear-Admiral Noel to Admiralty, 18 October 1898.

56. PRO, FO 881/7359, Turkey, Confidential Prints: Further Correspondence Affairs of Crete Part IV, Inclosure 5 in Doc. No. 15, British Civil Commissioner W. E. Fairlhome; PRO, FO 881/7392, Turkey, Confidential Prints: Further Correspondence Affairs of Crete Part III, Inclosure in No. 111, Instructions Addressed to District Commissioner, 17 November 1898.

57. On the experiment of Cretan Autonomy, Cretan politics, the policies of the high commissioner, and the events that led to the union of Crete with Greece, see Holland and Markides, *Britain and the Hellenes*, 108–61.

58. *Affaires de Crète, documents diplomatiques adressés par le Prince George de Grèce, Haut Commissaire en Crète, aux gouvernements des quatre puissances protectrices de la Crète, 1900–1905* (Paris: Imprimerie des Beaux-Arts, 1905).

59. MAE, CPC 1897–1914, Crète, vol. 93, Doc. No. 318, Cambon to the Ministry of Foreign Affairs.

60. PRO, FO 881/7452, Doc. No. 70*, Biliotti to Salisbury, 4 February 1899.

61. A. & P., Turkey No. 1, 1899, Doc. No. 157, Biliotti to Salisbury, 3 December 1898, received 15 December; PRO, FO 881/7250, Inclosure 2 in No. 475, Memorandum, Biliotti to the Foreign Office, 16 December 1898; MAE, CPC 1897–1914, Crète, vol. 95. In 1902 the European consuls formed a Commission centrael sur les indemnités des dommages causé par suite des événements politiques des années 1896 et en deça.

62. A. & P., Turkey No. 1, 1899, Doc. No. 187, Chermside to Salisbury, 2 January 1899; and Salisbury to Chermside, 10 January 1899.

63. Holland and Markides, *Britain and the Hellenes*, 160: "There was no significant emigration of Muslims after the consummation of Greek sovereignty—in 1913—(as there had been after the inauguration of autonomy in December 1898), and with the ensuing stability some returned to rural homes.

Yet given the underlying structures of local society and regional politics, the minority remained vulnerable to sudden external shocks. During 1921, the new war in Asia Minor was to take its toll in Crete. Armed men roamed the hills, evading conscription and harassing country people. As ever, Muslims bore the brunt of lawlessness. It was, moreover, never likely that their community could be the exception that proved the rule in the mass population exchange prescribed by the Treaty of Lausanne in July 1923. The first boatload of a total of 25,500 deportees left Rethymno for Turkey, a place most had never seen and whose language they did not speak, during January 1924."

64. MAE, CPC 1897–1914, Crète, vol. 4, Bureau International de la Paix to the Ministry of Foreign Affairs, 13 March 1897. French journalist Francis de Pressensé's views on the "The Cretan Question" were published in *The Nineteenth Century* 246 (1897): 339–42; and "The Powers and the East" 243 (1897): 681–84. Pressensé was a Protestant and a moderate Republican. In 1880 he was secretary of the French Embassy in Constantinople. He later became a journalist and wrote for *Le Temps* from 1888 and for *L'Aurore* from 1898. He became member of the French Socialist Party in 1902.

65. Georges Streit, "La question Crétoise au point de vue du droit international," *Revue Générale de Droit International Public* 4 (1897): 61–105, 447–83; 7 (1900): 5–52, 301–69; 10 (1903): 221–83, 345–418.

66. A. & P. *Correspondence Respecting the Affairs of Crete and the War Between Turkey and Greece, Turkey No. 11*, 1897, Doc. No. 133, Monson Salisbury, 21 February 1897, received 22 February.

67. CRAC, No. 11, 1897, Doc. No. 170, Salisbury to Monson, 24 February 1897; MAE, CPC 1897–1914, Crète, vol. 6.

68. CRAC, No. 10, 1897, Doc. No. 166, Salisbury to Biliotti, 19 February 1897.

69. Skinner, *Turkish Rule in Crete*. See also *Greece and the Powers*, Papers of the Greek Committee, New Series, 1897, No. ii. A Conference between Friends of Greece and Representatives of the Greek Residents in England was held on May 12, 1897, in the Banqueting Room, St. James's Hall. Sir Arthur Arnold, chairman of the committee, presided the executive committee comprised Sir Arthur Arnold, G. J. Shaw Lefevre, James Bryce, C. W. Dilke, John Gennadius, and Lewis Sergeant, the author of *Greece in the Nineteenth Century. A Record of Hellenic Emancipation and Progress: 1821–1897* (London: T. Fisher Unwin, 1897). The general committee was composed of many college and university professors. Among those present were the bishop of Hereford, Sir C. W. Dilke, G. Shaw Lefevre, Sir Walter Phillimore, and Sir Rover Reid.

70. William Wright, "The Syrian Massacres: A Parallel and a Contrast," *Contemporary Review*, vol. 71 (1897): 130–42. In the same issue, also see J. Jennadius, "Cretan Struggles for Liberty," 477–91; M. E. Grant Duff, "The Cretan Imbroglio," 492–98; "The Sultan and the Powers," 623–30.

71. CRAC, No. 7, 1896, Doc. No. 263, Biliotti to Salisbury, 29 June 1896. The Cretan Relief Committee had been formed under the Duke of Westminster, and its secretary meddled in Cretan politics by trying to persuade the Cretans that Britain was their best friend—a proceeding that drew sharp reproof from Salisbury, who pointed out that he would have nothing to do with the committee unless it limited its activities to purely charitable purposes.

72. Bickford-Smith, *Cretan Sketches*, 166, 240.

73. Algernon Charles Swinburne, "For Greece and Crete," *Nineteenth Century* 246 (1897): 336–37.

74. Ernest N. Bennett, "Side-lights on the Cretan Insurrection," *Nineteenth Century* 243 (1897) 687–99.

75. Bennett, in ibid., 699, concluded his article by claiming that "the real salvation of this island, full as it is of manifold possibilities, would be its annexation by one of the Powers. If Lord Beaconsfield had asked the Sultan for Crete instead of the useless Cyprus! In case mutual jealousies and conflicting interests prevent the acquisition of Crete by some one of the Powers, then let them at any rate guarantee the establishment of a firm and just government. To hand over the island to Greece would be to commit one of the gravest political mistakes, not to say crimes, of the century."

76. Bérard, *Les Affaires de Crète*, 218.

77. MAE, CPC 1897–1914, Crète, vol. 2, Télégramme de l'ambassadeur Cambon à Hanoutaux—MAE, Doc. No. 66, 15 February 1897.

78. Ibid., vol. 3, *Journal des Débats, Chambre des Députés*, 23 February 1897. "[C]e miracle de l'union de toute l'Europe dans un intérêt de pure humanité, il me semble que l'excès même des crimes qui ont été commis va le produire. . . . Oui l'horreur qui a soulevé la conscience de tous les peuples dicte aux hommes d'Etat leur devoir le plus pressant. Pour un instant—pour pas longtemps—il sera possible de faire trêve à toute autre considération. . . . Oui, dans ce moment, une initiative généreuse, entraînant toutes les nations de l'Europe, est facile ou du moins possible, à la condition qu'elle soit décidée et énergique."

79. Documents Diplomatiques Français, 1re série, 1871–1900, Tome 14, Doc. No. 152, Paul Cambon to Delcassé, French minister of foreign affairs, 15 September 1898.

80. Holland and Markides, *Britain and the Hellenes*, 120.

81. British Documents on Foreign Affairs, Part I, Series B, the Near and Middle East, vol. 19, Doc. No. 42, Memorand by Lord Percy, November 1903.

82. Documents Diplomatiques Français, 1re série, 1871–1900, Tome 13, Doc. No. 193, Hanotaux to Mr. Montebello, French ambassador at St. Petersburg, Paris, 10 April 1897.

Chapter Ten: Nonforcible Intervention in the Ottoman Macedonian Provinces (1903–08)

1. Vemund Aarbakke, *Ethnic Rivalry and the Quest for Macedonia 1870–1913*, East European Monographs, Boulder (New York: distributed by Columbia University Press, 2003), 8. Aarbakke's study combines and systematizes the available sources, especially the Greek and Bulgarian ones.

2. British Documents on Foreign Affairs, Part I, Series B, the Near and Middle East, vol. 19, Doc. No. 42, Memorand by Lord Percy, November 1903.

3. Aarbakke, *Ethnic Rivalry*, 82.

4. It would change name several times; in 1905 it became VMRO; "V" stands for *vîtreshna*, meaning inner.

5. Aarbakke, *Ethnic Rivalry*, 97.

6. Simeon Damianov, "La diplomatie française et les réformes en Turquie d'Europe (1895–1903)," *Etudes Balkaniques* 2–3 (1974): 130–53; "Aspects économiques de la politique française dans les Balkans au début du XXe siècle," *Etudes Balkaniques* 4 (1974): 8–26.

7. See *pro-memoria lists* in bibliography.

8. Pinon, *L'Europe*, 202–3, refers to the deportation of political prisoners to Northern Africa and Tripoli (of Lebanon). A. & P., Further Correspondence Respecting the Affairs of South-Eastern Europe [hereafter FCRASEE], Turkey No. 4, 1904, Inclosure in Doc. No. 151, Report by Dr. Thom of the American Mission at Mardin, Constantinople, 5 April 1904, received 11 April: "On the 31st November [1903] some 258 prisoners from Macedonia were brought to [Diarbekir]."

9. FCRASEE, Turkey No. 3, 1903, Inclosures 1 to 3 in Doc. No. 29, Biliotti to O'Conor, Salonica, 15 January 1903; and Doc. No. 54, Consul General Biliotti to Mr. Whitehead, Salonica, 31 January 1903, received at the Foreign Office, 23 February.

10. Ibid., Inclosure in Doc. No. 56, Biliotti to Whitehead, Salonica, 14 February 1903.

11. Ibid., Turkey No. 1, 1903, Doc. No. 333, O'Conor to Lansdowne, 3 December 1902, received 8 December; Aarbakke, *Ethnic Rivalry*, 107; Dakin, *Greek Struggle*, 86–91.

12. FCRASEE, No. 3, 1903, Inclosure in Doc. No. 347, Biliotti to O'Conor, 1 December 1902; MAE, CPC nouvelle série 1897–1914, vol. 29, Doc. No. 254, 30 December 1902.

13. MAE, CPC nouvelle série 1897–1914, vol. 30, Doc. No. 254, 23 January 1903.

14. Aarbakke, *Ethnic Rivalry*, 108.

15. Nadine Lange-Akhund, *The Macedonian Question, 1893–1908 from Western Sources*, trans. Gabriel Topor, East European Monographs, Boulder (New York: distributed by Columbia University Press, 1998), 132–33. Nadine Lange-Akhund has thoroughly researched the Quai d'Orsay and Austrian archives as well as the Archives du Service Historique de l'Armée de Terre.

16. "La situation en Macédoine—Le décret de réformes ottoman du 8 décembre 1902—Les réformes necessaires," *Revue Générale de Droit International Public* 10 (1903): 112–60; E. Engelhardt, "La Question Macédonienne," *Revue Générale de Droit International Public* 12 (1905): 544–51, 636–44; 13 (1906) 29–40, 64–174.

17. Pinon, *L'Europe*, 107.

18. Lange-Akhund, *Macedonian Question*, 111. A number of these articles are quoted by Gaston Routier, *La question Macédonienne* (Paris: Librairie H. Le Soudier, 1903).

19. André Chéradame, *Douze ans de propagande en faveur des peuples Balkaniques* (Paris: Plon, 1913), 60.

20. Routier, *Question Macédonienne*, i–ii: "des races [d'] une intelligence des plus vives, un esprit très ouvert, très déSireux d'apprendre, un sentiment extraordinaire de leurs droits à la liberté, à la sécurité, à la civilisation."

21. *Pour l'Arménie et la Macédoine: Manifestations Franco-Anglo-Italiennes* (Paris: Société Nouvelle de Librairie, 1904).

22. Ibid., 6. A number of prominent French public figures adhered to that initiative. D'Estournelles was a French diplomat and anticolonialist who would become president of the European Centre of the Carnegie Endowment for International Peace. Among the other public figures were the vice presidents of the Chamber of Deputies Etienne, Lockroy, and Guillain; Lavisse; Gaston Paris, administrator of the Collège de France; Anatole France; Sully-Prudhomme; Vandal, of the Académie Française; Passy; dean of the Facultés de Lettres of Paris Croisiet; Bérard, editor of the *Revue de Paris*; Etienne Lamy, editor of the *Revue des Deux Mondes*; Gaston Deschamps, editor of *Le Temps*; Quillard, chief editor of *Pro Armenia*; and Herold, editor of *L'Européen*. Among the thirty-seven deputies and senators were Clemenceau, Poincaré, and Aristide Briand. Vandal was also involved in the pro-Macedonia activities. He was among the organizers of the conferences of the Ecole Libre des Sciences Politiques, which in 1907 invited René Pinon to give a conference on that issue. *Les questions actuelles de politique etrangère en Europe*, Conférences organisés à la Société des Anciens Élèves de l'Ecole Libre des Sciences Politiques (Paris: Alcan, 1907), 161–211.

23. *Pour l'Arménie et la Macédoine*, 40.

24. See, for instance, H.F.B. Lynch, author of *Armenia*, published in 1901, and of many articles in the *Contemporary Review*, who wrote a series of articles in the *Morning Post* that were later reprinted under the title *Europe in Macedonia: Being Five Articles Reprinted from the "Morning Post"* (London: Edward Stanford, 1908).

25. Dakin, *Greek Struggle*, 150; Noel Buxton, *Europe and the Turks* (London: John Murray, 1907), 134–35, provides the committee's organization chart. Among the first publications of the Balkan Committee was *The Macedonian Crisis* (London, Balkan Committee, 1903) which contained newspaper clippings from the *Times, Spectator, Pilot, Speaker, Guardian, Daily News, Westminster Gazette*, and *Daily Chronicle*.

26. AMAE, CPC nouvelle série 1897–1914, vol. 46, Doc. No. 234, Diplomatic Agent in Bulgaria to Mr. Rouvier, Président du Conseil, and to the MAE, Sophia, 24 September 1905.

27. Henry Noel Brailsford, *Macedonia: Its Races and Their Future* (London: Methuen, 1906).

28. The bishop of Rochester in the Chair, *Report of the Proceedings at the National Conference on the Macedonian Question held at Caxton Hall, Westminster, S.W., on Tuesday, March 29th, 1904* (London: Balkan Committee, 1904).

29. Dakin, *Greek Struggle*, 151.

30. Buxton, *Europe and the Turks*, 130, 19, 60–74.

31. Ibid., 99–103, 119, 120, 131.

32. Victor Bérard's involvement in the Macedonian Question began very early indeed. In 1893 he published *La Turquie et l'Héllenisme Contemporain* (Paris: Ancienne Librairie Germer Baillière et Cie), followed by *Pro Macedonia* (Paris: Librairie Armand Colin, 1904).

33. *Pour l'Arménie et la Macédoine*, 248–50.

34. Mark Mazower, *Salonika—City of Ghosts: Christians, Muslims and Jews 1430–1950* (London: HarperCollins, 2005), 267.

35. Lange-Akhund, *Macedonian Question*, 122. See also MAE, CPC nouvelle série 1897–1914, vol. 36, Doc. No. 138, Ambassade de France près de la Porte Ottomane à la Direction Politique MAE, Therapia, 22 August 1903.

36. Antoine Rougier, "L'intervention de l'Europe dans la question de Macé-doine," *Revue Générale de Droit International Public* 13 (1906): 178–200, at 181.

37. Lange-Akhund, *Macedonian Question*, 147.

38. FCRASEE, Turkey No. 4, 1904.

39. Dakin, *Greek Struggle*, 160–61.

40. Draganof, *Macedonia and the Reforms* (preface by M. Victor Bérard) (London: Hazell, Watson and Viney, 1908), 86.

41. Dakin, *Greek Struggle*, 245. The Ottoman Public Debt Administration was established in 1881 as a direct consequence of the empire's 1875 default on its loan repayments contracted with European creditors since 1854. It was an independent, European-controlled organization set up to collect the payments that the Ottoman Empire owed to European companies. It was run by the creditors and employed five thousand officials who collected taxes that were then turned over to the creditors. By the turn of the century the Ottoman Public Debt Administration was also financing many railways and other European investment projects.

42. FCRASEE, Turkey No. 2, 1906, Inclosure "Règlement" for the Financial Service of the Three Vilayets of Roumelia.

43. Ibid., Turkey No. 1, Inclosures 1 to 3, Collective Note Communicated by the Ambassadors of the Great Powers to the Ottoman Government, dated 6 October 1905; Instructions Communicated by the Ambassadors of the Great Powers to the Financial Agents; Telegram to Be Communicated by the Ambassadors of the Great Powers to Their Respective Governments.

44. Ibid., Turkey No. 1, 1906, Doc. No. 122, O'Conor to Lansdowne, Constantinople, 14 November 1905, received 20 November.

45. Dakin, *Greek Struggle*, 248–49. Sir Edward Grey became secretary of state for foreign affairs on December 11, 1905.

46. Rougier, "L'intervention de l'Europe," 191–200.

47. Dakin, *Greek Struggle*, 344; NTA, FO 371/581, Secret memorandum [6742—26 February 1908] January 1908. There was a motion against the government in February 1908, which was eventually withdrawn. In his reply Grey repeated what he had said in the secret memorandum. See the *Times*, February 26, 1908.

48. M. B. Cooper, "British Policy in the Balkans, 1908–9," *Historical Journal* 7 (1964): 258–79, at 260.

49. Dakin, *Greek Struggle*, 359.

50. Roberts, *Europe*, 212.

51. Ibid.

52. Ibid., 213.

53. NTA, FO 371/581, South-Eastern Europe, Confidential, Doc. No. 1, Grey to Sir F. Bertie, Sir F. Lascelles, Sir. E. Egerton, Sir A. Nicolson, Sir E. Goschen, Sir N. O'Conor, Foreign Office, 3 March 1908.

54. Ibid, The Action of the Great Powers in Macedonia Up to the End of 1907, the Balkan Committee, signed by Westlake, Moore, and Buxton, 10 January 1908.

55. Ibid., Macedonia in the Winter of 1907–1908, the Balkan Committee: "Some 30,000 have left the country is in itself an adequate test of the failure of the so-called reforms. Shipping agents and bankers have found the emigration business the most prosperous trade in Macedonia. The [Ottoman] government approves of emigration, because the most active men are thereby removed, and because additional security that the taxes will be paid is always obtained before a passport is given. Sufficient guarantee is obtained for payment by the rule that wives and families must be left behind. Emigrants commonly return in about three years and the government gains in the end by the wealth they bring back."

56. Ibid., The Action of the Great Powers in Macedonia Up to the End of 1907, the Balkan Committee, signed by Westlake, Moore, and Buxton, 10 January 1908.

57. Lange-Akhund, *Macedonian Question*, 146.

58. NTA, FO 371/581, The Action of the Great Powers in Macedonia Up to the End of 1907, the Balkan Committee, signed by Westlake, Moore, and Buxton, 10 January 1908; Pinon, *L'Europe*, 237–24: "Tant que les agents et les officiers européens n'auront pas eux-mêmes la direction pratique des réformes, les populations seront en défiance. . . . Lorsqu'on aura ainsi crée les divers organes d'une administration autonome qui sera placée sous la haute surveillance d'Européens, il se pourrait qu'il parût opportun de couronner l'édifice en choisissant un chrétien pour gouverner ces populations en majorité chrétiennes. . . . On aboutirait ainsi à un régime qui se rapprocherait de celui qui a été organisé pour le Liban . . . en 1861."

59. Lange-Akhund, *Macedonian Question*, 146, quotes Pinon, *L'Europe*, 164.

60. FCRASEE, Turkey No. 2, 1904, Doc. No. 24, Lansdowne to O'Conor, 24 September 1903.

61. Ibid., No. 25, O'Conor to Lansdowne, 25 September 1903; AMAE, CPC nouvelle série 1897–1914, vol. 38, Doc. No. 222, Ambassade de France près de la Porte Ottomane à la Direction Politique MAE, Constantinople, 28 December 1903.

62. FCRASEE, Turkey No. 2, 1904, Inclosure in Doc. No. 119, Instructions Sent by Sir N. O'Conor to His Majesty's Consular Officers at Salonica and Monastir, 23 October 1903.

63. Ibid., Inclosure in No. 159, Graves to N. O'Conor, Salonica, 14 November 1903.

64. Ibid., Turkey No. 4, 1904, Inclosure in Doc. No. 1, Consul McGregor to Graves, Monastir, 9 December 1903.

65. Ibid., Inclosure in Doc. No. 133, Graves to O'Conor, Salonica, 29 March 1904. Among the agents there were a conspicuous number of women, including Mrs. Brailsford, Miss Durham, who then left Monastir for the Albanian coast, and Miss Bruce. On her work in Monastir, see Rosslyn Bruce (and his sister Kathleen), *Letters from Turkey: Being Glimpses of Macedonian Misery* (Nottingham: Henry B. Saxton, 1907).

66. NTA, FO 881/8119, Confidential Print: Memoranda by Lord Percy on Special Arrangements Made for the Government of the Lebanon and Crete, November 1903.

67. NTA, FO 371/581, The Action of the Great Powers in Macedonia Up to the End of 1907, the Balkan Committee, signed by Westlake, Moore, and Buxton, 10 January 1908.

EPILOGUE

1. Trevor Wilson, "Lord Bryce's Investigation into Alleged German Atrocities in Belgium, 1914–15," *Journal of Contemporary History* 14 (1979): 369–83; John Horne and Alan Kramer, *German Atrocities, 1914: A History of Denial* (New Haven: Yale University Press, 2001); Alan Kramer, *Dynamic of Destruction: Culture and Mass Killing in the First World War* (Oxford: Oxford University Press, 2007).

2. M. R. Marrus, "International Bystanders to the Holocaust and Humanitarian Intervention," in *Humanitarianism and Suffering*, 164.

3. Peter Haggenmacher, "Pensiero Umanitario e Intervento in Gentili," in *Azione Umanitaria ed Intervento Umanitario. Il Parere del Comitato Internazionale della Croce Rossa. Pensiero Umanitario e Intervento Umanitario in Gentili*, Atti del Convegno, Sesta Giornata Gentiliana, September 17, 1994 (Milano: Giuffré, 1994), 20–45.

4. Malbone W. Graham, "Humanitarian Intervention in International Law as Related to the Practice of the United States," *Michigan Law Review* 22 (1924): 312–28, at 320.

5. Ibid., 321.

6. Ibid., 325.

7. Mark Mazower, "An International Civilization? Empire, Internationalism and the Crisis of the Mid-twentieth Century," *International Affairs* 82 (2006): 553–66, at 558. See also Eric D. Weitz, "From the Vienna to the Paris System: International Politics and the Entangled Histories of Human Rights, Forced Deportations, and Civilizing Missions," *American Historical Review* 113 (2008): 1313–43.

8. Mazower, "International Civilization?" 559.

9. Marrus, "International Bystanders," 166.

10. André Liebich, "Minority as Inferiority: Minority Rights in Historical Perspective," *Review of International Studies* 34 (2008): 243–63.

11. Mazower, "International Civilization?" 560.

12. Marrus, "International Bystanders," 165, 167.

13. Anghie, *Imperialism, Sovereignty and International Law*, 137.

14. Quincy Wright, *Mandates under the League of Nations* (Chicago: University of Chicago Press, 1930), vii; Susan Pedersen, "Review Essay: Back to the League of Nations," *American Historical Review* 112 (2007): 1091–17; Pedersen, "The Meaning of the Mandates System: An Argument," *Geschicte und Gesellschaft* 32 (2006): 560–82.

15. Thomas Buergenthal, "The Evolving International Human Rights System," *American Journal of International Law* 100 (2006): 783–807, at 783.

16. Anne Orford, *Reading Humanitarian Intervention* (Cambridge: Cambridge University Press, 2003), 25–26.

17. Ellery C. Stowell, "Humanitarian Intervention," *American Journal of International Law* 33 (1939): 733–36, at 733. For an overview of the early-twentieth-century doctrine on intervention, see Fenwick, "Intervention: Individual and Collective."

18. Graham, "Humanitarian Intervention," 326, argues that if the United States had undertaken a humanitarian intervention in the Ottoman provinces inhabited by Armenian populations such as it did in Cuba in 1898, such action would ultimately have led to the establishment of something like a type A mandate over those Ottoman provinces, regardless of the existence or nonexistence of the league itself.

19. Ibid.

20. Stowell, "Humanitarian Intervention," 736.

21. Writing to Prime Minister Chamberlain on September 23, 1938, Hitler noted that ethnic Germans and various nationalities in Czechoslovakia had been maltreated in the unworthiest manner, tortured, economically destroyed, and, above all, prevented from realizing for themselves the right of nations to self-determination. They were subject to the "brutal will to destruction of the Czechs," whose behavior was "madness" and had led to over 120,000 refugees being forced to flee the country in recent days, while the "security of more than 3,000,000 human beings" was at stake.

22. Samuel Moyn's book *The Last Utopia* dismantles a number of myths and wrong assumptions about the birth of post-1945 human rights in his excellent chapter entitled "Death from Birth."

23. Noam Chomsky, *The New Military Humanism: Lessons from Kosovo* (Monroe: Common Courage, 1999), 15.

24. Anghie, *Imperialism*, 248–54, 263–64. On pages 190–91, Anghie argues that we might see in both the Mandate System and its successor, the United Nations Trusteeship System, as well as the Bretton Woods institutions, the World Bank and the International Monetary Fund, the reproduction of the basic premises of the civilizing mission and the dynamic of difference embodied in the very structure, logic and identity of international institutions.

25. Mahmood Mamdani, "The New Humanitarian Order," *Nation*, September 29, 2008.

26. Ibid.

27. David Forsythe, "Contemporary Humanitarianism: The Global and the Local," in *Humanitarianism and Suffering*, 58–87, at 63.

28. Samantha Power, *A Problem from Hell: America in the Age of Genocide* (New York: Perennial, 2002), 362–63;Wilson and Brown, "Introduction," in *Humanitarianism and Suffering*, 4.

29. In February 2000 troop levels were increased to 11,100 and the peacekeepers' mandate further extended to include the provision of security at key locations in and near the capital, Freetown. When the situation worsened, the British government sent to Sierra Leone some 700 troops with a robust mandate to protect the capital and to create the conditions for the release of about 500 hostages. Further strengthening of the UNAMSIL followed, as well as a program of disarmament, demobilization, and reintegration, the extension of state authority beyond the capital, and the establishment of a war crimes tribunal.

30. Mahmood Mamdani, *Saviours and Survivors: Darfur, Politics and the War on Terror* (Verso: New York, 2009), 25–39. Powell declared that "genocide has been committed in Darfur and that the Government of Sudan and the Janjaweed [Sudanese government-equipped militias] bear responsibility—and that genocide may still be occurring." Colin Powell, "The Crisis in Darfur," Testimony Before the Senate Foreign Relations Committee, Washington, DC, 2004. Available at http://2001-2009.state.gov/secretary/former/powell/remarks/36042.htm (accessed October 18, 2010).

31. Scott Straus, "Darfur and the Genocide Debate," *Foreign Affairs* 84 (2005): 123–33, at 128.

32. Mamdani, *Saviours and Survivors*, 42–44, quotes the *Report of the International Commission of Inquiry on Darfur for the United Nations Security-General Pursuant to Security Council Resolution 1564*, September 18, 2004. Thomas G. Weiss, "Cosmopolitan Force and the Responsibility to Protect," in *Roundtable: Humanitarian Intervention After 9/11*, special issue, *International Relations* 19 (2005): 211–50, at 237; *Genocide in Darfur: Investigating the Atrocities in the Sudan*, ed. Samuel Totten and Eric Markusen (New York, Routledge, 2006).

33. Nicholas Wheeler, "A Victory for Common Humanity? The Responsibility to Protect after the 2005 World Summit," paper presented to the conference on The UN at Sixty: Celebration or Wake?" Faculty of Law, University of Toronto, Canada, October 6–7, 2005. On page 10 he quotes Robert Legvold, "Foreword" to the Como Workshop, *Pugwash Occasional Papers*, September 2000, 10.

34. Taylor B. Seybolt, *Humanitarian Military Intervention: The Conditions for Success and Failure* (Oxford: Oxford University Press and Stockholm International Peace Research Institute, 2007), 273, notes that United Nations must cobble together a force with the often-inadequate troops and equipment that member states offer. In 1998 Stanley Hoffman argued in favor of the setting up in the United Nations of a peace-enforcing potential, initially provided by only by a handful of states, who would be motivated by a sense of duty or an expectation of prestige and a desire to make sure that Security Council resolutions always match the means to well-considered ends and aim at settlements that protect human rights, punish the guilty, and safeguard chances of reconciliation. He supported a reform of the council's composition so as to increase the legitimacy of its edicts and to reduce the risks of its paralysis, and provision of the UN with resources at least partly independent of the whims of governments and parliaments. Given the indispensable nature of domestic political and financial support, political leaders should remember that they have been elected to persuade and to lead, and not just to accept as fixed the momentary moods and pernicious prejudices of the public. Stanley Hoffmann, *World Disorders: Troubled Peace in the Post–Cold War Era* (Lanham: Rowman and Littlefield, 1998), 174–76.

35. See, for example, Dianne Johnston, "Humanitarian War: Making the Crime Fit the Punishment," in *Master of the Universe?* ed. Tariq Ali (London, Verso, 2000).

36. Nicholas Wheeler, "Review Article. Humanitarian Intervention after Kosovo: Emergent Norm, Moral Duty or the Coming Anarchy?" *International Affairs* 77 (2001): 113–28, at 113.

37. Richard Falk, "Legality and Legitimacy: The Quest for Principled Flexibility and Restraint," in *Force and Legitimacy in World Politics*, ed. David Armstrong, Theo Farell, and Bice Maiguashca (Cambridge: Cambridge University Press, 2005), 33–50.

38. Mary Kaldor, *Human Security* (Cambridge, Polity Press, 2007), 53.

39. Bass, *Freedom's Battle*, 229.

40. Andrew Wallis, *Silent Accomplice: The Untold Story of France's Role in the Rwandan Genocide* (London: I. B. Tauris, 2006); Daniela Kroslak, *The Role of France in the Rwandan Genocide* (London: Hurst, 2007); Stephen Kinzer, "Rwanda's Genocide: A Report on the Devastating Role of France," *International Herald Tribune*, August 15, 2008.

41. Jianming Shen, "The Non-Intervention Principle and Humanitarian Interventions under International Law," *International Legal Theory* 7 (2001): 10–11.

42. Marcus Cox, "The Right to Return Home: International Intervention and Ethnic Cleansing in Bosnia and Herzegovina," *International and Comparative Law Quarterly* 47 (1998): 599–631.

43. Richard Falk, "Humanitarian Intervention after Kosovo," in *Human Rights & Conflict: Exploring the Links between Rights, Law, and Peacebuilding*, ed. Julie A. Mertus and Jeffrey W. Helsing (Washington, DC: United States Institute of Peace, 2006), 185–208, at 202–3.

44. John Ruggie, "Multilateralism: The Anatomy of an Institution," *International Organization* 46 (1992): 561–98.

45. Nicholas J. Wheeler and Justin Morris, "Humanitarian Intervention and State Practice at the End of the Cold War," in *International Society after the Cold War*, ed. Rick Fawn and Jeremy Larkins (New York: St. Martin's Press, 1996), 135–71, at 148.

46. Cox, "Right to Return," 624.

47. Deen K. Chatterjee and Don E. Scheid, *Ethics and Foreign Intervention* (Cambridge: Cambridge University Press, 2003), 4; Nicholas J. Wheeler, "The Humanitarian Responsibilities of Sovereignty: Explaining the Development of a New Norm of Military Intervention for Humanitarian Purposes in International Society," in *Humanitarian Intervention and International Relations*, ed. Jennifer Walsh (Oxford: Oxford University Press, 2003), 32; N. Wheeler, "Humanitarian Intervention after September 11, 2001," in *Just Intervention*, ed. Tony Lang (Washington, DC: Georgetown University Press, 2003), 192–216, at 196–97. See also Gary J. Bass, "Jus Post Bellum," *Philosophy & Public Affairs* 32 (2004): 384–413.

48. Bass, *Freedom's Battle*, 366; Neta C. Crawford, "To Intervene or Not to Intervene? What Duties?" *Roundtable*, 232–33: "[H]ow can the practice of both humanitarian intervention and of transnational administration be made less paternalistic? Both practices are clearly imbued with a civilization narrative, a discourse of benevolent assistance to those who are incapable of helping themselves. We need to examine all the ways that even we benevolent academics fall into this discourse. And we must surely admit that the great powers have different obligations with respect to humanitarian interventions than do other powers. The language of "coalitions of the willing" belies the inequality of the

international system. In particular, the responsibility of the US must be more clearly debated within the US and outside it."

49. Robert O. Keohane, "Political Authority after Intervention: Gradations in Sovereignty," in *Humanitarian Intervention: Ethical, Legal and Political Dilemmas,* 296. In the same volume, see also Michael Ignatieff, "State Failure and Nation-Building," 299–321.

50. Keohane, "Political Authority after Intervention," 296–97.

51. Bass, *Freedom's Battle,* 371.

52. Ibid.

53. Ibid., 373.

54. Todorova, *Imagining the Balkans,* 118. I thank Rebecca Gill for letting me read her thesis, submitted to the University of Manchester in 2005, entitled "Calculating Compassion in War: The 'New Humanitarian' Ethos in Britain 1870–1918." The thesis will be published by Manchester University Press.

55. David Rieff, "Humanitarian Intervention," in *Crimes of War: What the Public Should Know,* ed. Roy Gutman and David Rieff (New York: Norton, 1999), 181–84.

56. Fiona Fox, "A New Humanitarianism: A New Morality for the 21st Century?" *Disasters* 5 (2001): 275–89.

57. Mamdani, *Saviours and Survivors,* particularly chapter 2, "The Politics of the Movement to Save Darfur," 48–74.

58. Fox, "A New Humanitarianism," 284, quoting Kirstin Sellar, "The New Imperialists," *Spectator,* October 23, 1999.

59. David Chandler, *From Kosovo to Kabul: Human Rights and International Intervention* (London: Pluto Press, 2002), 22.

60. *The Responsibility to Protect: Report of the International Commission on Intervention and State Sovereignty* (Ottawa: International Development Research Centre, 2001).

61. To head the commission, the Canadian government invited Gareth Evans, president of the International Crisis Group and former Australian foreign inister, and Mohamed Sahnoun of Algeria, special advisor to the UN secretary general and formerly his special representative for Somalia and the Great Lakes of Africa, and nominated ten other commissioners from a diverse range of regional backgrounds, perspectives, and experiences.

62. ICISS, "R2P," 35.

63. Laurence Boisson de Chazournes and Luigi Condorelli, "De la 'Responsabilité de Protéger,' ou d'une nouvelle Parure pour une notion déjà bien établie," *Revue Générale de Droit International Public* (2005): 11–18.

64. Ibid., 17.

65. *A More Secure World: Our Shared Responsibility, Report of the High-Level Panel on Threats, Challenges and Change,* 2004, UN Doc. A/59/565 available at http://www.un.org/secureworld/report.pdf; *In Larger Freedom: Towards Development, Security and Human Rights for All, Report of the Secretary-General,* 2005, UN Doc. A/59/2005, available at http://www.un.org/largerfreedom.htm, *2005 World Summit Outcome,* 2005, General Assembly (GA) Res. 60/1, 24 October 2005 (accessed October 18, 2010).

66. Carsten Stahn, "Responsibility to Protect: Political Rhetoric or Emerging Legal Norm?" *American Journal of International Law* 101 (2007): 99–120, at 107.

67. Ibid., 108.

68. Wheeler, "A Victory for Common Humanity?" 4.

69. Stahn, "Responsibility." See also Ban Ki Moon, *Implementing the Responsibility to Protect—Report of the Secretary General*, January 12, 2009, A/63/677.

70. Stahn, "Responsibility," 122–23.

71. Alex J. Bellamy, "Responsibility to Protect or Trojan Horse? The Crisis in Darfur and Humanitarian Intervention in Iraq," *Ethics & International Affairs* 19 (2005): 31–53, at 52.

72. Michael Ignatieff, *Virtual War: Kosovo and Beyond* (New York: Metropolitan Books, 2000), 176.

73. Kofi Annan, "Two Concepts of Sovereignty," *Economist*, September 18, 1999; and *We the Peoples: The Role of the United Nations in the 21st Century*, Millennium Report of the Secretary General (New York: UN Department of Public Information, 2000).

Bibliography

Note on Sources

In the British and French archives I looked for confidential documents, ambassadorial and consular reports, as well as documents concerning other powers' foreign policies. I have also relied on the French *Livres Jaunes* and their British equivalent the *Blue Books*, though I am aware— as contemporaries often were—that they were edited and censored by the Foreign Office or the French Ministry of Foreign Affairs. For instance, in his *La France et la Question d'Orient*, 7ff, Comte de Chaudordy claims that the foreign minister kept the Chambers and public opinion ignorant about the "horrors" taking place in the Ottoman provinces inhabited by the Armenians. In his *Les Affaires de Crète*, 97–99, Victor Bérard contrasts the attitude of the French government, which had kept silent on the operations in Crete, with the many available letters and dispatches published by the British authorities that give a detailed account of the events in the Ottoman island. Despite being edited and censored, the *Blue Books* and the *Livres Jaunes* are important for they were presented and discussed in the Parliament and were read in foreign chancelleries and cabinets. The foreign press extensively quoted them when revealing facts and events concerning the Eastern Question or when commenting on or criticizing British or French foreign policy. In their original format these sources reveal how the Foreign Office or the Quai d'Orsay wished to portray its own work and what each wanted to be known about its respective policies. Of course, while studying these documents I kept in mind that they deliberately overemphasized "humanitarian" aspects of foreign policy and tended to conceal other less noble motives driving state decisions and acts. The archives of the Quai d'Orsay allow the historian to see how a given *Livre Jaune* was conceived and what undesirable parts of documents were omitted from the published document. The intervention of the foreign ministers was decisive, for they ultimately sanctioned every document before its publication. After 1870, under the Third Republic regime, the foreign ministers learned how to protect "their" foreign policy from the attacks of the Chambres des Députés when entire séances were devoted to the discussion of a single passage of a *Livre Jaune*. Foreign ministers became experts at omitting parts of the documents considered as potentially compromising.

Finally, I made use of the very extensive literature that covers many now well-known aspects of the Eastern Question and of the relations between the European powers and the Ottoman Empire. Take, for instance, the work of Temperley and other historians of British foreign policy who delved deeply into the omissions of the *Blue Books* and brought suppressed passages to light. Other scholarly works important for the amount of primary sources they include are Arman Kirakossian's *The Armenian Question and British Foreign Policy*, which reflects an exhaustive search of the British archives, and Leila Tarazi Fawaz's *An Occasion for War*, which is based extensively on the French Army archives (Service Historique de l'Armée de Terre, located in Vincennes, Paris), including the personal papers of the French general Beaufort. Douglas Dakin's *The Greek Struggle for Independence 1821–1833* is based on a thorough analysis of British archives. Most of the British consular reports from Macedonia were published in the *Blue Books*, but Dakin refers to the unpublished sources, which contain important details, especially on the Ottoman atrocities, that neither the Conservative nor the Liberal government was prepared to reveal. Many diplomatic history volumes contain detailed information about the events I deal with in this study. Among them is R. W. Seton-Watson's classic study, *Disraeli, Gladstone, and the Eastern Question: A Study in Diplomacy and Party Politics*. I found further information in the diplomatic documents volumes, in contemporary collections of documents, and in the memoirs of European policy-makers, which, like the *Livres Jaunes* and the *Blue Books*, have to be consulted *cum grano salis*.

ARCHIVAL SOURCES

French Foreign Office Archives

Correspondance Consulaire et Commerciale: Alep, vol. 32; Alexandretta, vols. 1, 2; Athens, vol. 4; Beyrouth, vol. 7; Bucharest, vol. 20; Damas, vol. 4; Erzerum, vols. 28, 30; Schio (Chios), vols. 7, 8.

Correspondance Politique (CP) Origines—1871—Turkey: 234, 244–50, 256–58 (on Greece); 343–52 (on Syria); 367–76 (on Crete).

Correspondance Politique (CP) 1871–1896—Turkey: 403–8 (on Bulgaria); 464–70 (Roumelia 1885); 520–31 (covering the years 1895–96).

Correspondance Politique des Consuls (CP Consuls) Origines–1871: Alep, vol. 3; Damas, vol. 6; La Canée (Crete), vols. 5, 6.

Correspondance Politique des Consuls (CP Consuls) 1871–1896: Alep and Diarbékir, vol. 10; Erzeroum, vol. 7; La Canée (Crete), vol. 18–20.

Correspondance Politique et Commerciale (CPC) 1897–1918—Crete: 1–10 (war); 11–20 (médiation of the powers); 22–36 (Greco-Turkish peace); 39–47 (relations with the powers).

Correspondance Politique et Commerciale 1897–1918—Greece: 20–28 (international control commission)

Correspondance Politique et Commerciale 1897–1918—Rumania: 4 ("Jewish Question").

Correspondance Politique et Commerciale 1897–1918—Turkey: 23–29 (Macedonia 1898–1902); 30–50 (Macedonia 1903–1907); 51–61 (Macedonia 1908–1911); 71–85 (Armenian affairs); 86–90 (Armenian affairs after 1911); and 1918

Correspondance Politique et Commerciale 1897–1918—*"supplement"*—Crete: 85, 90, 91; 92–94 (Force Armée Internationale), 95, 96, 97, 101, 102.

Correspondance Politique et Commerciale 1897–1918—*"supplement"*—Turquie: 409–16 (Macedonia, including *Livres Jaunes*, photos, and papers of the Financial Commission); 417 (Armenian affairs); 471–74 (Commission de la Dette Publique).

Correspondance Politique Grèce: vols. 1–3.

Mémoires et Documents—*Turkey*: tomes 19–23, 33, 35, 39, 40, 47, 56, 62, 89–97, 106–9, 116–123, 126, 133, 134. Tome 126 has been lost since 2001. Equally lost is the microfilm copy of it devoted to the Armenian Question (Affaires Arméniennes) in 1896.

Great Britain National Archives (NTA)—Kew, London

GREECE

FO 881, FO 198/1, FO 286, FO 352 Stratford Canning Papers.

LEBANON AND SYRIA

FO 78/1384, 1385, 1386, 1387, 1389, 1447, 1448, 1449, 1450, 1451, 1452, 1453, 1454, 1464, 1519, 1557, 1624, 1625, 1626, 1627, 1628, 1629, 1630, 1706, 1707, 1708, 1709, 1710, 2068.

FO 84/691.

FO 195/: 648, 655.

FO 198/28.

FO 226/131, 133, 135, 136, 139, 140, 143, 144, 145, 147, 149, 152, 158.

FO 881/879, 982, 983.

NA 30/2/3/5.

NA 30/22/14; 30/22/21; 30/22/24; 30/22/30; 30/22/40; 30/22/46; 30/22/54; 30/22/55; 30/22/56; 30/22/62; 30/22/73; 30/22/83; 30/22/88; 30/22/89; 30/22/94; 30/22/99; 30/22/102; 30/22/104; 30/22/113; 30/22/114; 30/22/116.

CRETE (1866–68)

FO 78/574, 616, 656, 704, 1536, 1599, 1683, 1767, 1987, 1988, 2049, 2102, 2149, 2227, 2240, 3128, 3313, 3343, 3538, 3650, 3779, 3901, 4012, 4219, 4220, 4890, 4969, 4970, 5043, 5044, 5045, 5046, 5386.

FO 84/647, 691, 815, 1674, 1720.

FO 160/74.

FO 195/102, 307, 457, 600, 795, 878, 904, 936, 1003, 1078, 1146, 1191–92, 1248, 1318–19, 1449, 1483, 1513, 1551, 1582, 1616, 1650–51, 1685–86, 1726, 1764,

1803, 1845, 1890, 1933, 1939, 1970, 1983, 2023, 2058, 2079, 2102, 2121, 2136, 2160, 2169, 2193, 2220, 2248, 2279, 2314.

FO 198/25, 32.

FO 286/240, 248, 249, 254, 263, 264.

FO 421/23, 25–26, 178, 183, 185, 189,192, 195, 200, 207, 214–218, 225–30, 237–39, 246–47, 255–56, 267–68.

FO 8811545, 8483, 1462, 1550, 1499, 1581A, 1589, 1634, 2884, 2976, 3241, 3579, 3685X, 4369, 4453, 4581 5846X, 6739, 6858X, 7068X, 7250, 7452, 7392, 7359, 7589, 8230, 8187, 8232, 8119, 8287, 8288, 8303, 8302.

FO 925/3168.

NA 30/22/88, 92.

EASTERN CRISIS (1875–78) AND TREATY OF BERLIN

CAB 41/9/13.

CAB 41/11/3.

CAB 41/11/8.

FO 78/2437, 2551, 2552, 2553, 2554, 2555, 2993, 2998, 3085, 3175X.

FO 881/459, 2904, 2916, 2936A, 2936B, 2990, 2993, 3066, 3450, 3451, 3685X, 4236.

NA 30/22/40, 41, 43, 54, 58, 66, 70 78, 80, 84, 98, 104, 105, 114.

NA 30/29/22A/7.

NA 30/40/3.

NA 30/57/31.

SECOND INTERVENTION IN CRETE AND NONINTERVENTION ON BEHALF OF
OTTOMAN ARMENIANS

CAB 37/3/42, 4/79, 7/6, 7/28, 10/43, 38/17, 38/22, 91/5, 95/137.

FO 78/5254.

FO 881/3337, 3339, 3410, 3742X, 3735, 4012, 4358, 6645, 8227.

FO 925/1982, 2139, 2258, 2801, 2887, 2888, 2926, 3085, 3152, 3157, 3196, 17108, 41139, 41219.

T 1/13542.

OTTOMAN MACEDONIAN PROVINCES

CAB 37/64/26, 75/37, 75/52, 76/68, 91/5, 95/118, 96/140.

CAB 41/29/7, 29/43, 30/12, 30/15, 30/28, 31/45.

FO 96/183.

FO 371/379, 380, 381, 581,582, 583, 584, 585, 586.

FO 881/8337, 8339, 8376, 8785, 9027.

PRINTED PRIMARY SOURCES

British Blue Books—Accounts and Papers

GREECE AND CRETE

Papers Relative to the Affairs of Greece—Protocols of Conferences Held in London, 1830.

Correspondence Respecting the Disturbances in Crete: 1866–67, 1867.

Correspondence Respecting the Disturbance in Crete (in Continuation of Correspondence Presented to Parliament, December 2, 1867), 1868.

Further Correspondence Respecting the Disturbances in Crete: 1867 (in Continuation of Correspondence Presented to Parliament, February 11, 1867), 1868.

Turkey. No. 28 (1878). Correspondence Respecting the Affairs of Crete, 1878.

Turkey. No. 3 (1879). Further Correspondence Respecting the Affairs of Crete, 1879.

Turkey. No. 2 (1889). Correspondence Respecting the Affairs of Crete, 1889.

Turkey. No. 2 (1890). Further Correspondence Respecting the Affairs of Crete (in Continuation of Turkey No. 2, 1889), 1890.

Turkey. No. 4 (1891). Further Correspondence Respecting the Affairs of Crete (in Continuation of Turkey No. 2, 1890), 1891.

Turkey. No. 7 (1896), Correspondence Respecting the Affairs of Crete, 1896.

Turkey. No. 4 (1897), Notes Addressed by the Representatives of Great Britain, Austria-Hungary, France, Germany, Italy, and Russia, to the Turkish and Greek Governments in Regard to Crete, 1897.

Turkey. No. 5 (1897), Replies of the Turkish and Greek Governments to the Notes Addressed to Them on March 2, 1897, by the Representatives of Great Britain, Austria-Hungary, France, Germany, Italy, and Russia in Regard to Crete, 1897.

Turkey. No. 6 (1897), Reply of the Turkish Government to the Note Presented on March 5, 1897, by the Representatives of Great Britain, Austria-Hungary, France, Germany, Italy, and Russia in Regard to Crete, 1897.

Turkey. No. 8 (1897), Further Correspondence Respecting the Affairs of Crete (In Continuation of Turkey No. 7, 1896).

Turkey. No. 9 (1897), Reports on the Situation in Crete, 1897.

Turkey. No. 10 (1897), Further Correspondence Respecting the Affairs of Crete, 1897.

Turkey. No. 11 (1897), Correspondence Respecting the Affairs of Crete and the War Between Turkey and Greece, 1897.

Turkey. No. 12 (1897), Further Correspondence Respecting the Affairs of Crete, 1897.

Turkey. No. 3 (1898), Further Correspondence Respecting the Affairs of Crete, 1898.

Turkey. No. 4 (1898), Correspondence Respecting Relief Work in Crete, 1898.

Turkey. No. 5 (1898), Further Correspondence Respecting the Affairs of Crete (in Continuation of Turkey No. 3, 1898).

Turkey. No. 6 (1898), Further Correspondence Respecting the Affairs of Crete.

Turkey. No.1 (1899), Further Correspondence Respecting the Affairs of Crete (in Continuation of Turkey No. 7 1898).

Turkey. No. 2 (1899), Report by Her Majesty's Commissioner in Crete on the Provisional British Administration of the Province of Candia, 1899.

LEBANON AND SYRIA

Papers Relating to Administrative and Financial Reforms in Turkey, 1858–61.

Further Papers on the Disturbances in Syria, June 1860 (in Continuation of Papers Presented to Parliament July 23, 1860).

Despatches from Her Majesty's Consuls in the Levant, Respecting Past or Apprehended Disturbances in Syria 1858 to 1860, 1860.

Condition of Christians in Turkey (1860), 1861.

Convention between Great Britain, Austria, France, Prussia, Russia and Turkey, Respecting Measures to Be Taken for the Pacification of Syria, Signed at Paris, September 5, 1860, with Protocols Relating Thereto, 1861.

Convention between Great Britain, Austria, France, Prussia, Russia, and Turkey, Prolonging the Occupation of Syria to June 5, 1861, 1861.

Correspondence Relating to the Affairs of Syria, 1860–61, 1861.

REFORMS AND THE EASTERN CRISIS (1870s)

Papers Relating to Administrative and Financial Reforms in Turkey 1858–61, 1861.

Papers Respecting the Settlement of Circassian Emigrants in Turkey, 1864.

Despatch from Lord Lyons Respecting Reforms, and Treatment of Christians, in Turkey, 1867.

Correspondence respecting the Condition and Treatment of the Jews in Servia, 1867.

Reports Received from Her Majesty's Ambassador and Consuls Relating to the Condition of Christians in Turkey, 1867.

Turkey. No. 2 (1876), Correspondence Respecting the Affairs of Turkey, and the Insurrection in Bosnia and Herzegovina, 1876.

Principalities. No. 1 (1877), Correspondence Respecting the Condition and Treatment of the Jews in Servia and Roumania, 1867–76, 1877.

Turkey. No. 16 (1877), Reports by Her Majesty's Diplomatic and Consular Agents in Turkey Respecting the Condition of the Christian Subjects of the Porte: 1868–75, 1877.

State Papers—continued, Turkey, Session 8 February—14 August 1877.

Turkey. No. 31 (1878), Correspondence Respecting the Objections Raised by Populations Inhabiting Turkish Provinces Against the Territorial Changes Proposed in the Preliminary Treaty Signed at San Stefano 19 February/ 3 March, 1878, 1878.

Turkey. No. 49 (1878), Correspondence Respecting the Proceedings of the International Commission Sent to the Mount Rhodope District, 1878.

Turkey. No. 9 (1879), Part I, Correspondence Respecting the Proceedings of the European Commission for the Organization of Eastern Roumelia, 1879.

Turkey. No. 11 (1879), Return of Recent Consular Appointments in Asia Minor, 1879.

Turkey. No. 3 (1880), Return of Consular Appointments in Turkey in Asia Made Since January 1, 1879, 1880.

Turkey. No. 5 (1880), Correspondence Respecting the Mussulman, Greek, and Jewish Populations in Eastern Roumelia, 1880.

Turkey. No. 10 (1880), Report of the Commission Appointed to Inquire into the Occurrences in the Kirdjali District, 1880.

OTTOMAN ARMENIANS

Turkey. No. 51 (1878), Correspondence Respecting Reforms in Asiatic Turkey, 1878.

Turkey. No. 10 (1879), Correspondence Respecting the Condition of the Population in Asia Minor and Syria, 1879.

Turkey. No. 4 (1880), Correspondence Respecting the Condition of the Populations in Asia Minor and Syria, 1880.

Turkey. No. 23 (1880), Further Correspondence Respecting the Condition of the Populations in Asia Minor and Syria (in Continuation of Turkey No. 4, 1880), 1880.

Turkey. No. 6 (1881), Further Correspondence Respecting the Condition of the Populations in Asia Minor and Syria (in Continuation of Turkey No. 23, 1880), 1881.

Turkey. No. 1 (1889), Correspondence Respecting the Condition of the Populations of Asiatic Turkey: 1888–89, 1889.

Turkey. No. 1 (1890), Correspondence Respecting the Condition of the Populations of Asiatic Turkey and the Trial of Moussa Bey (in Continuation of Turkey No.1, 1899), 1890.

Turkey. No. 1 (1890–91), Correspondence Respecting the Condition of the Populations in Asiatic Turkey and the Proceedings in the Case of Moussa Bey (in Continuation of Turkey No. 1, 1890), 1891.

Turkey. No. 1 (1892), Further Correspondence Respecting the Condition of the Populations in Asiatic Turkey (in Continuation of Turkey No. 1, 1891), 1892.

Turkey. No. 3 (1896), Correspondence Relating to the Asiatic Provinces of Turkey: 1892–93, 1896.

Turkey. No. 1 (1895) (Part I), Correspondence Relating to the Asiatic Provinces of Turkey. Events at Sassoon, and the Commission of Inquiry at Moush, 1895.

Turkey. No. 8 (1896), Further Correspondence Relating to the Asiatic Provinces of Turkey (in Continuation of Turkey No. 2, 1896).

Turkey. No. 1 (1896), Correspondence Respecting the Introduction of Reforms in the Armenian Provinces of Asiatic Turkey, 1896.

Turkey. No. 2 (1896), Correspondence Relative to the Armenian Question, and Reports from Her Majesty's Consular Officers in Asiatic Turkey, 1896.

Turkey. No. 5 (1896), Correspondence Relating to the Asiatic Provinces of Turkey. Reports by Vice Consul Fitzmaurice from Birejik, Ourfa, Adiaman, and Behesni, 1896.

Turkey. No. 6 (1896), Correspondence Relating to the Asiatic Provinces of Turkey: 1894–95 (in Continuation of Turkey No. 3, 1896), 1896.

Turkey. No. 3 (1897), Further Correspondence Respecting the Asiatic Provinces of Turkey and Events in Constantinople (in Continuation of Turkey No. 8, 1896, and Turkey No.1, 1897), 1897.

Turkey. No. 1 (1898), Further Correspondence Respecting the Asiatic Provinces of Turkey (in Continuation of Turkey No. 7, 1897), 1898.

OTTOMAN MACEDONIA

Turkey. No. 1 (1903), Correspondence Respecting the Affairs of South-Eastern Europe, 1903.

Turkey. No. 2 (1903), Further Correspondence Respecting the Affairs of South-Eastern Europe, 1903.

Turkey. No. 3 (1903), Further Correspondence Respecting the Affairs of South-Eastern Europe, 1903.

Turkey. No. 1 (1904), Further Correspondence Respecting the Affairs of South-Eastern Europe, March–September 1903, 1904.

Turkey. No. 2 (1904), Further Correspondence Respecting the Affairs of South-Eastern Europe, 1904.

Turkey. No. 4 (1904), Further Correspondence Respecting the Affairs of South-Eastern Europe, 1904.

Turkey. No. 2 (1905), Further Correspondence Respecting the Affairs of South-Eastern, Europe, 1905.

Turkey. No. 3 (1905), Further Correspondence Respecting the Affairs of South-Eastern, Europe, 1905.

Turkey. No. 1 (1906), Further Correspondence Respecting the Affairs of South-Eastern Europe, 1906.

Turkey. No. 1. (1906), Further Correspondence Respecting the Affairs of South-Eastern Europe, 1906.

Turkey. No. 2. (1906), Further Correspondence Respecting the Affairs of South-Eastern Europe, 1906.

Turkey. No. 1. (1907), Further Correspondence Respecting the Affairs of South-Eastern Europe, 1907.

Turkey. No. 3 (1907), Despatches from the British Adviser on the Macedonian Financial Commission, 1907.

Turkey. No. 1 (1908), Further Correspondence Respecting Proposal by His Majesty's Government for Reforms in Macedonia, 1908.

Turkey. No. 2 (1908), Further Correspondence Respecting Proposal by His Majesty's Government for Reforms in Macedonia, 1908.

Turkey. No. 3. (1908), Further Correspondence Respecting the Affairs of South-Eastern Europe, 1908.

Turkey. No. 1 (1909), Correspondence Respecting the Constitutional Movement in Turkey, 1908, 1909.

CONGO

Africa. No. 14 (1903), Despatch to Certain of His Majesty's Representatives Abroad in Regard to Alleged Cases of Ill-treatment of Natives and to the Existence of Trade Monopolies in the Independent State of the Congo, 1903.

Africa. No. 1 (1904), Correspondence and Report from His Majesty's Consul at Boma Respecting the Administration of the Independent State of the Congo, 1904.

Africa. No. 7 (1904), Correspondence and Report from His Majesty's Consul at Boma Respecting the Administration of the Independent State of the Congo, 1904.

Africa, No. 1, (1905) Correspondence and Report from His MajIndependent State of the Congo; Further Correspondence, 1905.

Africa, No. 1, (1906), Correspondence Respecting the Report of the Commission of Inquiry into the Administration of the Independent State of the Congo.

PUTUMAYO

Special Report from the Select Committee on Putumayo Atrocities, 1912.

Miscellaneous No. 8 (1912), Correspondence Respecting the Treatment of British Colonial Subjects and Native Indians Employed in the Collection of Rubber in the Putumayo District.

Miscellaneous. No. 6 (1913), Report by His Majesty's Consul at Iquitos on His Tour in the Putumayo District.

Other Printed Sources

CHIOS, LEBANON, AND SYRIA

Argenti, Philippe. *The Massacres of Chios, Described in Contemporary Diplomatic Reports.* London: John Lane, 1932.

Hurewitz, J. C. *Diplomacy in the Near and Middle East, A Documentary Record: 1535–1914,* vol. 2. London: Macmillan 1956.

Lane-Poole, Stanley. *The Life of the Right Honourable Stratford Canning. Viscount Stratford de Redcliffe,* 2 vols. London: Longman, Green, 1888.

Noradounghian, Gabriel (Effendi). *Recueil d'Actes Internationaux de l'Empire Ottoman,* 4 vols. Paris: Pichon, 1897–1903.

Rochemonteix, Camille de. *Le Liban et l'expédition française en Syrie (1860–1861): documents inédits du Général A. Ducrot.* Paris: A. Picard, 1921.

EASTERN CRISIS (1875–78) AND TREATY OF BERLIN

Bourne, Kenneth, and D. Cameron Watts, eds. *The Ottoman Empire in the Balkans 1856–1875,* Part 1, Series B, Vol. 18 of *British Documents on Foreign Affairs: Reports and Papers from the Foreign Office Confidential Prints.* Frederick, MD: University Press of America, 1984.

Commission technique européenne formée en vertu d'un accord intervenu entre les puissances signataires du Traite de Berlin, 1879. Paris: Imprimerie nationale, 1880.

France, Ministère des Affaires Etrangères. *Documents diplomatiques. Affaires d'Orient, 1875–1876–1877.* Paris: Imprimerie nationale, 1877.

———. *Documents diplomatiques. Affaires d'Orient. Congres de Berlin, 1878.* Paris: Imprimerie nationale, 1878.

Taylor, Sedley. *The Conduct of Her Majesty's Ministers on the Eastern Question: A Statement of Facts Based on Official Documents.* London, 1877.

SECOND INTERVENTION IN CRETE

Affaires de Crète. [Documents diplomatiques adressés par le prince Georges de Grèce, haut commissaire en Crète, aux gouvernements des quatre puissances protectrices de la Crète, la France, la Russie, l'Italie et la Grande-Bretagne. 1900–1905.]

France, Ministère des Affaires Etrangères. *Documents diplomatiques: affaires d'Orient. Affaire de Crète, juin 1894–février 1897.* Paris: Imprimerie nationale, 1897.

———. *Documents, diplomatiques: affaires d'Orient. Affaire de Crète—conflit greco-turc. situation de l'empire Ottoman, février–mai 1897.* Paris: Imprimerie nationale, 1897.

———. *Documents diplomatiques: affaires d'Orient. Affaire de Crète: conflit grèco-turc: situation de l'Empire Ottoman*. Paris: Imprimerie nationale, 1897.

———. *Documents diplomatiques: affaires d'Orient: autonomie crétoise, janvier–octobre 1898*. Paris: Imprimerie nationale, 1898.

———. *Documents diplomatiques: affaires d'Orient: évacuation de la Crète par les troupes ottomanes: installation d'un haut commissaire: octobre–novembre 1898*. Paris: Imprimerie nationale, 1898.

ARMENIAN QUESTION

France, Ministère des Affaires Etrangères. *Documents diplomatiques: affaires arménieenes. Projets de réformes dans l'Empire Ottoman, 1893–1897*. Paris: Ministère des Affaires Etrangères, 1897.

———. *Documents diplomatiques: affaires arméniennes (supplément): 1895–1896*. Paris: Imprimerie nationale, 1897.

OTTOMAN MACEDONIAN PROVINCES

France, Ministère des Affaires Etrangères. *Documents diplomatiques: affaires de Macédoine: 1902*. Paris: Imprimerie nationale, 1903.

———. *Affaires de Macédoine: documents diplomatiques: janvier –février 1903*. Paris: Imprimerie nationale, 1903.

———. *Documents diplomatiques: affaires de Macédoine 1903–1905*. Paris: Imprimerie nationale, 1905.

CONTEMPORARY WRITINGS

International Legal Scholars

Amari Carnazza, Giuseppe. "Nouvel exposé du principe de non-intervention." *Revue de Droit Onternational et de Législation Comparée* 5 (1873): 352–565.

Amos, Sheldon. *Political and Legal Remedies for War*. London: Cassell, Petter and Galpin, 1880.

Bernard, Montagu. *On the Principle of Non-intervention. A Lecture Delivered in the Hall of All Souls' College by Mountague Bernard*. Oxford: J. H. & J. Parker, 1860.

Bluntschli, Johann C. *Le droit international codifié*. Paris: Librairie de Guillau-min, 1870.

Borchard, Edwin M. *The Diplomatic Protection of Citizen Abroad*. New York: Banks Law Publishing Co., 1915.

Boutourlin, Dimitirij Petrovich comte de (M.L.C.D.B.). *Des Grecs, des Turcs, et de l'esprit public Européen, opuscule de 1821*. Paris: Jules Renouard, 1828.

Creasy, Edward S. *First Platform of International Law*. London: John Van Voorst, 1876.

de Martens, George Frédéric. *Traité de droit international*. 3 vols. Paris: Librairie Marescq Ainé, 1886.

Despagnet, Frantz. *Cours de droit international public*, 3d ed. (updated). Paris: Librairie de la Société du Recueil Général des Lois et des Arrêts, 1905.

Dickinson, Edwin De Witt. *The Equality of States in International Law*. Cambridge: Harvard University Press, 1920.

Engelhardt, Edouard. "L'Angleterre et la Russie. A propos de la question Arménienne." *Revue de Droit International et de Législation Comparée* 15 (1883): 146–59.

———. "La question Macédonienne." *Revue Générale de Droit International Public* 12 (1905): 544–51, 636–44; 13 (1906): 29–40, 164–74.

———. *La Turquie et le Tanzimat ou histoire des réformes dans l'Empire Ottoman depuis 1826 jusqu'à nos jours*. 2 vols. Paris: A. Cotillon, 1882.

———. "Le droit d'intervention et la Turquie." *Revue de Droit International et de Législation Comparée* 12 (1880): 363–88.

Harcourt, William Vernon. *Letters by Historicus on Some Questions of International Law: Reprinted from "The Times" with Considerable Additions*. London: Macmillan, 1863.

Heffter, Augustus W. *Le droit international public de l'Europe. Nouvelle édition revue et augmentée après le décès du traducteur par l'auteur*, trans. Bergson. Paris: Cotillon, 1866; London: Elibron Classic Replica edition, 2004.

Hodges, Henry G. *The Doctrine of Intervention*. Princeton: Banner Press, 1915.

Hornung, Joseph. "Civilisés et barbares." *Revue Générale du Droit International Public* 16 (1884): 79; 17 (1885): 1–18, 447–70, 539–60; 18 (1886): 188–206, 281–98.

Ion, Theodore. "The Cretan Question." *American Journal of International Law* 4 (1910): 276–84.

Jooris, Joseph. "La question du Liban." *Revue de Droit International et de Législation Comparée* 15 (1883): 243–53.

Lawrence, Thomas J. *The Principles of Interntional Law*. 2 vols. 4th ed., rev. London: Macmillan, 1911; London: Elibron Classics Replica Edition, 2003.

Lingelbach, William E. "The Doctrine and Practice of Intervention in Europe." *Annals of the American Academy of Political and Social Science* 16 (1900); 1–32.

Lorimer, James. *Institutes of the Law of Nations: A Treatise of the Juridical Relations of Separate Political Communities* 2 vols. London: Blackwood, 1883.

Mahan, Alfred T. *Some Neglected Aspects of War*. Boston: Little Brown, 1907.

andelstam, André-N. *La Société des Nations et les puissances devant le problème Arménien*. Edition Spéciale de la *Revue Générale de Droit International Public*. Paris: Pédone, 1926.

Manning, William Oke. *Commentaries on the Law of Nations*, ed. Sheldon Amos. London: Sweet, 1875.

Mill, J. S. "A Few Words on Non-Intervention." In *Dissertations and Discussions*. 3 vols., 1867. Reprinted from *Fraser's Magazine* 60 (December 1859).

Nys, Ernest. *Le droit international: Les principes, les théories, les faits*. Brussels: Castaigne, 1904.

Oppenheim, Lassa F. *International Law*. New York: Longman, Green, 1905.

Phillimore, Robert. *Commentaries upon International Law*. 3d ed. London, Butterworths, 1879; London: Elibron Classics Replica Edition, 2004.

Reddie, James. *Inquiries in International Law: Public and Private*. 2d ed. Edinburgh: William Blackwood, 1851.

Rolin-Jaequemyns, Gustave. *Armenia, the Armenians, and the Treaties*. London: John Heywood, 1891.

———. "L'Arménie, les Arméniens et les traités." *Revue de Droit Internationale et de Législation Comparée* 19 (1887): 284–25; 21 (1889): 291–353.

———. *Le droit international et la question d'Orient, extrait de la Revue de Droit International et de Législation Comparée, 1876.* Gand: Bureau de la Revue de Droit International, 1876. http://www.archive.org/stream/ledroitinternat00jaegoog#page/n8/mode/1up.

———. "Note sur la théorie du droit d'intervention: A propos d'une lettre de M. le Professeur Arntz." *Revue de Droit International et de Législation Comparée* 8 (1876): 673–82.

Rougier, Antoine. "Théorie de l'intervention d'humanité." *Revue Générale du Droit International* 17 (1910): 468–526.

Stapleton, Augustus G. *Intervention and Non-Intervention or the Foreign Policy of Great Britain from 1790 to 1865.* London: J. Murray, 1866.

Stowell, Ellery. *Intervention in International Law.* Washington DC: Byrne, 1921.

Streit, Georges. "La question Crétoise au point de vue du droit international." *Revue Générale de Droit International Public* 4 (1897): 61–105, 447–83.

Thompson, Carslake. *Public Opinion and Lord Beaconsfield 1875–1880.* 2 vols. London: Macmillan, 1886.

Vie, Louis. *Des principales applications du droit d'intervention des puissances Européennes dans les affaires des Balkans depuis le Traité de Berlin de 1878 jusqu'à nos jours.* Toulouse: Imprimerie Lagarde & Sebille, 1900.

Westlake, John. *Chapters on the Principles of International Law.* Cambridge: Cambridge University Press, 1894 (London: Elibron Classic Replica Edition, 2003).

Wheaton, Henry. *Elements of International Law: With a Sketch of the History of Science.* 2 vols. London: Fellowes, 1836.

Wildman, Richard. *Institutes of International Law.* London: William Benning, 1849.

Woolsey, Theodore D. *Introduction to the Study of International Law.* 4th ed. London: Sampson, Low Marston, Low & Searle, 1875.

The Ottoman Empire and the Eastern Question (Including Memoirs and Recollections)

Cauhet, Albéric. *La question d'Orient dans l'histoire contemporaine (1821–1905), préface de Frédéric Passy.* Paris: Dujarric, 1905.

Chateaubriand, François-René de. *Itinéraire de Paris à Jérusalem et de Jérusalem à Paris: Oeuvres complètes de Chateaubriand.* 5 vols. Paris: Garnier, 1861.

Choublier, Max. *La question d'Orient depuis le Traité de Berlin. Deuxième édition revue, corrigée et augmentée.* Paris: Arthur Rousseau, 1899.

Cobden, Richard. *The Political Writings of Richard Cobden.* 2 vols. London: T. Fisher Unwin, 1903.

De Girardin, Emile. *Solutions de la Question d'Orient.* Paris: Librairie Nouvelle, 1854.

Djuvara, Trandafir G. *Cent projets de partage de la Turquie (1281–1913).* Paris: F. Alcan, 1914.

Guizot, François Pierre Guillaume. *Mémoires pour servir á l'histoire de mon temps.* Paris: Michel Lévy Freres, 1861.

Guizot, F. *Histoire de la civilisation en Europe (1828).* Paris, Hachette, 1985.

Lamartine, Alphonse de. *Histoire de la Turquie / par A. de Lamartine*. 3 vols. Paris: A. Delahays, 1861.

———. *Souvenirs, impressions, pensées et paysages pendant un voyage en Orient, 1832–1833, ou, notes d'un voyageur*. Paris: C. Gosselin, 1854.

———. *Voyage en Orient*. Paris: Nizet, 1960.

———. *Vues, discours et articles sur la question d'Orient*. Paris: C. Gosselin, 1840.

Lamy, Étienne. *La France du Levant* [1900]. London: Elibron Classics, 2003.

MacColl, Malcolm. *The Eastern Question: Its Facts & Fallacies*. London: Longman, Green, 1877.

Mathieu, Henri. *La Turquie et ses différents peuples*. Paris: E. Dentu, 1857.

Mill, J. S. "Civilization." In *Dissertations and Discussions: Political, Philosophical, and Historical*, vol. 1. London, 1869.

Millet, René. *Souvenirs des Balkans; de Salonique à Belgrade et du Danube à l'Adriatique*. Paris: Hachette, 1891.

Morel, Eugène. *La Turquie et ses réformes*. Paris: Dentu, 1866.

Palgrave, William G. *Essay on Eastern Questions*. London: Macmillan, 1872.

Sancerme, Charles. *La question d'Orient populaire*. Paris: Librairie Ch. Delagrave, 1897.

Solution de la question d'Orient proposée au Congrès de Berlin par un publiciste d'Orient. Paris: Charles Schiller, 1878.

Spencer, Edmund. *Travels in European Turkey*. 2 vols. London: Colubrun, 1851

Ubicini, Abdolonyme. *Lettres sur la Turquie ou tableau statistique, religieux, politique, administratif, militaire, commercial, etc. de l'Empire Ottoman depuis le Khatti-Cherif de Gulkhané (1839)*, vol. 1 (1853), vol. 2 (1854). Paris: Librairie Militaire de J. Dumaine, 1853–54.

Wellesley, Arthur, Duke of Wellington. *Despatches, Correspondence, and Memorandum of Field Marshal Arthur, Duke of Wellington*. 3 vols. London: John Murray, 1867.

Woods, Henry C. *Washed by Four Seas, an English Officer's Travels in the Near East*. London, T. F. Unwin, 1908.

———. *The Danger Zone of Europe: Changes and Problems in the Near East*. Boston: Little, Brown, 1911.

Greece and Crete

Benjamin, S.G.W. "Crete, Historical Sketch of." *Harper's New Monthly Magazine* 34 (1866–67): 758.

Bérard, Victor. *Les affaires de Crète*. Paris: Calmann Lévy, 1898.

Berton, J. M. *Les Turcs dans la Balance Politique de l'Europe au dix-neuvième siècle ou considérations sur l'usurpation et sur l'indépendance de la Grèce. Suivies d'une nouvelle traduction des Lettres de Lady Montague sur la Turquie*. Paris: La Librairie Nationale et Etrangère, 1822.

Bickford-Smith, Roandeu Albert H. *Cretan Sketches*. London: R. Bentley and Son, 1898.

Blaquiere, Edward. *Report on the Present State of the Greek Confederation, and on Its Claims to the Support of the Christian World: Read to the Greek Committee on Saturday, September 13, 1823*. Athens: Istorikê kai Ethnologikê Etairía tês Elládo, 1974.

Bunbury, E. H. "Crete." *Contemporary Review* 1 (1866): 551–67.

Chateaubriand, François-René. "Note sur la Grèce." In *Oeuvres completes de M. le vicomte de Chateaubriand, tome* 9. Paris: Pourrat Frères, 1836–39.

Constant, Benjamin. *Political Writings,* trans. and ed. Biancamaria Fontana. Cambridge: Cambridge University Press, 1988.

"Cretan Insurrection, The (a Resident in Crete)." *Macmillan's Magazine* 15 (1866–67): 257.

Facts on the Candian Question and the Hatt-I-Humayoun. London, 1867.

Finlay, George. *History of the Greek Revolution.* London: William Blackwood and Sons, 1861.

Green, R. L. *Sketches of the War in Greece.* London, Hurst, 1827.

Pellion, Jean P. *La Grèce et les Capodistrias: Pendant l'occupation Française de 1828 à 1834 / par le Général de division Pellion.* Paris: J. Dumaine, 1855.

Phillips, W. Alison. *The War of Greek Independence, 1821 to 1833.* New York: Smith Elder, 1897.

Pouqueville, François. *Histoire de la régénération de la Grèce.* 4 vols. Paris: Firmin Didot, 1827.

La Question d'Orient et l'insurrection Crétoise. Paris: E. Dentu, 1868.

Raffenel, M.C.D. *Histoire des événements de la Grèce, depuis les premiers troubles jusqu'à ce jour, avec des notes critiques et topographiques.* 3 vols. Paris: Dondey-Dupré, 1822–28.

R** (Alexandros R. Rankaves). *La solution de la question d'Orient.* Paris: E. Dentu, 1866.

Raybaud, Maxime. *Mémoires sur la Grèce, pour servir a l'histoire de la guerre de l'Indépendance, accompagnés de plans topographiques.* 2 vols. Paris: Tournachon-Molin, Libraire, 1824–25.

Skinner, James E. H. *Turkish Rule in Crete.* London: Cassell, Petter and Galpin for the Eastern Question Association, 1877.

Stanhope, H.L.F.C. *Greece, in 1823 and 1824: Geing a Series of Letters, and Other Documents, on the Greek Revolution, Written during a Visit to That Country.* London: Sherwood, Gilbert, and Piper, 1825.

Turot, M. H. *L'insurrection Crétoise et la guerre Gréco-Turque.* Paris: Hachette, 1898.

Waddington, George. *A Visit to Greece, in 1823 and 1824.* London: J. Murray, 1825.

W. H. Humphreys' First "Journal of the Greek Independence" (July 1821–February 1822), ed. Sture Linnér. Stockholm: Almqvist & Wiksell, 1967.

Lebanon and Syria

Calland, Henry. *Les massacres de Syrie: A Monsieur de Pongerville, membre de l'Académie Française.* Paris: Les Principaux Libraire, 1860.

Churchill, Charles Henry. *The Druzes and the Maronites under Turkish Rule from 1840 to 1860.* [London, 1862] Reading: Garnet, 1994.

Courcelle-Seneuil, J. L. *Les massacres du Liban: Au profit des Chrétiens de Syrie.* Paris: Albessard et Bérard, 1860.

Esquisse de l'état politique et commercial de la Syrie. Paris: Chez France, 1862.

La France en Syrie. Paris: E. Dentu, 1860.

Guy, Henry. *Beyrouth et le Liban: Relation d'un séjour de plusieurs années dans ce pays.* [Paris: Comptoir des Imprimeurs, 1850] Beirut: Lahd Khater, 1985.

———. *Esquisse de l'etat politique et commercial de la Syrie*. Paris: Chez France Libraire, 1862.

Jouan, Auguste. *Les massacres de Syrie en 1860* [poem]. Valogne impr. de Vve Carette-Bondessein, 1864.

Jullien, M. *La nouvelle mission de la Compagnie de Jésus en Syrie (1831–1895)*, vol. 2. Tours: Imprimerie A. Mame et Fils, 1898.

Lamy, Etienne. *La France du Levant*. Paris: Plon-Nourrit, 1900.

The Lebanon in Turmoil: Syria and the Powers in 1860. Book of the Marvels of the Time Concerning the Massacres in the Arab Country by Iskander Ibn Yakq'ub Abkarius, trans. and ann. J. F. Scheltema. New Haven: Yale University Press, 1920.

Lenormant, François. *Les derniers evénements de Syrie: Une persécution du Christianisme en 1860*. Paris: Ch. Duniol, 1860.

Louet, Ernest. *L'expédition de Syrie, 1860–1861*. Paris: Amyot, 1862.

Lyall, Alfred. *The Life of the Marquis of Dufferin and Ava*. 2 vols. London: Murray, 1905.

Les Massacres des chrétiens de la Syrie en 1860, précédés d'un aperçu géographique et historique. Paris: Librairie populaire des villes et des campagnes rue d'Ulm, 1861.

Massacres de Syrie, récit véridique et circonstancié des atrocités commises par les Druses et les Turcs sur les Maronites Chrétiens du Liban. Epouvantables détails. Montpellier, 1860.

Poujade, Eugène. *Chrétiens et Turcs: Scènes et souvenirs de la vie politique, militaire et religieuse en Orient*, 3d ed. Paris: Didier, 1859.

———. *Le Liban et la Syrie, 1845–1860*. Paris: A. Bourdilliat, 1860.

Réflexions sur les fonctions des consuls de France en Turquie, au point de vue moral. Marseille: Imprimerie de Barlatier-Feissat et Demonchy, 1867.

Thouvenel, Louis. *Pages de l'histoire du second Empire, d'après les papiers de M. Thouvenel, ancien ministre des affaires étrangères (1854–1866)*. Paris: Plon-Nourrit, 1903.

Bulgarian Atrocities

Arnold, Arthur R. *The Promises of Turkey*. London: Cassell, 1877.

Austin, Alfred. *Tory Horrors or the Question of the Hour. A Letter to the Right Hon. W. E. Gladstone, M.P.* 2d ed. London: Chatto and Windus, 1876.

Baker, James. *Turkey in Europe*. 2d ed. London: Cassell, 1877.

Barnwell, R. Grant. *The Russo-Turkish War: Comprising an Account of the Servian Insurrection, the Dreadful Massacre of Christians in Bulgaria and Other Turkish Atrocities*. Philadelphia: J. E. Potter, [1878?].

Bianconi, F. *La question d'Orient dévoilée, ou la vérité sur la Turquie. Mussulmans, Raias, Slaves et Grecs, Tcherkess et Tziganes*. Paris: Librairie Générale, 1876.

Blunt, Fanny Janet. *The People of Turkey: Twenty Years' Residence among Bulgarians, Greeks, Albanians, Turks, and Armenians. By a Consul's Daughter and Wife*, ed. Stanley Lane Poole. 2 vols. London: John Murray, 1878; London: Elibron Classics Series edition, 2005.

Brassey, Thomas. *The Eastern Question and the Political Situation at Home*. London: Longmans, Green, 1877.

Campbell, George. *The Blue Books, and What Is to Come Next*. Eastern Question Association, Papers on the Eastern Question, no. 12. London: Cassell, Petter and Galpin, 1877.

———. *The Races, Religions, and Institutions of Turkey and the Neighbouring Countries. Being the Substance of Two Lecturers Delivered in The Kirkcaldy Burghs*. Eastern Question Association, Papers on the Eastern Question, no. 3. London: Cassell, Petter and Galpin, 1877.

———. *The Resettlement of the Turkish Dominions*. Eastern Question Association. London: Cassell, 1878.

———. *What the Turks Are, and How We Have Been Helping Them: Speech . . . in the City Hall, Glasgow, September 19, 1876*. Glasgow: Maclehose, 1876.

Chesson, Frederick William. *Turkey and the Slave Trade: A Statement of Facts*. London: Petter and Galpin, 1877.

Davies, John L. *Religious Aspects of the Eastern Question*. London: Cassell, 1877.

Denton, William. *Fallacies of the Eastern Question*. London: Petter and Galpin, 1877.

Duff, Grant M. E. *The Eastern Question: A Lecture Delivered at Inverurie on 14th November 1876*. Edinburgh: Edmonston and Douglas, 1876.

Farley, John. *Turks and Christians: A Solution of the Eastern Question*. London: Simpkin, Marshall, 1876.

Fawcett, Millicent G. *The Martyrs of Turkish Misrule*. London: Petter and Galpin, 1877.

Freeman, Edward A. *The Eastern Question in Its Historical Bearings. An Address Delivered in Manchester, November, 15, 1876*. Manchester: Taylor Garnett Evans, 1897.

Gallenga, Antonio Carlo Napoleone. *Two Years of the Eastern Question*. 2 vols. London: Samuel Tinsley, 1877.

Gladstone, William E. *Bulgarian Horrors and the Question of the East*. London: Murray, 1876.

———. *England's Mission*. London: Hodges, 1878.

———. *Lessons in Massacre, or, The Conduct of the Turkish Government in and about Bulgaria since May, 1876: Chiefly from the Papers Presented by Command*. London: Murray, 1877.

———. *The Sclavonic [sic] Provinces of the Ottoman Empire: Address at Hawarden*. London: Petter and Galpin, 1877.

La guerre en Orient (1875–1878). Paris: J. Dumaine, 1877–78.

Holms, John. *Commercial & Financial Aspects of the Eastern Question*. Eastern Question Association, Papers on the Eastern Question, no. 3. London: Cassell, Petter and Galpin, 1877.

Kinnear, John Boyd. *The Mind of England on the Eastern Question. What England Thinks. What England Wishes. What England Can Do*. London: Chapman and Hall, 1877.

Munro-Butler-Johnstone, H. A. *The Turks: Their Character, Manners, and Institutions, as Bearing on the Eastern Question*. Oxford: James Parker, 1876.

The Question of the Day: Turk or Christian? An Answer to Mr. Gladstone's Pamphlet: [entitled: Bulgarian Horrors and the Question of the East] with, a True Narrative of the Bulgarian Horrors / by an Englishman. London: Diprose, 1876.

Richard, Henry. *Evidence of Turkish Misrule*. Eastern Question Association, Papers on the Eastern Question, no. 1. London: Cassell, Petter and Galpin, 1876.

Scudamore, F. E. *France in the East; a Contribution towards the Consideration of the Eastern Question*. London: W. H. Allen, 1882.

Wilson, John. *England's Duty in Relation to the Christians of Turkey*. London: Guest, [c. 1878].

Massacre of Ottoman Armenians

Armenia and the Forward Movement. Mr. George W. E. Russell's Speech at Manchester, November 19, 1895.

Brézol, Georges. *Les Turcs ont passé là . . . Recueil de documents, dossiers, rapports, requêtes, protestations, suppliques et enquêtes, établissant la vérité sur les massacres d'Adana en 1909*. Paris: [en vente chez l'auteur,] 1911.

Bryce, James. *The Case for the Armenians, with an Introduction by Francis Seymour Stevenson, M.P. (President of the Anglo-Armenian Association), and a Full Report of the Speeches Delivered at the Banquet in Honour of the Right. Hon. James Bryce, M.P., D.C.L., on Friday, May 12th, 1893*. London: Printed for the Anglo-Armenian Association, Harrison and Son, 1893.

Buxton, Noel, and Rev. Harold Buxton. *Travel and Politics in Armenia with an Introduction by Viscount Bryce and a Contribution on Armenian History and Culture by Aram Raffi*. London: Smith, Elder, 1914

Cambon, Paul. *Corréspondance 1870–1924*. 3 vols. Paris: Bernard Grasset, 1940–46.

Campbell, G. *Our Responsibilities for Turkey. Facts and Memories of Forty Years*. London: John Murray, 1896.

Carlier, Émilie. *Au milieu des massacres: Journal de la femme d'un consul de France en Arménie*. Paris: Félix Juven, 1903.

Charmetant, Père F. *Martyrologue Arménien: Tableau officiel des massacres d'Arménie dressé après enquêtes par les six ambassades de Constantinople et atatistique dressée par des témoins oculaires Grégoriens et Protestants des profanations, d'Eglises, massacres d'ecclésiastiques, apostasies forcées, enlèvements de femmes et jeunes vierges avec carte de la région des massacres*. Paris: Bureau des Oeuvres d'Orient, 1896.

Clemenceau, George. *L'iniquité*. Paris: P.-V. Stock, 1899.

Cochin, Denys. *Contre les barbares*. Paris: C. Lévy, 1899.

Decazis, Anaïs. *Les voix éplorées de l'Arménie*. Paris: Shmidt, 1897.

Dillon, Emil J. "Armenia: An Appeal." *Contemporary Review* 69 (1896): 1–19.

———. "Armenia and the Powers: From Behind the Scenes." *Contemporary Review* 69 (1896): 628–43.

———. "The Condition of Armenia." *Contemporary Review* 68 (1895): 153–89.

Dixon-Johnson, C. F. *The Armenians*, Blackburn: G. Toulmin, 1916.

Driault, Édouard. *La Question d'Orient depuis ses origines jusqu'à la Paix de Sèvres*, 8th ed. Paris: F. Alcan, 1921.

The Eastern Question and the Armenians. London, April 1878.

Edwards, H. S. *Sir William White, K.C.B., K.C.M.G., for Six Years Ambassador at Constantinople; His Life and Correspondence*. London: Murray, 1902.

Eliot, Charles. *Turkey in Europe*, 2d rev. ed. [1908]. New York: Barnes and Noble, 1965 .

France, Anatole. "Pour l'Arménie et la Macédoine (discours prononcé à Rome, le 21 mai 1903)." *Nuova antologia*, Fasc. 754, May 1903.

Gladstone, William E. *The Eastern Crisis: A Letter to the Duke of Westminster, K.G.* London, Murray, 1897.

———. *Verbatim Report of the . . . Great Speech on the Armenian Atrocities, Delivered at Liverpool, September 24th, 1896.* London: Sears, [1896?].

Graves, Robert. *Storm Centres of the Near East: Personal Memories, 1879–1929.* London: Hutchinson, 1933.

Greene, Frederick Davis. *The Armenian Crisis and the Rule of the Turk.* London: Hodder and Stoughton, 1895.

Harris, James Rendel, and Helen B. Harris. "Armenia's Desolation and Woe; Review of Letters from Armenia." *Review of Reviews* (May 1897): 626–27.

Harris, Walter B. "An Unbiased View of the Armenian Question." *Blackwood's Edinburgh Magazine* 158 (1895): 483–92.

[An Old Indian.] *Historical Sketch of Armenian and the Armenians in Ancient and Modern Times with Special Reference to the Present Crisis.* London: Elliot Stock, 1896.

Kimberley, J. W. *The Journal of John Wodehouse, First Earl of Kimberley, 1862–1902,* ed. A. Hawkins and J. Powell. London, Royal Historical Society, 1997.

Ernest Lavisse, "Notre politique orientale, I." *Revue de Paris* 13 (1897): 274–311.

———. "Notre politique orientale, II." *Revue de Paris* 13 (1897): 872–914.

———. "La paix d'Orient." *Revue de Paris* 14 (1898): 865–94.

Lepsius, Johannes. *Armenia and Europe: An Indictment*, trans. Rendel Harris. London: Hodder and Stoughton, 1897.

Lynch H.F.B. "The Armenian Question in Russia." *Contemporary Review* 65 (1895): 847–65; 66 (1895): 91–107, 435–56.

———. "The Armenian Question: Europe or Russia?" *Contemporary Review* 69 (1896): 271–76.

———. *Armenia: Travels and Studies.* 2 vols. Beirut: Khayats, 1965 (reprint London, 1901).

MacColl, Malcolm. *England's Responsibility Towards Armenia.* London: Longmans, Green, 1895.

———. *Memoirs and Correspondence,* ed. G.W.E. Russell. London: Smith, Elder, 1914.

Maclaren, Rev. Alex. *A Demand for the Emancipation of the Armenian, Macedonian, Minor Asian, Syrian, and Other Christian Subjects of the Porte in Conformity with the Treaty of Berlin. Report with Appendices of the Great Meeting of Christians of All Denominations and Political Parties on Turkish Misrule and Massacre Held in the Central Hall, Manchester, on May 21, 1895.* Manchester: James Edward Cornish, 1895.

Massacres d'Adana et nos missionnaires, récit de témoins. Lyon: Imprimerie Vve M. Paquet, 1909.

Les Massacre d'Arménie: Témoignages des victimes. Paris: Edition du Mercure de France, 1896.

"The Massacres in Turkey." *Nineteenth Century Review* 236 (1896).

Meyrier, Gustave. *Les massacres de Diarbekir: Correspondance diplomatique du vice-consul de France, 1894–1896*, ed. Claire Mouradian and Michèle Durand-Meyrier. Caen: L'Inventaire, 2000.

Passy, Paul E. *La vérité sur l'Arménie*. Paris: Lievens, 1896.

Pears, Edwin. *Forty Years in Constantinople: The Recollections of Sir Edwin Pears, 1873–1915*. London, Herbert Jenkins; New York: D. Appleton, 1916.

Pinon, René. *L'Europe et l'Empire Ottoman: Les aspects actuels de la Question d'Orient*. 7th ed. Paris: Perrin, 1913.

Pro Armenia. From 1st to [8th] year. November 25, 1900 [–September 20, 1908].

Probyn, J. W. *Armenia and the Lebanon*. Eastern Question Association, Papers on the Eastern Question, no. 10. London: Cassell, Petter and Galpin, 1877.

Quillard, Pierre. "L'extermination d'une race." *La Contemporaine* 8 (1901): 520–31.

Quillard, Pierre, and Louis Margery. *La question d'Orient et la politique personnelle de M. Hanotaux*. Paris: P.-V. Stock, 1897.

Ramsay, W. M. "Two Massacres in Asia Minor." *Contemporary Review* 70 (1896): 435–48.

Rolin-Jaequemyns, Gustave. *Armenia, The Armenians, and the Treaties*, trans. from the *Revue de Droit International et de Législation Comparée* and rev. by the author. London: John Heywood, 1891.

Stead, William T. *The Haunting Horrors in Armenia*. London: Review of Reviews Office, 1896.

Vandal, Albert. *Les Arméniens et la réforme de la Turquie. Conférence faite par M. Albert Vandal de l'Académie Française dans la Salle de la Société de Géographie, le 2 février 1897 sous la Présidence de M. Le Comte De Mun*. Paris: Librairie Plon, 1897.

Ottoman Macedonian Provinces

Bérard, Victor. *Pro Macedonia*. Paris: Librairie Armand Colin, 1904.

———. *La Turquie et l'Héllenisme contemporain*. Paris: Ancienne Librairie Germer Baillière, 1897.

Bishop of Rochester in the Chair. *Report of the Proceedings at the National Conference on the Macedonian Question Held at Caxton Hall, Westminster, S.W., on Tuesday, March 29th, 1904*. London: Balkan Committee, 1904.

Brailsford, Henry N. *Macedonia, Its Races and Their Future*. London: Methuen, 1906.

Brancoff, D. N. *La Macédoine et sa population Chrétienne, avec deux cartes ethnographiques*. Paris: Plon-Nourrit, 1905.

Bruce, Rosslyn (and his sister Kathleen). *Letters from Turkey: Being Glimpses of Macedonian Misery*. Nottingham: Henry B. Saxton, 1907.

Buxton, Noel. *Europe and the Turks*. London: John Murray, 1907.

Chéradame, André. *Douze ans de propagande en faveur des peuples Balkaniques*. Paris: Plon, 1913.

Engelhardt, E. "La question Macédonienne." *Revue Générale de Droit International Public* 12 (1905): 544–51, 636–44; 13 (1906), 29–40, 164–74.

"La situation en Macédoine—Le décret de réformes ottoman du 8 décembre 1902—Les réformes necessaires." *Revue Générale de Droit International Public* 10 (1903): 112–60.

Les questions actuelles de politique etrangère en Europe [Conférences organisés à la Société des Anciens Élèves de l'Ecole Libre des Sciences Politiques]. Paris: Alcan, 1907.

Pour l'Arménie et la Macédoine: Manifestations Franco-Anglo-Italiennes. Paris: Société Nouvelle de Librairie, 1904.

Routier, Gaston. *La question Macédonienne*. Paris: Librairie H. Le Soudier, 1903.

SOME PUBLICATIONS MENTIONING THE *PRO-MEMORIA LISTS*

Draganof. *Macedonia and the Reforms*. London: Hazell, Watson and Viney, 1908.

Focief, O. [alias Schopoff, Bulgarian commercial agent in Salonica]. *La justice Turque et les réformes en Macédoine: Aperçu sur leur histoire et leur organisation, leur fonctionnement et leur abus*. Paris: Plon, 1907.

Noirval, Gérard de. *Question Macédonienne et l'influence Française en Orient: Considérations sur le dernier "Livre Jaune."* Brussels: Société Belge de Librairie, 1903.

The Population of Macedonia: Evidence of the Christian Schools . . . Added to Which Is a List of the Greeks Killed at the Instance of the Bulgarian Committees in Macedonia, from 1897 to November 1904. London: Ede, Allom & Townsend, 1905.

Ruby, Jean. *La guerre d'Orient: Une race qu'on extermine. Témoignages et documents*. Np: nd.

The Tragedies of Macedonia: A Record of Greek Victims of Bulgarian Outrages in Macedonia between 1897 and February 1903. London: Ede, Allom & Townsend, 1903.

SECONDARY SOURCES

Nineteenth-Century European History (Including Imperialism and Foreign Policy)

Abbattista, Guido. "Empire, Liberty and the Rule of Difference: European Debates on British Colonialism in Asia at the End of the Eighteenth Century." *European Review of History—Revue Européenne d'Histoire* 13 (2006): 473–98.

Abbattista, Guido, and Rolando Minuti. *Le problème de l'Altérité dans la culture Européenne aux XVIIIe et XIXe siècles*. Naples: Bibliopolis, 2006.

Adelman, Paul. *Gladstone, Disraeli and Later Victorian Politics*. 3d ed. Harlow: Addison Wesley Longman, 1997.

Andrew, Donna T. *Philanthropy and Police: London Charity in the Eighteenth Century*. Princeton: Princeton University Press, 1989.

Arcidiacono, Bruno. "Les projets de réorganisation du système international au XIXe siècle (1871–1914)." *Relations Internationales* 123 (2005): 11–24.

———. "Pour une généalogie de la Charte des Nations Unies: la tradition directoriale." *Relations Internationales* 127 (2006): 5–23.

Ausubel, Herman. *John Bright, Victorian Reformer*. New York: Wiley, 1965.

Bayly, C. A. *Imperial Meridian. The British Empire and the World 1780–1830*. Harlow: Pearson Education, 1989.

Bebbington, D., and R. Swift. *Gladstone Centenary Essays*. Liverpool: Liverpool University Press, 2000.

Bell, Duncan, ed. *Victorian Visions of Global Order: Empire and International Relations in Nineteenth-Century Political Thought.* Cambridge: Cambridge University Press, 2007.

Bell, Herbert C. F. *Lord Palmerston.* 2 vols. London: Longman, 1936.

Bellamy, Richard, ed. *Victorian Liberalism.* Routledge: London, 1990.

Benot, Yves. *Les lumières, l'esclavage, la colonization: Textes réunis et présentés par Roland Desné et Macel Dorigny.* Paris: Editions La Découverte, 2005.

Bentley, Michael. *Lord Salisbury's World: Conservative Environments in Late-Victorian Britain.* Cambridge: Cambridge University Press, 2001.

Blake, Robert. *Disraeli.* New York: St. Martin's Press, 1967.

Billy, George J. *Palmerston's Foreign Policy: 1848,* New York: Peter Lang, 1993.

Bourne, Kenneth. *Palmerston. The Early Years. 1784–1841.* London, Allen Lane, 1982.

Briggs, Asa. *The Making of Modern England, 1784–1867: The Age of Improvement.* London: Harper Torchbook, 1965.

Buckle, George (in succession to W. F. Monypenny). *The Life of Benjamin Disraeli Earl of Beaconsfield,* vol. 4 (1855–68), vol. 5 (1868–76). London: Murray, 1916, 1920.

Burrow, J. W. *Whigs and Liberals: Continuity and Change in English Political Thought. The Carlyle Lectures 1985.* Oxford: Clarendon Press, 1985.

Byrne, Leo G. *The Great Ambassador: A Study of the Diplomatic Career of the Right Honourable Stratford Canning, K.G.: G.C.B., Viscount Stratford de Redcliffe, at the Epoch during Which He Served as the British Ambassador to the Sublime Porte of the Ottoman Sultan.* Columbus: Ohio State University Press, 1964.

Bull, Hedley, and Adam Watson. *The Expansion of International Society.* Oxford: Oxford University Press, 1985.

Cannadine, David. *Ornamentalism: How the British Saw Their Empire.* London: Penguin, 2002.

Chamberlain, Muriel E. *Lord Palmerston.* Cardiff: GPC, 1987.

Cecil, G. *Life of Robert, Marquis of Salisbury.* 4 vols. London: Hodder and Stoughton, 1921.

Colley, Linda. *Britons: Forging the Nation, 1707–1837.* 2d ed. London: Pimlico, 2003.

———. *Captives: Britain, Empire and the World 1600–1850.* London: Cape, 2002.

Collini, Stefan. *Public Moralists: Political Thought and Intellectual Life in Britain.* Oxford: Clarendon Press, 1991.

Collini, S., R. Whatmore, and B. Young, eds. *History, Religion, and Culture. British Intellectuals History 1750–1950.* Cambridge: Cambridge University Press, 2000.

Conklin, Alice. "Colonialism and Human Rights, a Contradiction in Terms? The Case of France and West Africa, 1895–1914." *American Historical Review* 103 (1998): 419–42.

———. *A Mission to Civilize: The Republican Idea of Empire in France and West Africa, 1895–1930.* Stanford: Stanford University Press, 1997.

Crossley, Ceri. *French Historians and Romanticism: Thierry, Guizot, the Saint-Simonians, Quinet, Michelet.* London: Routledge, 1993.

Cunningham, Hugh, and Joanna Innes. *Charity, Philanthropy, and Reform: From the 1690s to 1850.* New York: St. Martin's Press, 1998.

Davis, David Brion. *The Problem of Slavery in Western Culture*. Ithaca: Cornell University Press, 1966.

Ditchfield, Grayson M. *The Evangelical Revival*. London: UCL Press, 1998.

Driver, Felix. "Henry Morton Stanley and His Critics: Geography, Exploration and Empire." *Past and Present* 133 (1991): 134–66.

Echard, William E. *Napoleon III and the Concert of Europe*. Baton Rouge: Louisiana State University Press, 1983.

Elrod, Richard B. "The Concert of Europe: A Fresh Look at an International System." *World Politics* 28 (1976): 159–74.

Fink, Carol. *Defending the Rights of Others: The Great Powers, the Jews, and International Minority Protection, 1878–1938*. Cambridge: Cambridge University Press, 2004.

Fischer-Tiné, Harald, and Michael Mann, eds. *Colonialism as Civilizing Mission: Cultural Ideology in British India*. London: Anthen Press, 2004.

Fletcher, F.T.H. *Montesquieu and English Politics (1750–1800)*. Philadelphia: Porcupine Press, 1980 [1939].

Foot, M.R.D., and H.C.G. Matthew, eds. *The Gladstone Diaries*. 14 vols. Oxford: Clarendon Press, 1968–94.

Galbraith, John S. "Myths of the 'Little England' Era." *American Historical Review* 67 (1961): 34–48.

Ganiage, Jean. *L'expansion coloniale de la France sous la Troisième République (1871–1914)*. Paris: Payot, 1968.

Gong, Gerrit. *The Standard of "Civilization" in International Society*. Oxford: Clarendon Press, 1984.

Grenville, J.A.S. *Lord Salisbury and Foreign Policy: The Close of the Nineteenth Century*. London: Athlone Press, 1964.

Gueslin, André, and Dominique Kalifa. *Les exclus en Europe, 1830–1930*. Paris: Les Editions de l'Atelier, 1999.

Guillen, Pierre. *L'expansion 1881–1898*. Paris: Imprimerie nationale, 1984.

Hall, Catherine. *Civilising Subjects: Colony and Metropole in the English Imagination, 1830–1867*. Chicago: University of Chicago Press, 2002.

Hilton, Boyd. *The Age of Atonement: The Influence of Evangelicalism on Social and Economic Thought, 1795–1865*. Oxford: Clarendon Press, 1988.

Himmelfarb, Gertrude. *Victorian Minds: A Study of Intellectuals in Crisis and Ideologies in Transition*. Chicago: Elephant Paperbacks, 1995.

Holbraad, Carsten. *The Concert of Europe: A Study in German and British International Theory*. London: Longman, 1970.

Hollis, Patricia, ed. *Pressure from Without in Early Victorian England*. London: Arnold, 1974.

Hoppen, K. Theodore. *The Mid-Victorian Generation 1846–1886*. Oxford: Oxford University Press, 1998.

Howard, Christopher H. D. *Britain and the Casus Belli: A Study of Britain International Position from Canning to Salisbury*. London: Athlon Press, 1974.

Hyam, Ronald. *Britain's Imperail Century, 1815–1914*. 3d ed. Basingstoke: Palgrave, 2002.

Isser, Natalie. *The Second Empire and the Press: A Study of Government-Inspired Brochures on French Foreign Policy in Their Propaganda Milieu*. The Hague: Nijhoff, 1974.

Jackson-Preece, Jennifer. *National Minorities and the European Nation-States System*. Oxford: Clarendon Press, 1998.

Kennedy, Paul M. *The Realities Behind Diplomacy: Background Influences on British External Policy, 1865–1980*. London: Fontana Paperbacks, 1985.

Kingsley, Martin. *The Triumph of Lord Palmerston: A Study of Public Opinion in England before the Crimean War*. London: Hutchinson, 1963.

Kocabasoglu, U. "British Observations Regarding the Ottoman Empire in Nineteenth Century Periodicals." *Journal of Mediterranean Studies* 5 (1995): 247–58.

Koss, Stephen. *The Rise and Fall of the Political Press in Britain*, vol. 1: *The Nineteenth Century*. London: Hamish Hamilton, 1981.

Kostal, R. W. *A Jurisprudence of Power: Victorian Empire and the Rule of Law*. Oxford: Oxford University Press, 2008.

Levin, Michael. *J. S. Mill on Civilization and Barbarism*. Oxon: Routledge, 2004.

Lowe, C. J. *The Reluctant Imperialist: British Foreign Policy 1878–1902*. 2 vols. London: Routledge, 1967.

——— *Salisbury and the Mediterranean 1886–1896*. London: Routledge and Kegan Paul, 1965.

Lowe, Lisa. *Critical Terrains: French and British Orientalisms*. Ithaca: Cornell University Press, 1991.

Lyons, G. M., and M. Mastanduno, eds. *Beyond Westphalia? State Sovereignty and International Intervention*. Baltimore: Johns Hopkins University Press, 1995.

Makdisi, Saree. *Romantic Imperialism. Universal Empire and the Culture of Modernity*. Cambridge: Cambridge University Press, 1998.

Malchow, H. L. *Agitators and Promoters in the Age of Gladstone and Disraeli: A Biographical Dictionary of the Leaders of British Pressure Groups Founded between 1865 and 1886*. New York: Garland, 1983.

Mandler, Peter. *Aristocratic Government in the Age of Reform: Whigs and Liberals 1830–1852*. Oxford: Clarendon Press, 1990.

Matthew, H.C.G. *Gladstone 1809–1874*. Oxford: Clarendon Press, 1986.

———. *Gladstone 1875–1898*, Oxford: Clarendon Press, 1995.

Mazlish, Bruce. *Civilization and Its Contents*. Stanford: Stanford University Press, 2004.

Mazower, Mark. "An International Civilization? Empire, Internationalism and the Crisis of the Mid-Twentieth Century." *International Affairs* 82 (2006): 553–66.

Meyer, Jean, Jean Tarrade, Annie Rey-Goldzeiguer, and Jacques Tobie, eds. *Histoire de la France coloniale des origines à 1914*. Paris: Armand Colin, 1991.

Millman, Richard. *Britain and the Eastern Question, 1875–1878*. Oxford: Clarendon Press, 1979.

Muthu, Sankar. *Enlightenment Against Empire*. Princeton: Princeton University Press, 2003.

Owen, David Edward. *English Philanthropy, 1660–1960*. Cambridge: Belknap Press of Harvard University Press, 1964.

Padgen, Anthony. *European Encounters with the New World*. New Haven: Yale University Press, 1993.

———. *Lord of All the World: Ideologies of Empire in Spain, Britain and France c. 1500–1800*. New Haven: Yale University Press, 1995.

Parry, Jonathan P. *Democracy and Religion: Gladstone and the Liberal Party, 1867–1875*. Cambridge: Cambridge University Press, 1989.

Pécout, Gilles. *Penser les frontières de l'Europe*. Paris: Éditions Rue d'Ulm—PUF, 2003.

Philpott, Daniel. *Revolutions in Sovereignty: How Ideas Shaped Modern International Relations*. Princeton: Princeton University Press, 2001.

Pinto-Duschinsky, M. *The Political Thought of Lord Salisbury, 1854–68*. London: Constable, 1967.

Pitts, Jennifer. *A Turn to Empire: The Rise of Imperial Liberalism in Britain and France*. Princeton: Princeton University Press, 2005.

Porter, Andrew. "'Commerce and Christianity': The Rise and Fall of a Nineteenth-Century Missionary Slogan." *Historical Journal* 28 (1985): 579–621.

———. *Religion versus Empire? British Protestant Missionaries and Overseas Expansion, 1700–1914*. Manchester: Manchester University Press, 2004.

———. "Trusteeship, Anti-Slavery, and Humanitarianism." In *The Oxford History of the British Empire*, vol. 3: *The Nineteenth Century*, ed. Andrew Porter, 198–221. Oxford: Oxford University Press, 1999.

Porter, Roy. *Enlightenment: Britain and the Creation of the Modern World*. London: Penguin, 2001.

Prager, Carol A. L. "Intervention and Empire: John Stuart Mill and International Relations." *Political Studies* 53 (2005): 621–40.

Pratt, Michael. *Britain's Greek Empire: Reflections on the History of the Ionian Islands from the Fall of Byzantium*. London: Collings, 1978.

Read, Donald. *Cobden and Bright: A Victorian Political Partnership*. London: Edward Arnold, 1967.

Rendall, Matthew. "Restraint or Self-Restraint of Russia: Nicholas I, the Treaty of Unkiar Skelessi, and the Vienna System, 1832–1841." *International History Review* 24 (2002): 37–63.

Renton, James. "Changing Languages of Empire and the Orient: Britain and the Invention of the Middle East, 1917–1918." *Historical Journal* 50 (2007): 645–66.

Ridley, Jasper. *Lord Palmerston*. London: Constable, 1970.

Robbins, Keith. *Sir Edward Grey: A Biography of Lord Grey of Fallodon*. London: Cassell, 1971.

Roberts, David. *Paternalism in Early Victorian Britain*. New Brunswick: Rutgers University Press, 1979.

Roberts, J. M. *Europe 1880–1945*. 3d ed. London: Longman, 2001.

Ruggie, John. "Multilateralism: The Anatomy of an Institution." *International Organization* 46 (1992): 561–98.

Said, Edward W. *Orientalism. Western Conceptions of the Orient [with a New Afterword]*. London: Penguin Books, 1995.

Schroeder, Paul. W. *Austria, Great Britain, and the Crimean War: The Destruction of the European Concert*. Ithaca: Cornell University Press, 1972.

———. "Did the Vienna Settlement Rest on a Balance of Power?" *American Historical Review* 97 (1992): 683–706.

———. *The Transformation of European Politics 1763–1848*. Oxford: Oxford University Press, 1996.

Schultz, Bart, and Georgios Varouxakis. *Utilitarianism and Empire*. Oxford: Lexington Books, 2005.

Shannon, Richard. *Gladstone*. 2 vols. London. Hamish Hamilton, 1982; Penguin, 1999.

———. *God and Politics*. London: Hambledon Continuum, 2007.

Sherwood, Marika. *After Abolition. Britain and the Slave Trade since 1807*. London: I. B. Tauris, 2007.

Sigsworth, Eric. M. *In Search of Victorian Values. Aspects of Nineteenth-Century Thought and Society*. Manchester: Manchester University Press, 1988.

Singh Mehta, Uday. *Liberalism and Empire: A Study in Nineteenth-century British Liberal Thought*. Chicago: University of Chicago Press, 1999.

Skorupski, John, ed. *Cambridge Companion to Mill*. Cambridge: Cambridge University Press, 1998.

Steele, David. *Lord Salisbury: A Political Biography*. Routledge: London, 1999.

Stora, Benjamin. *Histoire de l'Algérie coloniale, 1830–1954*. Paris: Editions de la Découverte, 1991.

Swartz, Marvin. *The Politics of British Foreign Policy in the Era of Disraeli and Gladstone*. London: Macmillan, 1985.

Temperley, H.M.W. *A Century of Diplomatic Blue Books, 1814–1914*. Cambridge: Cambridge University Press, 1938.

———. *England and the Near East: The Crimea*. Hamden, CT: Archon Books, 1964.

———. *The Foreign Policy of Canning 1822–1827: England, the Neo-Holy Alliance, and the New World*. London: Frank Cass, 1966.

Thobie, Jacques. *Intérêts et impérialisme français dans l'Empire ottoman: 1895–1914*. Paris: Imprimerie nationale, 1977.

———. *La France et l'Est Méditerranéen depuis 1850: Economie, finance, diplomatie*. Istanbul: Editions Isis, 1993.

Thompson, F.M.L., ed. *The Cambridge Social History of Britain 1750–1950*, vol. 3. Cambridge: Cambridge University Press, 1990.

Varouxakis, Georgios. *Victorian Political Thought on France and the French*. Basingstoke: Palgrave, 2002.

Vital, David. *A People Apart: the Jews in Europe 1789–1939*. Oxford: Oxford University Press, 1999.

Webster, C. K. *The Foreign Policy of Castlereagh, 1812–1822*. London: G. Bell, 1925.

———. *The Foreign Policy of Palmerston, 1830–1841; Britain, the Liberal Movement, and the Eastern Question*. 2 vols. London: G. Bell, 1951.

Weil, Patrick, and Stéphane Dufoix, eds. *L'esclavage, la colonisation et après . . . France, Etats-Unis, Grande-Bretagne*. Paris: PUF, 2005.

Weitz, Eric D. "From the Vienna to the Paris System: International Politics and the Entangled Histories of Human Rights, Forced Deportations, and Civilizing Missions." *American Historical Review* 113 (2008): 1313–43.

Welsh, Jennifer M. *Edmund Burke and International Relations: The Commonwealth of Europe and the Crusade against the French Revolution*. Basingstoke: Macmillan, 1995.

Woolf, Stuart. "French Civilization and Ethnicity in the Napoleonic Empire." *Past and Present* 124 (1989): 96–120.

History of the Ottoman Empire (Including the Eastern Question)

Ageron, Charles-Robert. *Modern Algeria*, ed. and trans. Michael Brett. Trenton: Africa World Press, 1991.

Anderson, M. S. *The Eastern Question 1774–1923: A Study in International Relations*. London: Macmillan, 1966.

Barkey, Karen. *Empire of Difference: The Ottomans in Comparative Perspective.* New York: Cambridge University Press, 2008.

Baron, Salo W. "The Jewish Question in the Nineteenth Century." *Journal of Modern History* 10 (1938): 51–65.

Brett, Michael. "Legislating for Inequality in Algeria: The Senatus-Consulte of 14 July 1865." *Bulletin of the School of Oriental and African Studies, University of London* 51 (1988): 440–61.

Brown, L. Carl, ed. *Imperial Legacy: The Ottoman Imprint on the Balkans and the Middle East.* New York, Columbia University Press, 1996.

Cardini, Franco. *Europe and Islam*, trans. Caroline Beamish. Oxford: Blackwell, 2001.

Braude, Benjamin, and Bernard Lewis, eds. *Christians and Jews in the Ottoman Empire: The Functioning of a Plural Society.* Vol. 1: *The Central Lands.* London: Holmes & Meier, 1982.

Çırakman, Aslı. *From the "Terror of the World" to the Sick Man of Europe": European Images of Ottoman Empire and Society from the Sixteenth Century to the Nineteenth.* New York: Peter Lang, 2002.

Clayton, G. D. *Britain and the Eastern Question: Missolonghi to Gallipoli.* London: Lion Library, 1971.

Cohen, Lloyd A. "The Jewish Question during the Period of the Romanian National Renaissance and the Unification of the Two Principalities of Moldavia and Wallachia 1848–1866." In *Romania Between East and West. Historical Essays in Memory of Constantin C. Giurescu*, ed. Stephen Fischer-Galati, Radu R. Florescu, and George R. Ursul, 195–244. East European Monographs. New York: distributed by Columbia University Press, 1982.

Cunningham, Allan. *Eastern Questions in the Nineteenth Century: Collected Essays*, ed. Edward Ingram. 2 vols. London: Frank Cass, 1993.

Davison, Roderic. *Essays in Ottoman and Turkish History 1774–1923: The Impact of the West.* Austin: University of Texas Press, 1990

———. *Reform in the Ottoman Empire, 1856–1876.* Princeton: Princeton University Press, 1963.

Deringil, Selim. *The Well-Protected Domains: Ideology and the Legitimation of Power in the Ottoman Empire, 1876–1909.* London: I. B. Tauris, 1998.

Findley, Carter V. *Bureaucratic Reform in the Ottoman Empire: The Sublime Porte, 1789–1922.* Princeton: Princeton University Press, 1980.

———. *Ottoman Civil Officialdom: A Social History.* Princeton: Princeton University Press, 1989.

Dimakis, Jean. *P. Codrika et la question d'Orient sous l'Empire Français et la Restauration.* Paris: Edition Jean Maisonneuve et Presses de l'Université de Montréal, 1986.

Frémeaux, Jacques. *La France et l'Islam depuis 1789.* Paris: Presses Universitaires de France, 1991.

———. *Les bureaux arabes dans l'Algérie de la conquête.* Paris: Denoël, 1993.

Géorgeon, François. *Abdülhamid II: Le Sultan Calife (1876–1909).* Paris: Fayard, 2003.

Green, Molly. *A Shared World: Christians and Muslims in the Early Mediterranean World.* Princeton: Princeton University Press, 2000.

Hale, William. *Turkish Foreign Policy: 1774–2000.* London: Frank Cass, 2000.

Hentsh, Thierry. *L'Orient imaginaire: La vision politique Occidentale de l'Est Méditerranéen.* Paris: Les Editions de Minuit, 1988.

Holland, T. E. *The European Concert in the Eastern Question: A Collection of Treaties and Other Public Acts.* Aalen: Scientia Verlag, 1979.

Inalcik, Halil, and Donald Quataert. *An Economic History of the Ottoman Empire 1300–1914.* Cambridge: University Press, 1994.

Jelavich, Barbara. *Russia's Balkan Entanglements, 1806–1914.* Cambridge: Cambridge University Press, 1991.

Joubin, Rebecca. "Islam and Arabs through the Eyes of the Encyclopédie: The 'Other' as a Case of French Cultural Self-Criticism." *International Journal of Middle East Studies* 32 (2000): 197–217.

Karpat, Kemal. *Ottoman Population 1830–1914: Demographic and Social Characteristics.* Madison: University of Wisconsin Press, 1985.

Kent, Marian, ed. *The Great Powers and the End of the Ottoman Empire.* London: Frank Cass, 1995.

Laurens, Henry. *Le rouyaume impossible: La France et la genèse du monde Arabe.* Paris: Armand Colin, 1990.

Levy, Avigdor, ed. *The Jews of the Ottoman Empire.* Princeton: Darwin Press, 1999.

Lewis, Bernard. *The Emergence of Modern Turkey.* 3d ed. Oxford: Oxford University Press, 2002.

———. *What Went Wrong? Western Impact and Middle Eastern Response.* London: Phoenix Paperback, 2002.

Lorcin, Patricia M. E. *Imperial Identities. Stereotyping, Prejudice and Race in Colonial Algeria.* London: I. B. Tauris, 1999.

Mantran, Robert, ed. *Histoire de l'Empire Ottoman.* Paris: Fayard, 1989.

Marshall P. J., and Glyndwr Williams. *The Great Map of Mankind. British Perceptions of the World in the Age of Enlightenment.* London: J. M. Dent, 1982.

McCarthy, Justin. *Death and Exile: The Ethnic Cleansing of Ottoman Muslims, 1821–1922.* Princeton: Darwin Press, 1995.

———. *Muslims and Minorities: The Population of Ottoman Anatolia and the End of the Empire.* New York: New York University Press, 1983.

Papadopoulos, G. S. *England and the Near East 1896–1898.* Thessaloniki: Institute for Balkan Studies, 1969.

Pamuk, Şevket. *The Ottoman Empire and European Capitalism, 1820–1913: Trade, Investment, and Production.* Cambridge: Cambridge University Press, 1987.

Pavlowitch, Stevan K. *A History of the Balkans 1804–1945.* London: Longman, 1999.

Pedersen, Susan. "The Meaning of the Mandates System: An Argument." *Geschichte und Gesellschaft* 32 (2006): 560–82.

———. "Review Essay: Back to the League of Nations." *American Historical Review* 112 (2007): 1091–1117.

Quataert, Donald. "Ottoman History Writing and Changing Attitudes towards the Notion of 'Decline.'" *History Compass* 1 (2003): 1–9.

———. *Social Disintegration and Popular Resistance in the Ottoman Empire: 1881–1908; Reactions to European Economic Penetration.* New York: New York University Press, 1983.

Rich, Paul. "European Identity and the Myth of Islam: A Reassessment." *Review of International Studies* 25 (1999): 435–51.

Roux, F. Charles. *France et Chrétiens d-Orient.* Paris: Flammarion, 1939.

Seton-Watson, R. W. *Disraeli, Gladstone, and the Eastern Question: A Study in Diplomacy and Party Politics.* New York: Norton, 1972.

Shorrock, William I. "Anti-Clericalism and French Policy in the Ottoman Empire, 1900–1914." *European Studies Review* 4 (1974): 33–55.

———. "Prelude to Empire: French Balkan Policy, 1878–1881." *Eastern European Quarterly* 16 (1982): 345–62.

Thomson, Ann. *Barbary and Enlightenment: European Attitudes towards the Maghreb in the 18th Century.* Leiden: Brill, 1987.

Todorova, Maria. *Imagining the Balkans.* New York: Oxford University Press, 1997.

Weiker, Walter F. *Ottoman Turks and the Jewish Policy: A History of the Jews of Turkey.* New York: University Press of America, 1992.

Wheatcroft, Andrew. *Infidels: A History of the Conflict between Christendom and Islam.* London: Penguin, 2004.

Yapp, M. E. "Europe in the Turkish Mirror." *Past and Present* 137 (1992): 134–55.

The Capitulations

Benoît, A. *Etude sur les Capitulations entre l'Empire Ottoman et la France et sur la réforme judiciaire en Egypte.* Paris: A. Rousseau, 1890.

Brunswik, Benoît. *Etudes pratiques sur la question d'Orient, les réformes et les Capitulations.* Paris, 1869.

Gavillot, J.C.A. *Essai sur les droits des Européens en Turquie et en Egypte. Les Capitulations et la réforme judiciaire.* Paris: E. Dentu, 1875.

Sousa, Nasim. *The Capitulatory Regime of Turkey: Its History, Origin, and Nature.* Baltimore: Johns Hopkins University Press, 1933.

van den Boogert, Maurits H. *The Capitulations and the Ottoman Legal System: Qadis, Consuls, and Beraths in the 18th Century.* Leiden: Brill, 2005.

van den Boogert, Maurits H., and Kate Fleet, ed. *The Ottoman Capitulations: Text and Context.* Rome: Istituto per l'Oriente C. A. Nallino, 2003.

History of Massacre, Extermination, Genocide, and Ethnic Cleansing

Andreopoulos, George J., ed. *Genocide: Conceptual and Historical Dimensions.* Philadelphia: University of Pennsylvania Press, 2004.

Bell-Fialkoff, Andrew. "A Brief History of Ethnic Cleansing." *Foreign Affairs* (Summer 1993): 110–23.

Brantlinger, Patrick. *Dark Vanishing: Discourse on the Extinction of Primitive Races, 1800–1930.* Ithaca: Cornell University Press, 2003.

Brown, Christopher Leslie. *Moral Capital: Foundations of British Abolitionism.* Chapel Hill: University of North Carolina Press, 2006.

Boustany, K., and D. Dormoy, eds. *Génocide(s)*. Brussels: Bruyant, 1999.

Carlton, Eric. *Massacres: An Historical Perspective*. Aldershot: Hants Scolar Press, 1994.

Chalk Frank, and Kurt Jonassohn. *The History and Sociology of Genocide*. New Haven: Yale University Press, 1990.

Currat, Philippe. *Les crimes contre l'humanité dans le Statut de la Cour pénale internationale*. Brussels: Bruylant, 2006.

Donnelly, Jack. "Human Rights: A New Standard of Civilization?" *International Affairs* 74 (1998): 1–24.

Ellingson, Ter. *The Myth of the Noble Savage*. Berkeley: University of California Press, 2001.

Gellately, R., and B. Kiernan, eds. *The Spectre of Genocide: Mass Murder in Historical Perspective*. Cambridge: Cambridge University Press, 2003.

Kaufmann, Chaim D., and Robert A. Pape. "Explaining Costly International Moral Action: Britain's Sixty-Year Campaign against the Atlantic Slave Trade." *International Organization* 53 (1999): 631–68.

Kent, David El, ed. *Le massacre, objet d'histoire*. Paris: Gallimard, 2005.

Levene, Mark. "Creating a Modern 'Zone of Genocide': The Impact of Nation- and State-Formation on Eastern Anatolia, 1878–1923." *Holocaust and Genocide Studies* 12 (1998): 393–433.

———. *The Meaning of Genocide*. 2 vols. London: I. B. Tauris, 2005.

Lieberman, Benjamin. *Terrible Fate: Ethnic Cleansing in the Making of Modern Europe*. Chicago: Ivan R. Dee, 2006.

Madley, Benjamin. "Patterns of Frontier Genocide 1803–1910: The Aboriginal Tasmanians, the Yuki of California, and the Herero of Namibia." *Journal of Genocide Research* 6 (2004): 167–92.

Mann, Michael. *The Dark Side of Democracy: Explaining Ethnic Cleansing*. Cambridge: Cambridge University Press, 2005.

Moses, A. Dirk, ed. *Genocide and Settler Society: Frontier Violence and Stolen Indigenous Children in Australian History*. Oxford: Berghahn Books, 2004.

Moses, A. Dirk, and Dan Stone, eds. *Colonialism and Genocide*. Abingdon: Routledge, 2006.

Naimark, Norman. *Fires of Hatred: Ethnic Cleansing in Twentieth-Century Europe*. Cambridge: Harvard University Press, 2001.

Plomley, Norman J. B. *The Aboriginal/Settler Clash in Van Diemen's Land: 1803–1831*. Hobart: University of Tasmania, 1992.

Robertson, Geoffrey. *Crimes Against Humanity: The Struggle for Global Justice*. 2d ed. London: Penguin, 2002.

Roulot, Jean-François. *Le crime contre l'humanité*. Paris: L'Harmattan, 2002.

Sémelin, Jacques. *Purify and Destroy: The Political Uses of Massacre and Genocide*, trans. Cyntia Schoch. New York: Columbia University Press, 2007.

Sepinwall, Alyssa Goldstein. *The Abbé Grégoire and the French Revolution: The Making of Modern Universalism*. Berkeley: University of California Press, 2005.

Shaw, Martin. *What Is Genocide?* Cambridge: Polity Press, 2007.

Temperley, Howard. "Anti-Slavery." In *Pressure from Without in Early Victorian England*, ed. Patricia Hollis, 27–51. London: Arnold, 1974.

Ternon, Yves. *L'État criminel. Les genocides au XXème siècle*. Paris: Le Seuil, 2005.

———. *Guerre et genocides au XXème siècle*. Paris: Odile Jacob, 2007.

Walliman, Isador, and Michael N. Dobkowski, eds. *Genocide and the Modern Age: Etiology and Case Studies of Mass Death*. Syracuse: Syracuse University Press, 2000.

Greece and Crete

Athanassoglou-Kallmyer, Nina. *French Images from the Greek War of Independence 1821–1830: Art and Politics under the Restoration*. New Haven: Yale University Press, 1989.

Bourne, Kenneth. "Great Britain and the Cretan Revolt, 1866–1869." *Slavonic and East European Review* 35 (1956–57): 74–94.

Brewer, David. *The Flame of Freedom: The Greek War of Independence, 1821–1833*. London: John Murray, 2003.

Crawley, C. W. *The Question of Greek Independence: A Study of British Policy in the Near East 1821–1833* [reprint of the 1930 edition with a new preface by the author]. New York: H. Fertig, 1973.

Dakin, Douglas. *The Greek Struggle for Independence 1821–1833*. Berkeley: University of California Press, 1973.

Derry, J. W. *Castlereagh*. London: A. Lane, 1976.

Dimakis, Jean. *La guerre de L'indépendance Grecque vue par la presse Française (période de 1821 à 1824): Contribution à l'étude de l'opinion publique et du mouvement philhellénique en France*. Salonica: Institute for Balkan Studies, 1968.

Ganiage, Jean. "Les affaires de Crète (1895–1899)." *Revue d'Histoire Diplomatique* 88 (1974): 86–111.

Holland, Robert, and Diana Markides. *The British and the Hellenes: Struggles for Mastery in the Eastern Mediterranean 1850–1960*. Oxford: Oxford University Press, 2006.

Iseminger, Gordon L. "The Old Turkish Hands: The British Levantine Consuls, 1856–76." *Middle East Journal* 22 (1968): 297–316.

Lloyd, C. *Lord Cochrane: Seaman-Radical-Liberator. A Life of Thomas, Lord Cochrane 10th Earl of Dundonald*. London: Longman, 1947.

Long, Helen. *Greek Fire: The Massacre of Chios*. Bristol: Abson, 1992.

Marcopopoulos, G. J. "The Selection of Prince George of Greece as High Commissioner in Crete." *Balkan Studies* 10 (1969): 335–50.

Purvanova, Zorka. "Changes in the Political Status of the Island of Crete 1894–1899." *Etudes Balkaniques* 25 (1989): 64–84.

Puryear, Vernon John. *France and the Levant: From the Bourbon Restoration to the Peace of Kutiah*. Berkeley: University of California Press, 1941.

Robson, Maureen M. "Lord Clarendon and the Cretan Question, 1868–9." *Historical Journal* 3 (1960): 38–55.

Rosen, Frederick. *Bentham, Byron, and Greece: Constitutionalism, Nationalism, and Early Liberal Political Thought*. Oxford: Clarendon Press, 1992.

Saab, Ann Pottinger. "The Doctor's Dilemma: Britain and the Cretan Crisis, 1866–69." *Journal of Modern History* 49 (On Demand Supplement, December).

St. Clair, W. *That Greece Might Still Be Free: The Philhellenes in the War of Independence*. London: Oxford University Press, 1972.

Stivachtis, Yannis. *The Enlargement of International Society: Culture versus Anarchy and Greece's Entry into International Society*. New York: St. Martin's Press, 1998.

Temperley, H.W.V. *The Foreign Policy of Canning 1822–1827*. Hamden: Archon Book, 1966.

Woodhouse, Christopher M. *The Battle of Navarino*. London: Hodder and Stoughton, 1965.

Ottoman Syria and Lebanon

Arboit, Gérald. *Aux sources de la politique Arabe de la France: Le Second Empire au Machrek*. Paris: L'Harmattan, 2000.

Chevallier, Dominique. *La Société du Mont Liban à l'epoque de la révolution industrielle en Europe*. Paris: Geunther, 1971.

David, Renée. *Lamartine: La politique et l'histoire*. Paris: Imprimerie nationale, 1993.

Dib, Pierre. *L'Eglise Maronite*. 2 vols. Beirut: L'Imprimerie Catholique, 1962.

Farah, Caesar E. *The Politics of Interventionism in Ottoman Lebanon, 1830–1861*. London: I. B. Tauris, 2000.

———. "Protestantism and British Diplomacy in Syria." *International Journal of Middle East Studies* 7 (1976): 321–44.

Fawaz, Leila Tarazi. *An Occasion for War: Civil Conflict in Lebanon and Damascus in 1860*. Berkeley: University of California Press, 1994.

Forcade, Olivier. "Les premières expériences militaires françaises de l'humanitaire sous le Second Empire: Le moment originel de l'expédition française de Syrie en 1860–61." *Quatrième Journe Guerre et Médecine—12 mai 2007—Paris* (2007): 1–8.

Forcade, Olivier, and Frédéric Guelton. "L'expédition en Syrie en août 1860–juin 1861." *Revue Internationale d'Histoire Militaires* 75 (1995): 49–62.

Frankel, Jonathan. *The Damascus Affair: "Ritual Murder," Politics, and the Jews in 1840*. Cambridge: Cambridge University Press, 1997.

Issawi, Charles. "British Trade and the Rise of Beirut, 1830–1860." *International Journal of Middle East Studies* 8 (1977): 91–101.

Makdisi, Ussama. *The Culture of Sectarianism: Community, History, and Violence in Nineteenth-Century Ottoman Lebanon*. Berkeley: University of California Press, 2000.

Mange, Alyce E. *The Near Eastern Policy of the Emperor Napoleon III*. Westport, CT: Greenwood Press, 1975.

Masters, Bruce. *Christians and Jews in the Ottoman Arab World: The Roots of Sectarianism*. Cambridge: Cambridge University Press, 2001.

The Missionary Herald: Reports from Ottoman Syria, 1819–1870. 5 vols. Amman: Royal Institute for Inter-Faith Studies, 1995.

Shorrock, William I. *French Imperialism in the Middle East: The Failure of Policy in Syria and Lebanon 1900–1914*. Madison: University of Wisconsin Press, 1976.

Spagnolo, John P. *France & Ottoman Lebanon 1861–1914*. Published for the Middle East Centre, St. Antony's College, Oxford. London: Ithaca Press, 1977.

Tibawi, A. L. *American Interests in Syria 1800–1901: A Study of Educational, Literary and Religious Work*. Oxford: Clarendon Press, 1966.

Bulgarian Atrocities and the Eastern Crisis (1875–78)

Baron, Salo W. "The Jewish Question in the Nineteenth Century." *Journal of Modern History* 10 (1938): 51–65.

Cohen, Lloyd A. "The Jewish Question during the Period of the Romanian National Renaissance and the Unification of the Two Principalities of Moldavia and Wallachia 1848–1866." In *Romania Between East and West: Historical Essays in Memory of Constantin C. Giurescu*, ed. Stephen Fischer-Galati, Radu R. Florescu, and George R. Ursul, 195–244. East European Monographs. New York: distributed by Columbia University Press, 1982.

Damianov, Simeon. "The Great Powers and the Eastern Crisis of 1875–1876." *Southeastern Europe* 4 (1977): 201–16.

Harris, David. *Britain and the Bulgarian Horrors of 1876*. Chicago: University of Chicago Press, 1939.

Lee, Dwight E. *Great Britain and the Cyprus Convention Policy of 1878*. Cambridge: Harvard University Press, 1934.

Matikainen, Satu. "Great Britain, British Jews, and the International Protection of Romanian Jews, 1900–1914. A Study of Jewish Diplomacy and Minority Rights." Doctoral thesis, Jyväskylä Studies in Humanities 56 (2006).

Medlicott, W. N. *The Congress of Berlin and After: A Diplomatic History of the Near Eastern Settlement 1878–1880*. London: Frank Cass, 1963.

Rey, Francis. "La Question Israélite en Roumanie." *Revue Générale de Droit International Public* 10 (1903): 460–526.

Saab, Ann Pottinger. *Reluctant Icon: Gladstone, Bulgaria, and the Working Classes, 1856–1878*. Cambridge: Harvard University Press, 1991.

Shannon, Richard. *Gladstone and the Bulgarian Agitation*. London: Nelson, 1963.

Temperley, H.W.V. *The Bulgarian and Other Atrocities, 1875–8, in the Light of Historical Criticism*. London: H. Milford, 1931.

Ottoman Armenians

Balakian, Peter. *The Burning Tigris: A History of the Armenian Genocide*. London: Pimlico, 2005.

Bloxham, Donald. *The Great Game of Genocide: Imperialism, Nationalism, and the Destruction of the Ottoman Empire*. Oxford: Oxford University Press, 2005.

Courtois, Sébastien de. *Le génocide oublié. Chrétiens d'Orient, les derniers Araméens*. Paris: Ellipses, 2002.

Dadrian, Vahakn N. *The History of the Armenian Genocide: Ethnic Conflict from the Balkans to Anatolia to the Caucasus*. Oxford: Berghahn Books, 1995.

Douglas, Roy. "Britain and the Armenian Question, 1894–7." *Historical Journal* 19 (1976): 113–33.

Hovannisian, Richard G., ed. *The Armenian Genocide: History, Politics, Ethics*. London: Macmillan, 1992.

———. *The Armenian Genocide in Perspective*. New Brunswick: Transaction Books, 1986.

———. *The Armenian People from Ancient Times to Modern Times*. Vol. 2: *Foreign Domination to Statehood: The Fifteenth to the Twentieth Century*. London: Macmillan, 1997.

Kévorkian, Raymond. *Les Arméniens dans l'Empire Ottoman à la veille du génocide*. Paris: Arhis, 1992.

———, ed. *La Cilicie (1909–1921) des massacres d'Adana au mandat Français*. Special issue of *Revue d'Histoire Arménienne Contemporaine* 3 (1999).

Kieser, Hans-Lukas. *Der verpasste Friede. Mission, Ethnie und Staat in den Ost-provinzen der Türkei 1839–1938.* Zurich: Chronos, 2000.

Kirakossian, Arman J. *British Diplomacy and the Armenian Question, from the 1830s to 1914.* Princeton: Gomidas Institute Books, 2003.

Marsh, Paul. "Lord Salisbury and the Ottoman Massacres." *Journal of British Studies* 11 (1972): 63–83.

Melson, Robert. *Revolution and Genocide: On the Origins of the Armenian Geno-cide and the Holocaust.* Chicago: University of Chicago Press, 1992.

Minassian, A. Ter. *La question Arménienne.* Roquevaire: Parenthèse, 1983.

Sanjian, Avedis K. *The Armenian Communities in Syria under Ottoman Dominion.* Cambridge: Harvard University Press, 1965.

Sarkissian, Arshag O. *History of the Armenian Question to 1885.* Urbana: Univer-sity of Illinois Press, 1938.

Somakian, Manoug J. *Empires in Conflict: Armenia and the Great Powers, 1895–1920.* London: I. B. Tauris, 1995.

Ternon, Yves. *Les Arméniens: Histoire d'un génocide.* Paris: Le Seuil, 1996.

Wilson, Ann Marie. "In the Name of God, Civilization, and Humanity: The United States and the Armenian Massacres of the 1890s." *Le Mouvement Social* 227 (2009): 27–44.

Zeidner, Robert. "Britain and the Launching of the Armenian Question." *Inter-national Journal of Middle East Studies* 7 (1976): 465–83.

Macedonian Provinces of the Ottoman Empire

Aarbakke, Vemund. *Ethnic Rivalry and the Quest for Macedonia 1870–1913.* East European Monographs. New York: distributed by Columbia University Press, 2003.

Bonnefoi, Nadine. "*Le Temps* (1903–1913) et *Le Monde* (1990–1993): Miroirs d'une crise balkanique et européenne." *Guerres Mondiales et Conflits Contem-porains* 184 (1996): 15–28.

Dakin, Douglas. *The Greek Struggle in Macedonia 1897–1913.* Salonica: Institute for Balkan Studies, 1966.

Damianoc, Simeon. "Aspects économiques de la politique française dans les Balkans au début du XXe siècle." *Etudes Balkaniques* 4 (1974): 8–26.

———. "La diplomatie française et les réformes en Turquie d'Europe (1895–1903)." *Etudes Balkaniques* 2–3 (1974): 130–53.

Lange-Akhund, Nadine. *The Macedonian Question, 1893–1908 from Western Sources.* East European Monographs. New York: distributed by Columbia University Press, 1998.

Leo, Michel. *La Bulgarie et son peuple sous la domination ottoman: Tels que les ont vus les voyageurs Anglo-Saxons. Découverte d'une nationalité.* Paris: Edition d'Etat "Science et Art," 1949.

Mazower, Mark. *Salonika—City of Ghosts: Christians, Muslims and Jews 1430–1950.* London: HarperCollins, 2005.

Ortakovski, Vladimir. *Minorities in the Balkans.* New York: Transnational, 2000.

Roudometof, Victor, ed. *The Macedonian Question: Culture, Historiography, Politics.* East European Monographs. New York: distributed by Columbia University Press, 2000.

Toumarkine, Alexandre. *Les migrations des populations musulmanes balkaniques en Anatolie (1876–1913)*. Istanbul: Les Editions Isis, 1995.

U.S. War against Spain

Clymer, Kenton J. "Humanitarian Imperialism: David Prescott Barrows and the White Man's Burden in the Philipinnes." *Pacific Historical Review* 45 (1976): 495–517.

Coletta, Paolo E. "McKinley, the Peace Negotiations, and the Acquisition of the Philippines." *Pacific Historical Review* 30 (1961): 341–50.

Kramer, Paul A. *The Blood of Government. Race, Empire, the United States, & the Philippines*. Chapel Hill: University of North Carolina Press, 2006.

Lasch, Christopher. "The Anti-Imperialist, the Philippines, and the Inequality of Man." *Journal of Southern History* 24 (1958): 319–31.

Martin, Charles E. *The Policy of the United States as Regards Intervention*. New York: AMS Press, 1967.

Paterson, Thomas G. "United States Intervention in Cuba, 1898: Interpretations of the Spanish-American-Cuban-Filipino War." *History Teacher* 29 (1996): 341–61.

Tone, John Lawrence. *War and Genocide in Cuba, 1895–1898*. Chapel Hill: University of North Carolina Press, 2006.

Boer War (Pro-Boer Movement in Great Britain)

Auld, John W. "The Liberal Pro-Boers." *Journal of British Studies* 14 (1975): 78–101.

Haisan, Marouf. "The 'Histerical' Emily Hobhouse and Boer War Concentration Camp Controversy." *Western Journal of Communication* (2003): 138–63.

Hirshfield, Claire. "Liberal Women's Organizations and the War against the Boers, 1899–1902." *Albion: A Quarterly Journal Cncerned with British Studies* 14 (1982): 27–49.

Judd, Dennis, and Keith Surridge. *The Boer War*. New York: Palgrave Macmillan, 2003.

Krebs, Paula M. "The Last of the Gentlemen's Wars: Women in the Boer War Concentration Camp Controversy," *History Workshop* 33 (1992): 38–56.

Searle, G. R. *A New England? Peace and War 1886–1918*. Oxford: Clarendon Press, 2004.

Thompson, Andrew S. "The Language of Imperialism and the Meanings of Empire: Imperial Discourse in British Politics, 1895–1914." *Journal of British Studies* 36 (1997): 147–77.

Intervention in Leopold's Congo

Cline, Catherine Ann. "The Church and the Movement for Congo Reform." *Church History* 32 (1963): 46–56.

———. "E. D. Morel and the Crusade against the Foreign Office." *Journal of Modern History* 39 (1967): 126–37.

Cookey, S.J.S. *Britain and the Congo Question 1885–1913*. New York: Humanities Press, 1968.

Ewans, Martin *European Atrocity, African Catastrophe: Leopold II, the Congo Free State and its Aftermath*. London: Routledge, 2002.

Grant, Kevin. *A Civilised Savagery: Britain and the New Slaveries in Africa, 1884–1926*. New York: Routledge, 2005.

Hochschild, Adam. *King Leopold's Ghost: A Story of Greed, Terror, and Heroism in Colonial Africa*. Boston: Houghton Mifflin, 1998.

Louis, W. R. "Roger Casement and the Congo." *Journal of African History* 5 (1964): 99–120.

Pavlakis, Dean. "The Development of British Overseas Humanitarianism and the Congo Reform Campaign." *Journal of Colonialism and Colonial History* 11 (2010).

Stengers, Roger Louis and Jean, eds. *E.D. Morel's History of the Congo Reform Movement*. Oxford: Clarendon, 1968.

International Law

Angie, Anthony. "Finding the Peripheries: Sovereignty and Colonialism in the Nineteenth Century." *Harvard International Law Journal* 40 (1999): 1–80.

———. *Imperialism, Sovereignty and the Making of International Law*. Cambridge, Cambridge University Press, 2005.

Chesterman, Simon. *Just War or Just Peace? Humanitarian Intervention and International Law*. Oxford: Oxford University Press, 2001.

Dupuy, René-Jean. *L'humanité dans l'imaginaire des nations: Conférences essais et leçons du College de France*. Paris: Julliard, 1991.

Grewe, Wilhem G. *The Epochs of International Law*, trans. and rev. Michael Byers. Berlin: Walter de Gruyter, 2000.

Koskenniemi, Martti. *The Gentle Civilizer of Nations: The Rise and Fall of International Law 1870–1960*. Cambridge: Cambridge University Press, 2001.

Orakhelanshvili, Alexander. "The Idea of European International Law." *European Journal of International Law* 17 (2006): 315–47.

Schabas, William A. *Genocide in International Law*. Cambridge: Cambridge University Press, 2000.

Scupin, Hans-Ulrich. "History of the Law of Nations: 1815 to World War I." In *Encyclopaedia of Public International Law*, vol. 2, ed. R. Bernhardt, 767–93. Amsterdam: Elsevier, 2000.

Steiger, Heinhard. "From the International Law of Christianity to the International Law of the World Citizen—Reflections on the Formation of the Epochs of the History of International Law." *Journal of the History of International Law* 3 (2001): 180–93.

Sylvest, Caspet. "International Law in Nineteenth-Century Britain." *British Yearbook of International Law* (2005): 9–70.

Winfield, Percy H. "The History of Intervention in International Law." *British Yearbook of International Law* 3 (1922–23): 130–49.

Twentieth-Century Humanitarian Intervention

Abiew, Francis K. *The Evolution of the Doctrine and Practice of Humanitarian Intervention*. The Hague: Kluwer Law International, 1999.

Akehurst, Michael. "Humanitarian Intervention." In *Intervention in World Politics*, ed. Hedley Bull, 95–118. Oxford: Clarendon Press, 1984.

Annan, Kofi. *"We the Peoples": The Role of the United Nations in the 21st Century, Millennium Report of the Secretary-General of the United Nations*. 2000. http://www.un.org/millennium/sg/report/.

Archibugi, Daniele. "Cosmopolitan Guidelines for Humanitarian Intervention." *Alternatives. Global, Local, Political* 29 (2004): 1–21.

Armstrong, David, Theo Farell, and Bice Maiguashca, eds. *Force and Legitimacy in World Politics*. Cambridge: Cambridge University Press, 2005.

Barnett, M., and T. Weiss, eds. *Humanitarianism in Question*. Cornell: Cornell University Press, 2008.

Bass, Gary J. "Jus Post Bellum." *Philosophy & Public Affairs* 32 (2004): 384–413.

Boisson de Chazournes, Laurence, and Luigi Condorelli. "De la eesponsabilité de protéger ou d'une nouvelle parure pour une notion déjà bien étabie." *Revue Générale de Droit International Public* 110 (2006): 11–18.

Buergenthal, Thomas. "The Evolving International Human Rights System." *American Journal of International Law* 100 (2006): 783–807.

Bull, Hedley, ed. *Intervention in World Politics*. Oxford: Clarendon Press, 1984.

Cassese, Antonio. "Ex Iniuria Ius Oritur: Are We Moving towards International Legitimation of Forcible Humanitarian Countermeasures in the World Community?" *European Journal of International Law* 10 (1999): 23–30.

———. "A Follow-up: Forcible Humanitarian Countermeasures and Opinio Necessitatis." *European Journal of International Law* 10 (2000): 791–800.

Chandler, David. *From Kosovo to Kabul: Human Rights and International Intervention*. London: Pluto Press, 2002.

Chatterjee, Deen K., and Don E. Scheid, eds. *Ethics and Foreign Intervention*. Cambridge: Cambridge University Press, 2003.

Chomsky, Noam. *A New Generation Draws the Line: Kosovo, East Timor and the Lessons of the West*. New York: Verso, 2000.

———. *The New Military Humanism: Lessons from Kosovo*. Monroe: Common Courage, 1999.

Coady, C.A.J. *The Ethics of Armed Humanitarian Intervention*. Peaceworks no. 45. Washington, DC: United States Institute of Peace, 2002

Crawford, Timothy W., and Alan J. Kuperman, eds. *Gambling on Humanitarian Intervention*. London: Routledge, 2006.

Daalder, Ivo H., ed. *Beyond Preemption: Force and Legitimacy in a Changing World*. Washington, DC: Brookings Institution Press, 2007.

Danish Institution of International Affairs (DUPI). *Humanitarian Intervention: Legal and Political Aspects*. Copenaghen: DUPI, 1999.

Davis, Michael C., Wolfgang Dietrich, Bettina Scholdan, and Dieter Sepp, eds. *International Intervention in the Post–Cold War World*. London: M. E. Sharpe, 2004.

Devetak, Richard. "Between Kant and Pufendorf: Humanitarian Intervention, Statist Anti-Cosmopolitanism and Critical International Theory." *Review of International Studies* 33 (2007): 151–72.

Donnelly, Jack. "Human Rights: A New Standard of Civilization?" *International Affairs* 74 (1998): 1–24.

———. *Universal Human Rights in Theory and Practice*, 2d ed. Ithaca: Cornell University Press, 2003.

Evans, Gareth. *The Responsibility to Protect: Ending Mass Atrocity Crimes Once and for All*. Washington, DC: Brookings Institution Press, 2008.

Farer, Tom J., et al. "Roundtable: Humanitarian Intervention after 9/11." *International Relations* 19 (2005): 211–50.

Finnemore, Martha. "Constructing Norms of Humanitarian Intervention." In *The Culture of National Security: Norms and Identity in World Politics*, ed. Peter J. Katzenstein. New York: Columbia University Press, 1995.

———. *The Purpose of Intervention: Changing Beliefs about the Use of Force*. Ithaca: Cornell University Press, 2003.

Franck, Thomas M. "Lessons of Kosovo." *American Journal of International Law* 93 (1999): 857–59.

Franck, Thomas M., and Nigel S. Rodley. "After Bangladesh: The Law of Humanitarian Intervention by Military Force." *American Journal of International Law* 67 (1973): 275–305.

Frost, Mervyn. "The Ethics of Humanitarian Intervention: Protecting Civilians to Make Democratic Citizenship Possible." In *Ethics and Foreign Policy*, ed. Karen E. Smith and Margot Light, 33–54. Cambridge: Cambridge University Press, 2001.

Garrett, Stephen A. *Doing Good and Doing Well: An Examination of Humanitarian Intervention*. Westport, CT: Praeger, 1999.

Goodman, Ryan. "Humanitarian Intervention and Pretexts for War." *American Journal of International Law* 100 (2006): 107–41.

Hamilton, Rebecca J. "The Responsibility to Protect: From Document to Doctrine—but What of Implementation?" *Harvard Human Rights Journal* 19 (2006): 289–97.

Harriss, J., ed. *Politics of Humanitarian Intervention*. London: Pinter, 1995.

Helman, Gerald B., and Steven R. Ratner. "Saving Failed States." *Foreign Policy* 89 (1992–93): 3–20.

Henkin, Louis. "Kosovo and the Law of 'Humanitarian Intervention.'" *American Journal of International Law* 93 (1999): 824–28.

Hoffmann, Stanley. *The Ethics and Politics of Humanitarian Intervention*. Notre Dame: Notre Dame University Press, 1996.

———. *World Disorders: Troubled Peace in the Post–Cold War Era*. Lanham, MD: Rowman and Littlefield, 1998.

Holzgrefe, J. L., and Robert O. Keohane, eds. *Humanitarian Intervention: Ethical, Legal, and Political Dilemmas*. Cambridge: Cambridge University Press, 2003.

The Humanitarian Decade: Challenges for Humanitarian Assistance in the Last Decade and into the Future. New York: United Nations, Office for the Coordination of Humanitarian Affairs, 2002.

Humanitarian Intervention, International Legal Theory 7 (2001).

Humphrey, John. *No Distant Millennium: The International Law of Human Rights*. Paris: UNESCO, 1989.

Ishay, Micheline R. *The History of Human Right: From Ancient Times to the Globalization Era*. Berkeley: University of California Press, 2004.

Janzekovic, John. *The Use of Force in Humanitarian Intervention: Morality and Practicalities*. Burlington: Ashgate, 2006.

Kaldor, Mary. *Human Security*. Cambridge: Polity Press, 2007.

Kane, John. *The Politics of Moral Capital*. Cambridge: Cambridge University Press, 2001.

Keal, Paul. *European Conquest and the Rights of Indigenous Peoples: The Moral Backwardness of International Society*. Cambridge: Cambridge University Press, 2003.

Kennedy, David. *The Dark Sides of Virtue: Reassessing International Humanitarianism*. Princeton: Princeton University Press, 2004.

Kinzer, Stephen. "Rwanda's Genocide: A Report on the the Devastating Role of France." *International Herald Tribune*, August 15, 2008.

Köchler, Hans. *Humanitarian Intervention in the Context of Modern Power Politics: Is the Revival of the Doctrine of "Just War" Compatible with the International Rule of Law?* Vienna: International Progress Organization, 2001.

Kolb, Robert. "Note on Humanitarian intervention." *International Review of Red Cross* 85 (2003): 119–34.

Krasner, Stephen D. *Sovereignty. Organized Hypocrisy*. Princeton, Princeton University Press, 1999.

Kroslak, Daniela. *The Role of France in the Rwandan Genocide*. London: Hurst, 2007.

Lang, Tony, ed. *Just Intervention*. Washington, DC: Georgetown University Press, 2003.

Lepard, B. D. *Rethinking Humanitarian Intervention: A Fresh Legal Approach Based on Fundamental Ethical Principles in International Law and World Religions*. University Park: Pennsylvania State University Press, 2002.

Lillich, Richard B., ed. *Humanitarian Intervention and the United Nations*. Charlottesville: University Press of Virginia, 1973.

Löwenheim, Oded. "'Do Ourselves Credit and Render a Lasting Service to Mankind': British Moral Prestige, Humanitarian Intervention, and the Barbarity Pirates." *International Studies Quarterly* 47 (2003): 23–48.

Lu, Catherine. *Just and Unjust Interventions in World Politics*. Basingstoke: Palgrave Macmillan, 2006.

MacFarlane, S. N. *Intervention in Contemporary Politics*. Oxford: Adelphi Papers no. 350, 2002.

Mamdani, Mahmood. *Saviours and Survivors: Darfur, Politics and the War on Terror*. New York: Verso, 2009.

Matlary, Janne Haaland. *Values and Weapons: From Humanitarian Intervention to Regime Change?* London: Palgrave Macmillan, 2006.

Mazlish, Bruce. *The Idea of Humanity in a Global Era*. Basingstoke: Palgrave Macmillan, 2009.

Melvern, Linda. "Rwanda and Darfur: The Media and the Security Council." *International Relations* 20 (2006): 93–104.

Mertus, Jelie A., and Jeffrey W. Helsin, eds. *Human Rights and Conflict: Exploring the Links between Rights, Law, and Peacebuilding*. Washington, DC: United States Institute of Peace Press, 2006.

Moyn, Samuel. *The Last Utopia: Human Rights in History*. Cambridge: Belknap Press of Harvard University Press, 2010.

Nardin, Terry, and Melissa S. Williams, eds. *Humanitarian Intervention: Nomos XLVII—Yearbook of the American Society for Political and Legal Philosophy*. New York: New York University Press, 2006.

Orford, Anne.*Reading Humanitarian Intervention*. Cambridge: Cambridge University Press, 2003.

Otte, Thomas G. "Of Congresses and Gunboats: Military Intervention in the Nineteenth Century," in *Military Intervention: From Gunboat Diplomacy to Humanitarian Intervention*, ed. A. M. Dorman and T. G. Otte, 19–52. Aldershot: Darmouth, 1993.

Piiparinen, Touko. "The Lessons of Darfur for the Future of Humanitarian Intervention." *Global Governance* 13 (2007): 365–90.

Power, Samantha. *A Problem from Hell: America in the Age of Genocide*. New York: Perennial, 2002.

Ramsbothan, Oliver P. "Islam, Christianity, and Forcible Humanitarian Intervention." *Ethics & International Affairs* 12 (1998): 81–102.

Ramsbotham, Oliver, and Tom Woodhouse. *Humanitarian Intervention in Contemporary Conflict*. Cambridge: Polity Press, 1996.

Riemer, Neal, ed. *Protection Against Genocide: Mission Impossible?* Westport: Praeger, 1999.

Roberts, Adam. *Humanitarian Action in War: Aid, Protection and Impartiality in a Policy Vacuum*. Oxford: Oxford University Press, 1996.

———. "The So-Called Right of Humanitarian Intervention." *Trinity Papers* 13 (2000): 1–24.

Robertson, Geoffrey. *Crimes Against Humanity. The Struggle for Global Justice*. 2d ed. London: Penguin, 2002.

Sarooshi, Danesh. *The United Nations and the Development of Collective Security: The Delegation by the UN Security Council of Its Chapter VII Powers*. Oxford: Clarendon Press, 1999.

Schnabel, Albrecht, and Ramesh Thakur, eds. *Kosovo and the Challenge of Humanitarian Intervention: Selective Indignation, Collective Action, and International Citizenship*. Tokyo: United Nations University Press, 2000.

Seybolt, Taylor B. *Humanitarian Military Intervention: The Conditions for Success and Failure*. Oxford: Oxford University Press and Stockholm International Peace Research Institute, 2007.

Sherman, Nancy. "Empathy, Respect, and Humanitarian Intervention." *Ethics & International Affairs* 12 (1998): 103–20.

Smith, Michael J. "Humanitarian Intervention: An Overview of the Ethical Issues." *Ethics & International Affairs* 12 (1998): 63–80.

Sovereignty as Responsibility: Conflict Management in Africa. Washington, DC: Brookings Institution, 1996.

Stahn, Carsten. "Responsibility to Protect: Political Rhetoric or Emerging Legal Norm?" *American Journal of International Law* 101 (2007): 99–120.

Strobel, Warren P. *Late-Breaking Foreign Policy: The News Media's Influence on Peace Operations*. Washington: USIP, 1997.

Stromeseth, Jane, David Wippman, and Rosa Brooks. *Can Might Make Rights? Building the Rule of Law after Military Interventions*. Cambridge: Cambridge University Press, 2006.

Téson, Fernando. *Humanitarian Intervention: An Inquiry into Law and Morality*. New York: Dobbs Ferry Transnational Publishers, 1998.

Thornberry, Patrick. *International Law and the Rights of Minorities*. Oxford: Oxford University Press, 1991.

Trachtenberg, Marc. "Intervention in Historical Perspective." In *Emerging Norms of Justified Intervention*, ed. L. Reed and C. Kaysen. Cambridge, MA: American Academy of Arts and Sciences, 1993.

Tuck, Richard. *The Rights of War and Peace: Political Thought and the International Order from Grotius to Kant*. Oxford: Oxford University Press, 1999.

Vincent, R. J. *Non-Intervention and International Order*. Princeton: Princeton University Press, 1974.

Walzer, Michael. *Arguing About War*. New Haven: Yale University Press, 2004.

———. *Just and Unjust War*. New Haven: Yale University Press, 2004.

Weiss, Thomas G. "The Sunset of Humanitarian Intervention? The Responsibility to Protect in a Unipolar Era." *Security Dialogue* 35 (2004): 135–53.

Welsh, Jennifer, ed. *Humanitarian Intervention and International Relations*. Oxford: Oxford University Press, 2004.

Western, Jon. "Sources of Humanitarian Intervention: Beliefs, Information, and Advocacy in the U.S. Decisions on Somalia and Bosnia." *International Security* 26 (2002): 112–42.

Wheeler, Nicholas J. *Saving Strangers: Humanitarian Intervention in International Society*. Oxford, Oxford University Press 2000.

Wheeler, Nicholas J., and Justin Morris. "Humanitarian Intervention and State Practice at the End of the Cold War." In *International Society after the Cold War: Anarchy and Order Reconsidered*, ed. Rick Fawn and Jeremy Larkins, 135–71. Basingstoke: Macmillan, 1996.

Wallis, Andrew. *Silent Accomplice: The Untold Story of France's Role in the Rwandan Genocide*. London: I. B. Tauris, 2006.

William, Paul D., and Alex Bellamy. "The Responsibility to Protect and the Crisis in Darfur." *Security Dialogue* 36 (2005): 27–45.

Wilson, Richard Ashby, and Richard D. Brown, eds. *Humanitarianism and Suffering: The Mobilization of Empathy*. Cambridge: Cambridge University Press, 2009.

Zolo, Danilo. *Cosmopolis*. Cambridge: Polity Press, 1997.

———. *Invoking Humanity*. London: Continuum, 2002.

Index

Aarbakke, Vemund, 334 (n1)
Abd-el-Kader, 14
Abdul Hamid II (Sultan), 27, 155, 170–171, 173, 183, 185, 192–193, 199, 215–216, 232, 238, 322 (n22)
Abdul Mejid (Sultan), 26, 45
Aberdeen, Fourth Earl of (John Campbell Hamilton-Gordon), 46, 235
Achmed Aga, 149
Achmet Aga, 156
Ahmad Pasha (governor of Damascus), 112
Ährenthal, Alois Lexa von, 242
Albert de Saxe-Coburg-Gotha (Prince), 46
Albright, Madeleine, 261
Alexander I (Tsar), 81
Alexander II (Tsar), 142
Ali (Pasha of Ioannina), 64
Ali Pasha (sultan's Grand Vizier), 104, 118, 125–126, 131–133, 137–138, 291 (n43)
Amos, Sheldon, 89
Andrassy, Julius, 144–146, 166
Anghie, Anthony, 48, 249, 340 (n24)
Annan, Kofi, 260, 271, 273, 275
Arcidiacono, Bruno, 18, 282 (n1)
Argyll, Eighth Duke of (George Campbell), 123, 139, 153, 155, 157, 159, 205, 290 (n19), 315 (n42), 326 (n84)
Arnold, Arthur, 333 (n69)
Arntz, E.R.N., 55
Athanassoglou-Kallmeyer, Nina, 76
Atkin, Edward, 205

Bagot, Charles, 70
Balakian, Peter, 197, 204
Balladur, Edouard, 265
Baring, Walter, 148–149, 314 (n18)
Barron (British chargé d'affaires), 132
Bass, Gary, 1, 10–11, 16, 115, 267
Baudicour, Louis de, 96
Beaufort d'Hautpoul, Charles de, 106–107, 306 (n87)
Béclard, L., 109, 112
Bellamy, Alex, 275

Bennett, Ernest N., 225–226
Bentivoglio, Count de (Stanislas d'Aragon), 101, 106
Bérard, Victor, 207–208, 219, 226, 234, 237, 307 (n8), 336 (n22é 32)
Bernard, Montagu, 21, 49–50, 293 (n61)
Berton, Jean Michel, 38–39, 75
Bickford-Smith, R.A.H., 225
Biliotti, Alfred, 214, 216, 220–221, 223, 232, 322 (13), 329 (n10)
Bismarck, Otto von, 165, 173
Blair, Tony, 261
Blanc, Paul, 215, 219
Blaquiere, Edward, 74–75
Bloxham, Donald, 26, 140, 185, 200, 203, 210
Blunt, Fanny Janet, 40
Bluntschli, Johann Caspar, 57–58
Boisson de Chazournes, Laurence, 272
Bond, L., 245
Bonfils, Henri, 51
Borchard, Edwin M., 56
Bourne, Fox, 320 (n24)
Bourrée, Nicolas P., 126
Boutakoff, Commodore, 132
Boutourlin, Comte de. See Petrovitch, Dmitri (known as Comte de Boutourlin)
Boyer, Frédéric, 224
Brailsford, H. N., 235, 269–270
Brailsford, Mr. (relief worker), 245–246
Brailsford, Mrs. (relief worker), 245, 338 (n65)
Brant, James, 100–101
Brewer, David, 86
Brézol, Georges, 204
Briand, Aristide, 336 (n22)
Bright, John, 24
Brownlie, Ian, 89
Bruce, Kathleen, 338 (n65)
Bruce, Miss, 338 (n65)
Bruce, Rosslyn, 338 (n65)
Bryce, James, 157, 205, 235, 247, 316 (n53), 326 (n86), 328 (n111), 333 (n69)
Bulwer, Henry, 101

Burke, Edmund, 52
Bush, George W., 258
Buxton, Charles, 121
Buxton, Noel, 236–237
Buxton, Thomas Fowell, 121
Byron, Lord (George Gordon), 72, 76, 78

Calocherino, Calymachus, 128, 215, 221
Cambon, Paul, 185, 194, 208, 210, 227, 233
Campbell, George (Eighth Duke of
    Argyll). See Argyll, Eighth Duke of
    (George Campbell)
Canevaro, Napoleone, 217
Canfora, Luciana, v
Canning, George, 72, 79–80, 88
Canning, Stratford (First Viscount Strat-
    ford de Redcliffe), 24, 44, 46, 80, 154, 291
    (n43), 297 (n14), 310 (n39)
Caprini, Balduino, 223
Carlyle, Thomas, 121–122, 156
Carnarvon, Fourth Earl of (Henry
    Howard Molyneux), 11–12
Casement, Roger, 179–182
Castlereagh, Lord (Second Marquess of
    Londonderry; Robert Stewart), 69–72
Cavendish, Lucy Caroline (Lady Frederick
    Cavendish), 235
Cavendish, Spencer (Eighth Duke of
    Cavendish, known as Marquess of
    Hartington). See Hartington, Marquess
    of (Spencer Cavendish, Eighth Duke of
    Cavendish)
Cecil, Robert (Third Marquess of
    Salisbury). See Salisbury, Third
    Marquess of (Robert Cecil)
Chamberlain, Austen, 325 (n65)
Chambers, William, 204
Chandler, David, 271
Charmetant, Father, 207–208
Chateaubriand, René de, 24, 39, 63, 73–74
Chaudordy, Jean-Baptiste A. Damaze de,
    212
Chermside, Herbert, 193, 195, 219–220,
    322 (n13)
Chesson, F. W., 316 (n51)
Chesterman, Simon, 54, 60
Chomsky, Noam, 253–255
Chrétien, Jean, 271
Churchill, Charles Henry, 91, 96–100
Clayton, Captain, 322 (n13)
Clemenceau, Georges, 207–209, 328 (n111),
    336 (n22)

Clinton, Bill, 257, 263
Cobbett, William, 78
Cobden, Richard, 24, 40, 50
Cochin, Denys, 207–208, 226, 235, 305
    (n65), 328 (n111)
Cochrane, Lord, 78
Codrika, Panagiotis, 38–39
Codrington, Edward, 82–83
Cole, Madeleine, 326 (n80)
Condorelli, Luigi, 272
Conklin, Alice, 13–14, 282 (n40)
Constant, Benjamin, 24, 39
Cooper, Anthony Ashley (Seventh Earl of
    Shaftesbury), 97, 153
Cooper, H., 322 (n13)
Courcel, Geoffrey Chodron de, 199, 220
Cowley, Henry Wellesley, 103, 128
Cowley, Lord, 46
Cox, Marcus, 266
Craveri, Federico, 223
Crawford, Earl of, 283 (n4)
Creasy, Edward, 57
Creelman, James, 175
Crémieux, 305 (n65)
Currie, Philip, 192–193, 196, 200, 212

Dadrian, Vahakn, 63
Dakin, Douglas, 236, 240
Dalmatia, First Duke of (Nicolas Soult), 87
Darwin, Charles, 121, 156
David, Céléste Etienne, 297 (n17), 298
    (n19)
Decazis, Anaïs Caumel, 207
Dedering, Tilman, 288 (n52)
De Giorgis, Emilio, 240
Delacroix, Eugène, 76, 269
Delcassé, Théophile, 207, 235
Denton, William, 144, 153
Derby, Earl of. See Stanley, Edward (Fif-
    teenth Earl of Derby, known as Lord
    Stanley)
Deschamps, Gaston, 336 (n22)
Despagnet, Frantz, 58–59
Dickens, Charles, 121
Dickinson, Edwin de Witt, 56
Dickson, C. H., 125, 128, 133
Dilke, C. W., 333 (n69)
Dillon, Emil J., 193–194
Disraeli, Benjamin, 3, 11, 123, 145, 147–151,
    153–154, 161, 193
Doughty-Wiley, C.H.M., 203–204
Douvek (British vice counsel), 204

Drovetti, Bernardino, 84
Drury, Captain (British), 214
Duclert, Vincent, 208
Ducommun, Elie, 224
Ducrot, Auguste-Alexandre, 304 (n62)
Dufferin, Lord (Frederick Hamilton
    Temple Blackwood, First Marquess of
    Dufferin and Ava), 109, 112, 115, 190,
    303 (n35)
Dupuis, J. Hutton, 147
Durham, Miss, 338 (n65)

Eliot, Charles, 187–188, 321 (n4)
Elliot, Henry, 136, 147, 149–151
Engelhardt, Edouard, 27, 286 (n27)
Erskine, Edward, 124–125, 312 (n79)
d'Estournelles, Paul, 235, 328 (n111), 336
    (n22)
Etienne, 336 (n22)
Eugenie (Empress), 114
Evans, Arthur, 235
Evans, Gareth, 279 (n6), 343 (n61)
Everett, Captain, 322 (n13)
Eyre, Edward, 121–122, 156

Farley, J. Lewis, 153
Farley, Lewis, 144
Fauchille, Paul, 51
Fawaz, Leila Tarazi, 111
Fawcett, Millicent Garrett, 158
Ferdinand Coburg (Prince), 173
Ferguson, Adam, 13
Ferronays, Auguste de la, 85
Ferry, Jules, 286 (n27)
Findley, Carter V., 44
Fink, Carol, 166
Finlay, George, 87
Finnemore, Martha, 288 (n58)
Forsythe, David, 9, 256
Fox, Fiona, 270
France, Anatole, 207, 237, 336 (n22)
Francis-Joseph (Emperor of Austria-
    Hungary), 239
Fraser (Bishop of Manchester), 153
Freeman, Edward A., 158–160, 291 (n36)
Fuad Pasha, 102–103, 106–107, 109–112,
    128–129, 135–136, 291 (n43)
Fuller, Stuart J., 182

Gallenga, Antonio Carlo Napoleone, 148
Garrone, Egidio, 223
Gennadius, John, 333 (n69)

Gentili, Alberico, 5
George I (King of Greece), 216
George IV (King of England), 69
George of Greece (Prince), 216, 222–223
Gill, Rebecca, 343 (n54)
Girardin, Marc ("Saint"), 96, 305 (n65)
Gladstone, Herbert, 225, 235
Gladstone, William E., 15, 24–25, 150, 152–
    157, 169, 190–191, 196, 199, 224, 236
Glenny, Misha, 141–142, 144, 166, 313 (n3),
    314 (n14)
Goluchowski, Agenor Maria, 217, 233, 240
Gooch, G. P., 235
Gorchakov, Alexander M., 124, 131, 142,
    145–146
Graham, Cyril, 100–102, 303 (n35)
Graham, Malbone W., 248
Grant, Kevin, 179–180
Granville, Second Earl of (George Leveson
    Gower), 153, 155
Gratry, Father, 305 (n65)
Graves (Consul General), 246
Graves, Robert, 191
Green (member of Jamaica Committee),
    156
Gregory V (Greek Orthodox patriarch), 67
Grey, Edward, 204, 242–243, 337 (n47)
Grosvenor, Hugh (First Duke of
    Westminster), 205, 333 (n71)
Grosvenor, Robert (First Marquess of
    Westminster), 70–71, 73–74
Grotius, Hugo, 5
Guarracino, Frederick, 314 (n18)
Gueheneuc, Charles, 87
Guillain, 336 (n22)
Guilleminot, Armand
Guizot, François, 13–14, 24, 45
Guys, Henry, 96, 301 (n12), 302 (n18)

Habyarimana, Juvénal, 265
Hagopian, Karapet, 326 (n81)
Hall, Catherine, 122
Hall, William, 50–51, 59–60
Hallward, C. M., 192
Hamilton-Gordon, John Campbell (Fourth
    Earl of Aberdeen). See Aberdeen, Fourth
    Earl of (John Campbell Hamilton-
    Gordon)
Hammond, Edmund, 46
Hancourt, William, 293 (n61)
Hanotaux, Gabriel, 194, 208–209, 226–228
Harcourt, William, 59, 151

Harris, Alice, 180
Harris, H. (relief worker), 245
Harris, Helen, 206
Harris, J. Rendel, 206
Harris, John, 180
Hartington, Marquess of (Spencer Cavendish, Eighth Duke of Cavendish), 153
Haskell, Mr. (missionary), 245
Hay, John, 128
Heffter, Augustus, 58
Heiden, Lodewijk, 82–83
Henry, René, 234
Herold, 336 (n22)
Hilmi Pasha, Hussein, 233, 239, 241
Historicus. See Harcourt, William
Hitler, Adolph, 340 (n21)
Hoffmann, Stanley, 1, 341 (n34)
Holland, Robert, 138, 217, 221, 227
Hughes, Thomas S., 75
Humphreys, W. H., 66
Hussein Bey (Kurdish chief), 192
Huxley, Thomas, 121
Hyam, Ronald, 13

Ibrahim Ali (son of Mohamed Ali), 65, 79–80, 83, 85–86, 88–89, 91
Ibrahim Pasha (Egyptian general), 23, 106
Ignatyev, Nikolai Pavlovich, 131, 161–162, 164, 267
Isaac, Pierre, 207
Ismail Bey, 192
Ismail Pasha (governor of Crete), 119
Izvolsky, Alexander, 242–243

Jaurès, Jean, 207–208, 226, 235, 328 (n111)
Jooris, Joseph, 58

Kaldor, Mary, 260–261
Kane, John, 281 (n27)
Kant, Immanuel, 5
Kara Ali (Pasha). See Pasha Kara Ali (Captain)
Kaufmann, Chaim D., 281 (n28)
Kechriotis, Vangelis, 294 (n84)
Keohane, Robert O., 1, 267–268
Khurdish Pasha (governor of Morea), 64
Kimberley, John, 193, 225, 323 (n26)
Kingsley, Charles, 121
Kiria, Mr., 245
Kitchener, Horatio (Lord Kitchener), 221, 322 (n13)

Knox, Robert, 178
Krasner, Stephen D., 318 (n1)

Lamartine, Alphonse de, 24, 96, 284 (n15)
Lamsdorf, Vladimir, 233
Lamy, Etienne, 336 (n22)
Lane-Poole, Stanley, 80
Lange-Akhund, Nadine, 335 (n15)
Lansdowne, Fifth Marquess of (Henry Charles Keith Petty Fitz-Maurice), 233, 236, 239, 241, 245
Laurens, Henry, v
Lavalette, Charles Jean de, 25, 99, 101–102, 104, 127
Lavigerie, Charles Martial A., 40, 110
Lavisse, 328 (n111), 336 (n22)
Lawrence, Thomas J., 18, 21, 60
Layard, Austen, 46, 165, 189
Lazare, Bernard, 207
Lear, Edward, 96
Lecky, William, 156
Lefèvre-Pontalis, 305 (n65)
Legvold, Robert, 259
Lejeune, 328 (n111)
Lemaitre, Jules, 207
Lemkin, Raphael, 32
Lenormant, François, 96–97, 305 (n65)
Leopold II (King of Belgium), 178, 181
Lepsius, Johannes, 206
Levene, Mark, 171
Liddon, Henry Parry, 153
Lieven, Christopher, 79, 81
Lingelbach, W. E., 61
Liverpool, Lord (Robert Banks Jenkinson, Second Earl of Liverpool), 69–71
Lobanov-Rostovsky, Aleksei, 198, 324 (n51)
Lockroy, 336 (n22)
Logothetis, Lykourgos, 68
Longworth, H. Z., 197
Lorimer, James, 51–53, 293 (n61)
Lowther, Gerard, 202–203
Lyell, Charles, 121
Lyons (British ambassador), 123–126

Macaulay, Zachary, 280 (n20)
MacColl, Malcom, 40–41, 153, 157–158, 160, 205, 225, 235, 290 (n18), 326 (n84), 328 (n111)
MacCunn, John, v, 176–177
MacGahan, Januarius Aloysius, 150, 154

Mackintosh, James, 49
Mahmud (Sultan), 23
Maison, Nicholas Joseph de, 84–87
Maitland, "King Tom" (governor of Malta), 286 (n33)
Makdisi, Saree, 72
Makdisi, Ussama, 96, 111
Mamdani, Mahmood, 254–255, 258, 268
Mandelstam, André, 89
Mandler, Peter, 12–13
Mann, Michael, 32, 288 (n49)
Manning, William O., 58
Markides, Diana, 138, 217, 221, 227
Marrus, Michael R., 247–248
Martens, George de, 56
Martin (Rev.), 204
Mathieu, Henri, 297 (n13)
Mazower, Mark, 247–248
McKinley, William, 175, 319 (n12)
Mehemed V (Sultan), 183
Metternich, Klemens von, 81, 84, 297 (n14)
Mihaylovski, Stoyan, 231
Milan (Prince of Serbia), 146
Mill, John Stuart, 13, 28–29, 50, 52, 121–122, 317 (n61)
Millerand, Alexandre, 226
Mitterrand, François, 265–266
Mobutu (President of the Democratic Republic of the Congo [Zaire]), 266
Mohamed Ali (Pasha of Egypt), 23–24, 65, 79, 84–85, 91
Monk, Charles James, 134
Montesquieu, Charles-Louis de Secondat, Baron de la Brède, 38
Moore, Noel, 100–101, 110
Morel, Edmund Dene, 179–181, 320 (n24)
Moustier, Léonel de, 123, 125, 127, 130, 132
Moyn, Samuel, 6
Mun, Albert de, 207–208
Murray (Lieutenant), 134
Mustapha Pasha (Ottoman governor in Crete), 124–125

Naimark, Norman, 32, 288 (n49)
Napier, Robert, 3
Napoleon, Louis (Emperor Napoleon III), 16, 40, 46, 94, 104, 106–108, 114–115, 120, 127, 132
Napoleon Bonaparte, 13
Nelidov, Alexander, 198
Nelson, Horatio, 23

Nemours, Duke of, 81
Nesselrode, Karl Robert, 81
Nevinson (relief worker), 245
Nicholas I (Tsar), 81, 283 (n4)
Nicholas II (Tsar), 239
Novikow, E. P., 109
Nys, Ernest, 51, 292 (n53), 328 (n111)

O'Conor, Nicholas, 245
Omer Pasha, 131–132, 134
Oppenheim, Lassa Francis, 51, 60–62, 89
Outrey, Georges, 30, 129, 132
Outrey, Maxime, 111
Owen, David Edward, 280 (n15)

Paget (captain, *Dolphin*), 215
Paget, C. (vice-admiral), 134
Palmerston, Third Viscount (Henry John Temple), 32–33, 290 (n29)
Pape, Robert A., 281 (n28)
Paris, Gaston, 336 (n22)
Parry, William, 78
Pasha Kara Ali (Captain), 68
Passy, Paul, 207, 336 (n22)
Pavlowitch, Stevan, 141, 183
Paynter, J. A., 100, 303 (n36)
Pears, Edwin, 147–148
Pécout, Gilles, 208
Pellion (General), 86, 299 (n66)
Percy, Henry, 228, 246
Pétélot, Father, 305 (n65)
Petrovitch, Dmitri (known as Comte de Boutourlin), 54–55, 85), 294 (n84
Phillimore, Robert, 31, 59
Phillimore, Walter, 333 (n69)
Pinon, René, 61–62, 229, 336 (n22)
Pitts, Jennifer, 34, 48
Poincaré, 336 (n22)
Polignac, Jules A.A.M. de, 87
Pottier, Edouard, 216, 219
Potton (French consul), 204
Poujade, Eugène, 96
Poujoulat, Baptistin, 96, 301 (n12), 305 (n65)
Powell, Colin, 258, 341 (n30)
de Pressensé, Francis, 207, 235, 237, 305 (n65), 327 (n97)
Puaux, Franck, 208
Pufendorf, Samuel, 5
Pulitzer, Joseph, 175
Pym, Captain, 125

Quillard, Pierre, 207, 237, 336 (n22)

Rayneval, Maximilien de, 85
Reclus, Elie et Elisée, 328 (n111)
Recouly, Raymond, 234
Reid, Rover, 333 (n69)
Richard, Henry, 43
Rieff, David, 270
de Rigny, Henri, 82–83
Ripper (Austrian vice admiral), 241
Robert, David, 96
Roberts, J. M., 173
Roberty, E. de, 207
Robilant, Mario Nicolis di, 240
Rochefort, Henri, 207
Rochemonteix, Camille de, 304 (n62)
Rodecker von Rotteck, Herman, 59
Rolin-Jaequemyns, Gustave, 55
Roncière, Camille de la, 99
Rosebery, Archibald, 191, 193, 323 (n26)
Rougier, Antoine, 36, 53–54, 56–57, 239, 241
Routier, Gaston, 234–235
Ruggie, John, 264
Ruskin, John, 121, 156
Russell, John, 103, 105, 108, 144, 225

Saab, Ann Pottinger, 134, 152, 156
Sahnoun, Mohamed, 343 (n61)
Said, Edward, 36
Said Pasha (Ottoman Grand Vizier), 193
Salih (Major), 192
Salisbury, Third Marquess of (Robert Cecil), 155, 160–162, 165–166, 187–191, 195–196, 198–202, 205, 209, 213–214, 220, 225, 317 (n71), 321 (n9)
Samuel, Herbert, 179, 320 (n24)
Sazonov, Sergei, 184
Schneider, Virgile, 87
Schuyler, Eugene, 154
Scudamore, F. I., 193
Sellars, Kirsten, 270
Sembat, Marcel, 328 (n111)
Sémelin, Jacques, 4, 53, 288 (n49)
Sergeant, Lewis, 333 (n69)
Seymour, Hamilton, 283 (n4)
Shaftesbury, Earl of. See Cooper, Anthony Ashley (Seventh Earl of Shaftesbury)
Shaftesbury, Lord. See Cooper, Anthony Ashley (Seventh Earl of Shaftesbury)
Shannon, Richard, 153–154

Shaw Lefevre, G. J., 333 (n69)
Shore, John, 280 (n20)
Shuvalov, Pyotr A., 165
Simon, Admiral, 132
Smith, Adam, 13
Smith, Goldwin, 43, 316 (n52)
Somerset, Lady Henry, 327 (n87)
Soult, Nicolas, First Duke of Dalmatia. See Dalmatia, First Duke of (Nicolas Soult)
Spencer, Edmund, 43
Spencer, Herbert, 121, 156
Spuller, Eugène, 213
Stahn, Carsten, 273–274
Stanhope, Leicester, 78
Stanley, Edward (Fifteenth Earl of Derby, known as Lord Stanley), 122, 125–126, 134, 139, 145–146, 148–151, 156, 160–161, 193, 280 (n24)
Stapleton, Augustus Granville, 88–89
Stead, W. T., 153, 206
Steeg, Louis, 233
Stephen, James, 280 (n20)
Stevenson, Francis, 205, 225
Stewart, J.D.H., 322 (n13)
Stewart, Robert. See Castlereagh, Lord (second Marquess of Londonderry; Robert Stewart)
Stillman, William James, 125
Stowell, Ellery, 250, 294 (n82)
Strangford, Sixth Viscount (Percy C. S. Smythe), 68–69
Streit, Georges, 56, 224
Stroganov, Sergei, 68, 71–72
Sully-Prudhomme, 336 (n22)

Talbot, Edward (of Rochester), 201
Tashin Pasha (Ottoman governor), 191–192
Temperley, Harold, 297 (n14)
Temple, Frederik, 141
Tennyson, Alfred, 121
Tenterden, Lord, 147
Thompson, Carslake, 53, 150, 158
Thornton, Henry, 280 (n20)
Thouvenel, Edouard-Antoine de, 102–107, 114, 127, 291 (n43)
Tobia, Bishop, 97
Tocqueville, Alexis, 14
Todorov, Tzvetan, 4
Todorova, Maria, 176
Tone, John Lawrence, 175, 319 (n14)

Trézel, Camille Alphonse, 87
Trotter, Henry, 18, 322 (n13)
Tsiko, Mr. (relief worker), 246
Turner, J.M.W., 76
Twiss, Travers, 51, 293 (n61)

Vadervelde, Emile, 328 (n111)
Vandal, Albert, 207, 336 (n22)
Vassos (Greek Colonel), 216
Vattel, Emer de, 5, 21, 74, 318 (n1)
Venizelos, Eleftherios, 220, 223
Venn, Henry, 280 (n20)
Vernes, Louis, 208
Victoria (Queen of England), 197–198
Vie, Louis, 56
Villèle, Jean-Baptiste de, 81
Vitoria, Francisco de, 4
von Rehfues (Prussian commissioner in
    Lebanon), 109
von Trotha (General), 288 (n52)

Waddington, George, 299 (n42)
Weckbecker, P. von, 109
Wellington, Duke of (Arthur Wellesley),
    80–81
Westlake, John, 47, 51, 57
Westlake, K. C., 235
Westminster, First Duke of (Hugh
    Grosvenor), 205, 333 (n71)
Wheatcroft, Andrew, 288 (n54)
Wheaton, Henry, 49, 54, 56, 317 (n61)
Wheeler, Nicholas, 267
White, William, 321 (n5)
Wilberforce, William, 7, 70–71, 73
Wilson, Charles B., 18, 322 (n13)
Wood, Charles, 120, 204
Woolsey, Theodore D., 56

Ypsilantis, Alexander, 64

Zeki Pasha (Ottoman commander), 191

HUMAN RIGHTS AND CRIMES AGAINST HUMANITY

This series provides a forum for publication and debate on the most pressing issues of modern times: the establishment of human rights standards and, at the same time, their persistent violation. It features a broad understanding of human rights, one that encompasses democratic citizenship as well as concerns for social, economic, and environmental justice. Its understanding of crimes against humanity is similarly broad, ranging from large-scale atrocities like ethnic cleansings, genocides, war crimes, and various forms of human trafficking to lynchings, mass rapes, and torture. Some books in the series are more historically oriented and explore particular events and their legacies. Others focus on contemporary concerns, like instances of forced population displacements or indiscriminate bombings. Still others provide serious reflection on the meaning and history of human rights or on the reconciliation efforts that follow major human rights abuses. Chronologically, the series runs from around 1500, the onset of the modern era marked by European colonialism abroad and the Atlantic slave trade, to the present. Geographically, it takes in every area of the globe. It publishes significant works of original scholarship and major interpretations by historians, human rights practitioners, legal scholars, social scientists, philosophers, and journalists. An important goal is to bring issues of human rights and their violations to the attention of a wide audience and to stimulate discussion and debate in the public sphere as well as among scholars and in the classroom. The knowledge that develops from the series will also, we hope, help promote human rights standards and prevent future crimes against humanity.